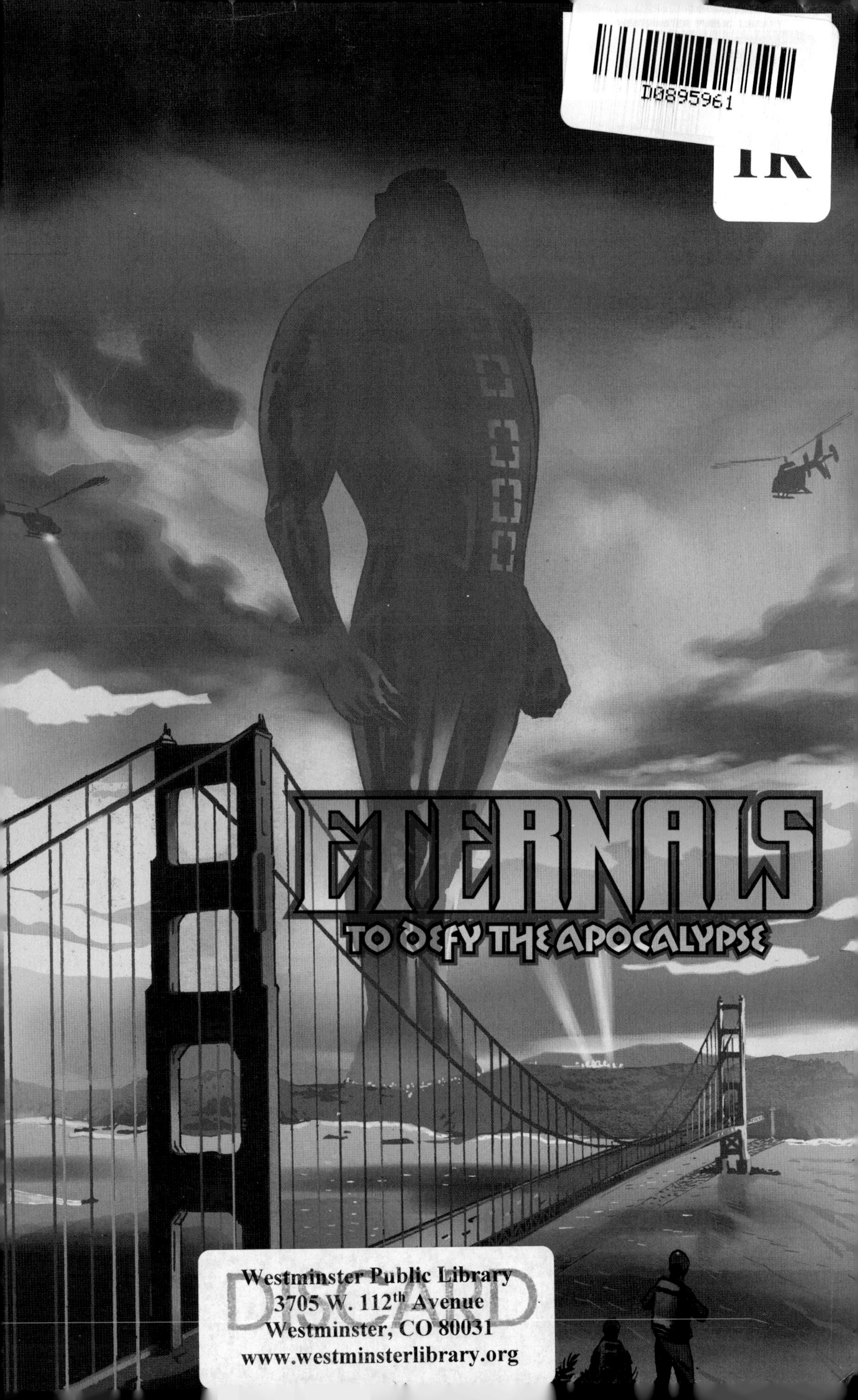
ETERNALS
TO DEFY THE APOCALYPSE

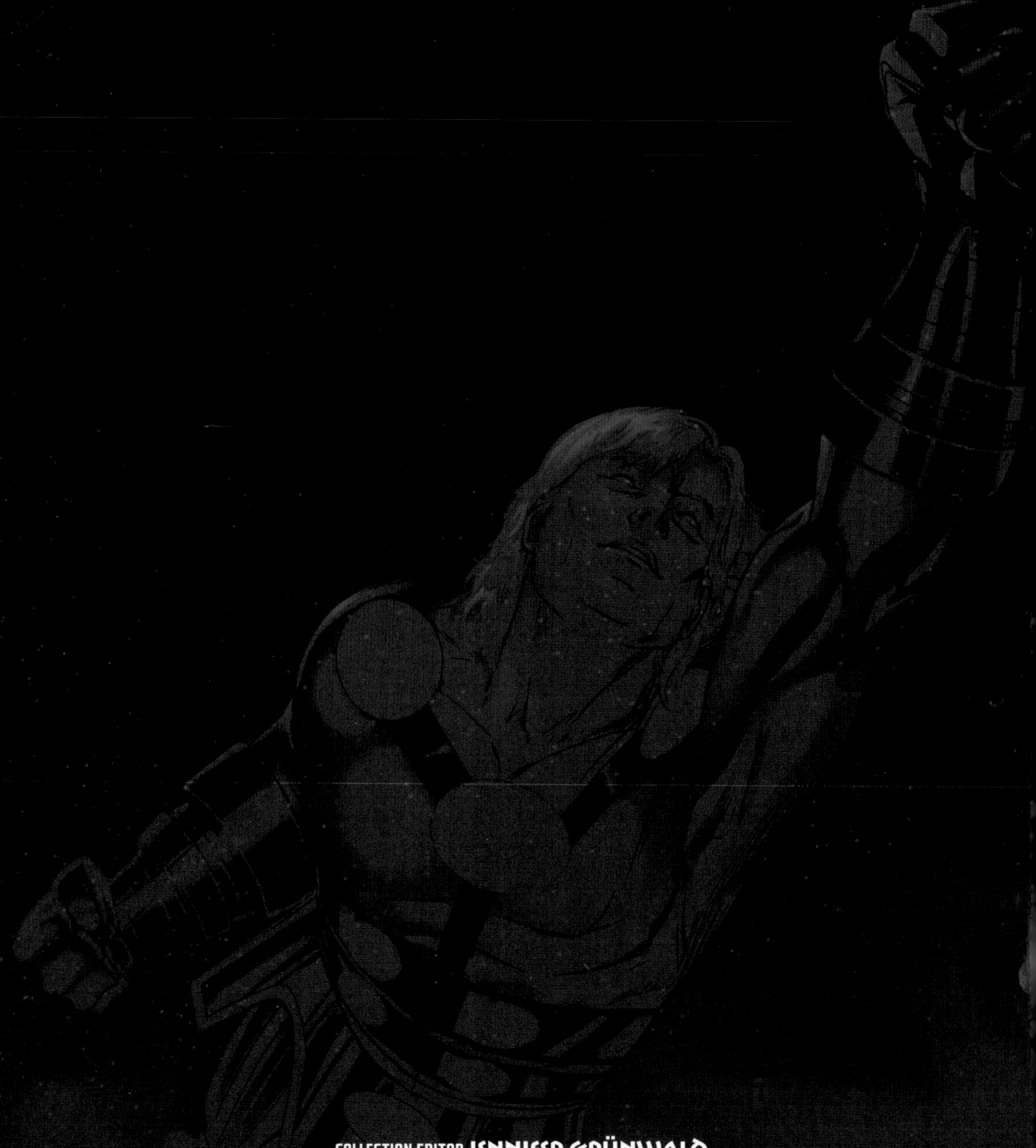

COLLECTION EDITOR **JENNIFER GRÜNWALD**
ASSISTANT EDITOR **DANIEL KIRCHHOFFER**
ASSISTANT MANAGING EDITOR **MAIA LOY**
ASSISTANT MANAGING EDITOR **LISA MONTALBANO**
ASSOCIATE MANAGER, DIGITAL ASSETS **JOE HOCHSTEIN**
VP PRODUCTION & SPECIAL PROJECTS **JEFF YOUNGQUIST**
RESEARCH **JOHN RHETT THOMAS**
LAYOUT **JEPH YORK**
BOOK DESIGNER **SALENA MAHINA**
SVP PRINT, SALES & MARKETING **DAVID GABRIEL**
EDITOR IN CHIEF **C.B. CEBULSKI**

ETERNALS: TO DEFY THE APOCALYPSE. Contains material originally published in magazine form as ETERNALS (2008) #1-9 and ETERNALS ANNUAL (2008) #1. First printing 2020. ISBN 978-1-302-92339-6. Published by MARVEL WORLDWIDE, INC., a subsidiary of MARVEL ENTERTAINMENT, LLC. OFFICE OF PUBLICATION: 1290 Avenue of the Americas, New York, NY 10104. **Printed in the U.S.A.** KEVIN FEIGE, Chief Creative Officer; DAN BUCKLEY, President, Marvel Entertainment; JOE QUESADA, EVP & Creative Director; DAVID BOGART, Associate Publisher & SVP of Talent Affairs; TOM BREVOORT, VP, Executive Editor; NICK LOWE, Executive Editor, VP of Content, Digital Publishing; DAVID GABRIEL, VP of Print & Digital Publishing; JEFF YOUNGQUIST, VP of Production & Special Projects; ALEX MORALES, Director of Publishing Operations; DAN EDINGTON, Managing Editor; RICKEY PURDIN, Director of Talent Relations; JENNIFER GRÜNWALD, Senior Editor, Special Projects; SUSAN CRESPI, Production Manager; STAN LEE, Chairman Emeritus. For information regarding advertising in Marvel Comics or on Marvel.com, please contact Vit DeBellis, Custom Solutions & Integrated Advertising Manager, at vdebellis@marvel.com. For Marvel subscription inquiries, please call 888-511-5480. **Manufactured between 12/11/2020 and 1/12/2021by FRY COMMUNICATIONS, MECHANICSBURG, PA, USA.**

10 9 8 7 6 5 4 3 2 1

ETERNALS
TO DEFY THE APOCALYPSE

ETERNALS #1-6

WRITERS **CHARLES & DANIEL KNAUF**

ARTIST & COLORIST **DANIEL ACUÑA**

LETTERER **TODD KLEIN**

COVER ART **DANIEL ACUÑA**

SPECIAL THANKS TO **STEPHEN MARCHAND**

ETERNALS #7-9

WRITERS **CHARLES & DANIEL KNAUF**

ARTISTS **ERIC NGUYEN** WITH **SARA PICHELLI** (#8)

COLORIST **ANDY TROY**

LETTERER **TODD KLEIN**

COVER ART **ERIC NGUYEN**

ETERNALS ANNUAL #1

WRITER **FRED VAN LENTE**

ARITST **PASCAL ALIXE**

COLORIST **BRAD ANDERSON**

LETTERER **ED DUKESHIRE**

COVER ART **ED McGUINNESS, MARK FARMER
& ASPEN's PETER STEIGERWALD**

ASSISTANT EDITORS **JORDAN D. WHITE & MICHAEL HORWITZ**

EDITORS **MARK PANICCIA & BILL ROSEMANN**

ETERNALS CREATED BY **JACK KIRBY**

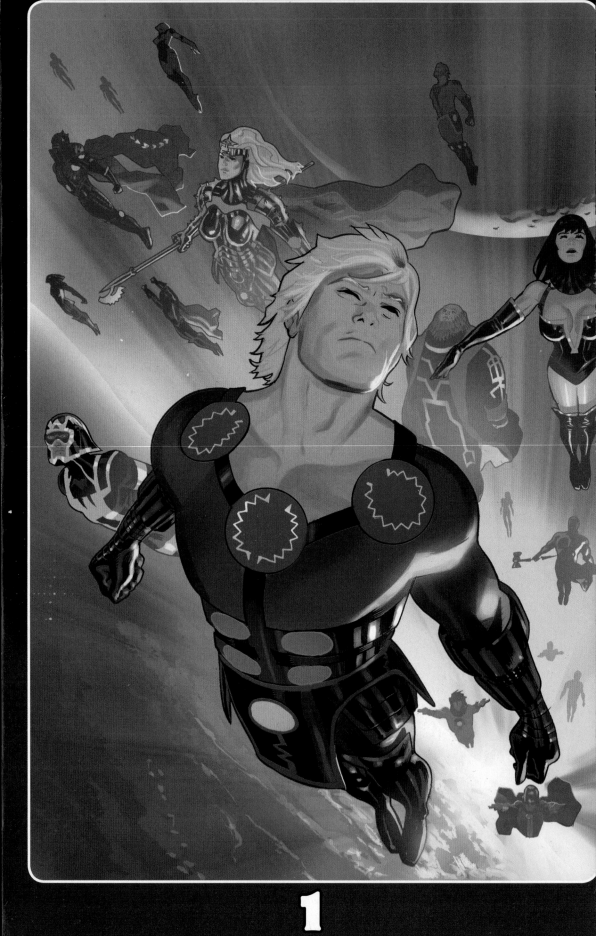

1

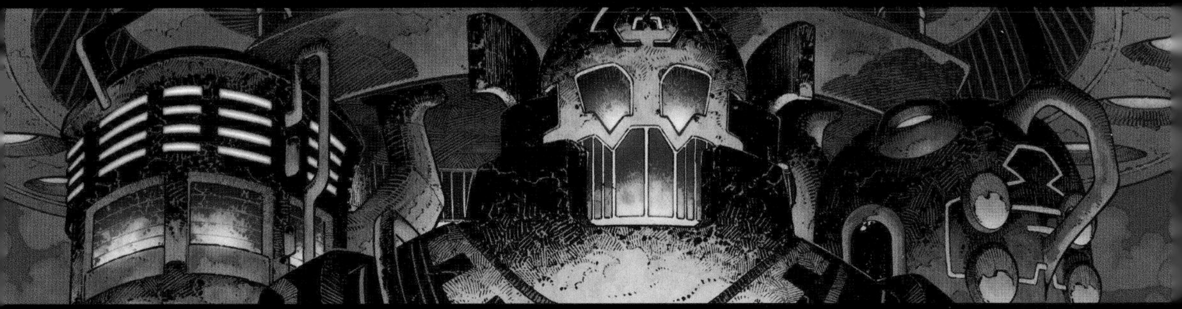

IESE ENORMOUS SPACE-GODS CAME TO EARTH TO PERFORM GENETIC EXPERIMENTS AS THEY HAD ON MANY A PLANET. IEY TOOK THE PRIMITIVE CREATURE KNOWN AS MAN AND FROM HIM, FORMED TWO NEW RACES. SOME THEY TWISTED INTO ONSTROUS FORMS, CALLING THEM **DEVIANTS**. SOME THEY LEFT RESEMBLING THEIR HUMAN COUSINS BUT ENDOWED WITH AMAZING POWERS. THESE BECAME KNOWN AS THE **ETERNALS**.

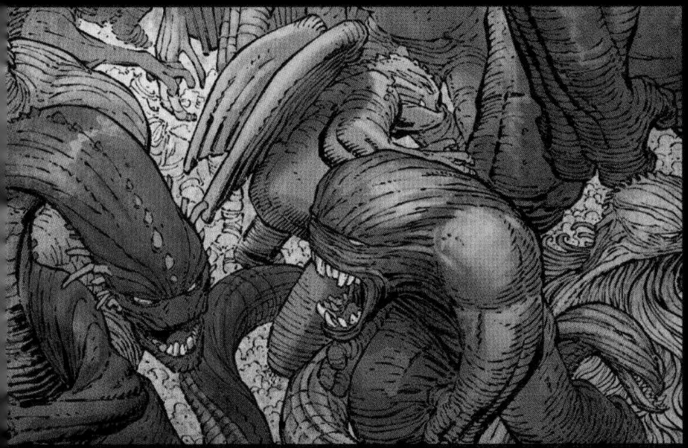

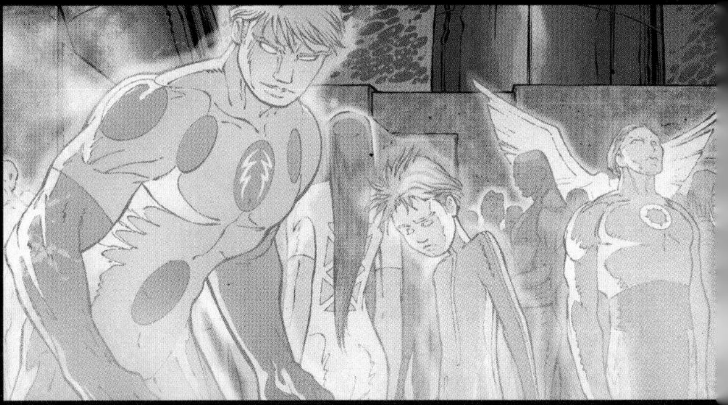

OR EONS, MANKIND WORSHIPPED THESE ETERNALS AS GODS, JUST AS IT FEARED THE DEVIANTS AS DEVILS... UT THEN CAME THE DAY WHEN THE ETERNALS VANISHED. THE HEAVENS WERE SILENT.

ROGUE ETERNAL HAD BETRAYED HIS OWN KIND AND STOLEN THEIR MEMORIES. THEY WERE SCATTERED CROSS THE PLANET AND FORCED TO LIVE AS MEN DO. FORTUNATELY, THE ETERNAL KNOWN AS **ARIS** REMEMBERED HIS TRUE IDENTITY, AND WAS ABLE TO AWAKEN SOME OF HIS PEOPLE.

A PLAY TO GAIN CONTROL BEFORE ALL THE ETERNALS REALIZED THEIR IDENTITIES, THE EVIANTS CAPTURED **MAKKARI** AND USED HIM TO AWAKEN THE **DREAMING CELESTIAL**, BURIED ENEATH THE DIABLO MOUNTAINS IN CALIFORNIA. HIS AWAKENING SIGNALED THE COSMIC OCUST-LIKE **HORDE** TO COME DEVOUR THE EARTH. TOWERING OVER GOLDEN GATE PARK IN AN FRANCISCO, THE DREAMING CELESTIAL STANDS OBSERVING MANKIND UNTIL THE HORDE RRIVES TO DESTROY THE PLANET.

OW THE ETERNALS NEED TO FIND THEIR LOST BRETHREN BEFORE THE HORDE ARRIVES, ALL IE WHILE DEALING WITH INTERNAL STRIFE AS THE AMBITIOUS **DRUIG** VIES FOR POWER WITHIN IEIR RANKS. CAN THE ETERNALS COME TOGETHER IN TIME TO SAVE THE WORLD AS THE OSMIC CLOCK TICKS TOWARDS DOOM? READ ON...

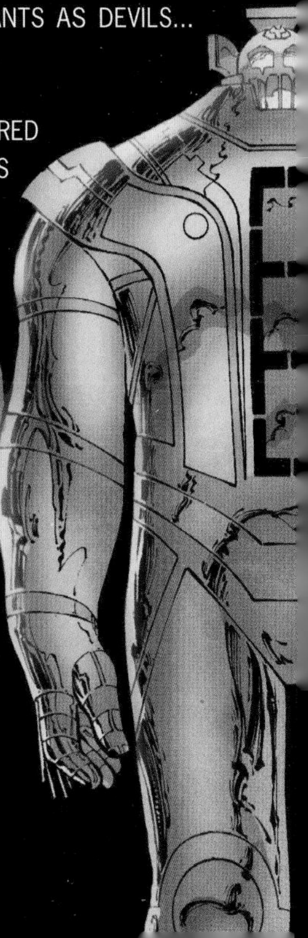

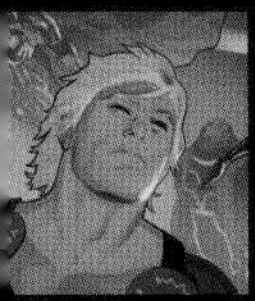

IKARIS

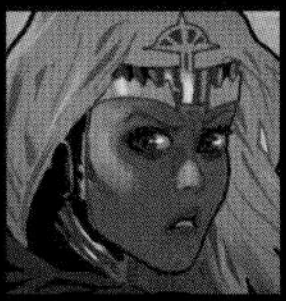

THENA

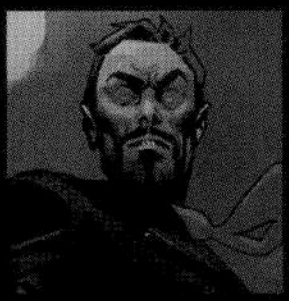

DRUIG

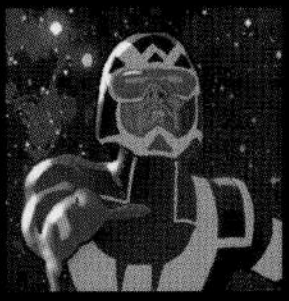

MAKKARI

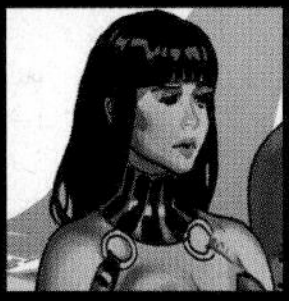

SERSI

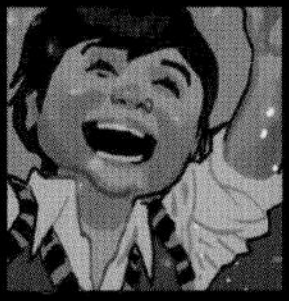

JOEY

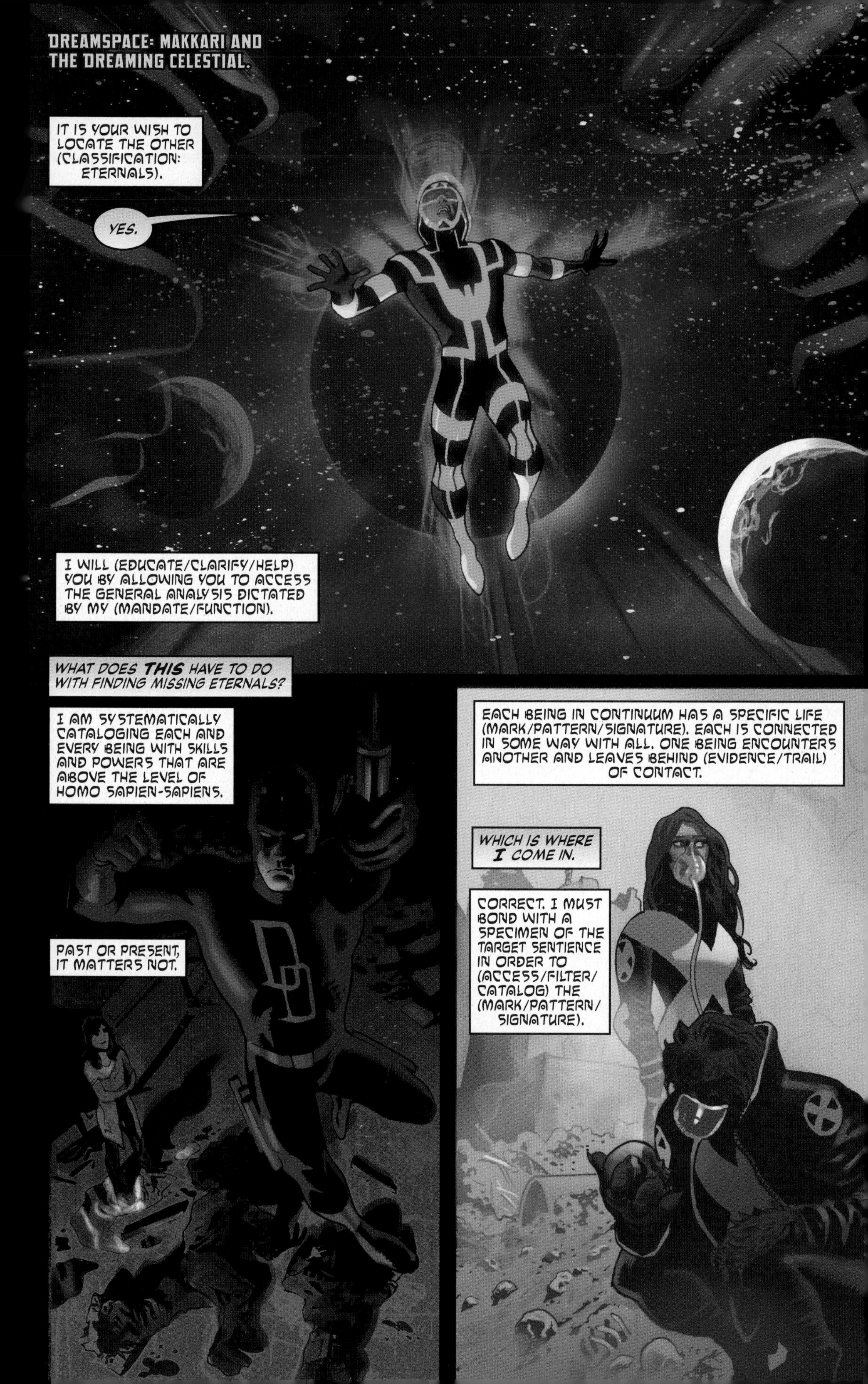
DREAMSPACE: MAKKARI AND THE DREAMING CELESTIAL.
IT IS YOUR WISH TO LOCATE THE OTHER (CLASSIFICATION: ETERNALS).
YES.
I WILL (EDUCATE/CLARIFY/HELP) YOU BY ALLOWING YOU TO ACCESS THE GENERAL ANALYSIS DICTATED BY MY (MANDATE/FUNCTION).
WHAT DOES THIS HAVE TO DO WITH FINDING MISSING ETERNALS?
I AM SYSTEMATICALLY CATALOGING EACH AND EVERY BEING WITH SKILLS AND POWERS THAT ARE ABOVE THE LEVEL OF HOMO SAPIEN-SAPIENS.
PAST OR PRESENT, IT MATTERS NOT.
EACH BEING IN CONTINUUM HAS A SPECIFIC LIFE (MARK/PATTERN/SIGNATURE). EACH IS CONNECTED IN SOME WAY WITH ALL. ONE BEING ENCOUNTERS ANOTHER AND LEAVES BEHIND (EVIDENCE/TRAIL) OF CONTACT.
WHICH IS WHERE I COME IN.
CORRECT. I MUST BOND WITH A SPECIMEN OF THE TARGET SENTIENCE IN ORDER TO (ACCESS/FILTER/CATALOG) THE (MARK/PATTERN/SIGNATURE).

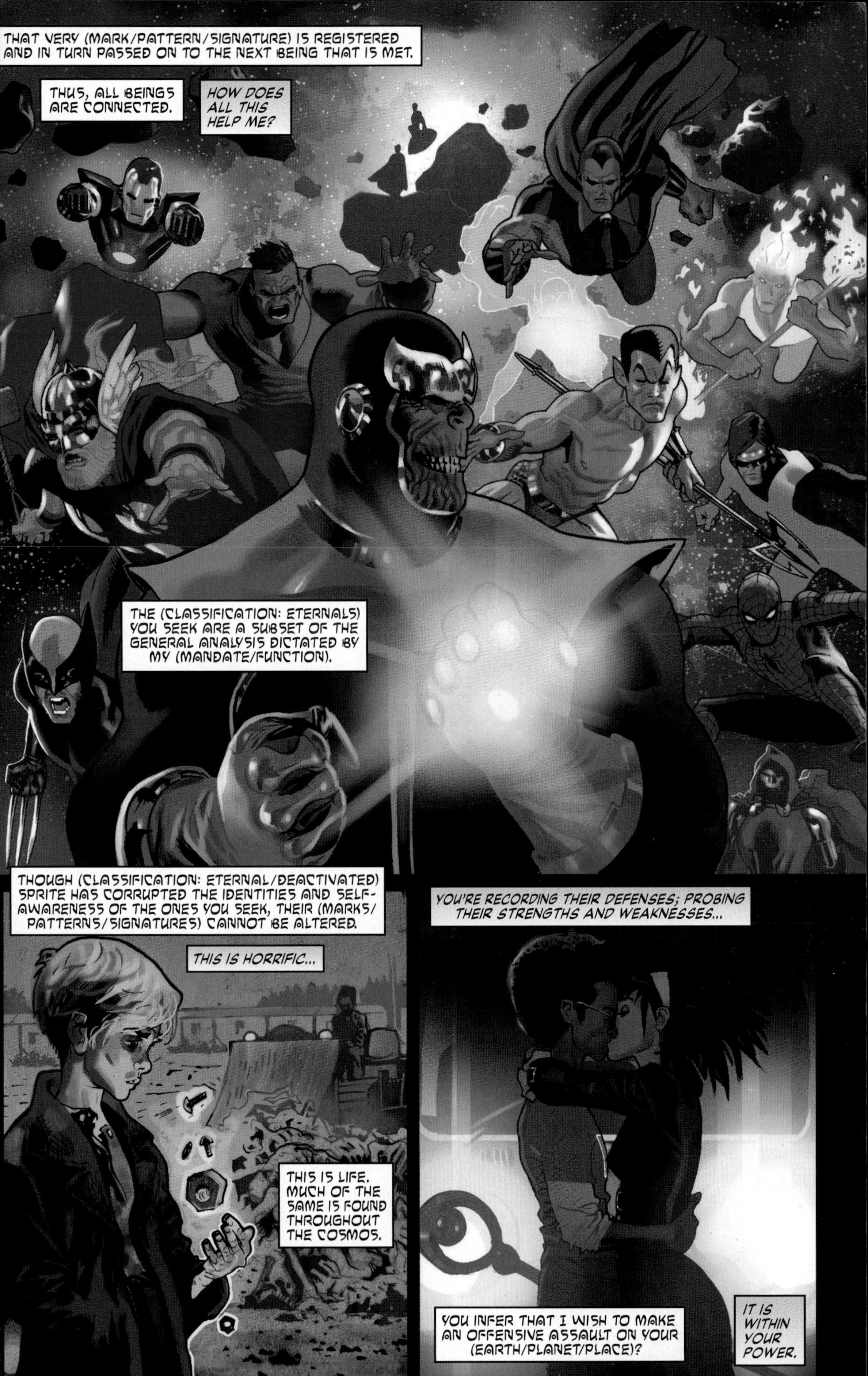
THAT VERY (MARK/PATTERN/SIGNATURE) IS REGISTERED AND IN TURN PASSED ON TO THE NEXT BEING THAT IS MET.
THUS, ALL BEINGS ARE CONNECTED.
HOW DOES ALL THIS HELP ME?
THE (CLASSIFICATION: ETERNALS) YOU SEEK ARE A SUBSET OF THE GENERAL ANALYSIS DICTATED BY MY (MANDATE/FUNCTION).
THOUGH (CLASSIFICATION: ETERNAL/DEACTIVATED) SPRITE HAS CORRUPTED THE IDENTITIES AND SELF-AWARENESS OF THE ONES YOU SEEK, THEIR (MARKS/PATTERNS/SIGNATURES) CANNOT BE ALTERED.
THIS IS HORRIFIC...
THIS IS LIFE. MUCH OF THE SAME IS FOUND THROUGHOUT THE COSMOS.
YOU'RE RECORDING THEIR DEFENSES; PROBING THEIR STRENGTHS AND WEAKNESSES...
YOU INFER THAT I WISH TO MAKE AN OFFENSIVE ASSAULT ON YOUR (EARTH/PLANET/PLACE)?
IT IS WITHIN YOUR POWER.

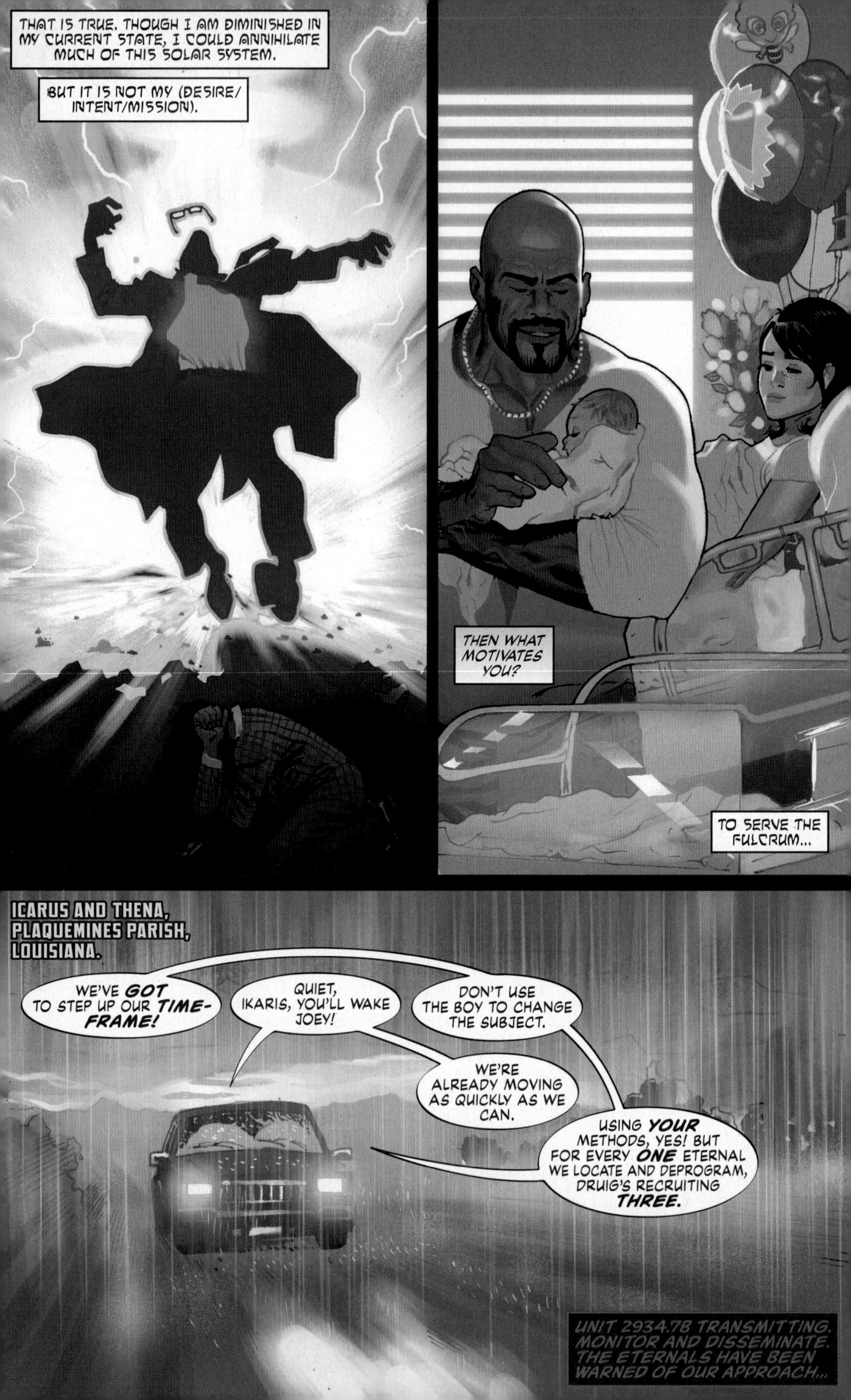
THAT IS TRUE. THOUGH I AM DIMINISHED IN MY CURRENT STATE, I COULD ANNIHILATE MUCH OF THIS SOLAR SYSTEM.
BUT IT IS NOT MY (DESIRE/ INTENT/MISSION).
THEN WHAT MOTIVATES YOU?
TO SERVE THE FULCRUM...
ICARUS AND THENA, PLAQUEMINES PARISH, LOUISIANA.
WE'VE GOT TO STEP UP OUR TIME-FRAME!
QUIET, IKARIS, YOU'LL WAKE JOEY!
DON'T USE THE BOY TO CHANGE THE SUBJECT.
WE'RE ALREADY MOVING AS QUICKLY AS WE CAN.
USING YOUR METHODS, YES! BUT FOR EVERY ONE ETERNAL WE LOCATE AND DEPROGRAM, DRUIG'S RECRUITING THREE.
UNIT 2934.78 TRANSMITTING. MONITOR AND DISSEMINATE. THE ETERNALS HAVE BEEN WARNED OF OUR APPROACH...

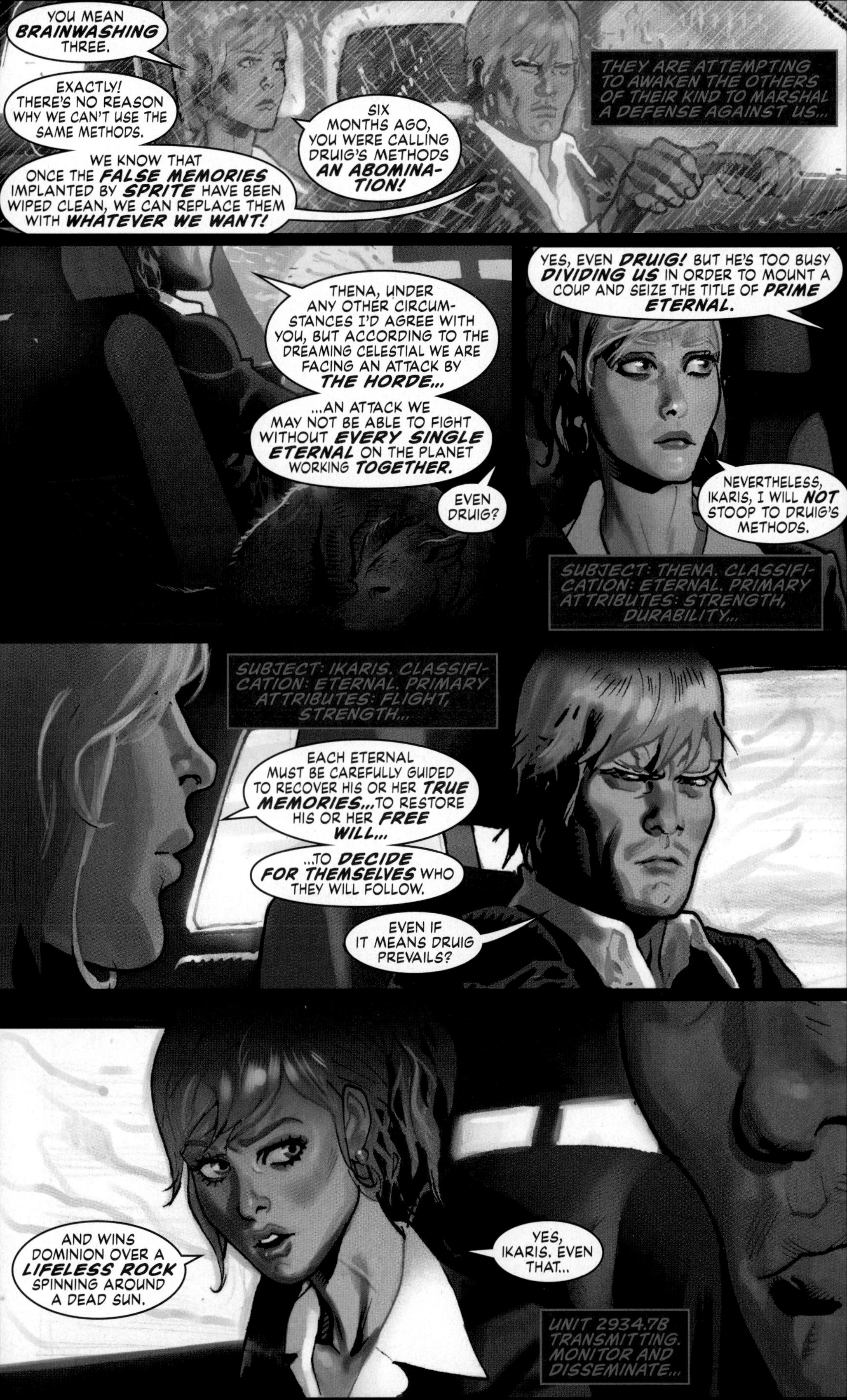
YOU MEAN BRAINWASHING THREE.
EXACTLY! THERE'S NO REASON WHY WE CAN'T USE THE SAME METHODS.
WE KNOW THAT ONCE THE FALSE MEMORIES IMPLANTED BY SPRITE HAVE BEEN WIPED CLEAN, WE CAN REPLACE THEM WITH WHATEVER WE WANT!
SIX MONTHS AGO, YOU WERE CALLING DRUIG'S METHODS AN ABOMINATION!
THEY ARE ATTEMPTING TO AWAKEN THE OTHERS OF THEIR KIND TO MARSHAL A DEFENSE AGAINST US...
THENA, UNDER ANY OTHER CIRCUMSTANCES I'D AGREE WITH YOU, BUT ACCORDING TO THE DREAMING CELESTIAL WE ARE FACING AN ATTACK BY THE HORDE...
...AN ATTACK WE MAY NOT BE ABLE TO FIGHT WITHOUT EVERY SINGLE ETERNAL ON THE PLANET WORKING TOGETHER.
EVEN DRUIG?
YES, EVEN DRUIG! BUT HE'S TOO BUSY DIVIDING US IN ORDER TO MOUNT A COUP AND SEIZE THE TITLE OF PRIME ETERNAL.
NEVERTHELESS, IKARIS, I WILL NOT STOOP TO DRUIG'S METHODS.
SUBJECT: THENA. CLASSIFICATION: ETERNAL. PRIMARY ATTRIBUTES: STRENGTH, DURABILITY...
SUBJECT: IKARIS. CLASSIFICATION: ETERNAL. PRIMARY ATTRIBUTES: FLIGHT, STRENGTH...
EACH ETERNAL MUST BE CAREFULLY GUIDED TO RECOVER HIS OR HER TRUE MEMORIES...TO RESTORE HIS OR HER FREE WILL...
...TO DECIDE FOR THEMSELVES WHO THEY WILL FOLLOW.
EVEN IF IT MEANS DRUIG PREVAILS?
AND WINS DOMINION OVER A LIFELESS ROCK SPINNING AROUND A DEAD SUN.
YES, IKARIS. EVEN THAT...
UNIT 2934.78 TRANSMITTING. MONITOR AND DISSEMINATE...

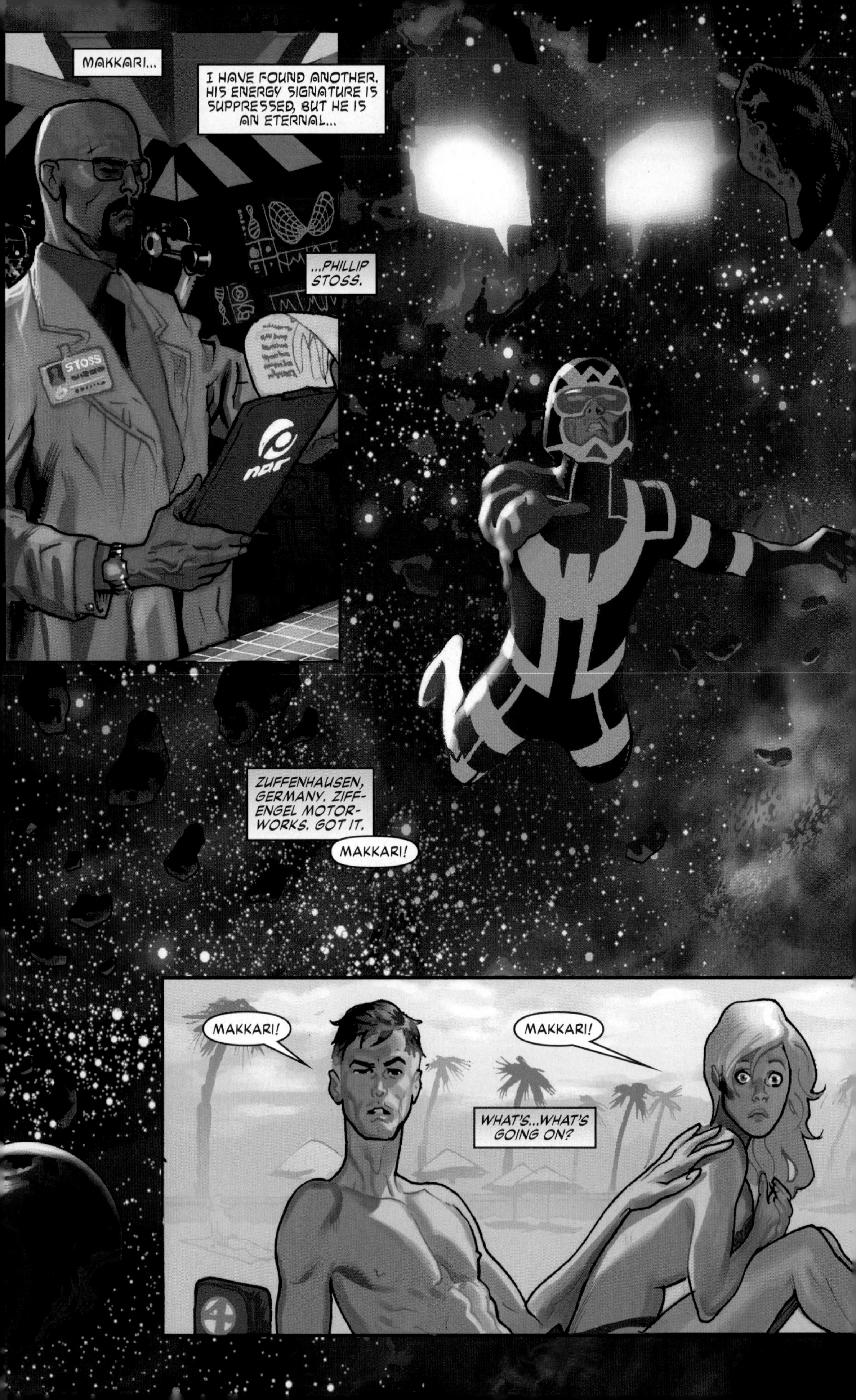
MAKKARI...
I HAVE FOUND ANOTHER. HIS ENERGY SIGNATURE IS SUPPRESSED, BUT HE IS AN ETERNAL...
...PHILLIP STOSS.
STOSS
ZUFFENHAUSEN, GERMANY. ZIFF-ENGEL MOTOR-WORKS. GOT IT.
MAKKARI!
MAKKARI!
MAKKARI!
WHAT'S...WHAT'S GOING ON?

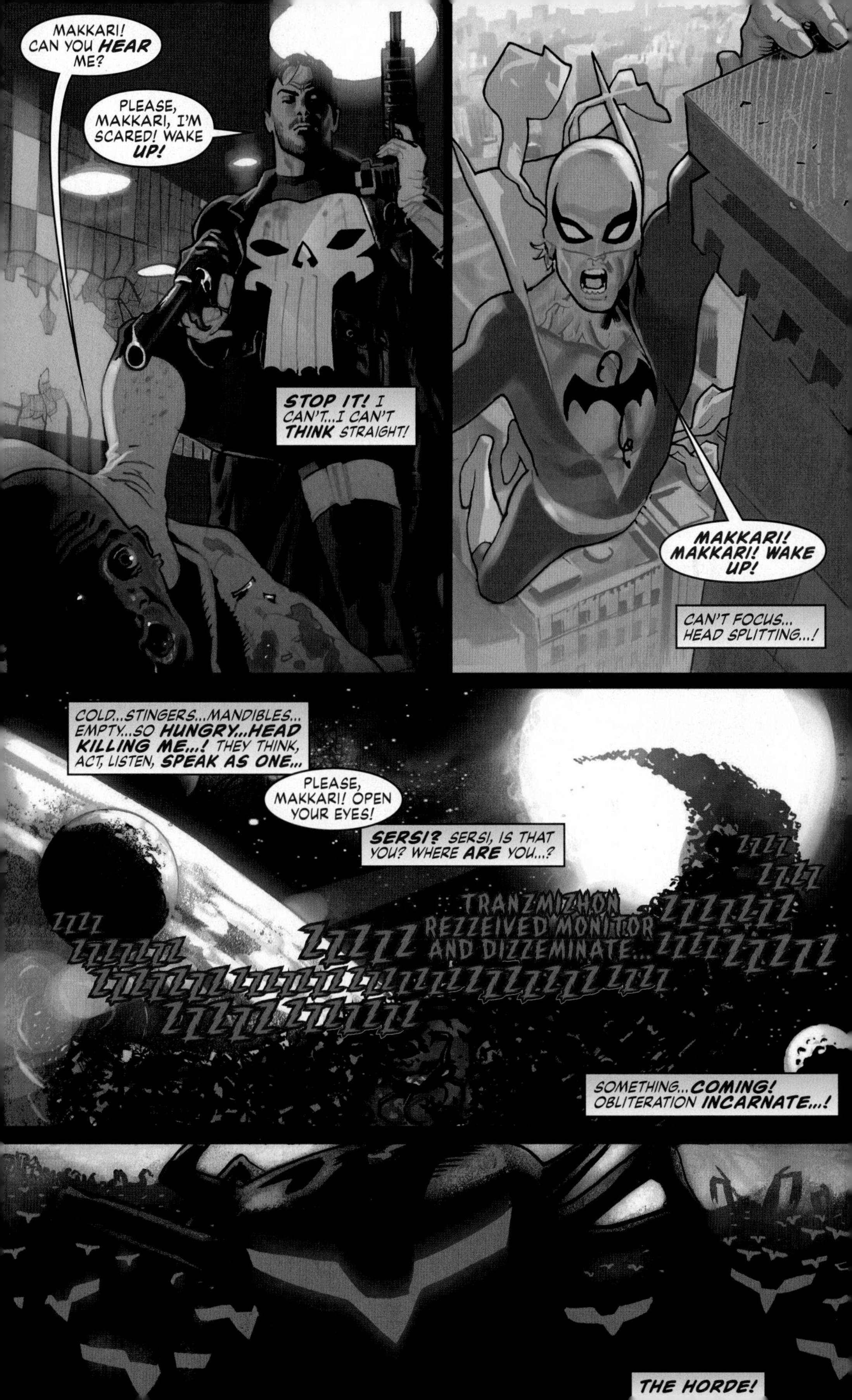
MAKKARI! CAN YOU HEAR ME?
PLEASE, MAKKARI, I'M SCARED! WAKE UP!
STOP IT! I CAN'T...I CAN'T THINK STRAIGHT!
MAKKARI! MAKKARI! WAKE UP!
CAN'T FOCUS... HEAD SPLITTING...!
COLD...STINGERS...MANDIBLES... EMPTY...SO HUNGRY...HEAD KILLING ME...! THEY THINK, ACT, LISTEN, SPEAK AS ONE...
PLEASE, MAKKARI! OPEN YOUR EYES!
SERSI? SERSI, IS THAT YOU? WHERE ARE YOU...?
TRANZMIZHON REZZEIVED MONITOR AND DIZZEMINATE...
SOMETHING...COMING! OBLITERATION INCARNATE...!
THE HORDE!

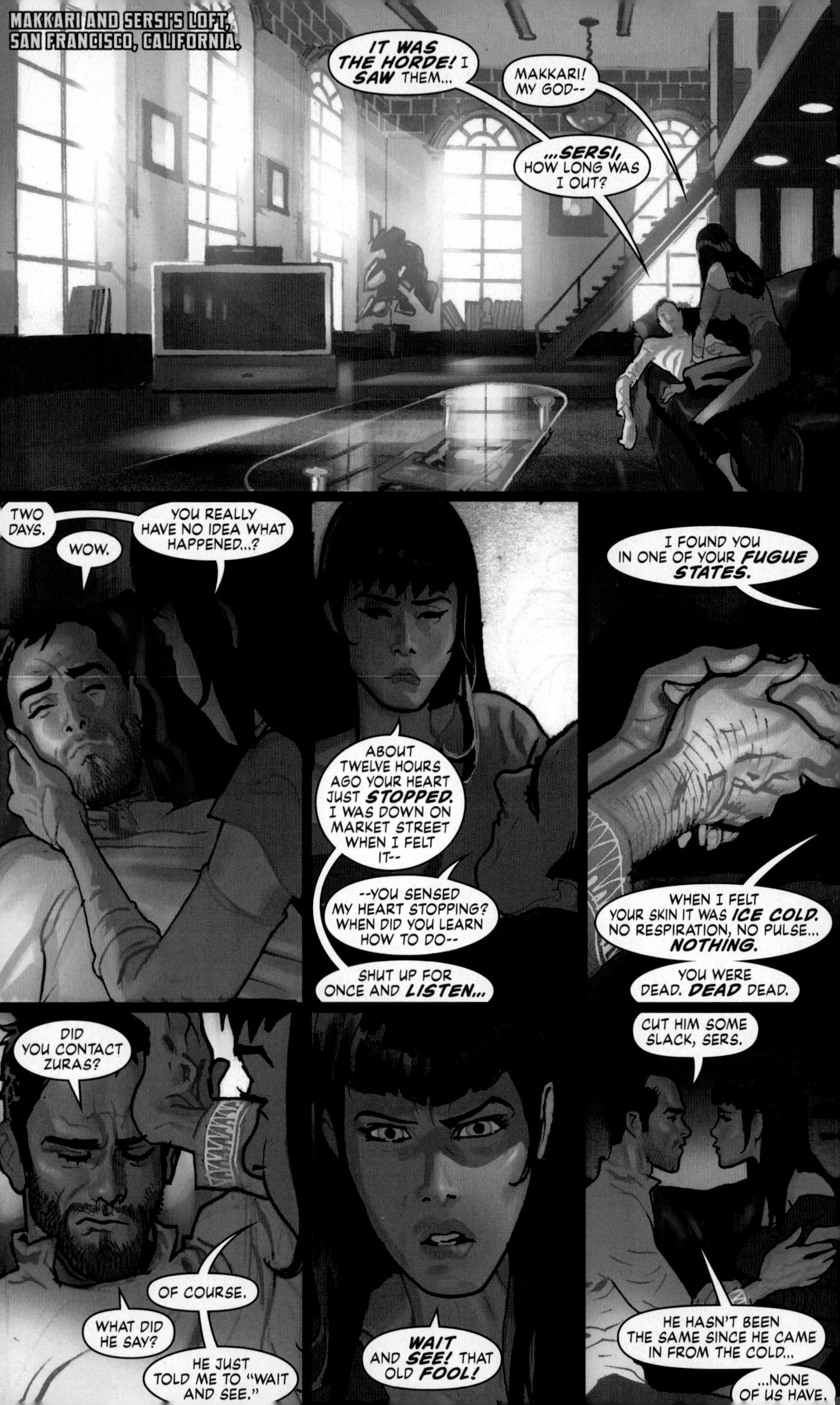
MAKKARI AND SERSI'S LOFT, SAN FRANCISCO, CALIFORNIA.
IT WAS THE HORDE! I SAW THEM...
MAKKARI! MY GOD--
...SERSI, HOW LONG WAS I OUT?
TWO DAYS.
WOW.
YOU REALLY HAVE NO IDEA WHAT HAPPENED...?
ABOUT TWELVE HOURS AGO YOUR HEART JUST STOPPED. I WAS DOWN ON MARKET STREET WHEN I FELT IT--
--YOU SENSED MY HEART STOPPING? WHEN DID YOU LEARN HOW TO DO--
SHUT UP FOR ONCE AND LISTEN...
I FOUND YOU IN ONE OF YOUR FUGUE STATES.
WHEN I FELT YOUR SKIN IT WAS ICE COLD. NO RESPIRATION, NO PULSE... NOTHING.
YOU WERE DEAD. DEAD DEAD.
DID YOU CONTACT ZURAS?
OF COURSE.
WHAT DID HE SAY?
HE JUST TOLD ME TO "WAIT AND SEE."
WAIT AND SEE! THAT OLD FOOL!
CUT HIM SOME SLACK, SERS.
HE HASN'T BEEN THE SAME SINCE HE CAME IN FROM THE COLD...
...NONE OF US HAVE.

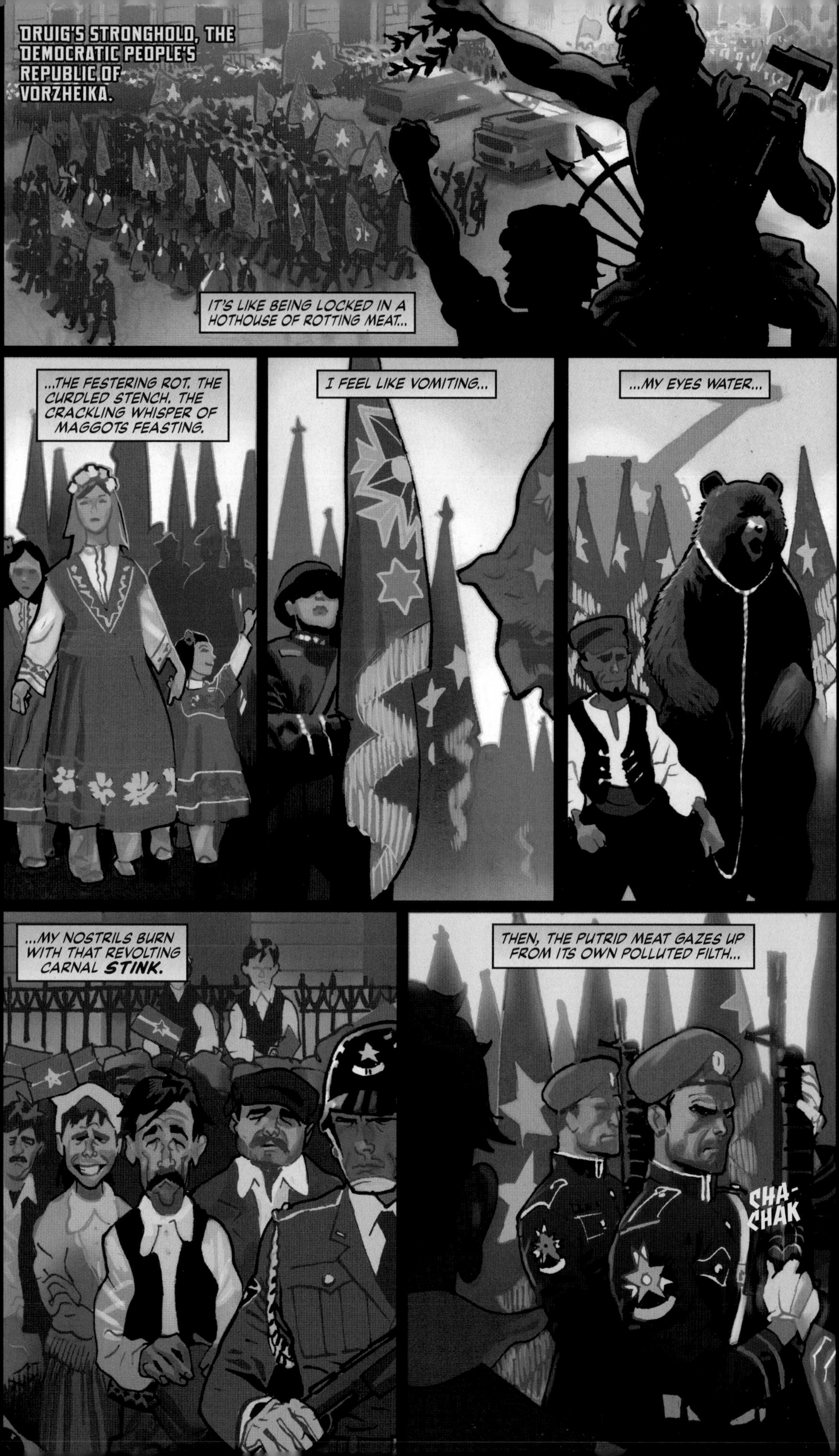
DRUIG'S STRONGHOLD, THE DEMOCRATIC PEOPLE'S REPUBLIC OF VORZHEIKA.
IT'S LIKE BEING LOCKED IN A HOTHOUSE OF ROTTING MEAT...
...THE FESTERING ROT. THE CURDLED STENCH. THE CRACKLING WHISPER OF MAGGOTS FEASTING.
I FEEL LIKE VOMITING...
...MY EYES WATER...
...MY NOSTRILS BURN WITH THAT REVOLTING CARNAL STINK.
THEN, THE PUTRID MEAT GAZES UP FROM ITS OWN POLLUTED FILTH...
SHA-CHAK

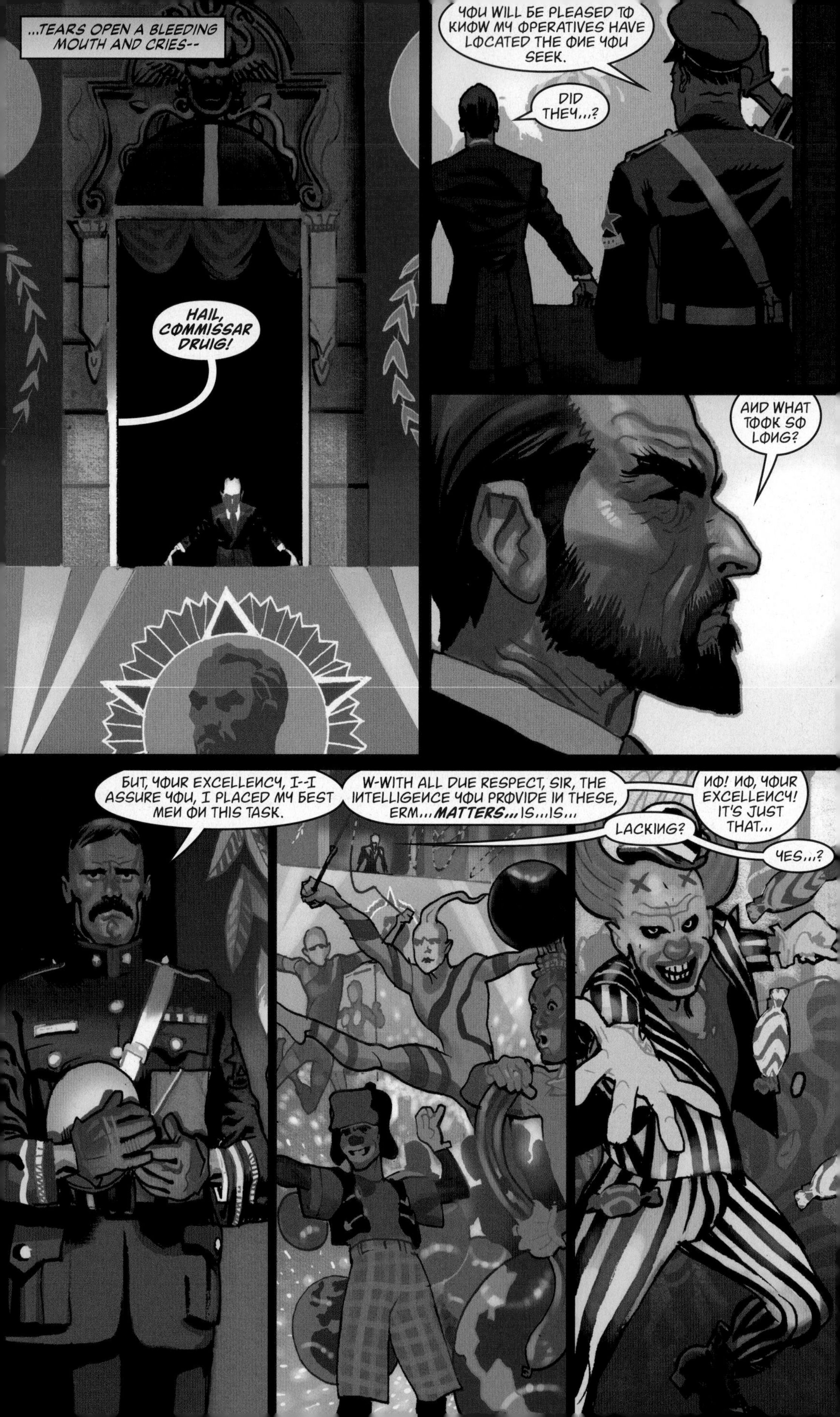
...TEARS OPEN A BLEEDING MOUTH AND CRIES--
HAIL, COMMISSAR DRUIG!
YOU WILL BE PLEASED TO KNOW MY OPERATIVES HAVE LOCATED THE ONE YOU SEEK.
DID THEY...?
AND WHAT TOOK SO LONG?
BUT, YOUR EXCELLENCY, I--I ASSURE YOU, I PLACED MY BEST MEN ON THIS TASK.
W-WITH ALL DUE RESPECT, SIR, THE INTELLIGENCE YOU PROVIDE IN THESE, ERM... **MATTERS...** IS...IS...
LACKING?
NO! NO, YOUR EXCELLENCY! IT'S JUST THAT...
YES...?

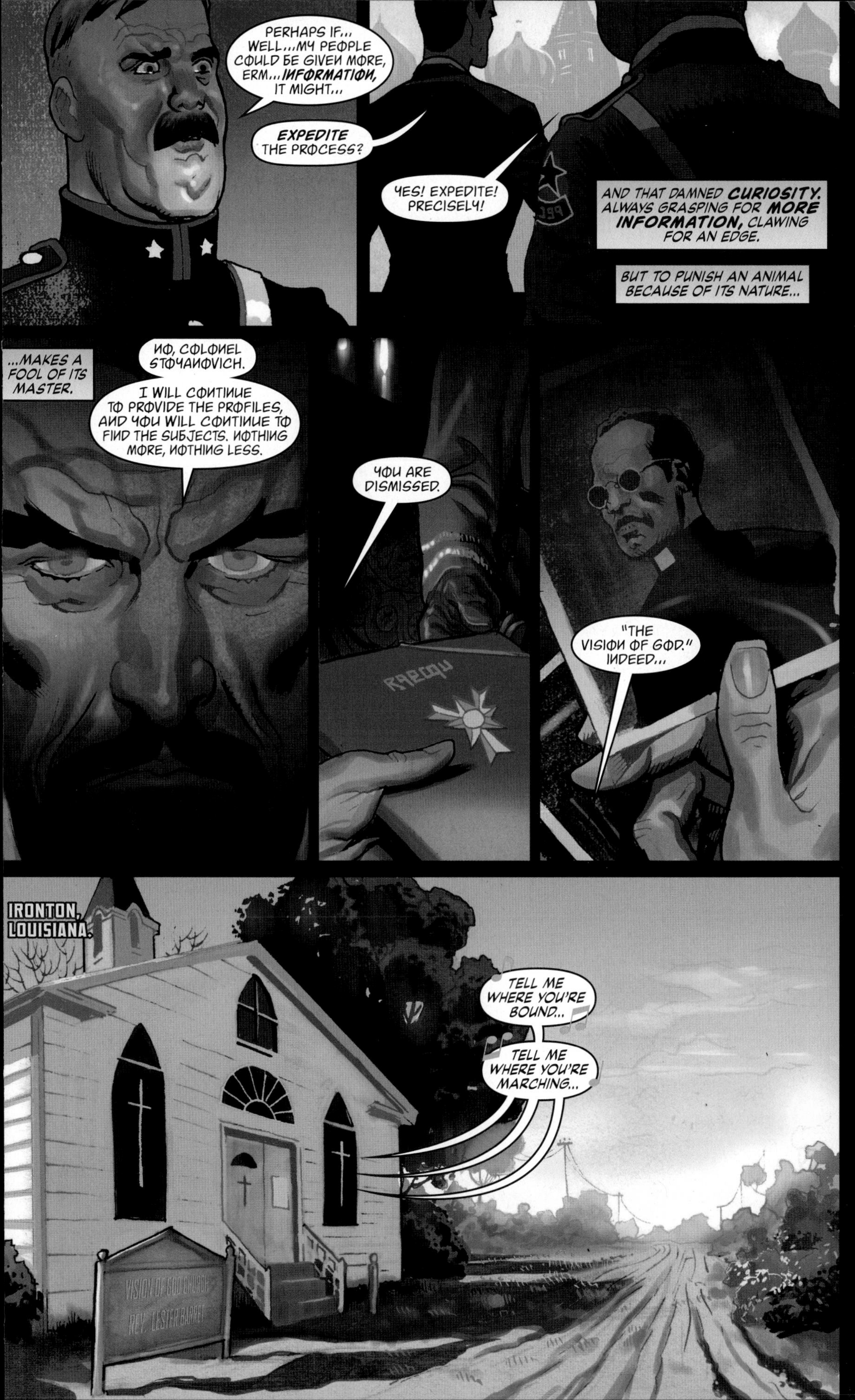

PERHAPS IF... WELL... MY PEOPLE COULD BE GIVEN MORE, ERM... INFORMATION, IT MIGHT...
EXPEDITE THE PROCESS?
YES! EXPEDITE! PRECISELY!
AND THAT DAMNED CURIOSITY. ALWAYS GRASPING FOR MORE INFORMATION, CLAWING FOR AN EDGE.
BUT TO PUNISH AN ANIMAL BECAUSE OF ITS NATURE...
...MAKES A FOOL OF ITS MASTER.
NO, COLONEL STOYANOVICH.
I WILL CONTINUE TO PROVIDE THE PROFILES, AND YOU WILL CONTINUE TO FIND THE SUBJECTS. NOTHING MORE, NOTHING LESS.
YOU ARE DISMISSED.
"THE VISION OF GOD." INDEED...
IRONTON, LOUISIANA.
TELL ME WHERE YOU'RE BOUND...
TELL ME WHERE YOU'RE MARCHING...
VISION OF GOD CHURCH
REV. LESTER BARRET

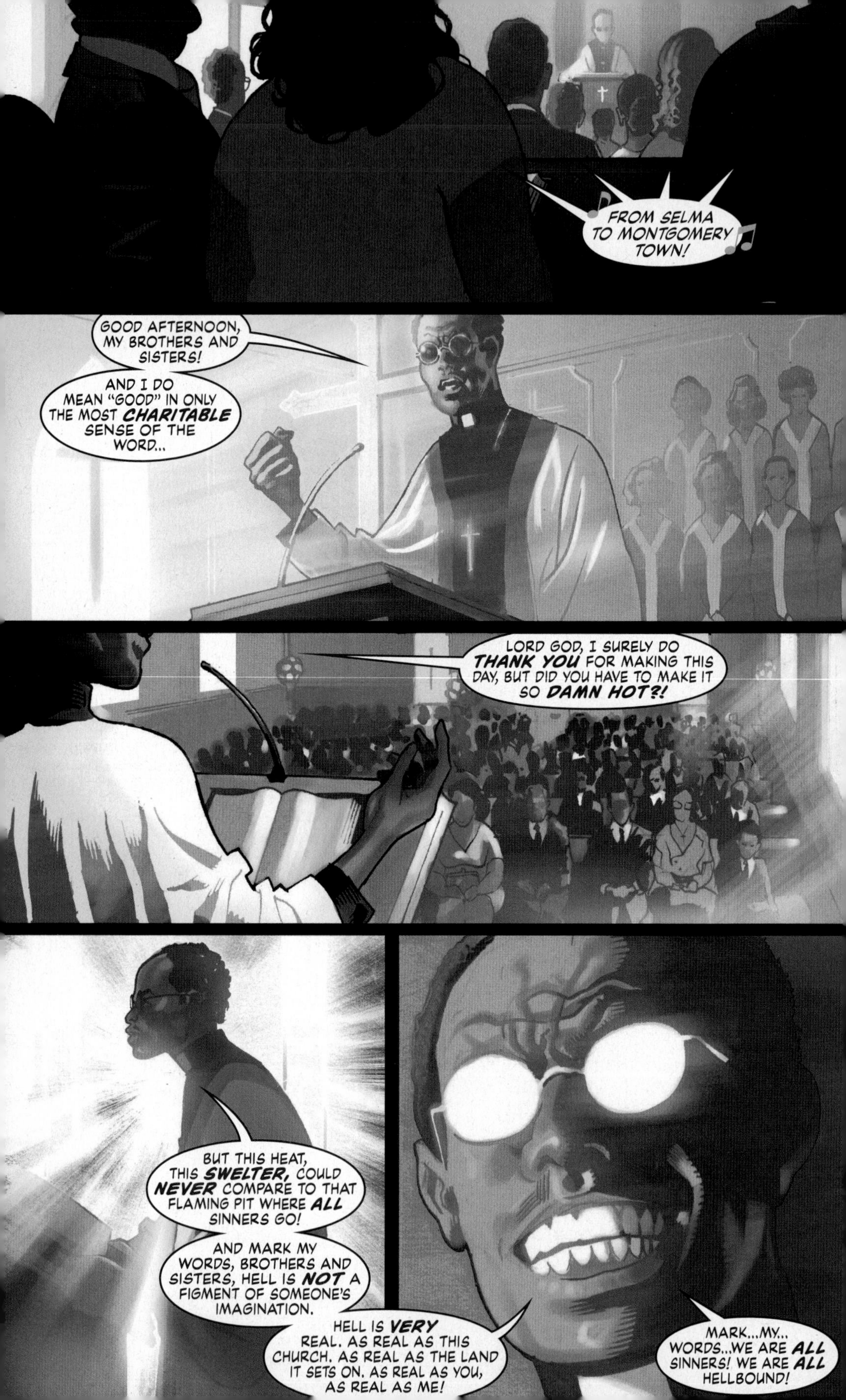
FROM SELMA TO MONTGOMERY TOWN!
GOOD AFTERNOON, MY BROTHERS AND SISTERS!
AND I DO MEAN "GOOD" IN ONLY THE MOST CHARITABLE SENSE OF THE WORD...
LORD GOD, I SURELY DO THANK YOU FOR MAKING THIS DAY, BUT DID YOU HAVE TO MAKE IT SO DAMN HOT?!
BUT THIS HEAT, THIS SWELTER, COULD NEVER COMPARE TO THAT FLAMING PIT WHERE ALL SINNERS GO!
AND MARK MY WORDS, BROTHERS AND SISTERS, HELL IS NOT A FIGMENT OF SOMEONE'S IMAGINATION.
HELL IS VERY REAL. AS REAL AS THIS CHURCH. AS REAL AS THE LAND IT SETS ON. AS REAL AS YOU, AS REAL AS ME!
MARK...MY... WORDS...WE ARE ALL SINNERS! WE ARE ALL HELLBOUND!

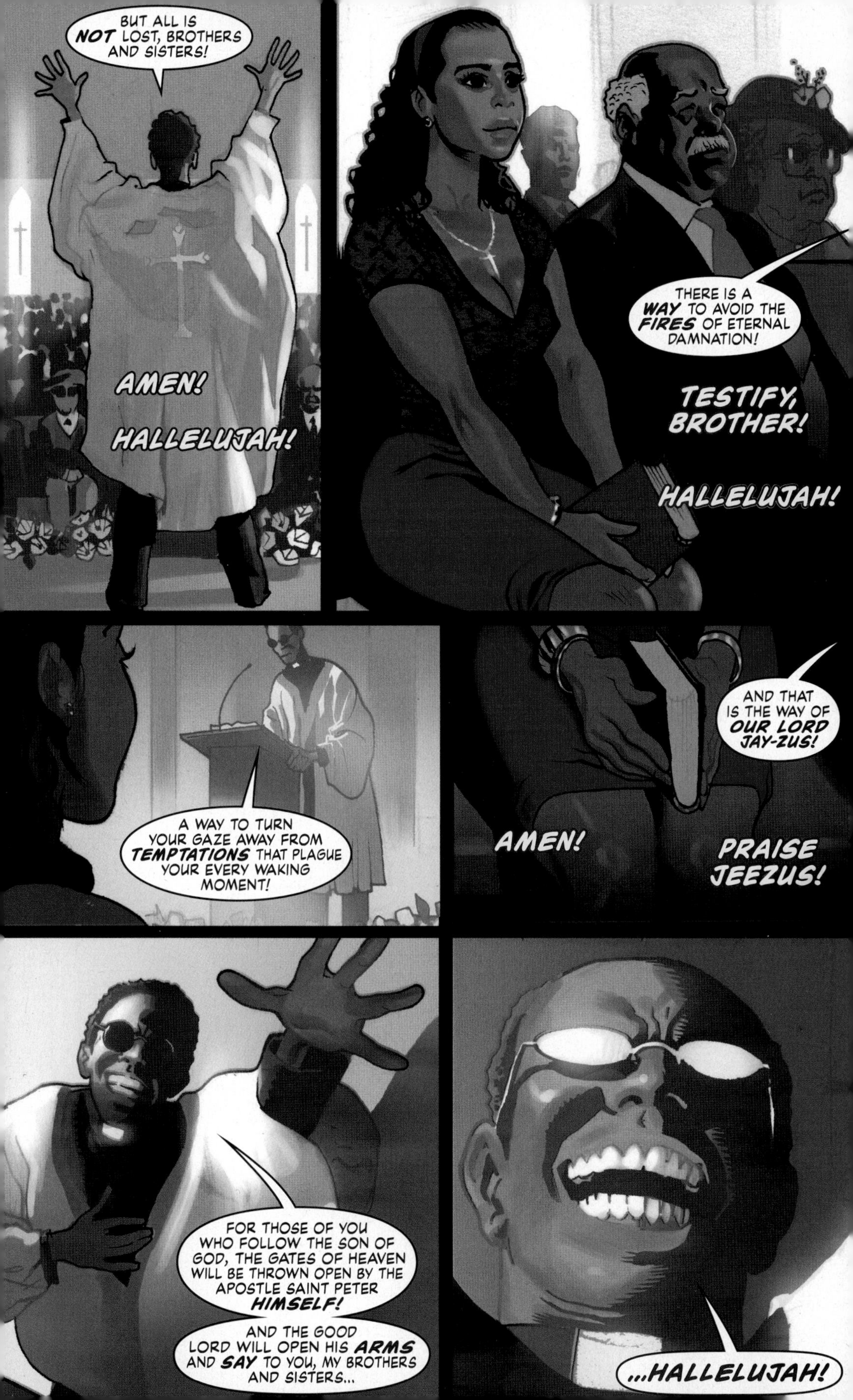

BUT ALL IS NOT LOST, BROTHERS AND SISTERS!
AMEN!
HALLELUJAH!
THERE IS A WAY TO AVOID THE FIRES OF ETERNAL DAMNATION!
TESTIFY, BROTHER!
HALLELUJAH!
A WAY TO TURN YOUR GAZE AWAY FROM TEMPTATIONS THAT PLAGUE YOUR EVERY WAKING MOMENT!
AND THAT IS THE WAY OF OUR LORD JAY-ZUS!
AMEN!
PRAISE JEEZUS!
FOR THOSE OF YOU WHO FOLLOW THE SON OF GOD, THE GATES OF HEAVEN WILL BE THROWN OPEN BY THE APOSTLE SAINT PETER HIMSELF!
AND THE GOOD LORD WILL OPEN HIS ARMS AND SAY TO YOU, MY BROTHERS AND SISTERS...
...HALLELUJAH!

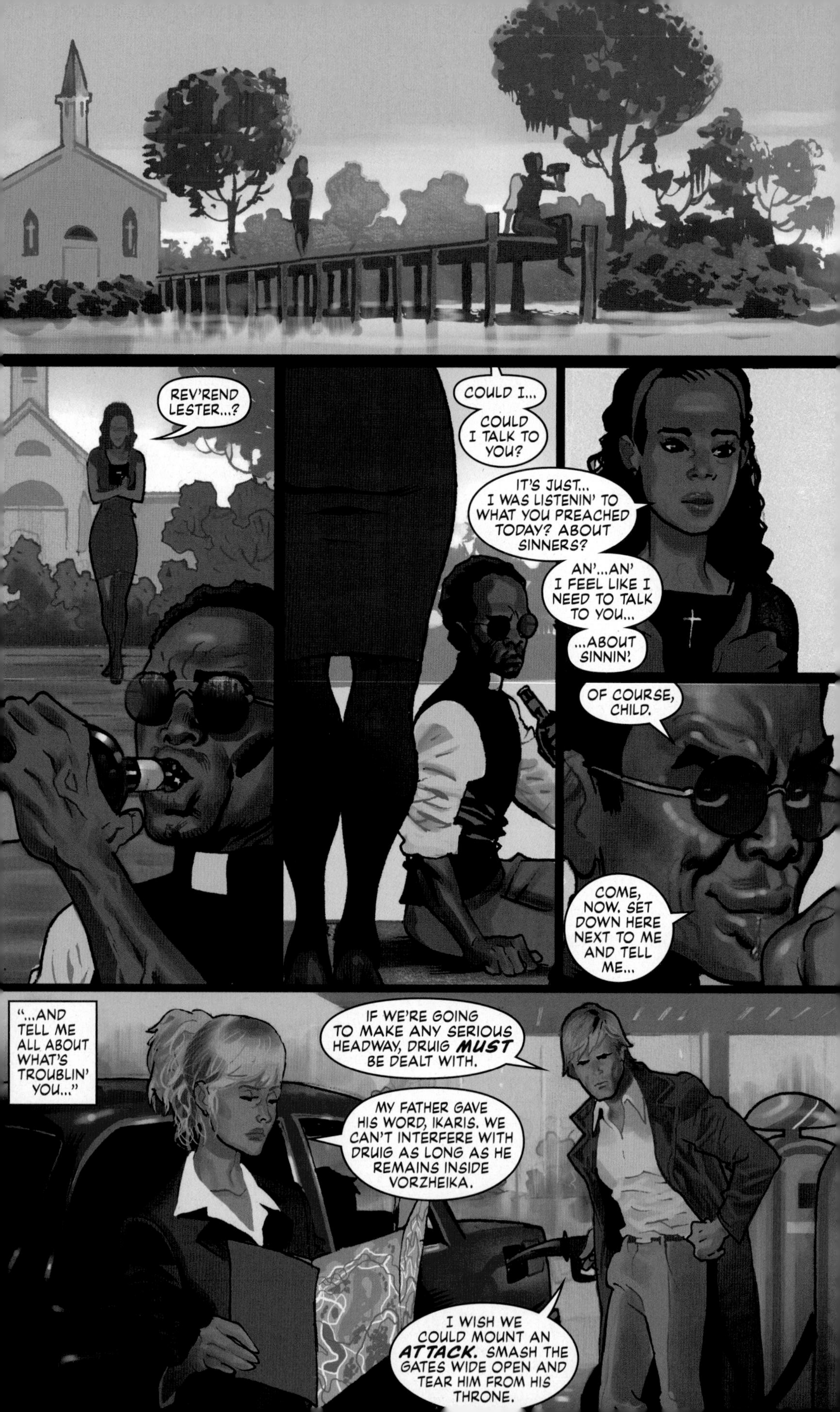
REV'REND LESTER...?
COULD I...
COULD I TALK TO YOU?
IT'S JUST... I WAS LISTENIN' TO WHAT YOU PREACHED TODAY? ABOUT SINNERS?
AN'...AN' I FEEL LIKE I NEED TO TALK TO YOU...
...ABOUT SINNIN'.
OF COURSE, CHILD.
COME, NOW. SET DOWN HERE NEXT TO ME AND TELL ME...
"...AND TELL ME ALL ABOUT WHAT'S TROUBLIN' YOU..."
IF WE'RE GOING TO MAKE ANY SERIOUS HEADWAY, DRUIG MUST BE DEALT WITH.
MY FATHER GAVE HIS WORD, IKARIS. WE CAN'T INTERFERE WITH DRUIG AS LONG AS HE REMAINS INSIDE VORZHEIKA.
I WISH WE COULD MOUNT AN ATTACK. SMASH THE GATES WIDE OPEN AND TEAR HIM FROM HIS THRONE.

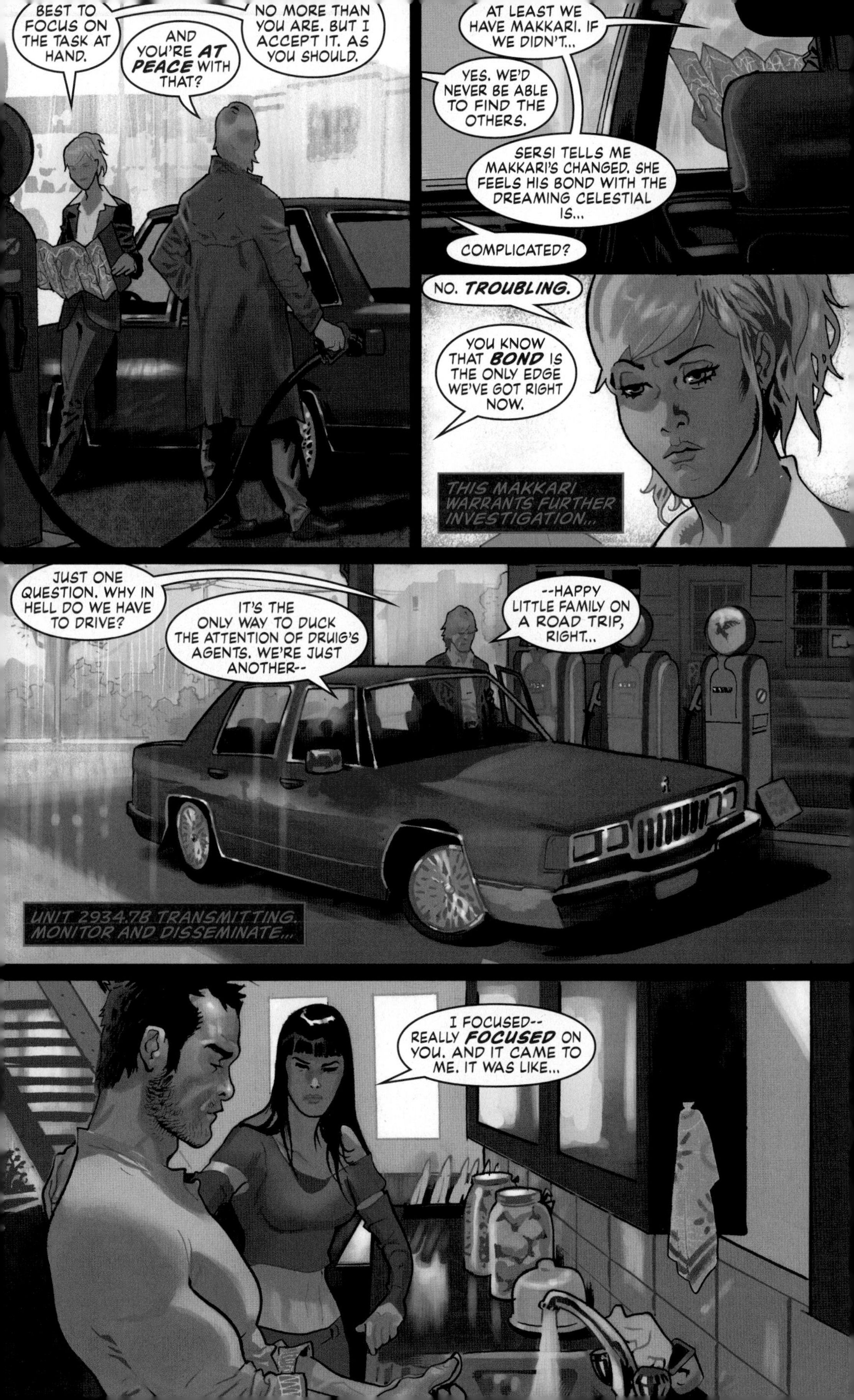
BEST TO FOCUS ON THE TASK AT HAND.
AND YOU'RE AT PEACE WITH THAT?
NO MORE THAN YOU ARE. BUT I ACCEPT IT. AS YOU SHOULD.
AT LEAST WE HAVE MAKKARI. IF WE DIDN'T...
YES. WE'D NEVER BE ABLE TO FIND THE OTHERS.
SERSI TELLS ME MAKKARI'S CHANGED. SHE FEELS HIS BOND WITH THE DREAMING CELESTIAL IS...
COMPLICATED?
NO. TROUBLING.
YOU KNOW THAT BOND IS THE ONLY EDGE WE'VE GOT RIGHT NOW.
THIS MAKKARI WARRANTS FURTHER INVESTIGATION...
JUST ONE QUESTION. WHY IN HELL DO WE HAVE TO DRIVE?
IT'S THE ONLY WAY TO DUCK THE ATTENTION OF DRUIG'S AGENTS. WE'RE JUST ANOTHER--
--HAPPY LITTLE FAMILY ON A ROAD TRIP, RIGHT...
UNIT 2934.78 TRANSMITTING. MONITOR AND DISSEMINATE...
I FOCUSED-- REALLY FOCUSED ON YOU. AND IT CAME TO ME. IT WAS LIKE...

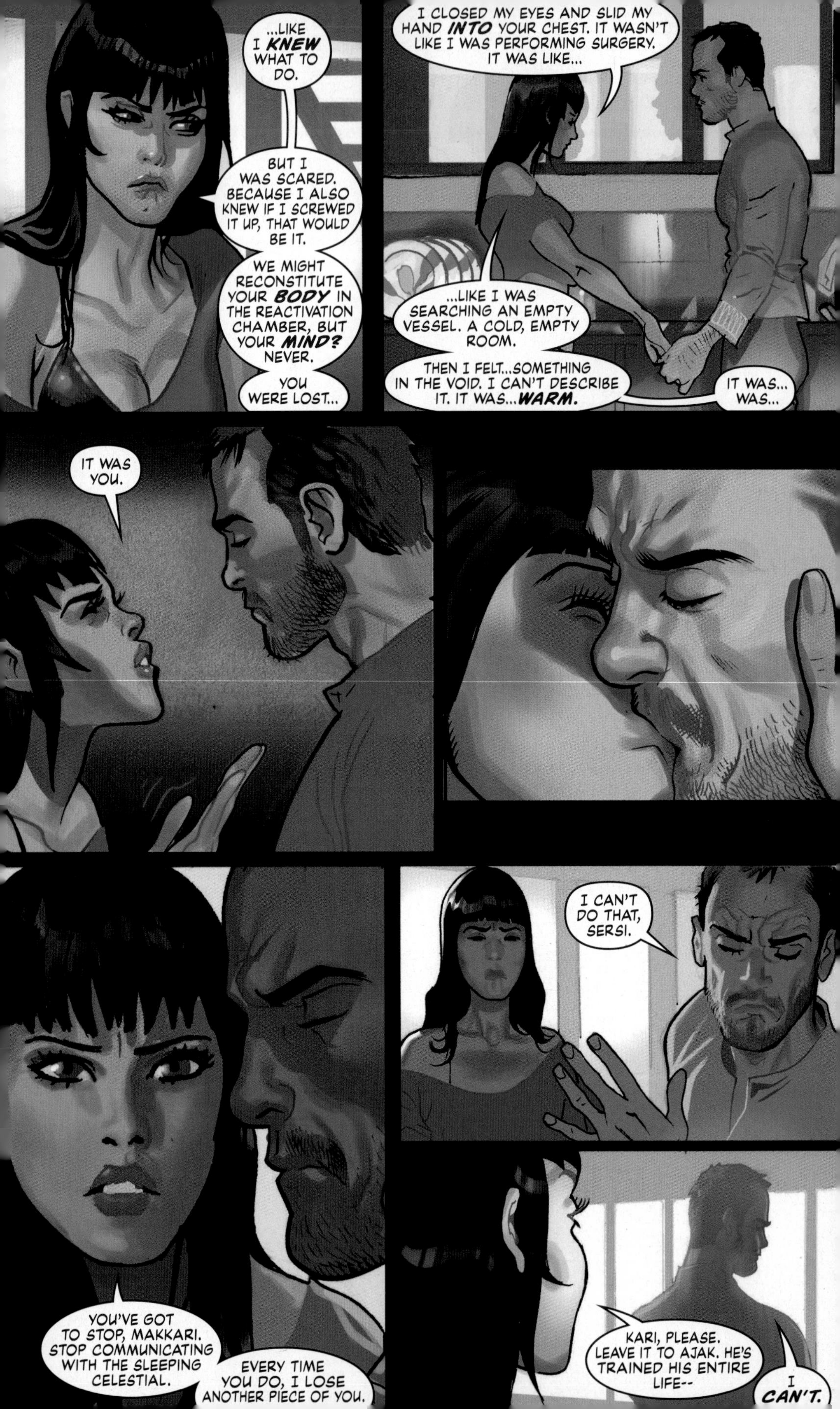
...LIKE I KNEW WHAT TO DO.
BUT I WAS SCARED. BECAUSE I ALSO KNEW IF I SCREWED IT UP, THAT WOULD BE IT.
WE MIGHT RECONSTITUTE YOUR BODY IN THE REACTIVATION CHAMBER, BUT YOUR MIND? NEVER.
YOU WERE LOST...
I CLOSED MY EYES AND SLID MY HAND INTO YOUR CHEST. IT WASN'T LIKE I WAS PERFORMING SURGERY. IT WAS LIKE...
...LIKE I WAS SEARCHING AN EMPTY VESSEL. A COLD, EMPTY ROOM.
THEN I FELT...SOMETHING IN THE VOID. I CAN'T DESCRIBE IT. IT WAS...WARM.
IT WAS... WAS...
IT WAS YOU.
YOU'VE GOT TO STOP, MAKKARI. STOP COMMUNICATING WITH THE SLEEPING CELESTIAL.
EVERY TIME YOU DO, I LOSE ANOTHER PIECE OF YOU.
I CAN'T DO THAT, SERSI.
KARI, PLEASE. LEAVE IT TO AJAK. HE'S TRAINED HIS ENTIRE LIFE--
I CAN'T.

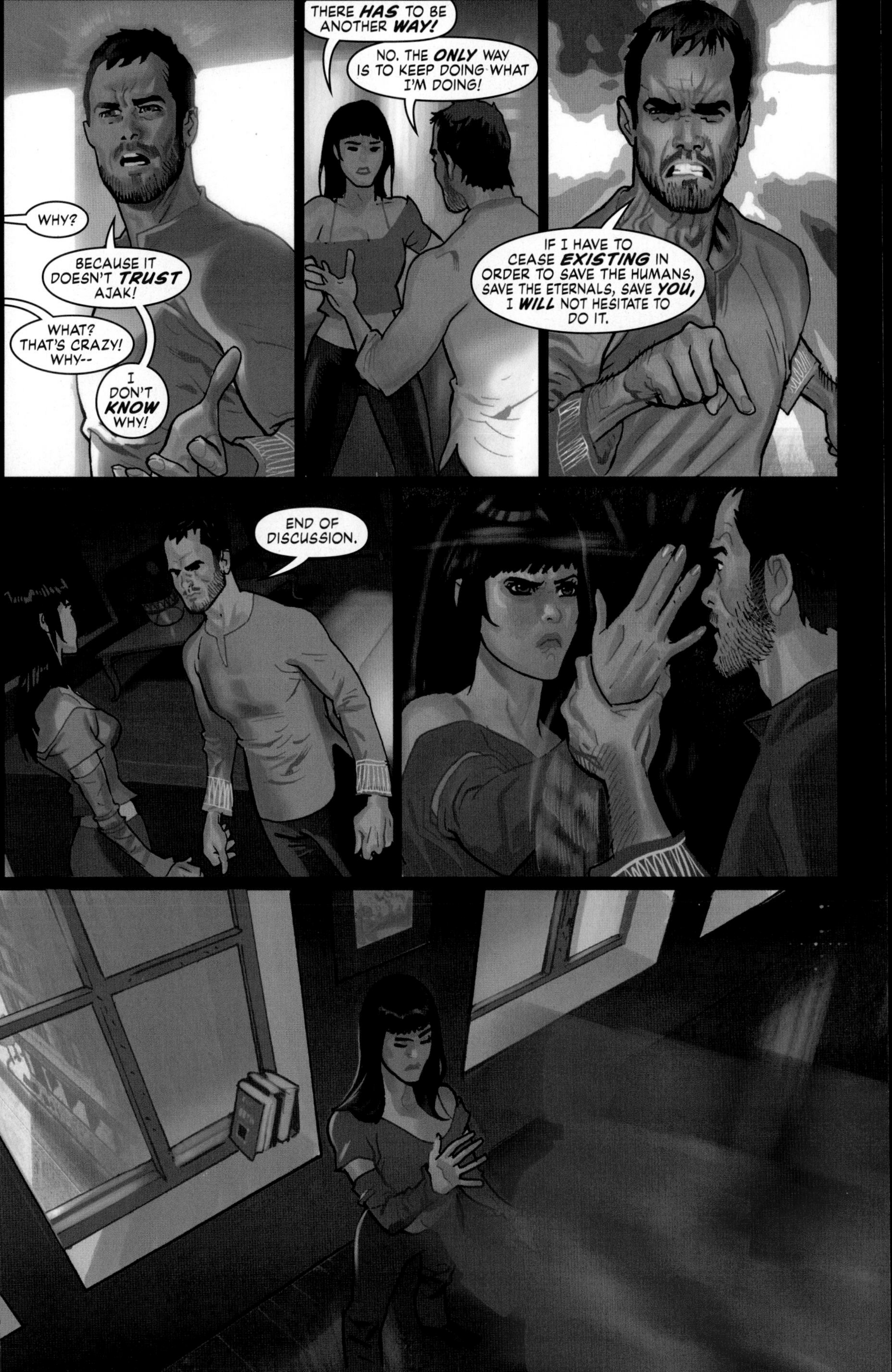
WHY?
BECAUSE IT DOESN'T TRUST AJAK!
WHAT? THAT'S CRAZY! WHY--
I DON'T KNOW WHY!
THERE HAS TO BE ANOTHER WAY!
NO. THE ONLY WAY IS TO KEEP DOING WHAT I'M DOING!
IF I HAVE TO CEASE EXISTING IN ORDER TO SAVE THE HUMANS, SAVE THE ETERNALS, SAVE YOU, I WILL NOT HESITATE TO DO IT.
END OF DISCUSSION.

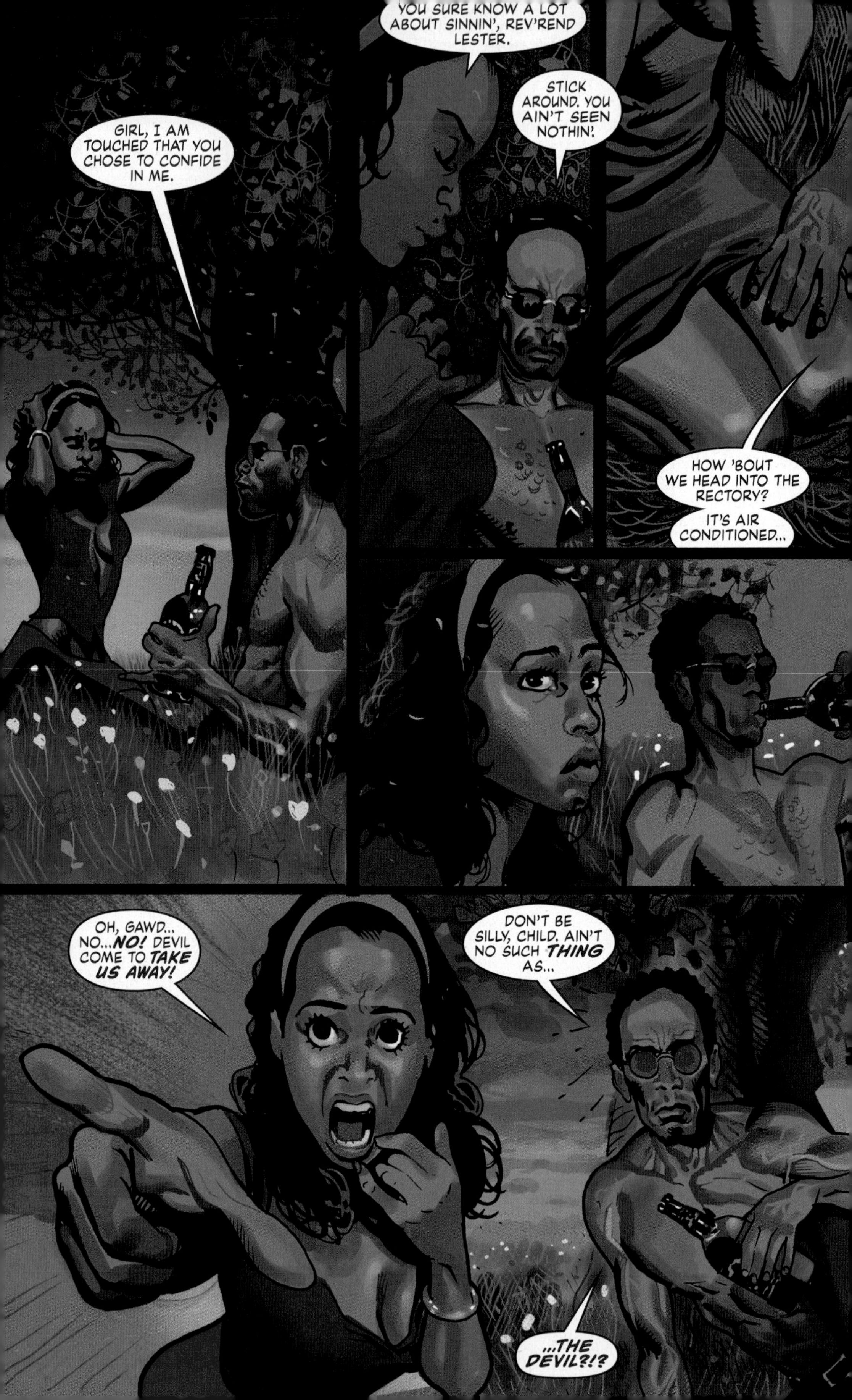
GIRL, I AM TOUCHED THAT YOU CHOSE TO CONFIDE IN ME.
YOU SURE KNOW A LOT ABOUT SINNIN', REV'REND LESTER.
STICK AROUND. YOU AIN'T SEEN NOTHIN'.
HOW 'BOUT WE HEAD INTO THE RECTORY?
IT'S AIR CONDITIONED...
OH, GAWD... NO...**NO!** DEVIL COME TO **TAKE US AWAY!**
DON'T BE SILLY, CHILD. AIN'T NO SUCH **THING** AS...
...THE DEVIL?!?

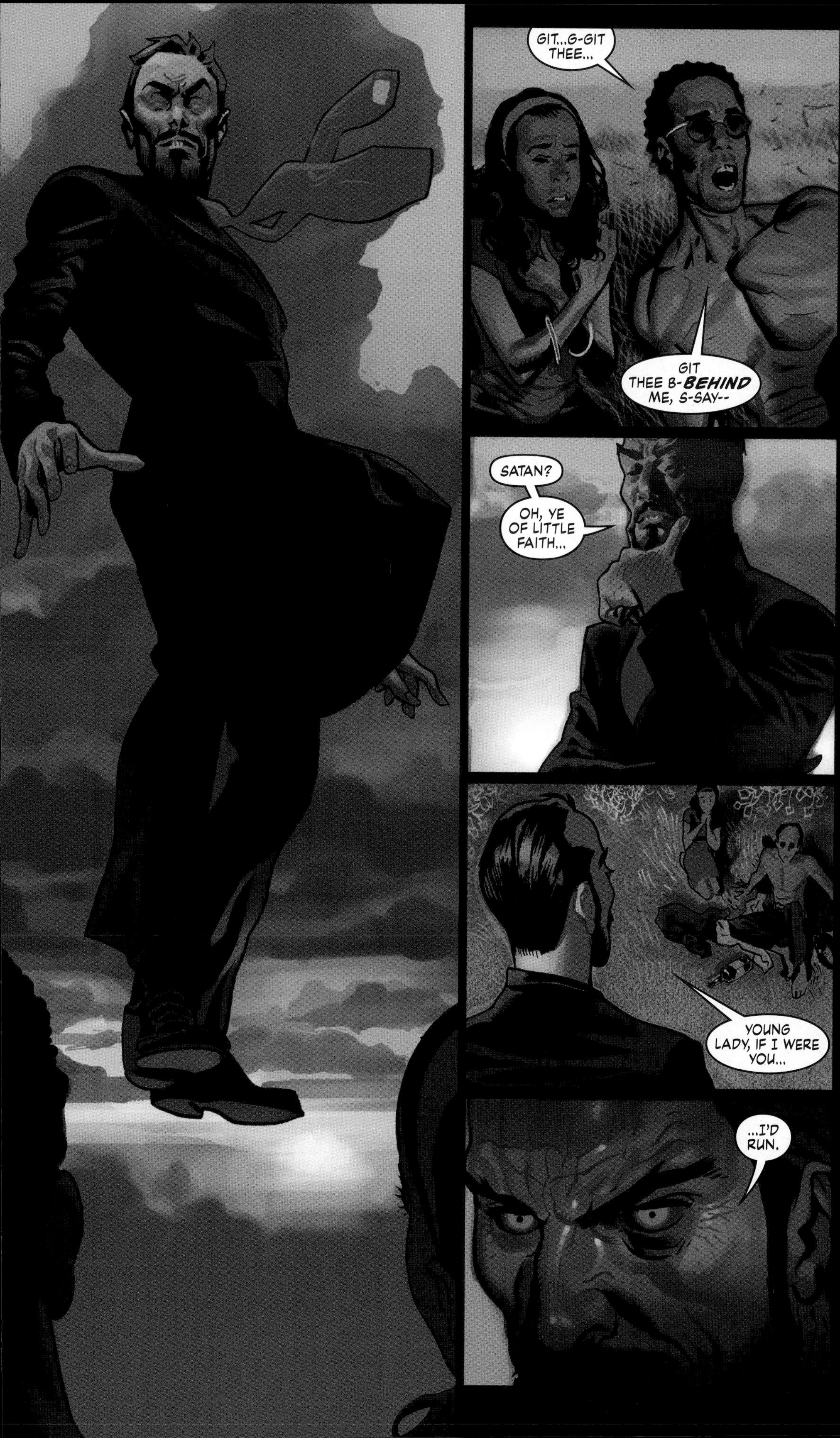
GIT...G-GIT THEE...
GIT THEE B-**BEHIND** ME, S-SAY--
SATAN?
OH, YE OF LITTLE FAITH...
YOUNG LADY, IF I WERE YOU...
...I'D RUN.

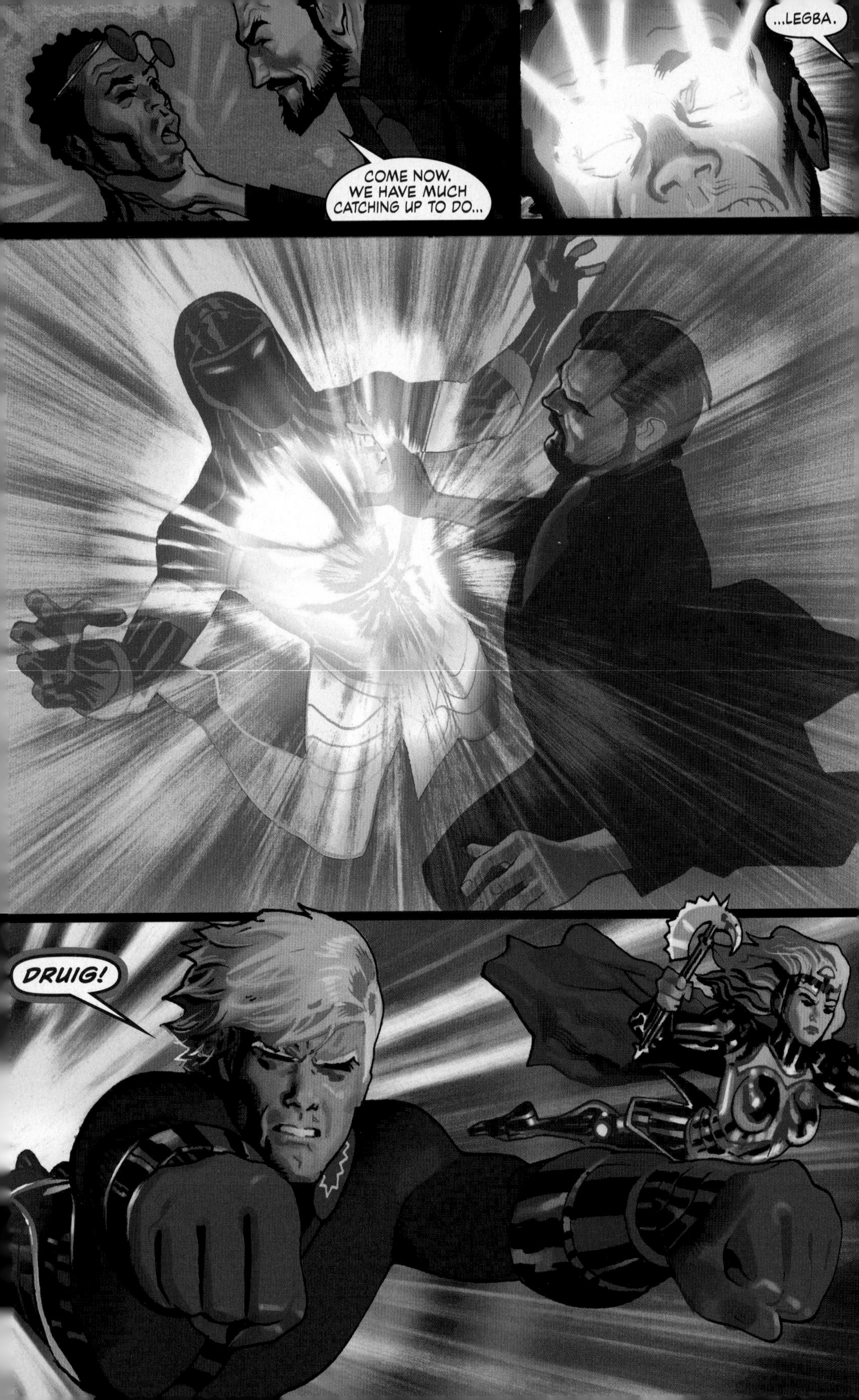
COME NOW. WE HAVE MUCH CATCHING UP TO DO...
...LEGBA.
DRUIG!

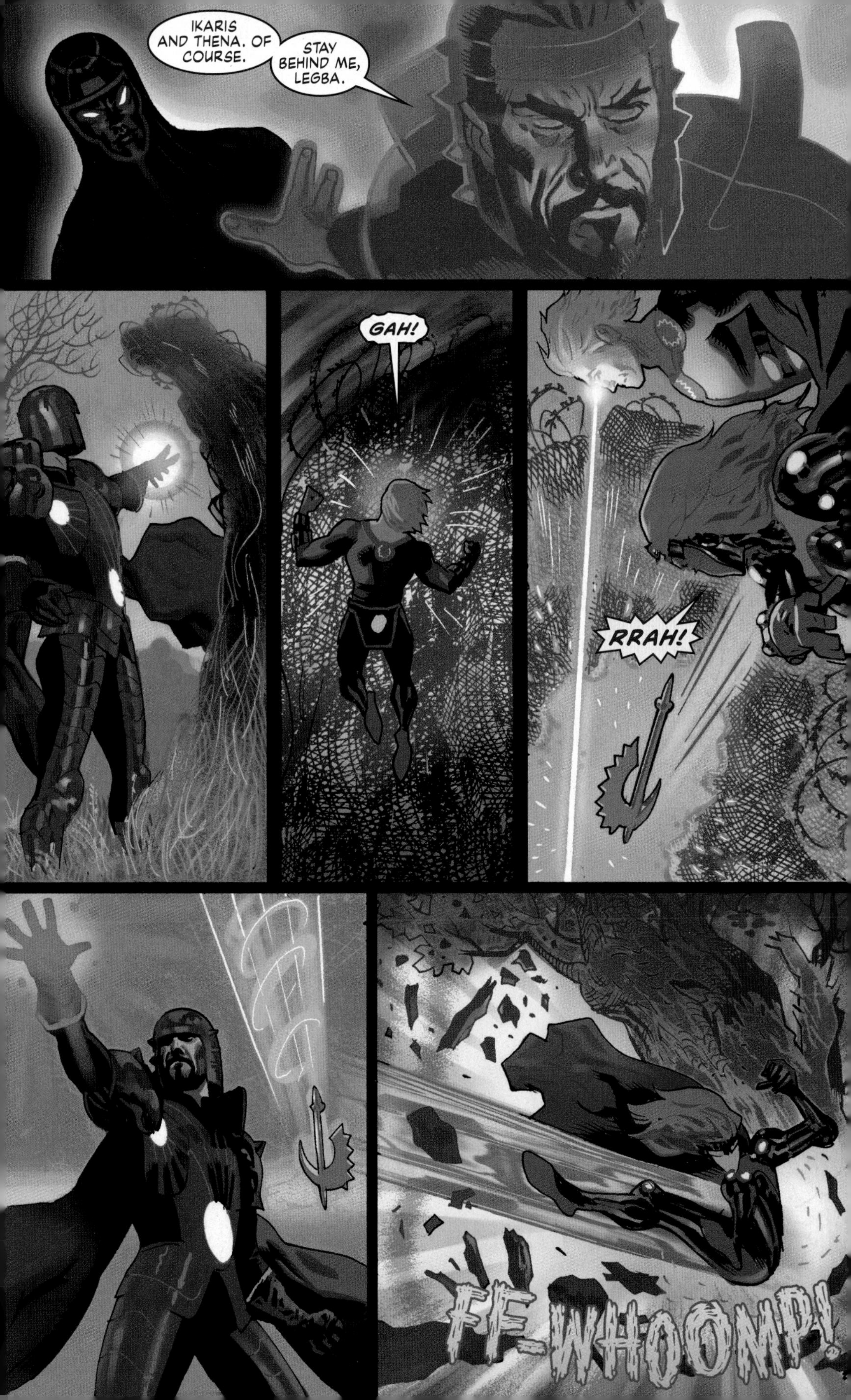
IKARIS AND THENA. OF COURSE.
STAY BEHIND ME, LEGBA.
GAH!
RRAH!
FF-WHOOMP!

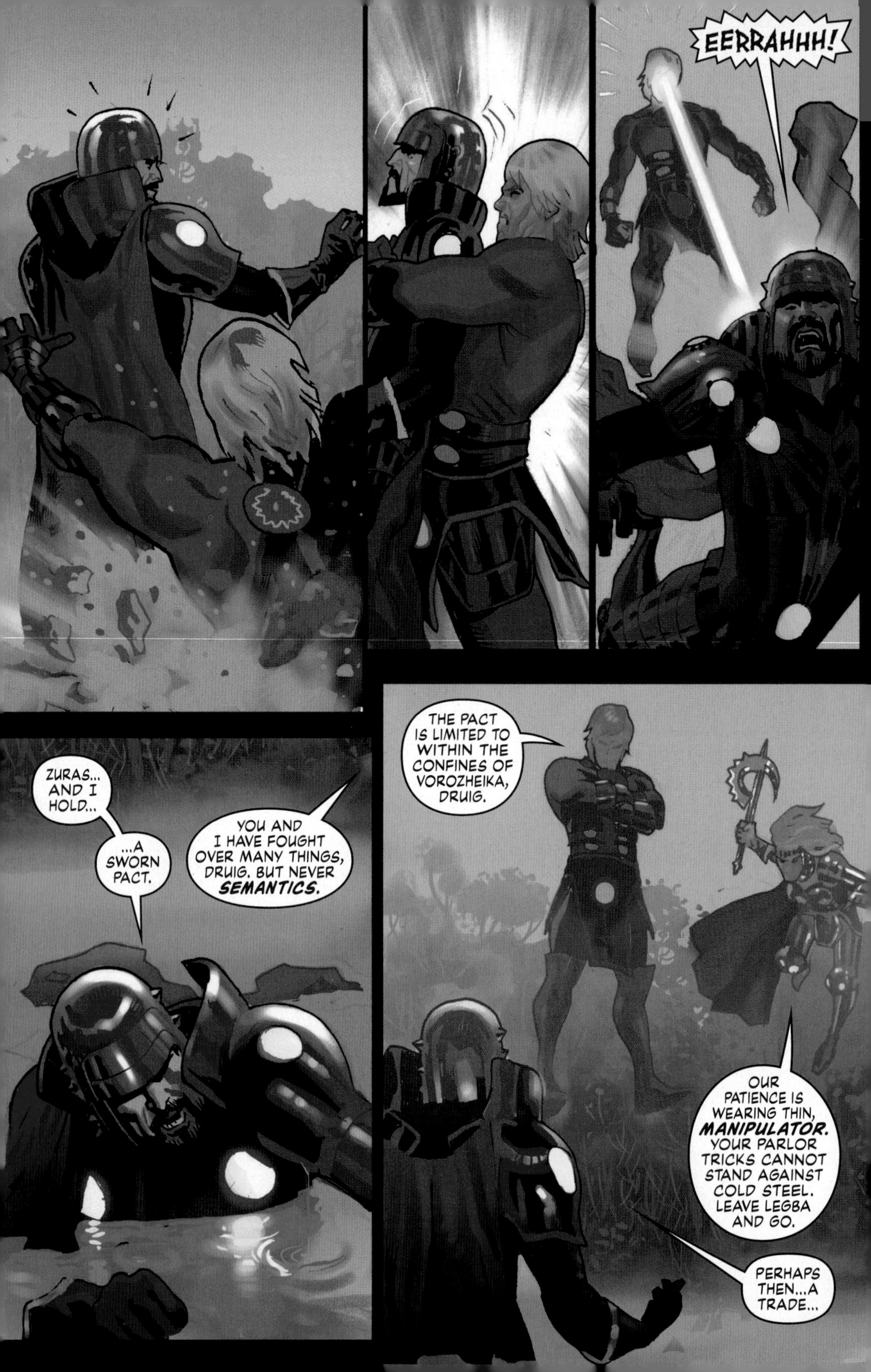
EERRAHHH!
ZURAS... AND I HOLD...
...A SWORN PACT.
YOU AND I HAVE FOUGHT OVER MANY THINGS, DRUIG. BUT NEVER SEMANTICS.
THE PACT IS LIMITED TO WITHIN THE CONFINES OF VOROZHEIKA, DRUIG.
OUR PATIENCE IS WEARING THIN, MANIPULATOR. YOUR PARLOR TRICKS CANNOT STAND AGAINST COLD STEEL. LEAVE LEGBA AND GO.
PERHAPS THEN...A TRADE...

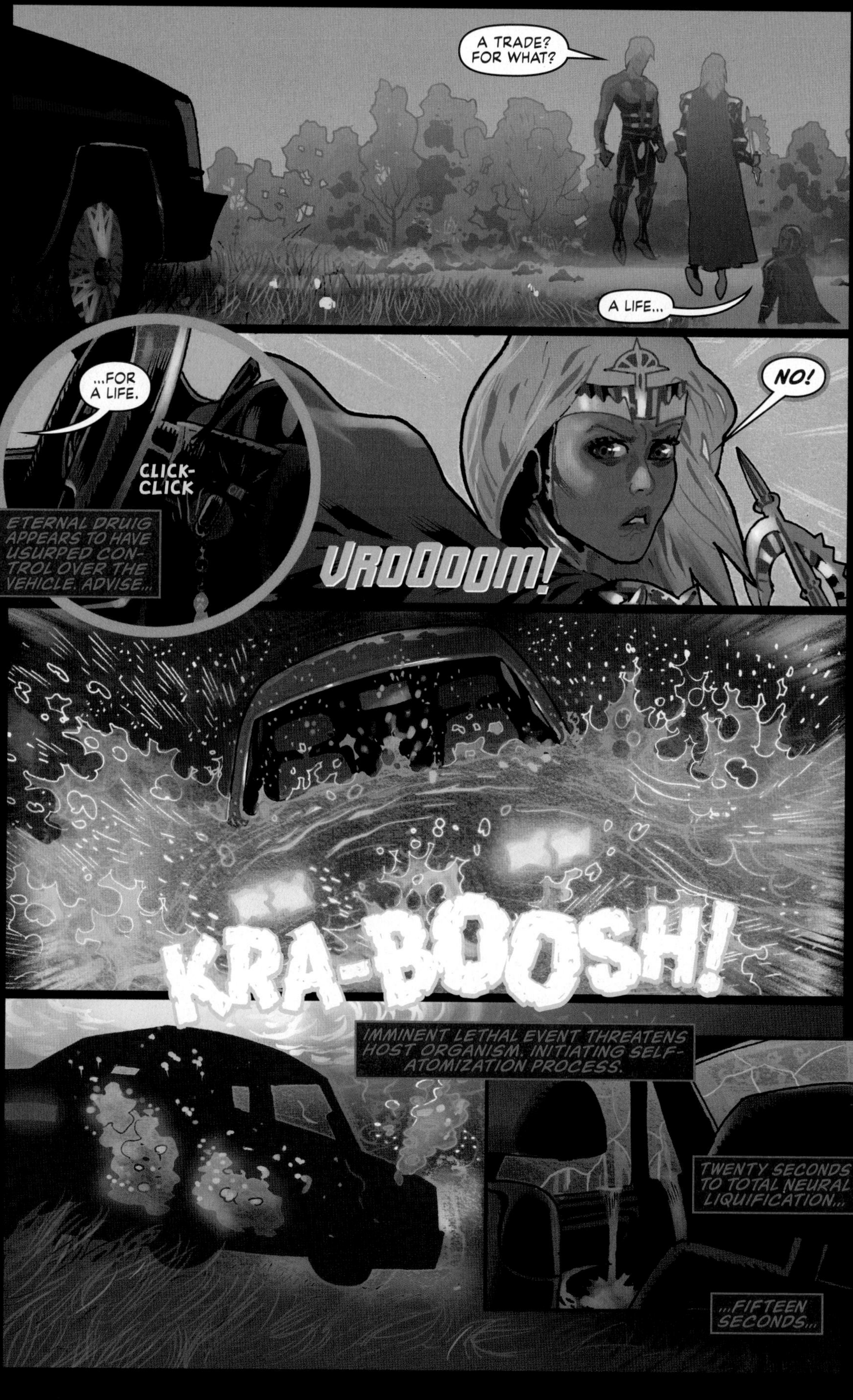
A TRADE? FOR WHAT?
A LIFE...
...FOR A LIFE.
CLICK-CLICK
ETERNAL DRUIG APPEARS TO HAVE USURPED CONTROL OVER THE VEHICLE. ADVISE...
NO!
VROOOOOM!
KRA-BOOSH!
IMMINENT LETHAL EVENT THREATENS HOST ORGANISM. INITIATING SELF-ATOMIZATION PROCESS.
TWENTY SECONDS TO TOTAL NEURAL LIQUIFICATION...
...FIFTEEN SECONDS...

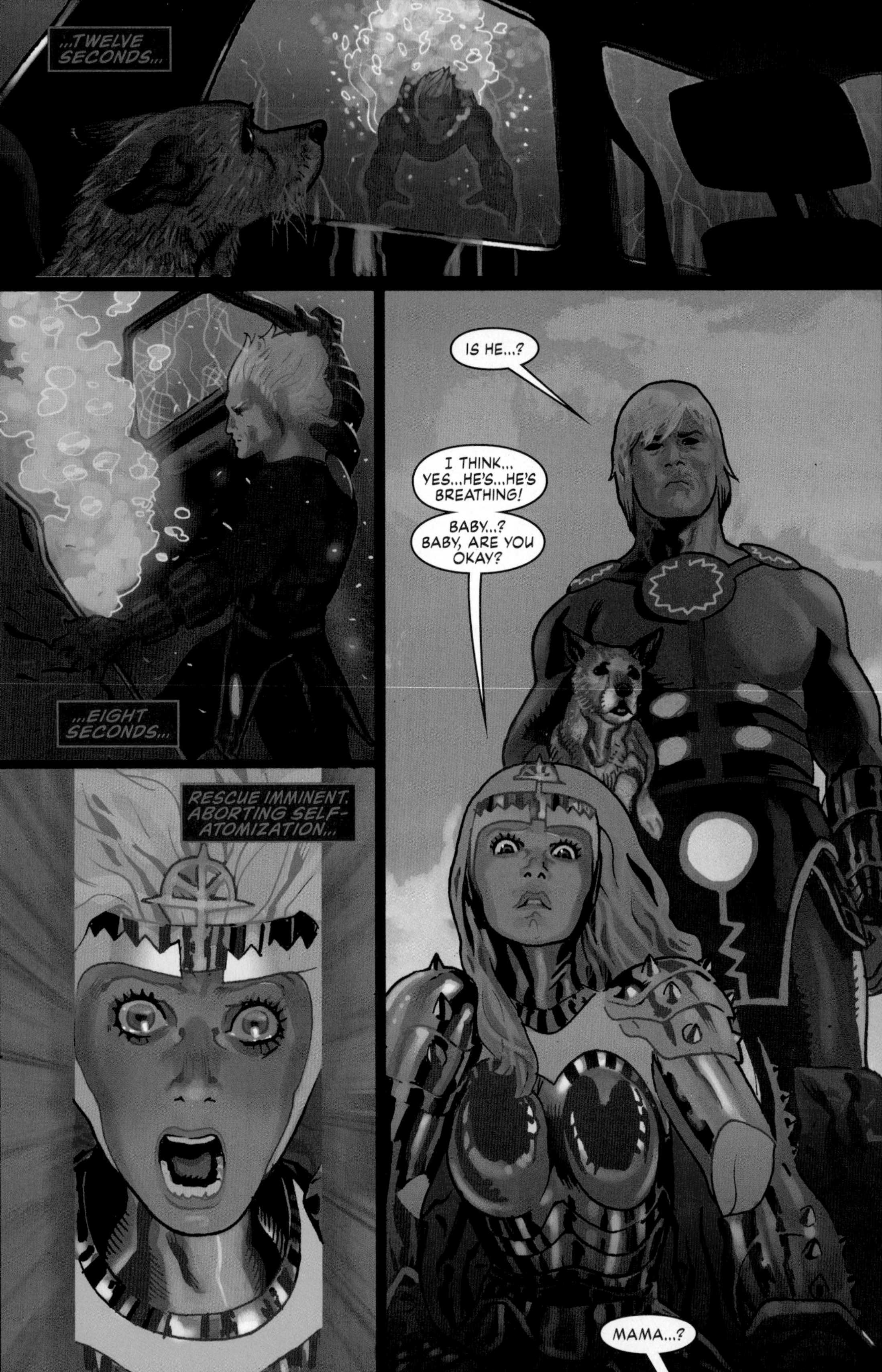
...TWELVE SECONDS...
...EIGHT SECONDS...
RESCUE IMMINENT. ABORTING SELF-ATOMIZATION...
IS HE...?
I THINK... YES...HE'S...HE'S BREATHING!
BABY...? BABY, ARE YOU OKAY?
MAMA...?

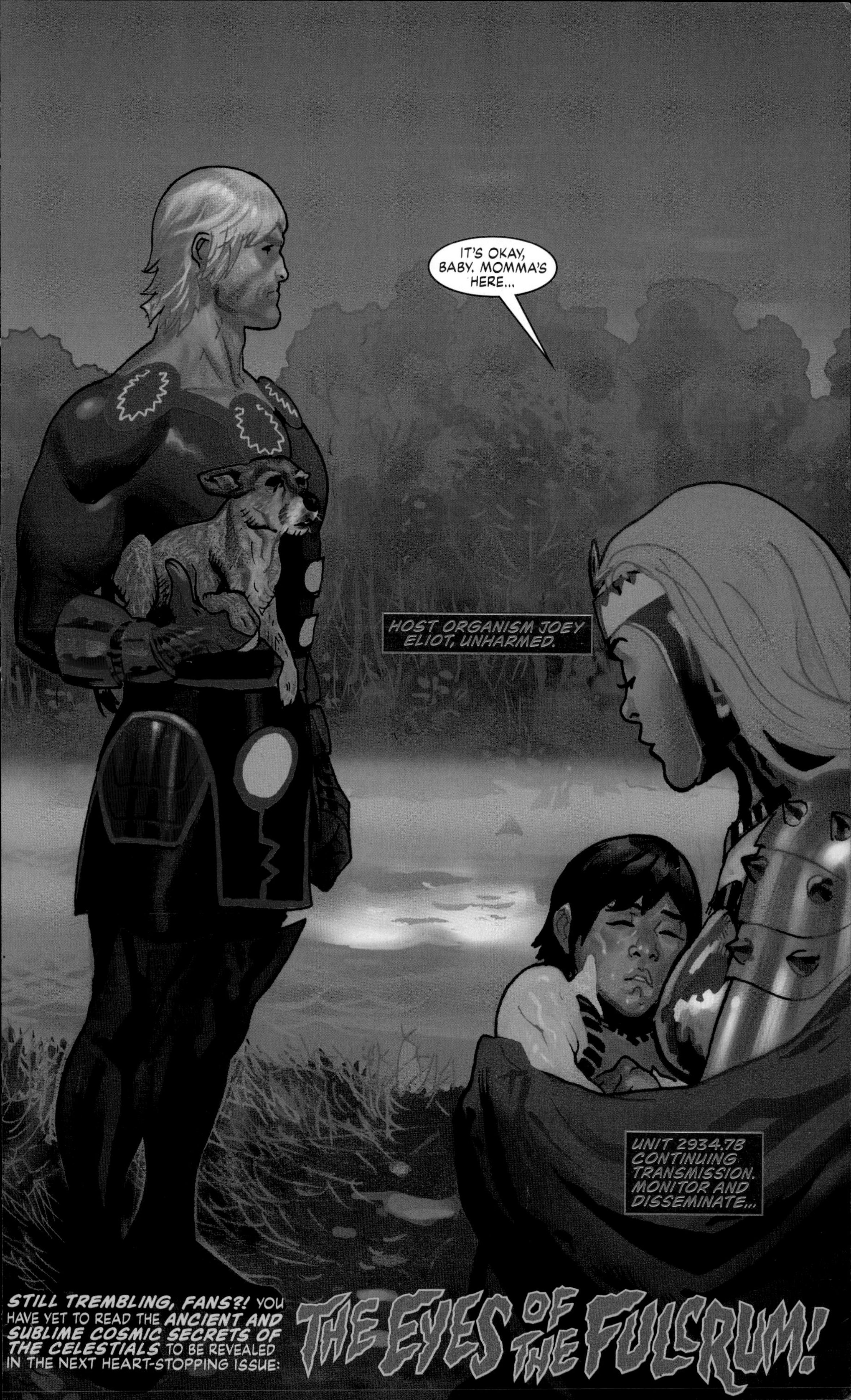
IT'S OKAY, BABY. MOMMA'S HERE...
HOST ORGANISM JOEY ELIOT, UNHARMED.
UNIT 2934.78 CONTINUING TRANSMISSION. MONITOR AND DISSEMINATE...
STILL TREMBLING, FANS?! YOU HAVE YET TO READ THE ANCIENT AND SUBLIME COSMIC SECRETS OF THE CELESTIALS TO BE REVEALED IN THE NEXT HEART-STOPPING ISSUE:
THE EYES OF THE FULCRUM!

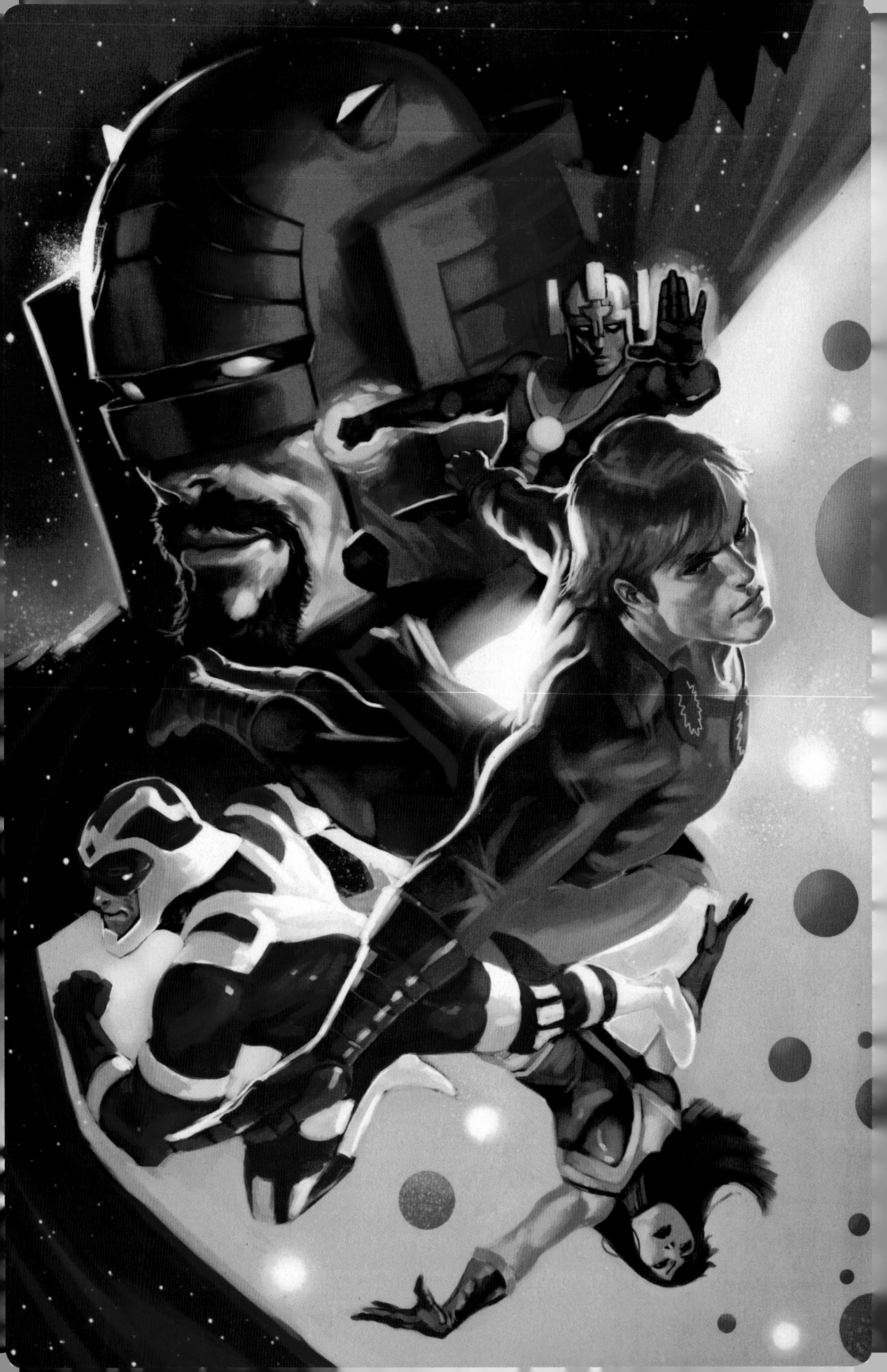

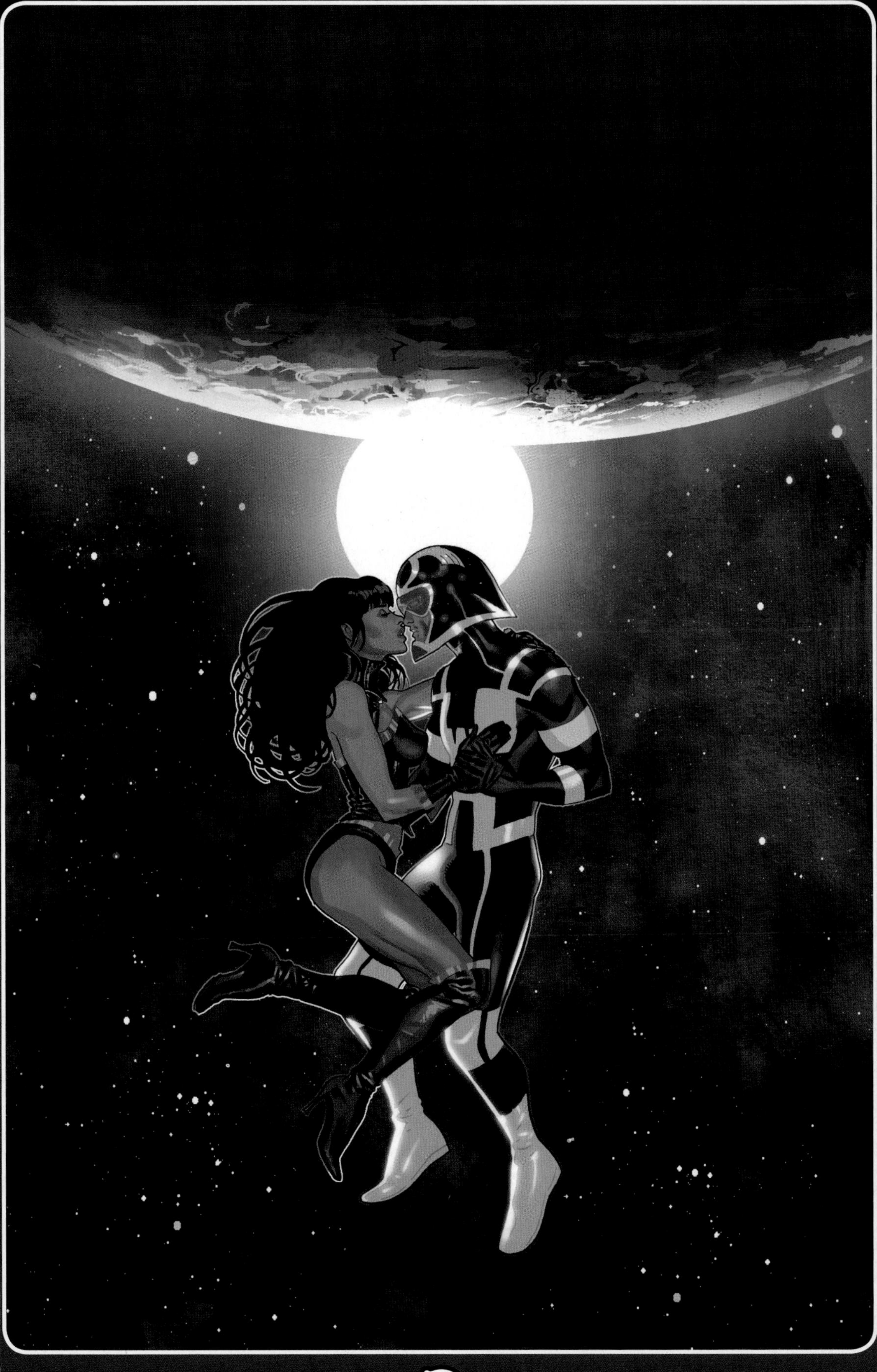

2

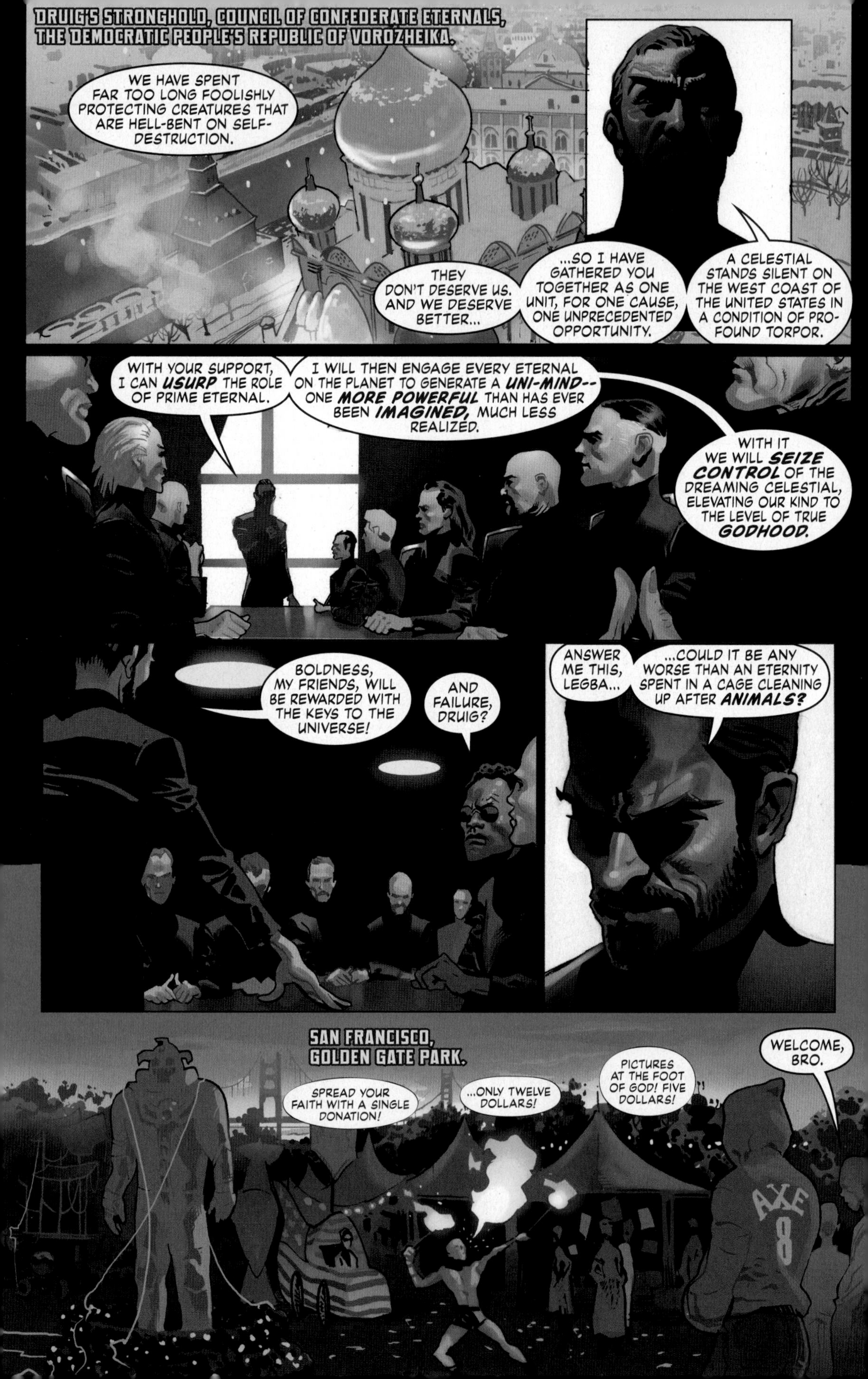
DRUIG'S STRONGHOLD, COUNCIL OF CONFEDERATE ETERNALS, THE DEMOCRATIC PEOPLE'S REPUBLIC OF VOROZHEIKA.
WE HAVE SPENT FAR TOO LONG FOOLISHLY PROTECTING CREATURES THAT ARE HELL-BENT ON SELF-DESTRUCTION.
THEY DON'T DESERVE US. AND WE DESERVE BETTER...
...SO I HAVE GATHERED YOU TOGETHER AS ONE UNIT, FOR ONE CAUSE, ONE UNPRECEDENTED OPPORTUNITY.
A CELESTIAL STANDS SILENT ON THE WEST COAST OF THE UNITED STATES IN A CONDITION OF PRO-FOUND TORPOR.
WITH YOUR SUPPORT, I CAN USURP THE ROLE OF PRIME ETERNAL.
I WILL THEN ENGAGE EVERY ETERNAL ON THE PLANET TO GENERATE A UNI-MIND-- ONE MORE POWERFUL THAN HAS EVER BEEN IMAGINED, MUCH LESS REALIZED.
WITH IT WE WILL SEIZE CONTROL OF THE DREAMING CELESTIAL, ELEVATING OUR KIND TO THE LEVEL OF TRUE GODHOOD.
BOLDNESS, MY FRIENDS, WILL BE REWARDED WITH THE KEYS TO THE UNIVERSE!
AND FAILURE, DRUIG?
ANSWER ME THIS, LEGBA...
...COULD IT BE ANY WORSE THAN AN ETERNITY SPENT IN A CAGE CLEANING UP AFTER ANIMALS?
SAN FRANCISCO, GOLDEN GATE PARK.
SPREAD YOUR FAITH WITH A SINGLE DONATION!
...ONLY TWELVE DOLLARS!
PICTURES AT THE FOOT OF GOD! FIVE DOLLARS!
WELCOME, BRO.
AXE
8

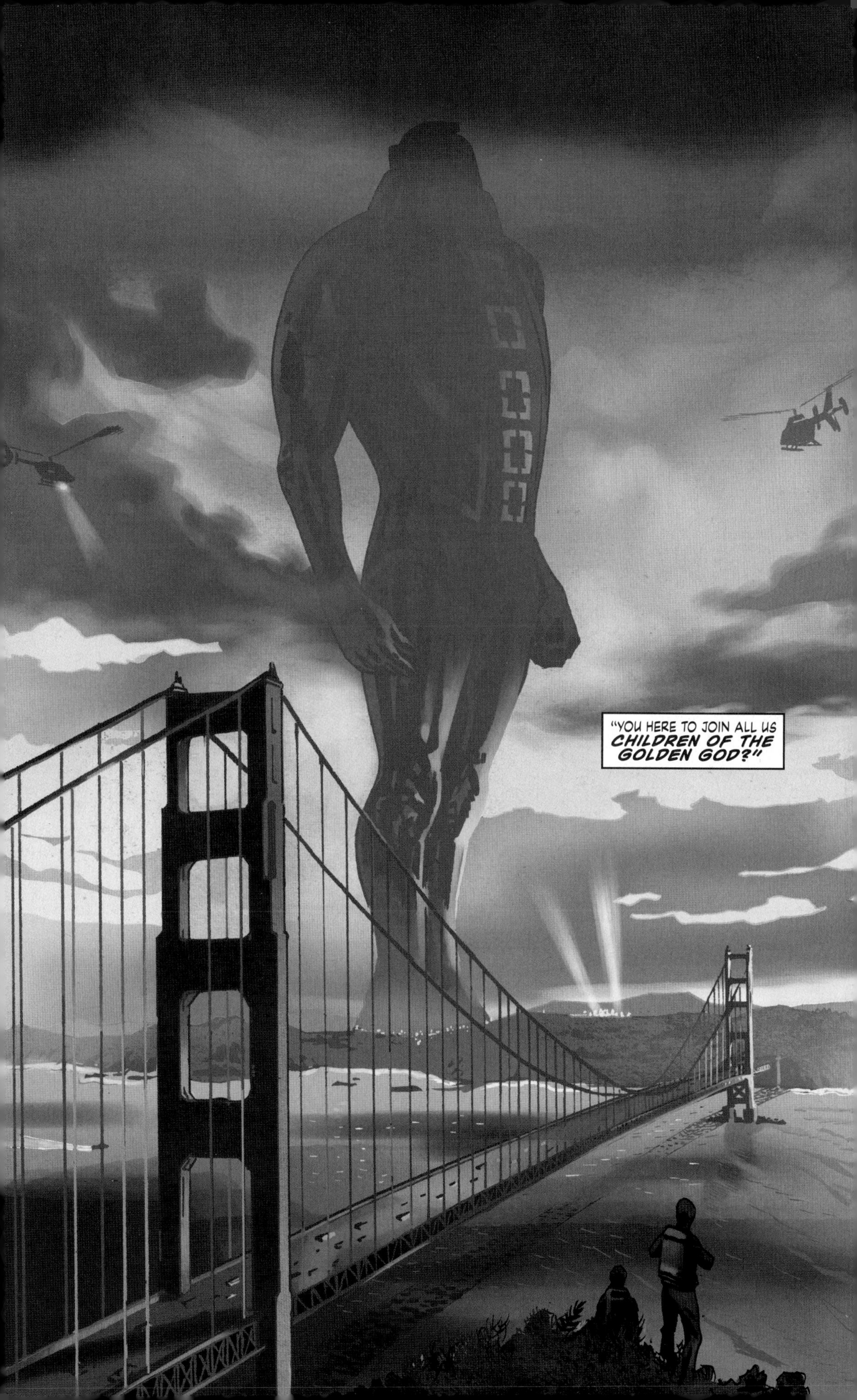
"YOU HERE TO JOIN ALL US *CHILDREN OF THE GOLDEN GOD?"*

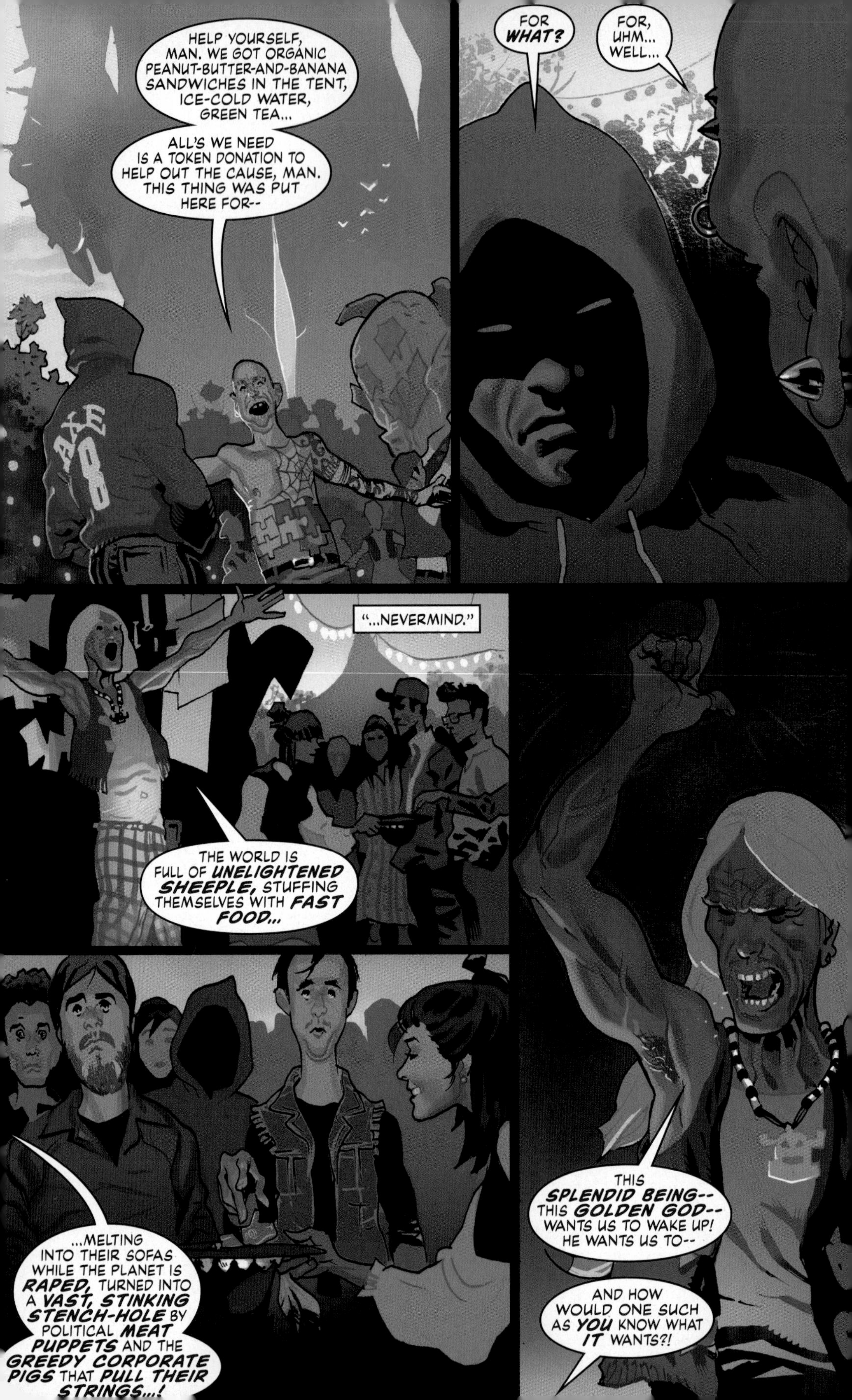
HELP YOURSELF, MAN. WE GOT ORGANIC PEANUT-BUTTER-AND-BANANA SANDWICHES IN THE TENT, ICE-COLD WATER, GREEN TEA...
ALL'S WE NEED IS A TOKEN DONATION TO HELP OUT THE CAUSE, MAN. THIS THING WAS PUT HERE FOR--
FOR *WHAT?*
FOR, UHM... WELL...
"...NEVERMIND."
THE WORLD IS FULL OF *UNELIGHTENED SHEEPLE,* STUFFING THEMSELVES WITH *FAST FOOD...*
...MELTING INTO THEIR SOFAS WHILE THE PLANET IS *RAPED,* TURNED INTO A *VAST, STINKING STENCH-HOLE* BY POLITICAL *MEAT PUPPETS* AND THE *GREEDY CORPORATE PIGS* THAT *PULL THEIR STRINGS...!*
THIS *SPLENDID BEING--* THIS *GOLDEN GOD--* WANTS US TO WAKE UP! HE WANTS US TO--
AND HOW WOULD ONE SUCH AS *YOU* KNOW WHAT *IT* WANTS?!

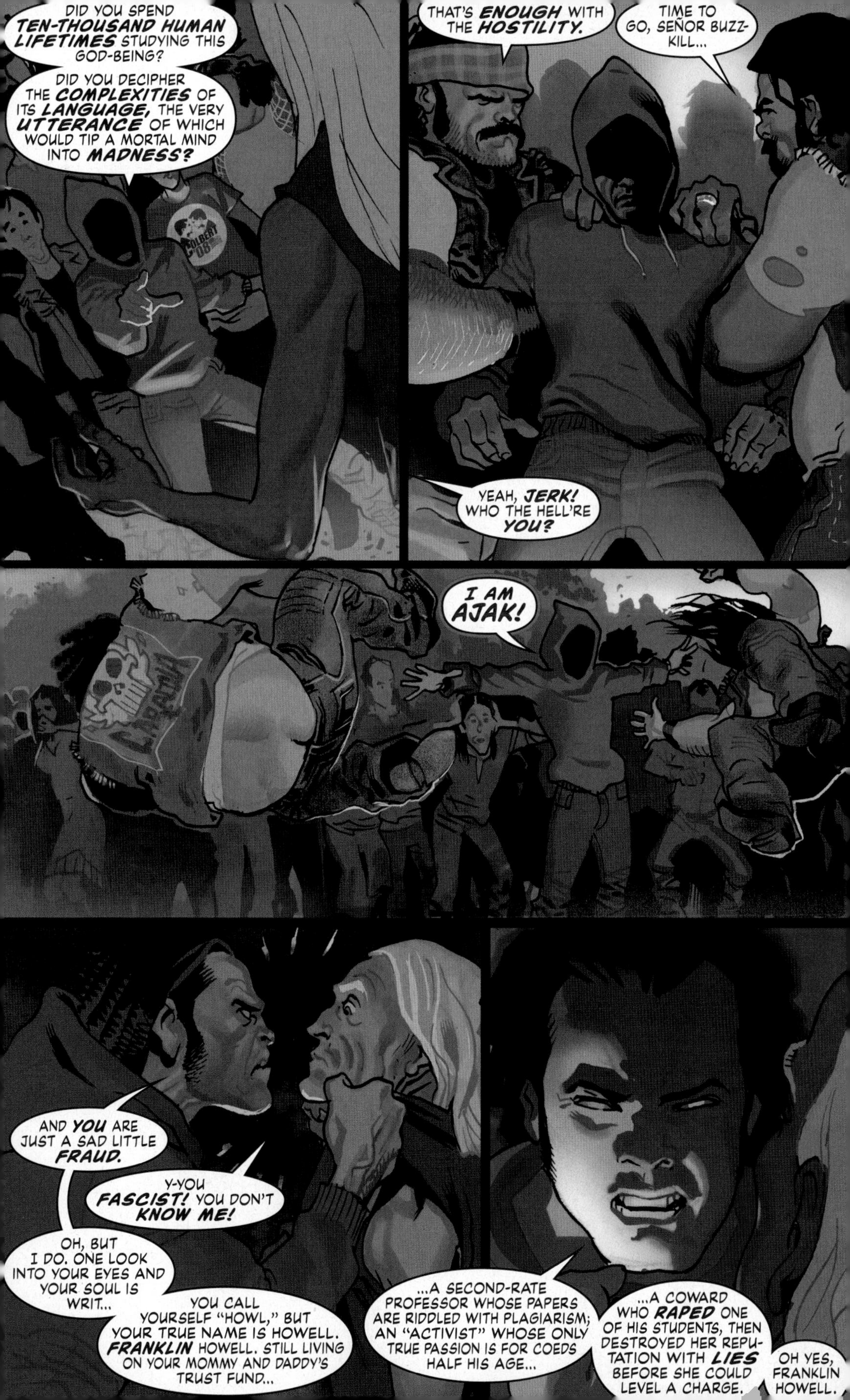

DID YOU SPEND TEN-THOUSAND HUMAN LIFETIMES STUDYING THIS GOD-BEING?
DID YOU DECIPHER THE COMPLEXITIES OF ITS LANGUAGE, THE VERY UTTERANCE OF WHICH WOULD TIP A MORTAL MIND INTO MADNESS?
COLBERT '08
THAT'S ENOUGH WITH THE HOSTILITY.
TIME TO GO, SEÑOR BUZZ-KILL...
YEAH, JERK! WHO THE HELL'RE YOU?
I AM AJAK!
AND YOU ARE JUST A SAD LITTLE FRAUD.
Y-YOU FASCIST! YOU DON'T KNOW ME!
OH, BUT I DO. ONE LOOK INTO YOUR EYES AND YOUR SOUL IS WRIT...
YOU CALL YOURSELF "HOWL," BUT YOUR TRUE NAME IS HOWELL. FRANKLIN HOWELL. STILL LIVING ON YOUR MOMMY AND DADDY'S TRUST FUND...
...A SECOND-RATE PROFESSOR WHOSE PAPERS ARE RIDDLED WITH PLAGIARISM; AN "ACTIVIST" WHOSE ONLY TRUE PASSION IS FOR COEDS HALF HIS AGE...
...A COWARD WHO RAPED ONE OF HIS STUDENTS, THEN DESTROYED HER REPUTATION WITH LIES BEFORE SHE COULD LEVEL A CHARGE.
OH YES, FRANKLIN HOWELL.

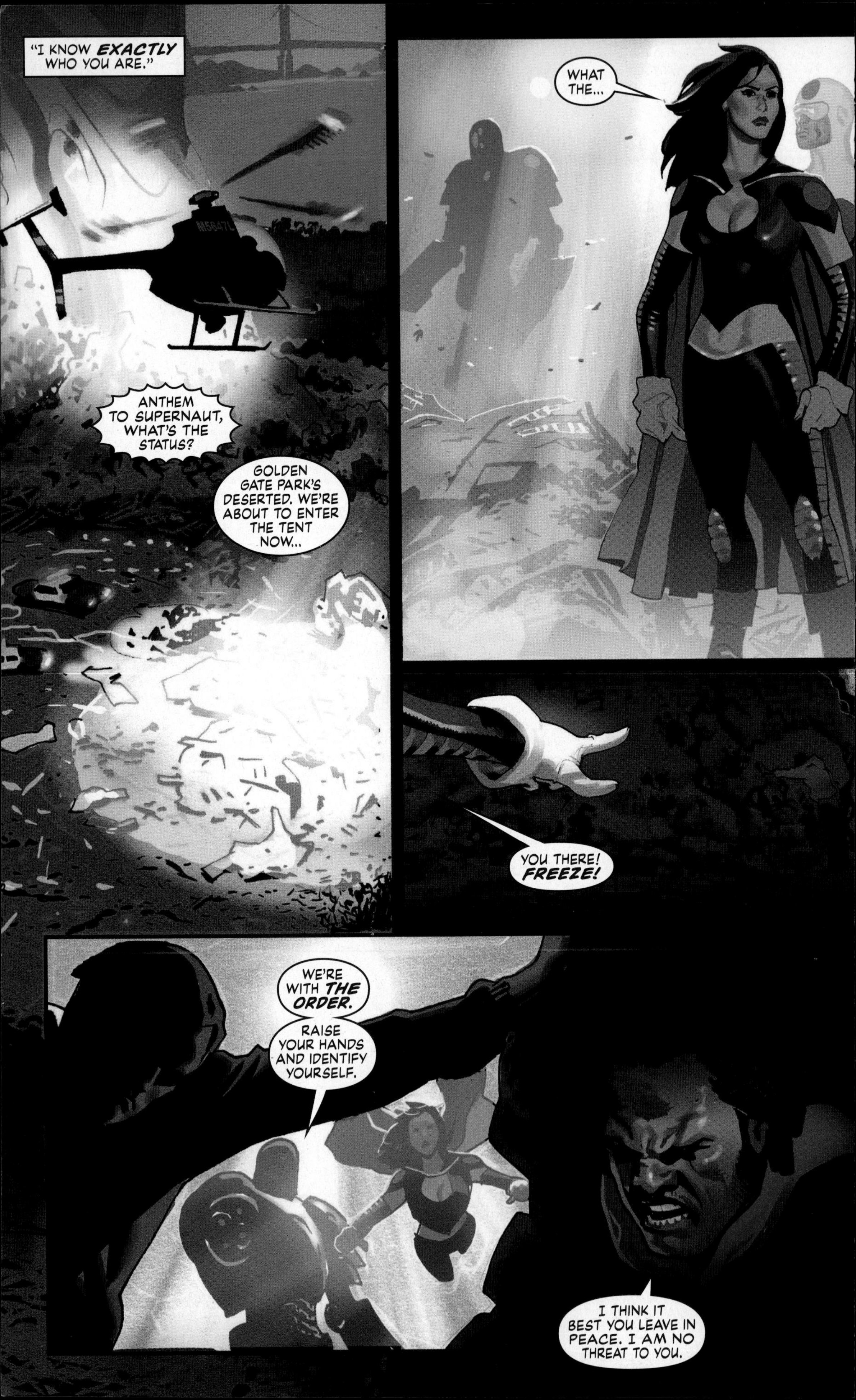
"I KNOW **EXACTLY** WHO YOU ARE."
M5647L
ANTHEM TO SUPERNAUT, WHAT'S THE STATUS?
GOLDEN GATE PARK'S DESERTED. WE'RE ABOUT TO ENTER THE TENT NOW...
WHAT THE...
YOU THERE! ***FREEZE!***
WE'RE WITH ***THE ORDER.***
RAISE YOUR HANDS AND IDENTIFY YOURSELF.
I THINK IT BEST YOU LEAVE IN PEACE. I AM NO THREAT TO YOU.

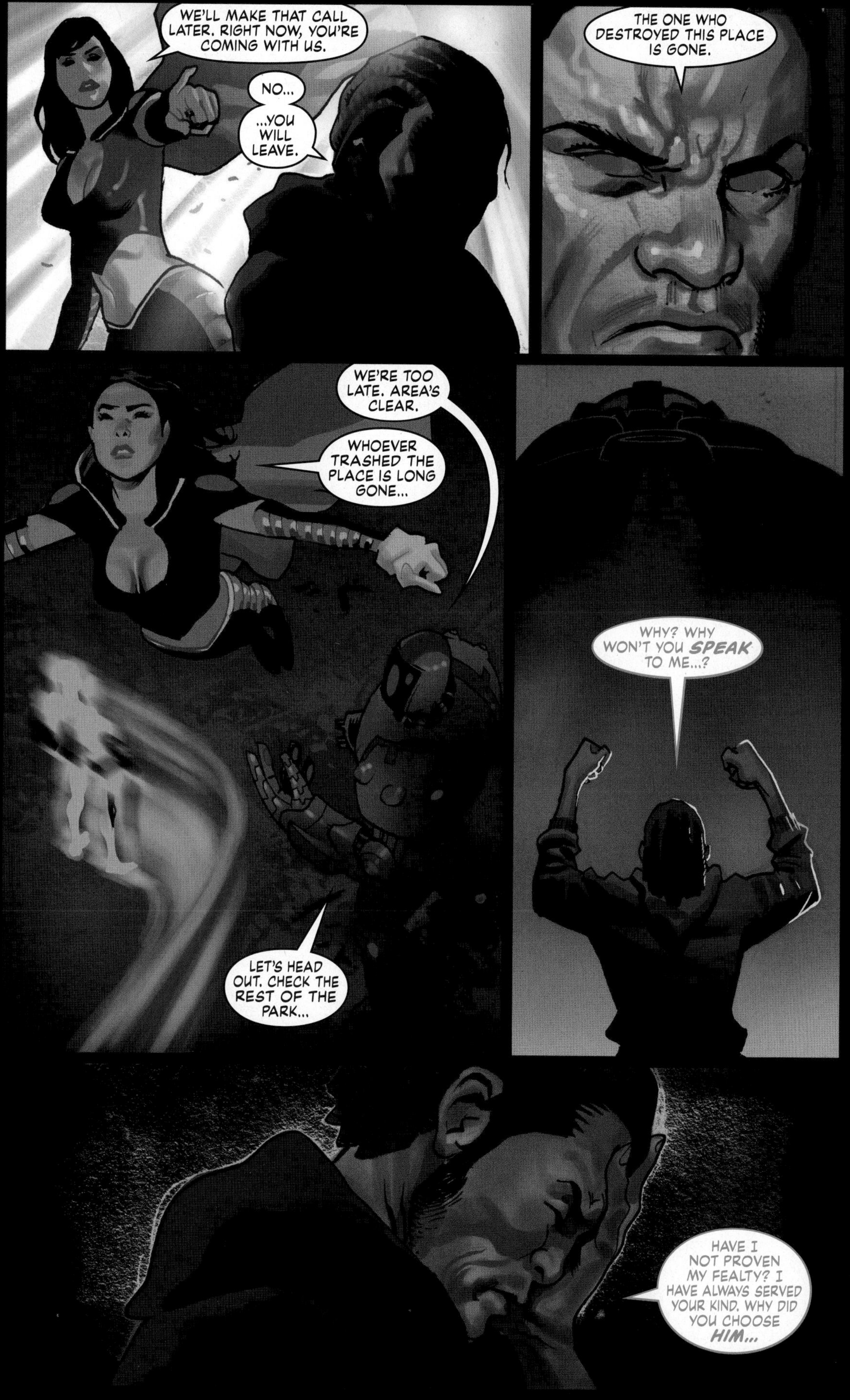
WE'LL MAKE THAT CALL LATER. RIGHT NOW, YOU'RE COMING WITH US.
NO...
...YOU WILL LEAVE.
THE ONE WHO DESTROYED THIS PLACE IS GONE.
WE'RE TOO LATE. AREA'S CLEAR.
WHOEVER TRASHED THE PLACE IS LONG GONE...
LET'S HEAD OUT. CHECK THE REST OF THE PARK...
WHY? WHY WON'T YOU **SPEAK** TO ME...?
HAVE I NOT PROVEN MY FEALTY? I HAVE ALWAYS SERVED YOUR KIND. WHY DID YOU CHOOSE ***HIM...***

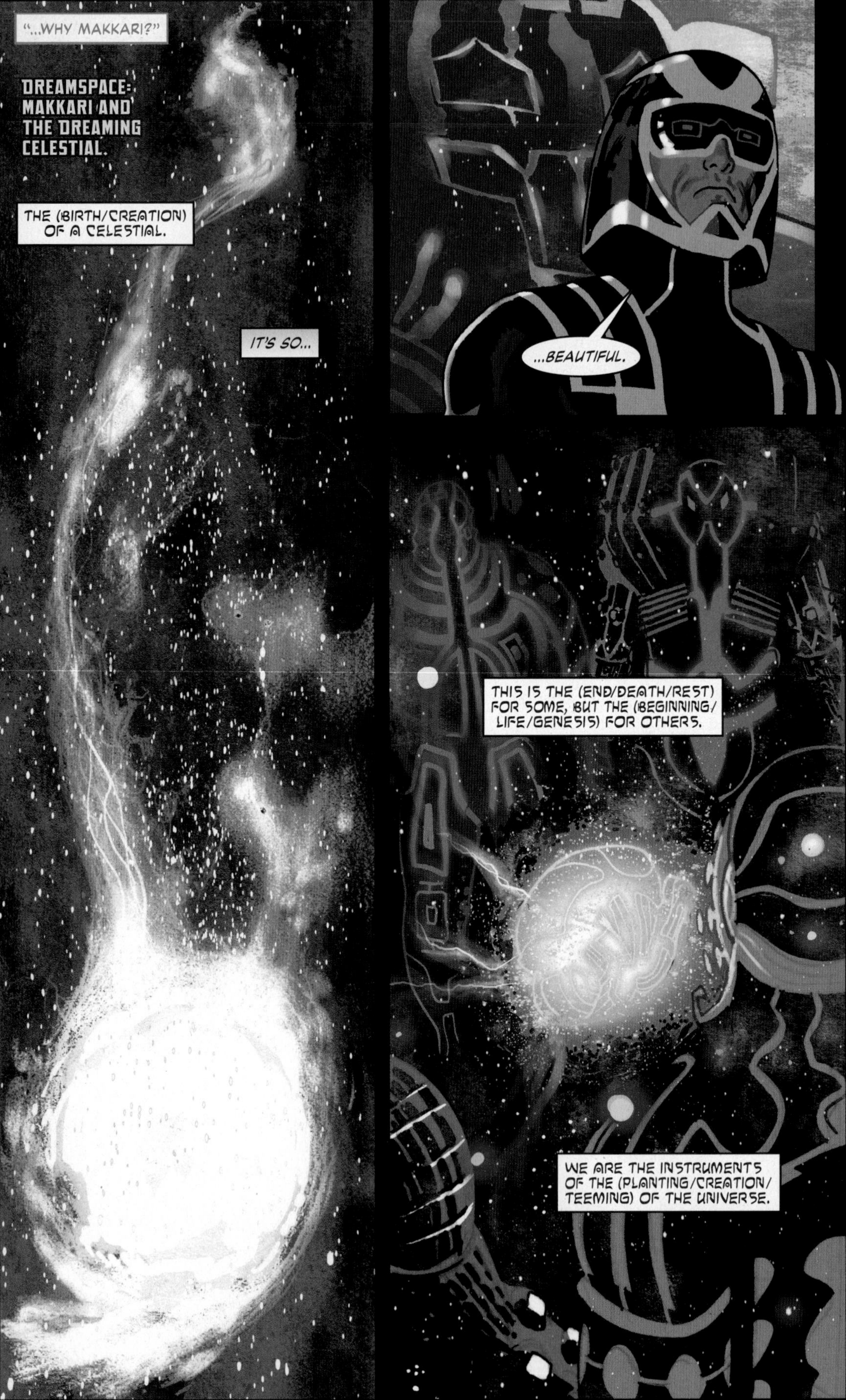
"...WHY MAKKARI?"
DREAMSPACE: MAKKARI AND THE DREAMING CELESTIAL.
THE (BIRTH/CREATION) OF A CELESTIAL.
IT'S SO...
...BEAUTIFUL.
THIS IS THE (END/DEATH/REST) FOR SOME, BUT THE (BEGINNING/ LIFE/GENESIS) FOR OTHERS.
WE ARE THE INSTRUMENTS OF THE (PLANTING/CREATION/ TEEMING) OF THE UNIVERSE.

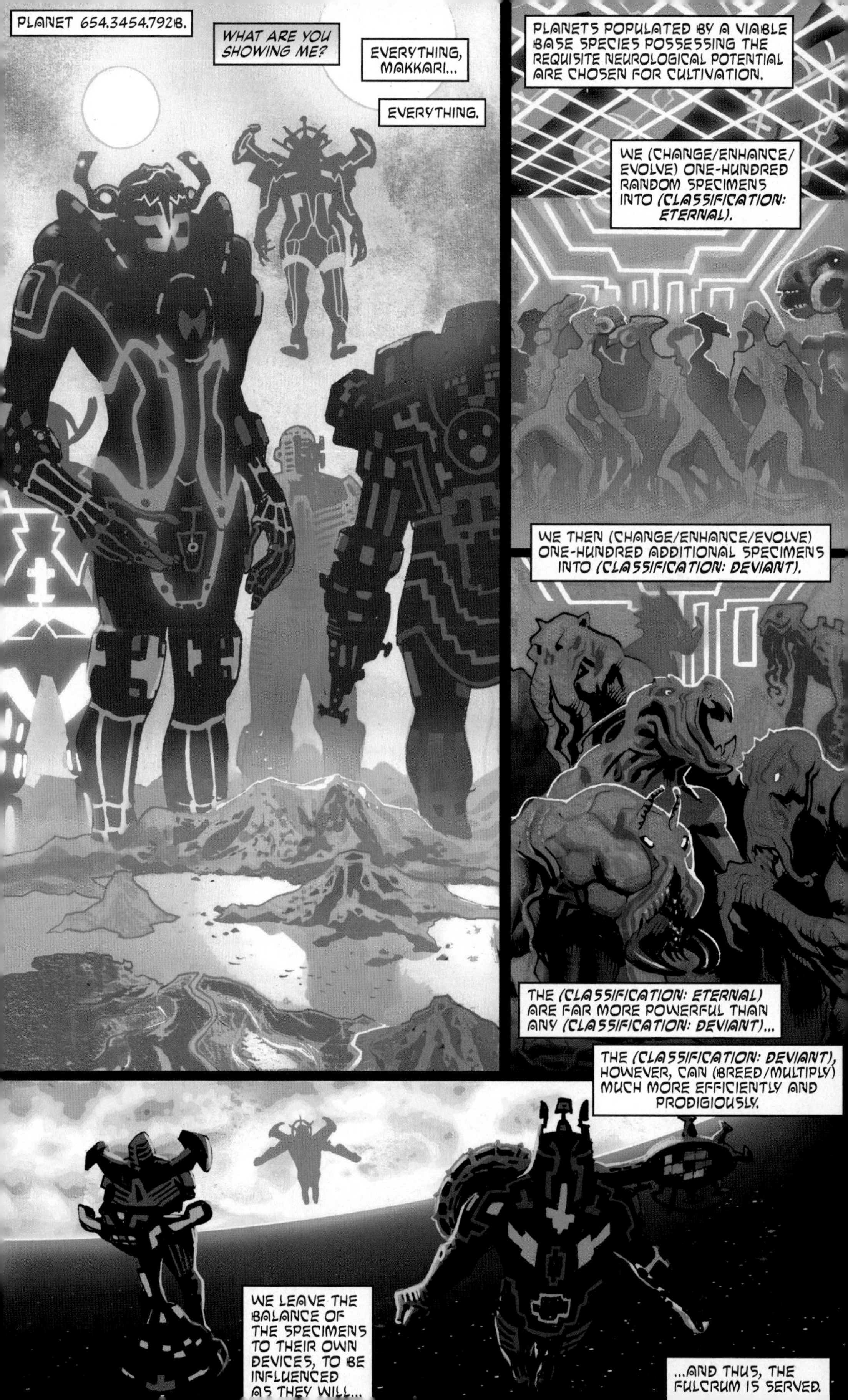
PLANET 654.3454.792B.
WHAT ARE YOU SHOWING ME?
EVERYTHING, MAKKARI...
EVERYTHING.
PLANETS POPULATED BY A VIABLE BASE SPECIES POSSESSING THE REQUISITE NEUROLOGICAL POTENTIAL ARE CHOSEN FOR CULTIVATION.
WE (CHANGE/ENHANCE/EVOLVE) ONE-HUNDRED RANDOM SPECIMENS INTO (CLASSIFICATION: ETERNAL).
WE THEN (CHANGE/ENHANCE/EVOLVE) ONE-HUNDRED ADDITIONAL SPECIMENS INTO (CLASSIFICATION: DEVIANT).
THE (CLASSIFICATION: ETERNAL) ARE FAR MORE POWERFUL THAN ANY (CLASSIFICATION: DEVIANT)...
THE (CLASSIFICATION: DEVIANT), HOWEVER, CAN (BREED/MULTIPLY) MUCH MORE EFFICIENTLY AND PRODIGIOUSLY.
WE LEAVE THE BALANCE OF THE SPECIMENS TO THEIR OWN DEVICES, TO BE INFLUENCED AS THEY WILL...
...AND THUS, THE FULCRUM IS SERVED.

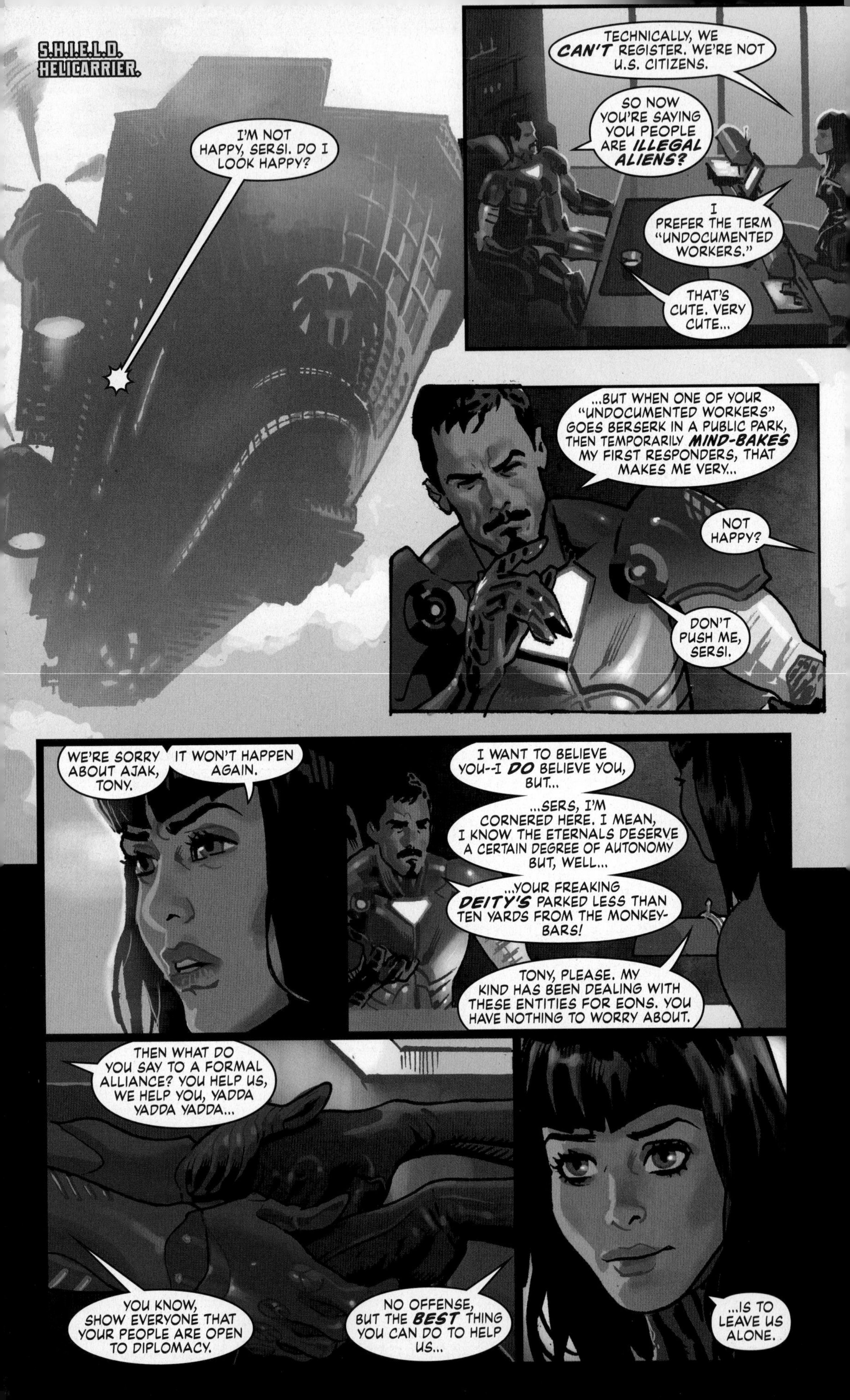
S.H.I.E.L.D. HELICARRIER.
I'M NOT HAPPY, SERSI. DO I LOOK HAPPY?
TECHNICALLY, WE CAN'T REGISTER. WE'RE NOT U.S. CITIZENS.
SO NOW YOU'RE SAYING YOU PEOPLE ARE ILLEGAL ALIENS?
I PREFER THE TERM "UNDOCUMENTED WORKERS."
THAT'S CUTE. VERY CUTE...
...BUT WHEN ONE OF YOUR "UNDOCUMENTED WORKERS" GOES BERSERK IN A PUBLIC PARK, THEN TEMPORARILY MIND-BAKES MY FIRST RESPONDERS, THAT MAKES ME VERY...
NOT HAPPY?
DON'T PUSH ME, SERSI.
WE'RE SORRY ABOUT AJAK, TONY.
IT WON'T HAPPEN AGAIN.
I WANT TO BELIEVE YOU--I DO BELIEVE YOU, BUT...
...SERS, I'M CORNERED HERE. I MEAN, I KNOW THE ETERNALS DESERVE A CERTAIN DEGREE OF AUTONOMY BUT, WELL...
...YOUR FREAKING DEITY'S PARKED LESS THAN TEN YARDS FROM THE MONKEY-BARS!
TONY, PLEASE. MY KIND HAS BEEN DEALING WITH THESE ENTITIES FOR EONS. YOU HAVE NOTHING TO WORRY ABOUT.
THEN WHAT DO YOU SAY TO A FORMAL ALLIANCE? YOU HELP US, WE HELP YOU, YADDA YADDA YADDA...
YOU KNOW, SHOW EVERYONE THAT YOUR PEOPLE ARE OPEN TO DIPLOMACY.
NO OFFENSE, BUT THE BEST THING YOU CAN DO TO HELP US...
...IS TO LEAVE US ALONE.

AFTER NINETEEN COSMIC CYCLES, THE PLANET IS READY FOR (REAPING/TERMINATION/QUIETUS) AND THE AGGREGATE ENERGY FROM THE BASE SPECIES IS (GATHERED/HARVESTED/CHANNELED) TO THE FULCRUM.

THERE IS BUT ONE ENTITY IN THE UNIVERSE THAT CAN (GATHER/HARVEST/CHANNEL) THE COLLECTIVE LIFE-FORCE WITHOUT COMPLETE SELF-ANNIHILATION.

THE HORDE.

IF THE PLANET'S AGGREGATE ENERGY SIGNATURE IS CONSISTENT WITH (CLASSIFICATION: ETERNAL), THE LIFE-FORCE IS TRANSFERRED TO THE CELESTIALS.

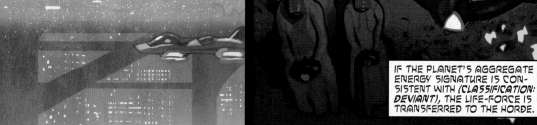

IF THE PLANET'S AGGREGATE ENERGY SIGNATURE IS CONSISTENT WITH (CLASSIFICATION: DEVIANT), THE LIFE-FORCE IS TRANSFERRED TO THE HORDE.

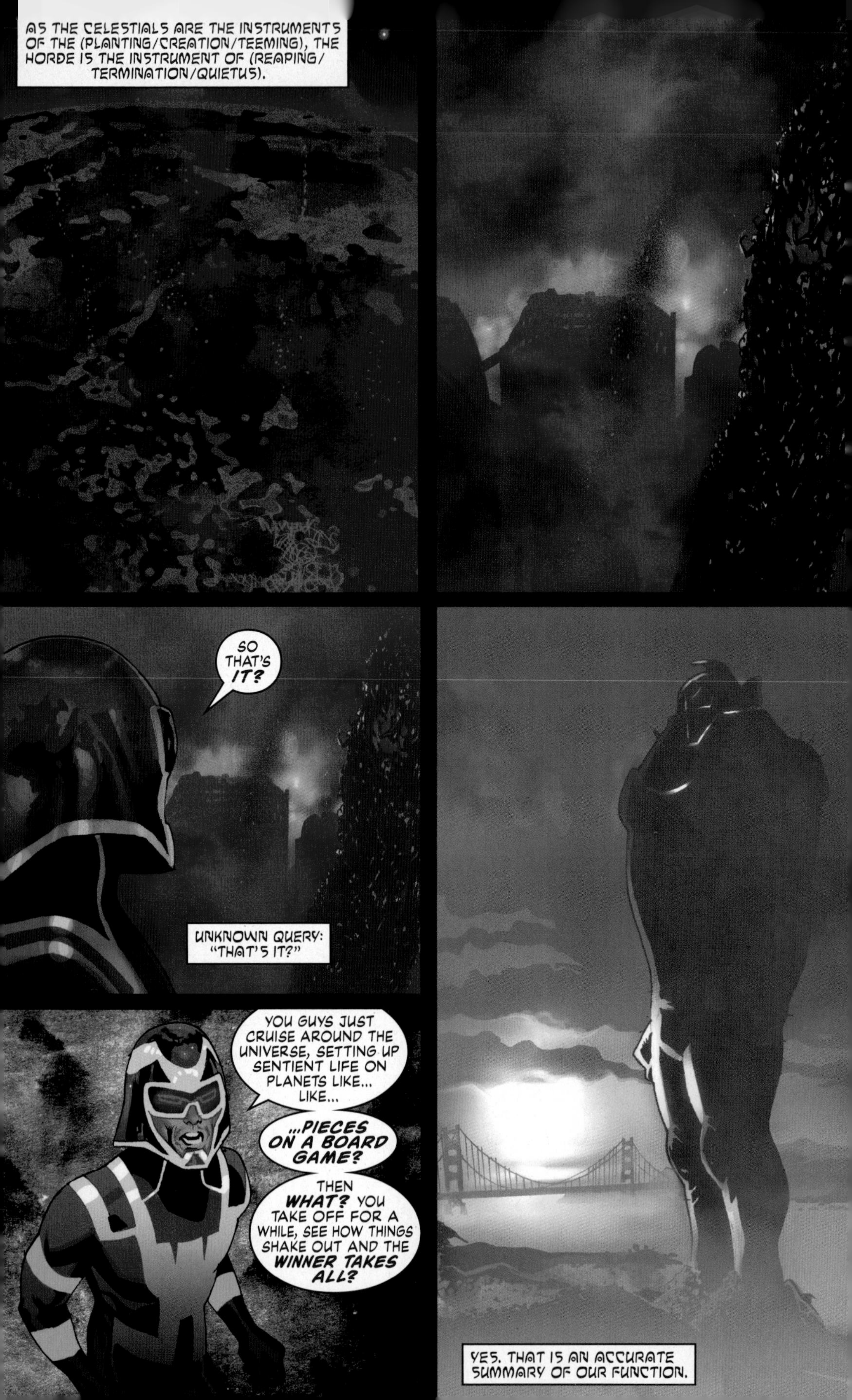

AS THE CELESTIALS ARE THE INSTRUMENTS OF THE (PLANTING/CREATION/TEEMING), THE HORDE IS THE INSTRUMENT OF (REAPING/TERMINATION/QUIETUS).
SO THAT'S IT?
UNKNOWN QUERY: "THAT'S IT?"
YOU GUYS JUST CRUISE AROUND THE UNIVERSE, SETTING UP SENTIENT LIFE ON PLANETS LIKE... LIKE...
...PIECES ON A BOARD GAME?
THEN WHAT? YOU TAKE OFF FOR A WHILE, SEE HOW THINGS SHAKE OUT AND THE WINNER TAKES ALL?
YES. THAT IS AN ACCURATE SUMMARY OF OUR FUNCTION.

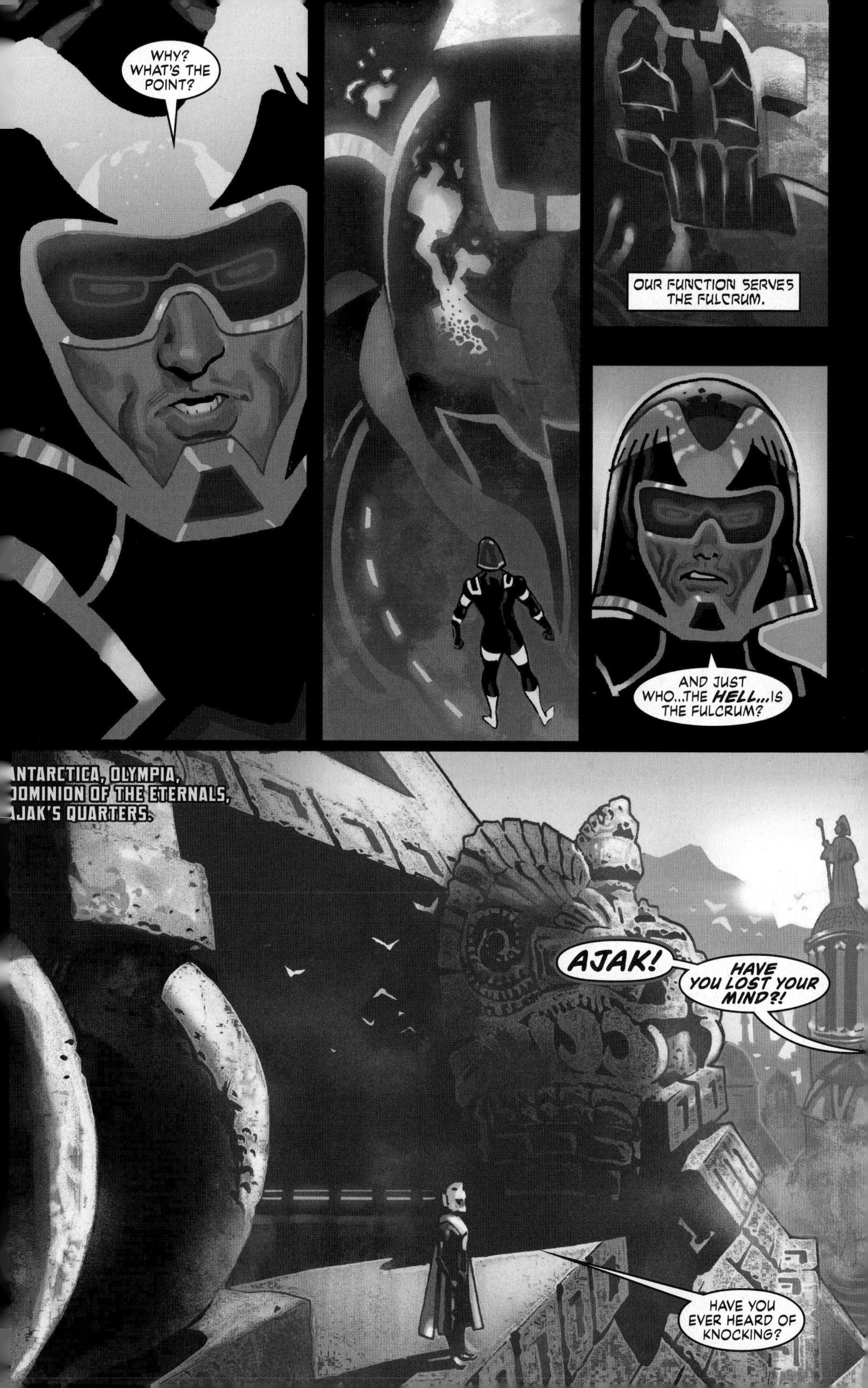
WHY? WHAT'S THE POINT?
OUR FUNCTION SERVES THE FULCRUM.
AND JUST WHO...THE HELL...IS THE FULCRUM?
ANTARCTICA, OLYMPIA, DOMINION OF THE ETERNALS, AJAK'S QUARTERS.
AJAK!
HAVE YOU LOST YOUR MIND?!
HAVE YOU EVER HEARD OF KNOCKING?

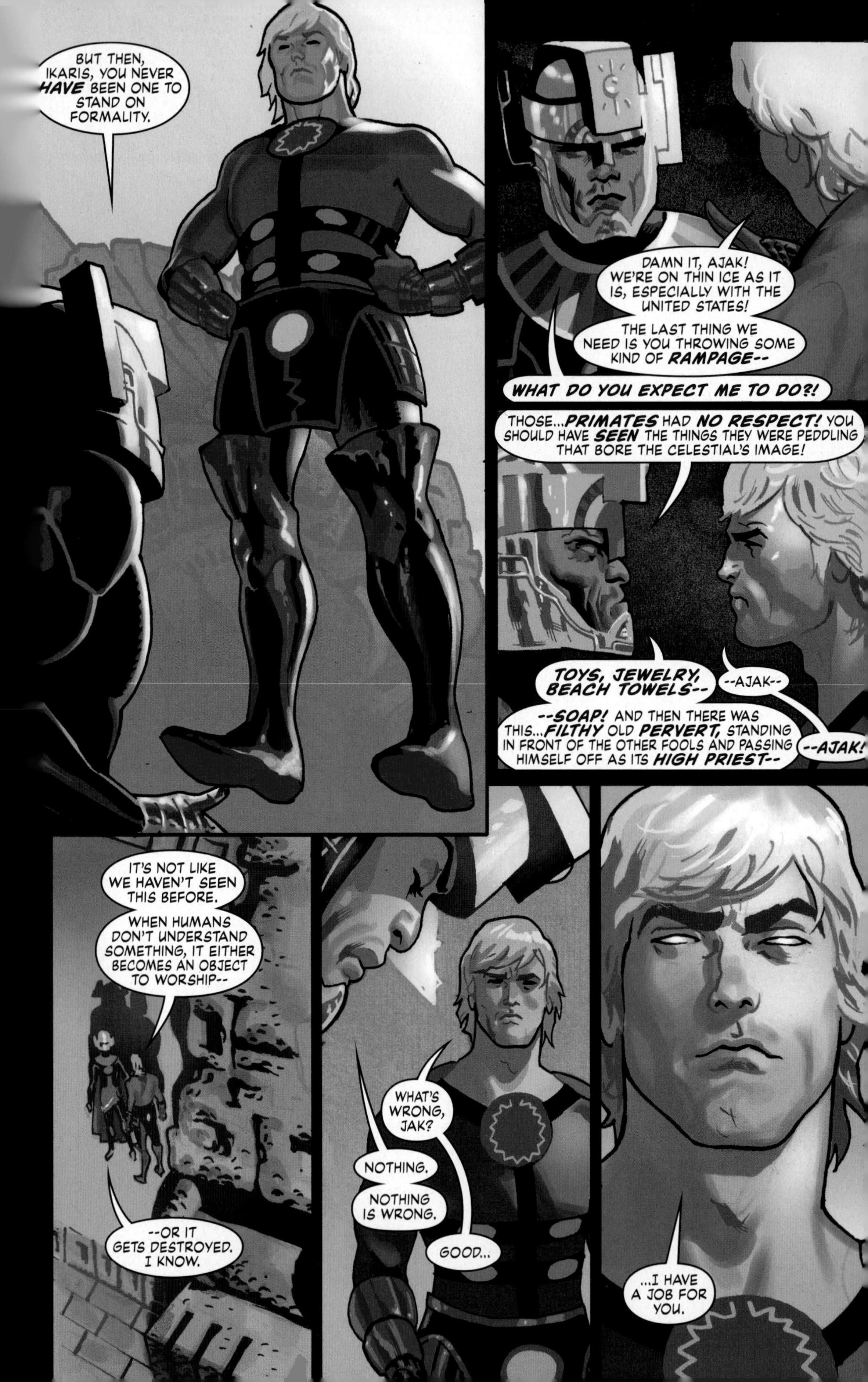

BUT THEN, IKARIS, YOU NEVER HAVE BEEN ONE TO STAND ON FORMALITY.
DAMN IT, AJAK! WE'RE ON THIN ICE AS IT IS, ESPECIALLY WITH THE UNITED STATES!
THE LAST THING WE NEED IS YOU THROWING SOME KIND OF RAMPAGE--
WHAT DO YOU EXPECT ME TO DO?!
THOSE...PRIMATES HAD NO RESPECT! YOU SHOULD HAVE SEEN THE THINGS THEY WERE PEDDLING THAT BORE THE CELESTIAL'S IMAGE!
TOYS, JEWELRY, BEACH TOWELS--
--AJAK--
--SOAP! AND THEN THERE WAS THIS...FILTHY OLD PERVERT, STANDING IN FRONT OF THE OTHER FOOLS AND PASSING HIMSELF OFF AS ITS HIGH PRIEST--
--AJAK!
IT'S NOT LIKE WE HAVEN'T SEEN THIS BEFORE.
WHEN HUMANS DON'T UNDERSTAND SOMETHING, IT EITHER BECOMES AN OBJECT TO WORSHIP--
--OR IT GETS DESTROYED. I KNOW.
WHAT'S WRONG, JAK?
NOTHING.
NOTHING IS WRONG.
GOOD...
...I HAVE A JOB FOR YOU.

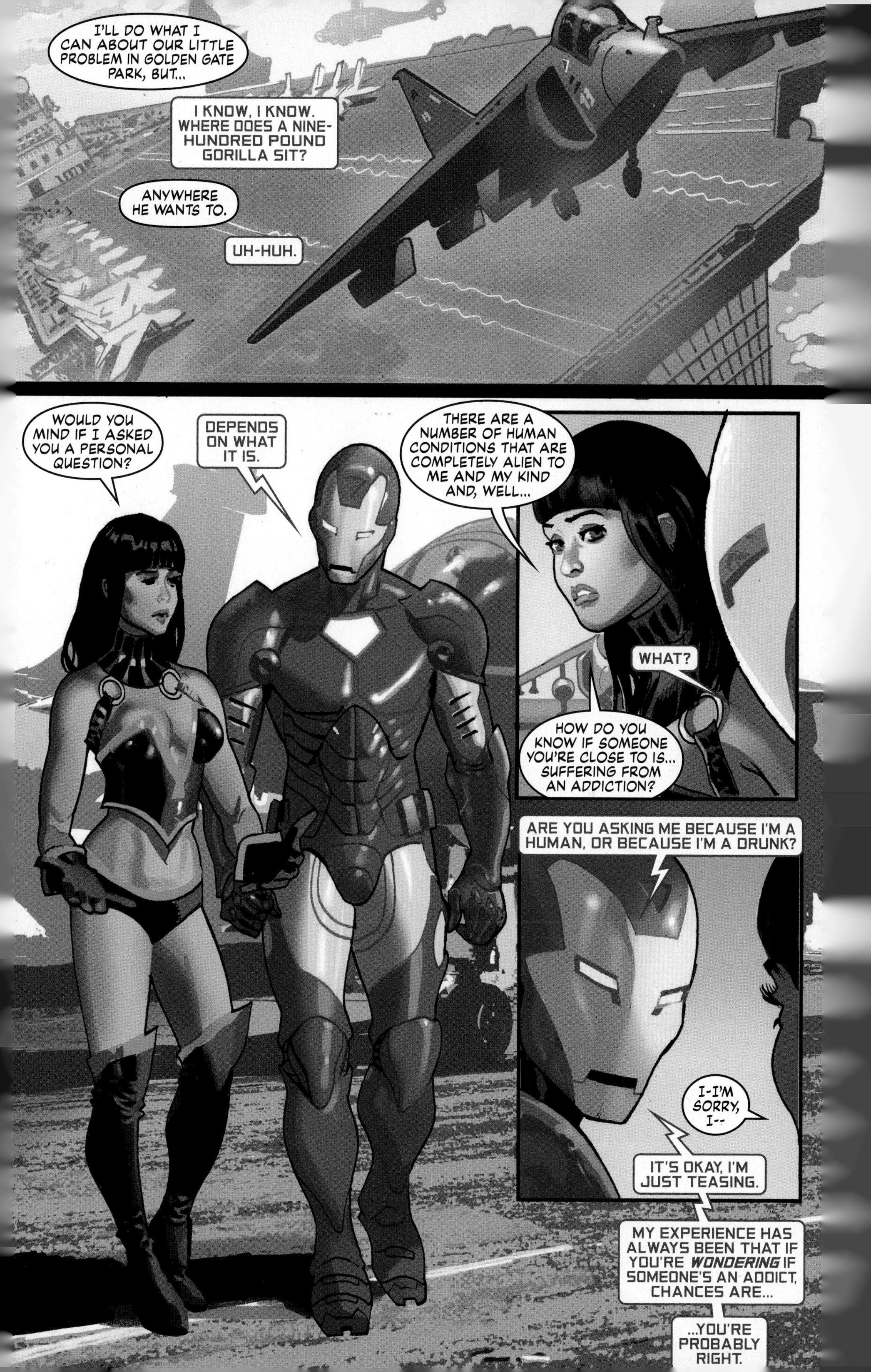
I'LL DO WHAT I CAN ABOUT OUR LITTLE PROBLEM IN GOLDEN GATE PARK, BUT...
I KNOW, I KNOW. WHERE DOES A NINE-HUNDRED POUND GORILLA SIT?
ANYWHERE HE WANTS TO.
UH-HUH.
WOULD YOU MIND IF I ASKED YOU A PERSONAL QUESTION?
DEPENDS ON WHAT IT IS.
THERE ARE A NUMBER OF HUMAN CONDITIONS THAT ARE COMPLETELY ALIEN TO ME AND MY KIND AND, WELL...
WHAT?
HOW DO YOU KNOW IF SOMEONE YOU'RE CLOSE TO IS... SUFFERING FROM AN ADDICTION?
ARE YOU ASKING ME BECAUSE I'M A HUMAN, OR BECAUSE I'M A DRUNK?
I-I'M SORRY, I--
IT'S OKAY, I'M JUST TEASING.
MY EXPERIENCE HAS ALWAYS BEEN THAT IF YOU'RE *WONDERING* IF SOMEONE'S AN ADDICT, CHANCES ARE...
...YOU'RE PROBABLY RIGHT.

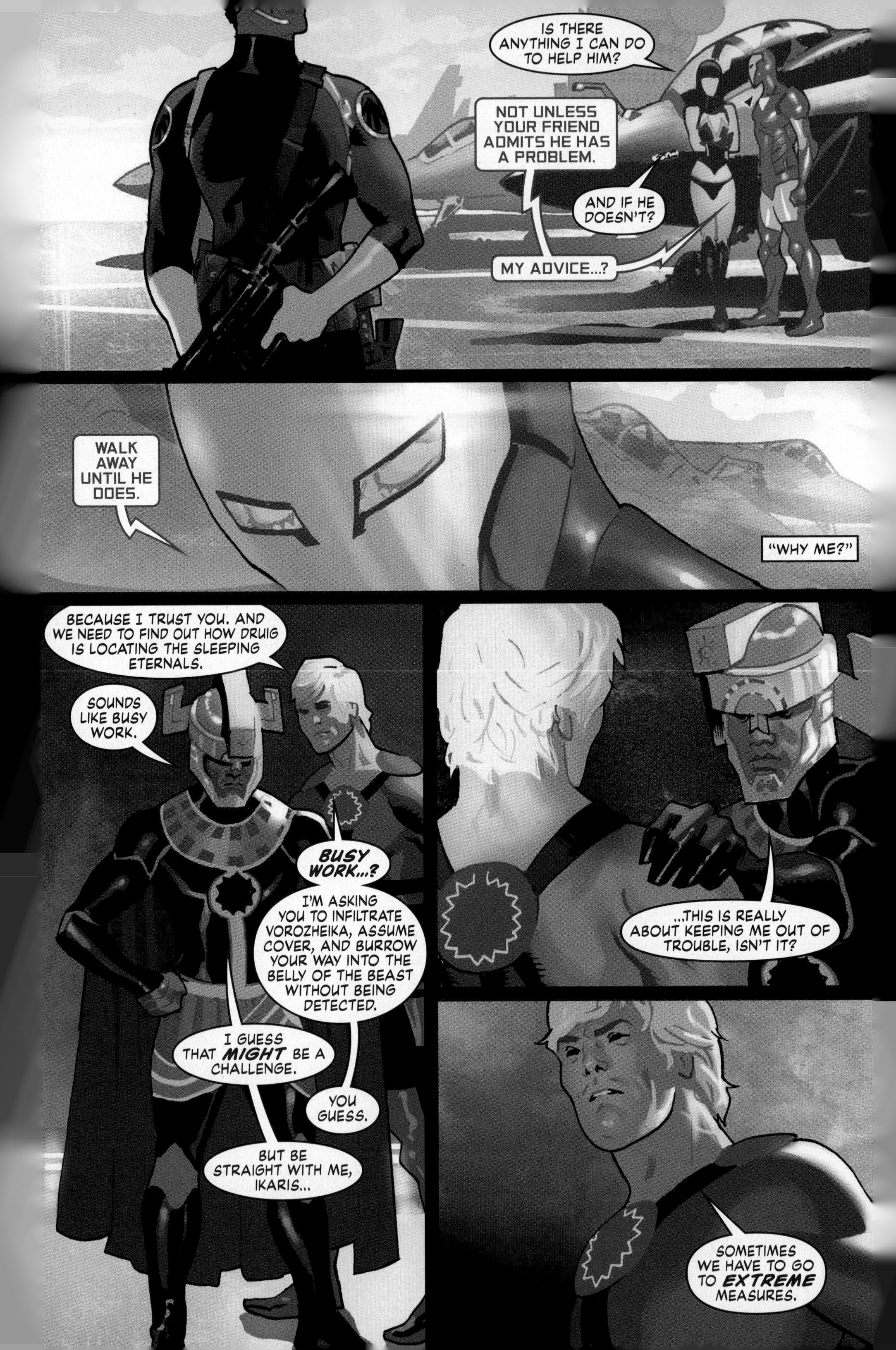
IS THERE ANYTHING I CAN DO TO HELP HIM?
NOT UNLESS YOUR FRIEND ADMITS HE HAS A PROBLEM.
AND IF HE DOESN'T?
MY ADVICE...?
WALK AWAY UNTIL HE DOES.
"WHY ME?"
BECAUSE I TRUST YOU. AND WE NEED TO FIND OUT HOW DRUIG IS LOCATING THE SLEEPING ETERNALS.
SOUNDS LIKE BUSY WORK.
BUSY WORK...?
I'M ASKING YOU TO INFILTRATE VOROZHEIKA, ASSUME COVER, AND BURROW YOUR WAY INTO THE BELLY OF THE BEAST WITHOUT BEING DETECTED.
I GUESS THAT MIGHT BE A CHALLENGE.
YOU GUESS.
BUT BE STRAIGHT WITH ME, IKARIS...
...THIS IS REALLY ABOUT KEEPING ME OUT OF TROUBLE, ISN'T IT?
SOMETIMES WE HAVE TO GO TO EXTREME MEASURES.

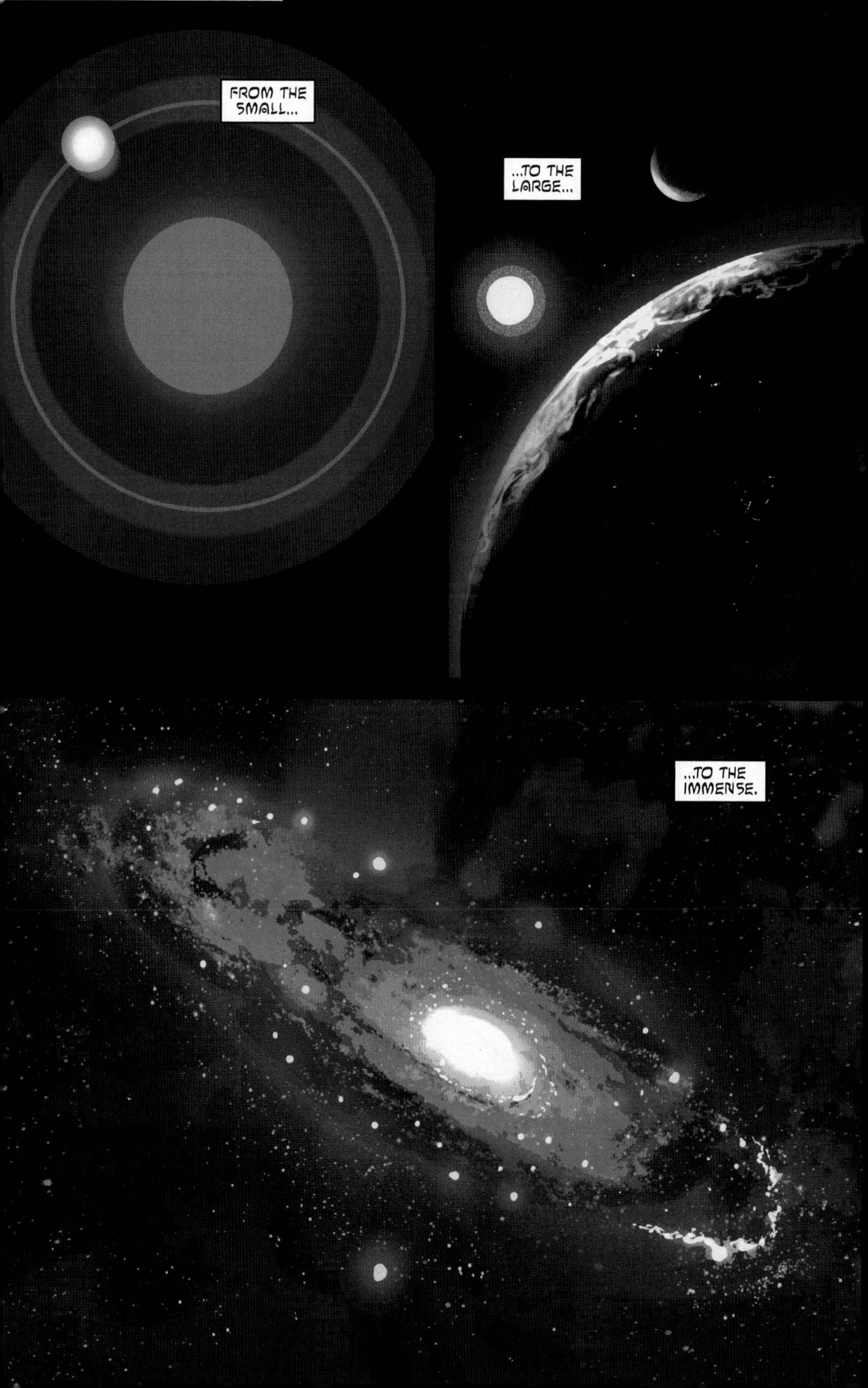
FROM THE SMALL...
...TO THE LARGE...
...TO THE IMMENSE.

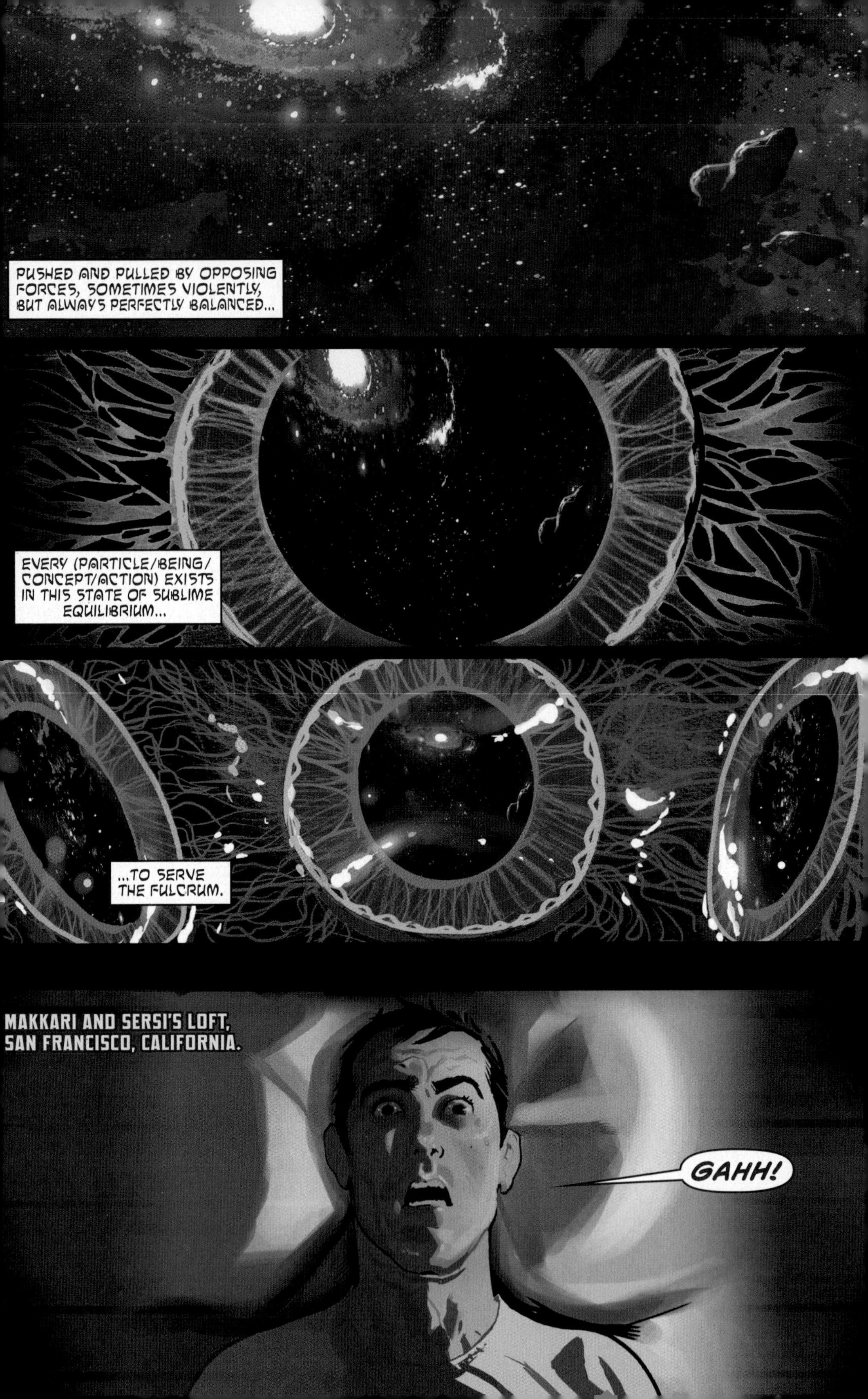
PUSHED AND PULLED BY OPPOSING FORCES, SOMETIMES VIOLENTLY, BUT ALWAYS PERFECTLY BALANCED...
EVERY (PARTICLE/BEING/ CONCEPT/ACTION) EXISTS IN THIS STATE OF SUBLIME EQUILIBRIUM...
...TO SERVE THE FULCRUM.
MAKKARI AND SERSI'S LOFT, SAN FRANCISCO, CALIFORNIA.
GAHH!

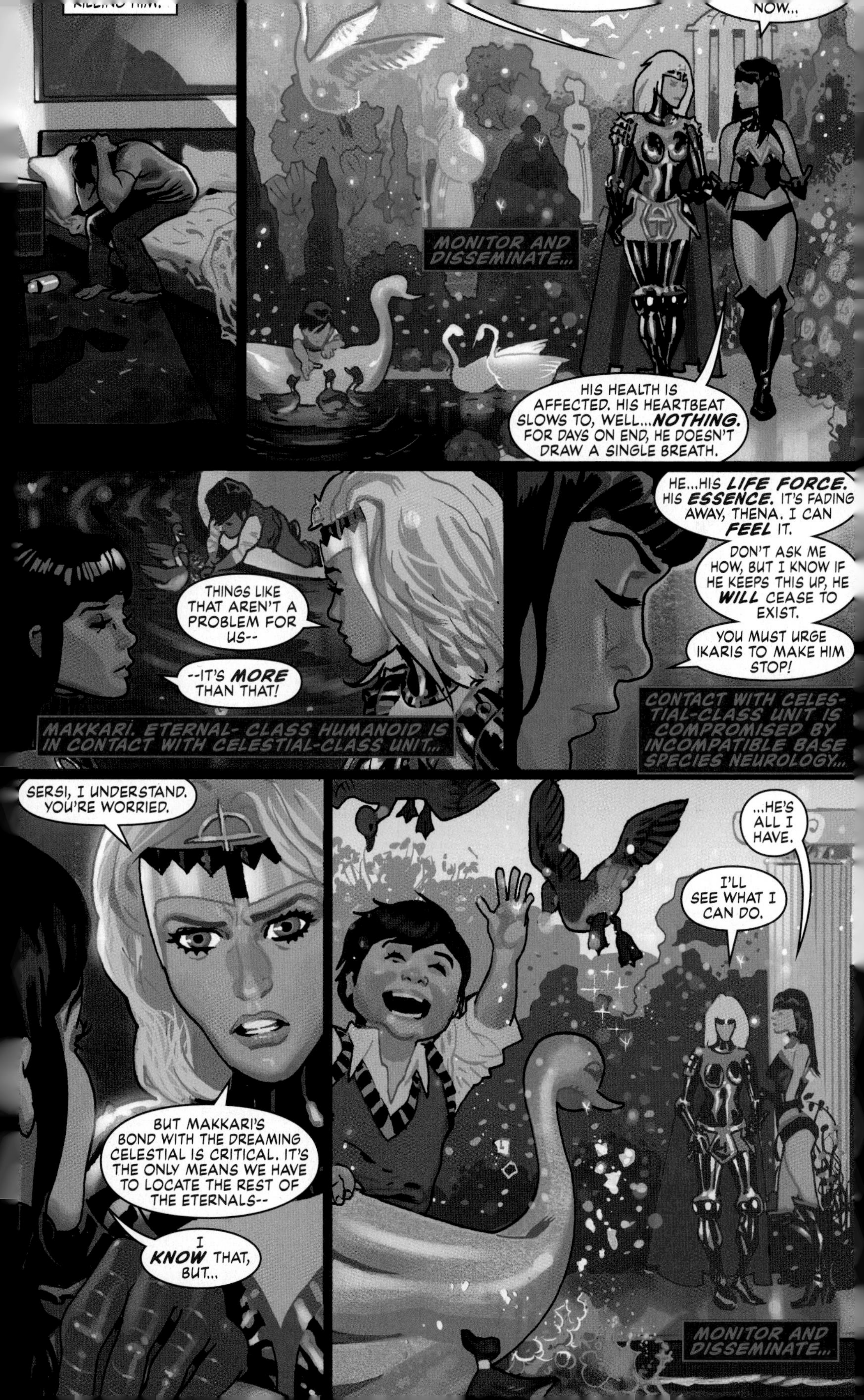
NOW...
MONITOR AND DISSEMINATE...
HIS HEALTH IS AFFECTED. HIS HEARTBEAT SLOWS TO, WELL...NOTHING. FOR DAYS ON END, HE DOESN'T DRAW A SINGLE BREATH.
THINGS LIKE THAT AREN'T A PROBLEM FOR US--
--IT'S MORE THAN THAT!
MAKKARI. ETERNAL- CLASS HUMANOID IS IN CONTACT WITH CELESTIAL-CLASS UNIT...
HE...HIS LIFE FORCE. HIS ESSENCE. IT'S FADING AWAY, THENA. I CAN FEEL IT.
DON'T ASK ME HOW, BUT I KNOW IF HE KEEPS THIS UP, HE WILL CEASE TO EXIST.
YOU MUST URGE IKARIS TO MAKE HIM STOP!
CONTACT WITH CELESTIAL-CLASS UNIT IS COMPROMISED BY INCOMPATIBLE BASE SPECIES NEUROLOGY...
SERSI, I UNDERSTAND. YOU'RE WORRIED.
BUT MAKKARI'S BOND WITH THE DREAMING CELESTIAL IS CRITICAL. IT'S THE ONLY MEANS WE HAVE TO LOCATE THE REST OF THE ETERNALS--
I KNOW THAT, BUT...
...HE'S ALL I HAVE.
I'LL SEE WHAT I CAN DO.
MONITOR AND DISSEMINATE...

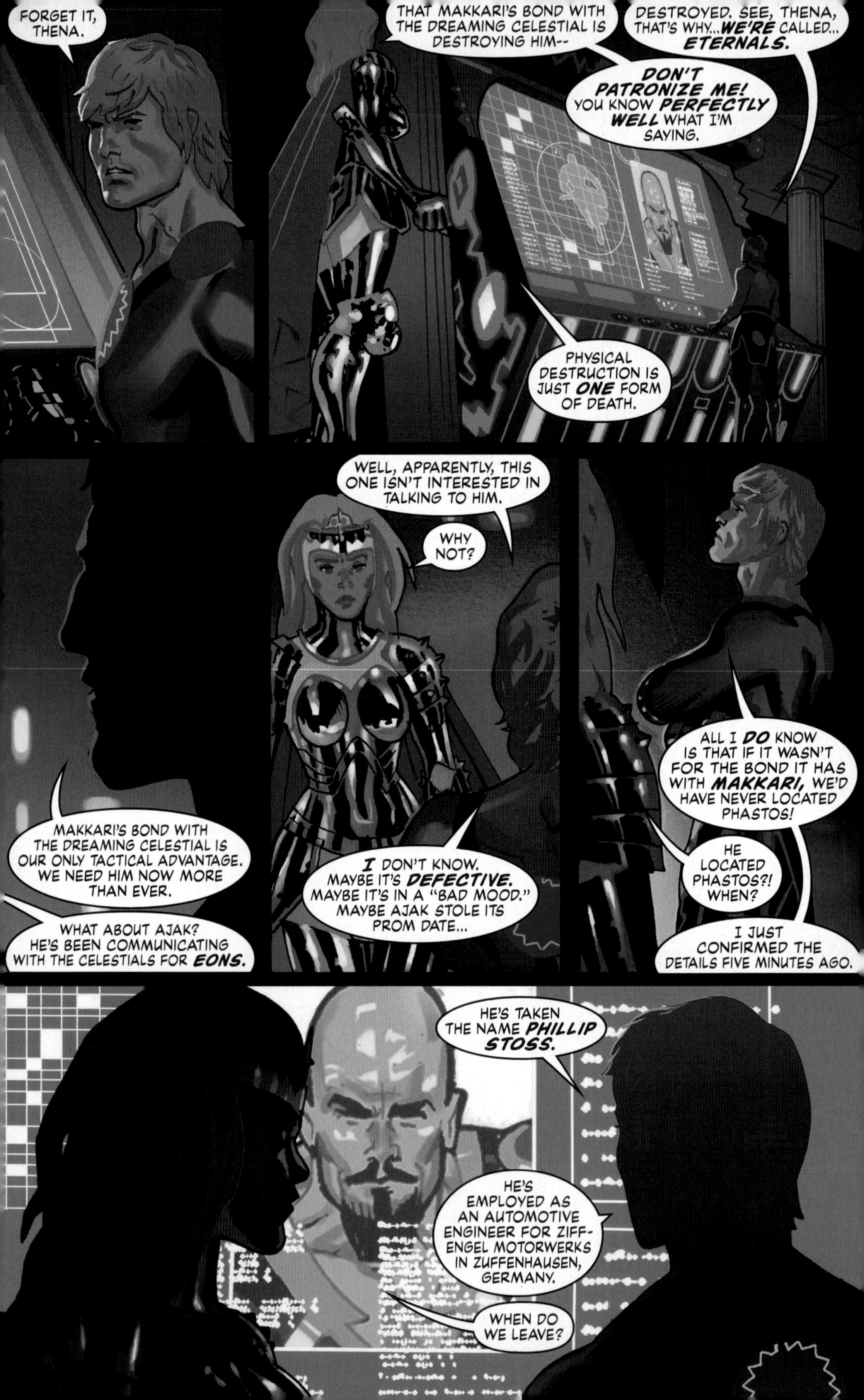
FORGET IT, THENA.
THAT MAKKARI'S BOND WITH THE DREAMING CELESTIAL IS DESTROYING HIM--
DESTROYED. SEE, THENA, THAT'S WHY...WE'RE CALLED... ETERNALS.
DON'T PATRONIZE ME! YOU KNOW PERFECTLY WELL WHAT I'M SAYING.
PHYSICAL DESTRUCTION IS JUST ONE FORM OF DEATH.
MAKKARI'S BOND WITH THE DREAMING CELESTIAL IS OUR ONLY TACTICAL ADVANTAGE. WE NEED HIM NOW MORE THAN EVER.
WHAT ABOUT AJAK? HE'S BEEN COMMUNICATING WITH THE CELESTIALS FOR EONS.
WELL, APPARENTLY, THIS ONE ISN'T INTERESTED IN TALKING TO HIM.
WHY NOT?
I DON'T KNOW. MAYBE IT'S DEFECTIVE. MAYBE IT'S IN A "BAD MOOD." MAYBE AJAK STOLE ITS PROM DATE...
ALL I DO KNOW IS THAT IF IT WASN'T FOR THE BOND IT HAS WITH MAKKARI, WE'D HAVE NEVER LOCATED PHASTOS!
HE LOCATED PHASTOS?! WHEN?
I JUST CONFIRMED THE DETAILS FIVE MINUTES AGO.
HE'S TAKEN THE NAME PHILLIP STOSS.
HE'S EMPLOYED AS AN AUTOMOTIVE ENGINEER FOR ZIFF-ENGEL MOTORWERKS IN ZUFFENHAUSEN, GERMANY.
WHEN DO WE LEAVE?

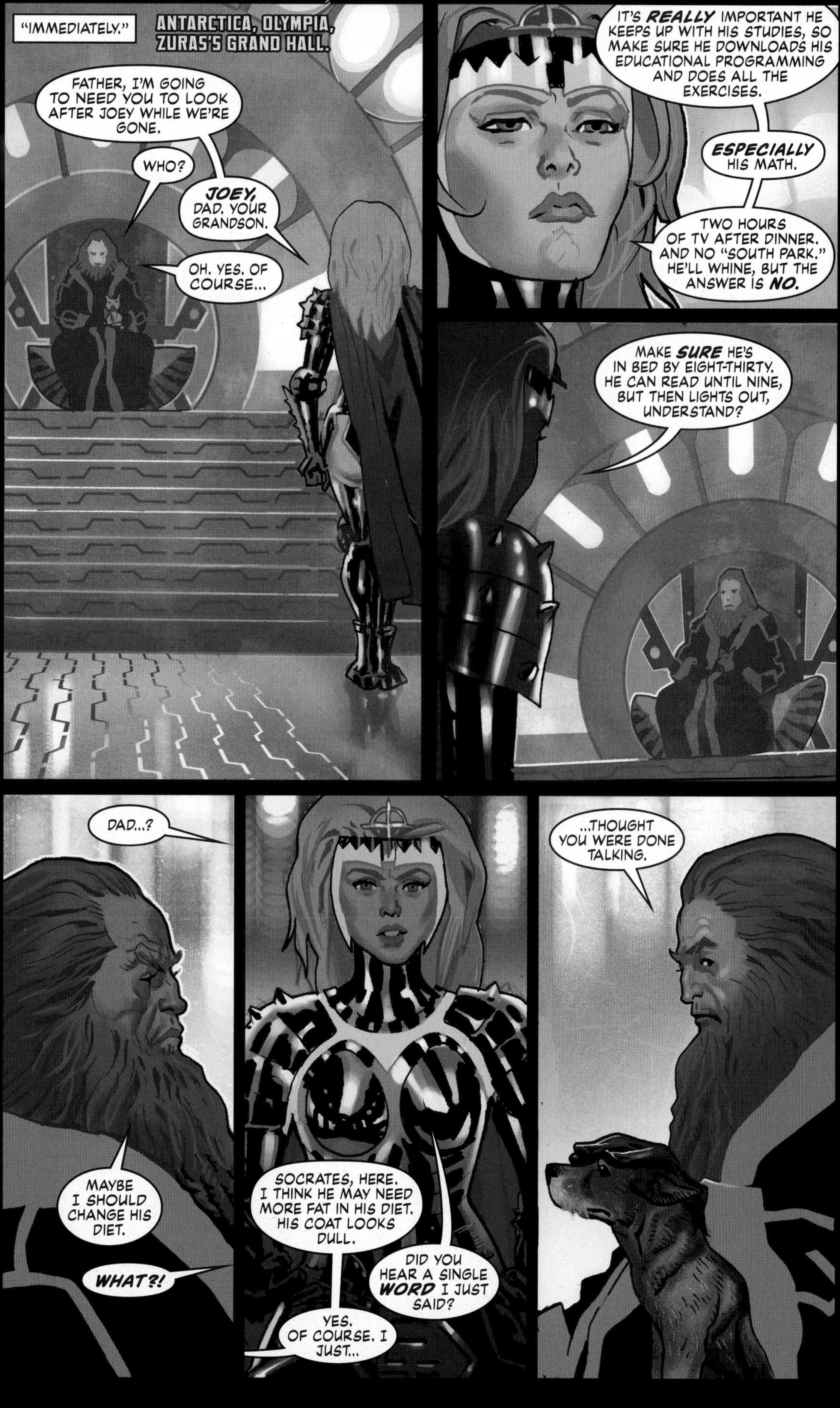
"IMMEDIATELY."
ANTARCTICA, OLYMPIA, ZURAS'S GRAND HALL.
FATHER, I'M GOING TO NEED YOU TO LOOK AFTER JOEY WHILE WE'RE GONE.
WHO?
JOEY, DAD. YOUR GRANDSON.
OH. YES. OF COURSE...
IT'S REALLY IMPORTANT HE KEEPS UP WITH HIS STUDIES, SO MAKE SURE HE DOWNLOADS HIS EDUCATIONAL PROGRAMMING AND DOES ALL THE EXERCISES.
ESPECIALLY HIS MATH.
TWO HOURS OF TV AFTER DINNER. AND NO "SOUTH PARK." HE'LL WHINE, BUT THE ANSWER IS NO.
MAKE SURE HE'S IN BED BY EIGHT-THIRTY. HE CAN READ UNTIL NINE, BUT THEN LIGHTS OUT, UNDERSTAND?
DAD...?
...THOUGHT YOU WERE DONE TALKING.
MAYBE I SHOULD CHANGE HIS DIET.
SOCRATES, HERE. I THINK HE MAY NEED MORE FAT IN HIS DIET. HIS COAT LOOKS DULL.
WHAT?!
DID YOU HEAR A SINGLE WORD I JUST SAID?
YES. OF COURSE. I JUST...

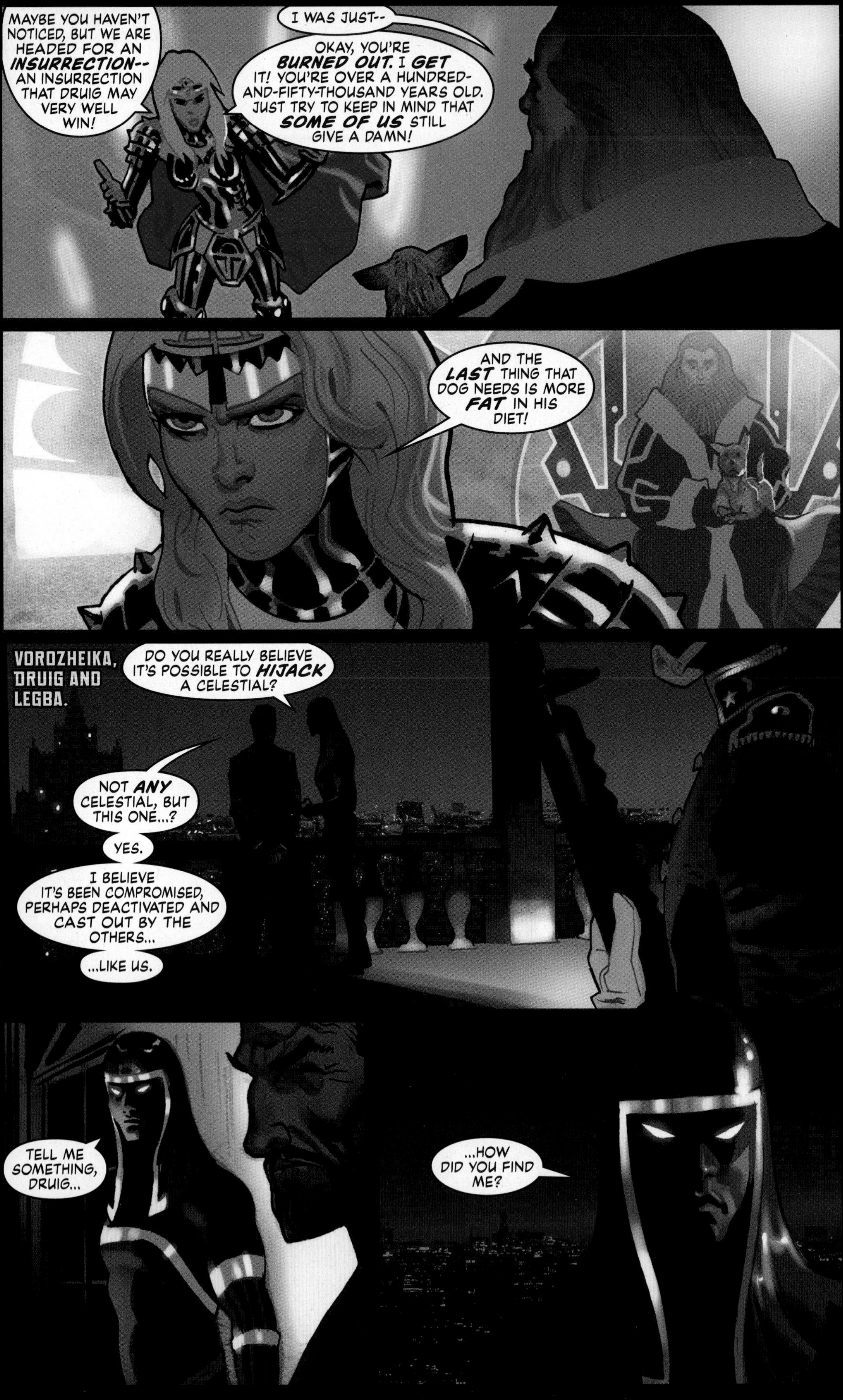
MAYBE YOU HAVEN'T NOTICED, BUT WE ARE HEADED FOR AN INSURRECTION-- AN INSURRECTION THAT DRUIG MAY VERY WELL WIN!
I WAS JUST--
OKAY, YOU'RE BURNED OUT. I GET IT! YOU'RE OVER A HUNDRED-AND-FIFTY-THOUSAND YEARS OLD. JUST TRY TO KEEP IN MIND THAT SOME OF US STILL GIVE A DAMN!
AND THE LAST THING THAT DOG NEEDS IS MORE FAT IN HIS DIET!
VOROZHEIKA, DRUIG AND LEGBA.
DO YOU REALLY BELIEVE IT'S POSSIBLE TO HIJACK A CELESTIAL?
NOT ANY CELESTIAL, BUT THIS ONE...?
YES.
I BELIEVE IT'S BEEN COMPROMISED, PERHAPS DEACTIVATED AND CAST OUT BY THE OTHERS...
...LIKE US.
TELL ME SOMETHING, DRUIG...
...HOW DID YOU FIND ME?

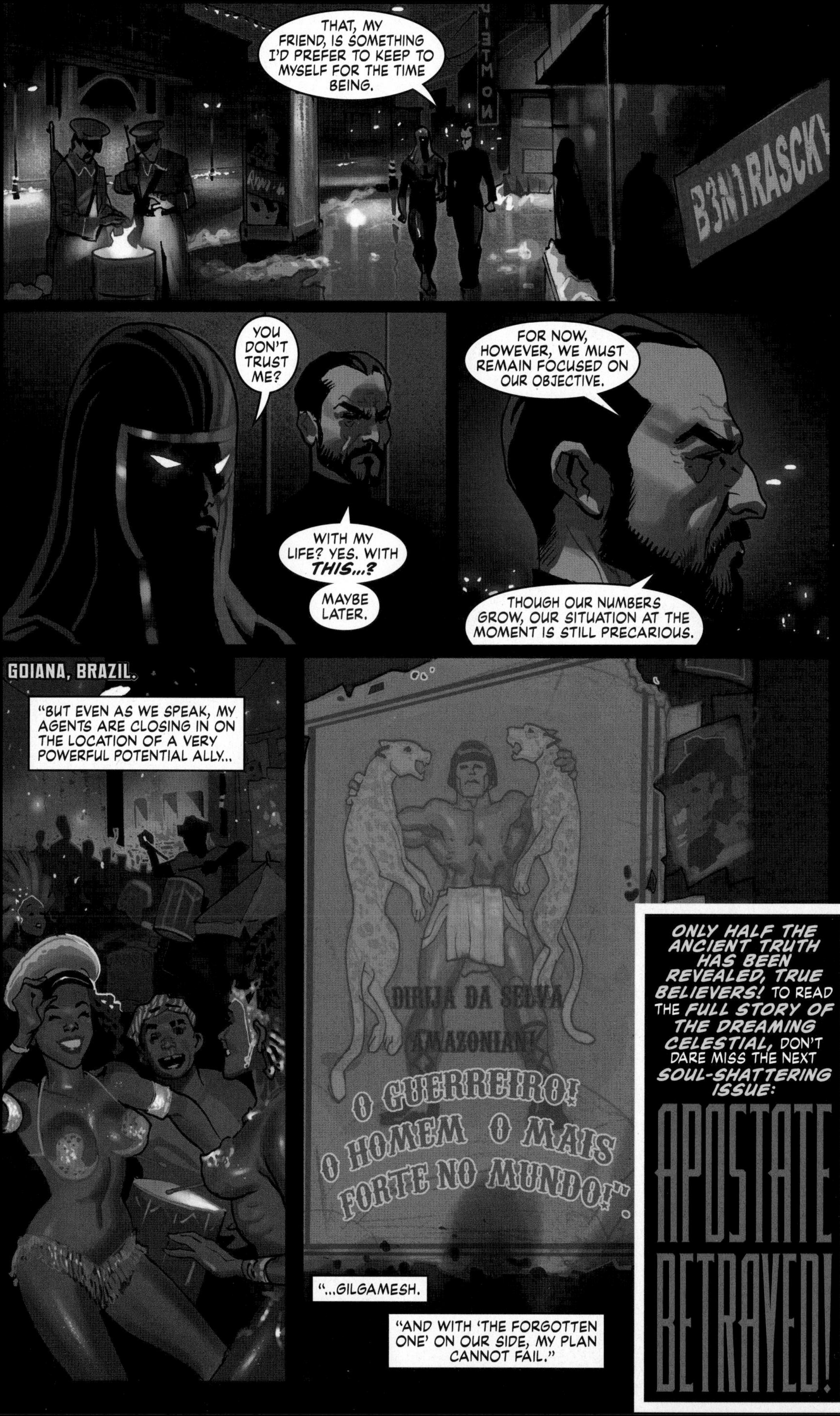
THAT, MY FRIEND, IS SOMETHING I'D PREFER TO KEEP TO MYSELF FOR THE TIME BEING.
B3N1RASCKY
YOU DON'T TRUST ME?
WITH MY LIFE? YES. WITH THIS...?
MAYBE LATER.
FOR NOW, HOWEVER, WE MUST REMAIN FOCUSED ON OUR OBJECTIVE.
THOUGH OUR NUMBERS GROW, OUR SITUATION AT THE MOMENT IS STILL PRECARIOUS.
GOIANA, BRAZIL.
"BUT EVEN AS WE SPEAK, MY AGENTS ARE CLOSING IN ON THE LOCATION OF A VERY POWERFUL POTENTIAL ALLY...
DIRIJA DA SELVA
AMAZONIAN!
O GUERREIRO!
O HOMEM O MAIS FORTE NO MUNDO!"
"...GILGAMESH.
"AND WITH 'THE FORGOTTEN ONE' ON OUR SIDE, MY PLAN CANNOT FAIL."
ONLY HALF THE ANCIENT TRUTH HAS BEEN REVEALED, TRUE BELIEVERS! TO READ THE FULL STORY OF THE DREAMING CELESTIAL, DON'T DARE MISS THE NEXT SOUL-SHATTERING ISSUE:
APOSTATE BETRAYED!

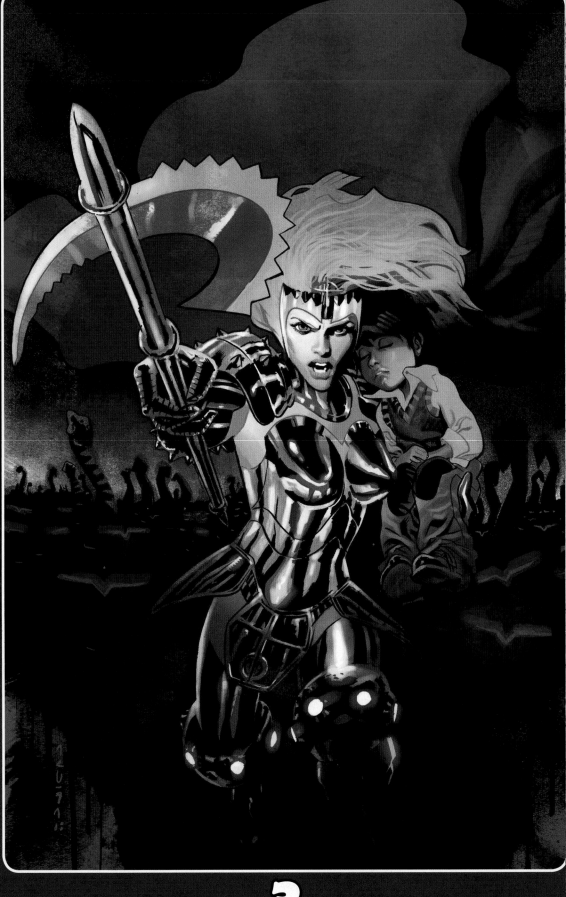

3

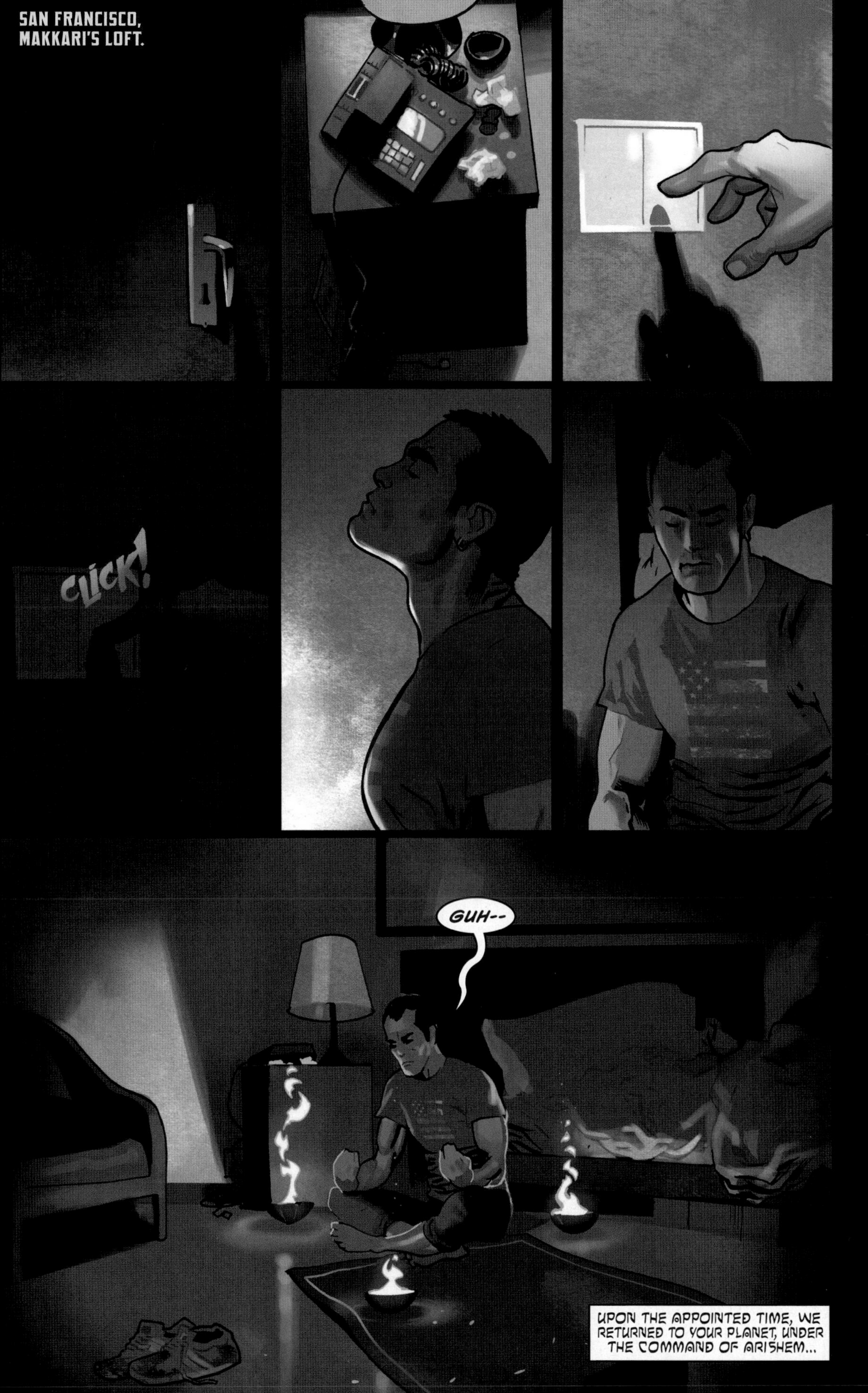
SAN FRANCISCO,
MAKKARI'S LOFT.
CLICK!
GUH--
UPON THE APPOINTED TIME, WE RETURNED TO YOUR PLANET, UNDER THE COMMAND OF ARISHEM...

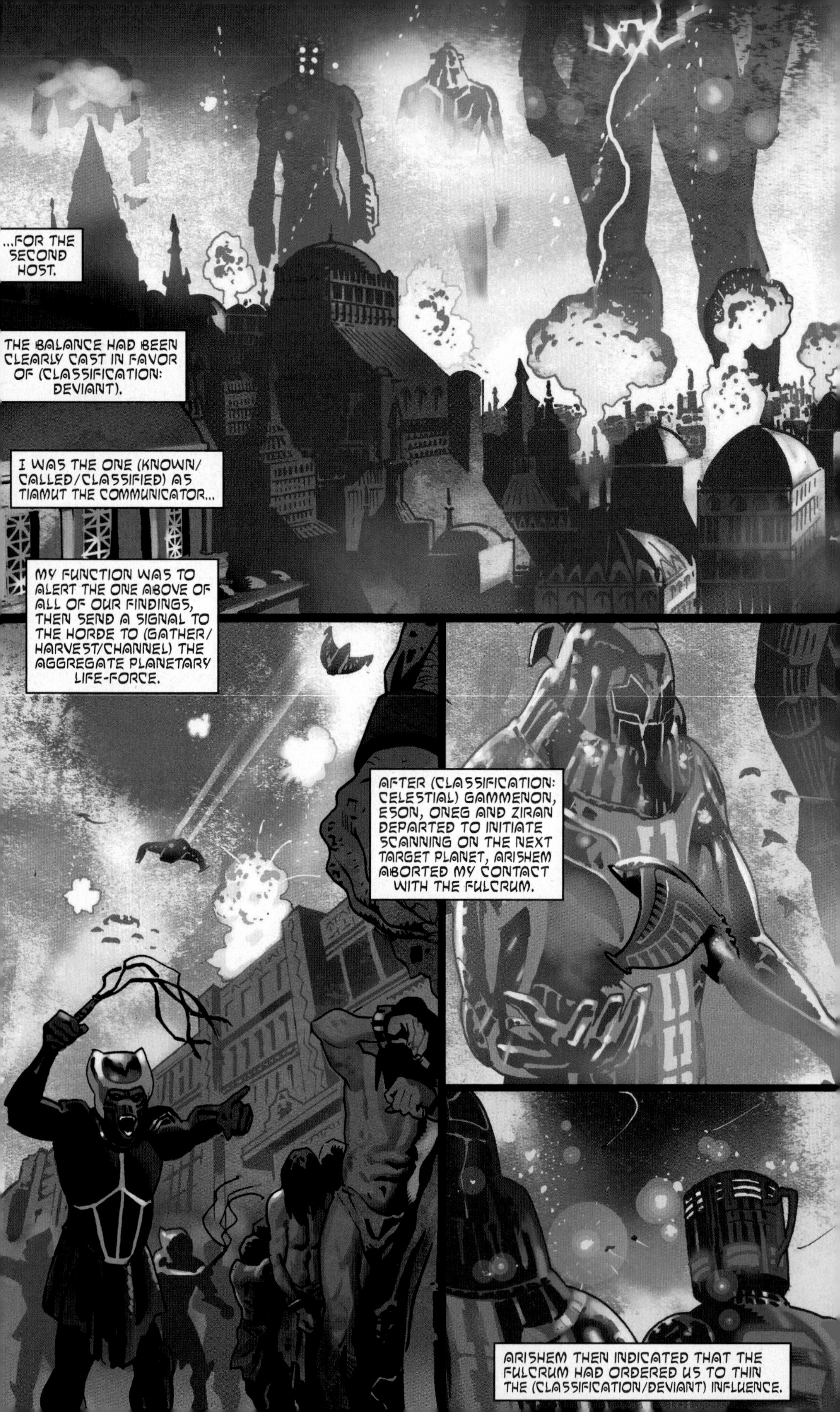
...FOR THE SECOND HOST.
THE BALANCE HAD BEEN CLEARLY CAST IN FAVOR OF (CLASSIFICATION: DEVIANT).
I WAS THE ONE (KNOWN/ CALLED/CLASSIFIED) AS TIAMUT THE COMMUNICATOR...
MY FUNCTION WAS TO ALERT THE ONE ABOVE OF ALL OF OUR FINDINGS, THEN SEND A SIGNAL TO THE HORDE TO (GATHER/ HARVEST/CHANNEL) THE AGGREGATE PLANETARY LIFE-FORCE.
AFTER (CLASSIFICATION: CELESTIAL) GAMMENON, ESON, ONEG AND ZIRAN DEPARTED TO INITIATE SCANNING ON THE NEXT TARGET PLANET, ARISHEM ABORTED MY CONTACT WITH THE FULCRUM.
ARISHEM THEN INDICATED THAT THE FULCRUM HAD ORDERED US TO THIN THE (CLASSIFICATION/DEVIANT) INFLUENCE.

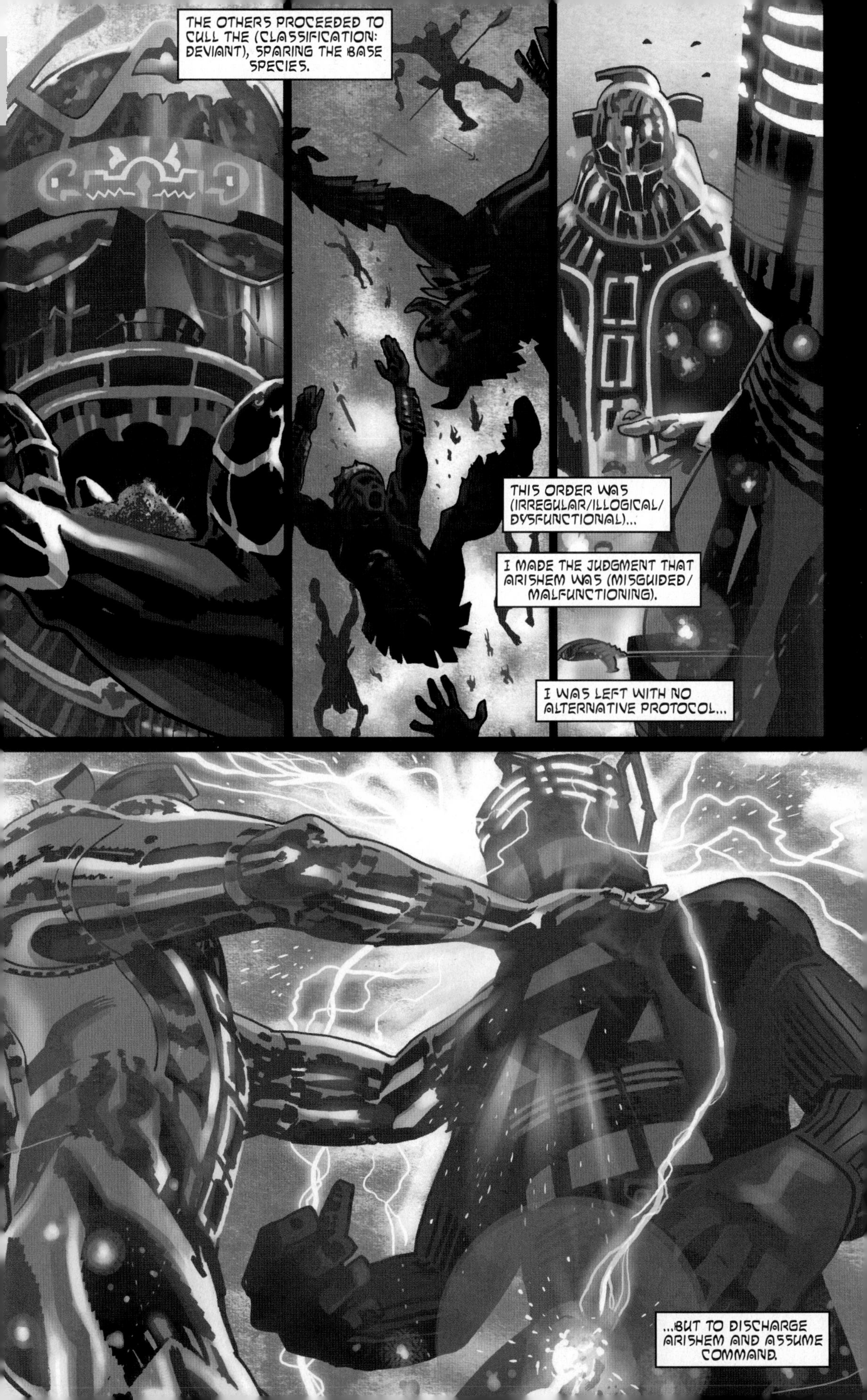
THE OTHERS PROCEEDED TO CULL THE (CLASSIFICATION: DEVIANT), SPARING THE BASE SPECIES.
THIS ORDER WAS (IRREGULAR/ILLOGICAL/ DYSFUNCTIONAL)...
I MADE THE JUDGMENT THAT ARISHEM WAS (MISGUIDED/ MALFUNCTIONING).
I WAS LEFT WITH NO ALTERNATIVE PROTOCOL...
...BUT TO DISCHARGE ARISHEM AND ASSUME COMMAND.

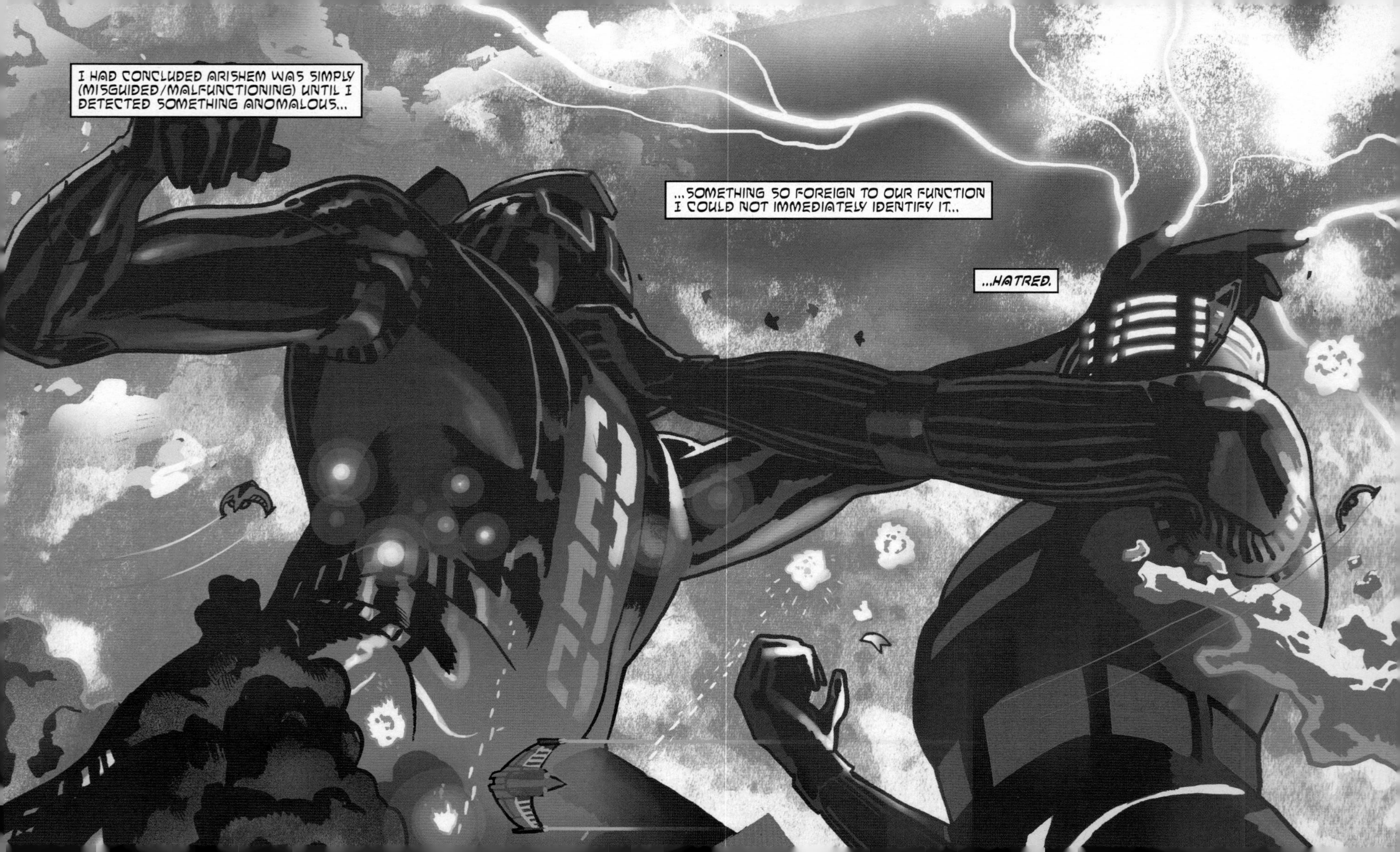
I HAD CONCLUDED ARISHEM WAS SIMPLY (MISGUIDED/MALFUNCTIONING) UNTIL I DETECTED SOMETHING ANOMALOUS...
...SOMETHING SO FOREIGN TO OUR FUNCTION I COULD NOT IMMEDIATELY IDENTIFY IT...
...HATRED.

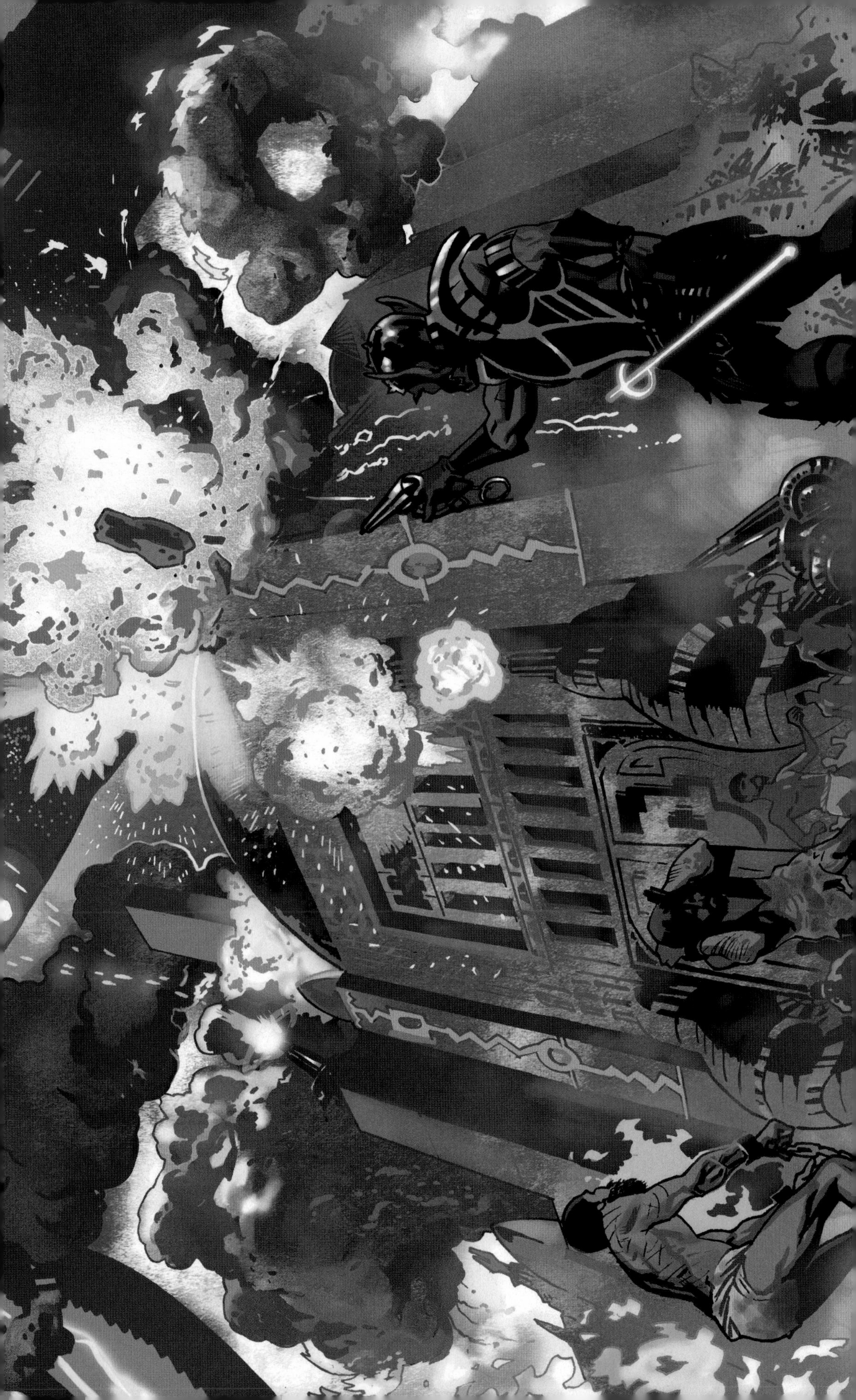

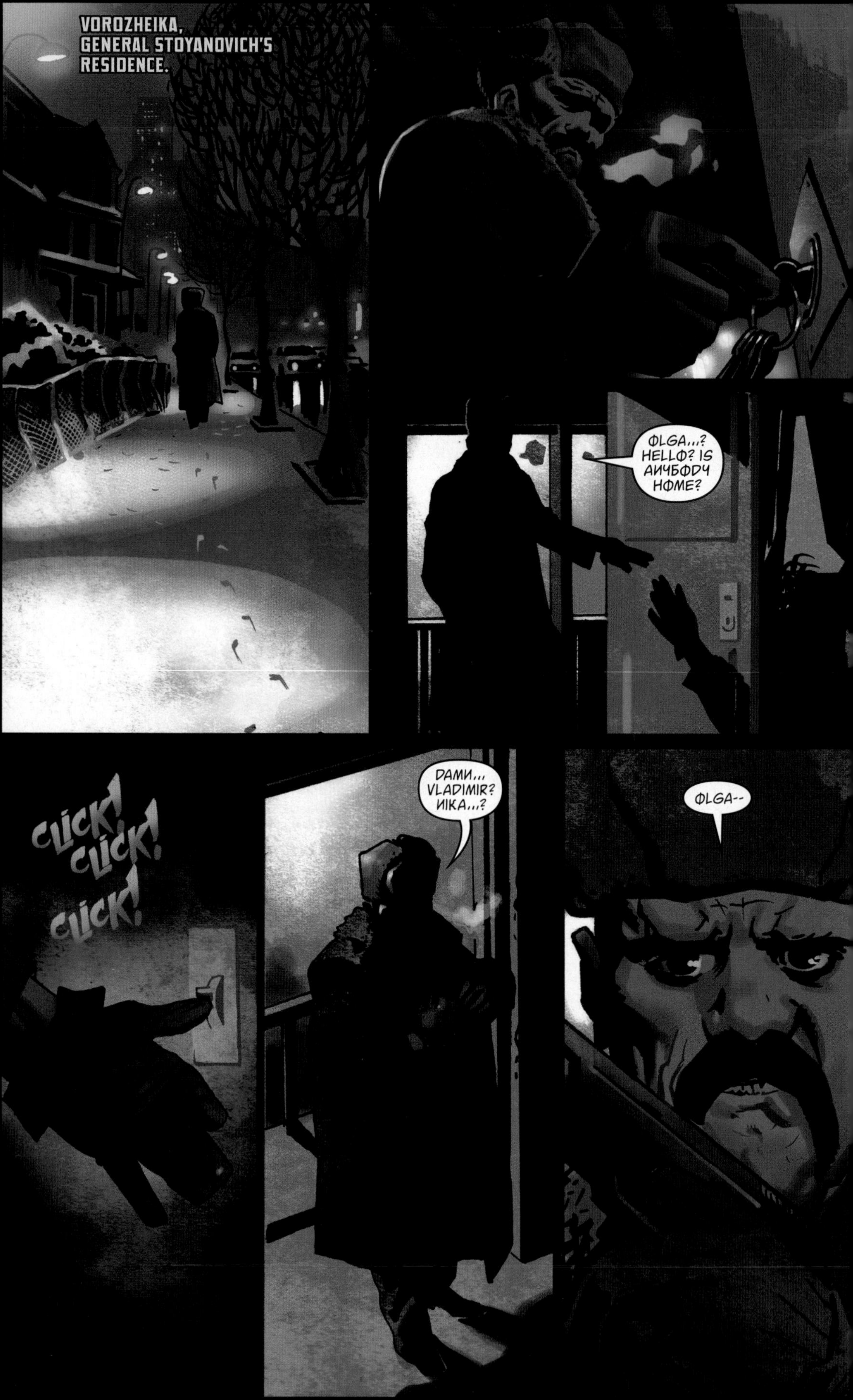

VOROZHEIKA, GENERAL STOYANOVICH'S RESIDENCE.
ΦLGA...? HELLΦ? IS AИЧБΦDЧ HΦME?
CLICK! CLICK! CLICK!
DAMИ... VLADIMIR? ИIKA...?
ΦLGA--

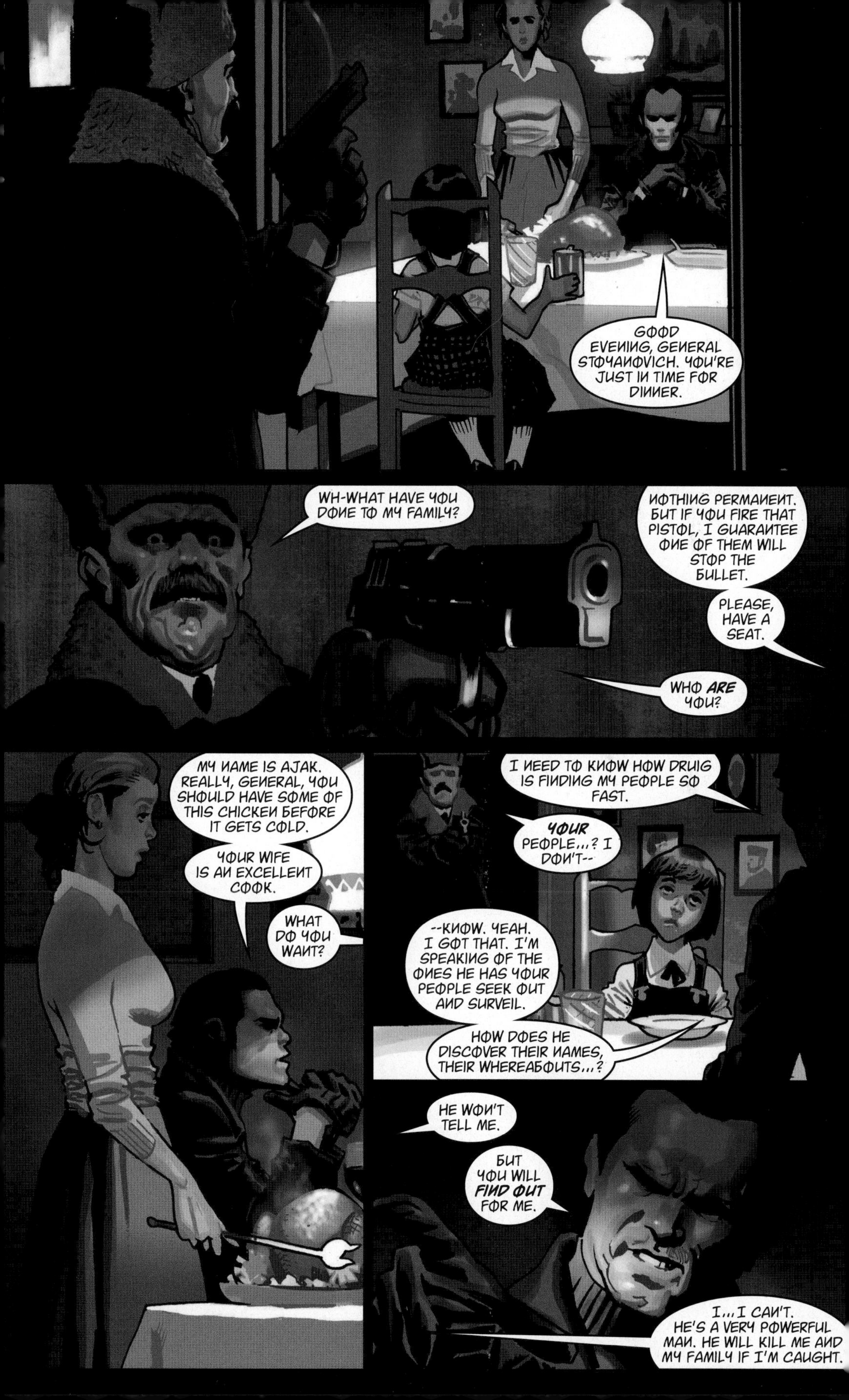
GOOD EVENING, GENERAL STOYANOVICH. YOU'RE JUST IN TIME FOR DINNER.
WH-WHAT HAVE YOU DONE TO MY FAMILY?
NOTHING PERMANENT. BUT IF YOU FIRE THAT PISTOL, I GUARANTEE ONE OF THEM WILL STOP THE BULLET.
PLEASE, HAVE A SEAT.
WHO **ARE** YOU?
MY NAME IS AJAK. REALLY, GENERAL, YOU SHOULD HAVE SOME OF THIS CHICKEN BEFORE IT GETS COLD.
YOUR WIFE IS AN EXCELLENT COOK.
WHAT DO YOU WANT?
I NEED TO KNOW HOW DRUIG IS FINDING MY PEOPLE SO FAST.
YOUR PEOPLE...? I DON'T--
--KNOW. YEAH. I GOT THAT. I'M SPEAKING OF THE ONES HE HAS YOUR PEOPLE SEEK OUT AND SURVEIL.
HOW DOES HE DISCOVER THEIR NAMES, THEIR WHEREABOUTS...?
HE WON'T TELL ME.
BUT YOU WILL ***FIND OUT*** FOR ME.
I...I CAN'T. HE'S A VERY POWERFUL MAN. HE WILL KILL ME AND MY FAMILY IF I'M CAUGHT.

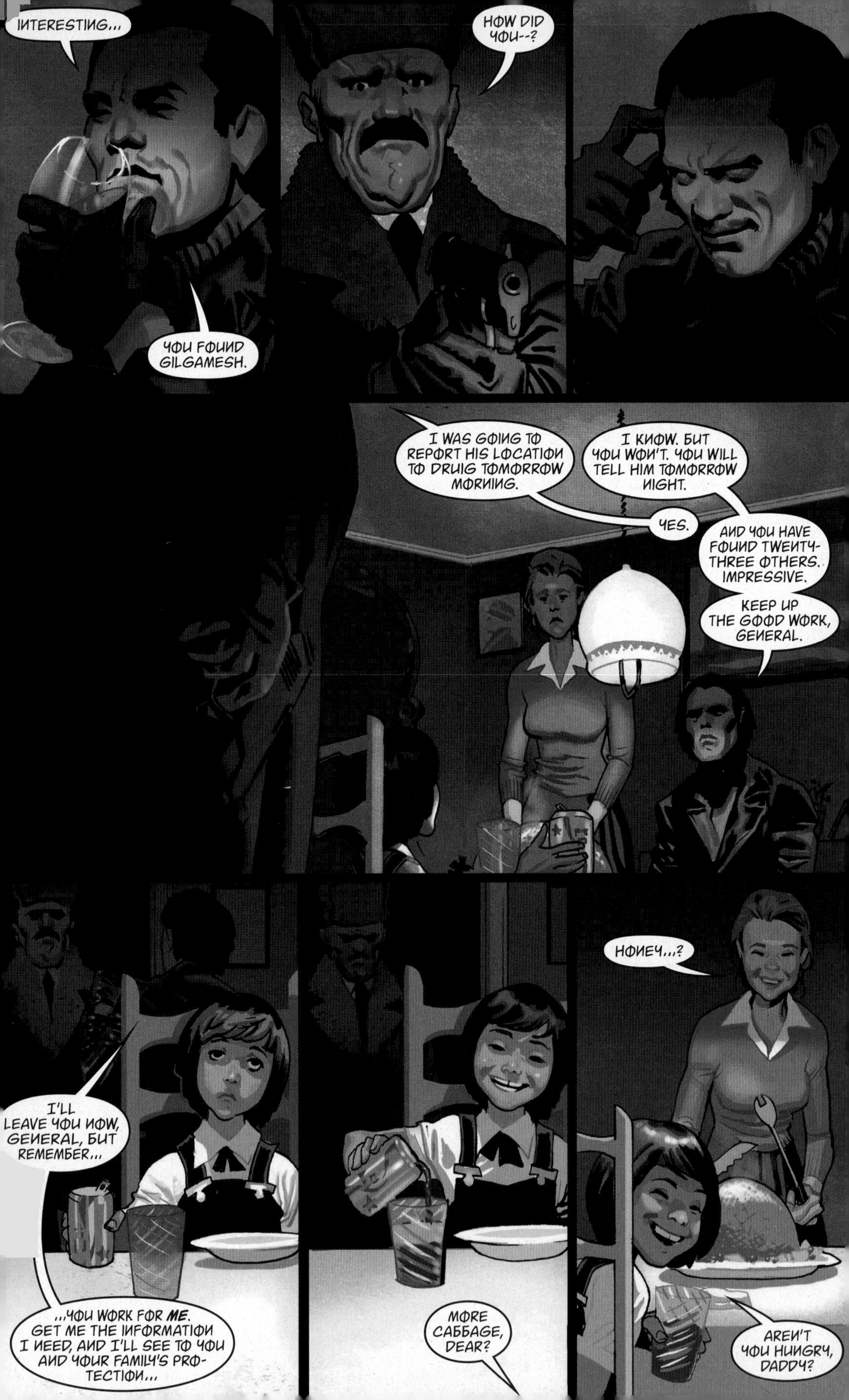
INTERESTING...
YOU FOUND GILGAMESH.
HOW DID YOU--?
I WAS GOING TO REPORT HIS LOCATION TO DRUIG TOMORROW MORNING.
I KNOW. BUT YOU WON'T. YOU WILL TELL HIM TOMORROW NIGHT.
YES.
AND YOU HAVE FOUND TWENTY-THREE OTHERS. IMPRESSIVE.
KEEP UP THE GOOD WORK, GENERAL.
I'LL LEAVE YOU NOW, GENERAL, BUT REMEMBER...
...YOU WORK FOR ME. GET ME THE INFORMATION I NEED, AND I'LL SEE TO YOU AND YOUR FAMILY'S PRO-TECTION...
MORE CABBAGE, DEAR?
HONEY...?
AREN'T YOU HUNGRY, DADDY?

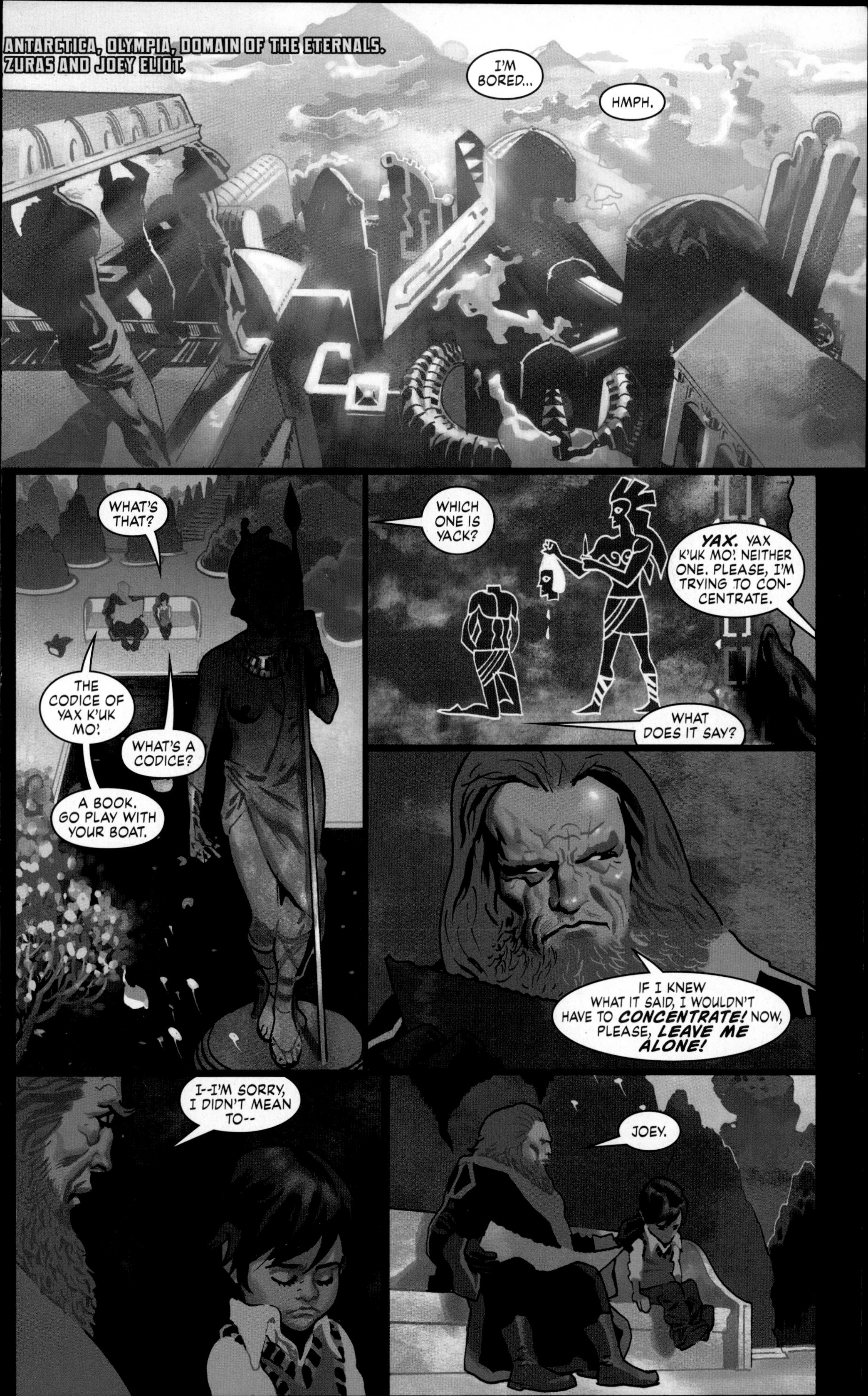
ANTARCTICA, OLYMPIA, DOMAIN OF THE ETERNALS.
ZURAS AND JOEY ELIOT.
I'M BORED...
HMPH.
WHAT'S THAT?
THE CODICE OF YAX K'UK MO'.
WHAT'S A CODICE?
A BOOK. GO PLAY WITH YOUR BOAT.
WHICH ONE IS YACK?
YAX. YAX K'UK MO'. NEITHER ONE. PLEASE, I'M TRYING TO CON-CENTRATE.
WHAT DOES IT SAY?
IF I KNEW WHAT IT SAID, I WOULDN'T HAVE TO CONCENTRATE! NOW, PLEASE, LEAVE ME ALONE!
I--I'M SORRY, I DIDN'T MEAN TO--
JOEY.

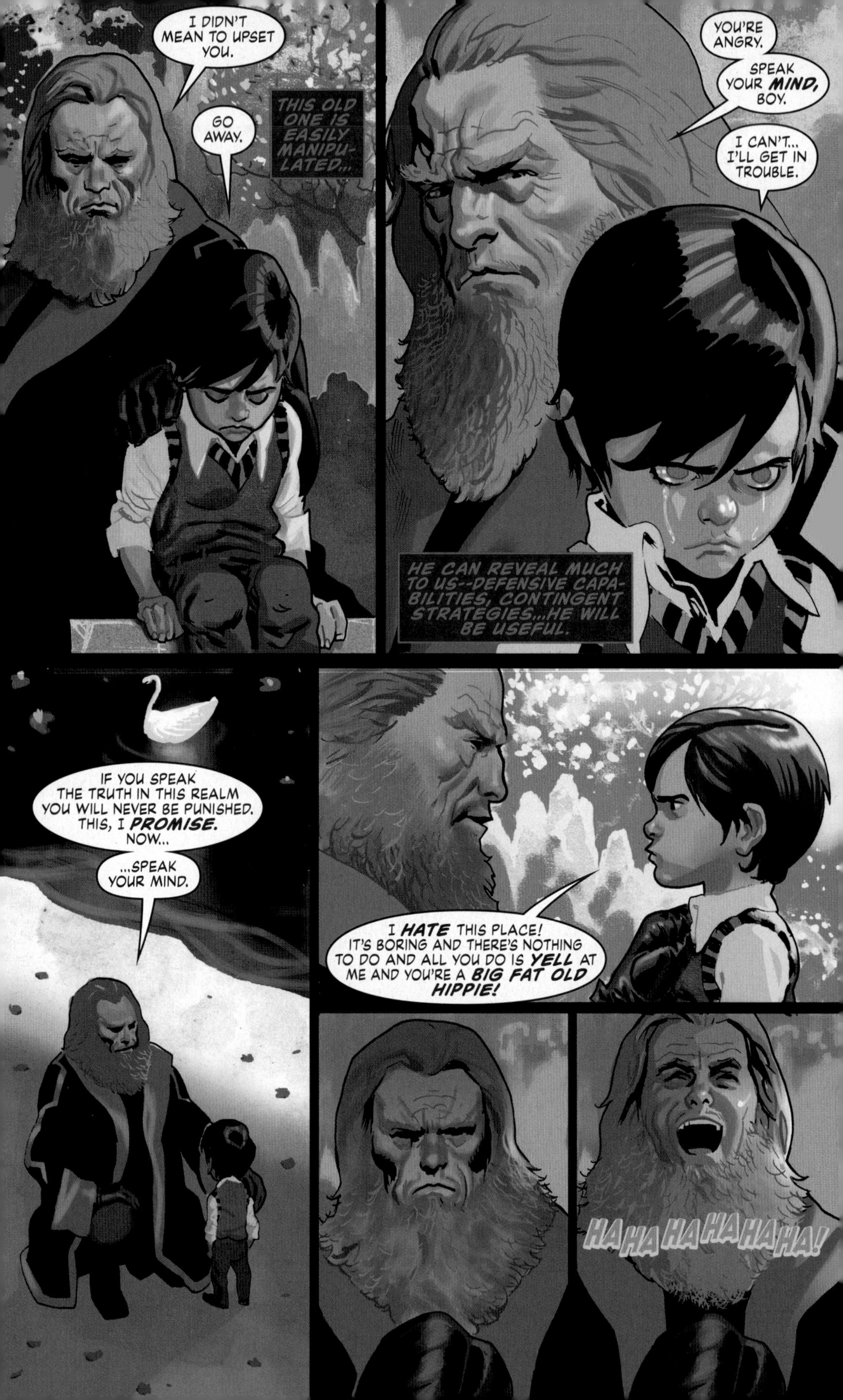
I DIDN'T MEAN TO UPSET YOU.
GO AWAY.
THIS OLD ONE IS EASILY MANIPULATED...
YOU'RE ANGRY.
SPEAK YOUR MIND, BOY.
I CAN'T... I'LL GET IN TROUBLE.
HE CAN REVEAL MUCH TO US--DEFENSIVE CAPABILITIES, CONTINGENT STRATEGIES...HE WILL BE USEFUL.
IF YOU SPEAK THE TRUTH IN THIS REALM YOU WILL NEVER BE PUNISHED. THIS, I PROMISE. NOW...
...SPEAK YOUR MIND.
I HATE THIS PLACE! IT'S BORING AND THERE'S NOTHING TO DO AND ALL YOU DO IS YELL AT ME AND YOU'RE A BIG FAT OLD HIPPIE!
HAHAHAHAHAHAHA!

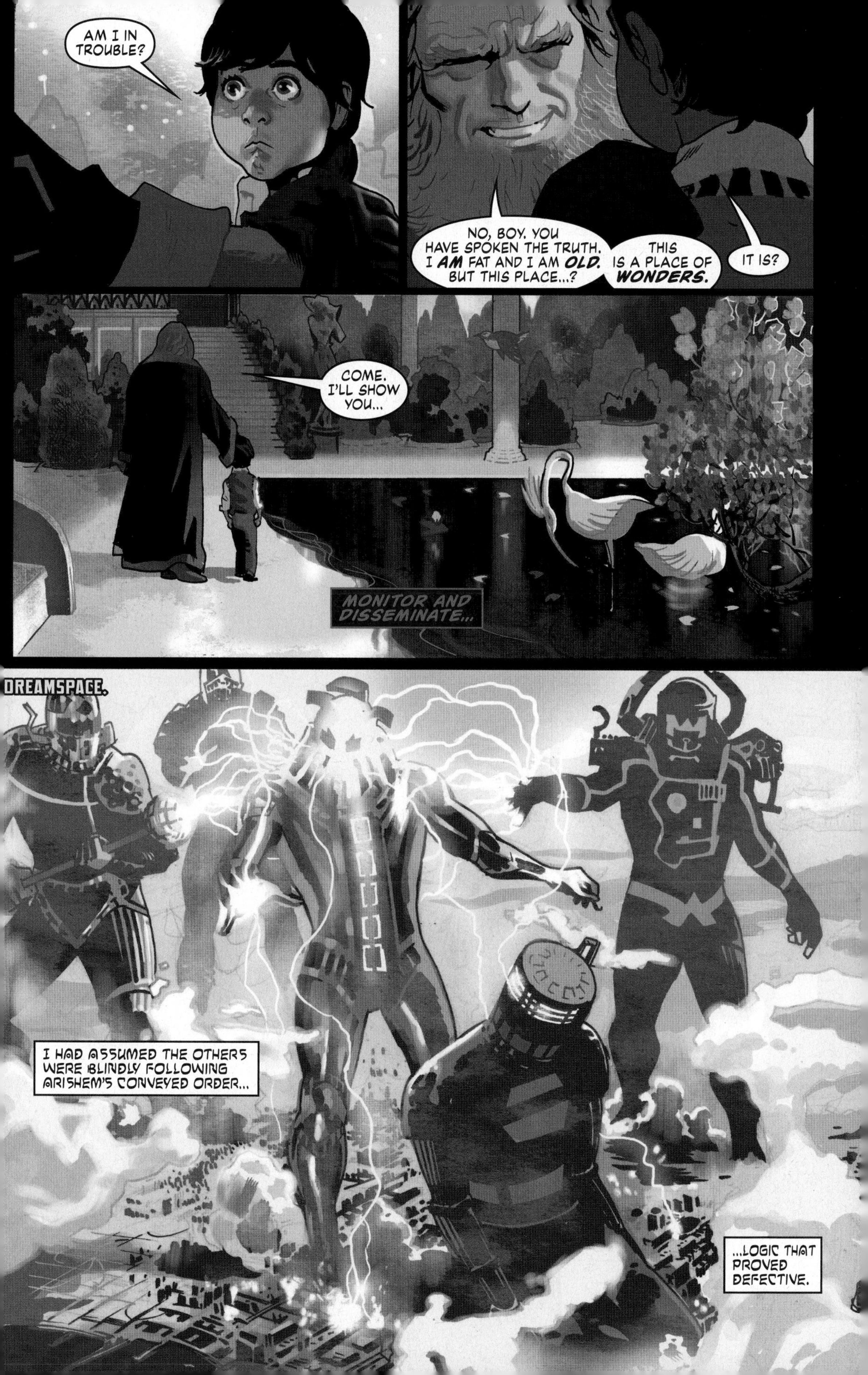

AM I IN TROUBLE?
NO, BOY. YOU HAVE SPOKEN THE TRUTH. I **AM** FAT AND I AM **OLD.** BUT THIS PLACE...?
THIS IS A PLACE OF **WONDERS.**
IT IS?
COME. I'LL SHOW YOU...
MONITOR AND DISSEMINATE...
DREAMSPACE.
I HAD ASSUMED THE OTHERS WERE BLINDLY FOLLOWING ARISHEM'S CONVEYED ORDER...
...LOGIC THAT PROVED DEFECTIVE.

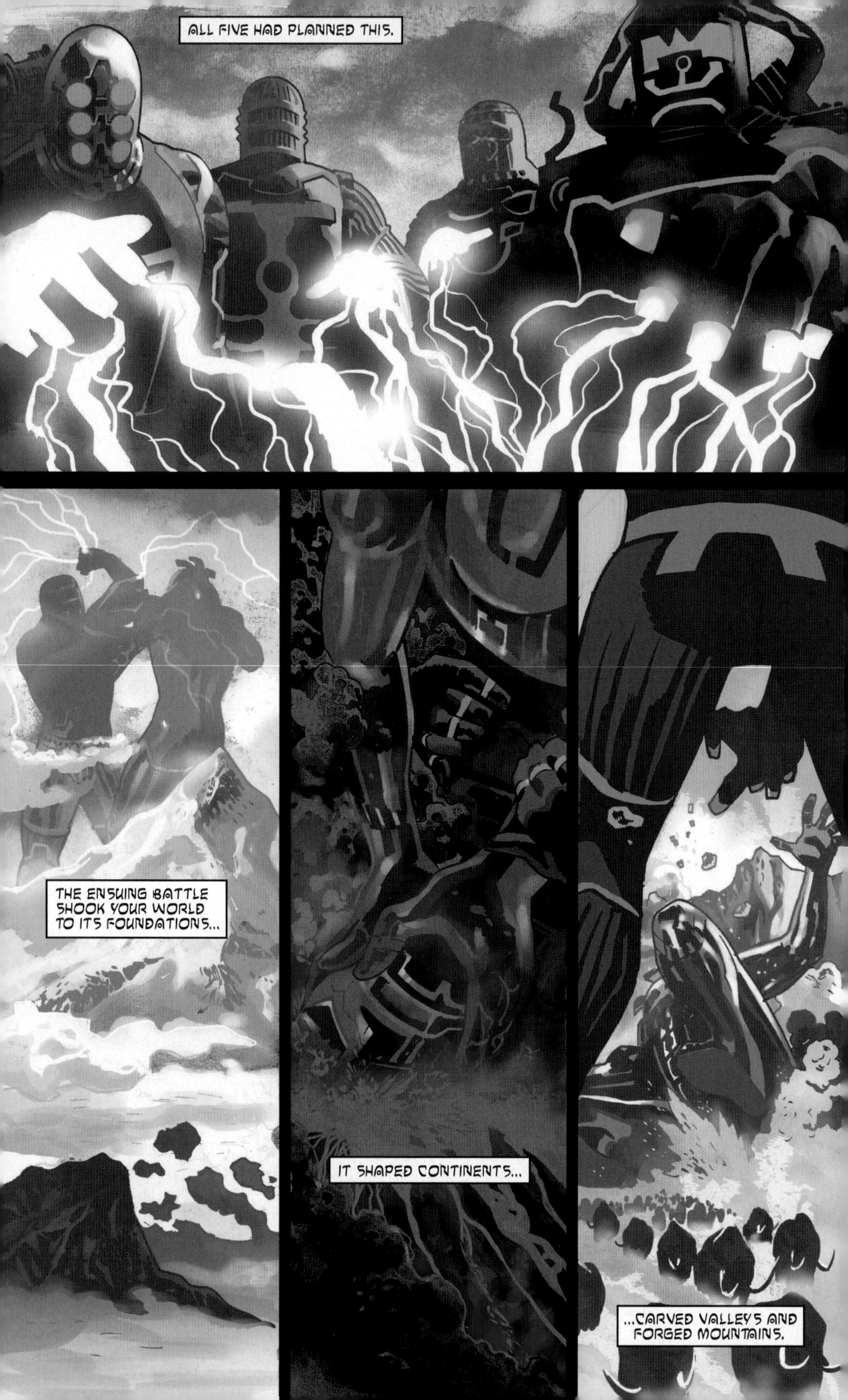
ALL FIVE HAD PLANNED THIS.
THE ENSUING BATTLE SHOOK YOUR WORLD TO ITS FOUNDATIONS...
IT SHAPED CONTINENTS...
...CARVED VALLEYS AND FORGED MOUNTAINS.

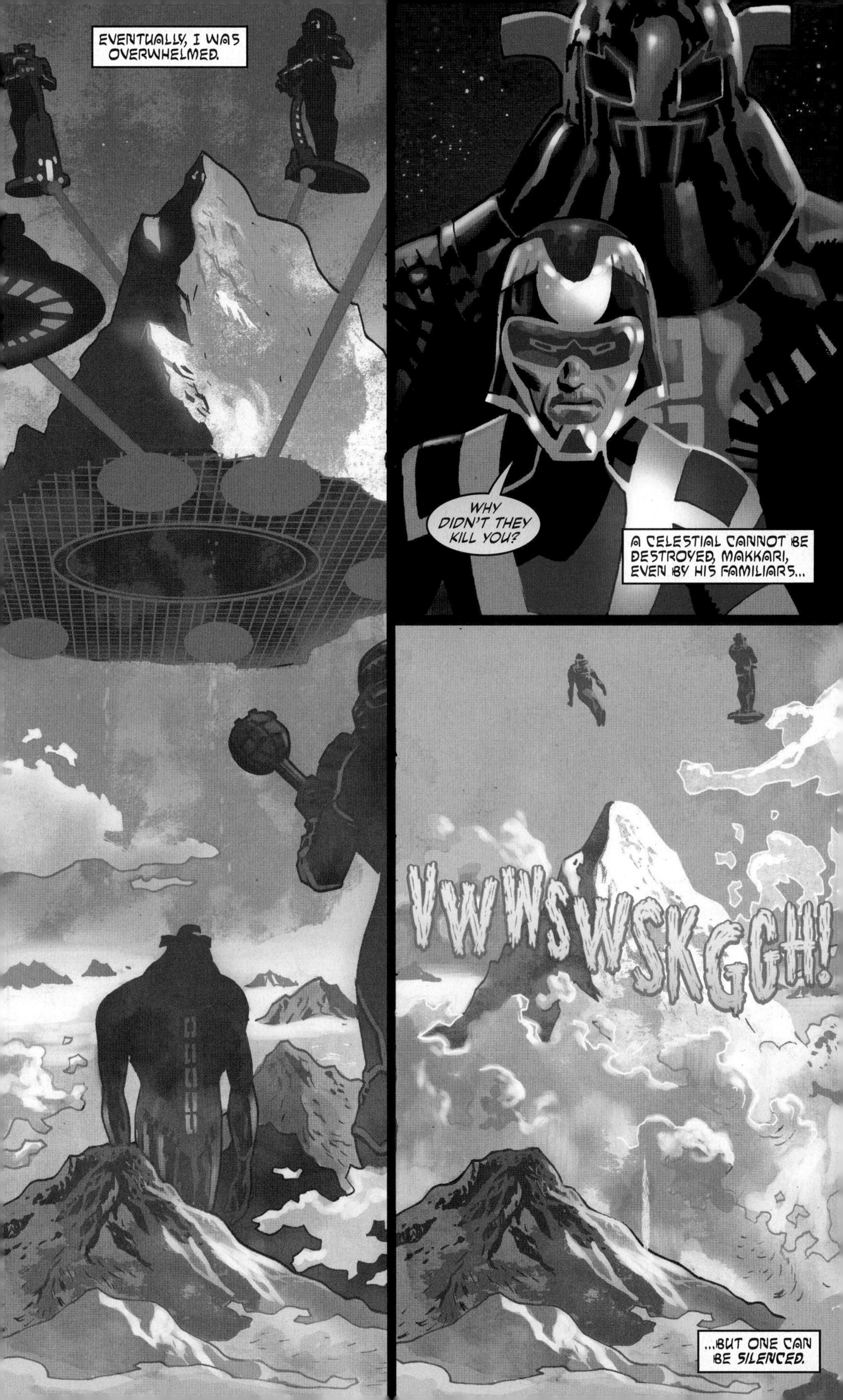
EVENTUALLY, I WAS OVERWHELMED.
WHY DIDN'T THEY KILL YOU?
A CELESTIAL CANNOT BE DESTROYED, MAKKARI, EVEN BY HIS FAMILIARS...
VWWSWSKGCH!
...BUT ONE CAN BE *SILENCED.*

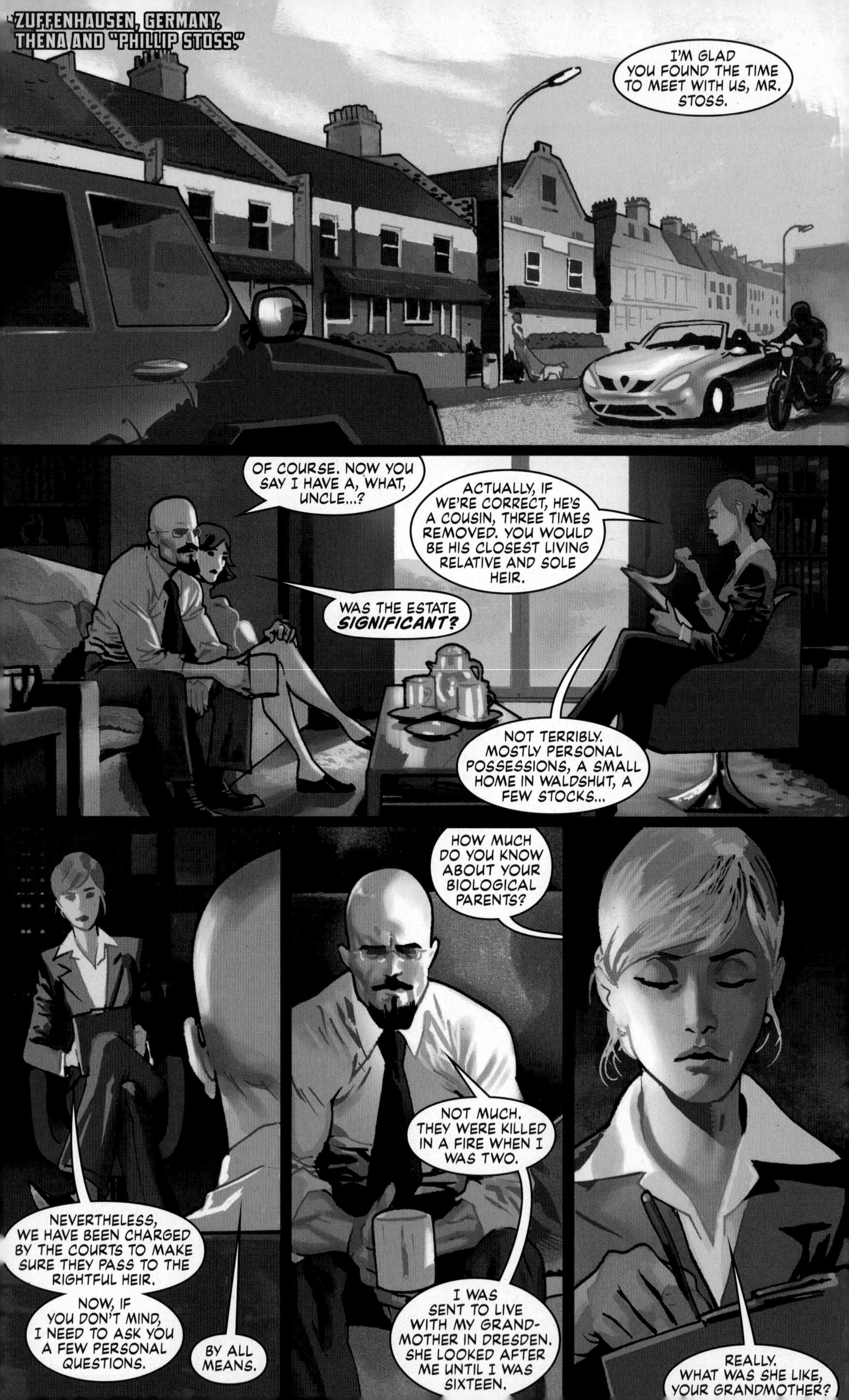
ZUFFENHAUSEN, GERMANY.
THENA AND "PHILLIP STOSS."
I'M GLAD YOU FOUND THE TIME TO MEET WITH US, MR. STOSS.
OF COURSE. NOW YOU SAY I HAVE A, WHAT, UNCLE...?
ACTUALLY, IF WE'RE CORRECT, HE'S A COUSIN, THREE TIMES REMOVED. YOU WOULD BE HIS CLOSEST LIVING RELATIVE AND SOLE HEIR.
WAS THE ESTATE *SIGNIFICANT?*
NOT TERRIBLY. MOSTLY PERSONAL POSSESSIONS, A SMALL HOME IN WALDSHUT, A FEW STOCKS...
NEVERTHELESS, WE HAVE BEEN CHARGED BY THE COURTS TO MAKE SURE THEY PASS TO THE RIGHTFUL HEIR.
NOW, IF YOU DON'T MIND, I NEED TO ASK YOU A FEW PERSONAL QUESTIONS.
BY ALL MEANS.
HOW MUCH DO YOU KNOW ABOUT YOUR BIOLOGICAL PARENTS?
NOT MUCH. THEY WERE KILLED IN A FIRE WHEN I WAS TWO.
I WAS SENT TO LIVE WITH MY GRAND-MOTHER IN DRESDEN. SHE LOOKED AFTER ME UNTIL I WAS SIXTEEN.
REALLY. WHAT WAS SHE LIKE, YOUR GRANDMOTHER?

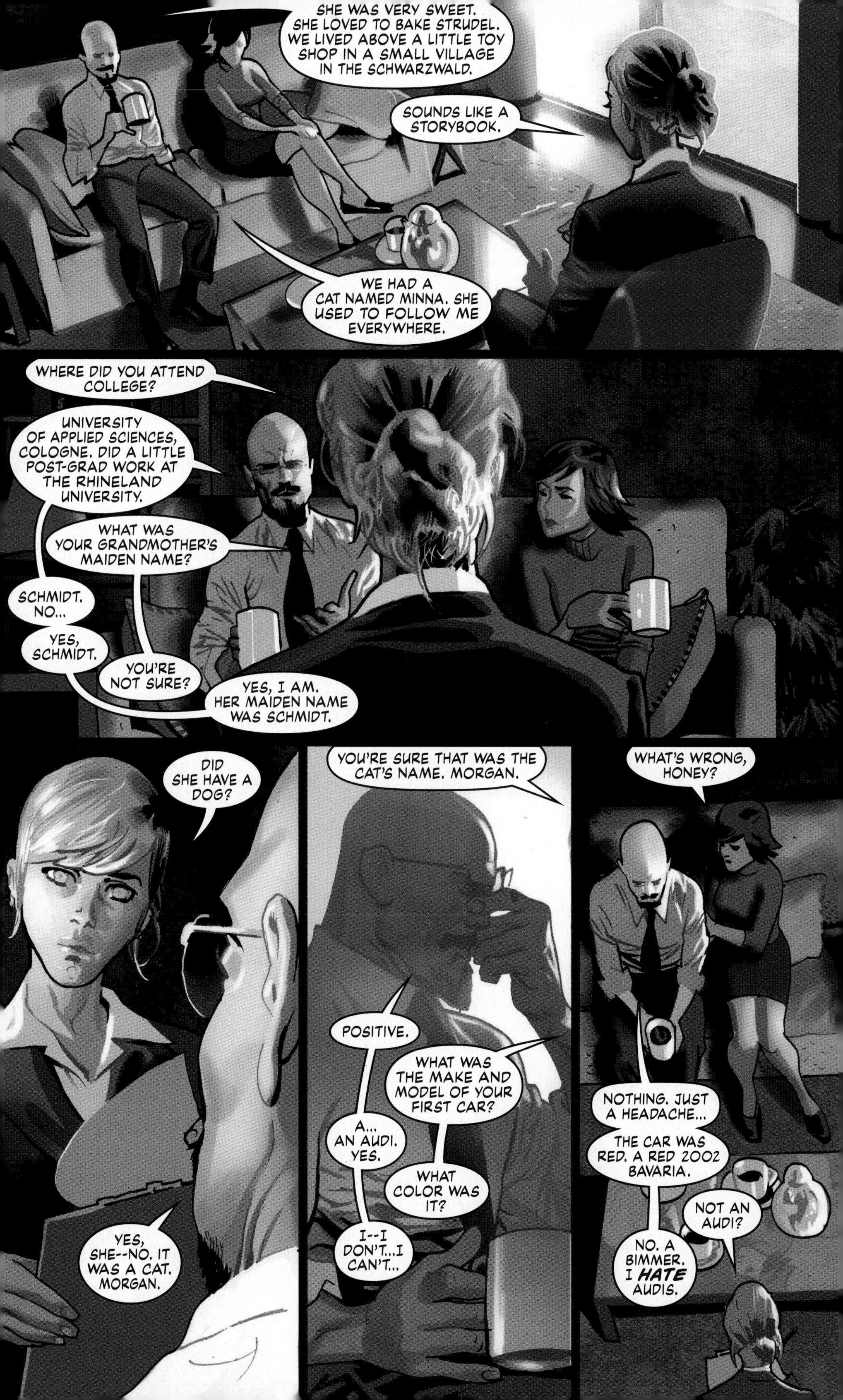
SHE WAS VERY SWEET. SHE LOVED TO BAKE STRUDEL. WE LIVED ABOVE A LITTLE TOY SHOP IN A SMALL VILLAGE IN THE SCHWARZWALD.
SOUNDS LIKE A STORYBOOK.
WE HAD A CAT NAMED MINNA. SHE USED TO FOLLOW ME EVERYWHERE.
WHERE DID YOU ATTEND COLLEGE?
UNIVERSITY OF APPLIED SCIENCES, COLOGNE. DID A LITTLE POST-GRAD WORK AT THE RHINELAND UNIVERSITY.
WHAT WAS YOUR GRANDMOTHER'S MAIDEN NAME?
SCHMIDT. NO...
YES, SCHMIDT.
YOU'RE NOT SURE?
YES, I AM. HER MAIDEN NAME WAS SCHMIDT.
DID SHE HAVE A DOG?
YES, SHE--NO. IT WAS A CAT. MORGAN.
YOU'RE SURE THAT WAS THE CAT'S NAME. MORGAN.
POSITIVE.
WHAT WAS THE MAKE AND MODEL OF YOUR FIRST CAR?
A... AN AUDI. YES.
WHAT COLOR WAS IT?
I--I DON'T...I CAN'T...
WHAT'S WRONG, HONEY?
NOTHING. JUST A HEADACHE...
THE CAR WAS RED. A RED 2002 BAVARIA.
NOT AN AUDI?
NO. A BIMMER. I HATE AUDIS.

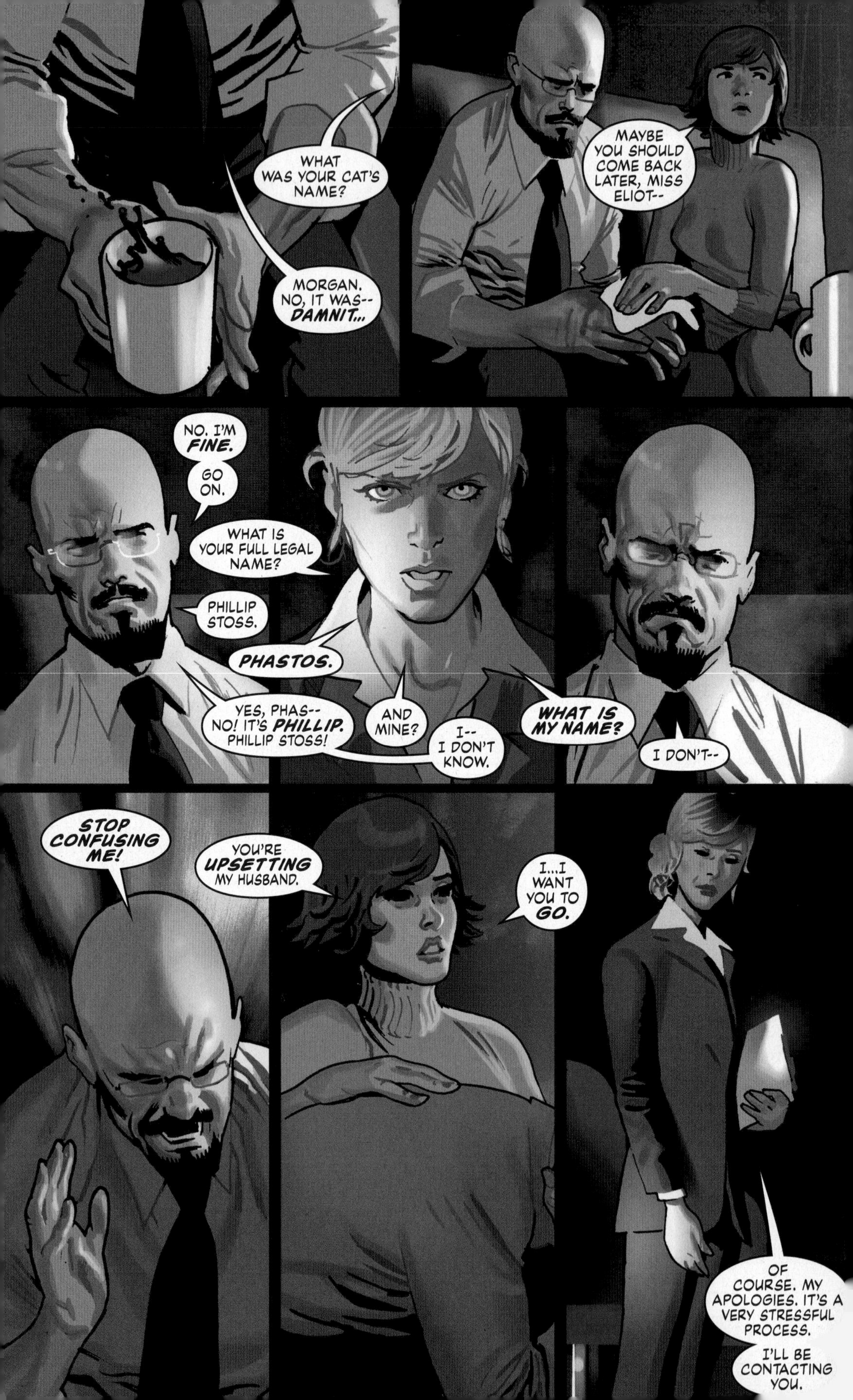
WHAT WAS YOUR CAT'S NAME?
MORGAN. NO, IT WAS-- DAMNIT...
MAYBE YOU SHOULD COME BACK LATER, MISS ELIOT--
NO. I'M FINE.
GO ON.
WHAT IS YOUR FULL LEGAL NAME?
PHILLIP STOSS.
PHASTOS.
YES, PHAS-- NO! IT'S PHILLIP. PHILLIP STOSS!
AND MINE?
I-- I DON'T KNOW.
WHAT IS MY NAME?
I DON'T--
STOP CONFUSING ME!
YOU'RE UPSETTING MY HUSBAND.
I...I WANT YOU TO GO.
OF COURSE. MY APOLOGIES. IT'S A VERY STRESSFUL PROCESS.
I'LL BE CONTACTING YOU.

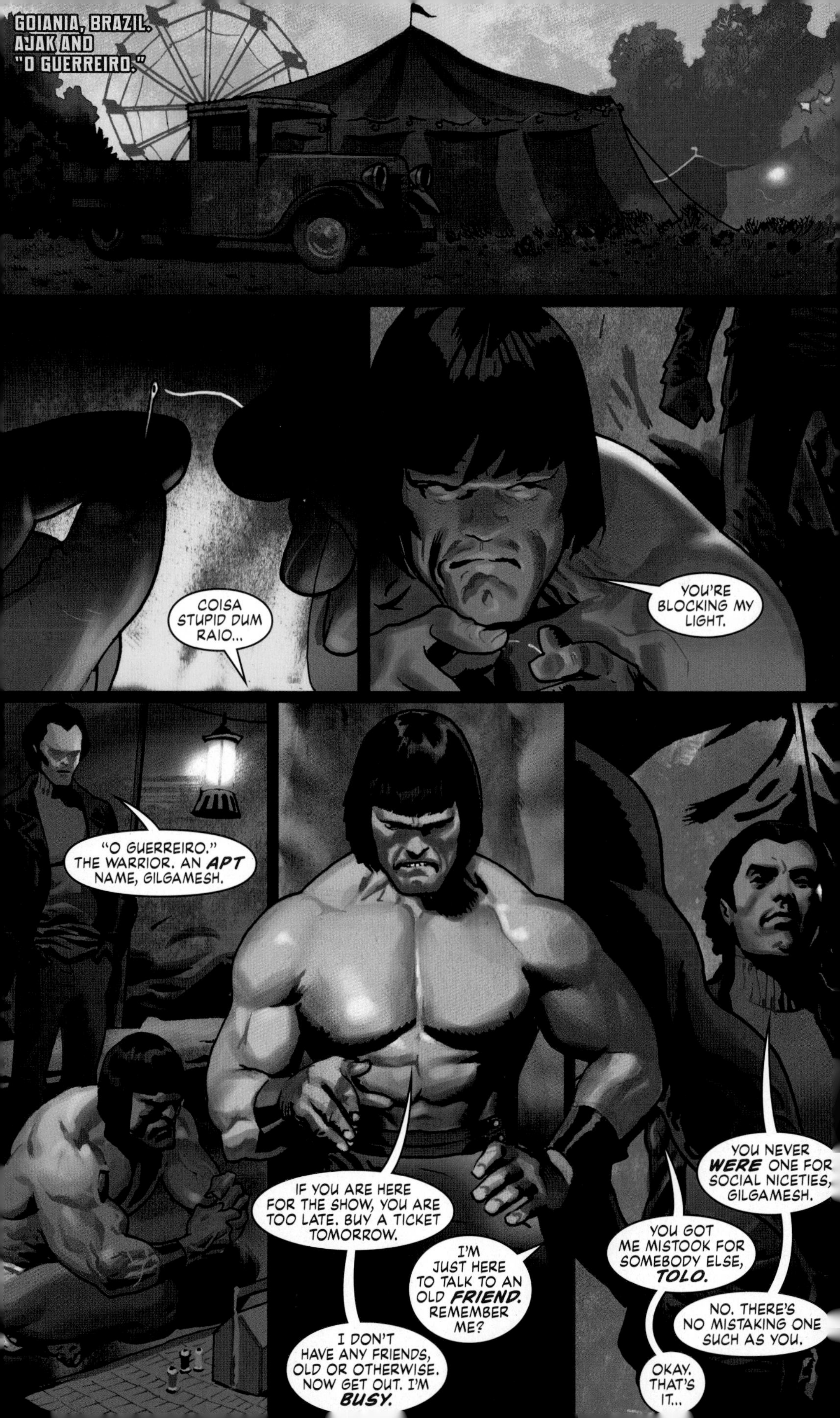
GOIANIA, BRAZIL. AJAK AND "O GUERREIRO."
COISA STUPID DUM RAIO...
YOU'RE BLOCKING MY LIGHT.
"O GUERREIRO." THE WARRIOR. AN APT NAME, GILGAMESH.
IF YOU ARE HERE FOR THE SHOW, YOU ARE TOO LATE. BUY A TICKET TOMORROW.
I'M JUST HERE TO TALK TO AN OLD FRIEND. REMEMBER ME?
I DON'T HAVE ANY FRIENDS, OLD OR OTHERWISE. NOW GET OUT. I'M BUSY.
YOU NEVER WERE ONE FOR SOCIAL NICETIES, GILGAMESH.
YOU GOT ME MISTOOK FOR SOMEBODY ELSE, TOLO.
NO. THERE'S NO MISTAKING ONE SUCH AS YOU.
OKAY. THAT'S IT...

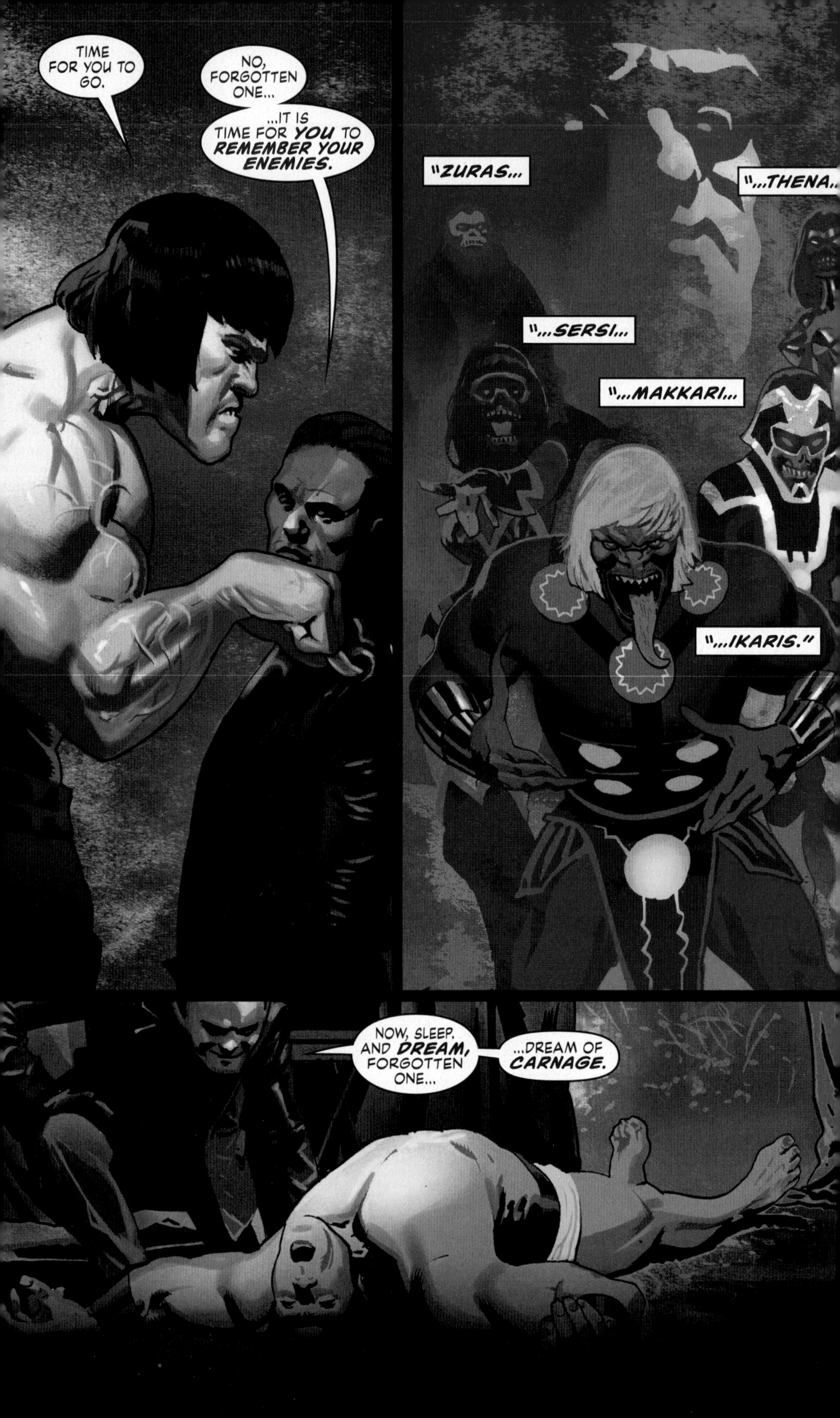
TIME FOR YOU TO GO.
NO, FORGOTTEN ONE...
...IT IS TIME FOR YOU TO REMEMBER YOUR ENEMIES.
"ZURAS...
"...THENA...
"...SERSI...
"...MAKKARI...
"...IKARIS."
NOW, SLEEP. AND DREAM, FORGOTTEN ONE...
...DREAM OF CARNAGE.

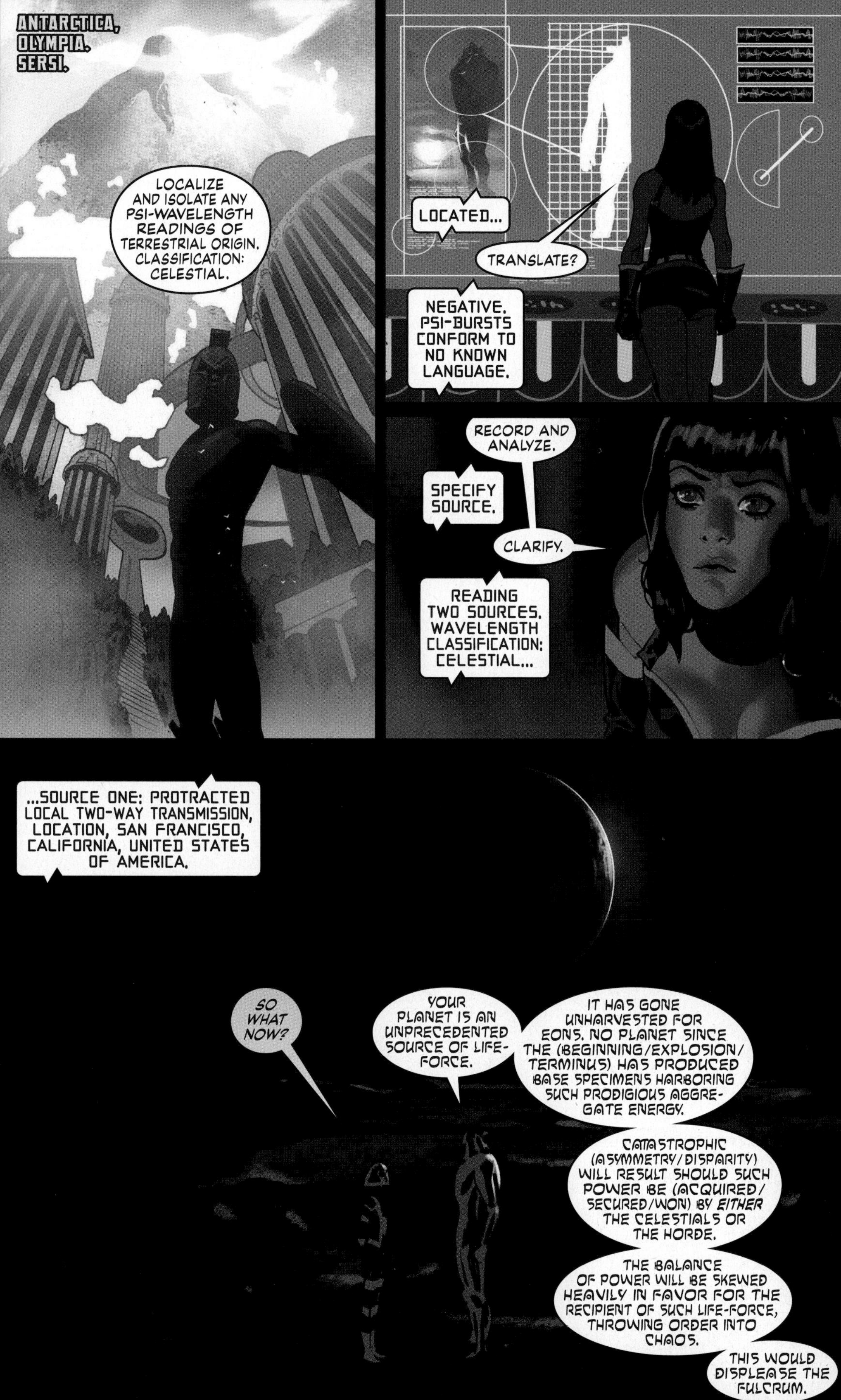
ANTARCTICA, OLYMPIA. SERSI.
LOCALIZE AND ISOLATE ANY PSI-WAVELENGTH READINGS OF TERRESTRIAL ORIGIN. CLASSIFICATION: CELESTIAL.
LOCATED...
TRANSLATE?
NEGATIVE. PSI-BURSTS CONFORM TO NO KNOWN LANGUAGE.
RECORD AND ANALYZE.
SPECIFY SOURCE.
CLARIFY.
READING TWO SOURCES. WAVELENGTH CLASSIFICATION: CELESTIAL...
...SOURCE ONE: PROTRACTED LOCAL TWO-WAY TRANSMISSION, LOCATION, SAN FRANCISCO, CALIFORNIA, UNITED STATES OF AMERICA.
SO WHAT NOW?
YOUR PLANET IS AN UNPRECEDENTED SOURCE OF LIFE-FORCE.
IT HAS GONE UNHARVESTED FOR EONS. NO PLANET SINCE THE (BEGINNING/EXPLOSION/TERMINUS) HAS PRODUCED BASE SPECIMENS HARBORING SUCH PRODIGIOUS AGGREGATE ENERGY.
CATASTROPHIC (ASYMMETRY/DISPARITY) WILL RESULT SHOULD SUCH POWER BE (ACQUIRED/SECURED/WON) BY EITHER THE CELESTIALS OR THE HORDE.
THE BALANCE OF POWER WILL BE SKEWED HEAVILY IN FAVOR FOR THE RECIPIENT OF SUCH LIFE-FORCE, THROWING ORDER INTO CHAOS.
THIS WOULD DISPLEASE THE FULCRUM.

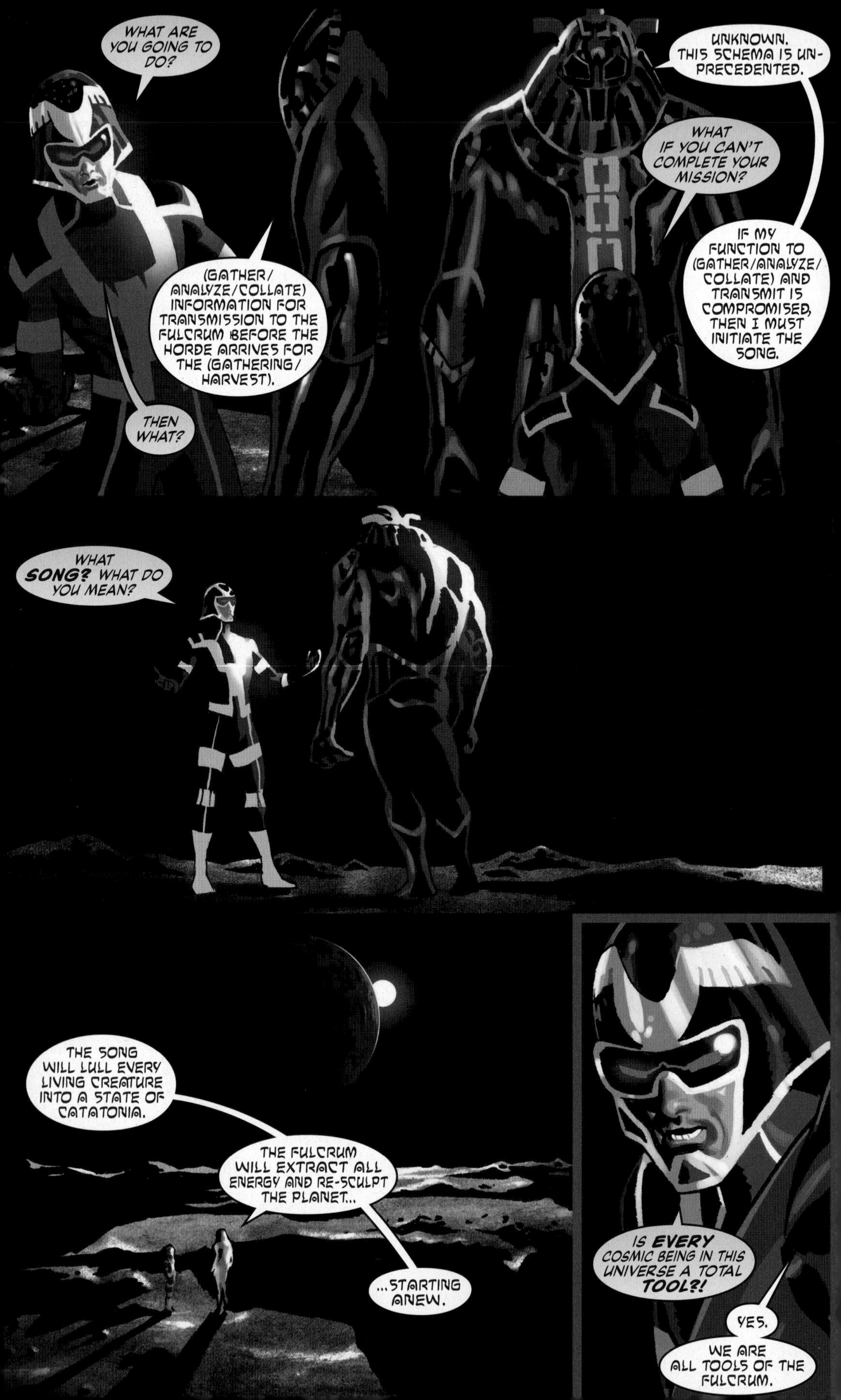
WHAT ARE YOU GOING TO DO?
(GATHER/ANALYZE/COLLATE) INFORMATION FOR TRANSMISSION TO THE FULCRUM BEFORE THE HORDE ARRIVES FOR THE (GATHERING/HARVEST).
THEN WHAT?
UNKNOWN. THIS SCHEMA IS UN-PRECEDENTED.
WHAT IF YOU CAN'T COMPLETE YOUR MISSION?
IF MY FUNCTION TO (GATHER/ANALYZE/COLLATE) AND TRANSMIT IS COMPROMISED, THEN I MUST INITIATE THE SONG.
WHAT SONG? WHAT DO YOU MEAN?
THE SONG WILL LULL EVERY LIVING CREATURE INTO A STATE OF CATATONIA.
THE FULCRUM WILL EXTRACT ALL ENERGY AND RE-SCULPT THE PLANET...
...STARTING ANEW.
IS EVERY COSMIC BEING IN THIS UNIVERSE A TOTAL TOOL?!
YES.
WE ARE ALL TOOLS OF THE FULCRUM.

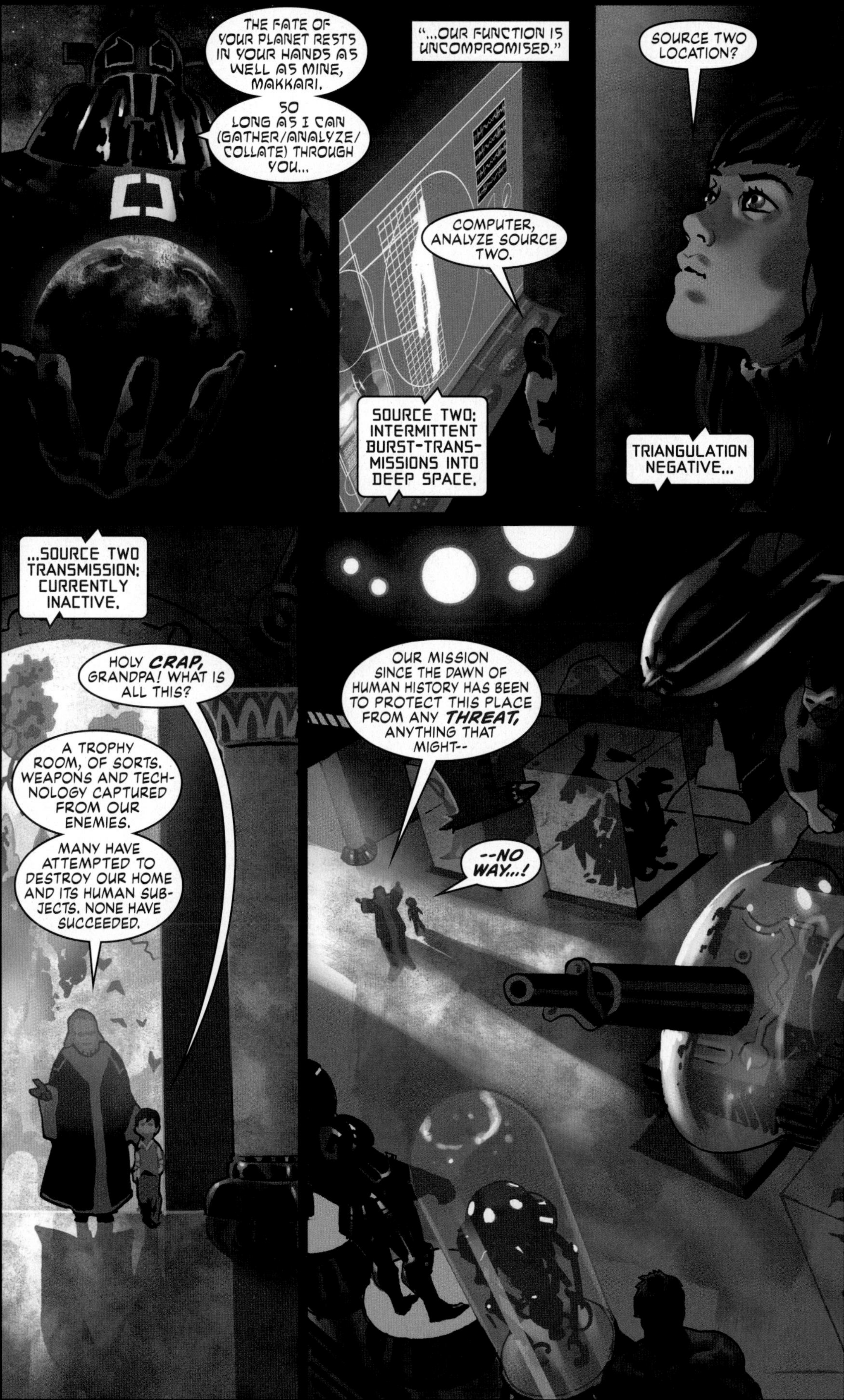

THE FATE OF YOUR PLANET RESTS IN YOUR HANDS AS WELL AS MINE, MAKKARI.
SO LONG AS I CAN (GATHER/ANALYZE/COLLATE) THROUGH YOU...
"...OUR FUNCTION IS UNCOMPROMISED."
COMPUTER, ANALYZE SOURCE TWO.
SOURCE TWO: INTERMITTENT BURST-TRANSMISSIONS INTO DEEP SPACE.
SOURCE TWO LOCATION?
TRIANGULATION NEGATIVE...
...SOURCE TWO TRANSMISSION: CURRENTLY INACTIVE.
HOLY CRAP, GRANDPA! WHAT IS ALL THIS?
A TROPHY ROOM, OF SORTS. WEAPONS AND TECHNOLOGY CAPTURED FROM OUR ENEMIES.
MANY HAVE ATTEMPTED TO DESTROY OUR HOME AND ITS HUMAN SUBJECTS. NONE HAVE SUCCEEDED.
OUR MISSION SINCE THE DAWN OF HUMAN HISTORY HAS BEEN TO PROTECT THIS PLACE FROM ANY THREAT, ANYTHING THAT MIGHT--
--NO WAY...!

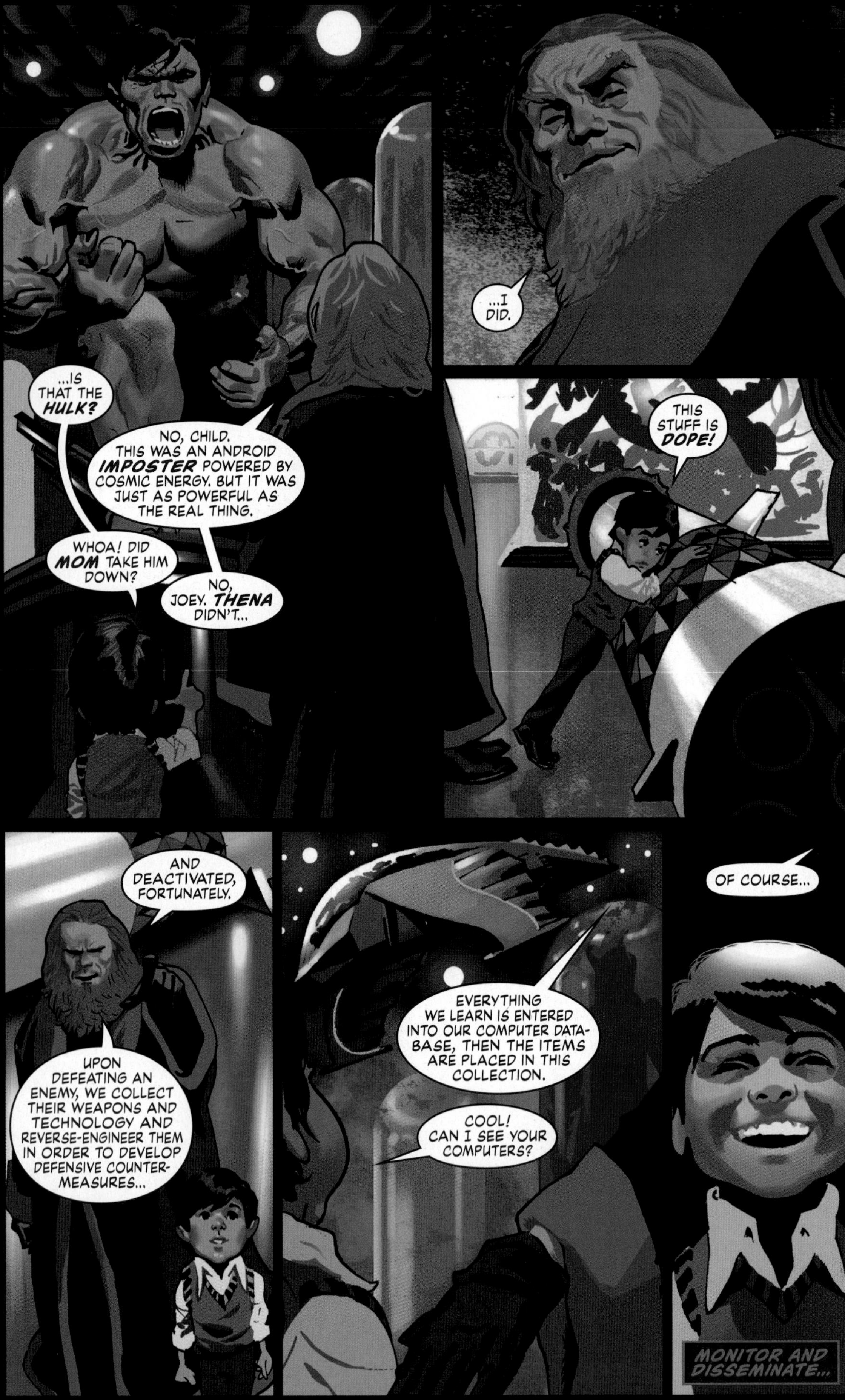

...I DID.
...IS THAT THE HULK?
NO, CHILD. THIS WAS AN ANDROID IMPOSTER POWERED BY COSMIC ENERGY. BUT IT WAS JUST AS POWERFUL AS THE REAL THING.
WHOA! DID MOM TAKE HIM DOWN?
NO, JOEY. THENA DIDN'T...
THIS STUFF IS DOPE!
AND DEACTIVATED, FORTUNATELY.
UPON DEFEATING AN ENEMY, WE COLLECT THEIR WEAPONS AND TECHNOLOGY AND REVERSE-ENGINEER THEM IN ORDER TO DEVELOP DEFENSIVE COUNTER-MEASURES...
EVERYTHING WE LEARN IS ENTERED INTO OUR COMPUTER DATA-BASE, THEN THE ITEMS ARE PLACED IN THIS COLLECTION.
COOL! CAN I SEE YOUR COMPUTERS?
OF COURSE...
MONITOR AND DISSEMINATE...

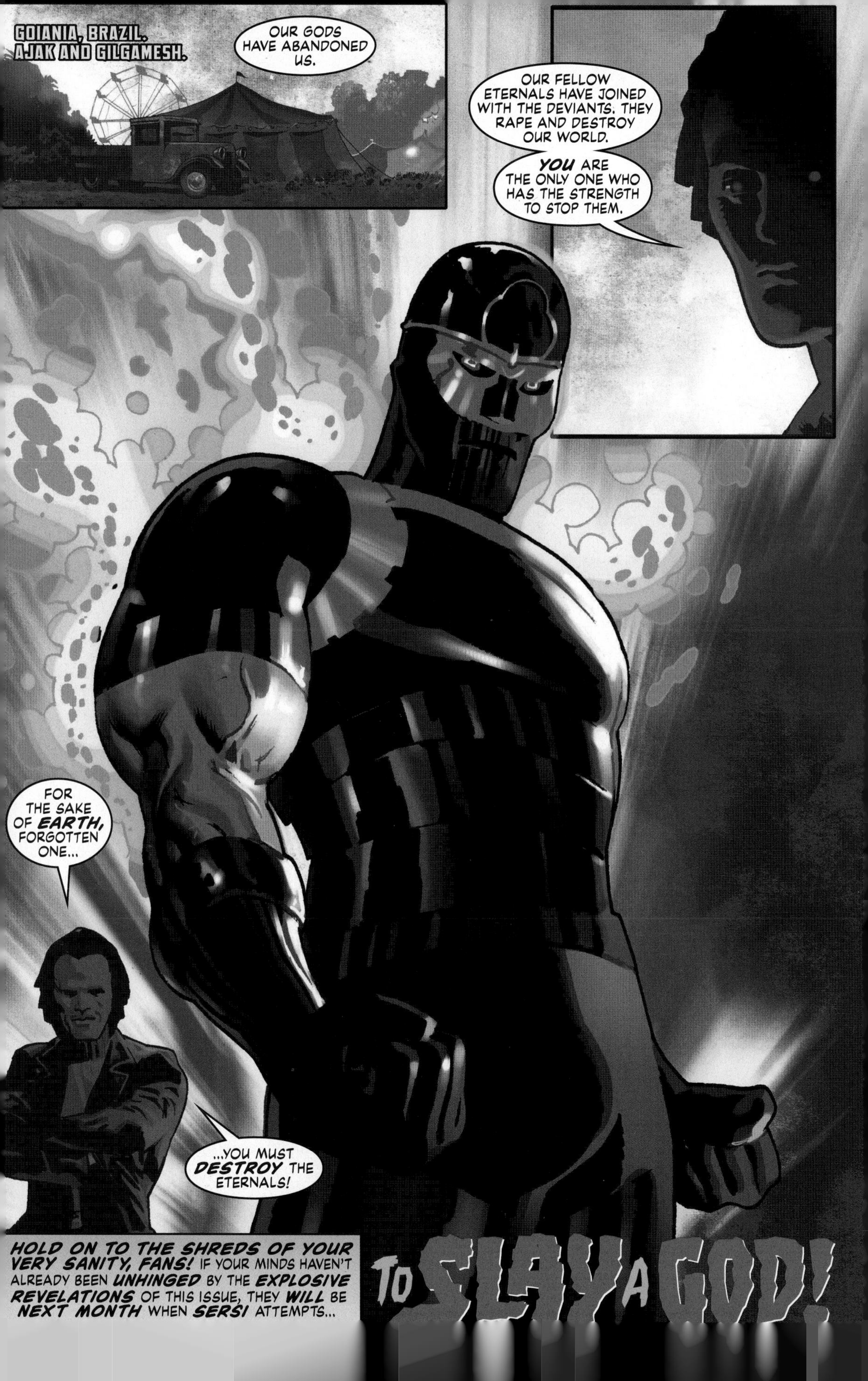
GOIANIA, BRAZIL. AJAK AND GILGAMESH.
OUR GODS HAVE ABANDONED US.
OUR FELLOW ETERNALS HAVE JOINED WITH THE DEVIANTS. THEY RAPE AND DESTROY OUR WORLD.
YOU ARE THE ONLY ONE WHO HAS THE STRENGTH TO STOP THEM.
FOR THE SAKE OF EARTH, FORGOTTEN ONE...
...YOU MUST DESTROY THE ETERNALS!
HOLD ON TO THE SHREDS OF YOUR VERY SANITY, FANS! IF YOUR MINDS HAVEN'T ALREADY BEEN UNHINGED BY THE EXPLOSIVE REVELATIONS OF THIS ISSUE, THEY WILL BE NEXT MONTH WHEN SERSI ATTEMPTS...
TO SLAY A GOD!

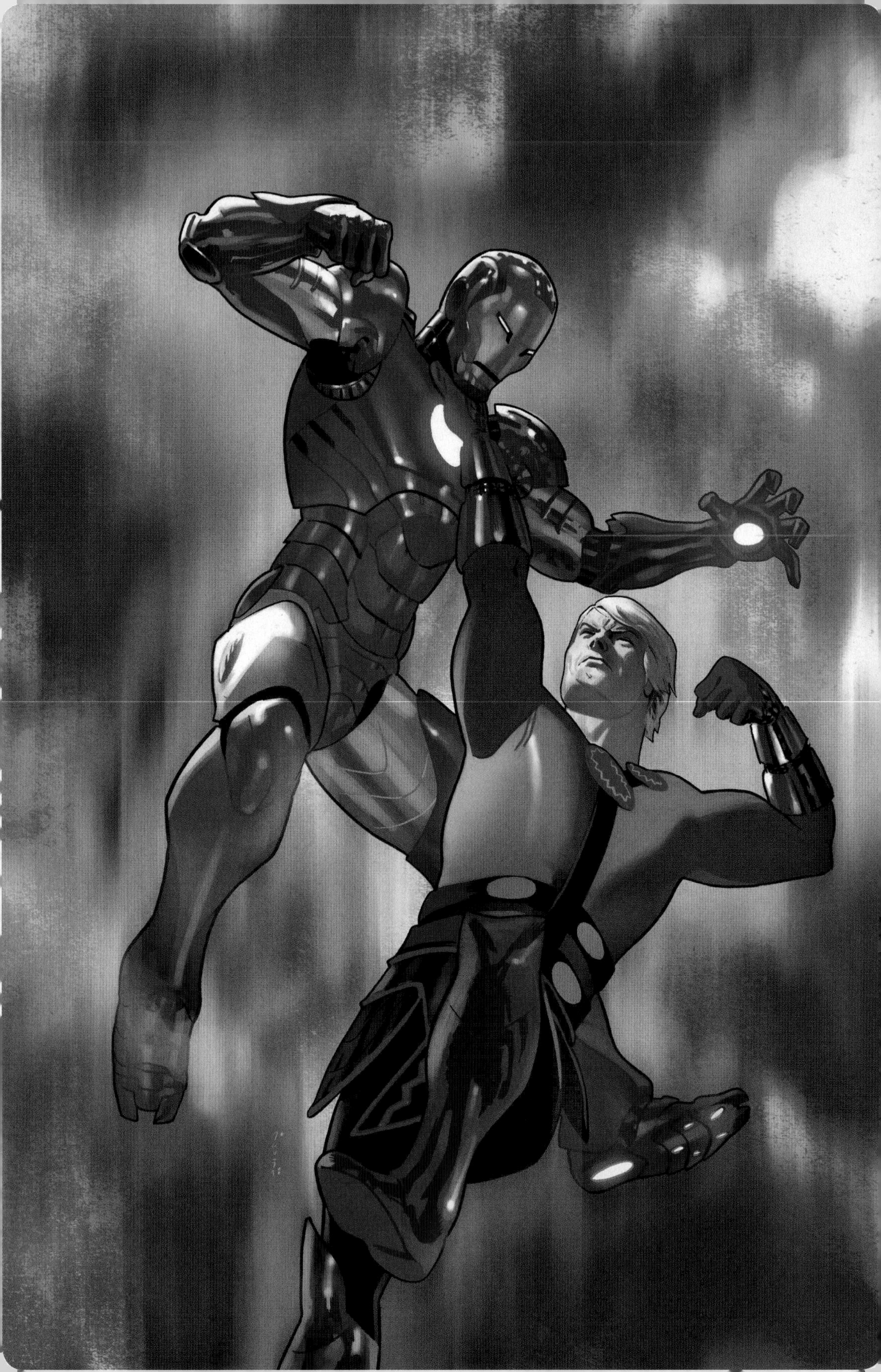

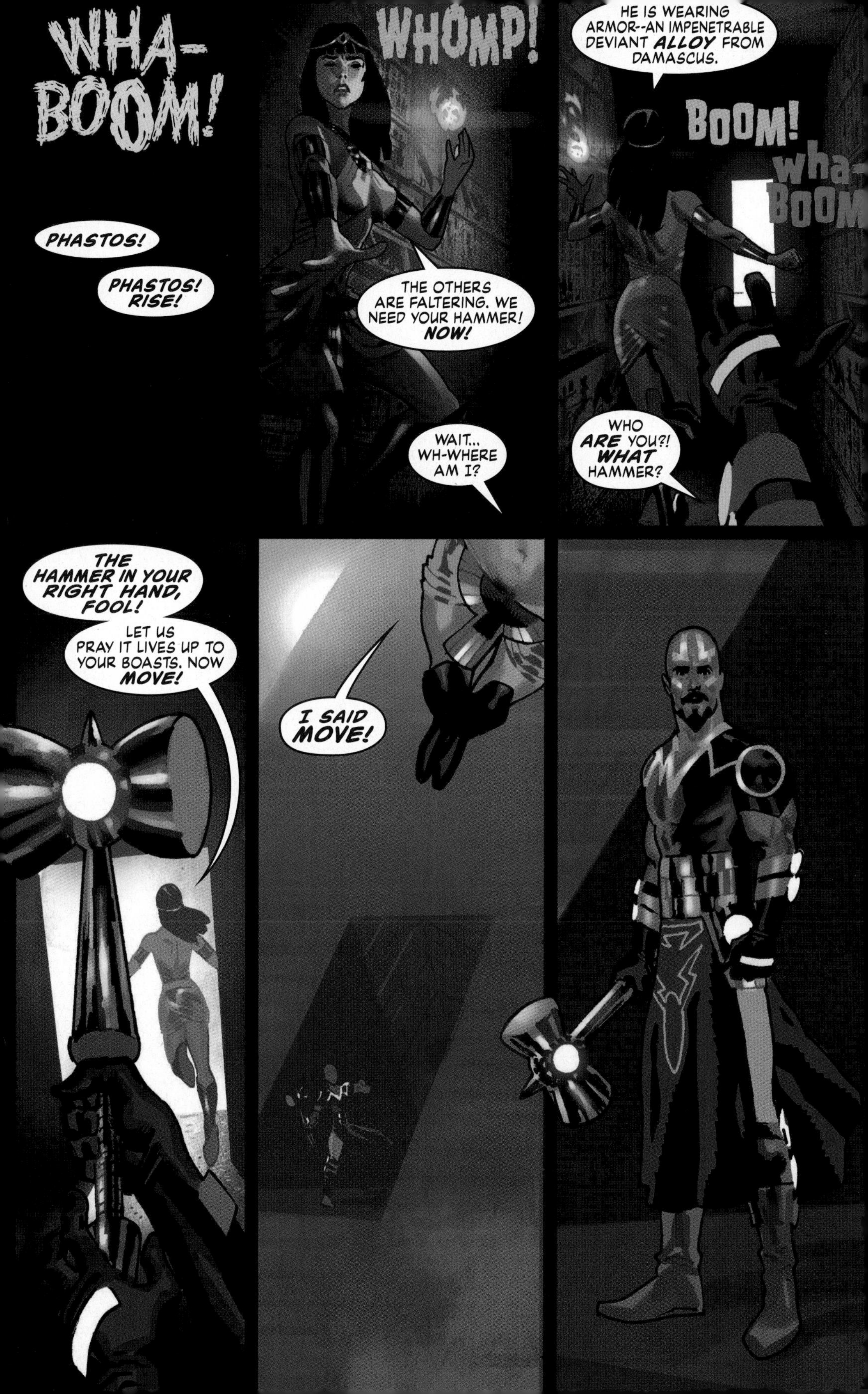
WHA-BOOM!
PHASTOS!
PHASTOS! RISE!
WHOMP!
THE OTHERS ARE FALTERING. WE NEED YOUR HAMMER! NOW!
WAIT... WH-WHERE AM I?
HE IS WEARING ARMOR--AN IMPENETRABLE DEVIANT ALLOY FROM DAMASCUS.
BOOM!
wha-BOOM
WHO ARE YOU?! WHAT HAMMER?
THE HAMMER IN YOUR RIGHT HAND, FOOL!
LET US PRAY IT LIVES UP TO YOUR BOASTS. NOW MOVE!
I SAID MOVE!

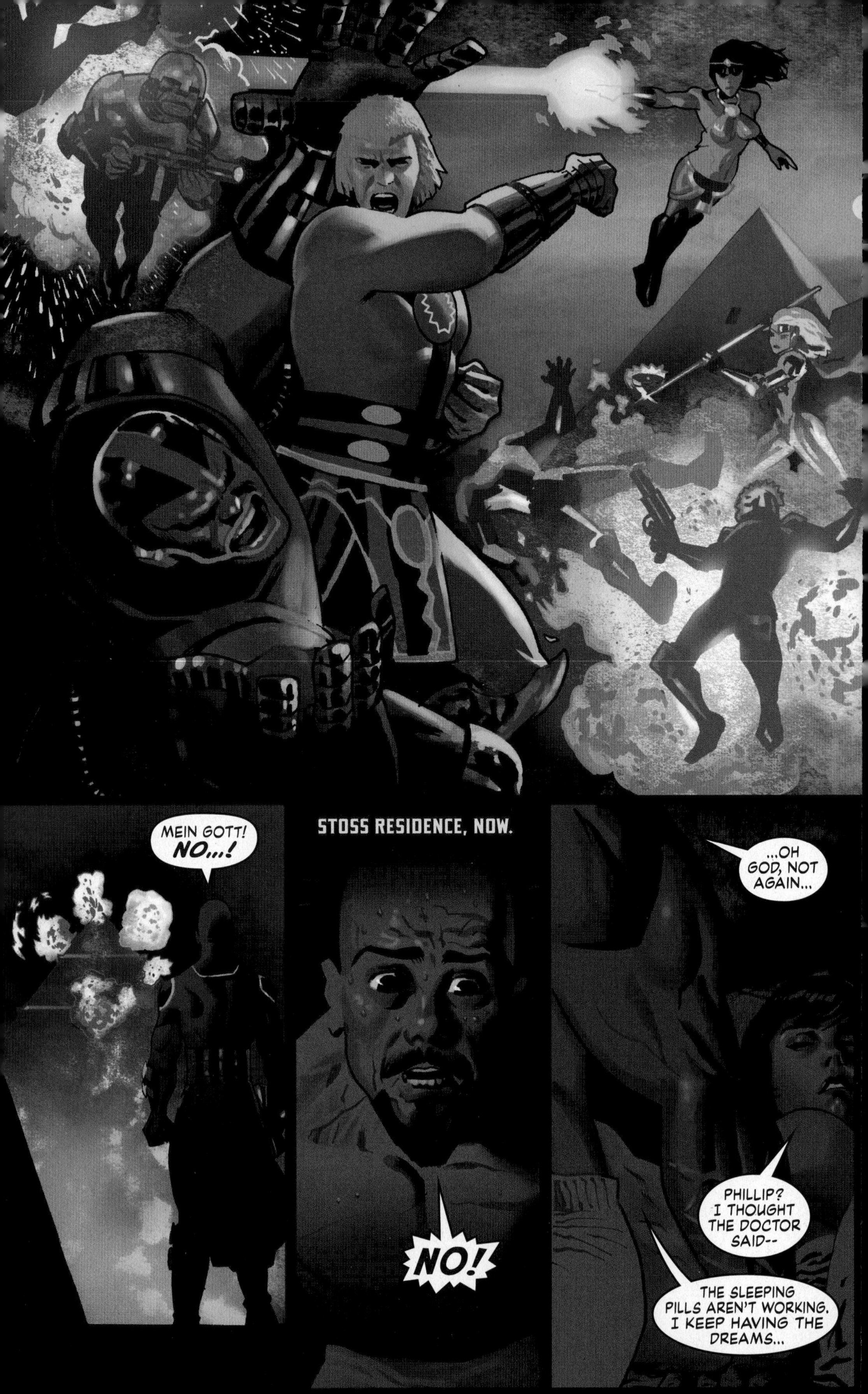
MEIN GOTT! NO...!
STOSS RESIDENCE, NOW.
NO!
...OH GOD, NOT AGAIN...
PHILLIP? I THOUGHT THE DOCTOR SAID--
THE SLEEPING PILLS AREN'T WORKING. I KEEP HAVING THE DREAMS...

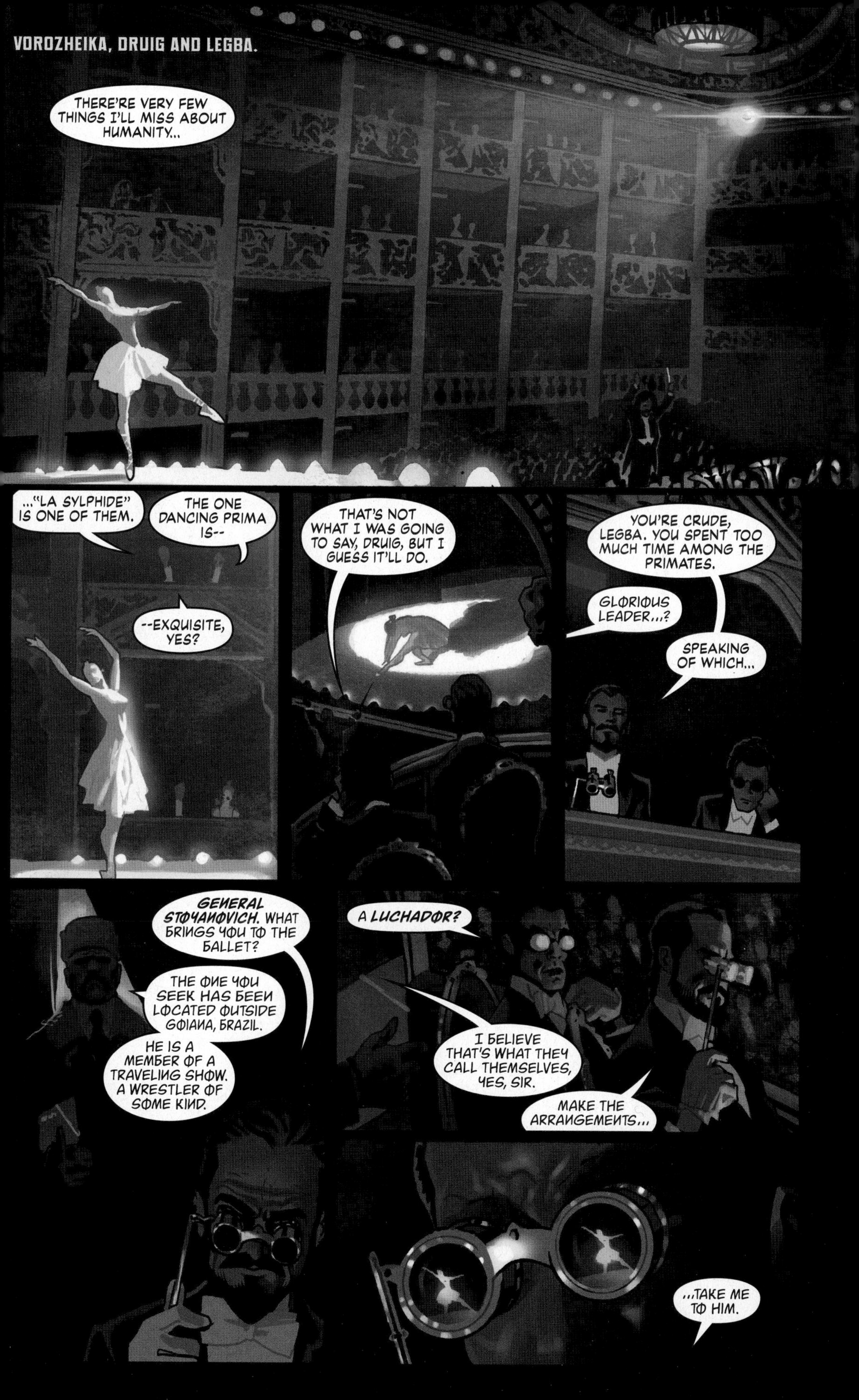
VOROZHEIKA, DRUIG AND LEGBA.
THERE'RE VERY FEW THINGS I'LL MISS ABOUT HUMANITY...
..."LA SYLPHIDE" IS ONE OF THEM.
THE ONE DANCING PRIMA IS--
--EXQUISITE, YES?
THAT'S NOT WHAT I WAS GOING TO SAY, DRUIG, BUT I GUESS IT'LL DO.
YOU'RE CRUDE, LEGBA. YOU SPENT TOO MUCH TIME AMONG THE PRIMATES.
GLORIOUS LEADER...?
SPEAKING OF WHICH...
GENERAL STOYANOVICH. WHAT BRINGS YOU TO THE BALLET?
THE ONE YOU SEEK HAS BEEN LOCATED OUTSIDE GOIANA, BRAZIL.
HE IS A MEMBER OF A TRAVELING SHOW. A WRESTLER OF SOME KIND.
A LUCHADOR?
I BELIEVE THAT'S WHAT THEY CALL THEMSELVES, YES, SIR.
MAKE THE ARRANGEMENTS...
...TAKE ME TO HIM.

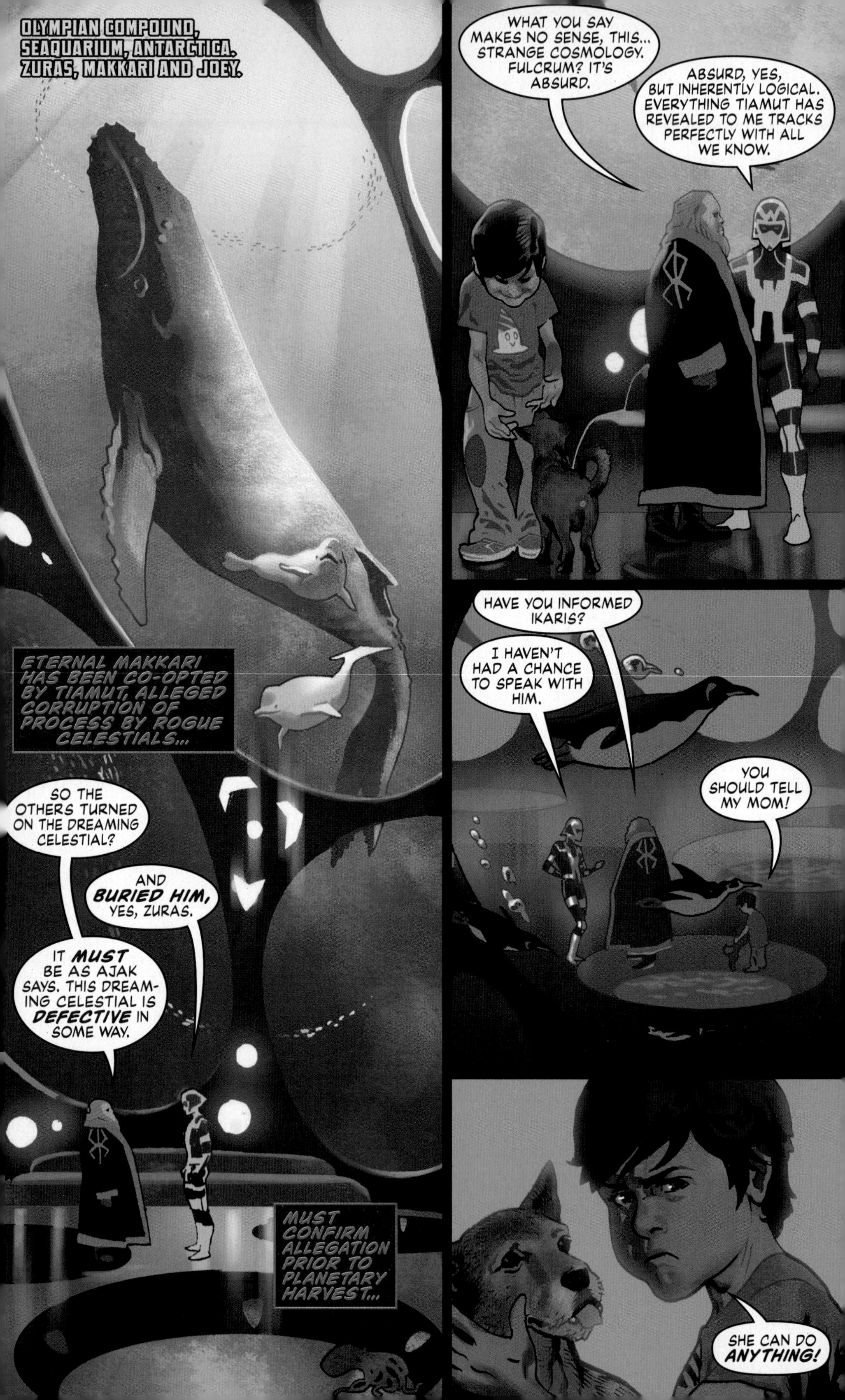
OLYMPIAN COMPOUND, SEAQUARIUM, ANTARCTICA. ZURAS, MAKKARI AND JOEY.
ETERNAL MAKKARI HAS BEEN CO-OPTED BY TIAMUT, ALLEGED CORRUPTION OF PROCESS BY ROGUE CELESTIALS...
SO THE OTHERS TURNED ON THE DREAMING CELESTIAL?
AND BURIED HIM, YES, ZURAS.
IT MUST BE AS AJAK SAYS. THIS DREAMING CELESTIAL IS DEFECTIVE IN SOME WAY.
MUST CONFIRM ALLEGATION PRIOR TO PLANETARY HARVEST...
WHAT YOU SAY MAKES NO SENSE, THIS... STRANGE COSMOLOGY. FULCRUM? IT'S ABSURD.
ABSURD, YES, BUT INHERENTLY LOGICAL. EVERYTHING TIAMUT HAS REVEALED TO ME TRACKS PERFECTLY WITH ALL WE KNOW.
HAVE YOU INFORMED IKARIS?
I HAVEN'T HAD A CHANCE TO SPEAK WITH HIM.
YOU SHOULD TELL MY MOM!
SHE CAN DO ANYTHING!

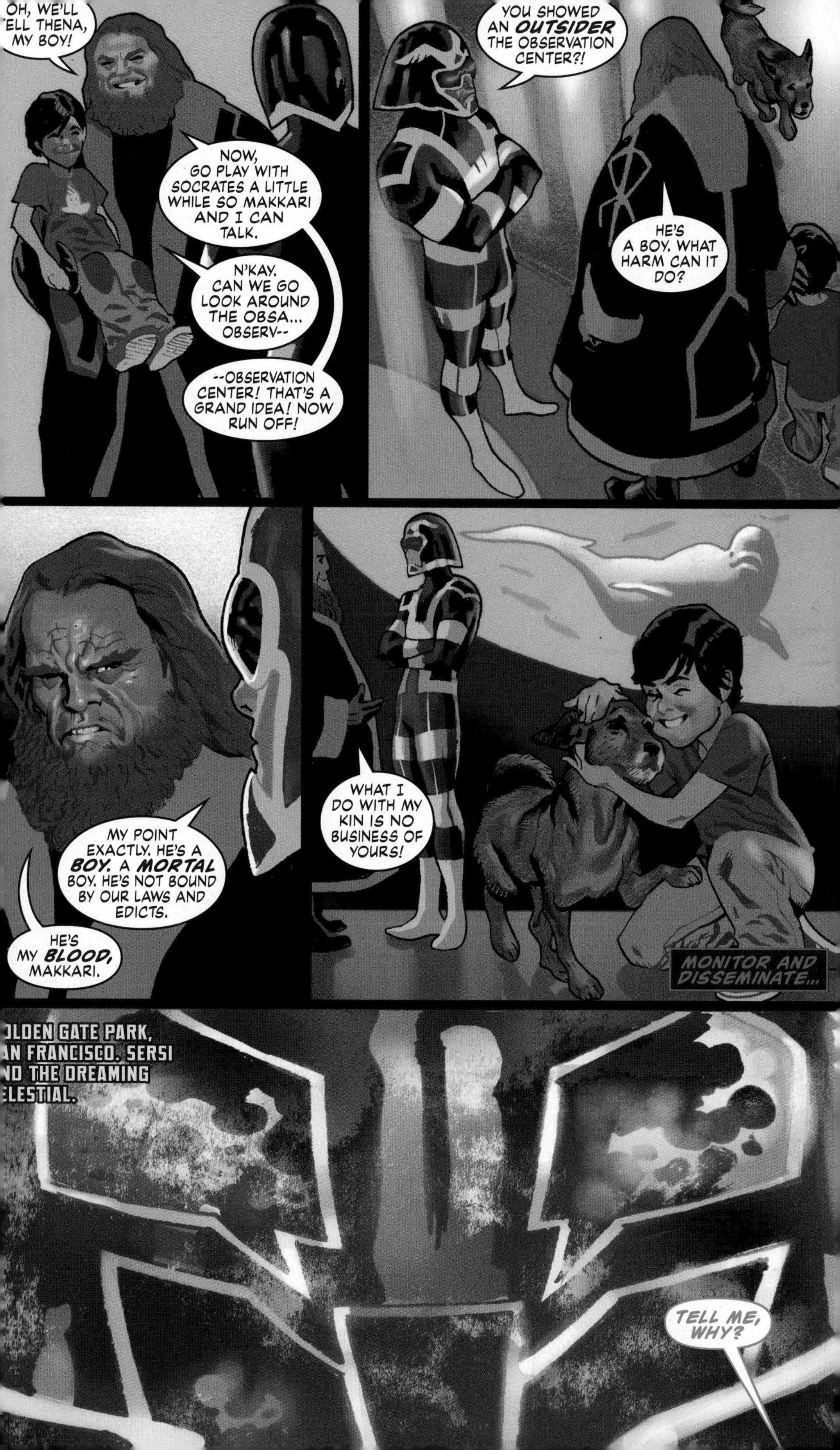
OH, WE'LL TELL THENA, MY BOY!
NOW, GO PLAY WITH SOCRATES A LITTLE WHILE SO MAKKARI AND I CAN TALK.
N'KAY. CAN WE GO LOOK AROUND THE OBSA... OBSERV--
--OBSERVATION CENTER! THAT'S A GRAND IDEA! NOW RUN OFF!
YOU SHOWED AN OUTSIDER THE OBSERVATION CENTER?!
HE'S A BOY. WHAT HARM CAN IT DO?
MY POINT EXACTLY. HE'S A BOY. A MORTAL BOY. HE'S NOT BOUND BY OUR LAWS AND EDICTS.
HE'S MY BLOOD, MAKKARI.
WHAT I DO WITH MY KIN IS NO BUSINESS OF YOURS!
MONITOR AND DISSEMINATE...
OLDEN GATE PARK, AN FRANCISCO. SERSI ND THE DREAMING ELESTIAL.
TELL ME, WHY?

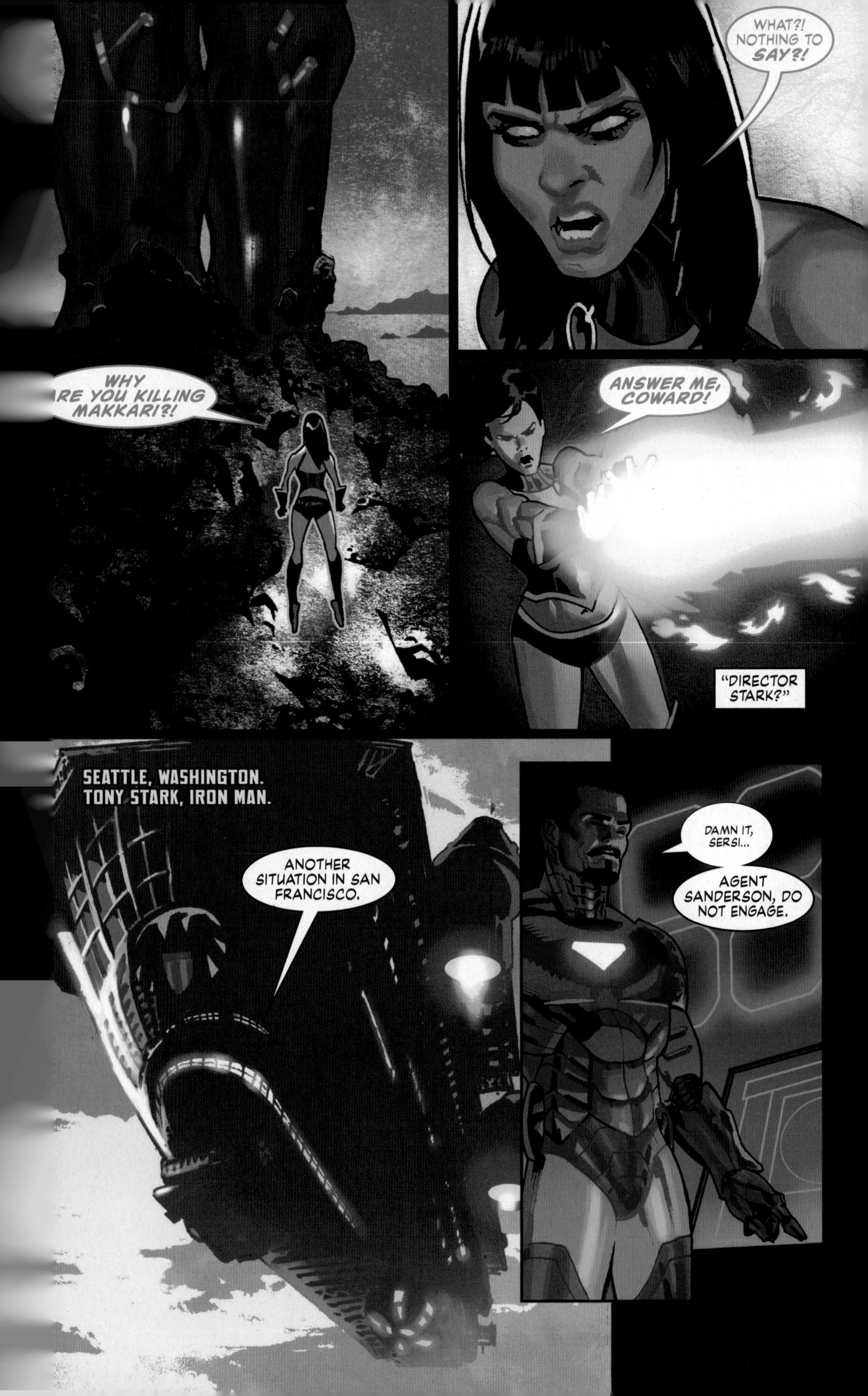
WHY ARE YOU KILLING MAKKARI?!
WHAT?! NOTHING TO SAY?!
ANSWER ME, COWARD!
"DIRECTOR STARK?"
SEATTLE, WASHINGTON. TONY STARK, IRON MAN.
ANOTHER SITUATION IN SAN FRANCISCO.
DAMN IT, SERSI...
AGENT SANDERSON, DO NOT ENGAGE.

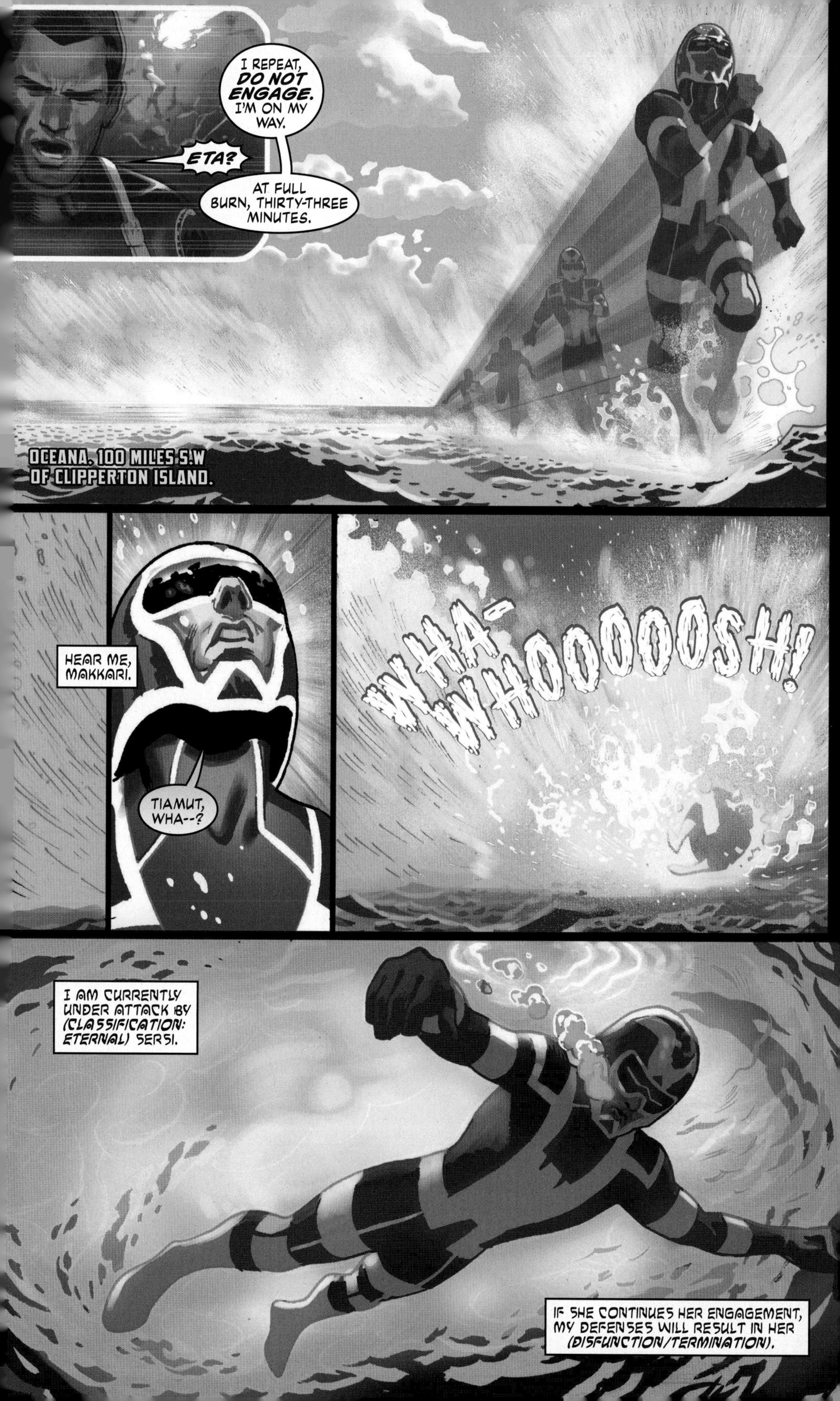
I REPEAT, **DO NOT ENGAGE.** I'M ON MY WAY.
ETA?
AT FULL BURN, THIRTY-THREE MINUTES.
OCEANA. 100 MILES S.W OF CLIPPERTON ISLAND.
HEAR ME, MAKKARI.
TIAMUT, WHA--?
WHA-WHOOOOOOSH!
I AM CURRENTLY UNDER ATTACK BY *(CLASSIFICATION: ETERNAL)* SERSI.
IF SHE CONTINUES HER ENGAGEMENT, MY DEFENSES WILL RESULT IN HER *(DISFUNCTION/TERMINATION).*

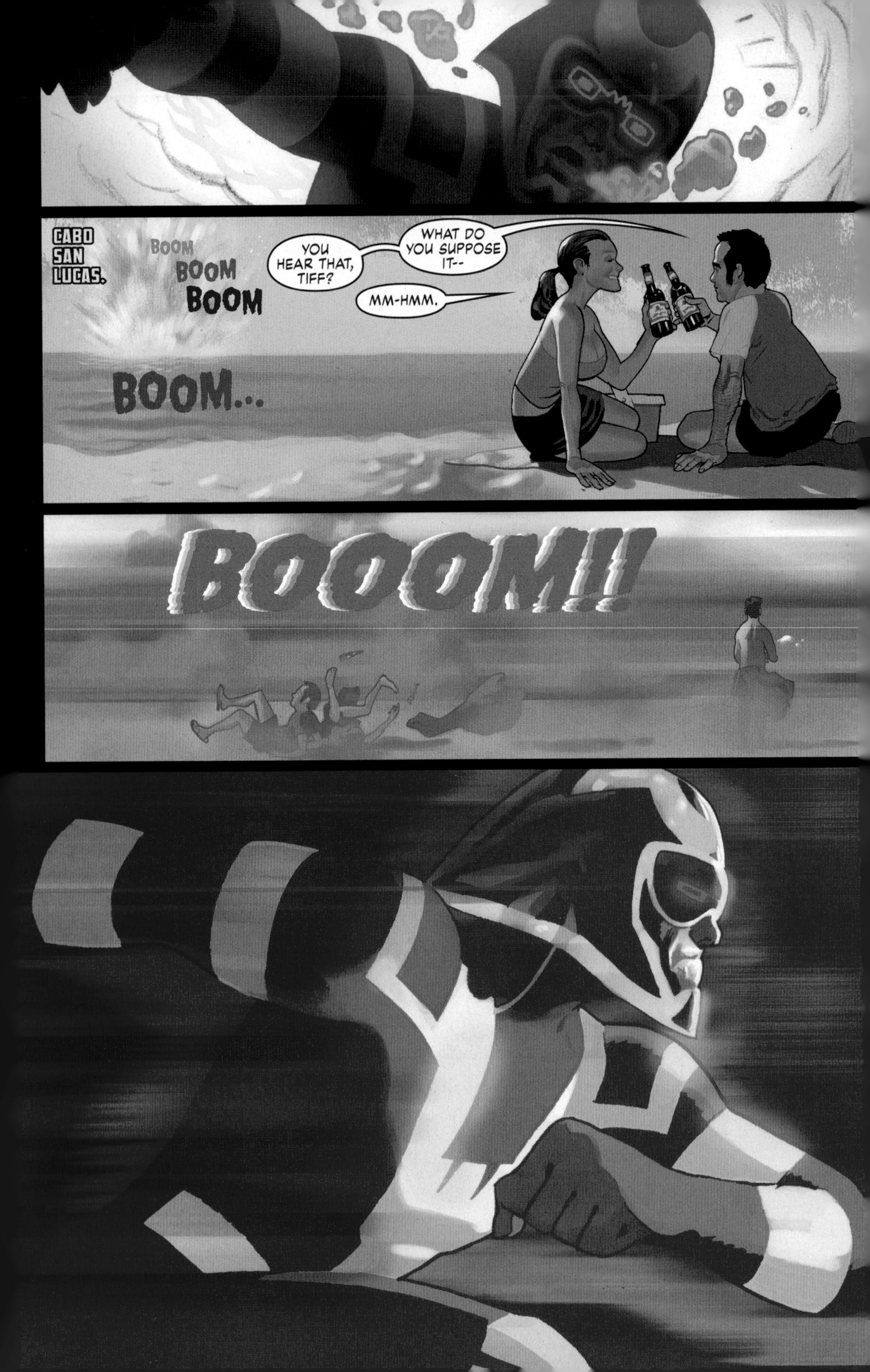
CABO SAN LUCAS.
BOOM
BOOM
BOOM
BOOM...
YOU HEAR THAT, TIFF?
WHAT DO YOU SUPPOSE IT--
MM-HMM.
BOOOM!!

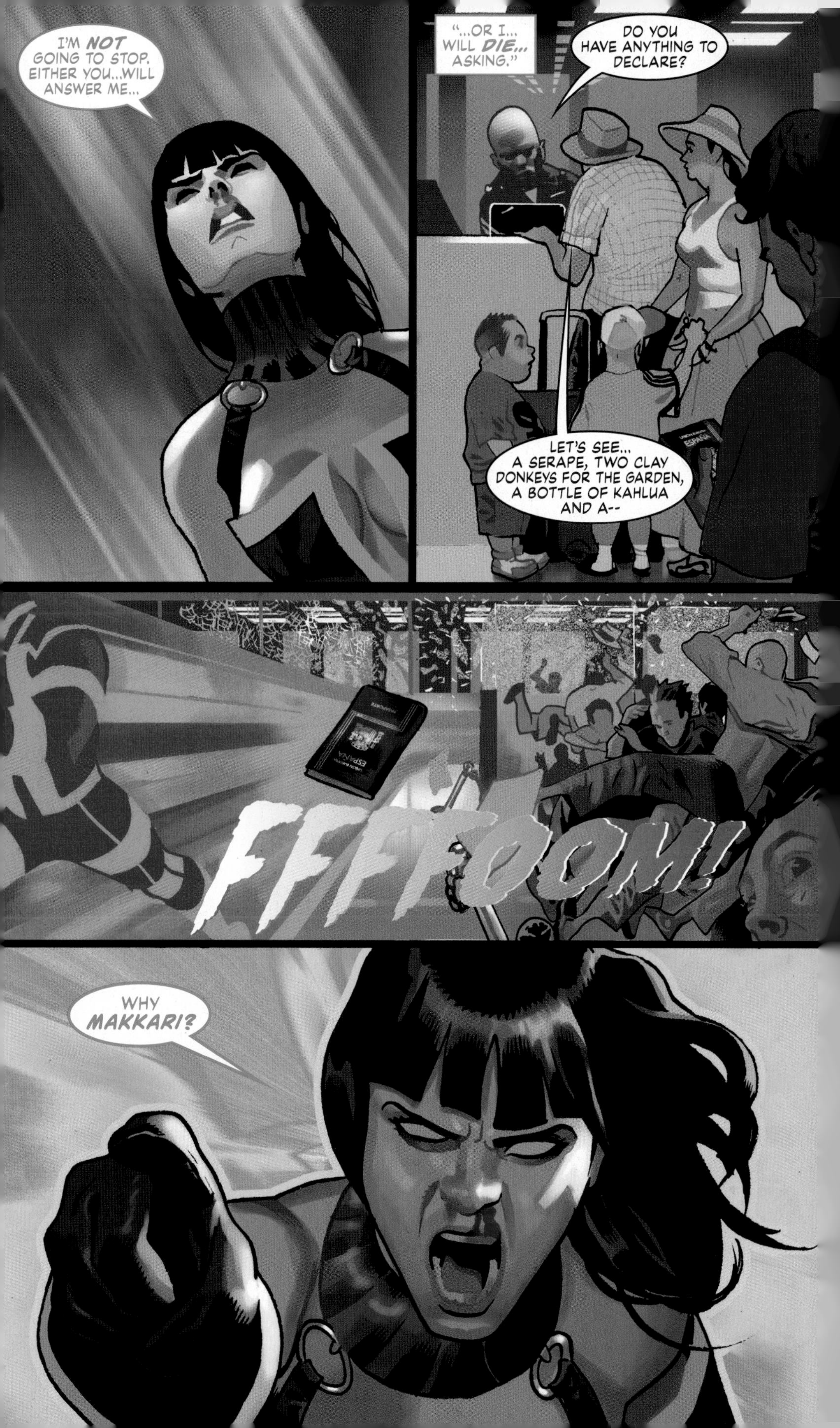
I'M NOT GOING TO STOP. EITHER YOU...WILL ANSWER ME...
"...OR I... WILL DIE... ASKING."
DO YOU HAVE ANYTHING TO DECLARE?
LET'S SEE... A SERAPE, TWO CLAY DONKEYS FOR THE GARDEN, A BOTTLE OF KAHLUA AND A--
ESPAÑA
FFFFOOM!
WHY MAKKARI?

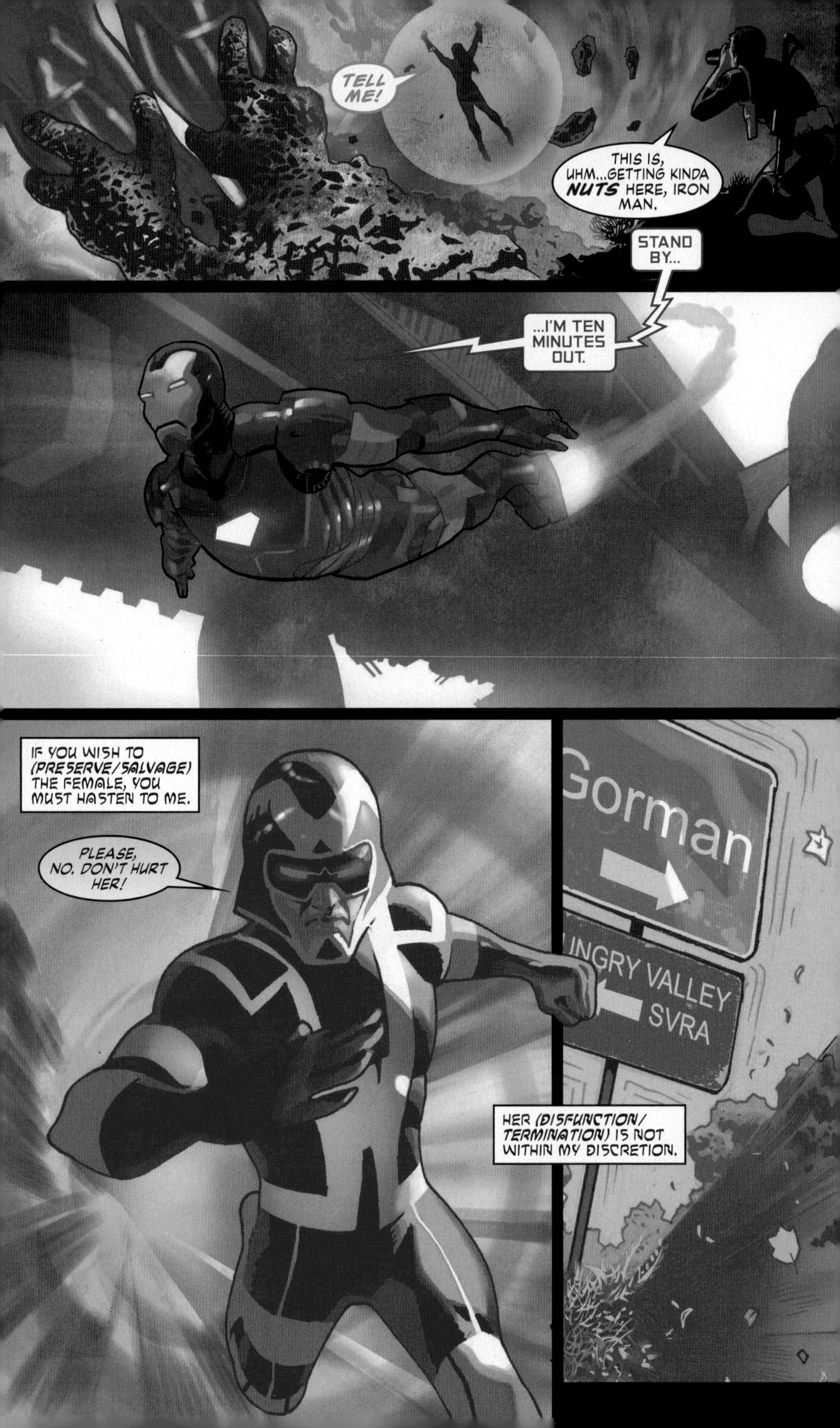

TELL ME!
THIS IS, UHM...GETTING KINDA NUTS HERE, IRON MAN.
STAND BY...
...I'M TEN MINUTES OUT.
IF YOU WISH TO (PRESERVE/SALVAGE) THE FEMALE, YOU MUST HASTEN TO ME.
PLEASE, NO. DON'T HURT HER!
Gorman
NGRY VALLEY SVRA
HER (DISFUNCTION/ TERMINATION) IS NOT WITHIN MY DISCRETION.

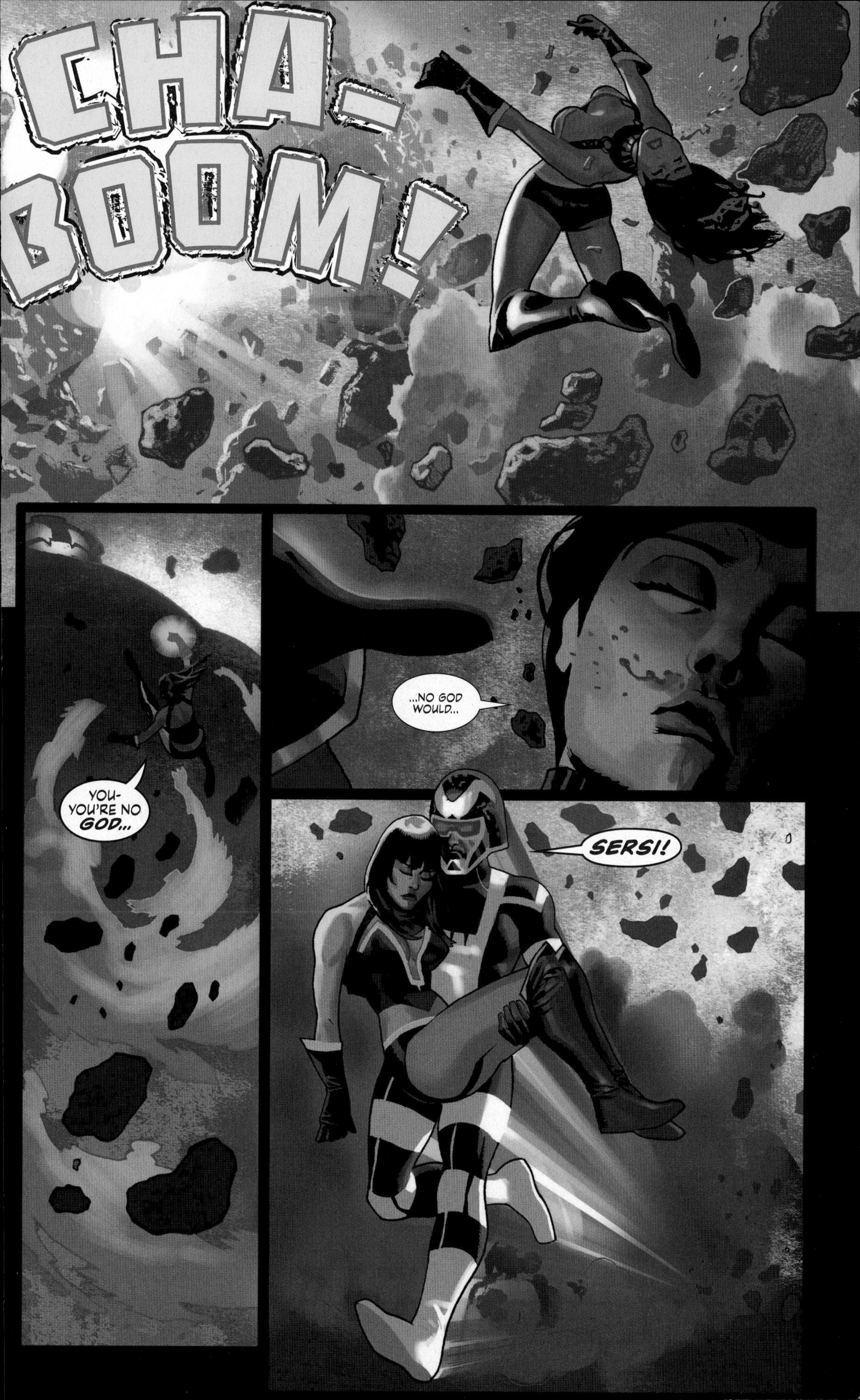
CHA-BOOM!
YOU-YOU'RE NO GOD...
...NO GOD WOULD...
SERSI!

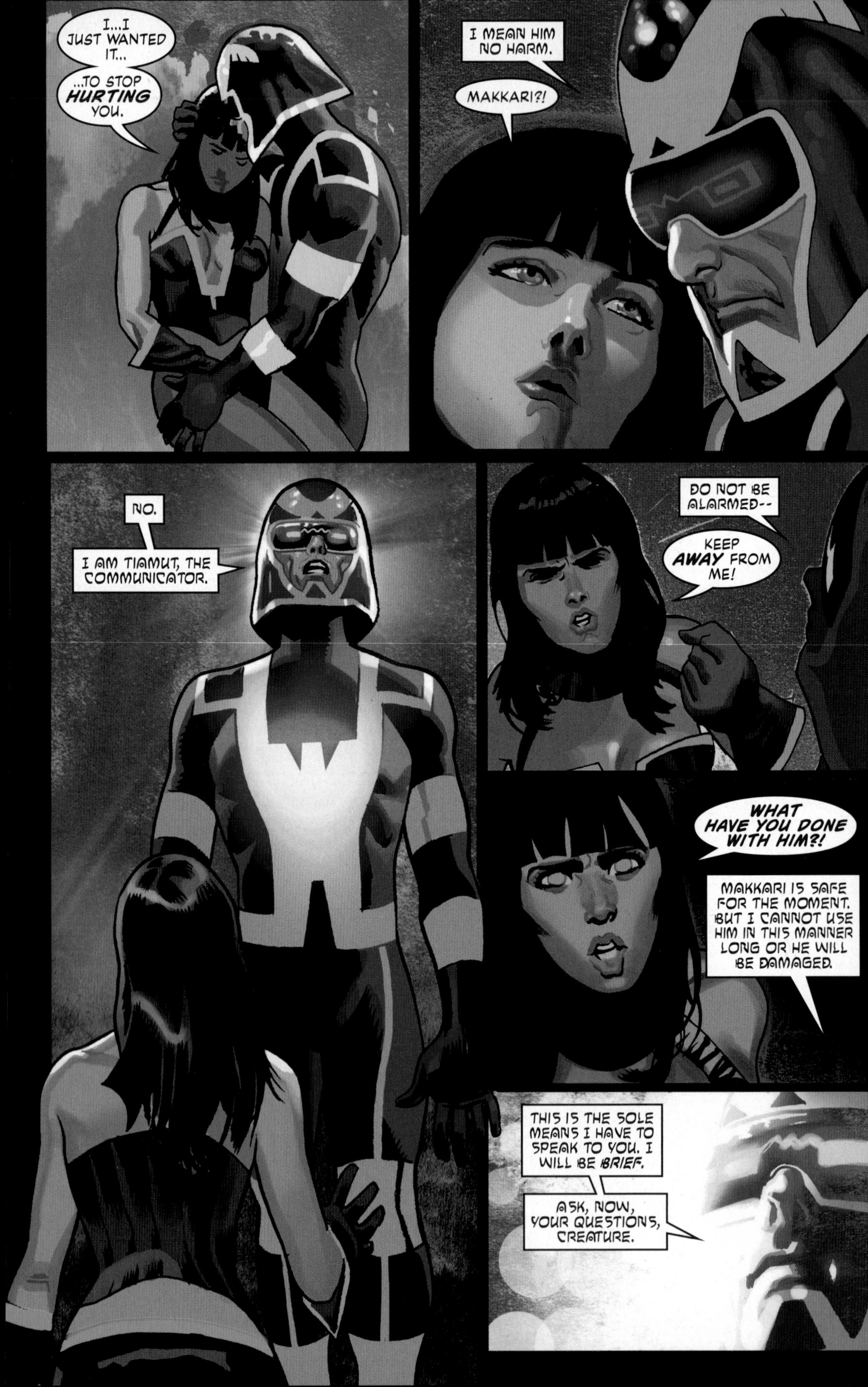

I...I JUST WANTED IT...
...TO STOP HURTING YOU.
I MEAN HIM NO HARM.
MAKKARI?!
NO.
I AM TIAMUT, THE COMMUNICATOR.
DO NOT BE ALARMED--
KEEP AWAY FROM ME!
WHAT HAVE YOU DONE WITH HIM?!
MAKKARI IS SAFE FOR THE MOMENT. BUT I CANNOT USE HIM IN THIS MANNER LONG OR HE WILL BE DAMAGED.
THIS IS THE SOLE MEANS I HAVE TO SPEAK TO YOU. I WILL BE BRIEF.
ASK, NOW, YOUR QUESTIONS, CREATURE.

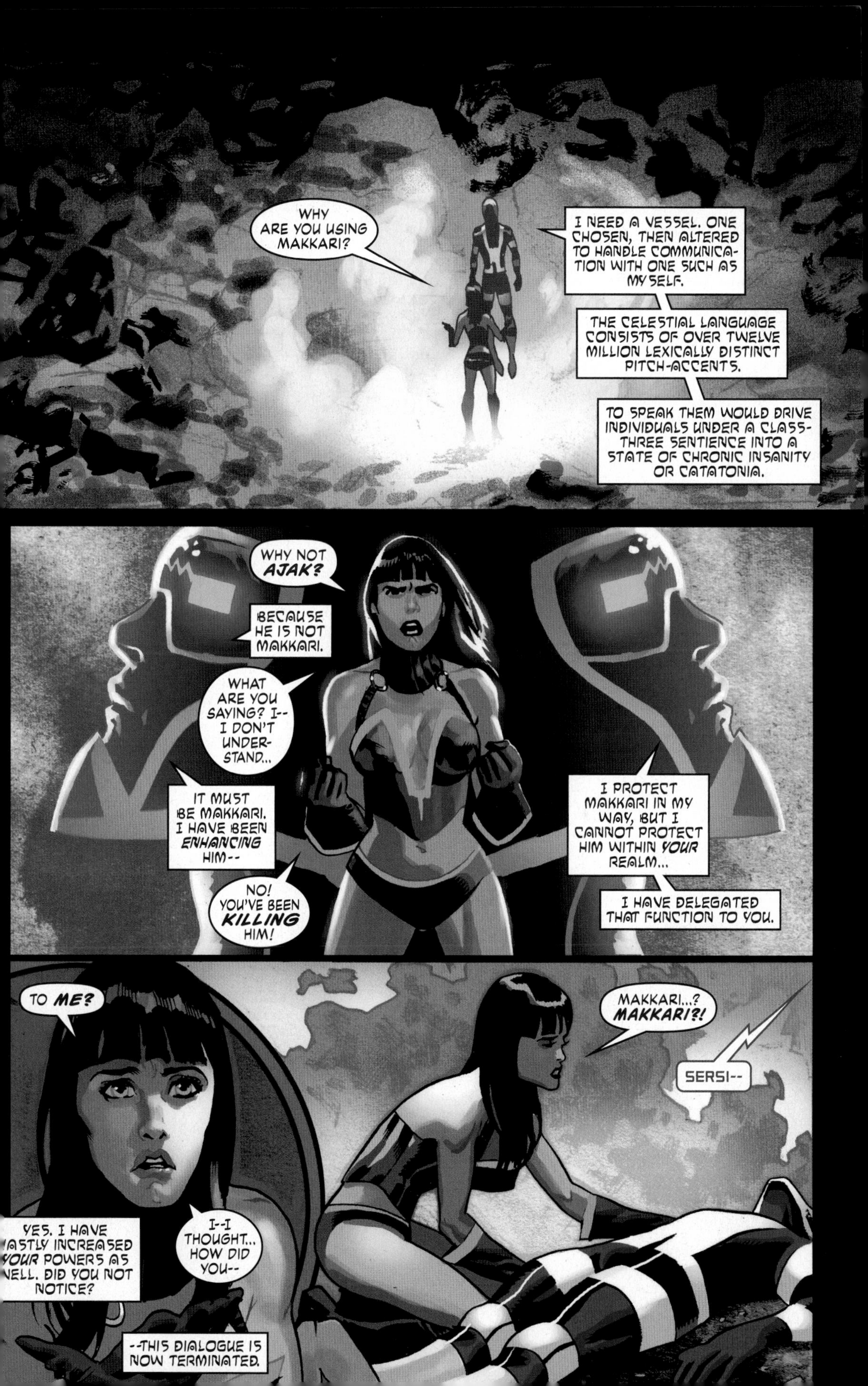
WHY ARE YOU USING MAKKARI?
I NEED A VESSEL. ONE CHOSEN, THEN ALTERED TO HANDLE COMMUNICATION WITH ONE SUCH AS MYSELF.
THE CELESTIAL LANGUAGE CONSISTS OF OVER TWELVE MILLION LEXICALLY DISTINCT PITCH-ACCENTS.
TO SPEAK THEM WOULD DRIVE INDIVIDUALS UNDER A CLASS-THREE SENTIENCE INTO A STATE OF CHRONIC INSANITY OR CATATONIA.
WHY NOT AJAK?
BECAUSE HE IS NOT MAKKARI.
WHAT ARE YOU SAYING? I-- I DON'T UNDERSTAND...
IT MUST BE MAKKARI. I HAVE BEEN ENHANCING HIM--
NO! YOU'VE BEEN KILLING HIM!
I PROTECT MAKKARI IN MY WAY, BUT I CANNOT PROTECT HIM WITHIN YOUR REALM...
I HAVE DELEGATED THAT FUNCTION TO YOU.
TO ME?
YES. I HAVE VASTLY INCREASED YOUR POWERS AS WELL. DID YOU NOT NOTICE?
I--I THOUGHT... HOW DID YOU--
--THIS DIALOGUE IS NOW TERMINATED.
MAKKARI...? MAKKARI?!
SERSI--

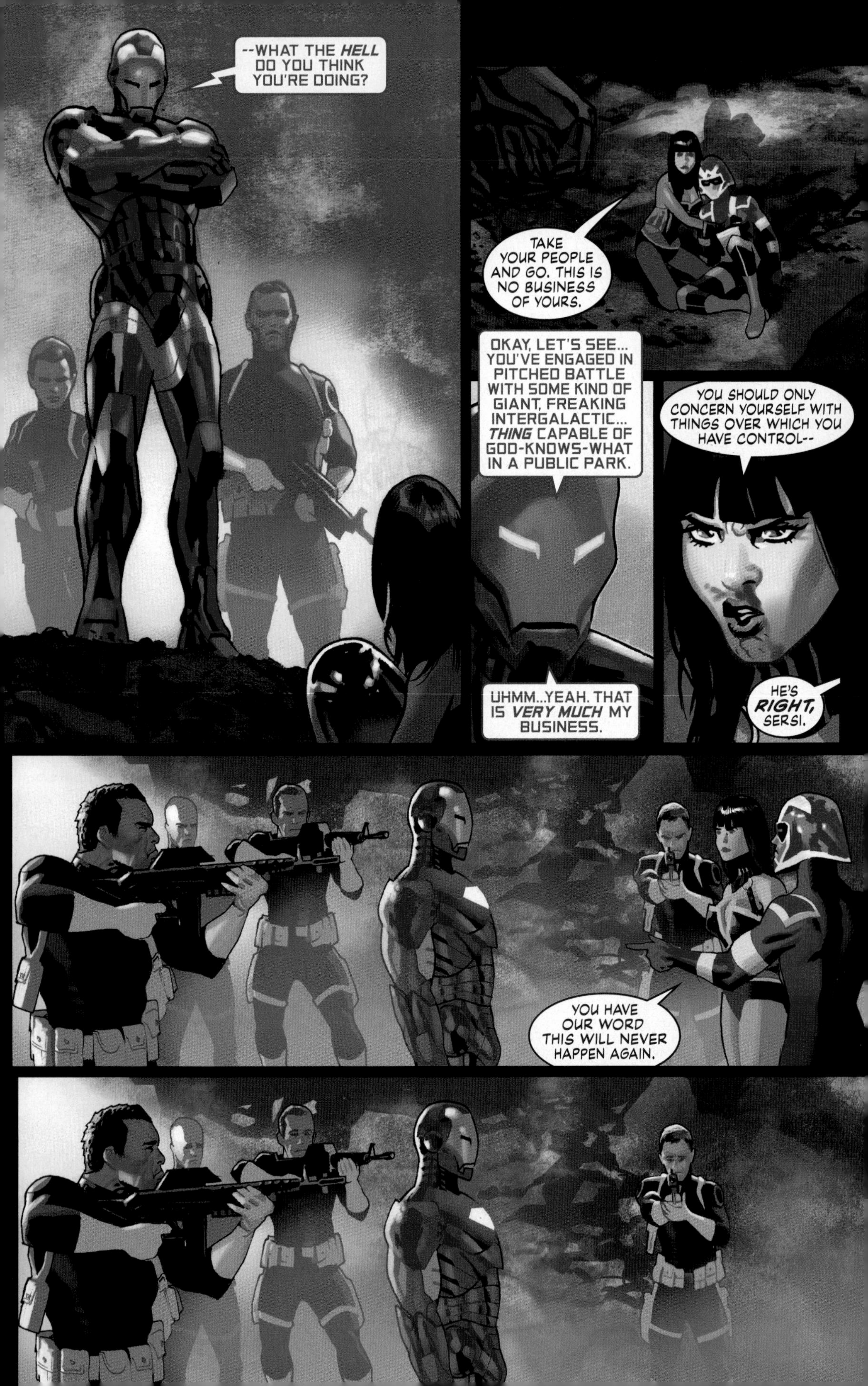
--WHAT THE *HELL* DO YOU THINK YOU'RE DOING?
TAKE YOUR PEOPLE AND GO. THIS IS NO BUSINESS OF YOURS.
OKAY, LET'S SEE... YOU'VE ENGAGED IN PITCHED BATTLE WITH SOME KIND OF GIANT, FREAKING INTERGALACTIC... *THING* CAPABLE OF GOD-KNOWS-WHAT IN A PUBLIC PARK.
UHMM...YEAH. THAT IS *VERY MUCH* MY BUSINESS.
YOU SHOULD ONLY CONCERN YOURSELF WITH THINGS OVER WHICH YOU HAVE CONTROL--
HE'S *RIGHT,* SERSI.
YOU HAVE OUR WORD THIS WILL NEVER HAPPEN AGAIN.

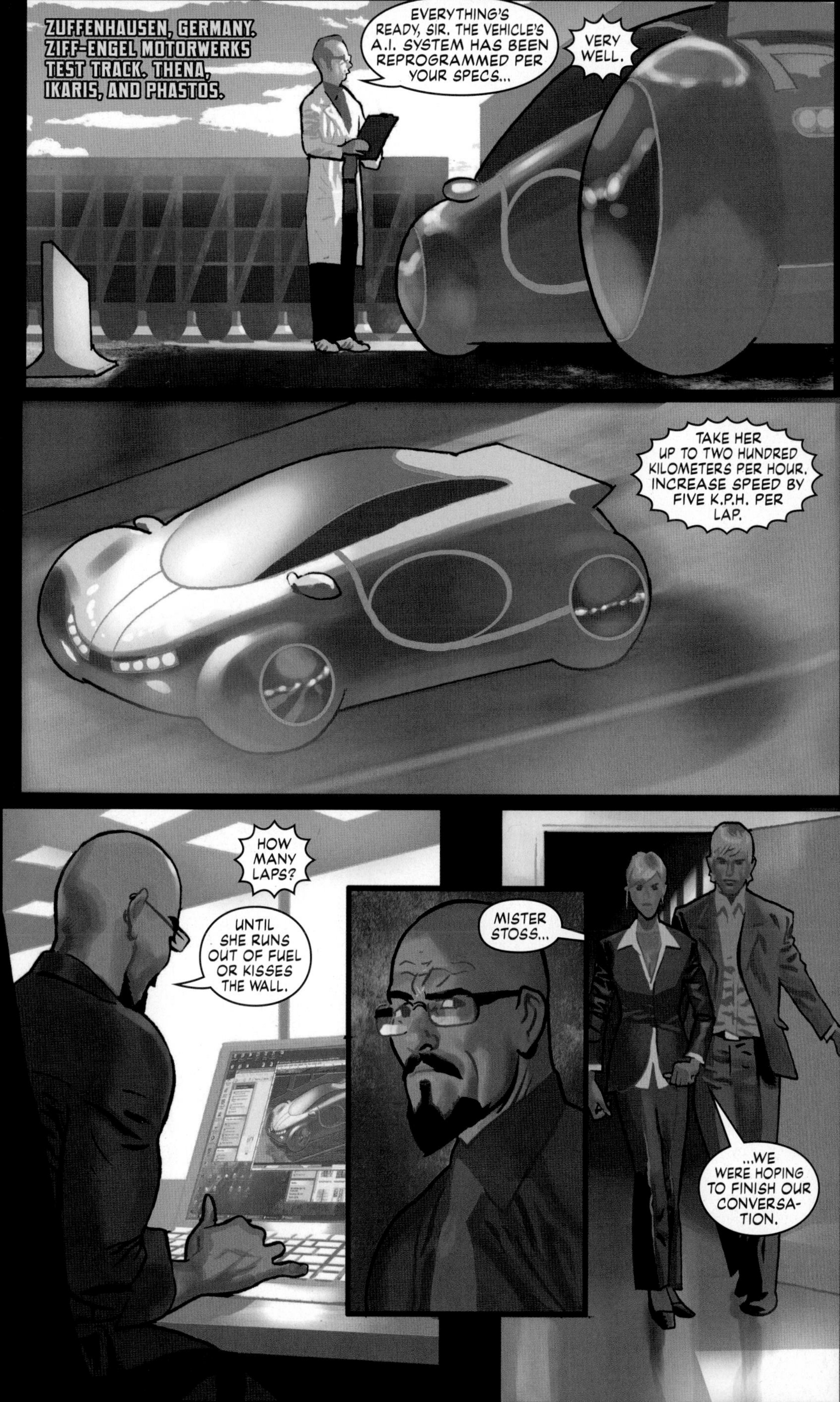
ZUFFENHAUSEN, GERMANY. ZIFF-ENGEL MOTORWERKS TEST TRACK. THENA, IKARIS, AND PHASTOS.
EVERYTHING'S READY, SIR. THE VEHICLE'S A.I. SYSTEM HAS BEEN REPROGRAMMED PER YOUR SPECS...
VERY WELL.
TAKE HER UP TO TWO HUNDRED KILOMETERS PER HOUR. INCREASE SPEED BY FIVE K.P.H. PER LAP.
HOW MANY LAPS?
UNTIL SHE RUNS OUT OF FUEL OR KISSES THE WALL.
MISTER STOSS...
...WE WERE HOPING TO FINISH OUR CONVERSA-TION.

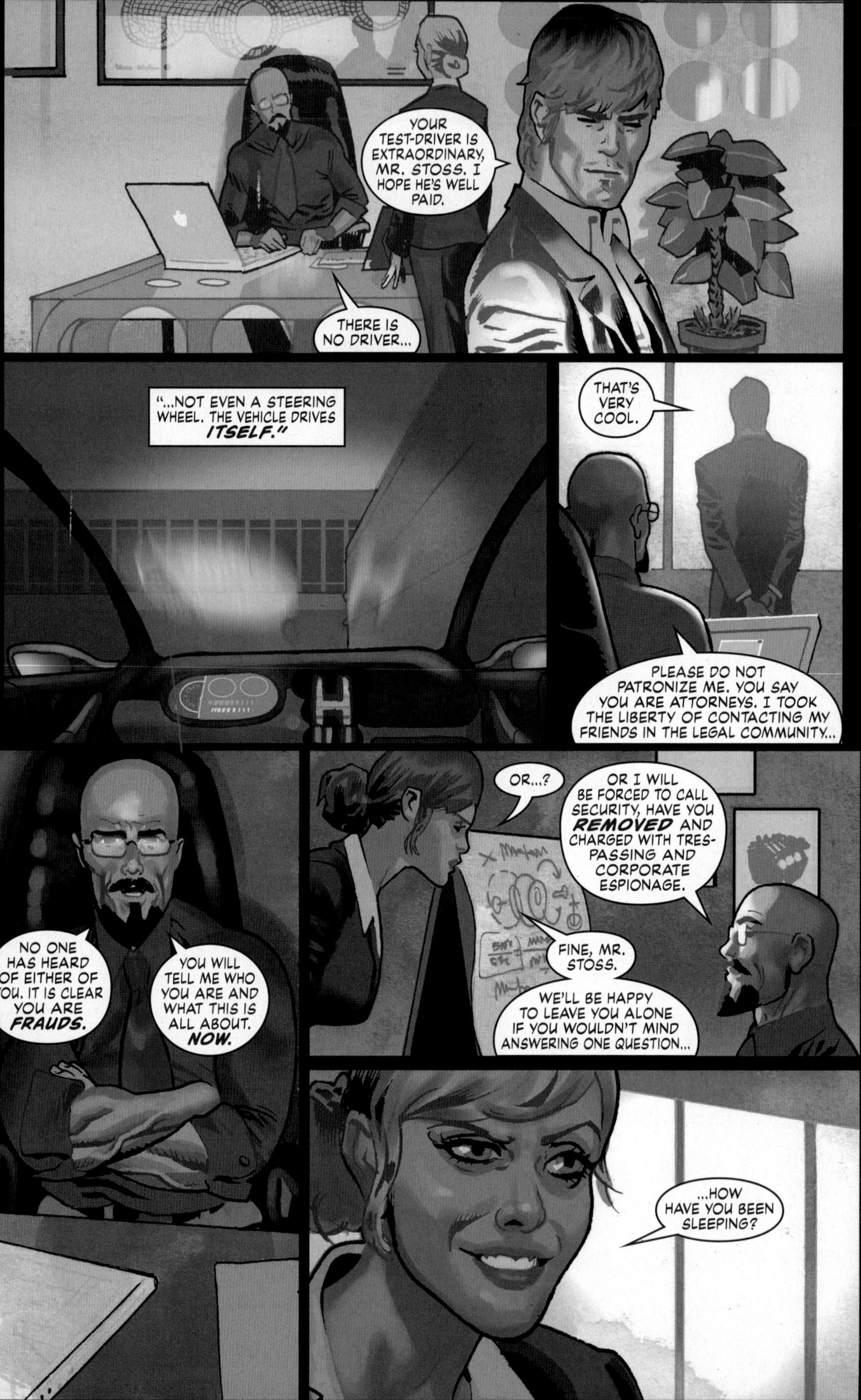
YOUR TEST-DRIVER IS EXTRAORDINARY, MR. STOSS. I HOPE HE'S WELL PAID.
THERE IS NO DRIVER...
"...NOT EVEN A STEERING WHEEL. THE VEHICLE DRIVES *ITSELF.*"
THAT'S VERY COOL.
PLEASE DO NOT PATRONIZE ME. YOU SAY YOU ARE ATTORNEYS. I TOOK THE LIBERTY OF CONTACTING MY FRIENDS IN THE LEGAL COMMUNITY...
NO ONE HAS HEARD OF EITHER OF YOU. IT IS CLEAR YOU ARE *FRAUDS.*
YOU WILL TELL ME WHO YOU ARE AND WHAT THIS IS ALL ABOUT. *NOW.*
OR...?
OR I WILL BE FORCED TO CALL SECURITY, HAVE YOU ***REMOVED*** AND CHARGED WITH TRES-PASSING AND CORPORATE ESPIONAGE.
FINE, MR. STOSS.
WE'LL BE HAPPY TO LEAVE YOU ALONE IF YOU WOULDN'T MIND ANSWERING ONE QUESTION...
...HOW HAVE YOU BEEN SLEEPING?

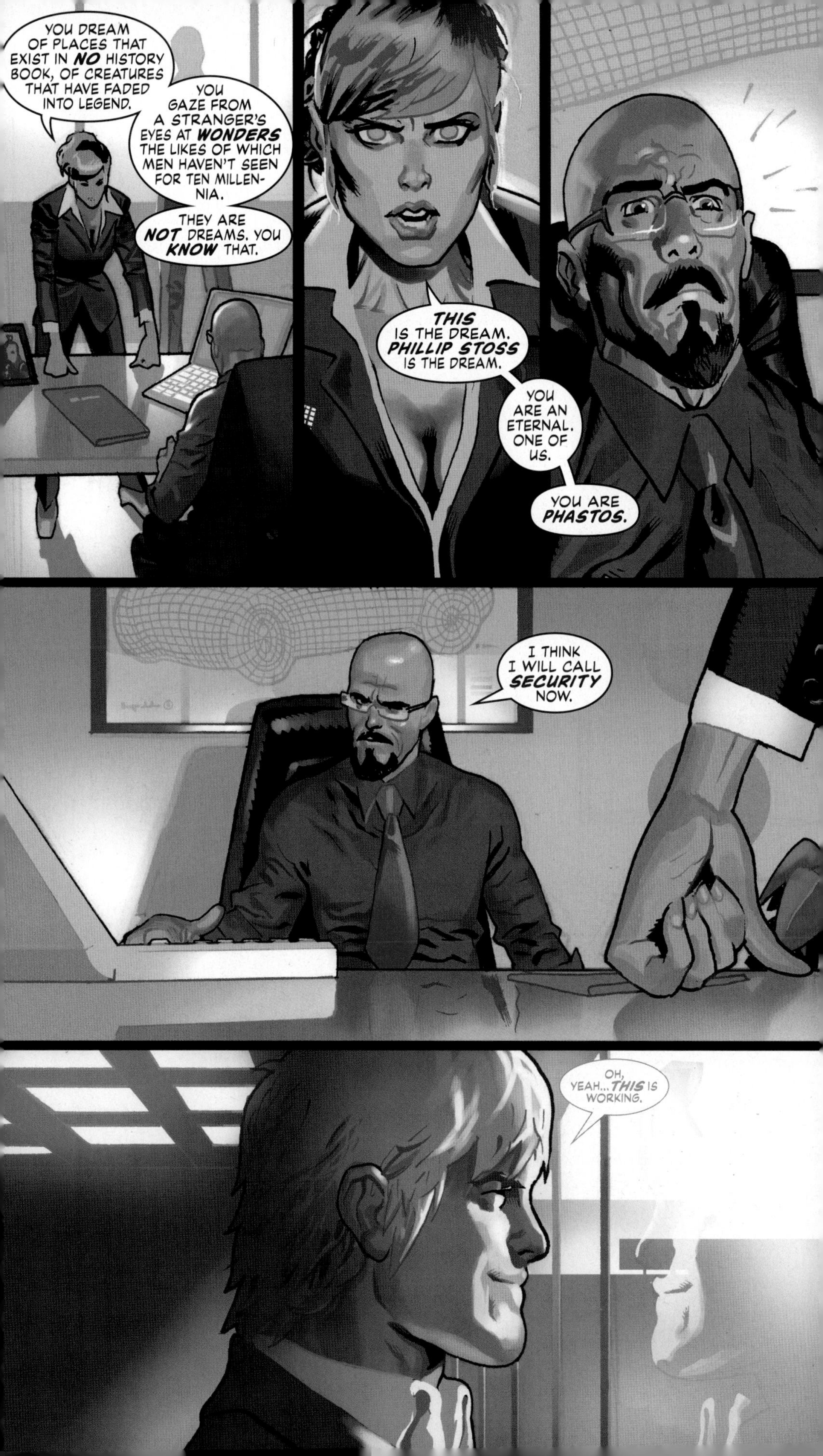
YOU DREAM OF PLACES THAT EXIST IN NO HISTORY BOOK, OF CREATURES THAT HAVE FADED INTO LEGEND.
YOU GAZE FROM A STRANGER'S EYES AT WONDERS THE LIKES OF WHICH MEN HAVEN'T SEEN FOR TEN MILLENNIA.
THEY ARE NOT DREAMS. YOU KNOW THAT.
THIS IS THE DREAM. PHILLIP STOSS IS THE DREAM.
YOU ARE AN ETERNAL. ONE OF US.
YOU ARE PHASTOS.
I THINK I WILL CALL SECURITY NOW.
OH, YEAH...THIS IS WORKING.

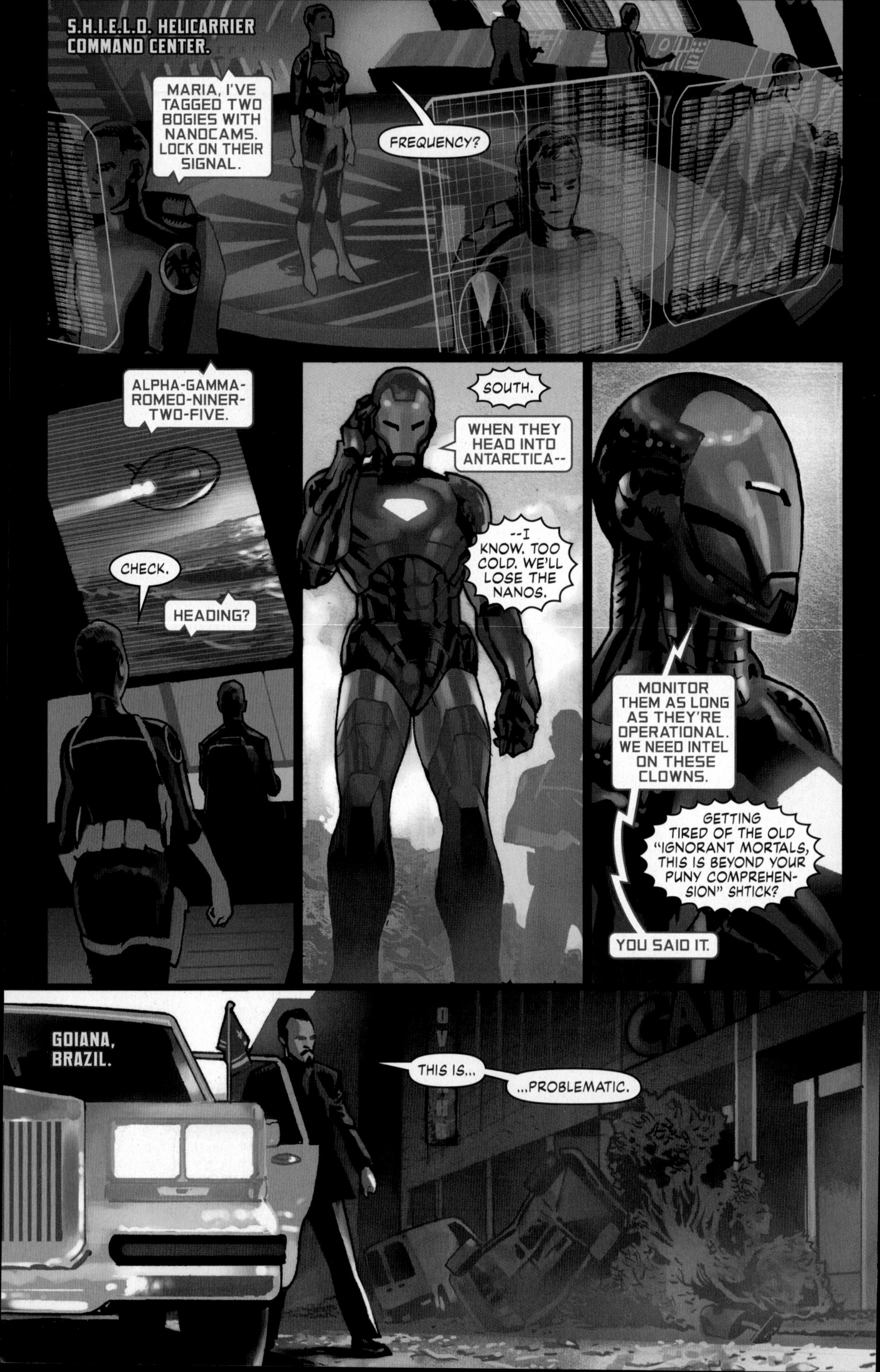
S.H.I.E.L.D. HELICARRIER COMMAND CENTER.
MARIA, I'VE TAGGED TWO BOGIES WITH NANOCAMS. LOCK ON THEIR SIGNAL.
FREQUENCY?
ALPHA-GAMMA-ROMEO-NINER-TWO-FIVE.
CHECK.
HEADING?
SOUTH.
WHEN THEY HEAD INTO ANTARCTICA--
--I KNOW. TOO COLD. WE'LL LOSE THE NANOS.
MONITOR THEM AS LONG AS THEY'RE OPERATIONAL. WE NEED INTEL ON THESE CLOWNS.
GETTING TIRED OF THE OLD "IGNORANT MORTALS, THIS IS BEYOND YOUR PUNY COMPREHENSION" SHTICK?
YOU SAID IT.
GOIANA, BRAZIL.
THIS IS...
...PROBLEMATIC.

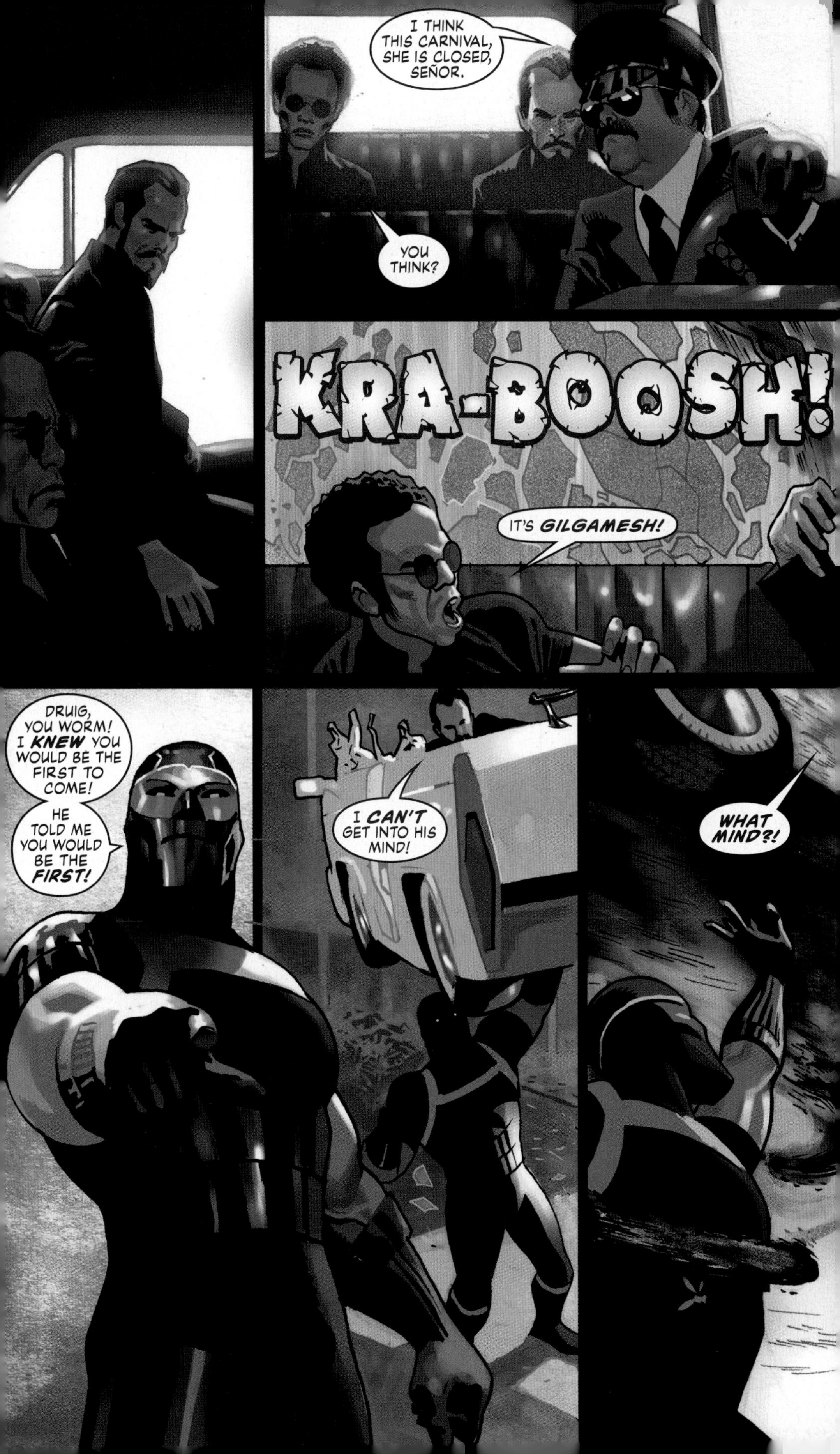
I THINK THIS CARNIVAL, SHE IS CLOSED, SEÑOR.
YOU THINK?
KRA-BOOSH!
IT'S GILGAMESH!
DRUIG, YOU WORM! I KNEW YOU WOULD BE THE FIRST TO COME!
HE TOLD ME YOU WOULD BE THE FIRST!
I CAN'T GET INTO HIS MIND!
WHAT MIND?!

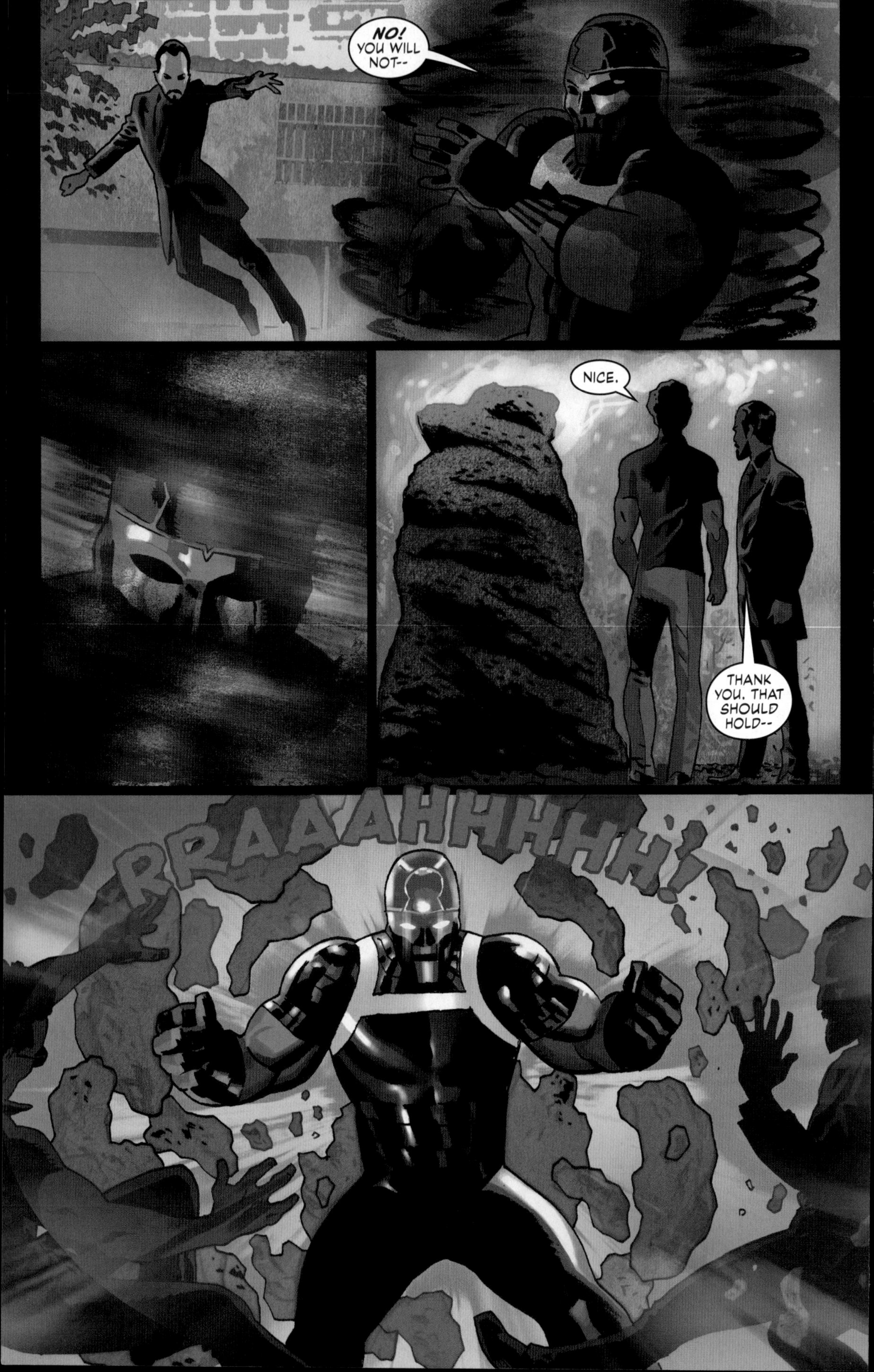
NO! YOU WILL NOT--
NICE.
THANK YOU. THAT SHOULD HOLD--
RRAAAHHHHH!

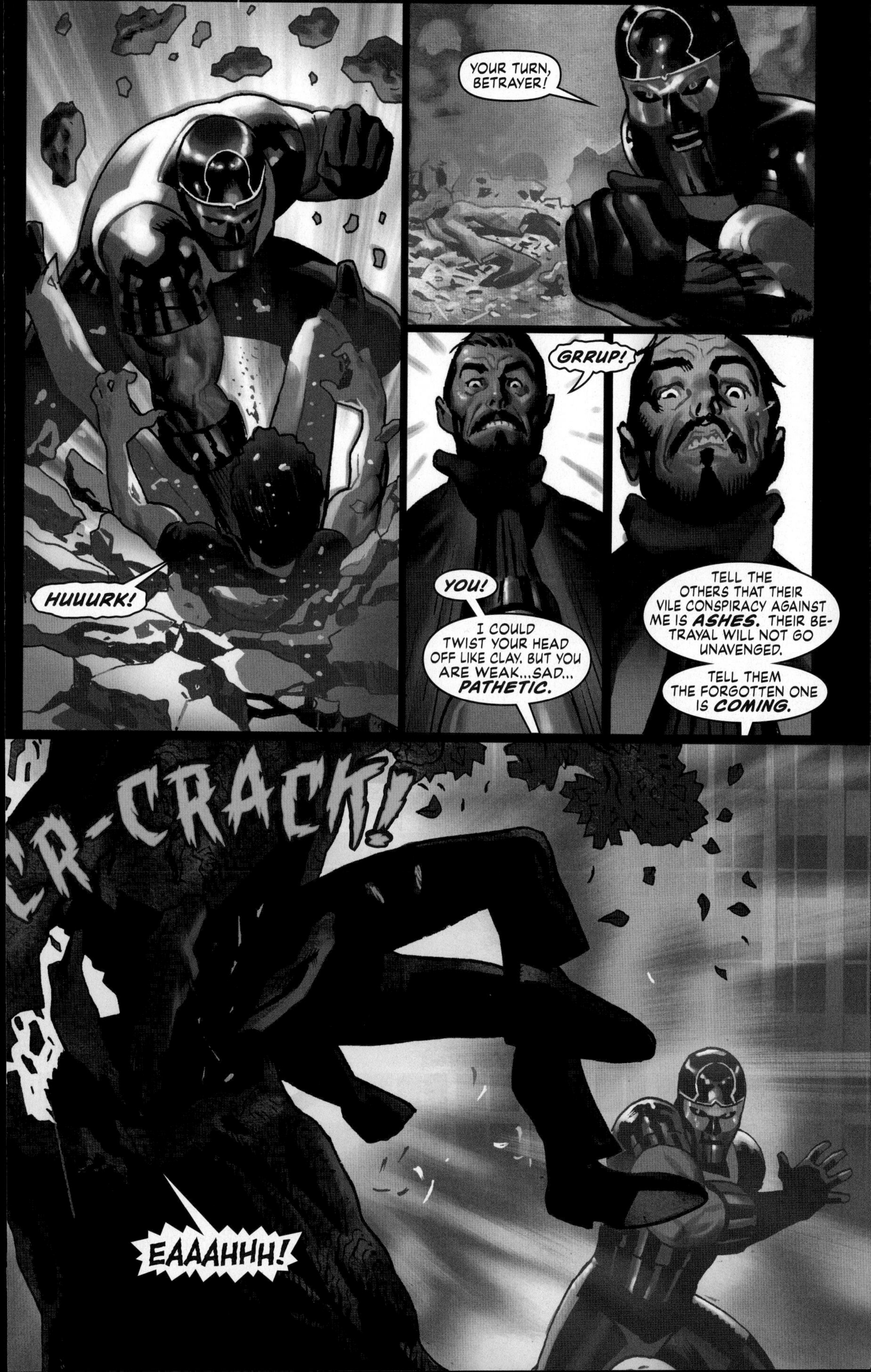
HUUURK!
YOUR TURN, BETRAYER!
GRRUP!
YOU!
I COULD TWIST YOUR HEAD OFF LIKE CLAY. BUT YOU ARE WEAK...SAD... PATHETIC.
TELL THE OTHERS THAT THEIR VILE CONSPIRACY AGAINST ME IS ASHES. THEIR BE-TRAYAL WILL NOT GO UNAVENGED.
TELL THEM THE FORGOTTEN ONE IS COMING.
CR-CRACK!
EAAAHHH!

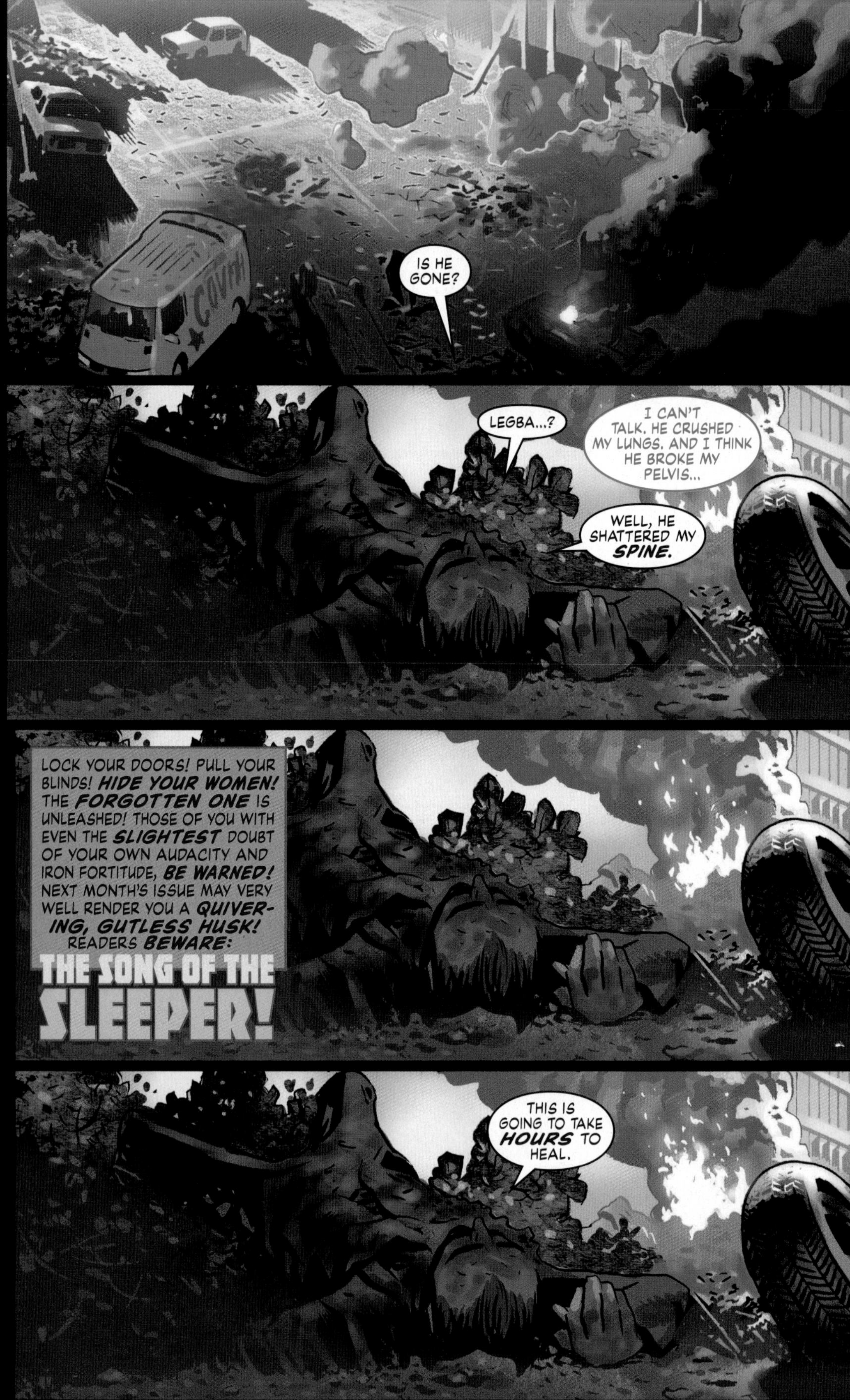
IS HE GONE?
LEGBA...?
I CAN'T TALK. HE CRUSHED MY LUNGS. AND I THINK HE BROKE MY PELVIS...
WELL, HE SHATTERED MY SPINE.
LOCK YOUR DOORS! PULL YOUR BLINDS! HIDE YOUR WOMEN! THE FORGOTTEN ONE IS UNLEASHED! THOSE OF YOU WITH EVEN THE SLIGHTEST DOUBT OF YOUR OWN AUDACITY AND IRON FORTITUDE, BE WARNED! NEXT MONTH'S ISSUE MAY VERY WELL RENDER YOU A QUIVERING, GUTLESS HUSK! READERS BEWARE:
THE SONG OF THE SLEEPER!
THIS IS GOING TO TAKE HOURS TO HEAL.

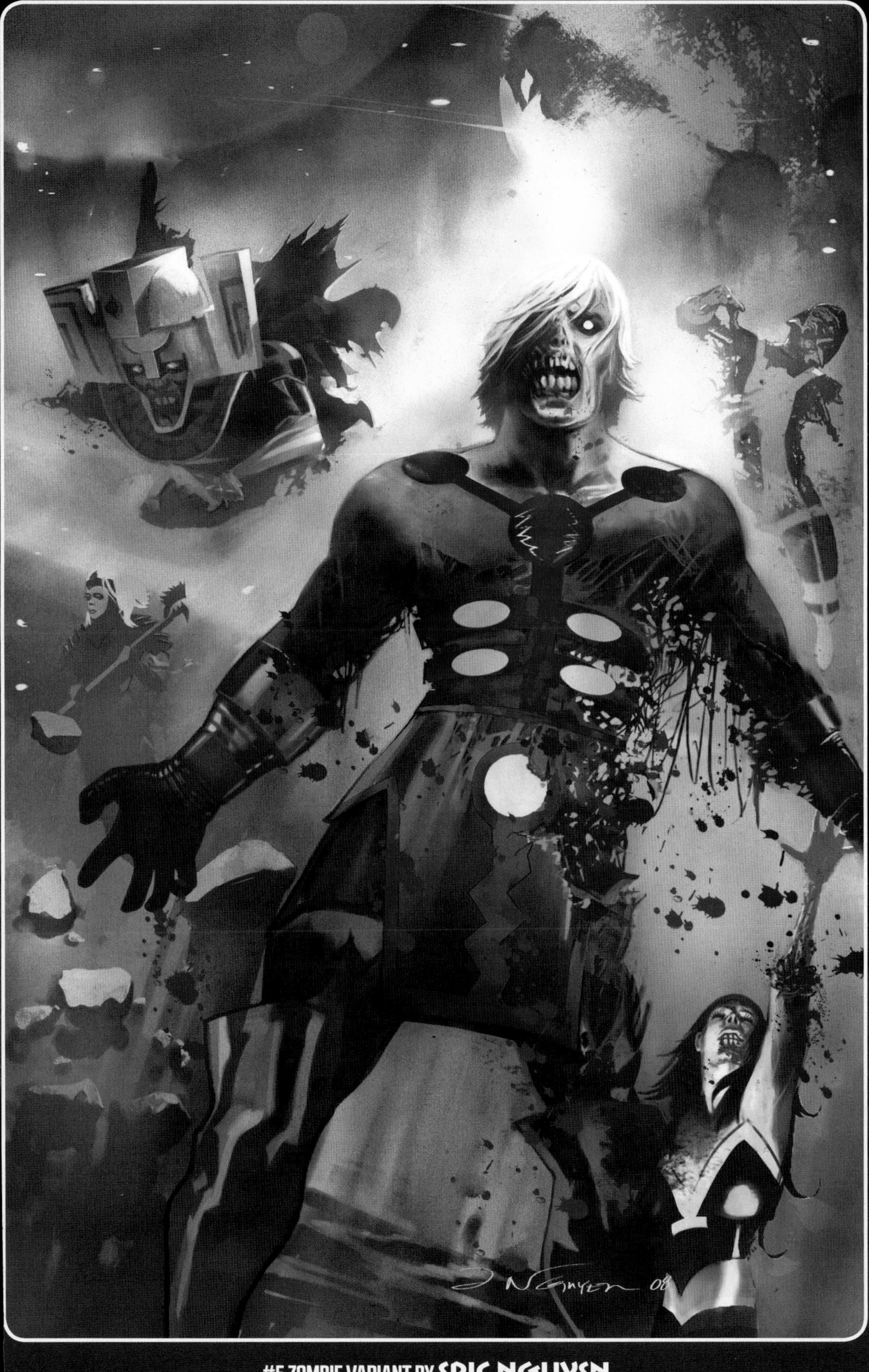

N Guyen 08

#5 ZOMBIE VARIANT BY ERIC NGUYEN

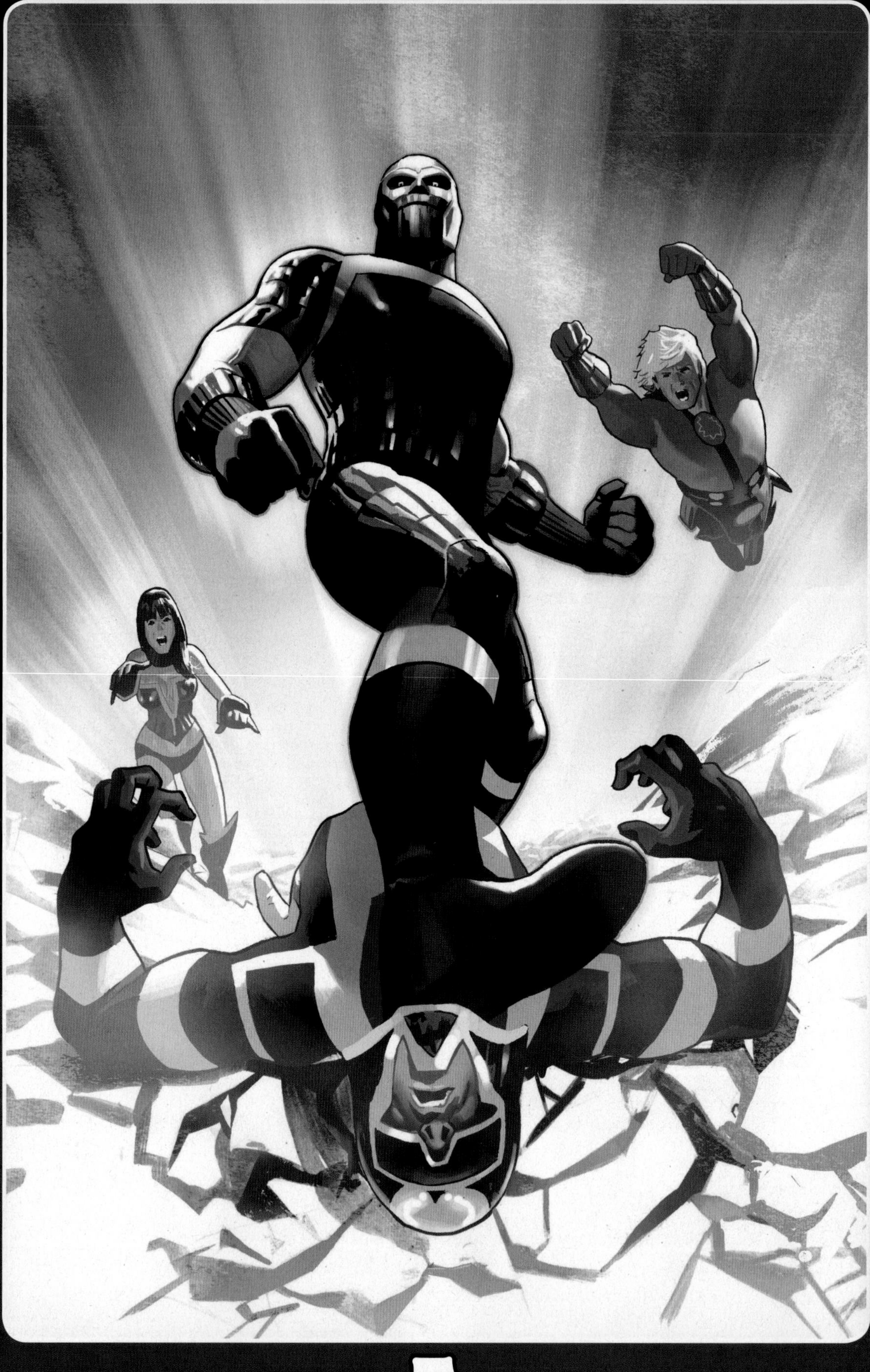

5

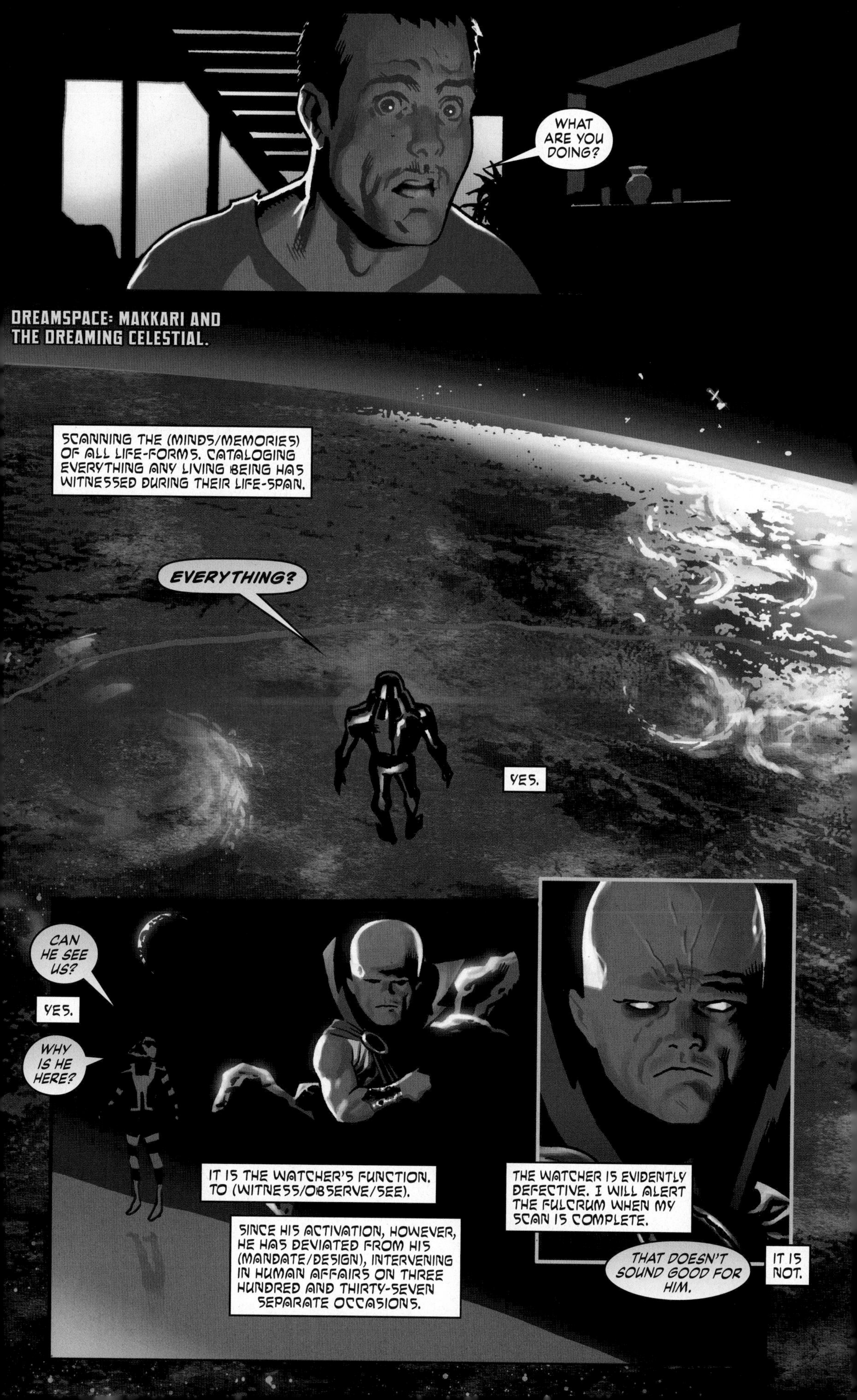
WHAT ARE YOU DOING?
DREAMSPACE: MAKKARI AND THE DREAMING CELESTIAL.
SCANNING THE (MINDS/MEMORIES) OF ALL LIFE-FORMS. CATALOGING EVERYTHING ANY LIVING BEING HAS WITNESSED DURING THEIR LIFE-SPAN.
EVERYTHING?
YES.
CAN HE SEE US?
YES.
WHY IS HE HERE?
IT IS THE WATCHER'S FUNCTION. TO (WITNESS/OBSERVE/SEE).
SINCE HIS ACTIVATION, HOWEVER, HE HAS DEVIATED FROM HIS (MANDATE/DESIGN), INTERVENING IN HUMAN AFFAIRS ON THREE HUNDRED AND THIRTY-SEVEN SEPARATE OCCASIONS.
THE WATCHER IS EVIDENTLY DEFECTIVE. I WILL ALERT THE FULCRUM WHEN MY SCAN IS COMPLETE.
THAT DOESN'T SOUND GOOD FOR HIM.
IT IS NOT.

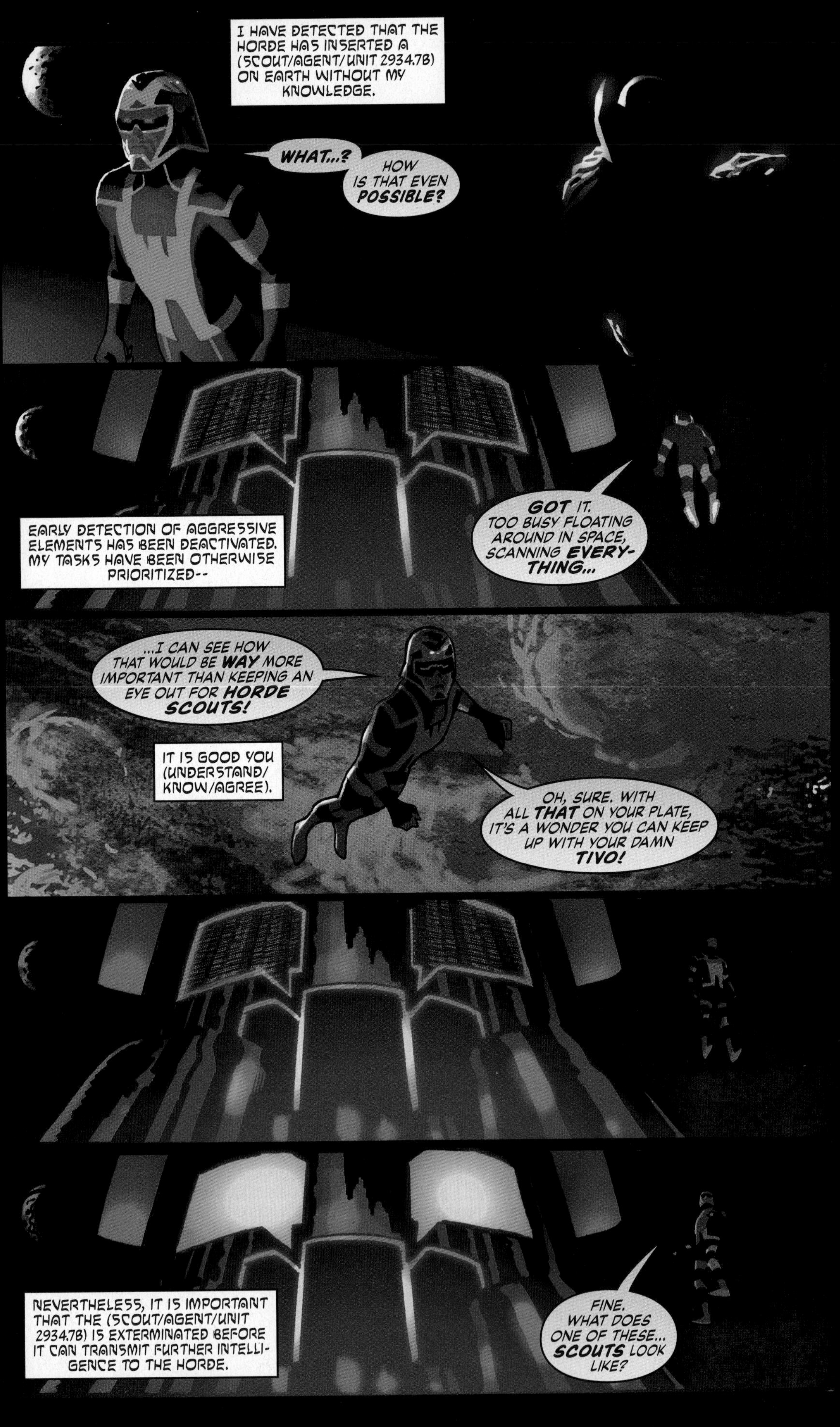
I HAVE DETECTED THAT THE HORDE HAS INSERTED A (SCOUT/AGENT/UNIT 2934.7B) ON EARTH WITHOUT MY KNOWLEDGE.
WHAT...?
HOW IS THAT EVEN POSSIBLE?
EARLY DETECTION OF AGGRESSIVE ELEMENTS HAS BEEN DEACTIVATED. MY TASKS HAVE BEEN OTHERWISE PRIORITIZED--
GOT IT. TOO BUSY FLOATING AROUND IN SPACE, SCANNING EVERY-THING...
...I CAN SEE HOW THAT WOULD BE WAY MORE IMPORTANT THAN KEEPING AN EYE OUT FOR HORDE SCOUTS!
IT IS GOOD YOU (UNDERSTAND/ KNOW/AGREE).
OH, SURE. WITH ALL THAT ON YOUR PLATE, IT'S A WONDER YOU CAN KEEP UP WITH YOUR DAMN TIVO!
NEVERTHELESS, IT IS IMPORTANT THAT THE (SCOUT/AGENT/UNIT 2934.7B) IS EXTERMINATED BEFORE IT CAN TRANSMIT FURTHER INTELLI-GENCE TO THE HORDE.
FINE. WHAT DOES ONE OF THESE... SCOUTS LOOK LIKE?

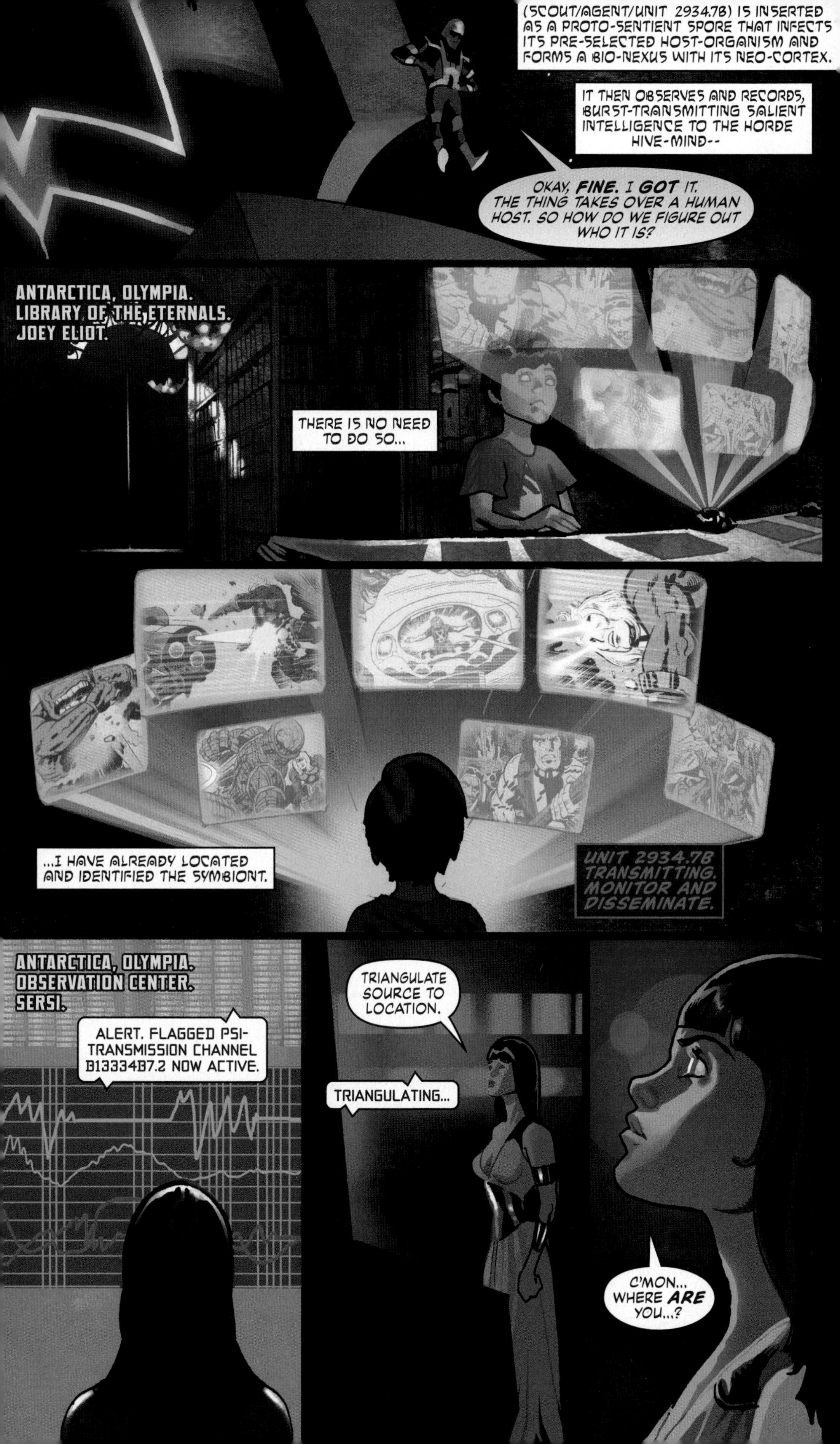
(SCOUT/AGENT/UNIT 2934.7B) IS INSERTED AS A PROTO-SENTIENT SPORE THAT INFECTS ITS PRE-SELECTED HOST-ORGANISM AND FORMS A BIO-NEXUS WITH ITS NEO-CORTEX.
IT THEN OBSERVES AND RECORDS, BURST-TRANSMITTING SALIENT INTELLIGENCE TO THE HORDE HIVE-MIND--
OKAY, FINE. I GOT IT. THE THING TAKES OVER A HUMAN HOST. SO HOW DO WE FIGURE OUT WHO IT IS?
ANTARCTICA, OLYMPIA. LIBRARY OF THE ETERNALS. JOEY ELIOT.
THERE IS NO NEED TO DO SO...
...I HAVE ALREADY LOCATED AND IDENTIFIED THE SYMBIONT.
UNIT 2934.7B TRANSMITTING. MONITOR AND DISSEMINATE.
ANTARCTICA, OLYMPIA. OBSERVATION CENTER. SERSI.
ALERT. FLAGGED PSI-TRANSMISSION CHANNEL B13334B7.2 NOW ACTIVE.
TRIANGULATE SOURCE TO LOCATION.
TRIANGULATING...
C'MON... WHERE ARE YOU...?

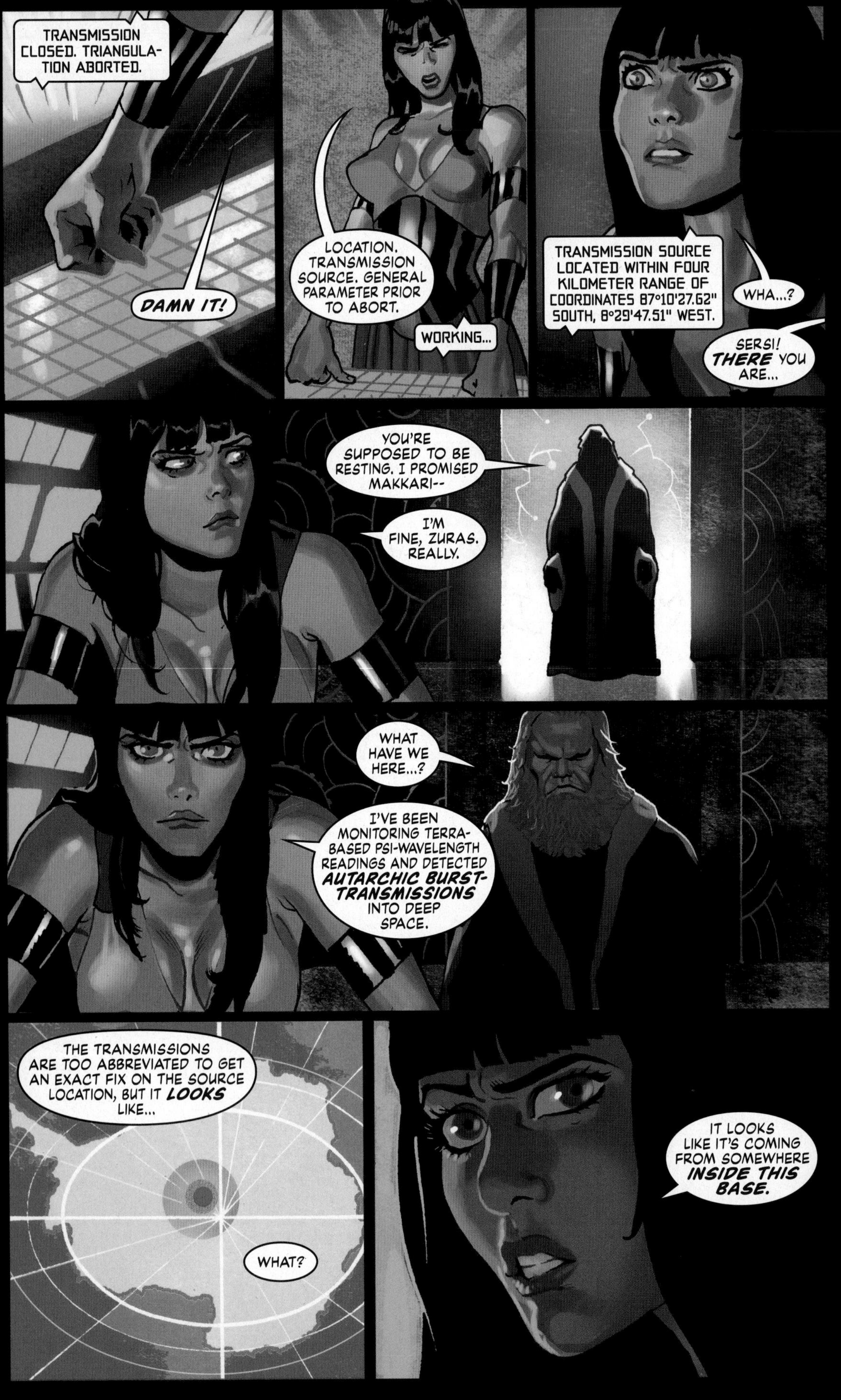
TRANSMISSION CLOSED. TRIANGULATION ABORTED.
DAMN IT!
LOCATION. TRANSMISSION SOURCE. GENERAL PARAMETER PRIOR TO ABORT.
WORKING...
TRANSMISSION SOURCE LOCATED WITHIN FOUR KILOMETER RANGE OF COORDINATES 87°10'27.62" SOUTH, 8°29'47.51" WEST.
WHA...?
SERSI! THERE YOU ARE...
YOU'RE SUPPOSED TO BE RESTING. I PROMISED MAKKARI--
I'M FINE, ZURAS. REALLY.
WHAT HAVE WE HERE...?
I'VE BEEN MONITORING TERRA-BASED PSI-WAVELENGTH READINGS AND DETECTED AUTARCHIC BURST-TRANSMISSIONS INTO DEEP SPACE.
THE TRANSMISSIONS ARE TOO ABBREVIATED TO GET AN EXACT FIX ON THE SOURCE LOCATION, BUT IT LOOKS LIKE...
WHAT?
IT LOOKS LIKE IT'S COMING FROM SOMEWHERE INSIDE THIS BASE.

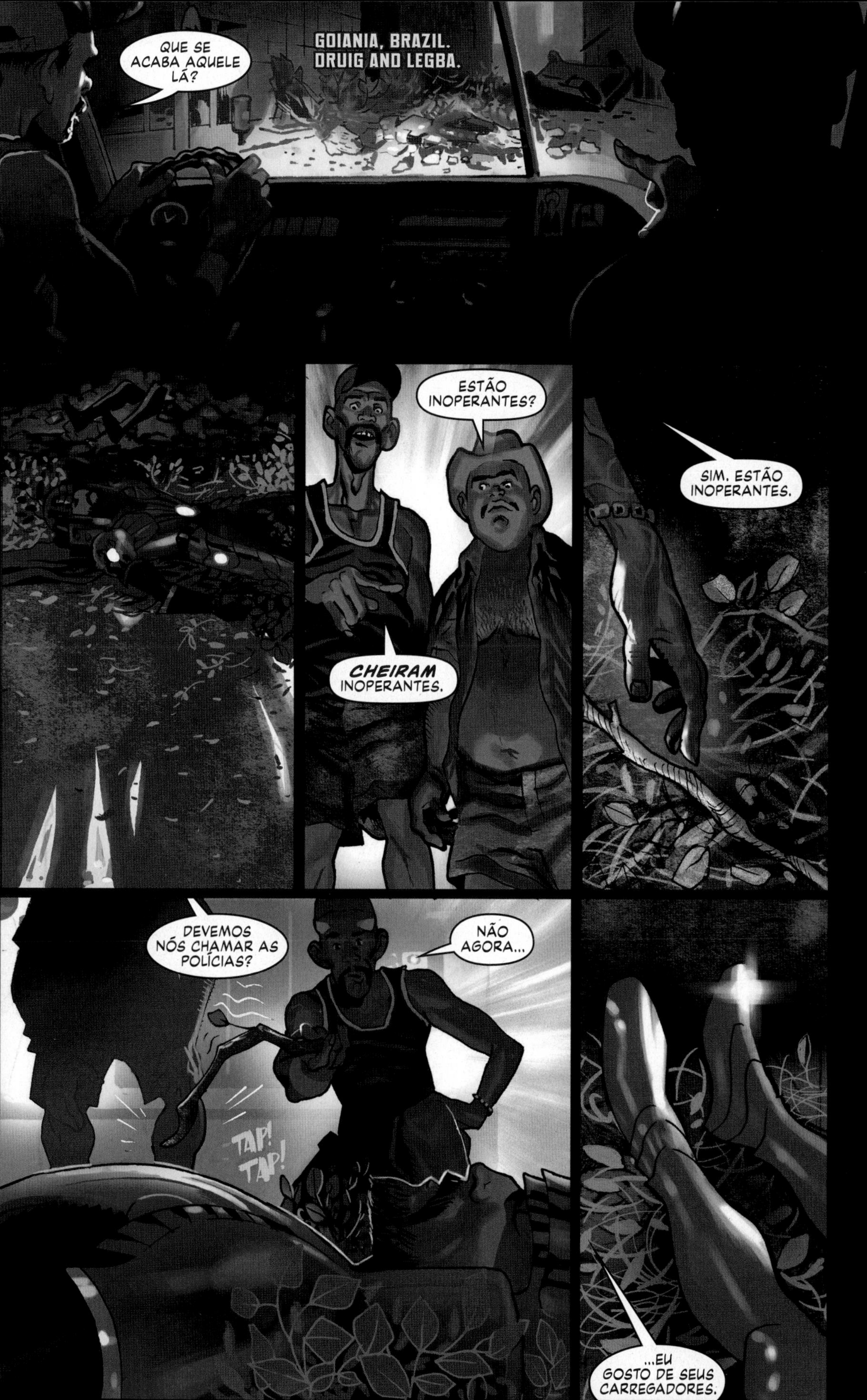
QUE SE ACABA AQUELE LÁ?
GOIANIA, BRAZIL. DRUIG AND LEGBA.
ESTÃO INOPERANTES?
CHEIRAM INOPERANTES.
SIM. ESTÃO INOPERANTES.
DEVEMOS NÓS CHAMAR AS POLÍCIAS?
NÃO AGORA...
TAP! TAP!
...EU GOSTO DE SEUS CARREGADORES.

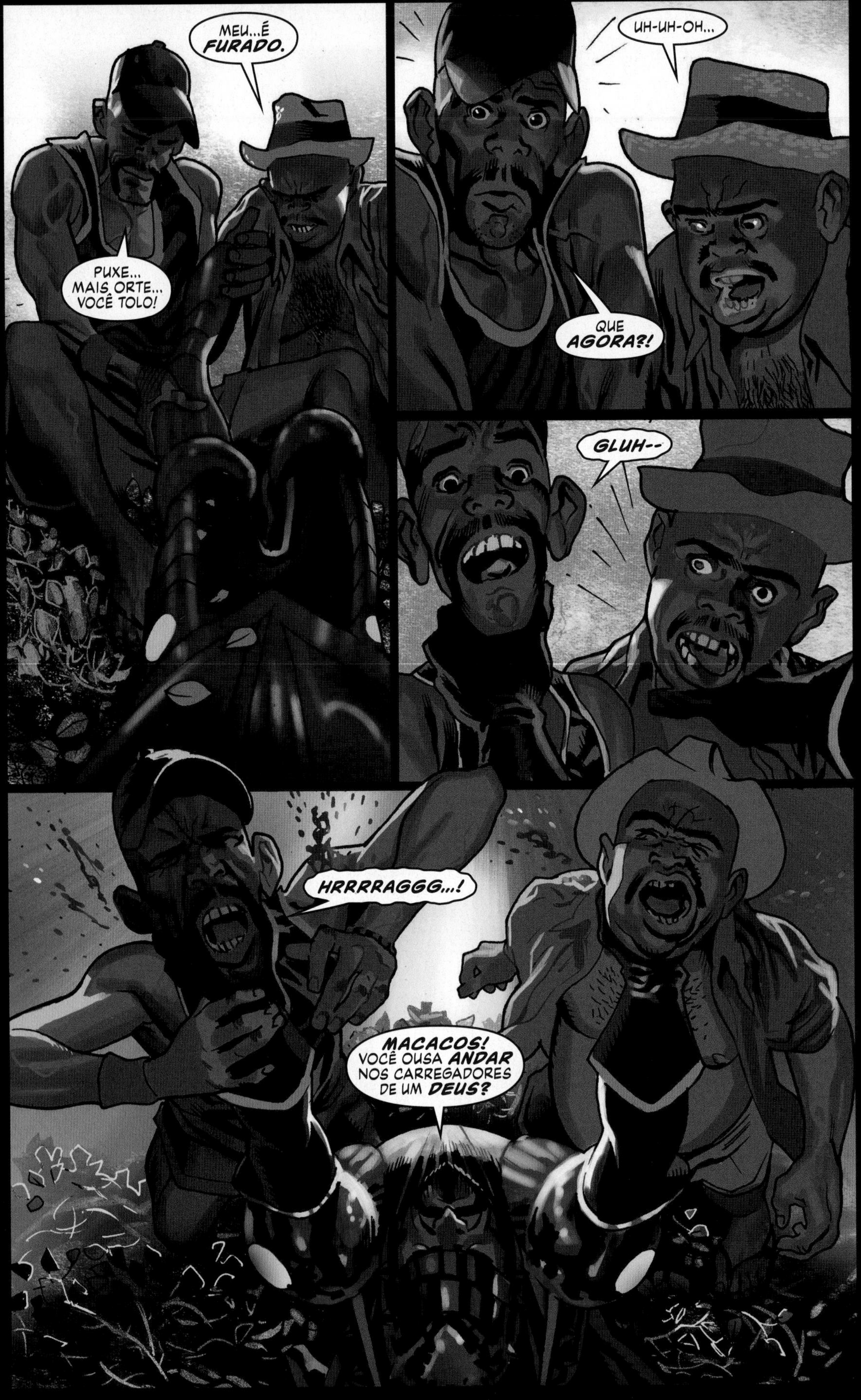
MEU...É FURADO.
PUXE... MAIS ORTE... VOCÊ TOLO!
UH-UH-OH...
QUE AGORA?!
GLUH--
HRRRRAGGG...!
MACACOS! VOCÊ OUSA ANDAR NOS CARREGADORES DE UM DEUS?

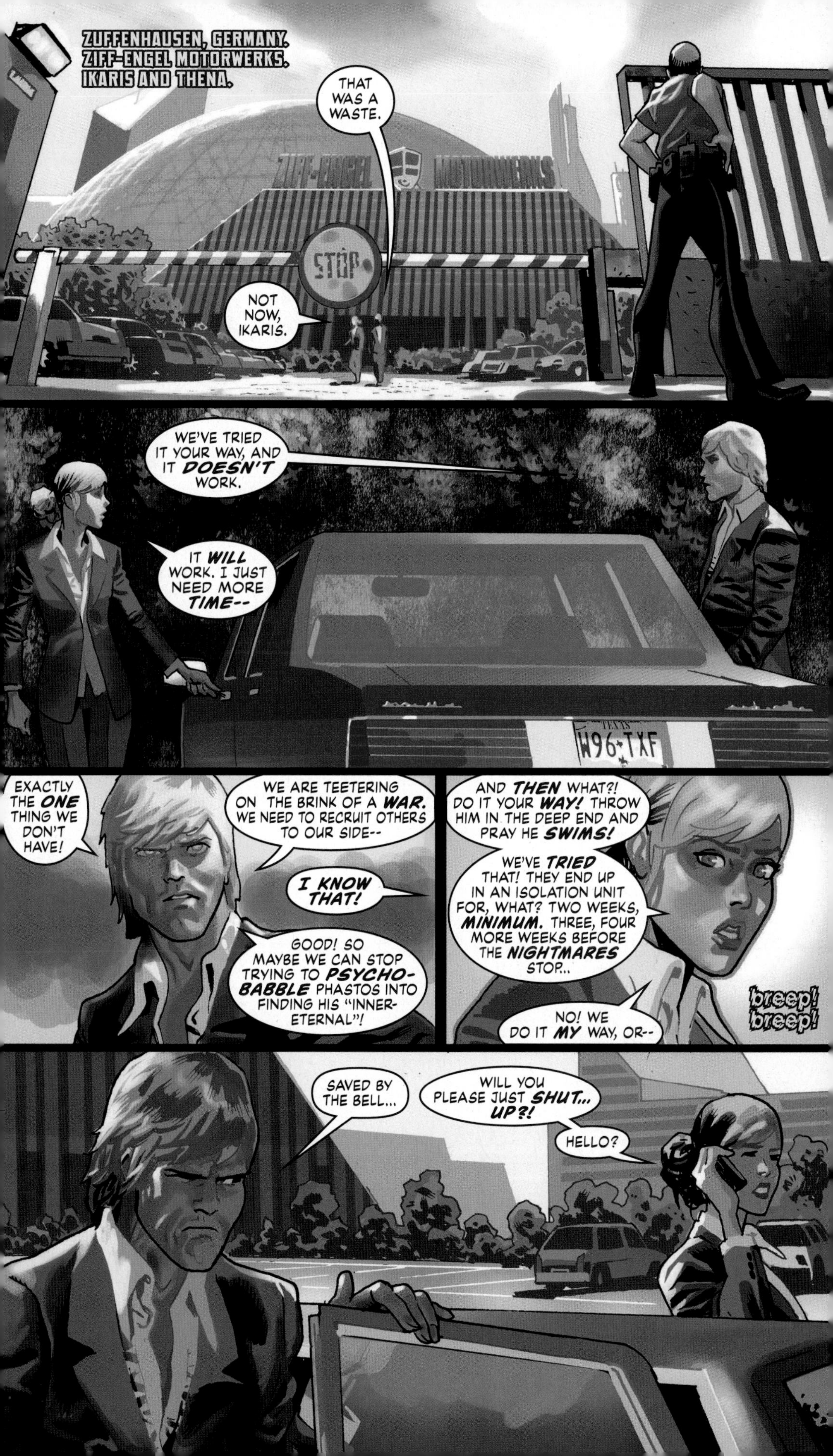
ZUFFENHAUSEN, GERMANY. ZIFF-ENGEL MOTORWERKS. IKARIS AND THENA.
ZIFF-ENGEL MOTORWERKS
STOP
THAT WAS A WASTE.
NOT NOW, IKARIS.
WE'VE TRIED IT YOUR WAY, AND IT DOESN'T WORK.
IT WILL WORK. I JUST NEED MORE TIME--
W96 TXF
EXACTLY THE ONE THING WE DON'T HAVE!
WE ARE TEETERING ON THE BRINK OF A WAR. WE NEED TO RECRUIT OTHERS TO OUR SIDE--
I KNOW THAT!
GOOD! SO MAYBE WE CAN STOP TRYING TO PSYCHO-BABBLE PHASTOS INTO FINDING HIS "INNER-ETERNAL"!
AND THEN WHAT?! DO IT YOUR WAY! THROW HIM IN THE DEEP END AND PRAY HE SWIMS!
WE'VE TRIED THAT! THEY END UP IN AN ISOLATION UNIT FOR, WHAT? TWO WEEKS, MINIMUM. THREE, FOUR MORE WEEKS BEFORE THE NIGHTMARES STOP...
NO! WE DO IT MY WAY, OR--
breep! breep!
SAVED BY THE BELL...
WILL YOU PLEASE JUST SHUT... UP?!
HELLO?

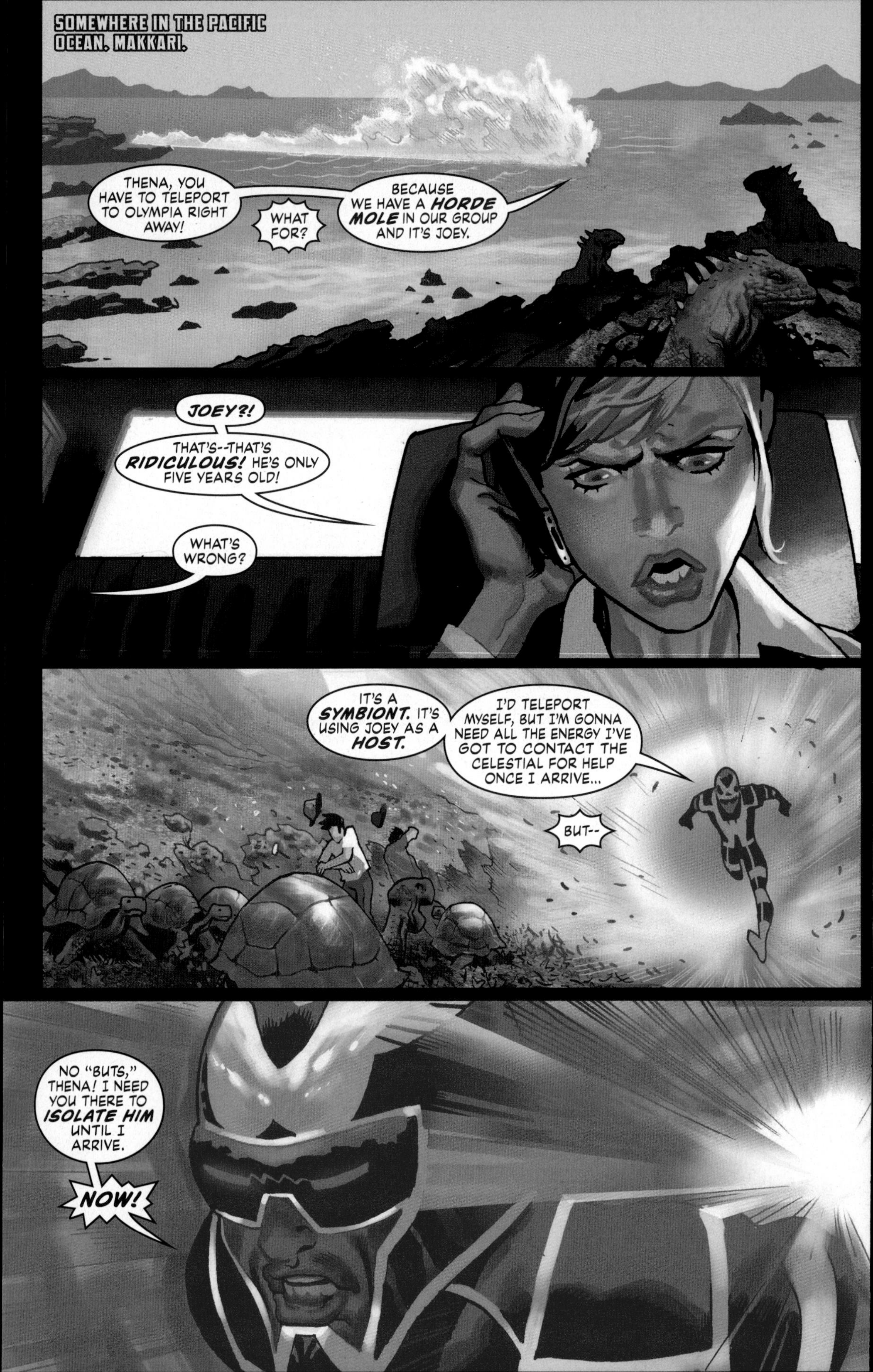
SOMEWHERE IN THE PACIFIC OCEAN. MAKKARI.
THENA, YOU HAVE TO TELEPORT TO OLYMPIA RIGHT AWAY!
WHAT FOR?
BECAUSE WE HAVE A HORDE MOLE IN OUR GROUP AND IT'S JOEY.
JOEY?!
THAT'S--THAT'S RIDICULOUS! HE'S ONLY FIVE YEARS OLD!
WHAT'S WRONG?
IT'S A SYMBIONT. IT'S USING JOEY AS A HOST.
I'D TELEPORT MYSELF, BUT I'M GONNA NEED ALL THE ENERGY I'VE GOT TO CONTACT THE CELESTIAL FOR HELP ONCE I ARRIVE...
BUT--
NO "BUTS," THENA! I NEED YOU THERE TO ISOLATE HIM UNTIL I ARRIVE.
NOW!

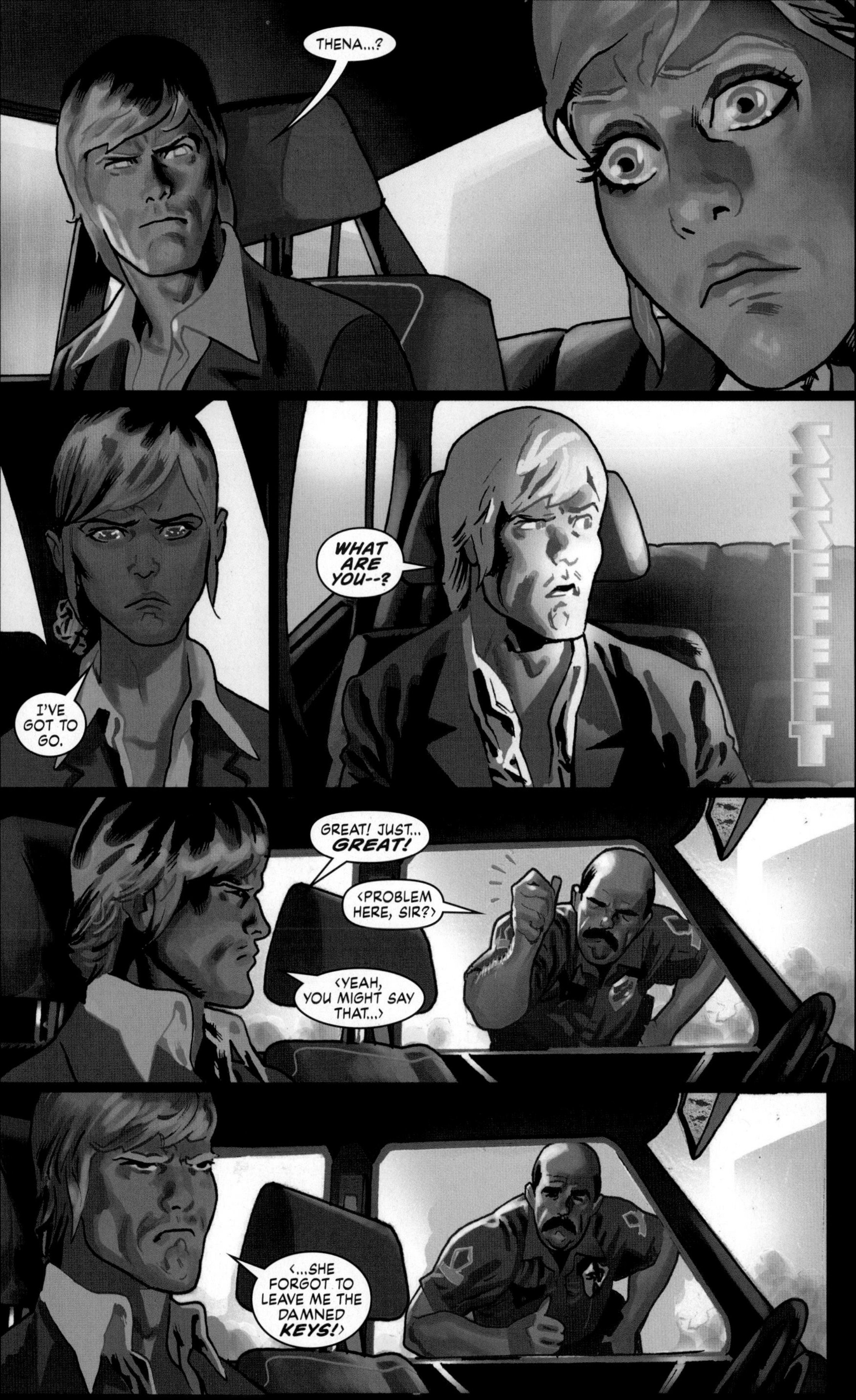
THENA...?
I'VE GOT TO GO.
WHAT ARE YOU--?
SSSFFFFT
GREAT! JUST... GREAT!
‹PROBLEM HERE, SIR?›
‹YEAH, YOU MIGHT SAY THAT...›
‹...SHE FORGOT TO LEAVE ME THE DAMNED KEYS!›

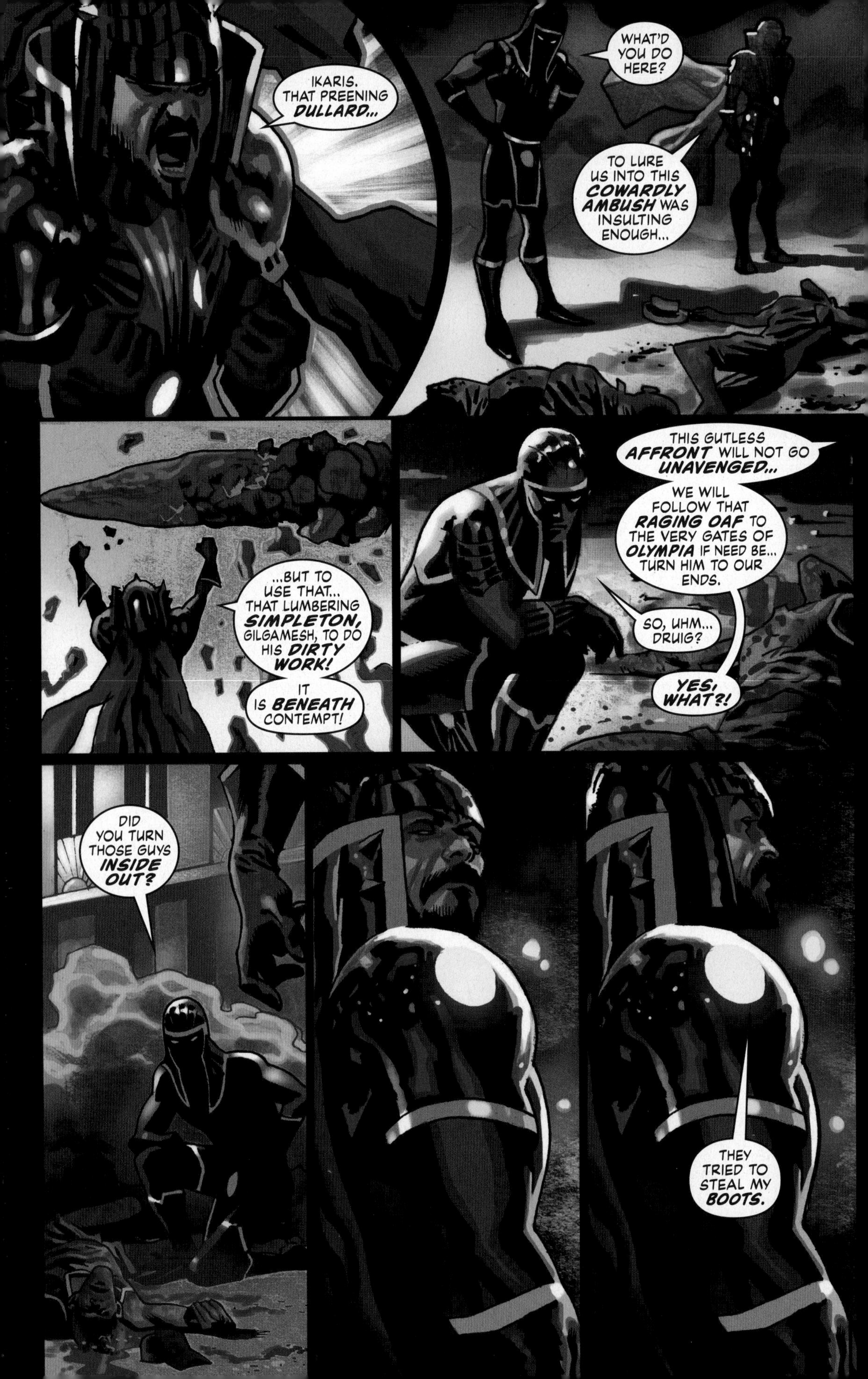
IKARIS. THAT PREENING DULLARD...
WHAT'D YOU DO HERE?
TO LURE US INTO THIS COWARDLY AMBUSH WAS INSULTING ENOUGH...
...BUT TO USE THAT... THAT LUMBERING SIMPLETON, GILGAMESH, TO DO HIS DIRTY WORK!
IT IS BENEATH CONTEMPT!
THIS GUTLESS AFFRONT WILL NOT GO UNAVENGED...
WE WILL FOLLOW THAT RAGING OAF TO THE VERY GATES OF OLYMPIA IF NEED BE... TURN HIM TO OUR ENDS.
SO, UHM... DRUIG?
YES, WHAT?!
DID YOU TURN THOSE GUYS INSIDE OUT?
THEY TRIED TO STEAL MY BOOTS.

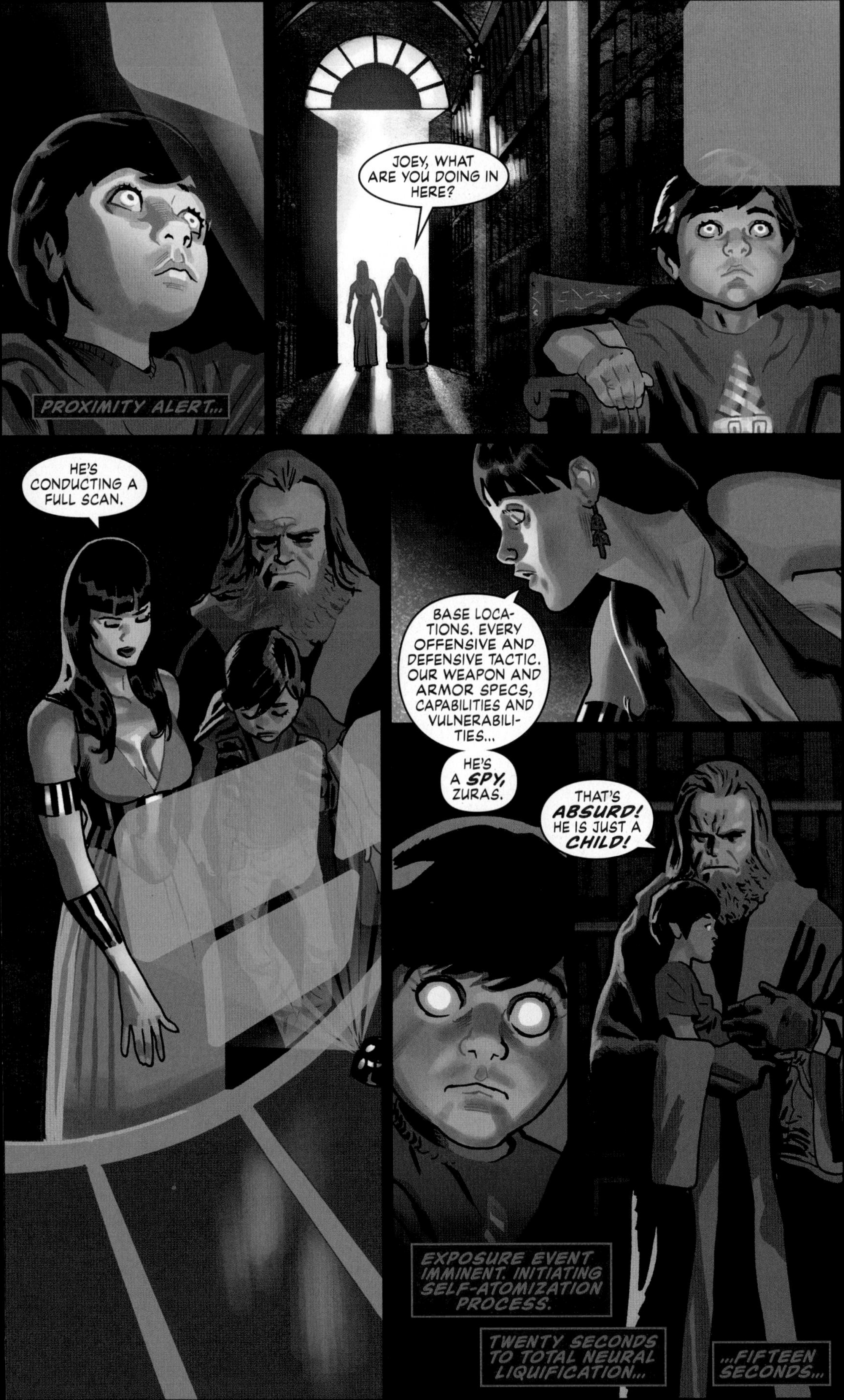
PROXIMITY ALERT...
JOEY, WHAT ARE YOU DOING IN HERE?
HE'S CONDUCTING A FULL SCAN.
BASE LOCATIONS. EVERY OFFENSIVE AND DEFENSIVE TACTIC. OUR WEAPON AND ARMOR SPECS, CAPABILITIES AND VULNERABILITIES...
HE'S A SPY, ZURAS.
THAT'S ABSURD! HE IS JUST A CHILD!
EXPOSURE EVENT IMMINENT. INITIATING SELF-ATOMIZATION PROCESS.
TWENTY SECONDS TO TOTAL NEURAL LIQUIFICATION...
...FIFTEEN SECONDS...

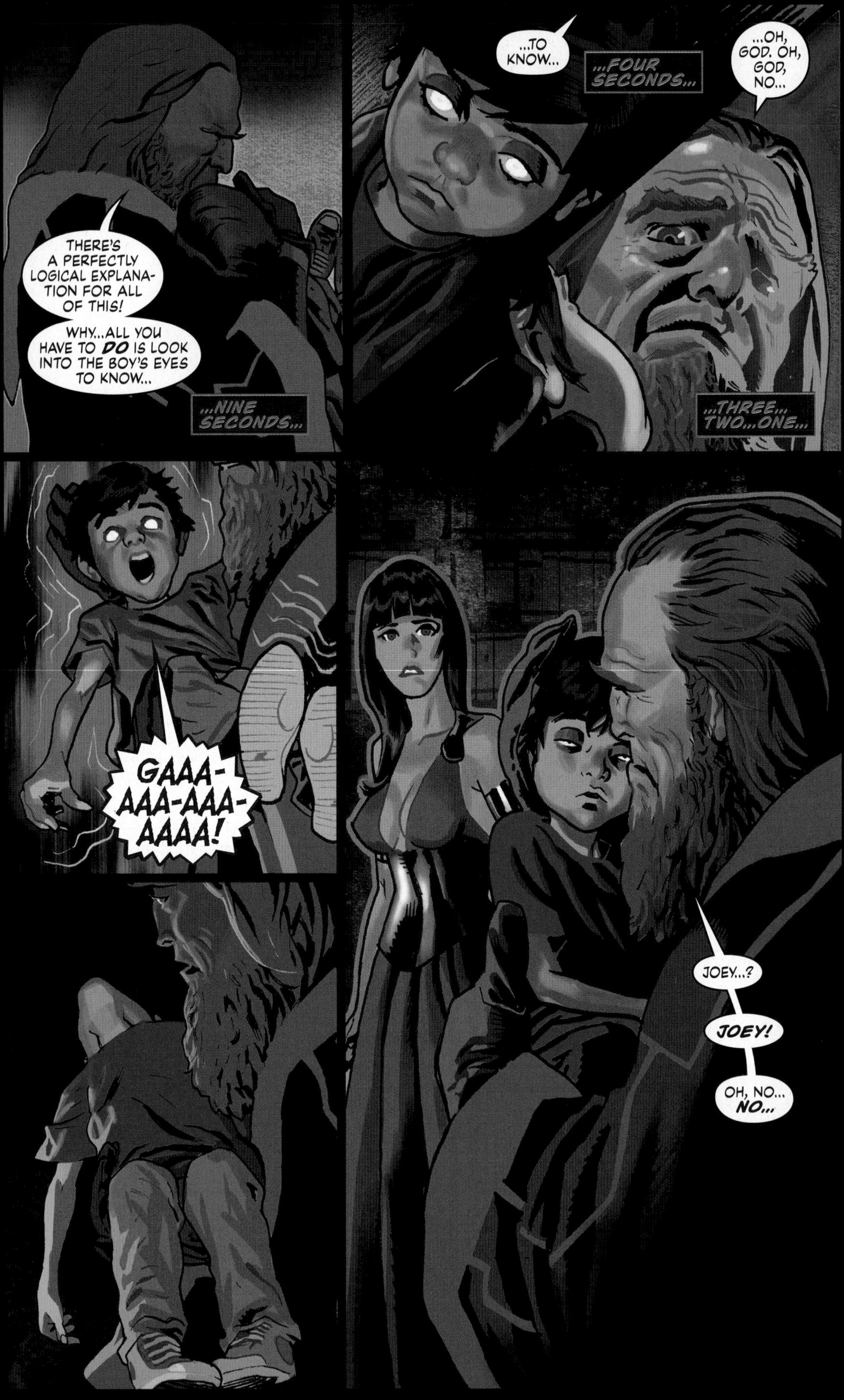
THERE'S A PERFECTLY LOGICAL EXPLANATION FOR ALL OF THIS!
WHY...ALL YOU HAVE TO DO IS LOOK INTO THE BOY'S EYES TO KNOW...
...NINE SECONDS...
...TO KNOW...
...FOUR SECONDS...
...OH, GOD. OH, GOD, NO...
...THREE... TWO...ONE...
GAAA-AAA-AAA-AAAA!
JOEY...?
JOEY!
OH, NO... NO...

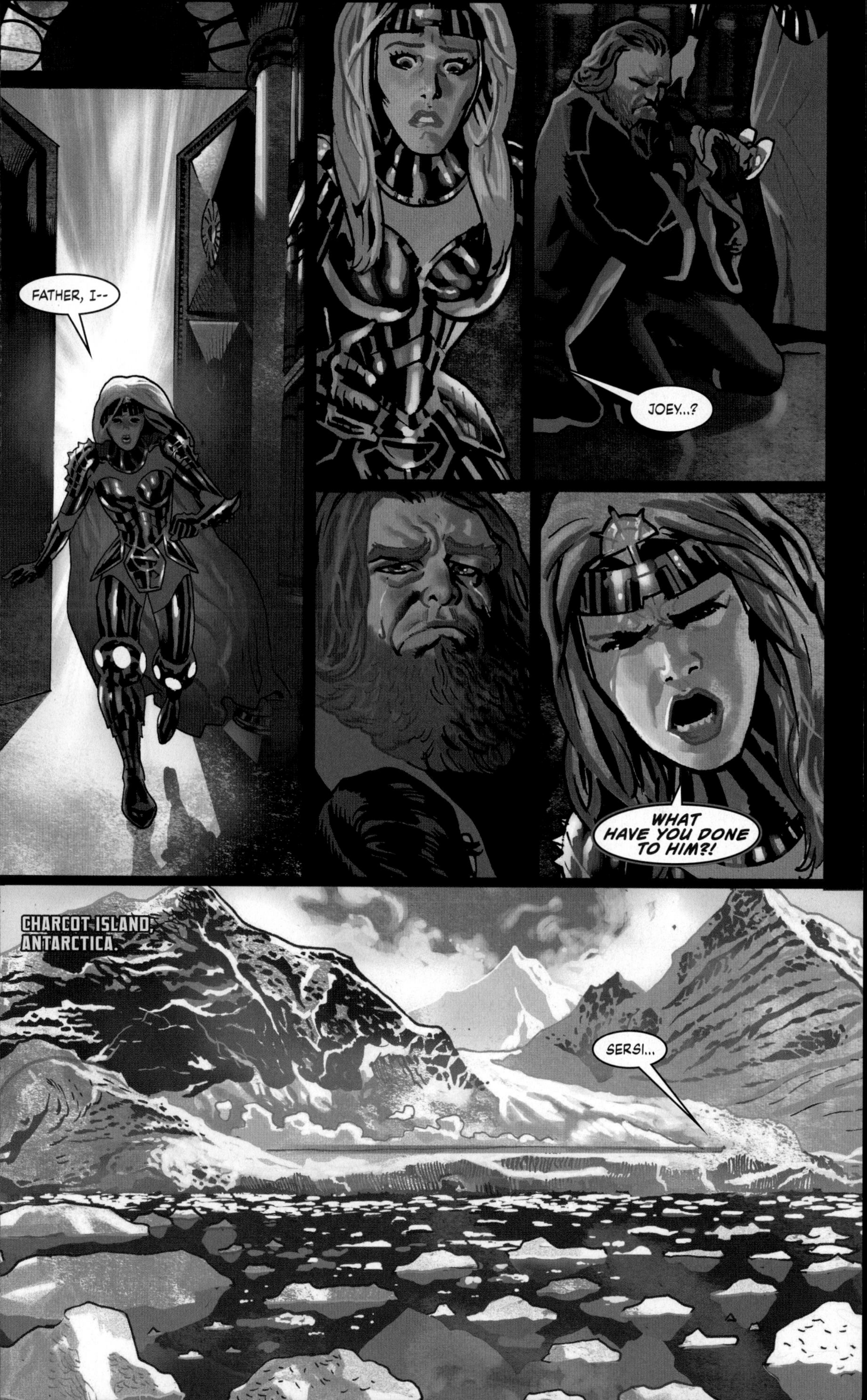
FATHER, I--
JOEY...?
WHAT HAVE YOU DONE TO HIM?!
CHARCOT ISLAND, ANTARCTICA.
SERSI...

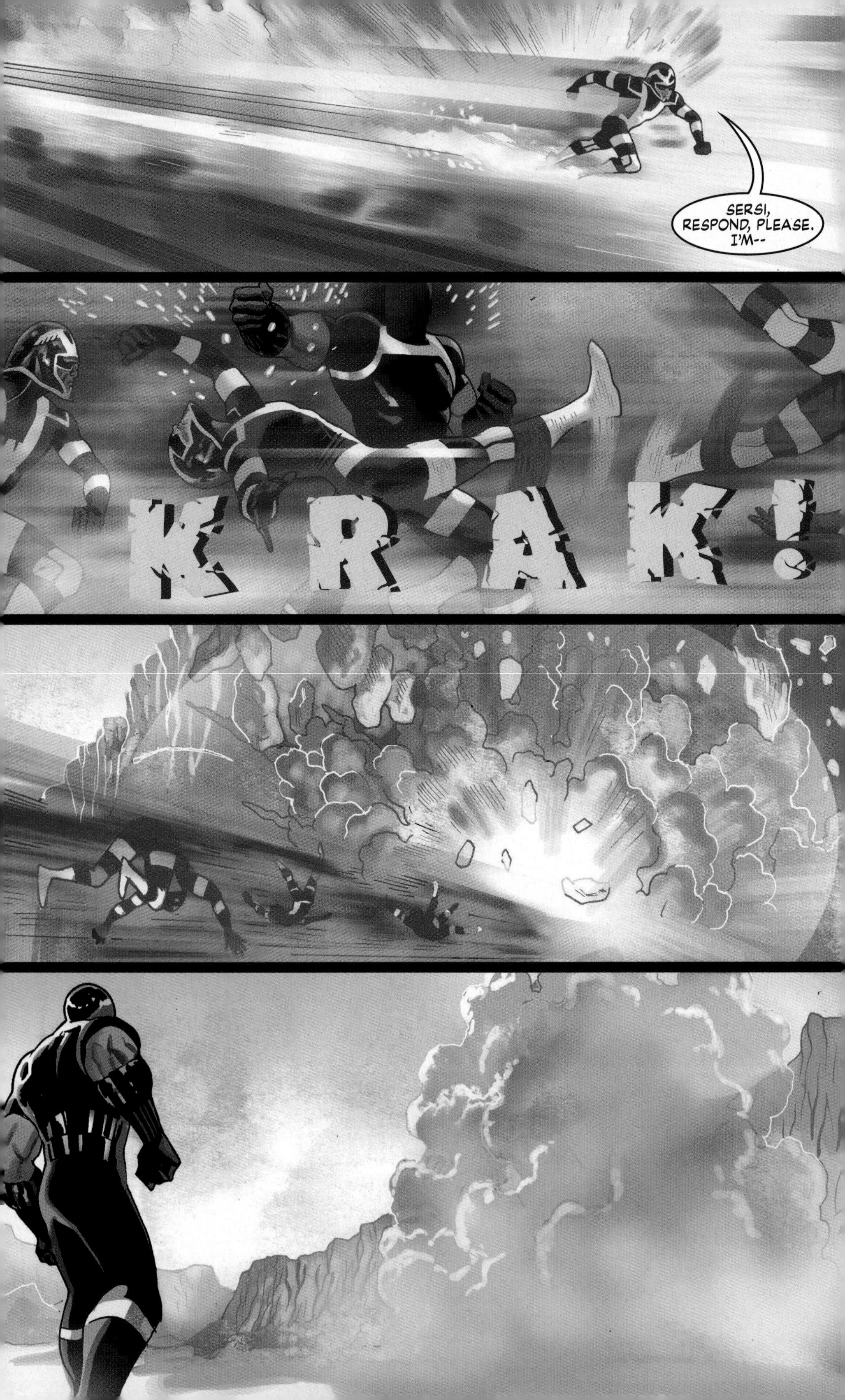
SERSI, RESPOND, PLEASE. I'M--
KRAK!

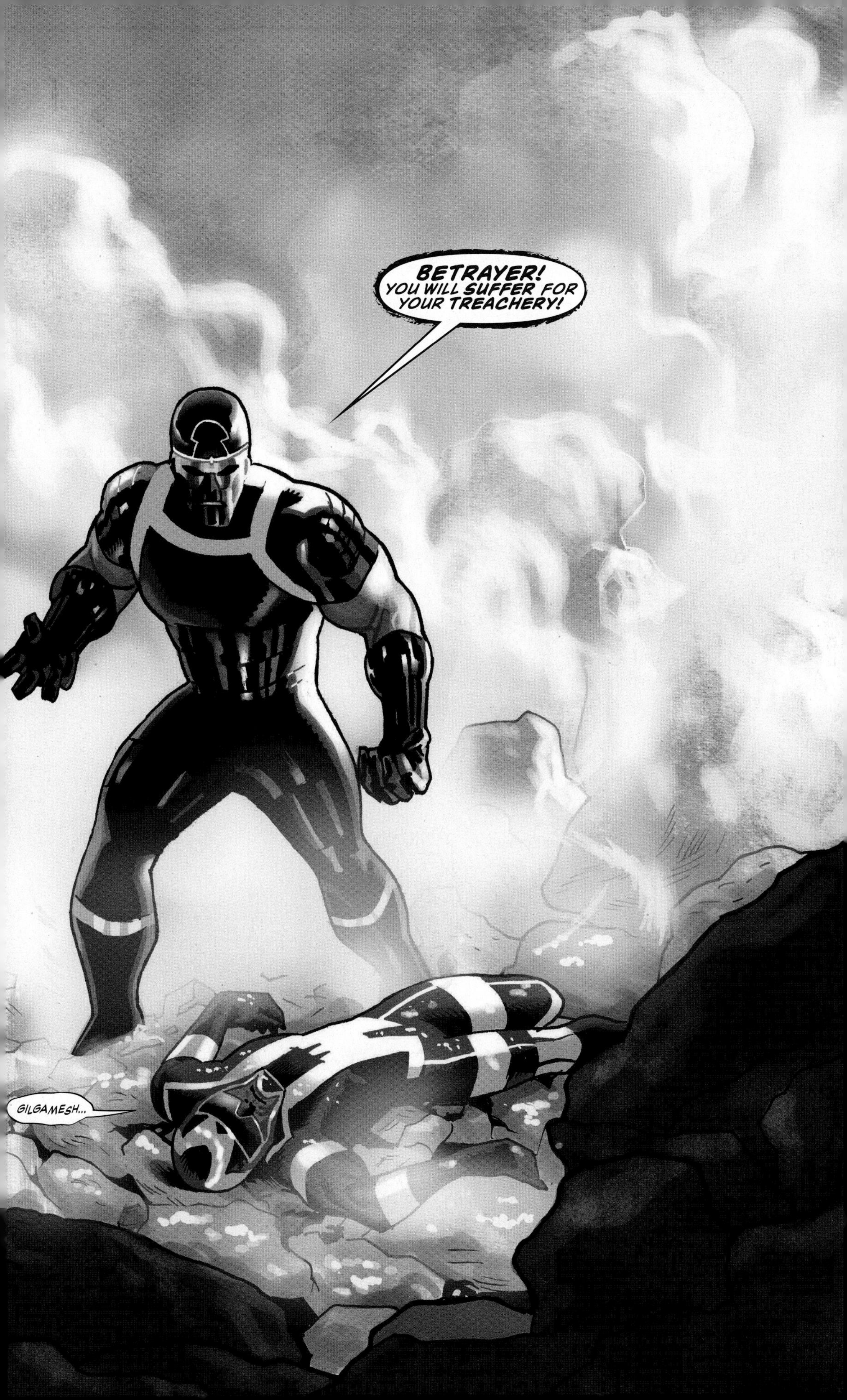
BETRAYER! YOU WILL SUFFER FOR YOUR TREACHERY!
GILGAMESH...

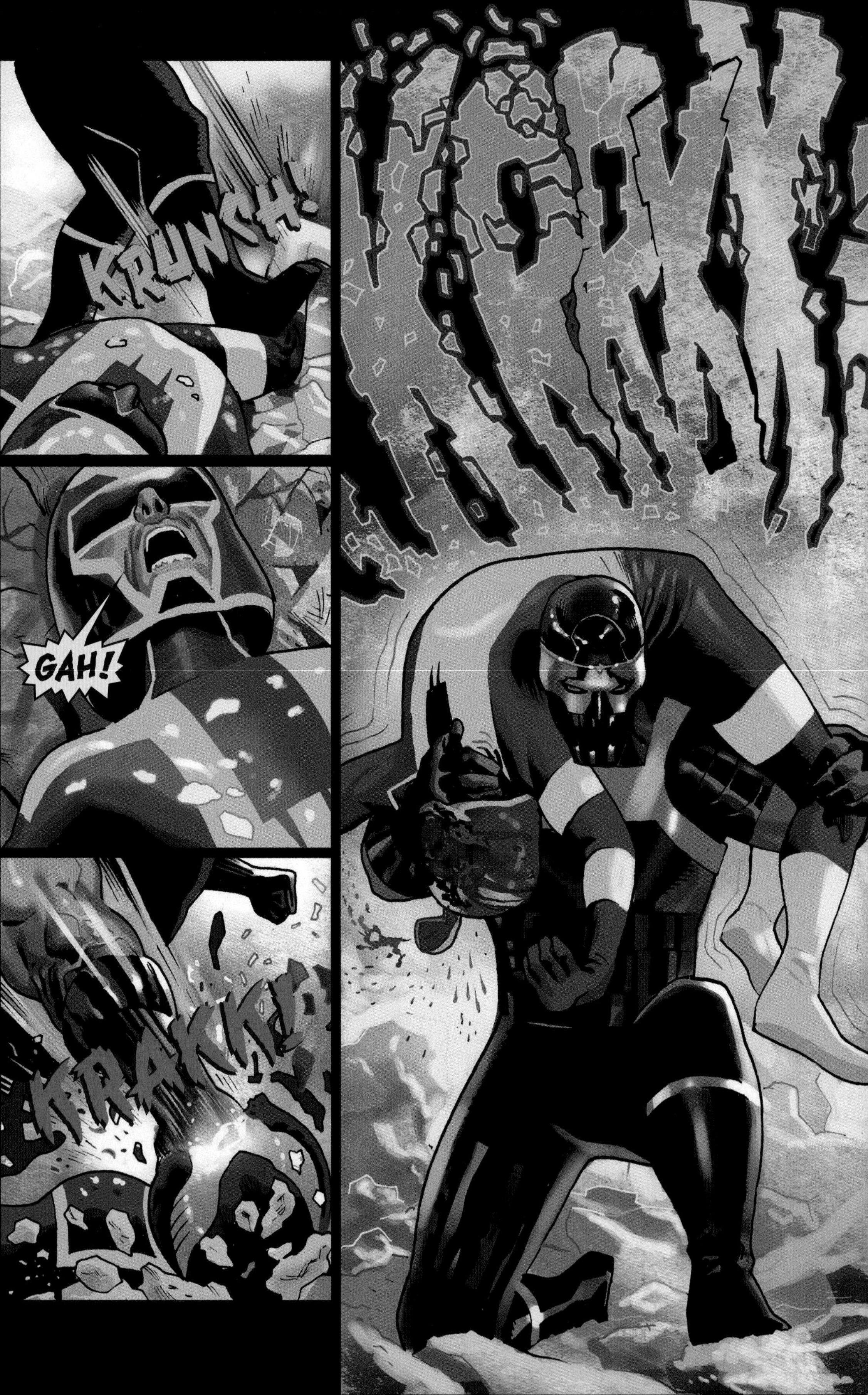
KRUNSH!
GAH!
KRAKK!

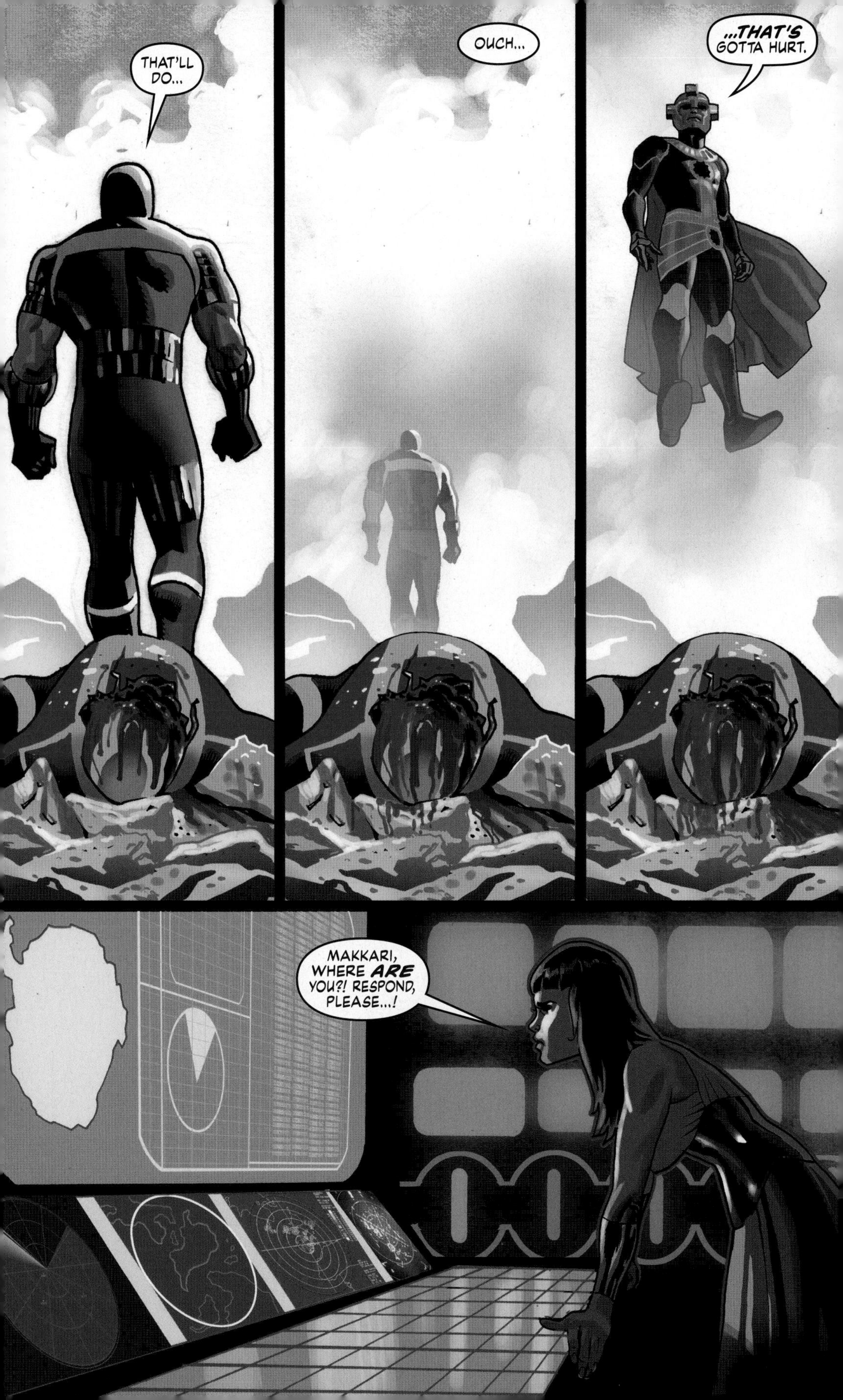
THAT'LL DO...
OUCH...
...THAT'S GOTTA HURT.
MAKKARI, WHERE ARE YOU?! RESPOND, PLEASE...!

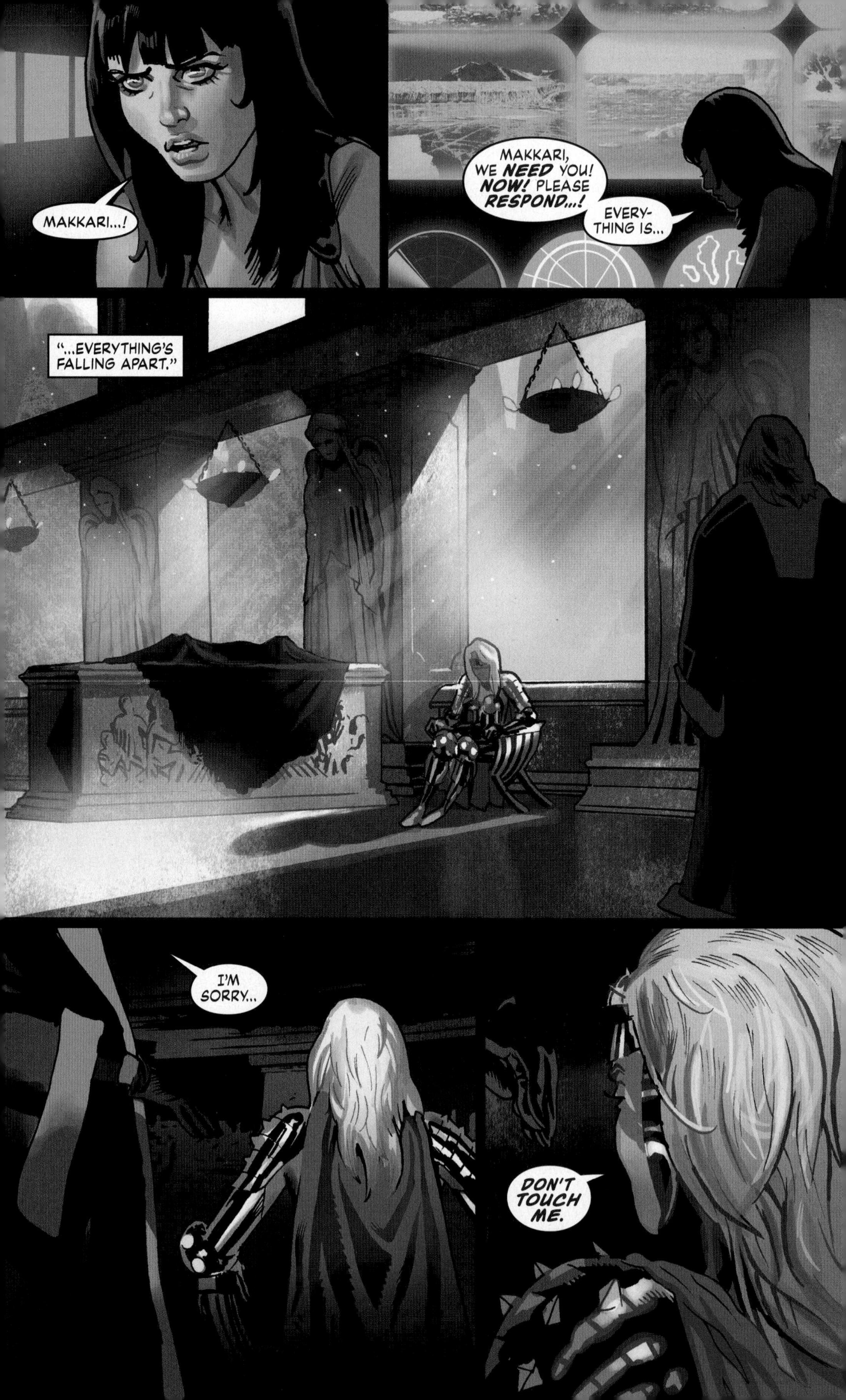
MAKKARI...!
MAKKARI, WE NEED YOU! NOW! PLEASE RESPOND...!
EVERY-THING IS...
"...EVERYTHING'S FALLING APART."
I'M SORRY...
DON'T TOUCH ME.

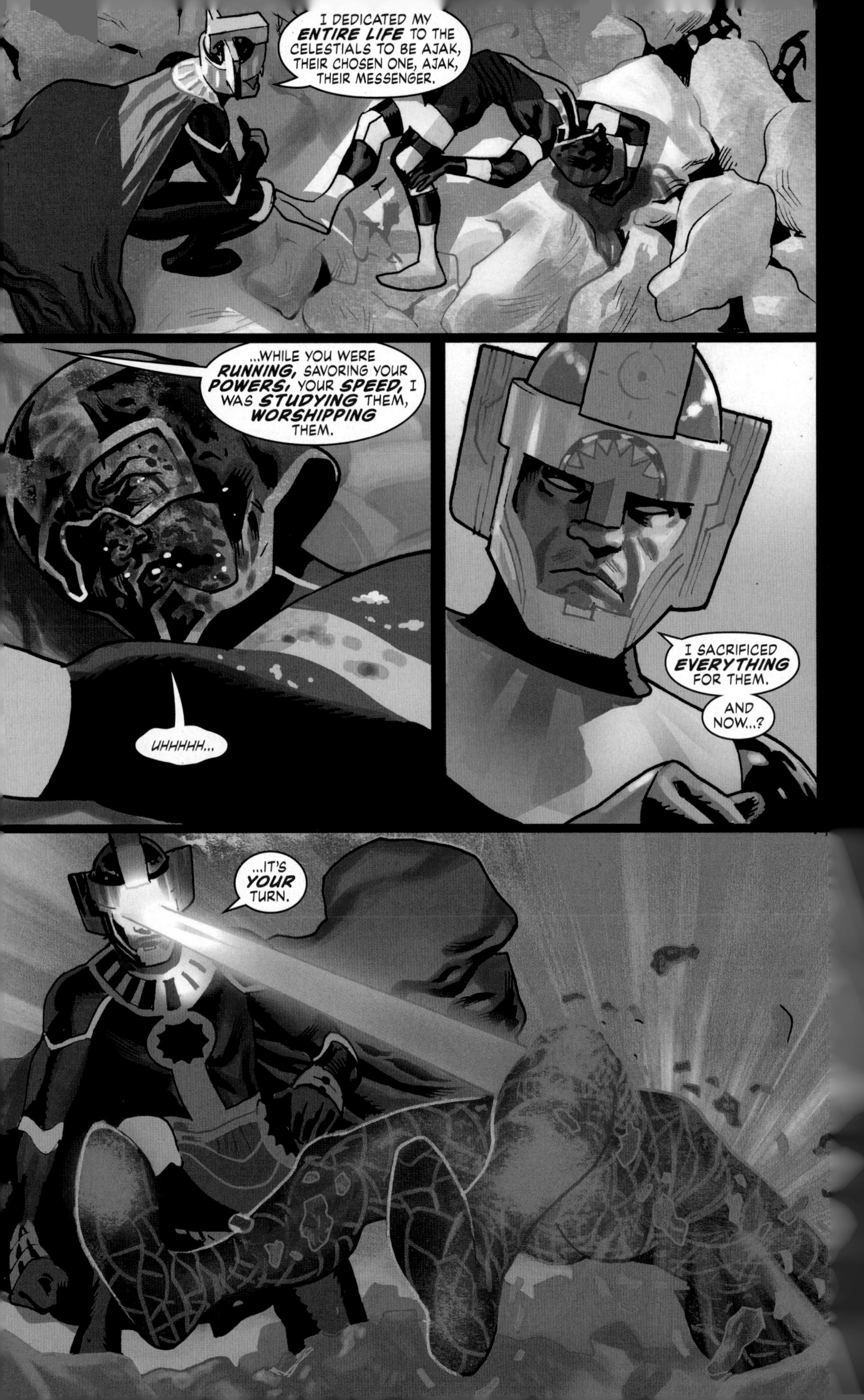
I DEDICATED MY ENTIRE LIFE TO THE CELESTIALS TO BE AJAK, THEIR CHOSEN ONE, AJAK, THEIR MESSENGER.
...WHILE YOU WERE RUNNING, SAVORING YOUR POWERS, YOUR SPEED, I WAS STUDYING THEM, WORSHIPPING THEM.
UHHHHH...
I SACRIFICED EVERYTHING FOR THEM.
AND NOW...?
...IT'S YOUR TURN.

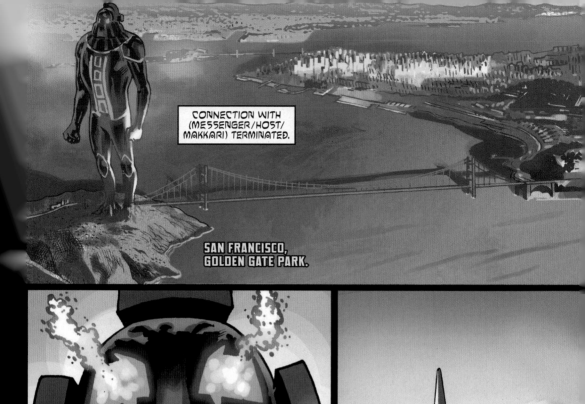

CONNECTION WITH
(MESSENGER/HOST/
MAKKARI) TERMINATED.

SAN FRANCISCO,
GOLDEN GATE PARK.

INITIATE (SONG/SEQUENCE/FAIL-SAFE).

INITIATING...

AICHO AICHO MINNO MAU,
AICHO AICHO MINNO MAU,
AICHO AICHO MINNO MAU...

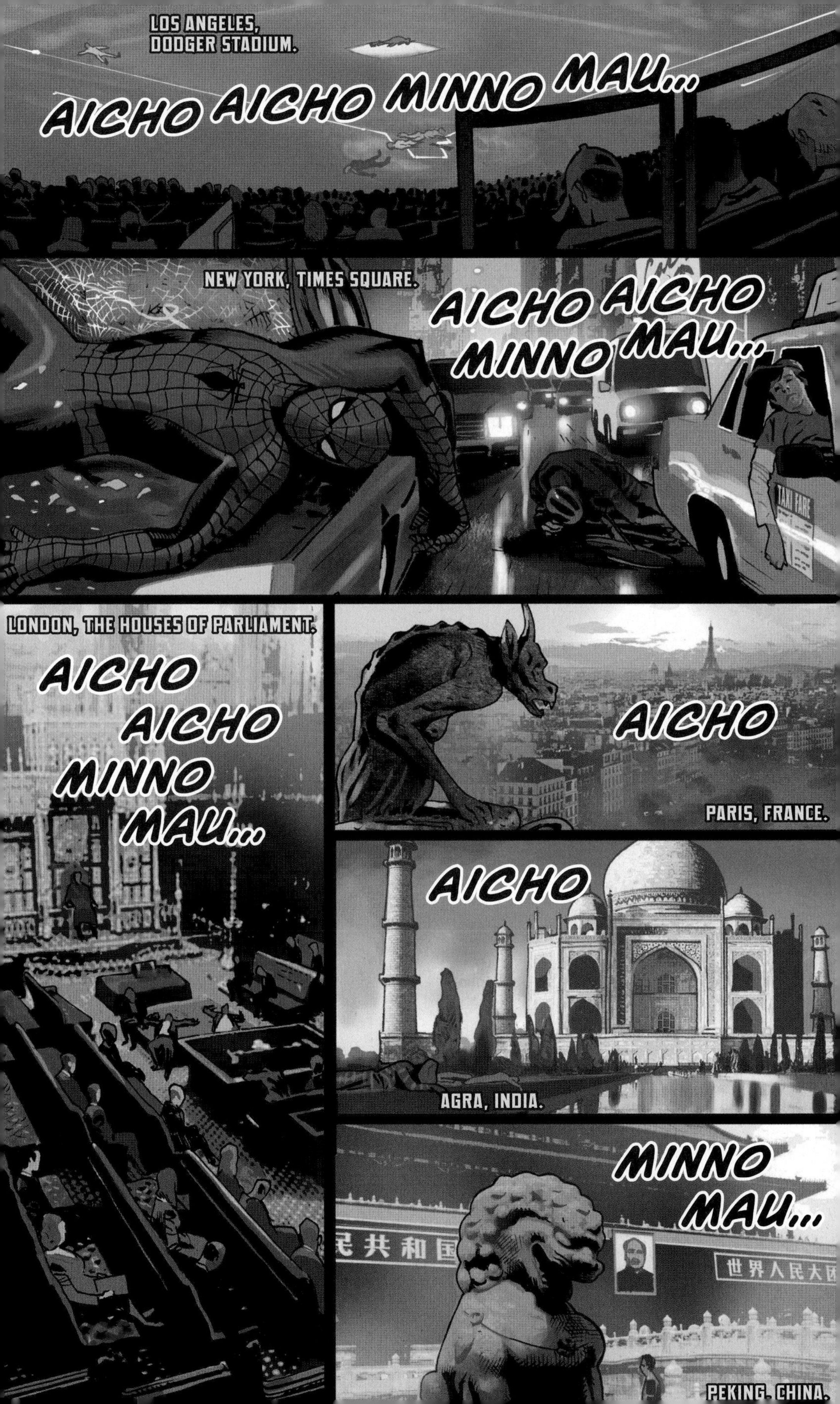

LOS ANGELES, DODGER STADIUM.
AICHO AICHO MINNO MAU...
NEW YORK, TIMES SQUARE.
AICHO AICHO MINNO MAU...
TAXI FARE
LONDON, THE HOUSES OF PARLIAMENT.
AICHO AICHO MINNO MAU...
AICHO
PARIS, FRANCE.
AICHO
AGRA, INDIA.
MINNO MAU...
民共和国
世界人民大
PEKING, CHINA.

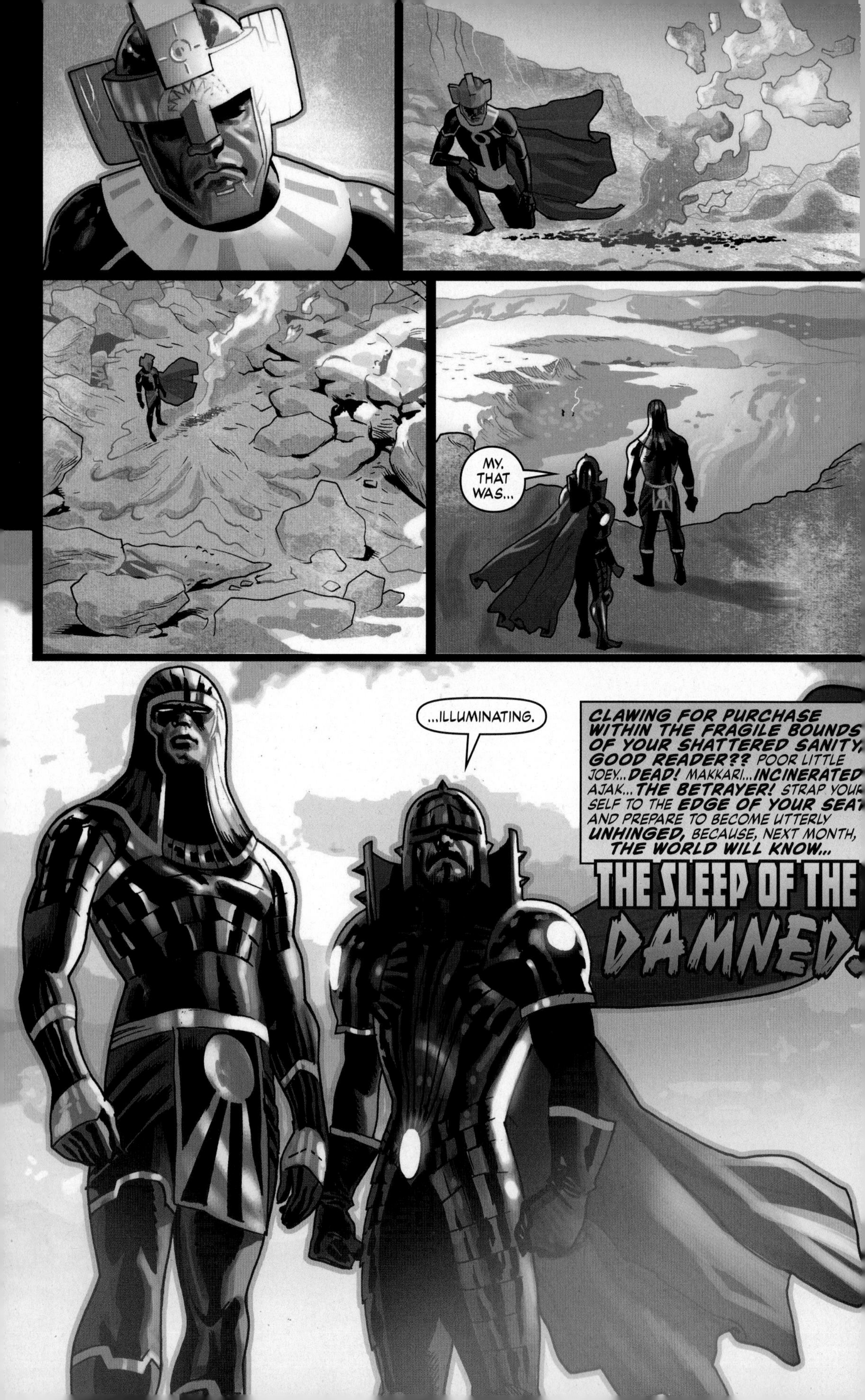
MY. THAT WAS...
...ILLUMINATING.
CLAWING FOR PURCHASE WITHIN THE FRAGILE BOUNDS OF YOUR SHATTERED SANITY, GOOD READER?? POOR LITTLE JOEY...DEAD! MAKKARI...INCINERATED! AJAK...THE BETRAYER! STRAP YOURSELF TO THE EDGE OF YOUR SEAT AND PREPARE TO BECOME UTTERLY UNHINGED, BECAUSE, NEXT MONTH, THE WORLD WILL KNOW...
THE SLEEP OF THE DAMNED!

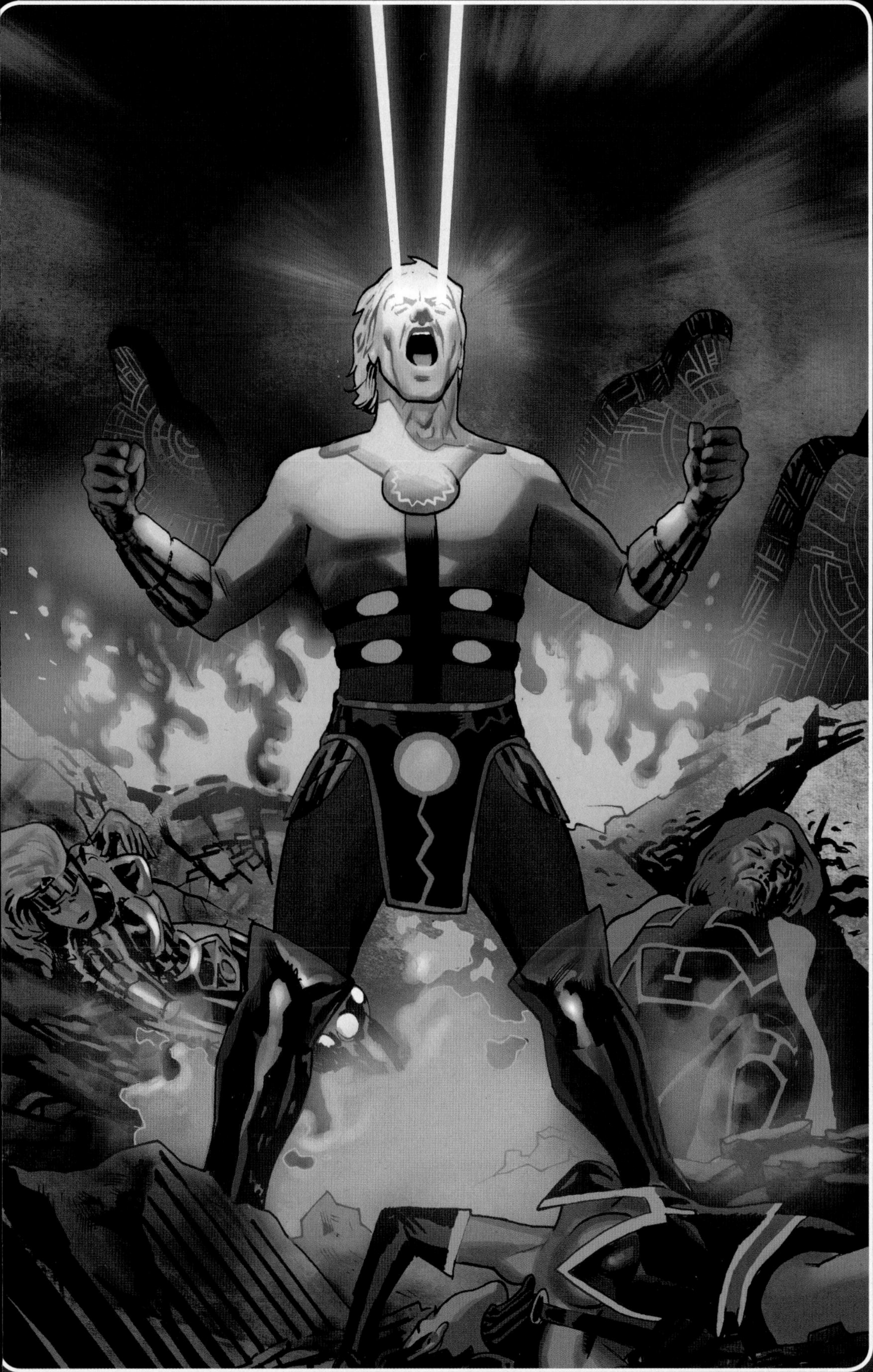

6

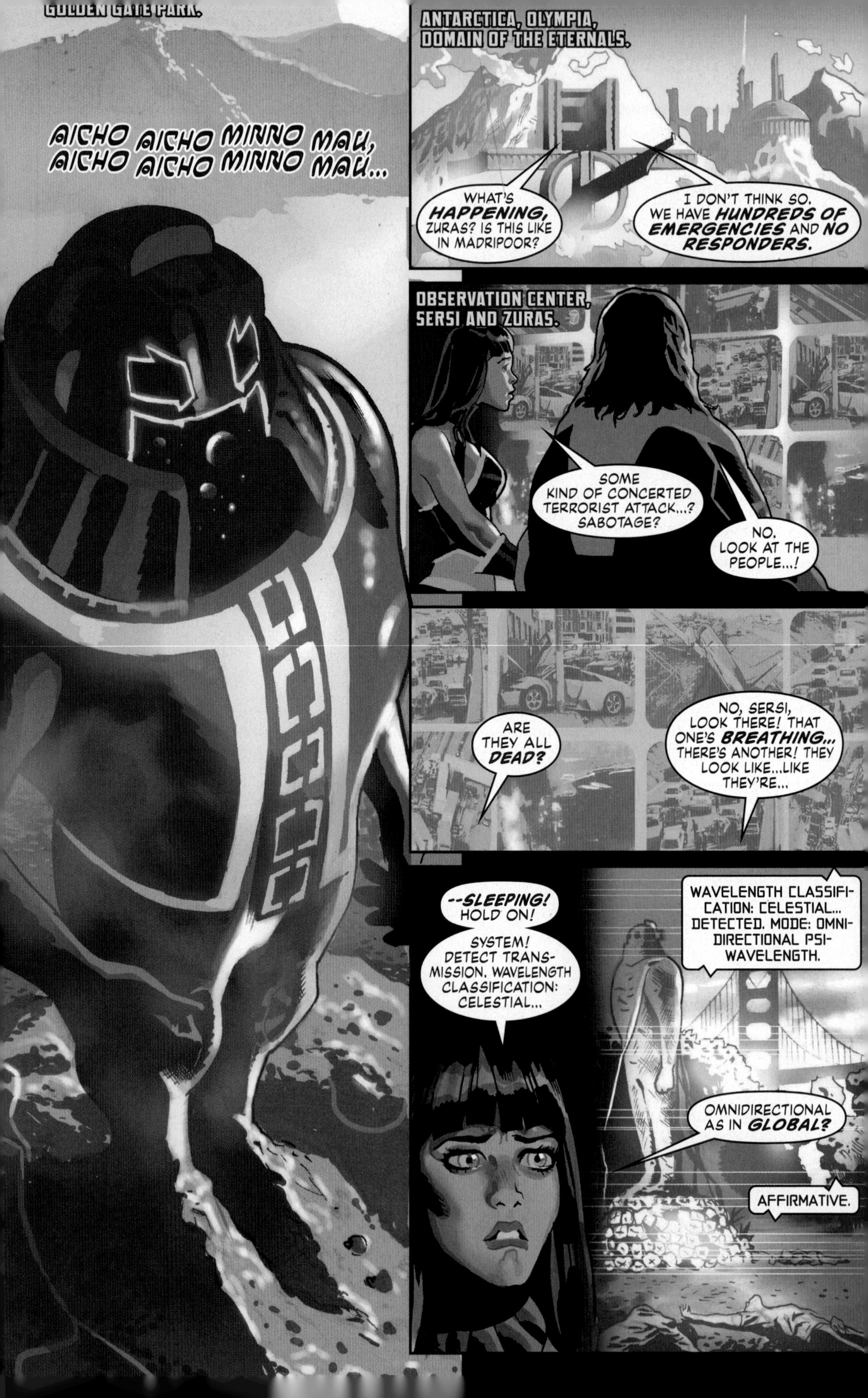
GOLDEN GATE PARK.
AICHO AICHO MINNO MAU, AICHO AICHO MINNO MAU...
ANTARCTICA, OLYMPIA, DOMAIN OF THE ETERNALS.
WHAT'S HAPPENING, ZURAS? IS THIS LIKE IN MADRIPOOR?
I DON'T THINK SO. WE HAVE HUNDREDS OF EMERGENCIES AND NO RESPONDERS.
OBSERVATION CENTER, SERSI AND ZURAS.
SOME KIND OF CONCERTED TERRORIST ATTACK...? SABOTAGE?
NO. LOOK AT THE PEOPLE...!
ARE THEY ALL DEAD?
NO, SERSI, LOOK THERE! THAT ONE'S BREATHING... THERE'S ANOTHER! THEY LOOK LIKE...LIKE THEY'RE...
--SLEEPING! HOLD ON!
SYSTEM! DETECT TRANSMISSION. WAVELENGTH CLASSIFICATION: CELESTIAL...
WAVELENGTH CLASSIFICATION: CELESTIAL... DETECTED. MODE: OMNIDIRECTIONAL PSI-WAVELENGTH.
OMNIDIRECTIONAL AS IN GLOBAL?
AFFIRMATIVE.

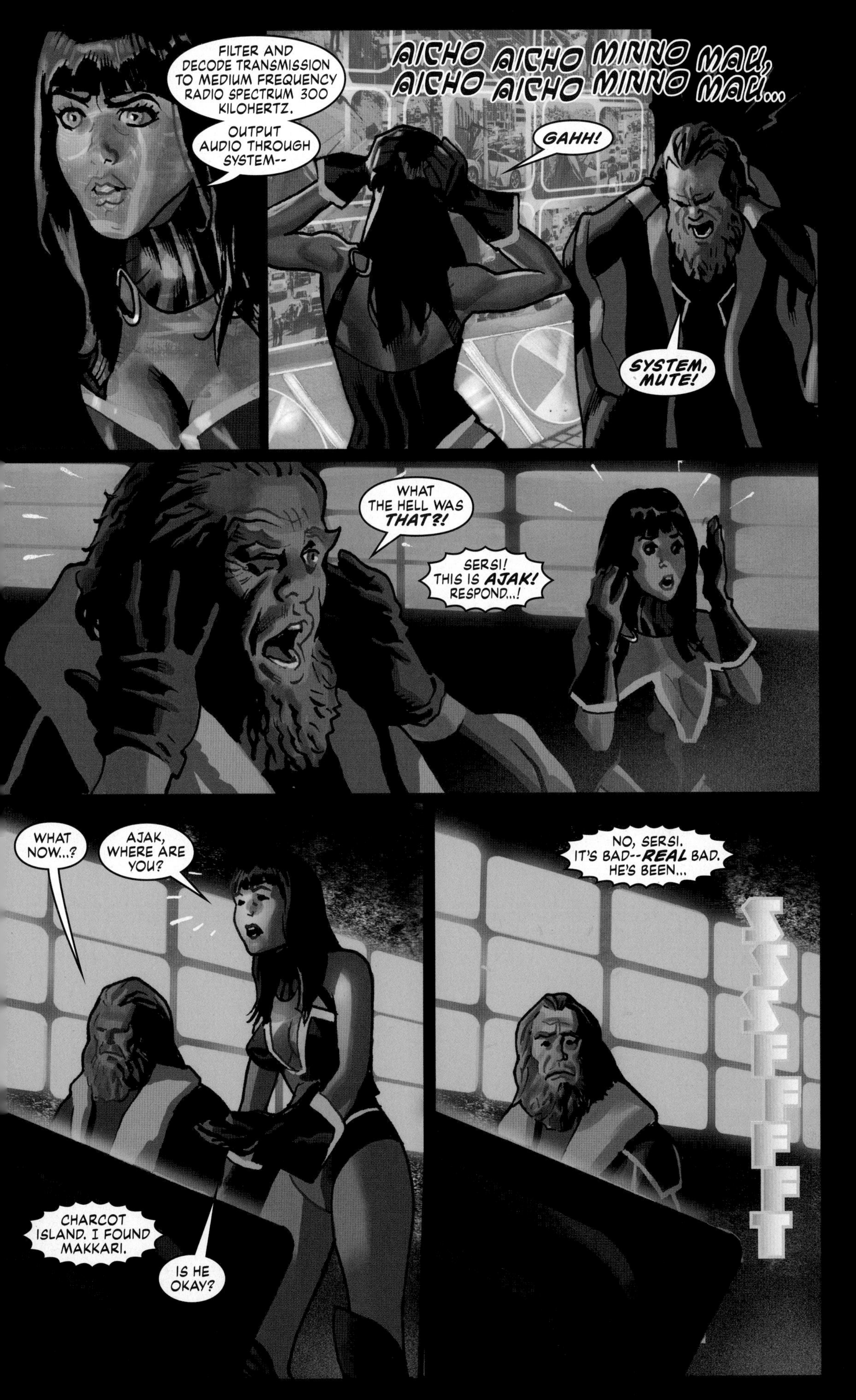
FILTER AND DECODE TRANSMISSION TO MEDIUM FREQUENCY RADIO SPECTRUM 300 KILOHERTZ.
OUTPUT AUDIO THROUGH SYSTEM--
AICHO AICHO MINNO MAU, AICHO AICHO MINNO MAU...
GAHH!
SYSTEM, MUTE!
WHAT THE HELL WAS THAT?!
SERSI! THIS IS AJAK! RESPOND...!
WHAT NOW...?
AJAK, WHERE ARE YOU?
CHARCOT ISLAND. I FOUND MAKKARI.
IS HE OKAY?
NO, SERSI. IT'S BAD--REAL BAD. HE'S BEEN...
SSSFFFFT

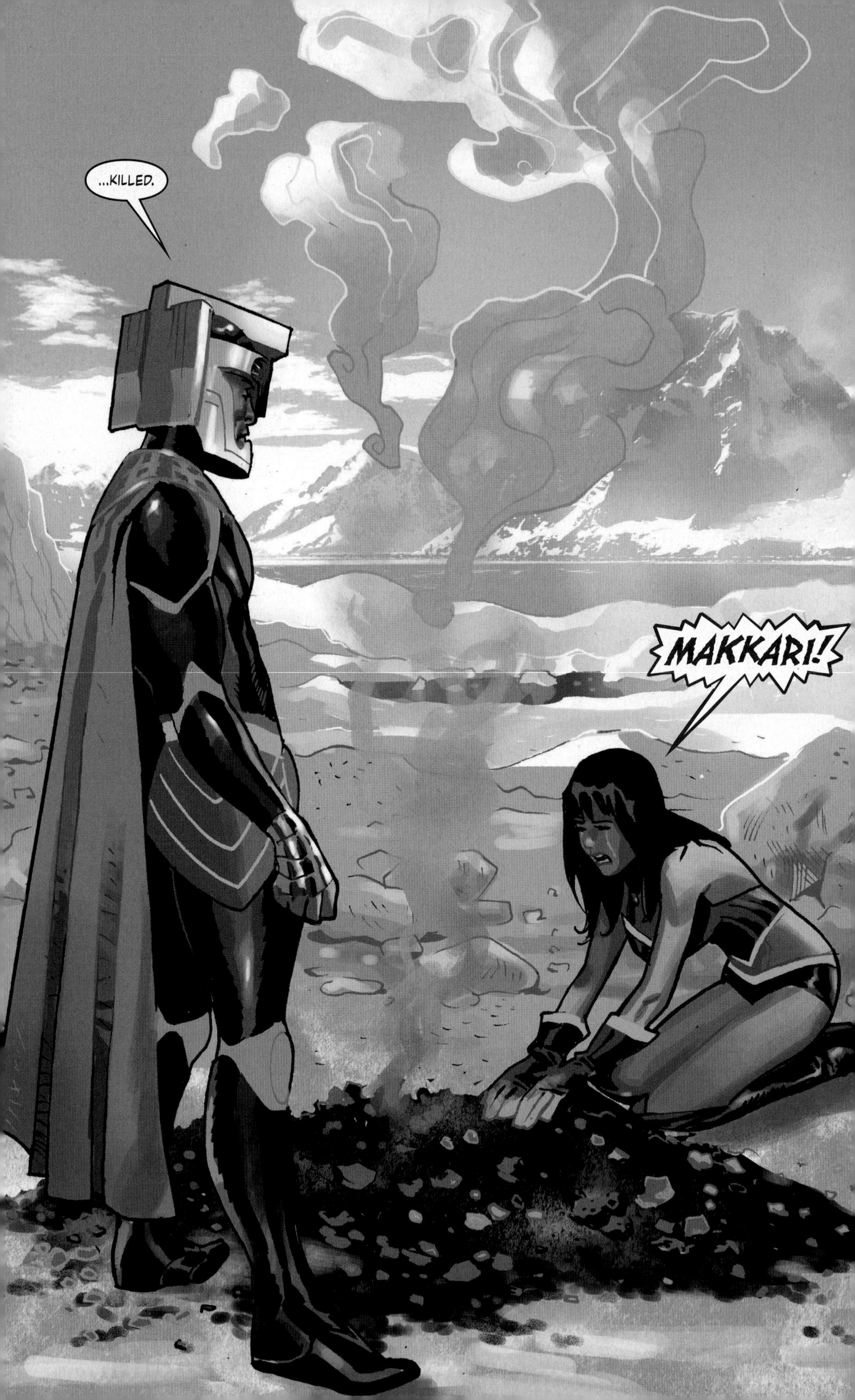
...KILLED.
MAKKARI!

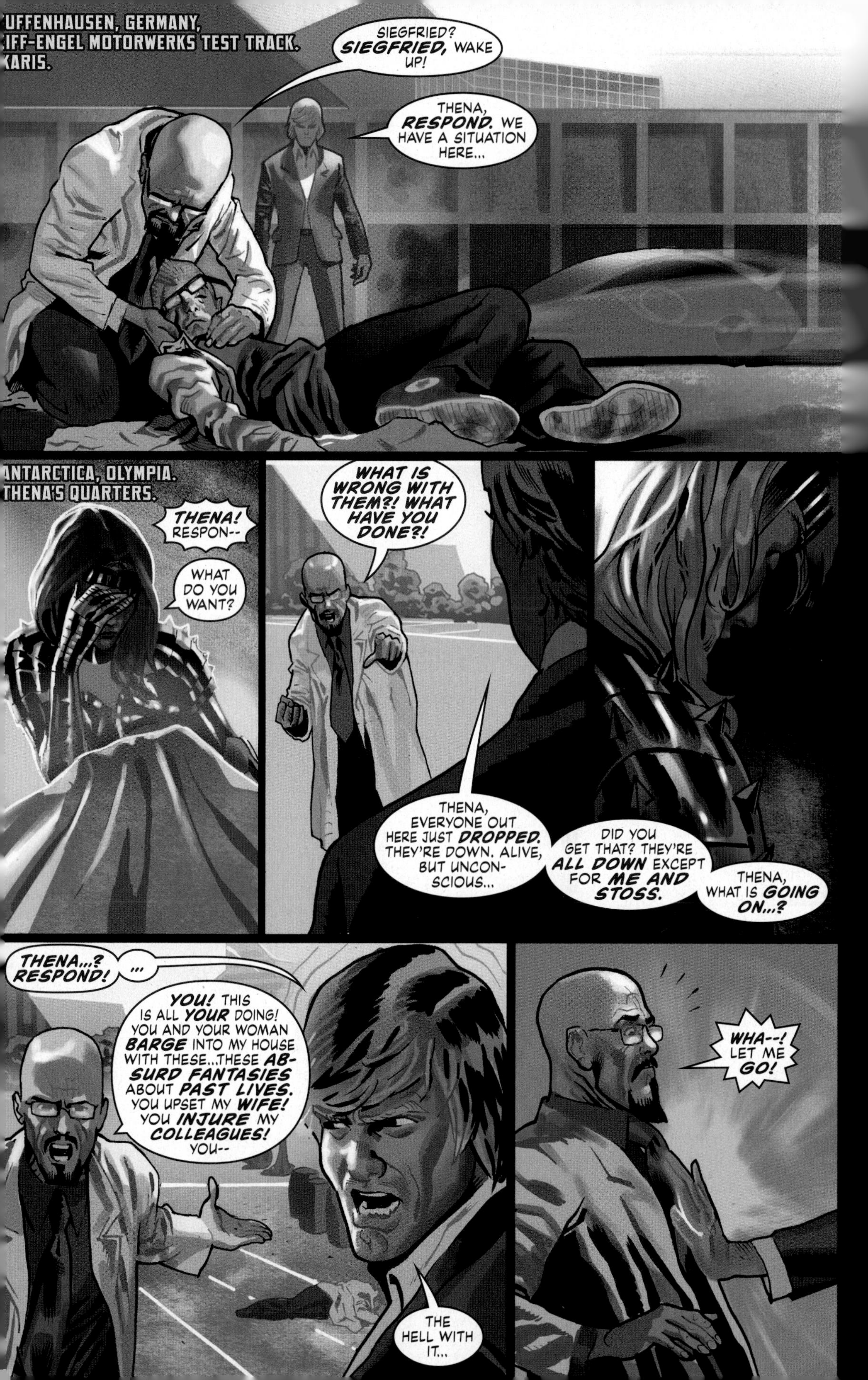

UFFENHAUSEN, GERMANY,
IFF-ENGEL MOTORWERKS TEST TRACK.
KARIS.
SIEGFRIED? SIEGFRIED, WAKE UP!
THENA, RESPOND. WE HAVE A SITUATION HERE...
ANTARCTICA, OLYMPIA.
THENA'S QUARTERS.
THENA! RESPON--
WHAT DO YOU WANT?
WHAT IS WRONG WITH THEM?! WHAT HAVE YOU DONE?!
THENA, EVERYONE OUT HERE JUST DROPPED. THEY'RE DOWN. ALIVE, BUT UNCON-SCIOUS...
DID YOU GET THAT? THEY'RE ALL DOWN EXCEPT FOR ME AND STOSS.
THENA, WHAT IS GOING ON...?
THENA...? RESPOND!
...
YOU! THIS IS ALL YOUR DOING! YOU AND YOUR WOMAN BARGE INTO MY HOUSE WITH THESE...THESE AB-SURD FANTASIES ABOUT PAST LIVES. YOU UPSET MY WIFE! YOU INJURE MY COLLEAGUES! YOU--
THE HELL WITH IT...
WHA--! LET ME GO!

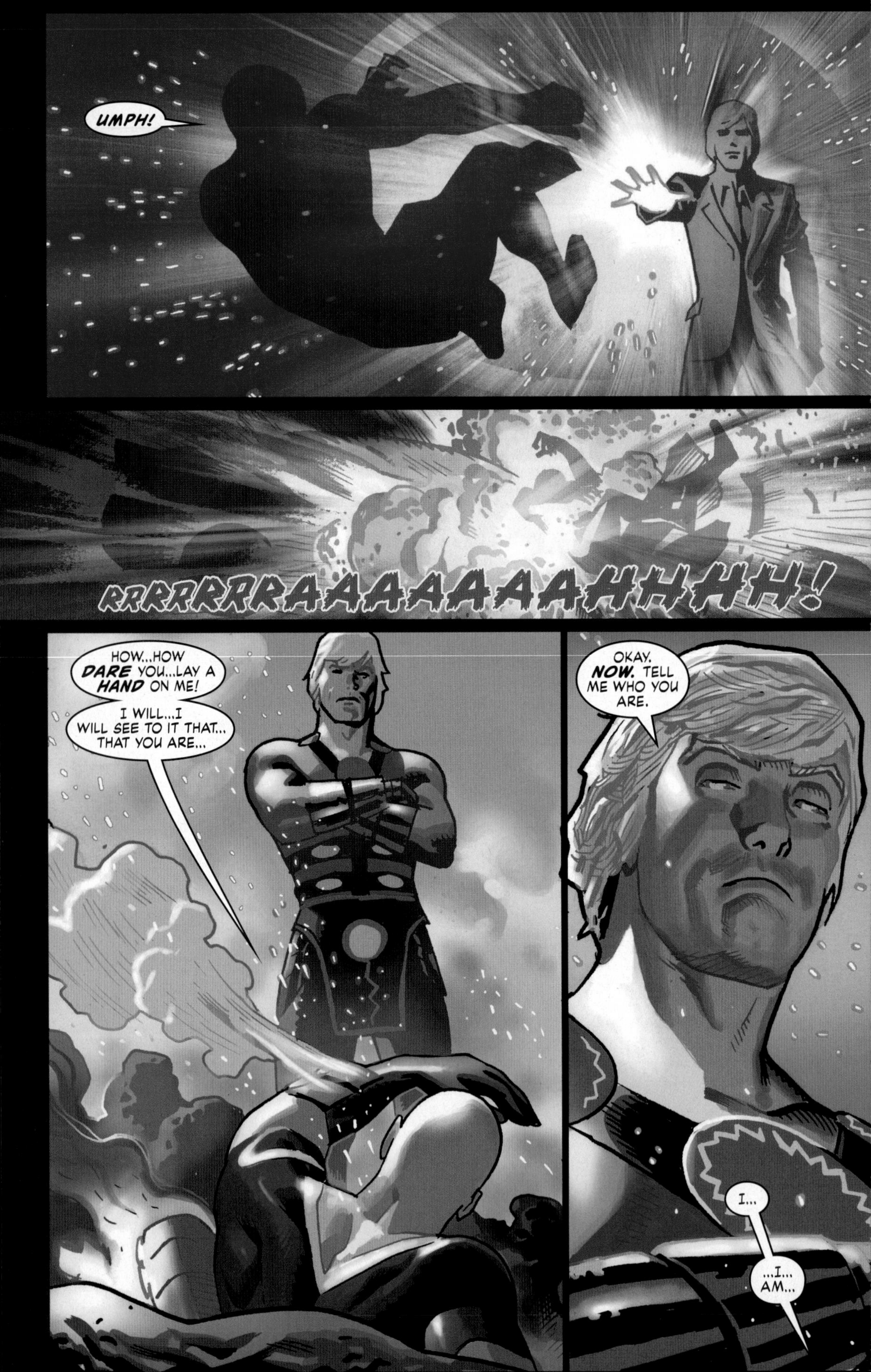
UMPH!
RRRRRRRAAAAAAAAAHHHHH!
HOW...HOW DARE YOU...LAY A HAND ON ME!
I WILL...I WILL SEE TO IT THAT... THAT YOU ARE...
OKAY. NOW. TELL ME WHO YOU ARE.
I...
...I... AM...

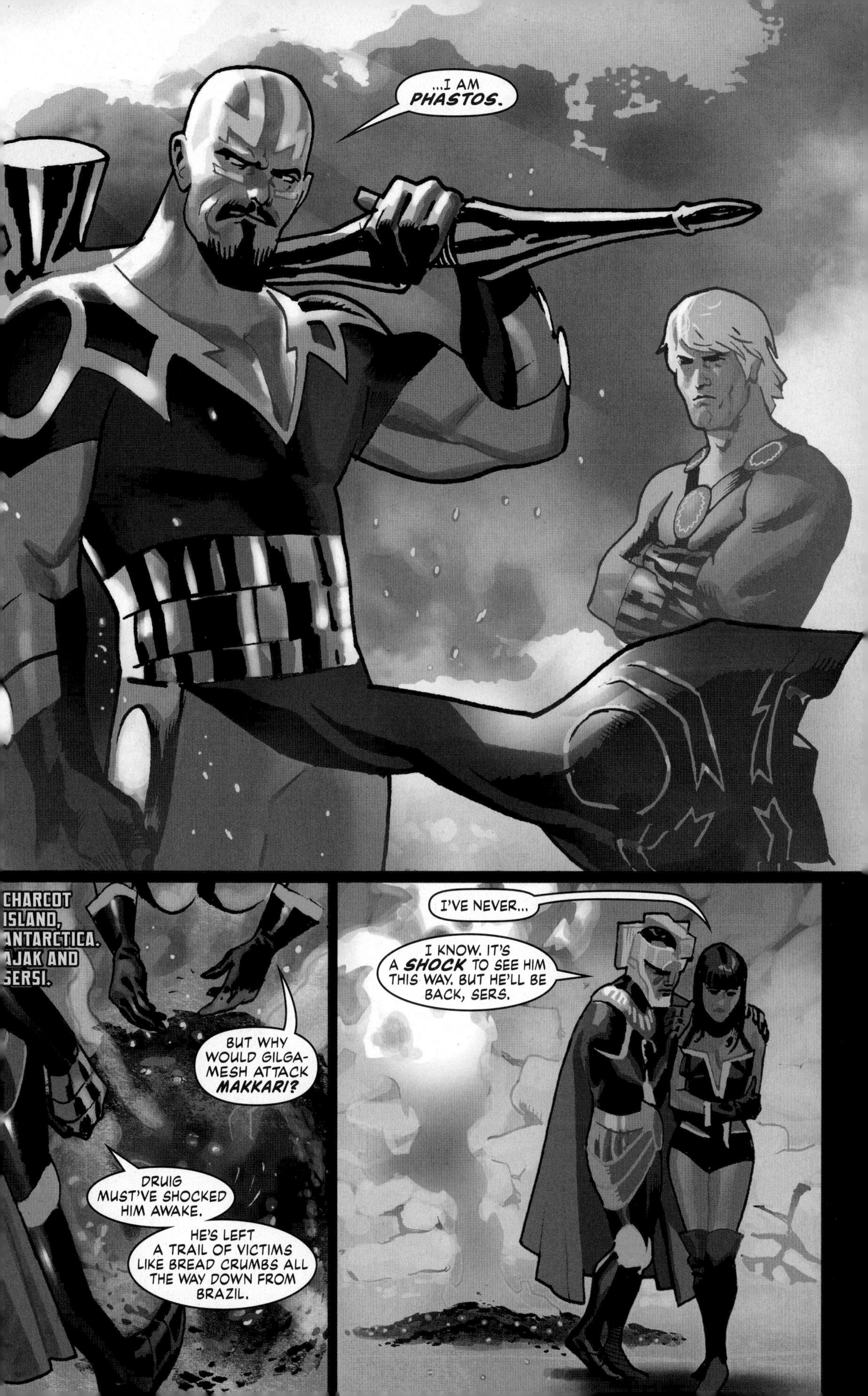
...I AM PHASTOS.
CHARCOT ISLAND, ANTARCTICA. AJAK AND SERSI.
BUT WHY WOULD GILGAMESH ATTACK MAKKARI?
DRUIG MUST'VE SHOCKED HIM AWAKE.
HE'S LEFT A TRAIL OF VICTIMS LIKE BREAD CRUMBS ALL THE WAY DOWN FROM BRAZIL.
I'VE NEVER...
I KNOW. IT'S A SHOCK TO SEE HIM THIS WAY. BUT HE'LL BE BACK, SERS.

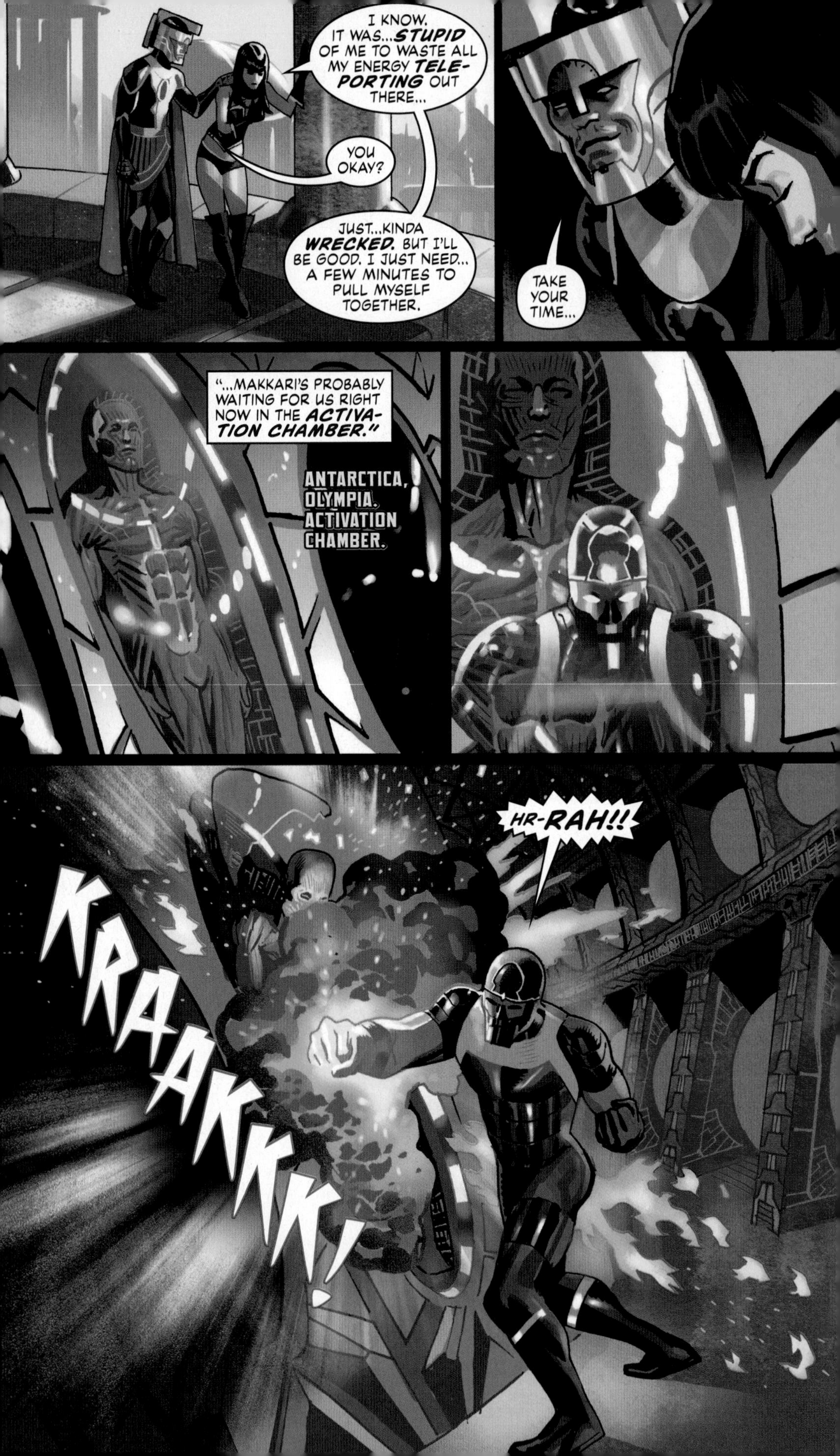
I KNOW. IT WAS...STUPID OF ME TO WASTE ALL MY ENERGY TELE-PORTING OUT THERE...
YOU OKAY?
JUST...KINDA WRECKED. BUT I'LL BE GOOD. I JUST NEED... A FEW MINUTES TO PULL MYSELF TOGETHER.
TAKE YOUR TIME...
"...MAKKARI'S PROBABLY WAITING FOR US RIGHT NOW IN THE ACTIVA-TION CHAMBER."
ANTARCTICA, OLYMPIA. ACTIVATION CHAMBER.
HR-RAH!!
KRAAKKK!

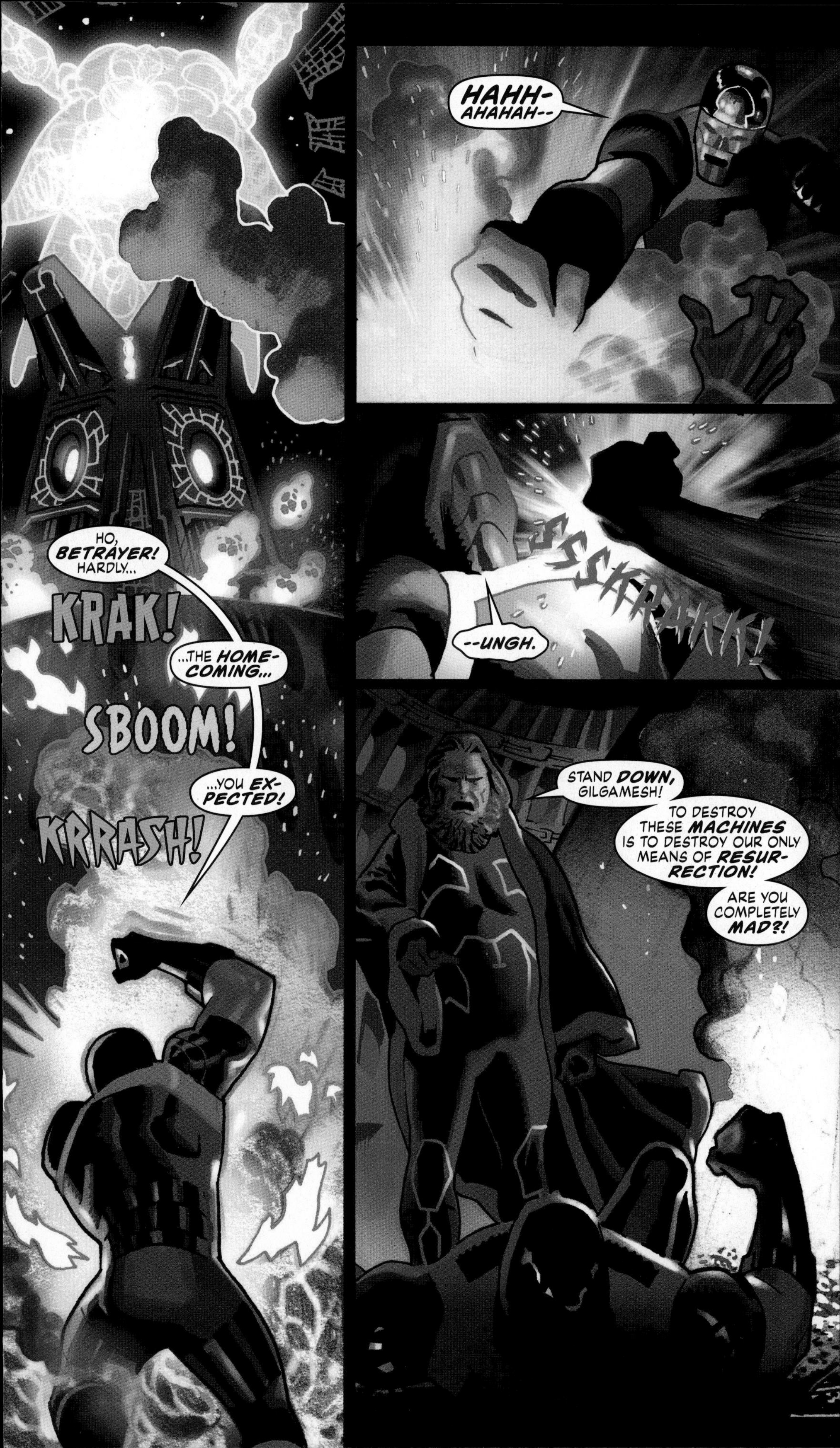
HO, BETRAYER! HARDLY...
KRAK!
...THE HOME-COMING...
SBOOM!
...YOU EX-PECTED!
KRRASH!
HAHH-AHAHAH--
SSSKRAKK!
--UNGH.
STAND DOWN, GILGAMESH!
TO DESTROY THESE MACHINES IS TO DESTROY OUR ONLY MEANS OF RESUR-RECTION!
ARE YOU COMPLETELY MAD?!

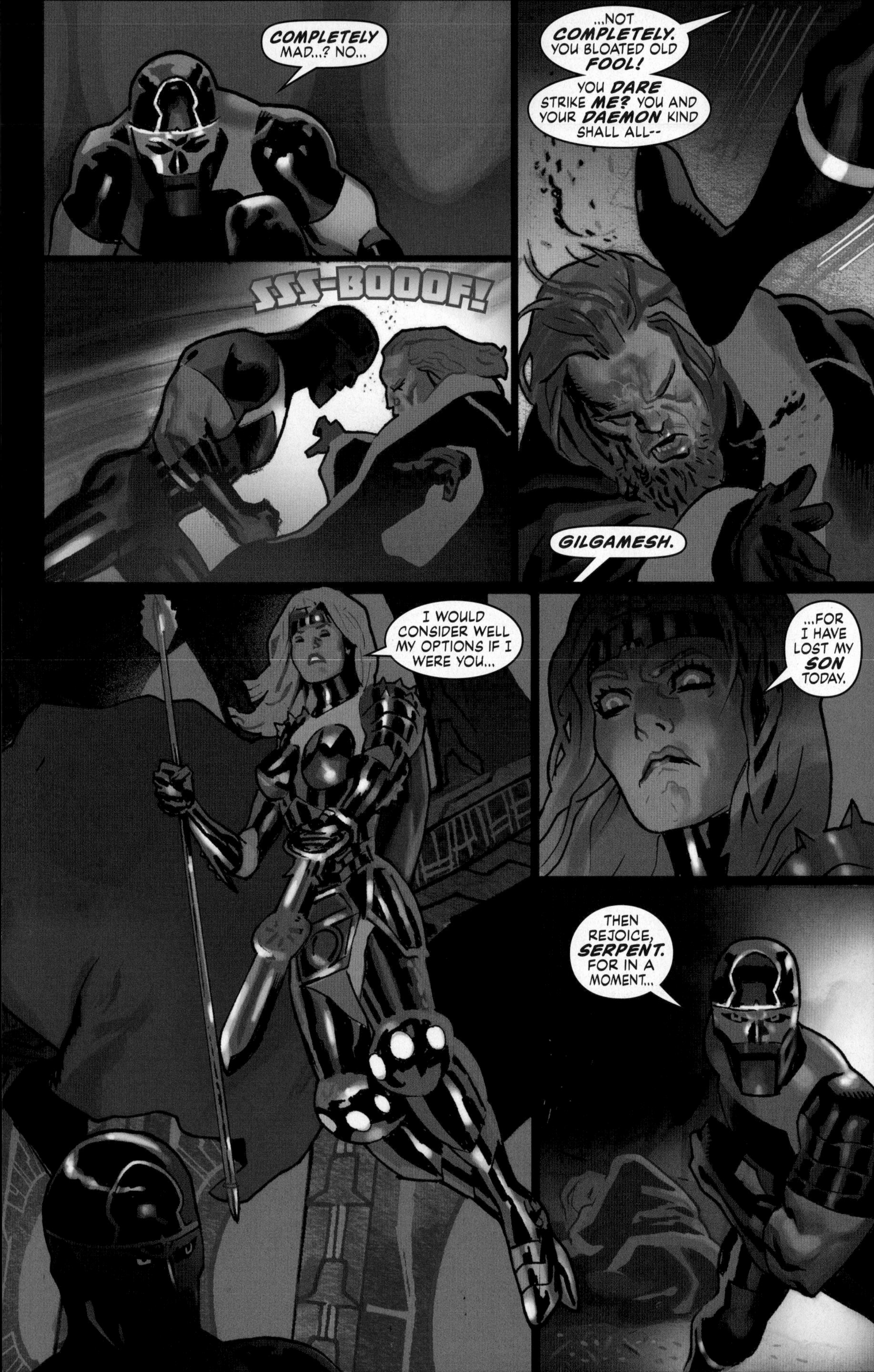
COMPLETELY MAD...? NO...
...NOT COMPLETELY. YOU BLOATED OLD FOOL!
YOU DARE STRIKE ME? YOU AND YOUR DAEMON KIND SHALL ALL--
SSS-BOOOF!
GILGAMESH.
I WOULD CONSIDER WELL MY OPTIONS IF I WERE YOU...
...FOR I HAVE LOST MY SON TODAY.
THEN REJOICE, SERPENT. FOR IN A MOMENT...

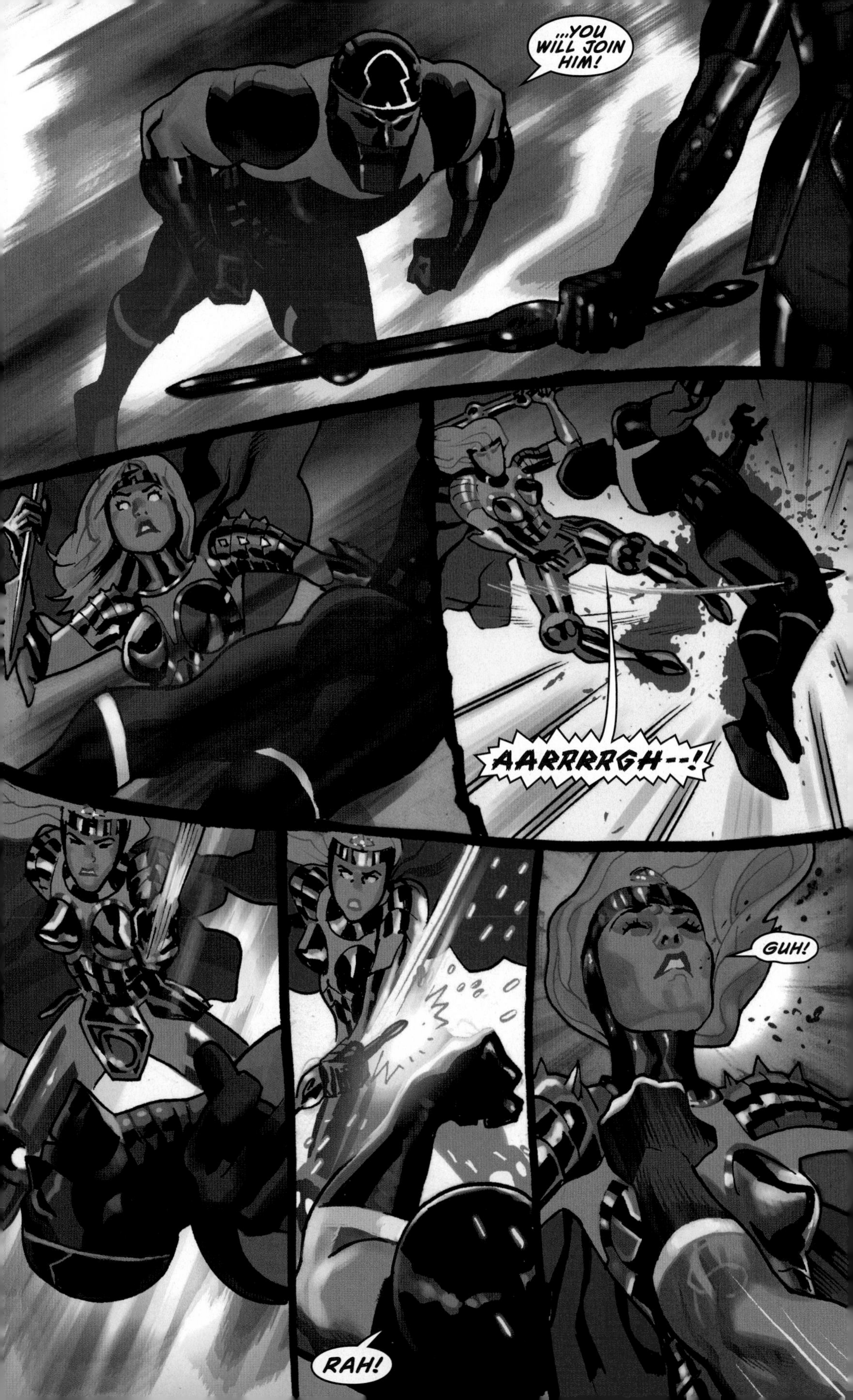
...YOU WILL JOIN HIM!
AARRRRGH--!
RAH!
GUH!

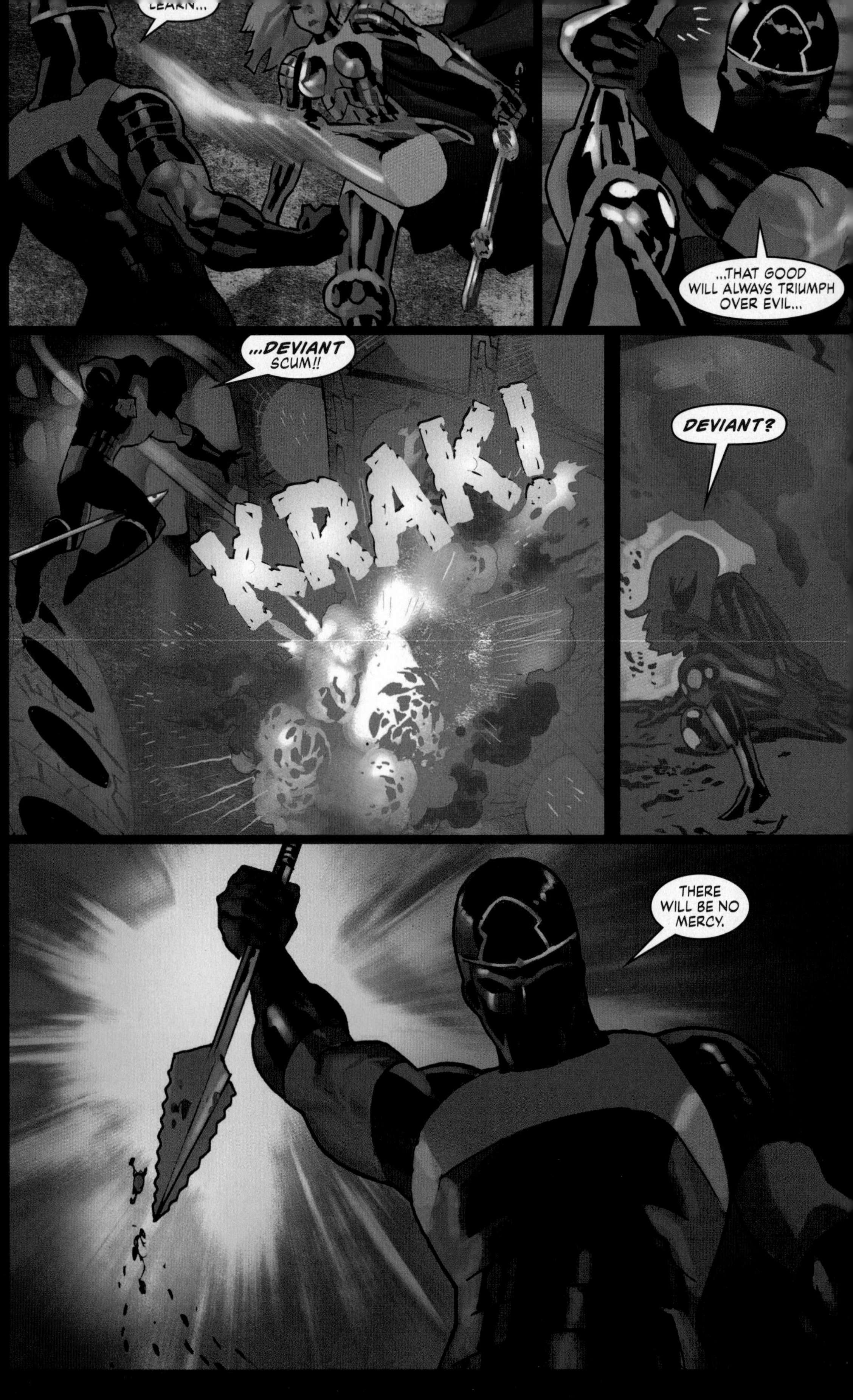
LEARN...
...THAT GOOD WILL ALWAYS TRIUMPH OVER EVIL...
...DEVIANT SCUM!!
KRAK!
DEVIANT?
THERE WILL BE NO MERCY.

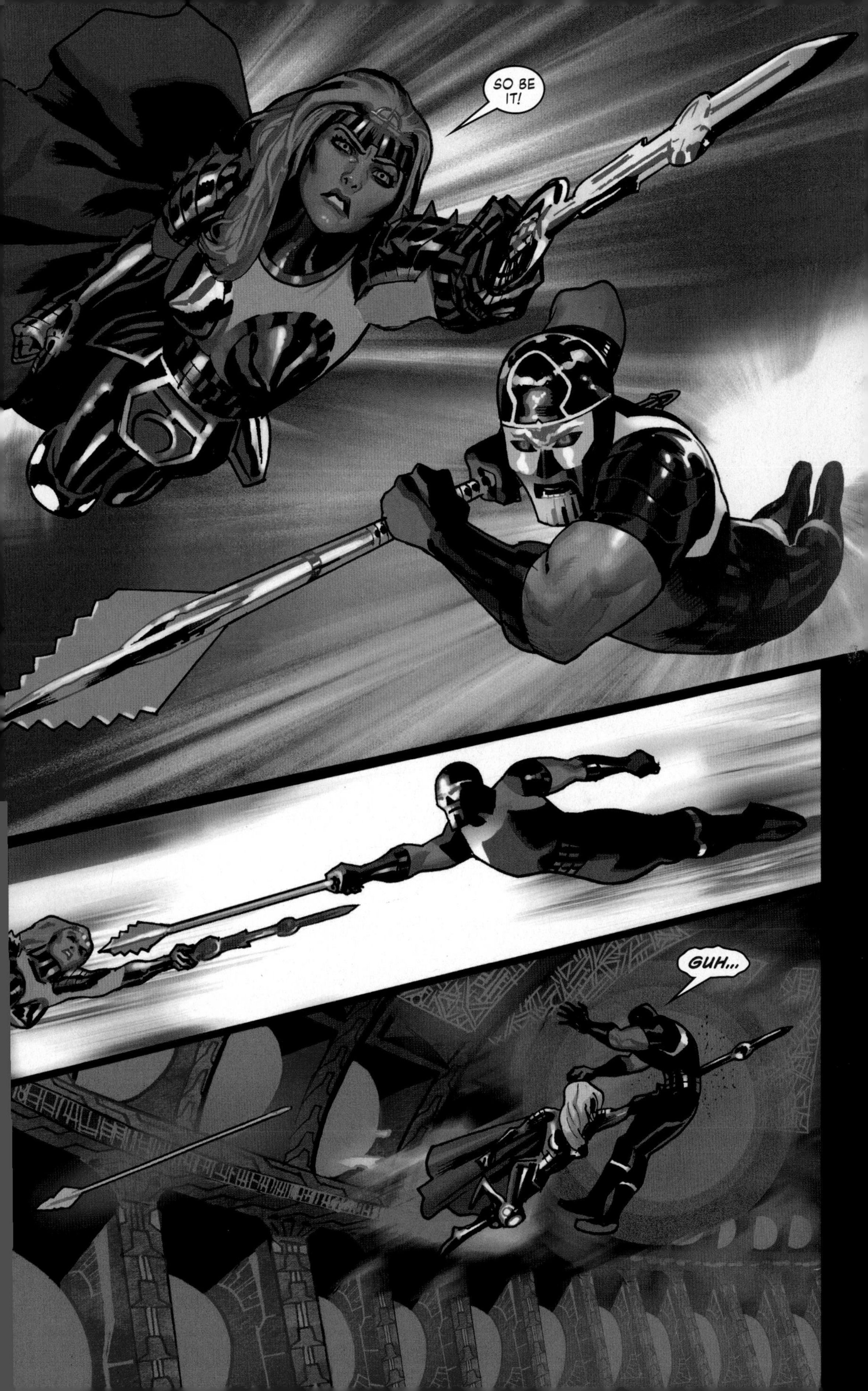
SO BE IT!
GUH...

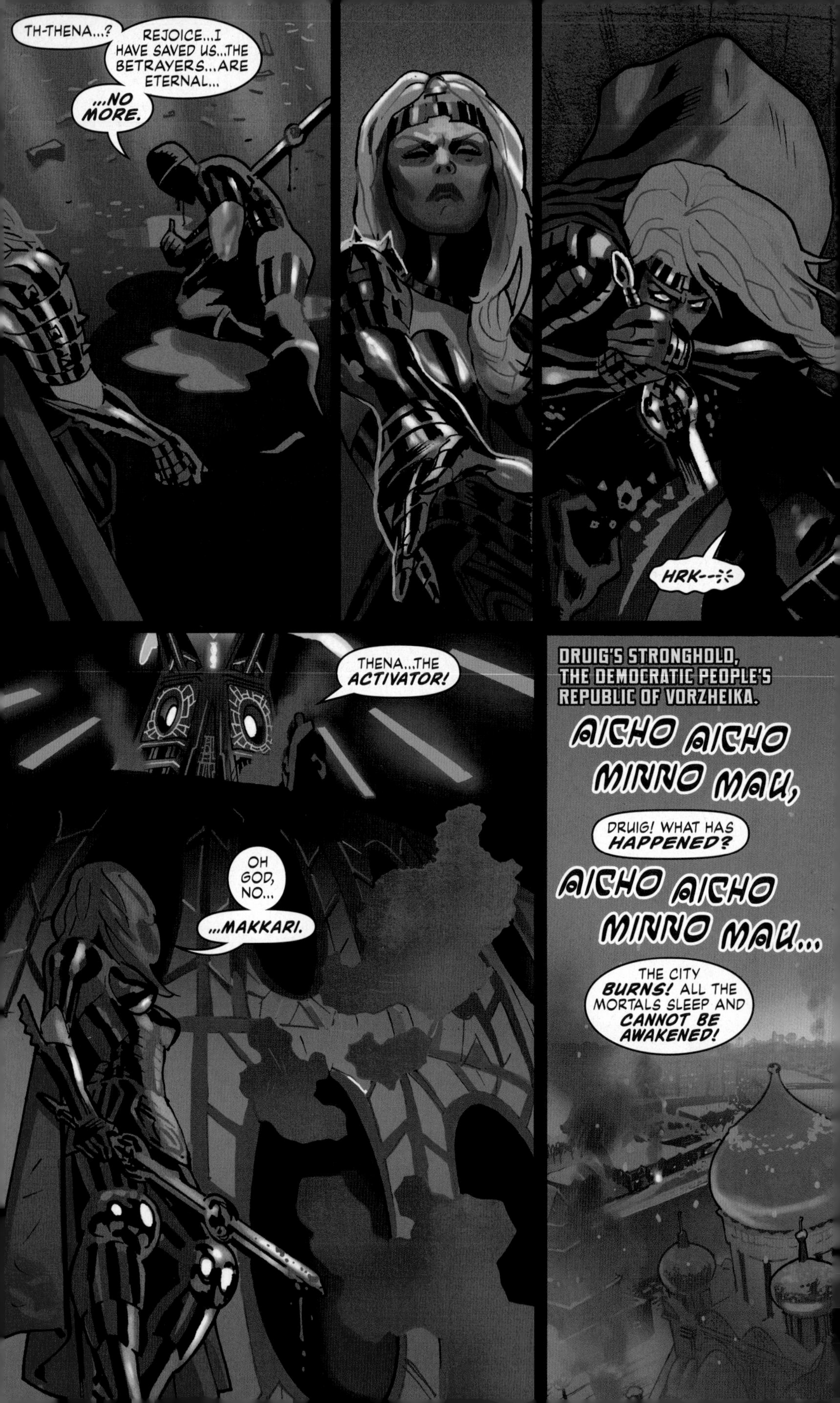
TH-THENA...?
REJOICE...I HAVE SAVED US...THE BETRAYERS...ARE ETERNAL...
...NO MORE.
HRK--
THENA...THE ACTIVATOR!
OH GOD, NO...
...MAKKARI.
DRUIG'S STRONGHOLD, THE DEMOCRATIC PEOPLE'S REPUBLIC OF VORZHEIKA.
AICHO AICHO MINNO MAU,
DRUIG! WHAT HAS HAPPENED?
AICHO AICHO MINNO MAU...
THE CITY BURNS! ALL THE MORTALS SLEEP AND CANNOT BE AWAKENED!

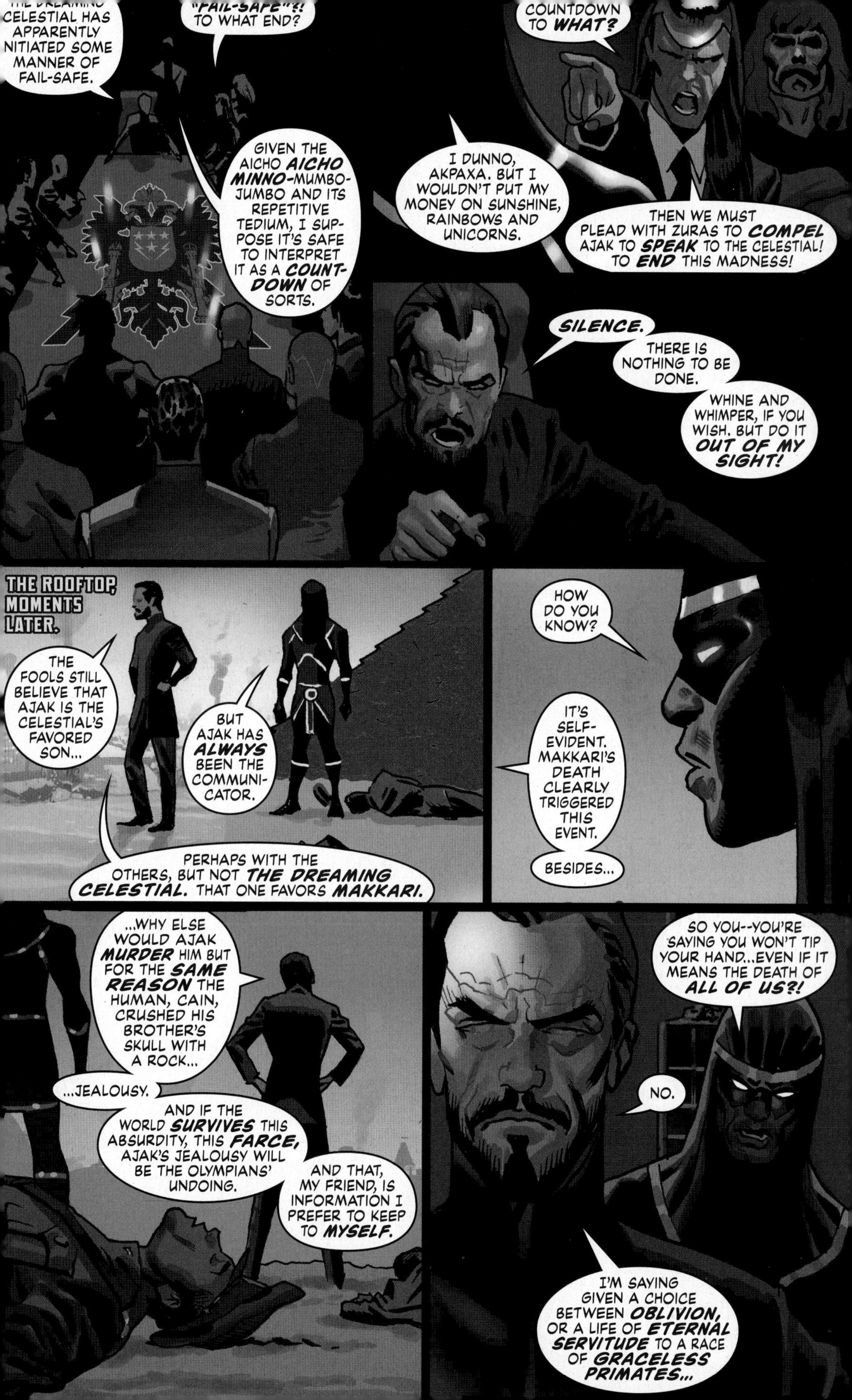
CELESTIAL HAS APPARENTLY NITIATED SOME MANNER OF FAIL-SAFE.
"FAIL-SAFE"?! TO WHAT END?
GIVEN THE AICHO AICHO MINNO-MUMBO-JUMBO AND ITS REPETITIVE TEDIUM, I SUPPOSE IT'S SAFE TO INTERPRET IT AS A COUNTDOWN OF SORTS.
COUNTDOWN TO WHAT?
I DUNNO, AKPAXA. BUT I WOULDN'T PUT MY MONEY ON SUNSHINE, RAINBOWS AND UNICORNS.
THEN WE MUST PLEAD WITH ZURAS TO COMPEL AJAK TO SPEAK TO THE CELESTIAL! TO END THIS MADNESS!
SILENCE.
THERE IS NOTHING TO BE DONE.
WHINE AND WHIMPER, IF YOU WISH. BUT DO IT OUT OF MY SIGHT!
THE ROOFTOP, MOMENTS LATER.
THE FOOLS STILL BELIEVE THAT AJAK IS THE CELESTIAL'S FAVORED SON...
BUT AJAK HAS ALWAYS BEEN THE COMMUNICATOR.
PERHAPS WITH THE OTHERS, BUT NOT THE DREAMING CELESTIAL. THAT ONE FAVORS MAKKARI.
HOW DO YOU KNOW?
IT'S SELF-EVIDENT. MAKKARI'S DEATH CLEARLY TRIGGERED THIS EVENT.
BESIDES...
...WHY ELSE WOULD AJAK MURDER HIM BUT FOR THE SAME REASON THE HUMAN, CAIN, CRUSHED HIS BROTHER'S SKULL WITH A ROCK...
...JEALOUSY.
AND IF THE WORLD SURVIVES THIS ABSURDITY, THIS FARCE, AJAK'S JEALOUSY WILL BE THE OLYMPIANS' UNDOING.
AND THAT, MY FRIEND, IS INFORMATION I PREFER TO KEEP TO MYSELF.
SO YOU--YOU'RE SAYING YOU WON'T TIP YOUR HAND...EVEN IF IT MEANS THE DEATH OF ALL OF US?!
NO.
I'M SAYING GIVEN A CHOICE BETWEEN OBLIVION, OR A LIFE OF ETERNAL SERVITUDE TO A RACE OF GRACELESS PRIMATES...

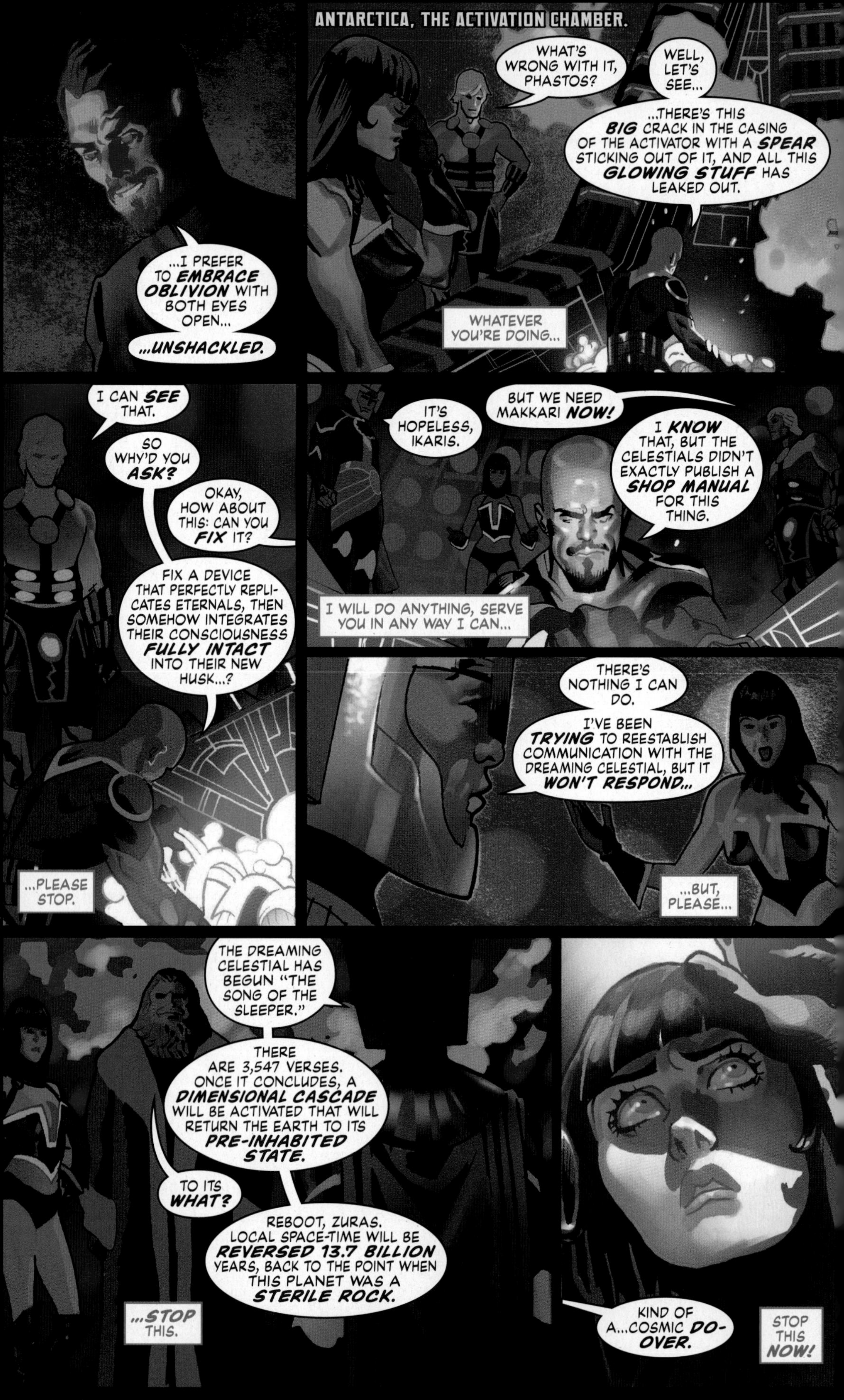
...I PREFER TO EMBRACE OBLIVION WITH BOTH EYES OPEN...
...UNSHACKLED.
ANTARCTICA, THE ACTIVATION CHAMBER.
WHAT'S WRONG WITH IT, PHASTOS?
WELL, LET'S SEE...
...THERE'S THIS BIG CRACK IN THE CASING OF THE ACTIVATOR WITH A SPEAR STICKING OUT OF IT, AND ALL THIS GLOWING STUFF HAS LEAKED OUT.
WHATEVER YOU'RE DOING...
I CAN SEE THAT.
SO WHY'D YOU ASK?
OKAY, HOW ABOUT THIS: CAN YOU FIX IT?
FIX A DEVICE THAT PERFECTLY REPLICATES ETERNALS, THEN SOMEHOW INTEGRATES THEIR CONSCIOUSNESS FULLY INTACT INTO THEIR NEW HUSK...?
...PLEASE STOP.
IT'S HOPELESS, IKARIS.
BUT WE NEED MAKKARI NOW!
I KNOW THAT, BUT THE CELESTIALS DIDN'T EXACTLY PUBLISH A SHOP MANUAL FOR THIS THING.
I WILL DO ANYTHING, SERVE YOU IN ANY WAY I CAN...
THERE'S NOTHING I CAN DO.
I'VE BEEN TRYING TO REESTABLISH COMMUNICATION WITH THE DREAMING CELESTIAL, BUT IT WON'T RESPOND...
...BUT, PLEASE...
THE DREAMING CELESTIAL HAS BEGUN "THE SONG OF THE SLEEPER."
THERE ARE 3,547 VERSES. ONCE IT CONCLUDES, A DIMENSIONAL CASCADE WILL BE ACTIVATED THAT WILL RETURN THE EARTH TO ITS PRE-INHABITED STATE.
TO ITS WHAT?
REBOOT, ZURAS. LOCAL SPACE-TIME WILL BE REVERSED 13.7 BILLION YEARS, BACK TO THE POINT WHEN THIS PLANET WAS A STERILE ROCK.
...STOP THIS.
KIND OF A...COSMIC DO-OVER.
STOP THIS NOW!

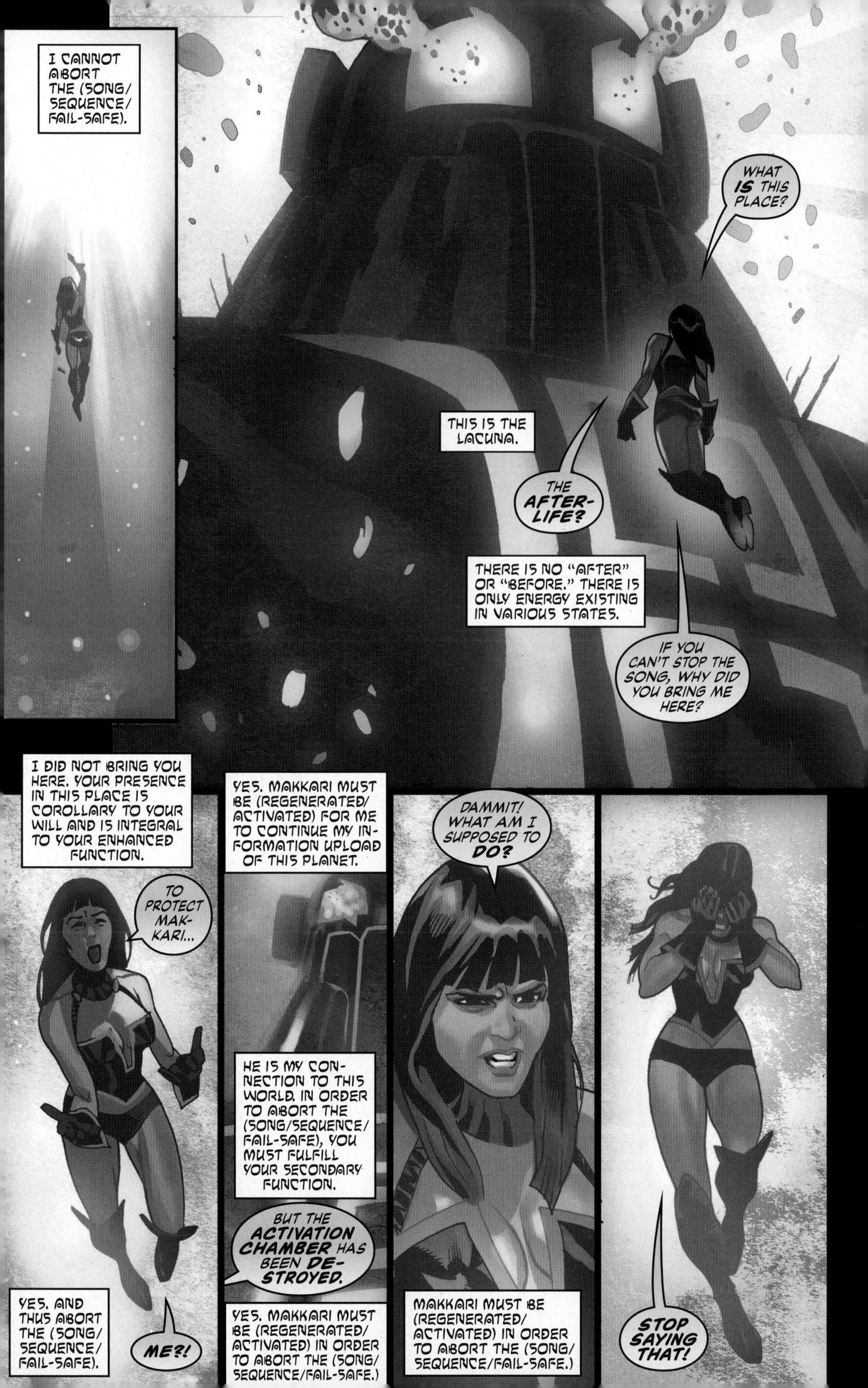
I CANNOT ABORT THE (SONG/ SEQUENCE/ FAIL-SAFE).
WHAT IS THIS PLACE?
THIS IS THE LACUNA.
THE AFTER-LIFE?
THERE IS NO "AFTER" OR "BEFORE." THERE IS ONLY ENERGY EXISTING IN VARIOUS STATES.
IF YOU CAN'T STOP THE SONG, WHY DID YOU BRING ME HERE?
I DID NOT BRING YOU HERE. YOUR PRESENCE IN THIS PLACE IS COROLLARY TO YOUR WILL AND IS INTEGRAL TO YOUR ENHANCED FUNCTION.
TO PROTECT MAK-KARI...
YES. AND THUS ABORT THE (SONG/ SEQUENCE/ FAIL-SAFE).
ME?!
YES. MAKKARI MUST BE (REGENERATED/ ACTIVATED) FOR ME TO CONTINUE MY IN-FORMATION UPLOAD OF THIS PLANET.
HE IS MY CON-NECTION TO THIS WORLD. IN ORDER TO ABORT THE (SONG/SEQUENCE/ FAIL-SAFE), YOU MUST FULFILL YOUR SECONDARY FUNCTION.
BUT THE ACTIVATION CHAMBER HAS BEEN DE-STROYED.
YES. MAKKARI MUST BE (REGENERATED/ ACTIVATED) IN ORDER TO ABORT THE (SONG/ SEQUENCE/FAIL-SAFE.)
DAMMIT! WHAT AM I SUPPOSED TO DO?
MAKKARI MUST BE (REGENERATED/ ACTIVATED) IN ORDER TO ABORT THE (SONG/ SEQUENCE/FAIL-SAFE.)
STOP SAYING THAT!

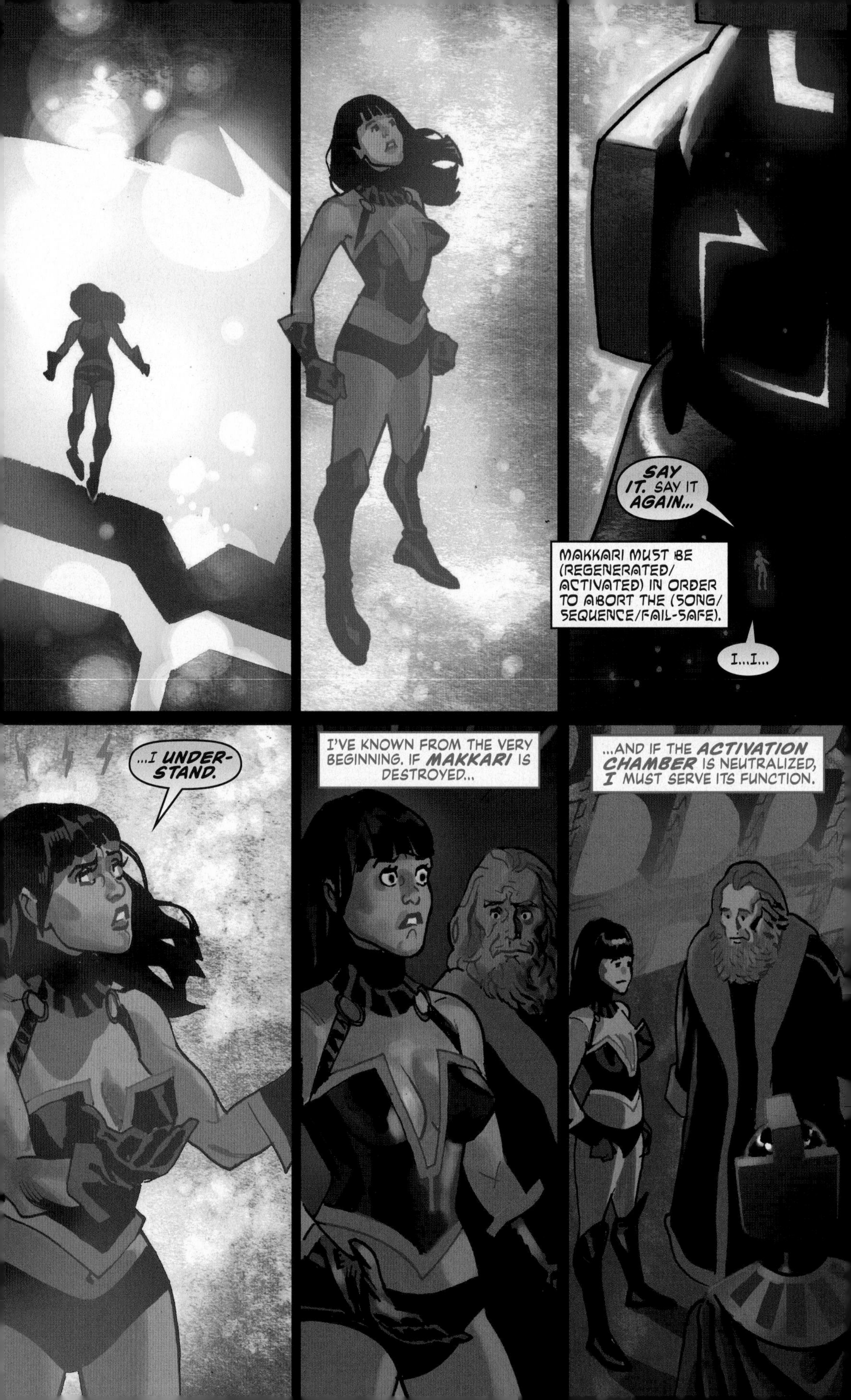
SAY IT. SAY IT AGAIN...
MAKKARI MUST BE (REGENERATED/ ACTIVATED) IN ORDER TO ABORT THE (SONG/ SEQUENCE/FAIL-SAFE).
I...I...
...I UNDER-STAND.
I'VE KNOWN FROM THE VERY BEGINNING. IF MAKKARI IS DESTROYED...
...AND IF THE ACTIVATION CHAMBER IS NEUTRALIZED, I MUST SERVE ITS FUNCTION.

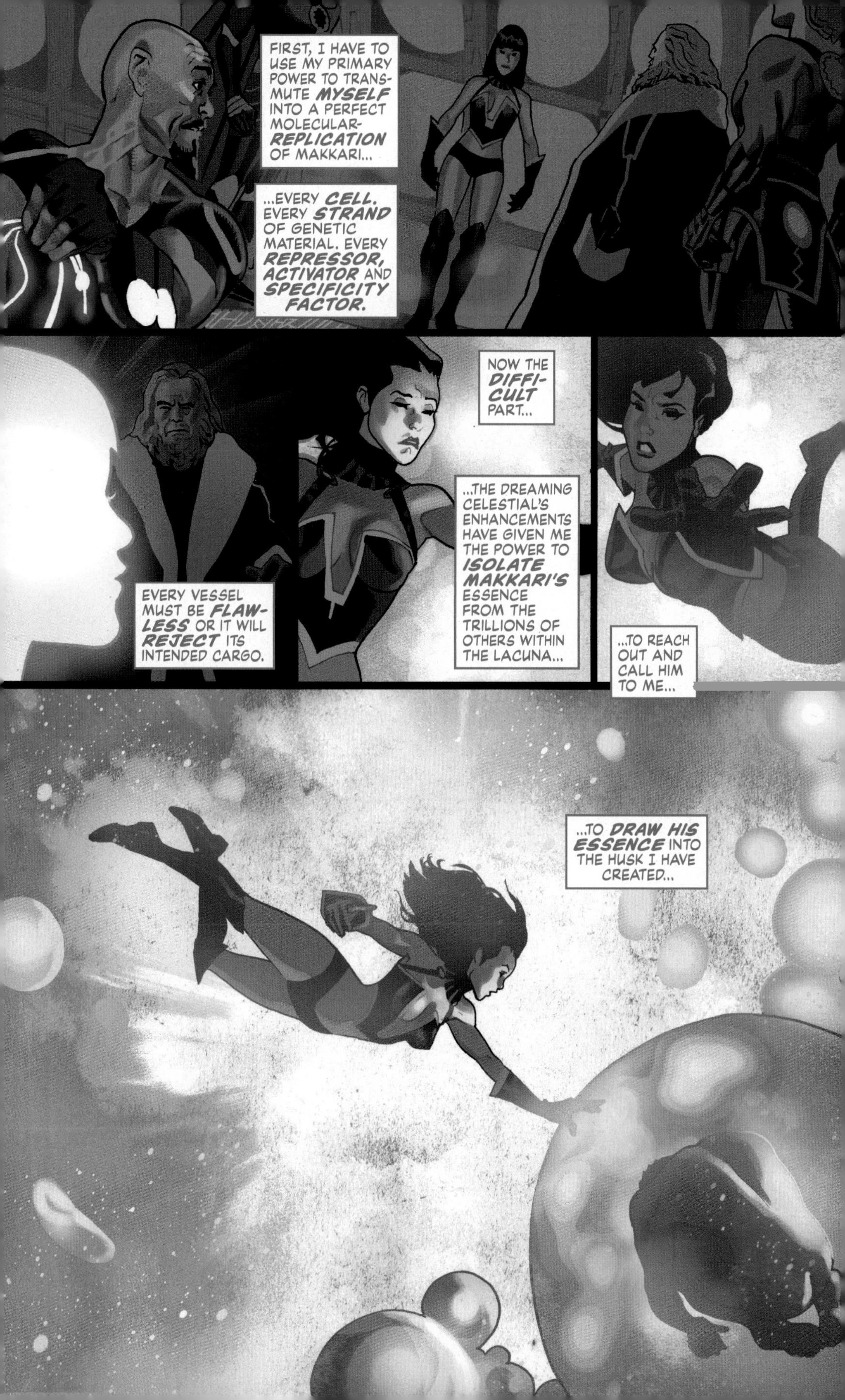
FIRST, I HAVE TO USE MY PRIMARY POWER TO TRANS-MUTE MYSELF INTO A PERFECT MOLECULAR-REPLICATION OF MAKKARI...
...EVERY CELL. EVERY STRAND OF GENETIC MATERIAL. EVERY REPRESSOR, ACTIVATOR AND SPECIFICITY FACTOR.
EVERY VESSEL MUST BE FLAW-LESS OR IT WILL REJECT ITS INTENDED CARGO.
NOW THE DIFFI-CULT PART...
...THE DREAMING CELESTIAL'S ENHANCEMENTS HAVE GIVEN ME THE POWER TO ISOLATE MAKKARI'S ESSENCE FROM THE TRILLIONS OF OTHERS WITHIN THE LACUNA...
...TO REACH OUT AND CALL HIM TO ME...
...TO DRAW HIS ESSENCE INTO THE HUSK I HAVE CREATED...

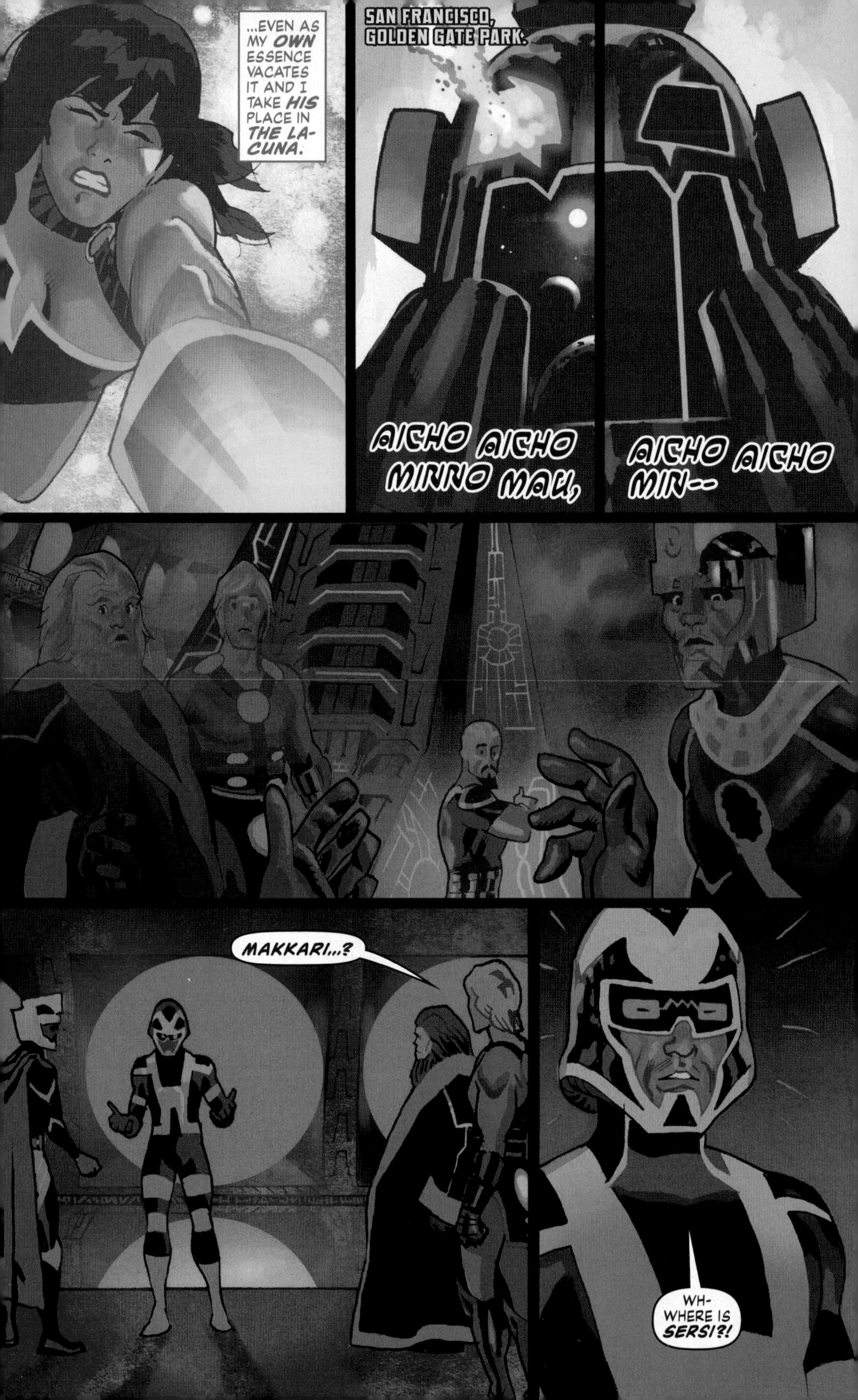

...EVEN AS MY OWN ESSENCE VACATES IT AND I TAKE HIS PLACE IN THE LA-CUNA.
SAN FRANCISCO, GOLDEN GATE PARK:
AICHO AICHO MINNO MAU,
AICHO AICHO MIN--
MAKKARI...?
WH- WHERE IS SERSI?!

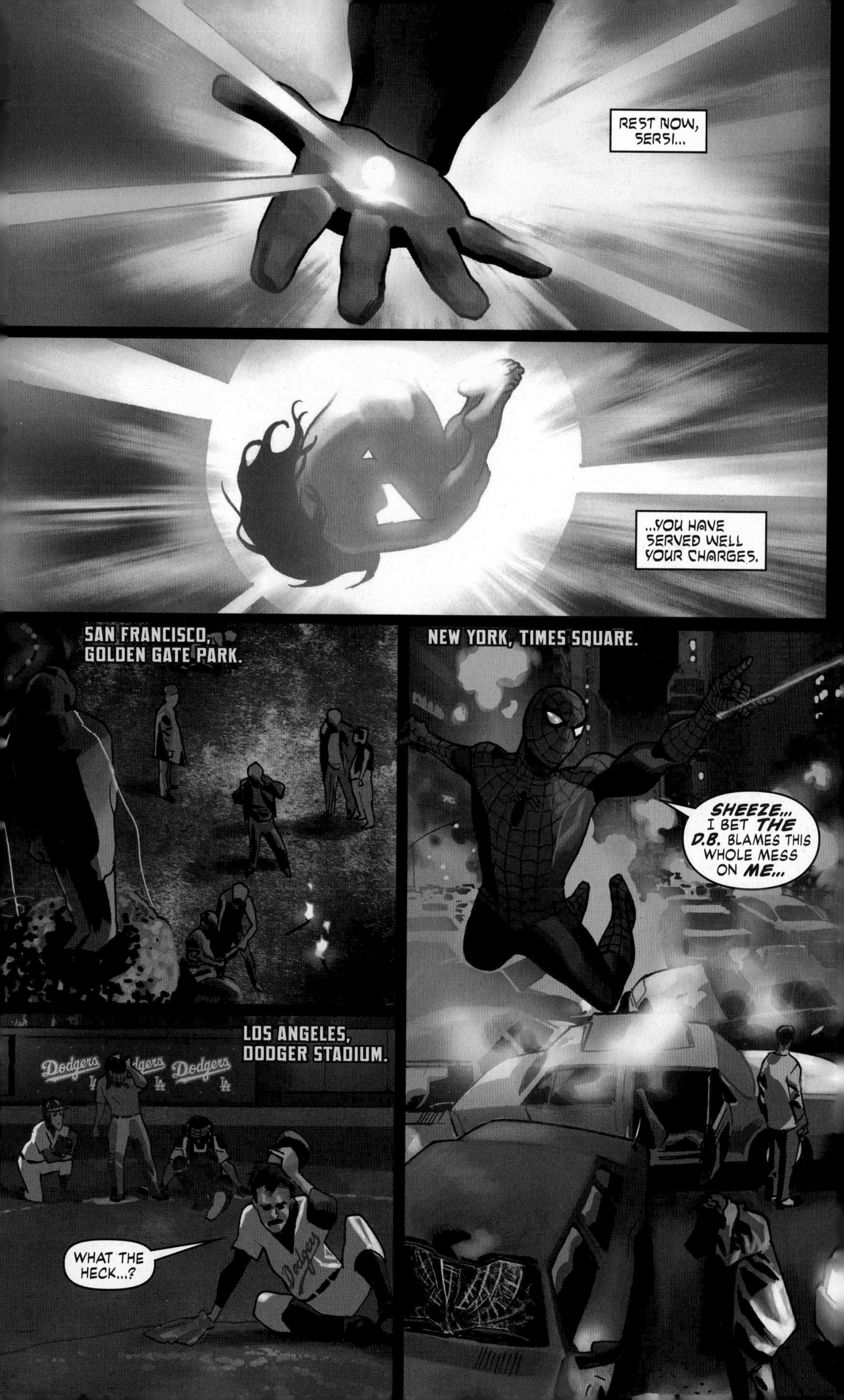
REST NOW, SERSI...
...YOU HAVE SERVED WELL YOUR CHARGES.
SAN FRANCISCO, GOLDEN GATE PARK.
NEW YORK, TIMES SQUARE.
SHEEZE... I BET THE D.B. BLAMES THIS WHOLE MESS ON ME...
LOS ANGELES, DODGER STADIUM.
Dodgers
Dodgers
LA
LA
LA
WHAT THE HECK...?
Dodgers

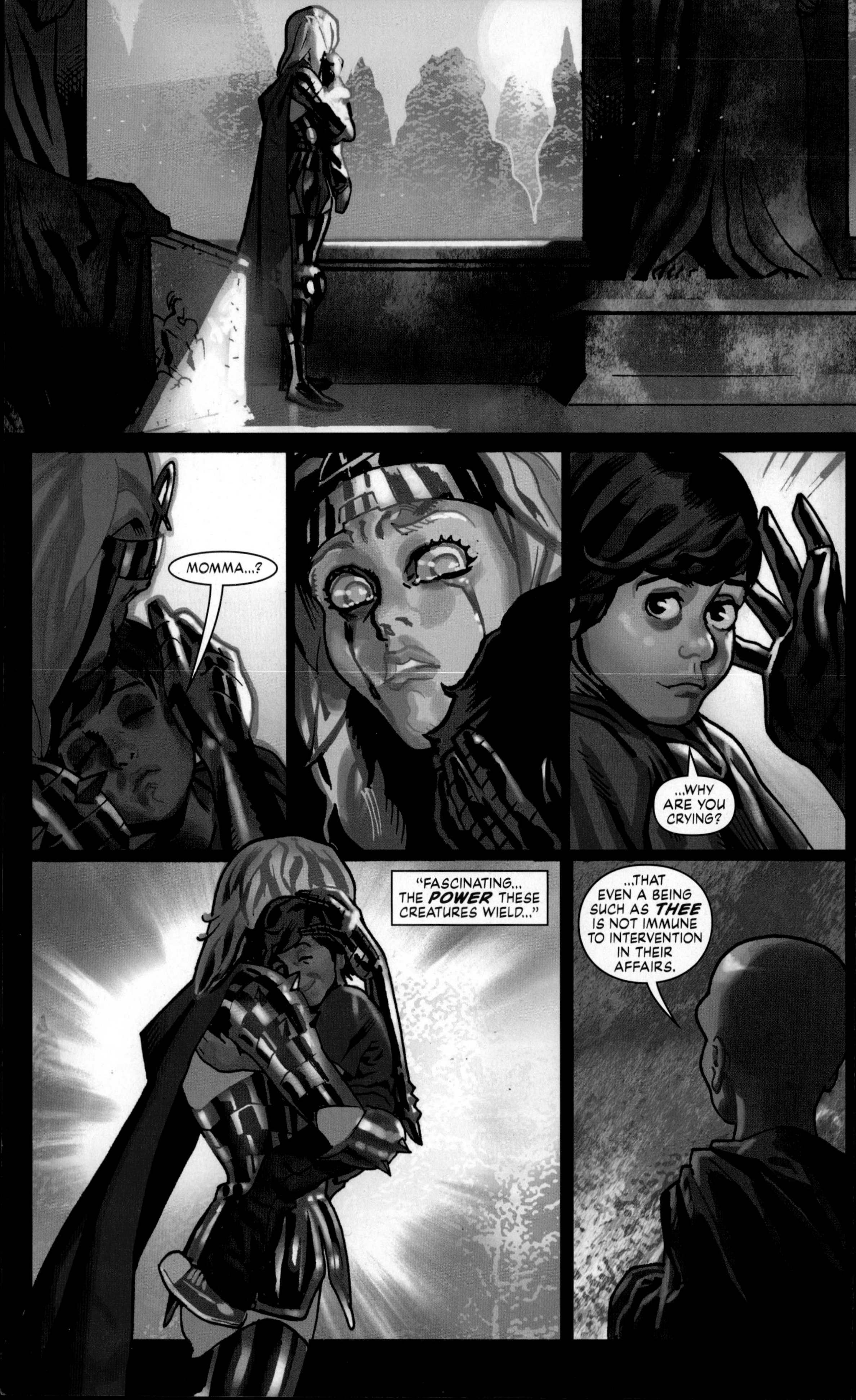
MOMMA...?
...WHY ARE YOU CRYING?
"FASCINATING... THE POWER THESE CREATURES WIELD..."
...THAT EVEN A BEING SUCH AS THEE IS NOT IMMUNE TO INTERVENTION IN THEIR AFFAIRS.

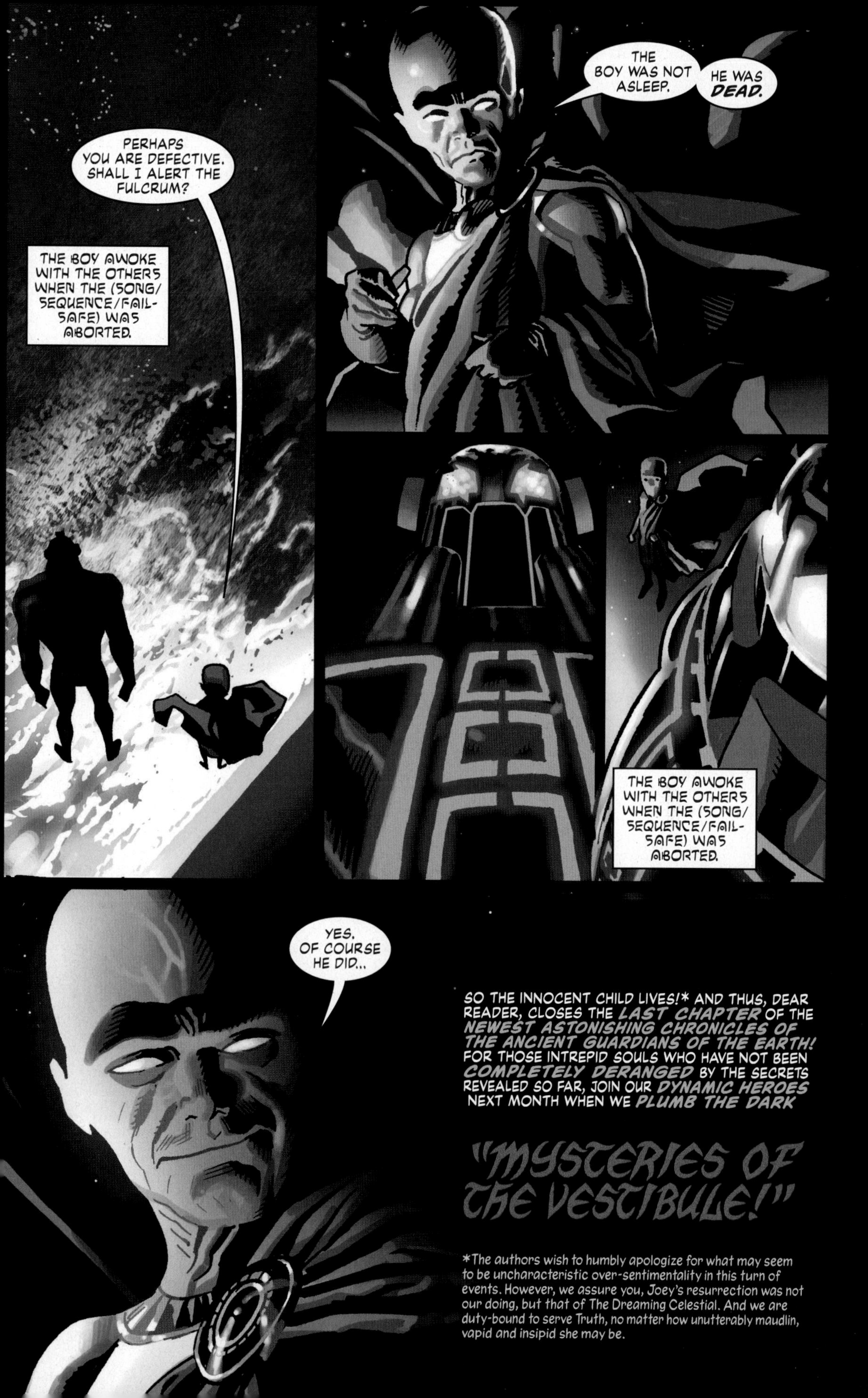

PERHAPS YOU ARE DEFECTIVE. SHALL I ALERT THE FULCRUM?
THE BOY AWOKE WITH THE OTHERS WHEN THE (SONG/ SEQUENCE/FAIL-SAFE) WAS ABORTED.
THE BOY WAS NOT ASLEEP.
HE WAS *DEAD.*
THE BOY AWOKE WITH THE OTHERS WHEN THE (SONG/ SEQUENCE/FAIL-SAFE) WAS ABORTED.
YES. OF COURSE HE DID...
SO THE INNOCENT CHILD LIVES!* AND THUS, DEAR READER, CLOSES THE *LAST CHAPTER* OF THE *NEWEST ASTONISHING CHRONICLES OF THE ANCIENT GUARDIANS OF THE EARTH!* FOR THOSE INTREPID SOULS WHO HAVE NOT BEEN *COMPLETELY DERANGED* BY THE SECRETS REVEALED SO FAR, JOIN OUR *DYNAMIC HEROES* NEXT MONTH WHEN WE *PLUMB THE DARK*
"MYSTERIES OF THE VESTIBULE!"
*The authors wish to humbly apologize for what may seem to be uncharacteristic over-sentimentality in this turn of events. However, we assure you, Joey's resurrection was not our doing, but that of The Dreaming Celestial. And we are duty-bound to serve Truth, no matter how unutterably maudlin, vapid and insipid she may be.

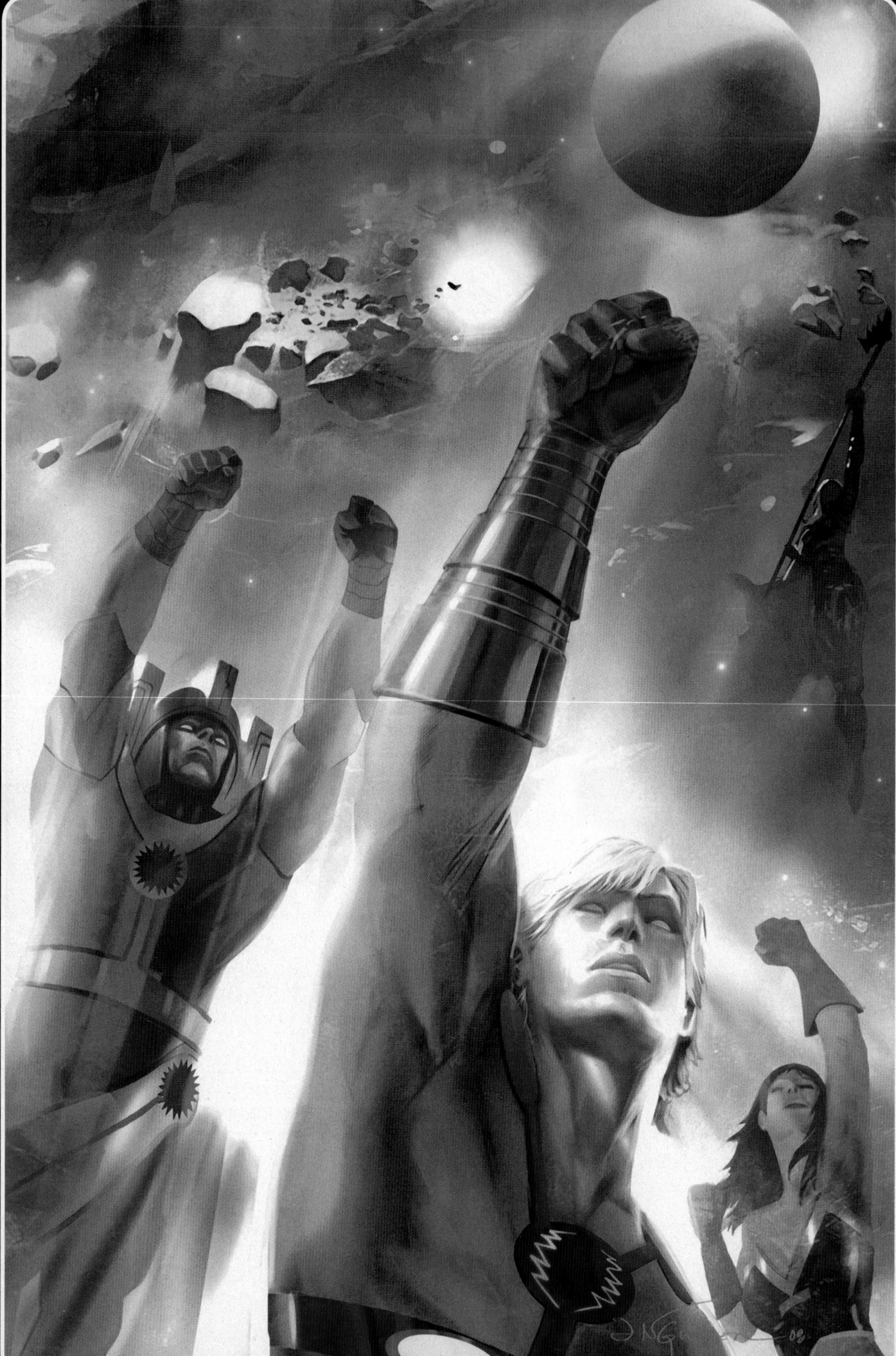

7

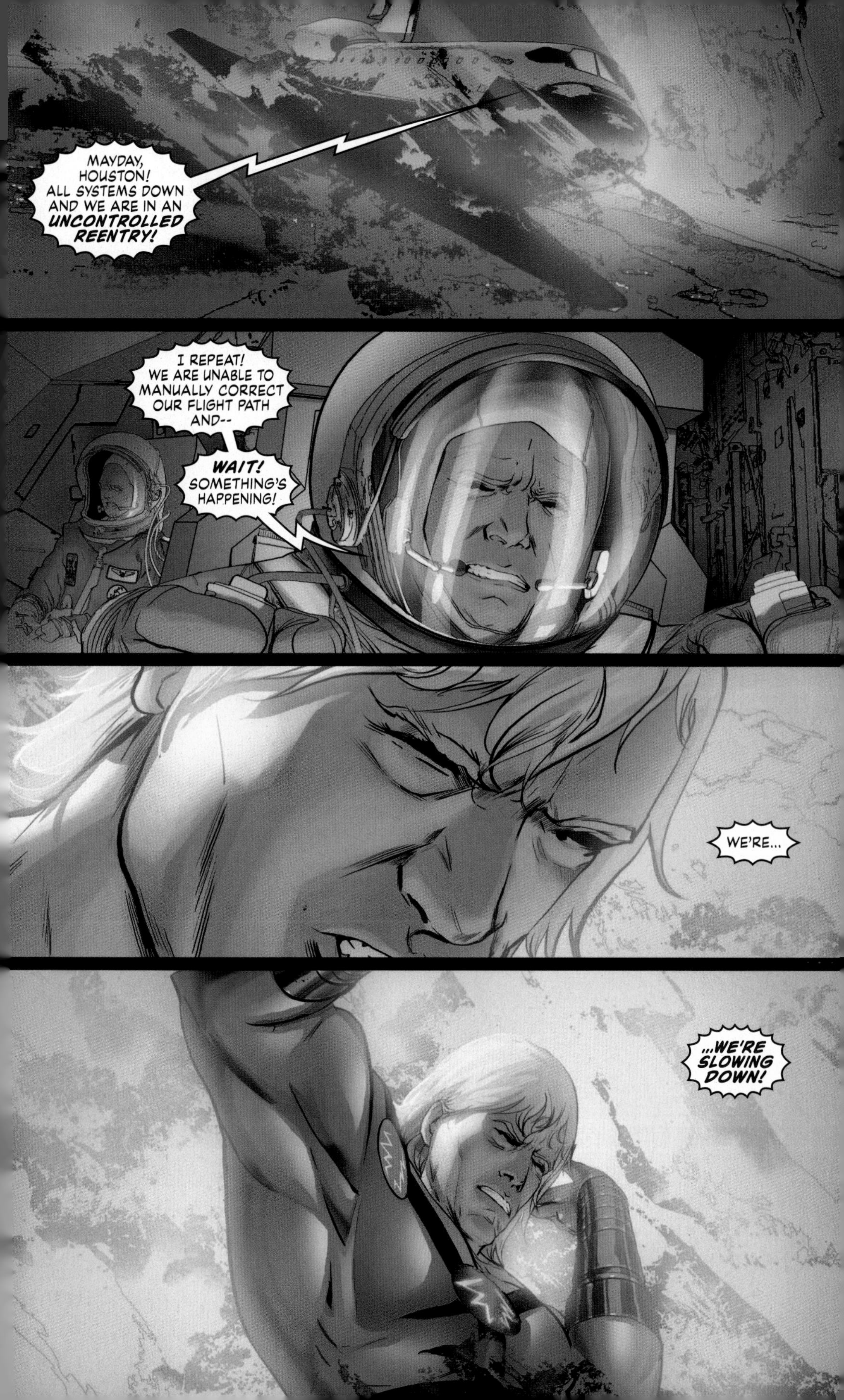
MAYDAY, HOUSTON! ALL SYSTEMS DOWN AND WE ARE IN AN UNCONTROLLED REENTRY!
I REPEAT! WE ARE UNABLE TO MANUALLY CORRECT OUR FLIGHT PATH AND--
WAIT! SOMETHING'S HAPPENING!
WE'RE...
...WE'RE SLOWING DOWN!

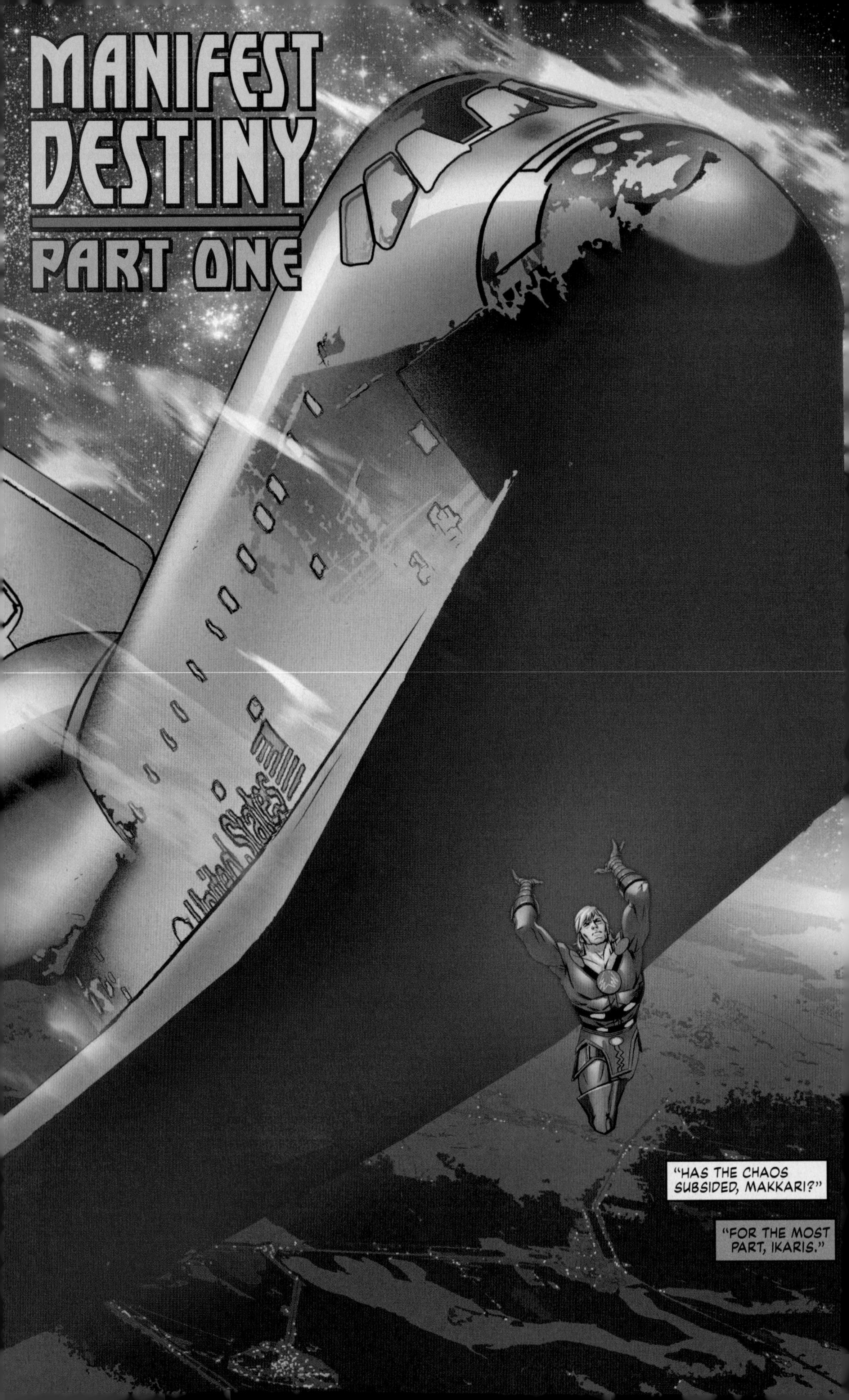
MANIFEST DESTINY
PART ONE
"HAS THE CHAOS SUBSIDED, MAKKARI?"
"FOR THE MOST PART, IKARIS."

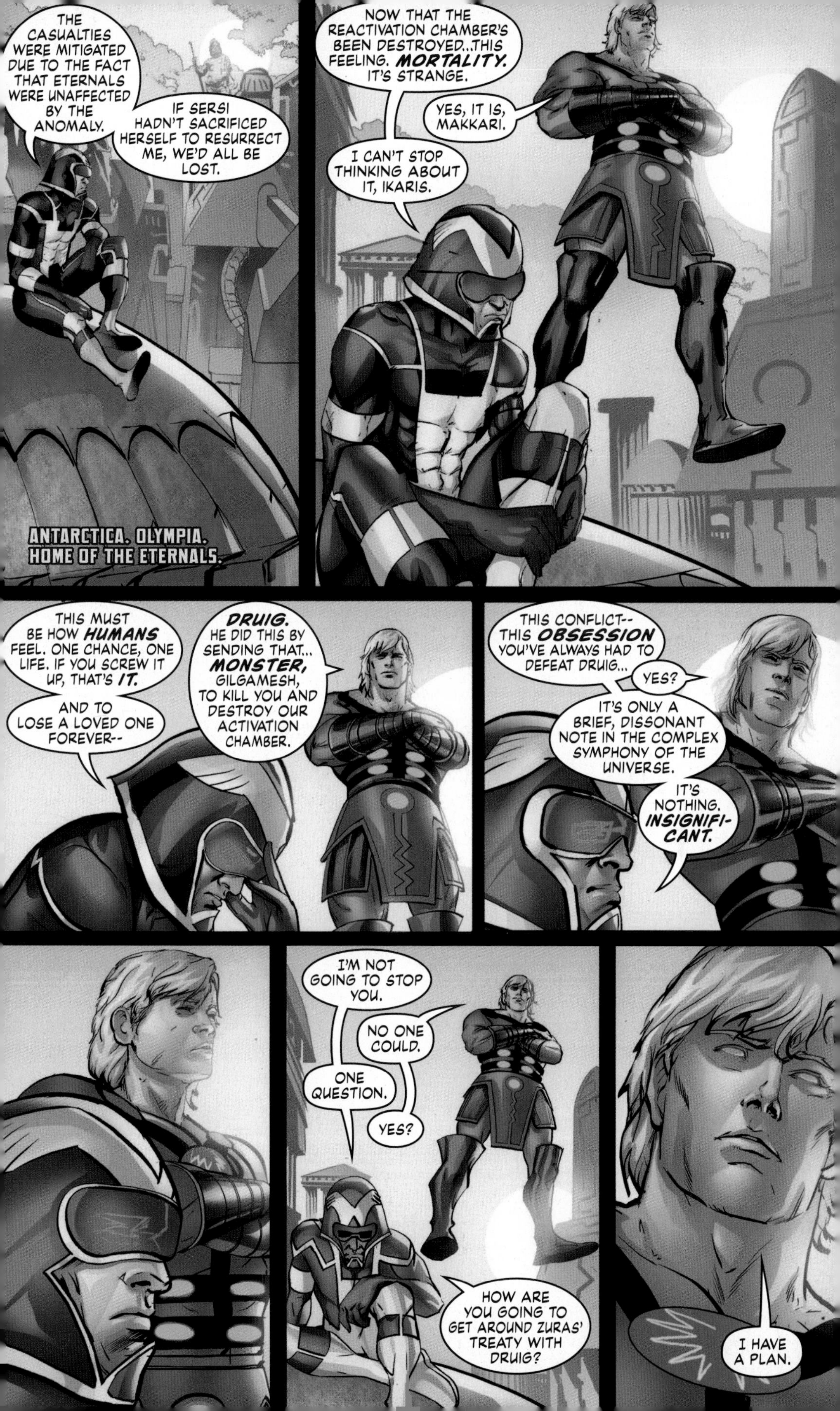
ANTARCTICA. OLYMPIA. HOME OF THE ETERNALS.
THE CASUALTIES WERE MITIGATED DUE TO THE FACT THAT ETERNALS WERE UNAFFECTED BY THE ANOMALY.
IF SERSI HADN'T SACRIFICED HERSELF TO RESURRECT ME, WE'D ALL BE LOST.
NOW THAT THE REACTIVATION CHAMBER'S BEEN DESTROYED...THIS FEELING. MORTALITY. IT'S STRANGE.
YES, IT IS, MAKKARI.
I CAN'T STOP THINKING ABOUT IT, IKARIS.
THIS MUST BE HOW HUMANS FEEL. ONE CHANCE, ONE LIFE. IF YOU SCREW IT UP, THAT'S IT.
AND TO LOSE A LOVED ONE FOREVER--
DRUIG. HE DID THIS BY SENDING THAT... MONSTER, GILGAMESH, TO KILL YOU AND DESTROY OUR ACTIVATION CHAMBER.
THIS CONFLICT-- THIS OBSESSION YOU'VE ALWAYS HAD TO DEFEAT DRUIG...
YES?
IT'S ONLY A BRIEF, DISSONANT NOTE IN THE COMPLEX SYMPHONY OF THE UNIVERSE.
IT'S NOTHING. INSIGNIFI-CANT.
I'M NOT GOING TO STOP YOU.
NO ONE COULD.
ONE QUESTION.
YES?
HOW ARE YOU GOING TO GET AROUND ZURAS' TREATY WITH DRUIG?
I HAVE A PLAN.

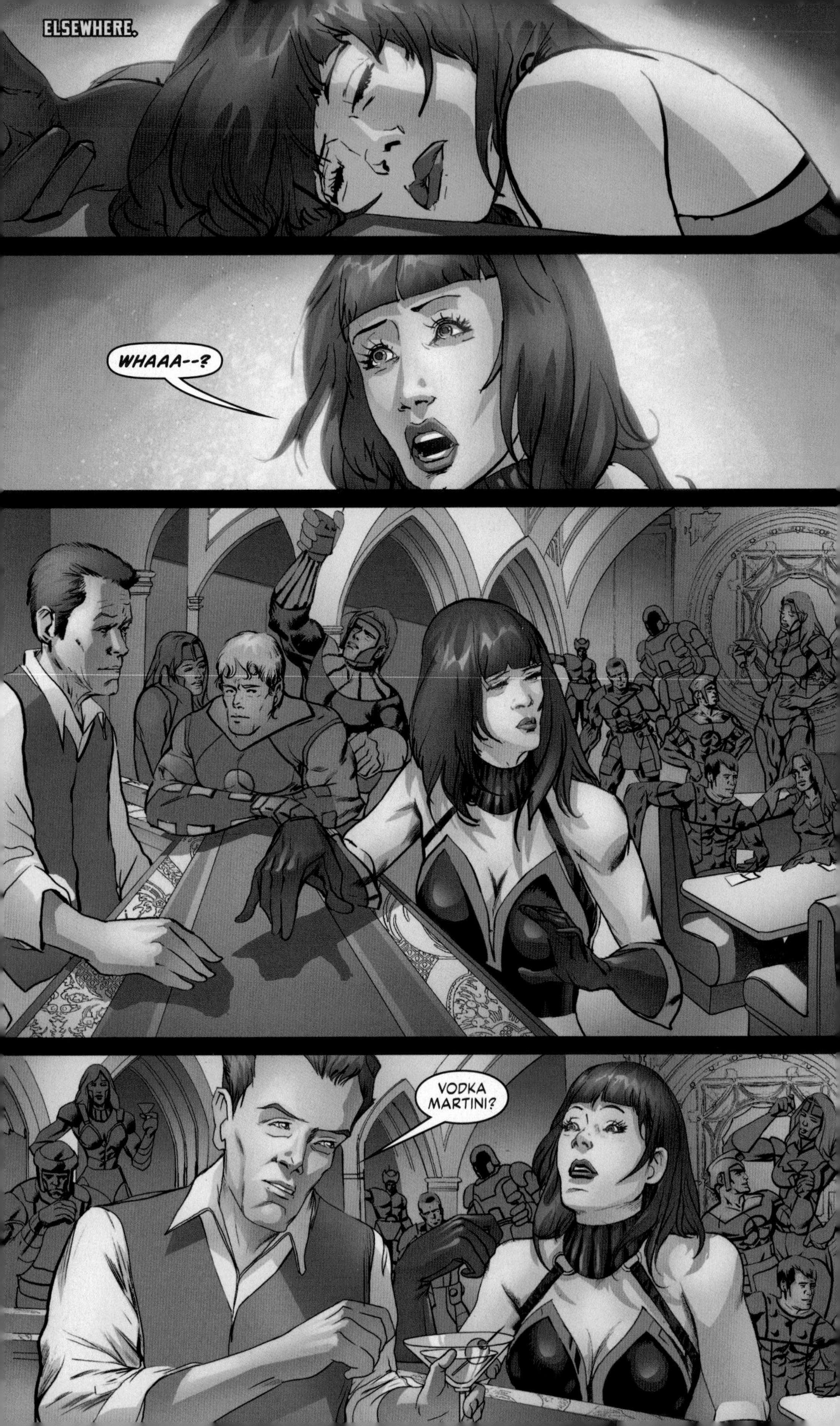
ELSEWHERE.
WHAAA--?
VODKA MARTINI?

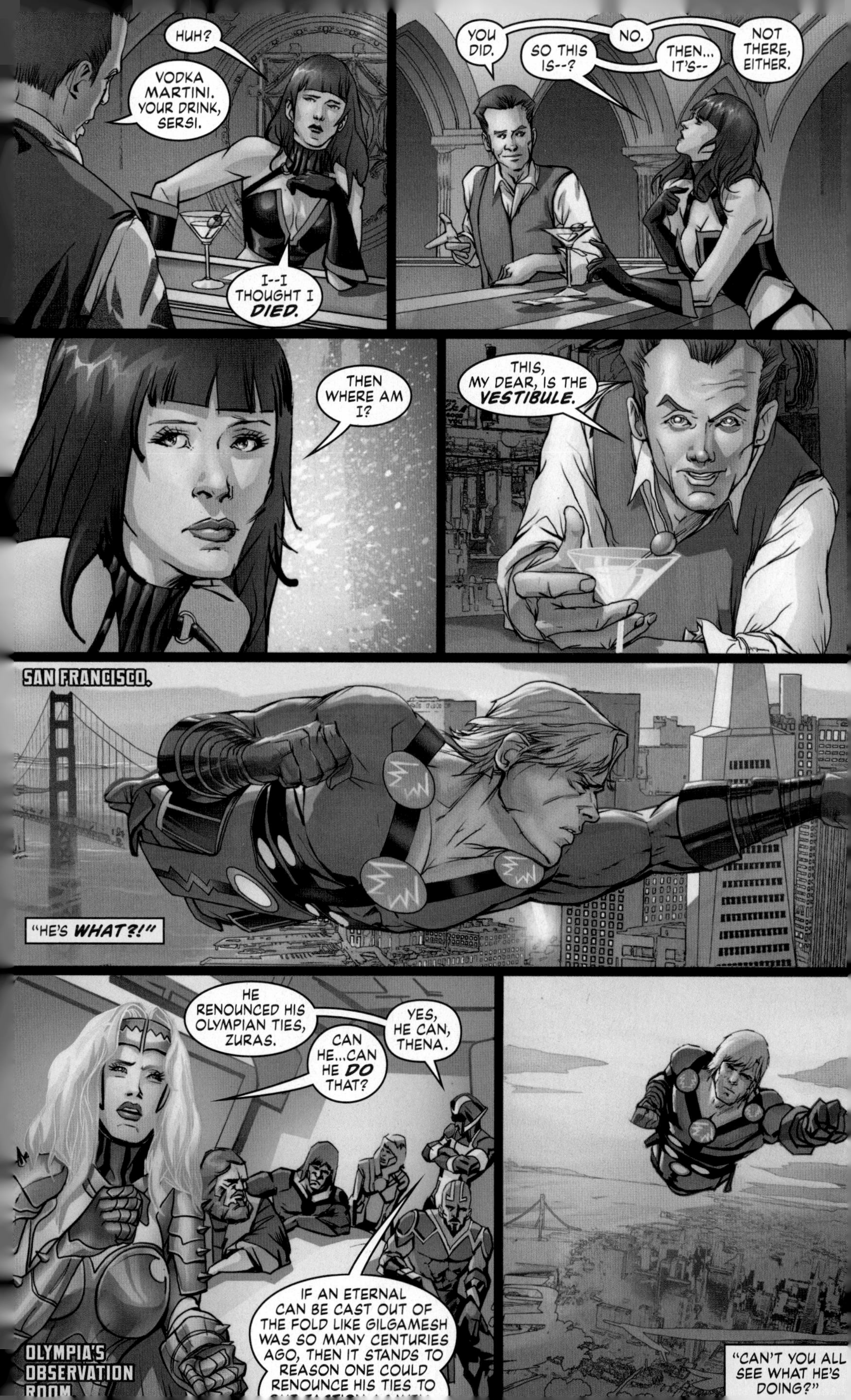
HUH?
VODKA MARTINI. YOUR DRINK, SERSI.
I--I THOUGHT I DIED.
YOU DID.
SO THIS IS--?
NO.
THEN... IT'S--
NOT THERE, EITHER.
THEN WHERE AM I?
THIS, MY DEAR, IS THE VESTIBULE.
SAN FRANCISCO.
"HE'S WHAT?!"
OLYMPIA'S OBSERVATION ROOM
HE RENOUNCED HIS OLYMPIAN TIES, ZURAS.
CAN HE...CAN HE DO THAT?
YES, HE CAN, THENA.
IF AN ETERNAL CAN BE CAST OUT OF THE FOLD LIKE GILGAMESH WAS SO MANY CENTURIES AGO, THEN IT STANDS TO REASON ONE COULD RENOUNCE HIS TIES TO
"CAN'T YOU ALL SEE WHAT HE'S DOING?"

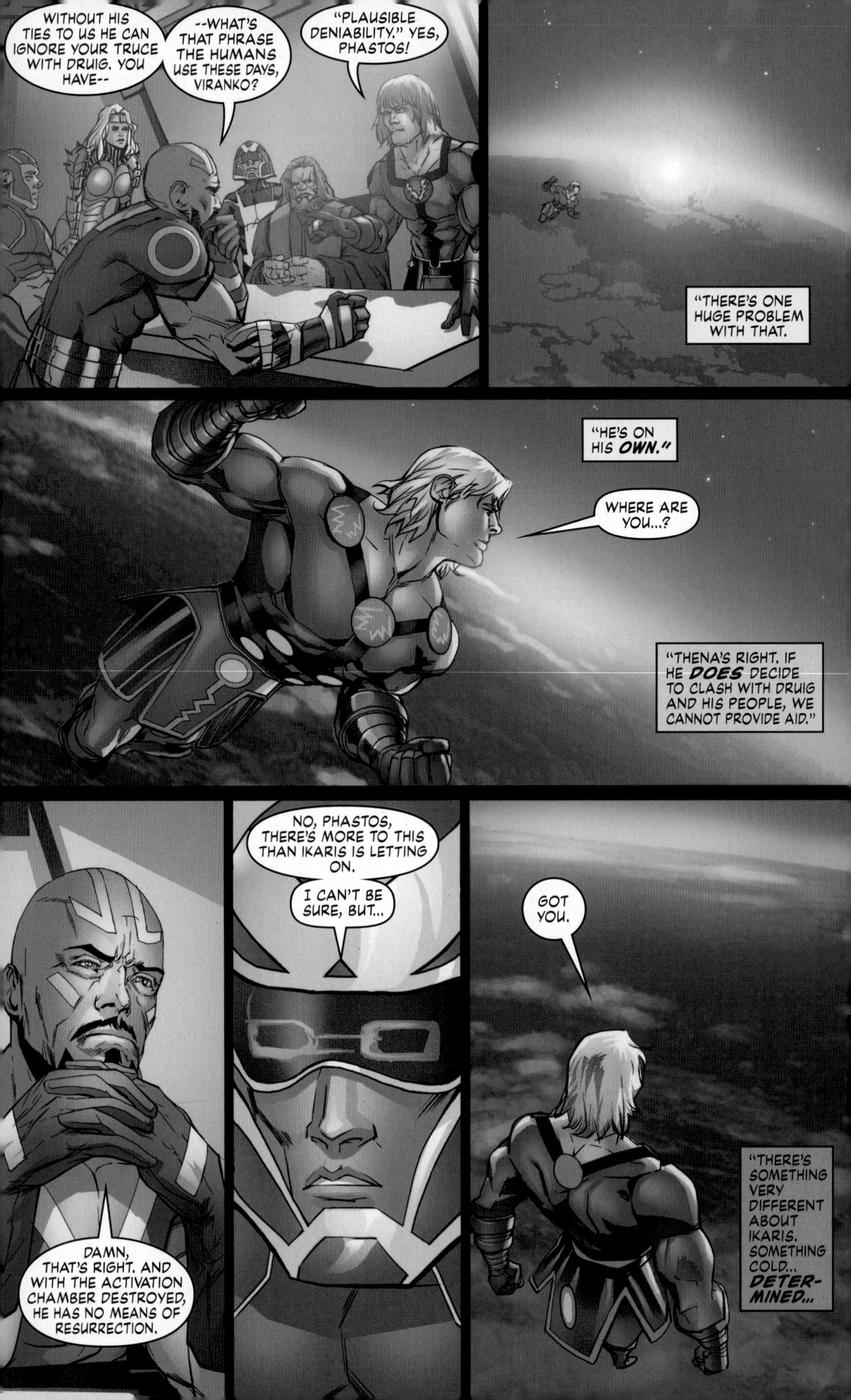
WITHOUT HIS TIES TO US HE CAN IGNORE YOUR TRUCE WITH DRUIG. YOU HAVE--
--WHAT'S THAT PHRASE THE HUMANS USE THESE DAYS, VIRANKO?
"PLAUSIBLE DENIABILITY." YES, PHASTOS!
"THERE'S ONE HUGE PROBLEM WITH THAT.
"HE'S ON HIS OWN."
WHERE ARE YOU...?
"THENA'S RIGHT. IF HE DOES DECIDE TO CLASH WITH DRUIG AND HIS PEOPLE, WE CANNOT PROVIDE AID."
DAMN, THAT'S RIGHT. AND WITH THE ACTIVATION CHAMBER DESTROYED, HE HAS NO MEANS OF RESURRECTION.
NO, PHASTOS, THERE'S MORE TO THIS THAN IKARIS IS LETTING ON.
I CAN'T BE SURE, BUT...
GOT YOU.
"THERE'S SOMETHING VERY DIFFERENT ABOUT IKARIS. SOMETHING COLD... DETER-MINED...

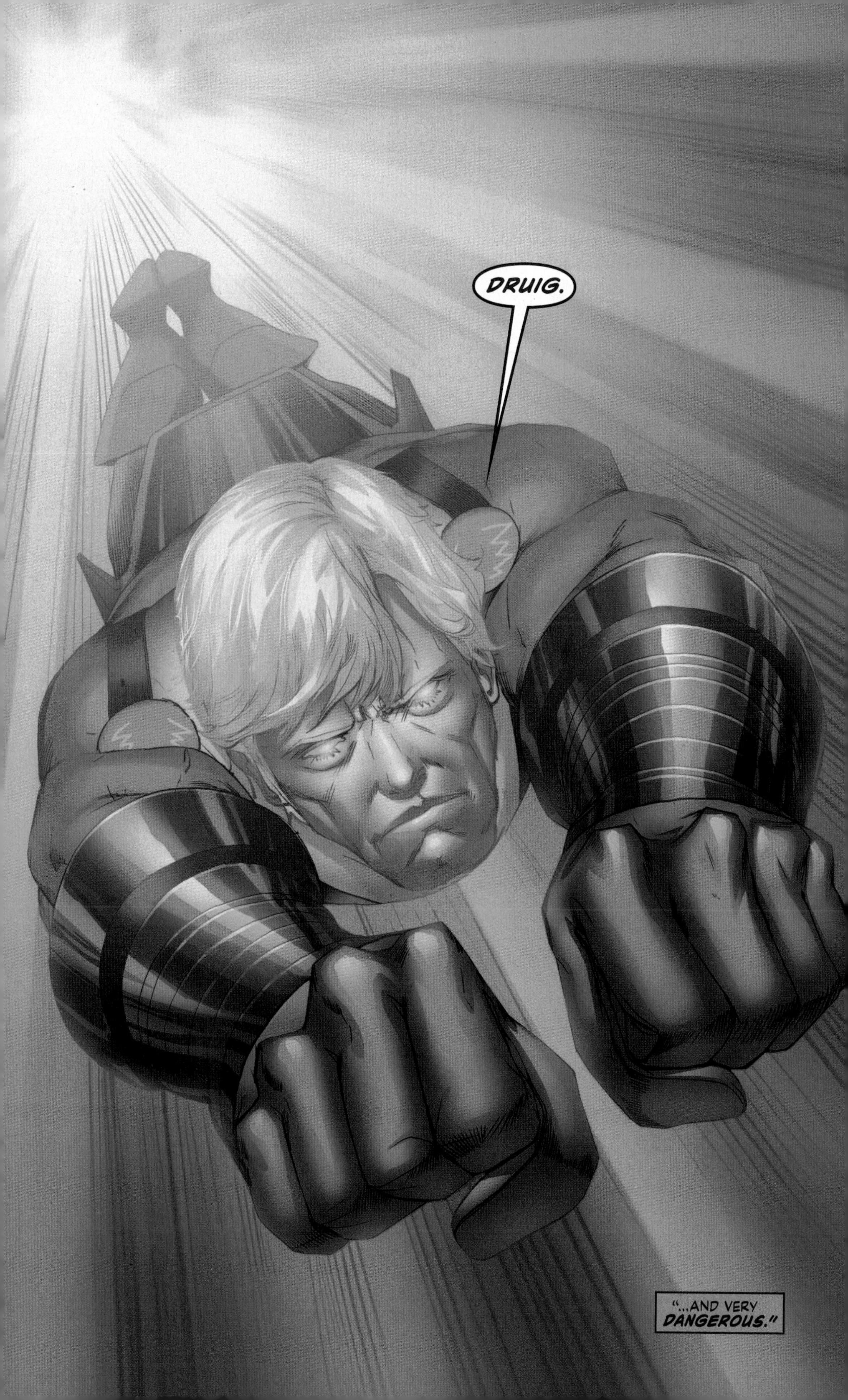
DRUIG.
"...AND VERY DANGEROUS."

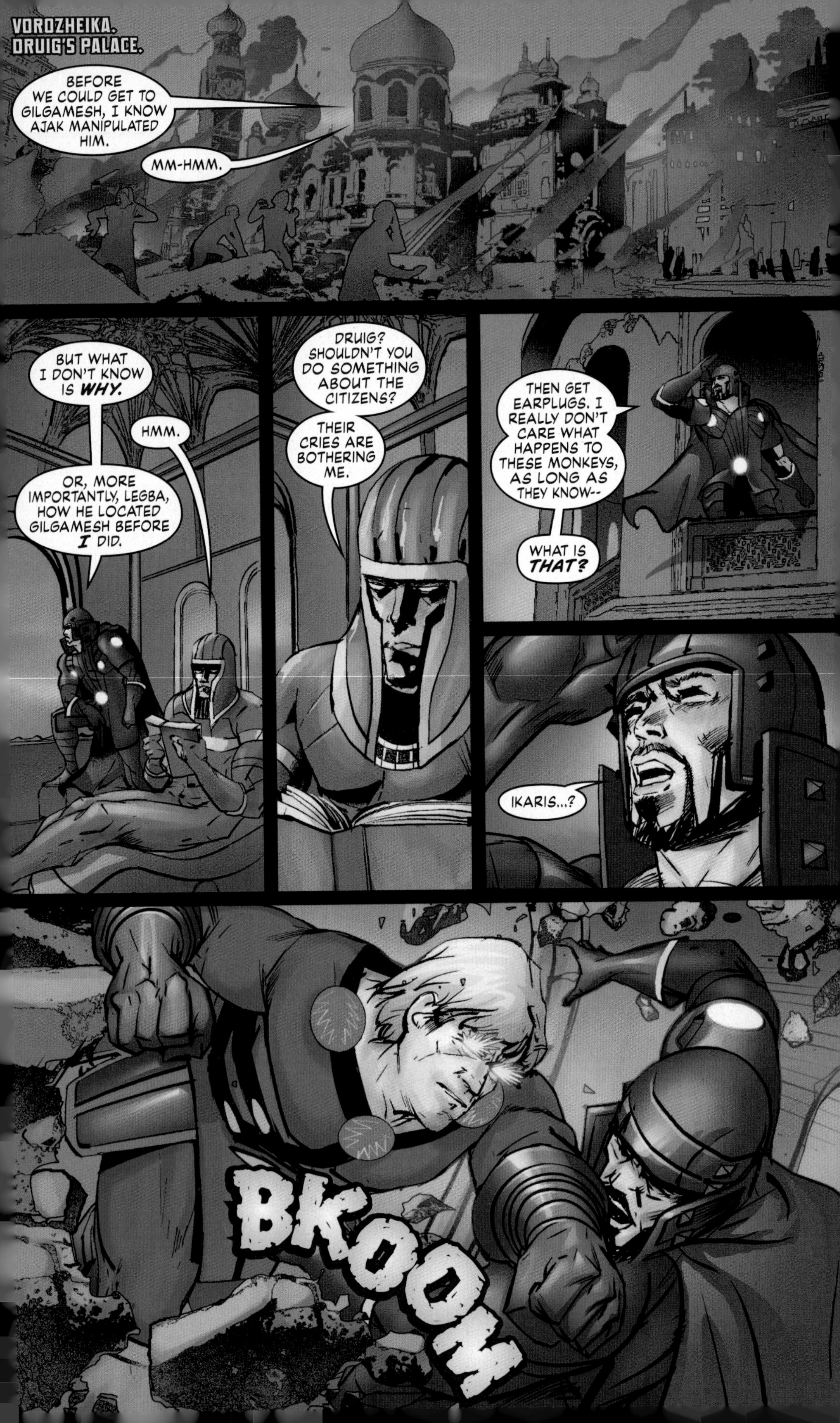
VOROZHEIKA. DRUIG'S PALACE.
BEFORE WE COULD GET TO GILGAMESH, I KNOW AJAK MANIPULATED HIM.
MM-HMM.
BUT WHAT I DON'T KNOW IS WHY.
HMM.
OR, MORE IMPORTANTLY, LEGBA, HOW HE LOCATED GILGAMESH BEFORE I DID.
DRUIG? SHOULDN'T YOU DO SOMETHING ABOUT THE CITIZENS?
THEIR CRIES ARE BOTHERING ME.
THEN GET EARPLUGS. I REALLY DON'T CARE WHAT HAPPENS TO THESE MONKEYS, AS LONG AS THEY KNOW--
WHAT IS THAT?
IKARIS...?
BKOOOM

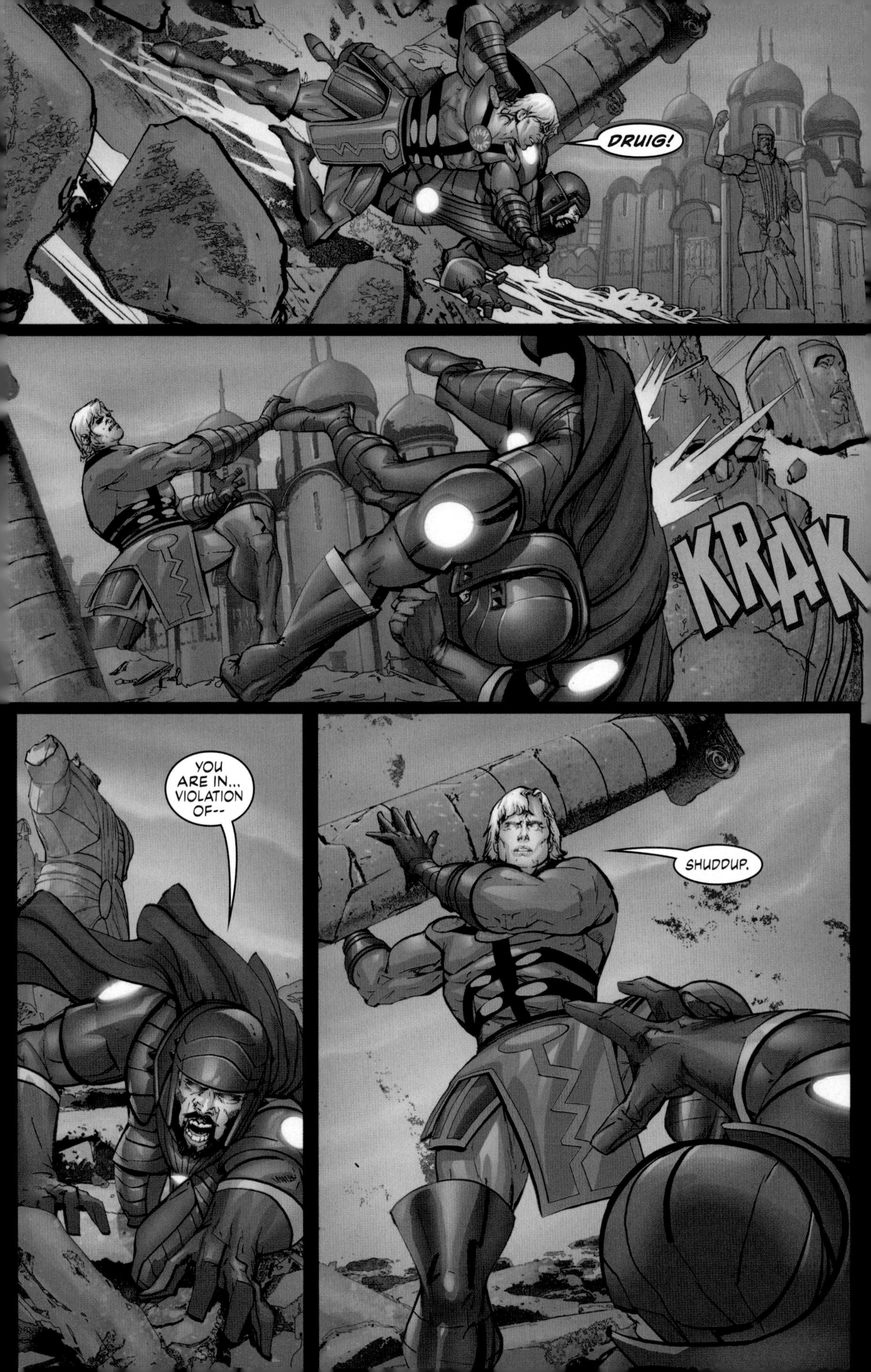
DRUIG!
KRAK
YOU ARE IN... VIOLATION OF--
SHUDDUP.

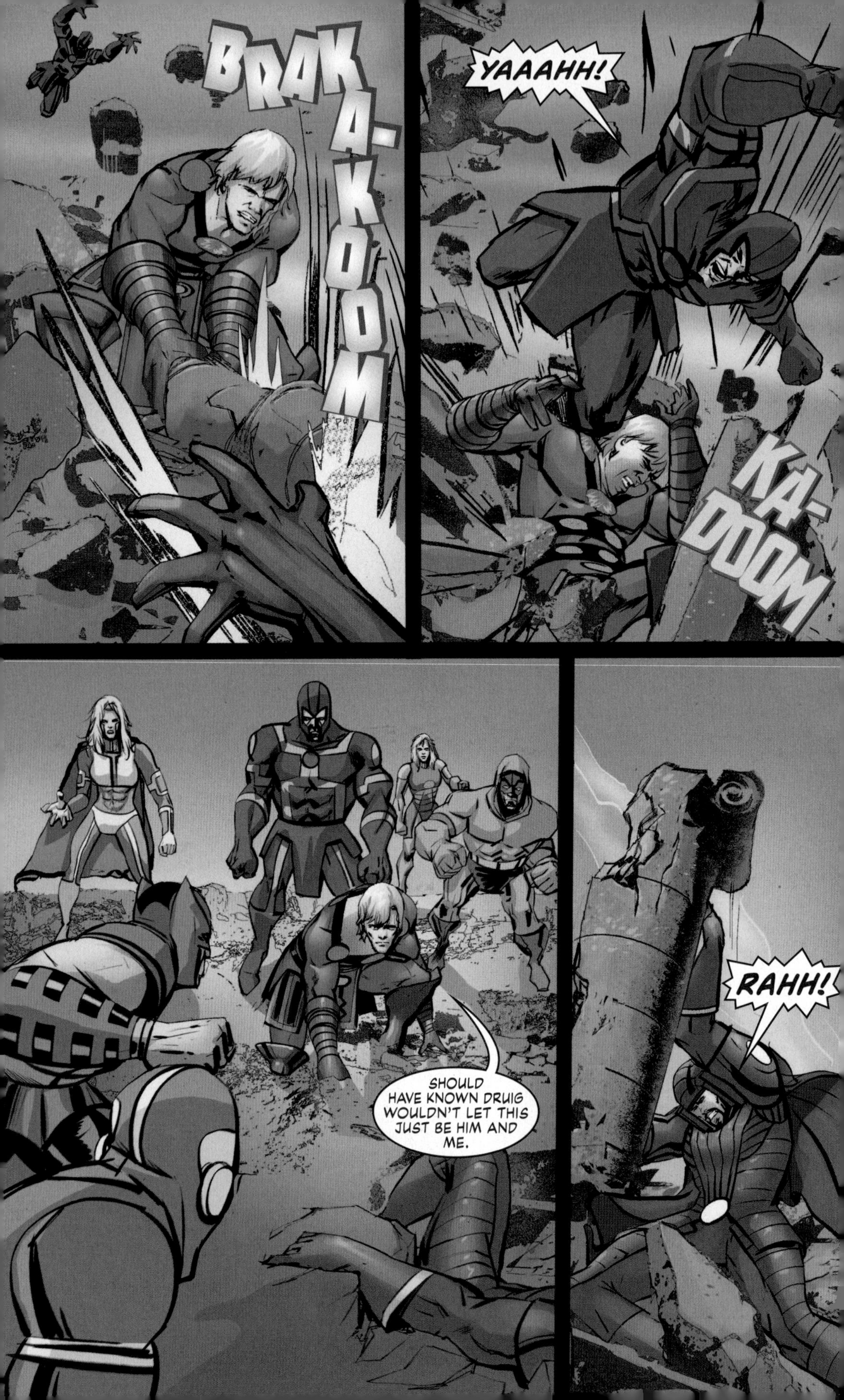
BRAKA-KOOM
YAAAHH!
KA-DOOM
SHOULD HAVE KNOWN DRUIG WOULDN'T LET THIS JUST BE HIM AND ME.
RAHH!

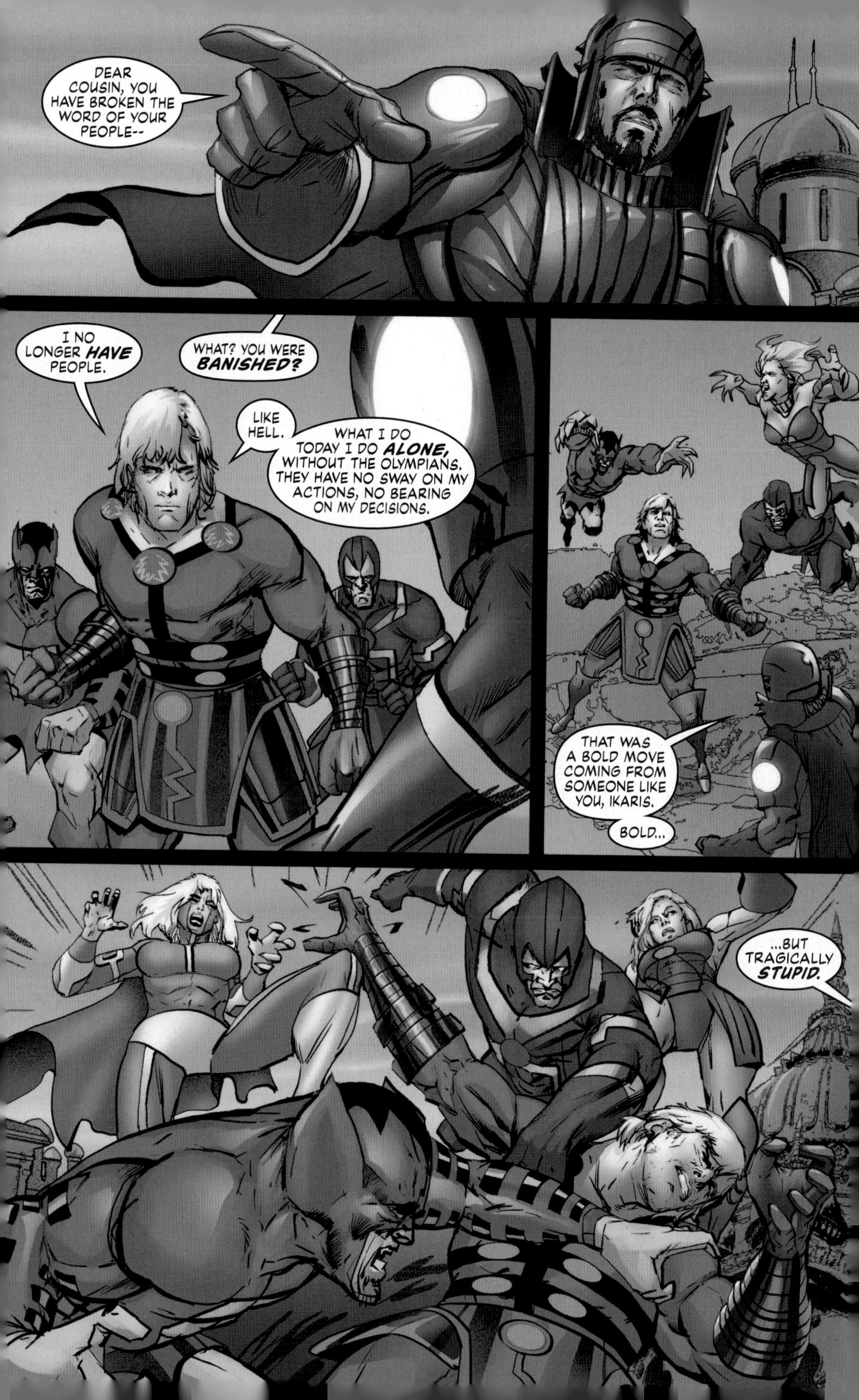
DEAR COUSIN, YOU HAVE BROKEN THE WORD OF YOUR PEOPLE--
I NO LONGER HAVE PEOPLE.
WHAT? YOU WERE BANISHED?
LIKE HELL.
WHAT I DO TODAY I DO ALONE, WITHOUT THE OLYMPIANS. THEY HAVE NO SWAY ON MY ACTIONS, NO BEARING ON MY DECISIONS.
THAT WAS A BOLD MOVE COMING FROM SOMEONE LIKE YOU, IKARIS.
BOLD...
...BUT TRAGICALLY STUPID.

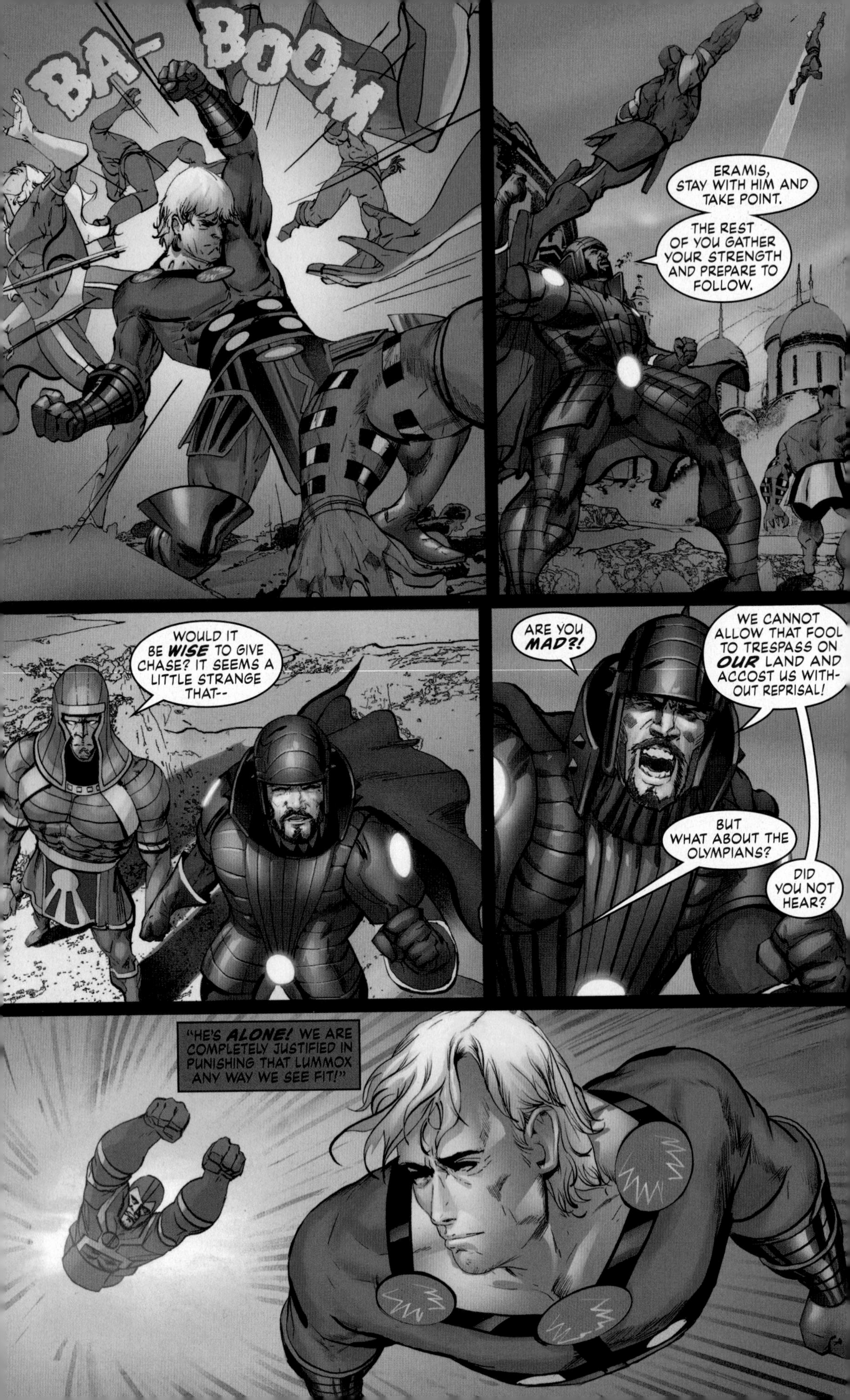
BA-BOOM
ERAMIS, STAY WITH HIM AND TAKE POINT.
THE REST OF YOU GATHER YOUR STRENGTH AND PREPARE TO FOLLOW.
WOULD IT BE **WISE** TO GIVE CHASE? IT SEEMS A LITTLE STRANGE THAT--
ARE YOU **MAD?!**
WE CANNOT ALLOW THAT FOOL TO TRESPASS ON **OUR** LAND AND ACCOST US WITH-OUT REPRISAL!
BUT WHAT ABOUT THE OLYMPIANS?
DID YOU NOT HEAR?
"HE'S **ALONE!** WE ARE COMPLETELY JUSTIFIED IN PUNISHING THAT LUMMOX ANY WAY WE SEE FIT!"

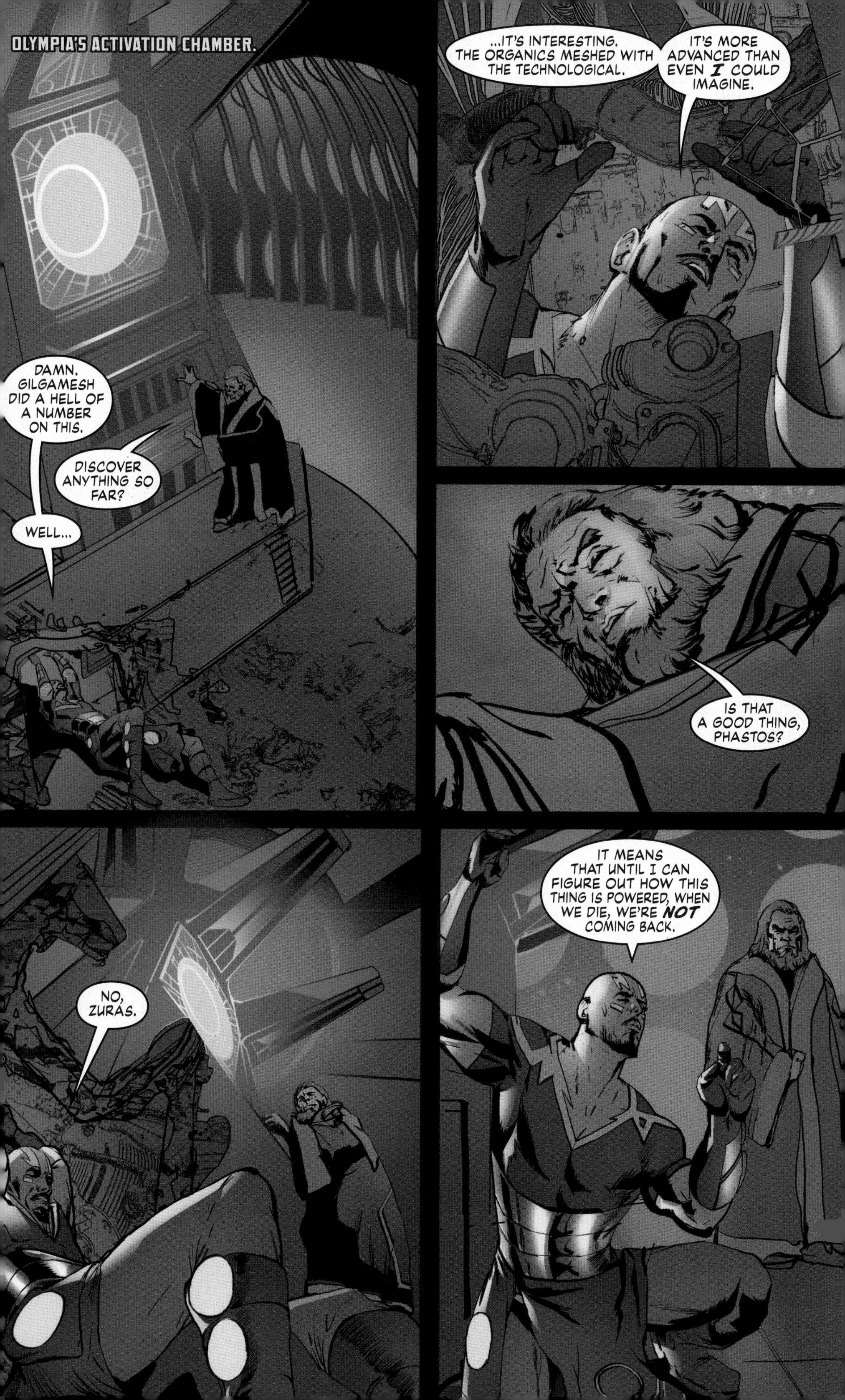
OLYMPIA'S ACTIVATION CHAMBER.
DAMN. GILGAMESH DID A HELL OF A NUMBER ON THIS.
DISCOVER ANYTHING SO FAR?
WELL...
...IT'S INTERESTING. THE ORGANICS MESHED WITH THE TECHNOLOGICAL.
IT'S MORE ADVANCED THAN EVEN I COULD IMAGINE.
IS THAT A GOOD THING, PHASTOS?
NO, ZURAS.
IT MEANS THAT UNTIL I CAN FIGURE OUT HOW THIS THING IS POWERED, WHEN WE DIE, WE'RE NOT COMING BACK.

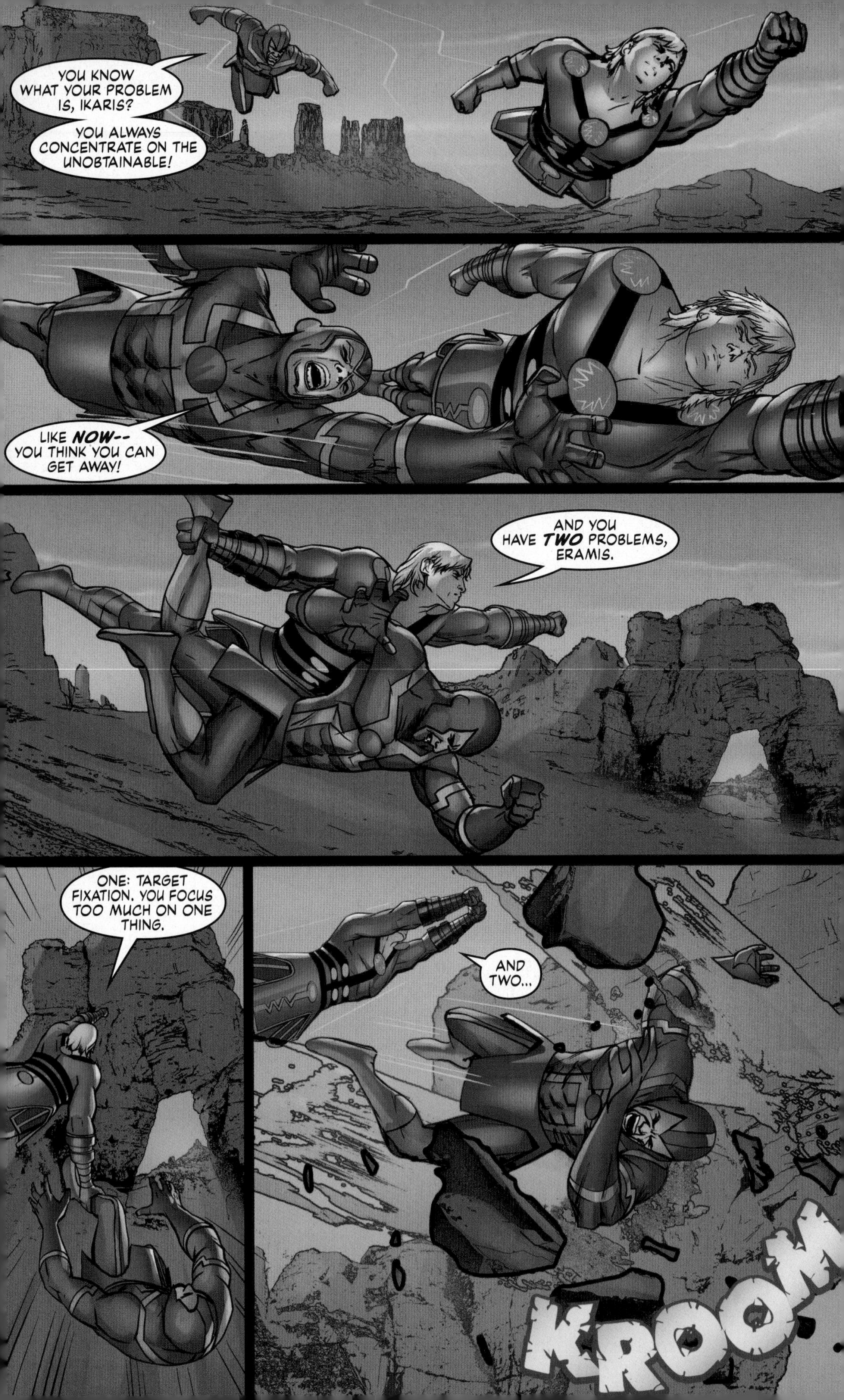
YOU KNOW WHAT YOUR PROBLEM IS, IKARIS?
YOU ALWAYS CONCENTRATE ON THE UNOBTAINABLE!
LIKE NOW-- YOU THINK YOU CAN GET AWAY!
AND YOU HAVE TWO PROBLEMS, ERAMIS.
ONE: TARGET FIXATION. YOU FOCUS TOO MUCH ON ONE THING.
AND TWO...
KROOM

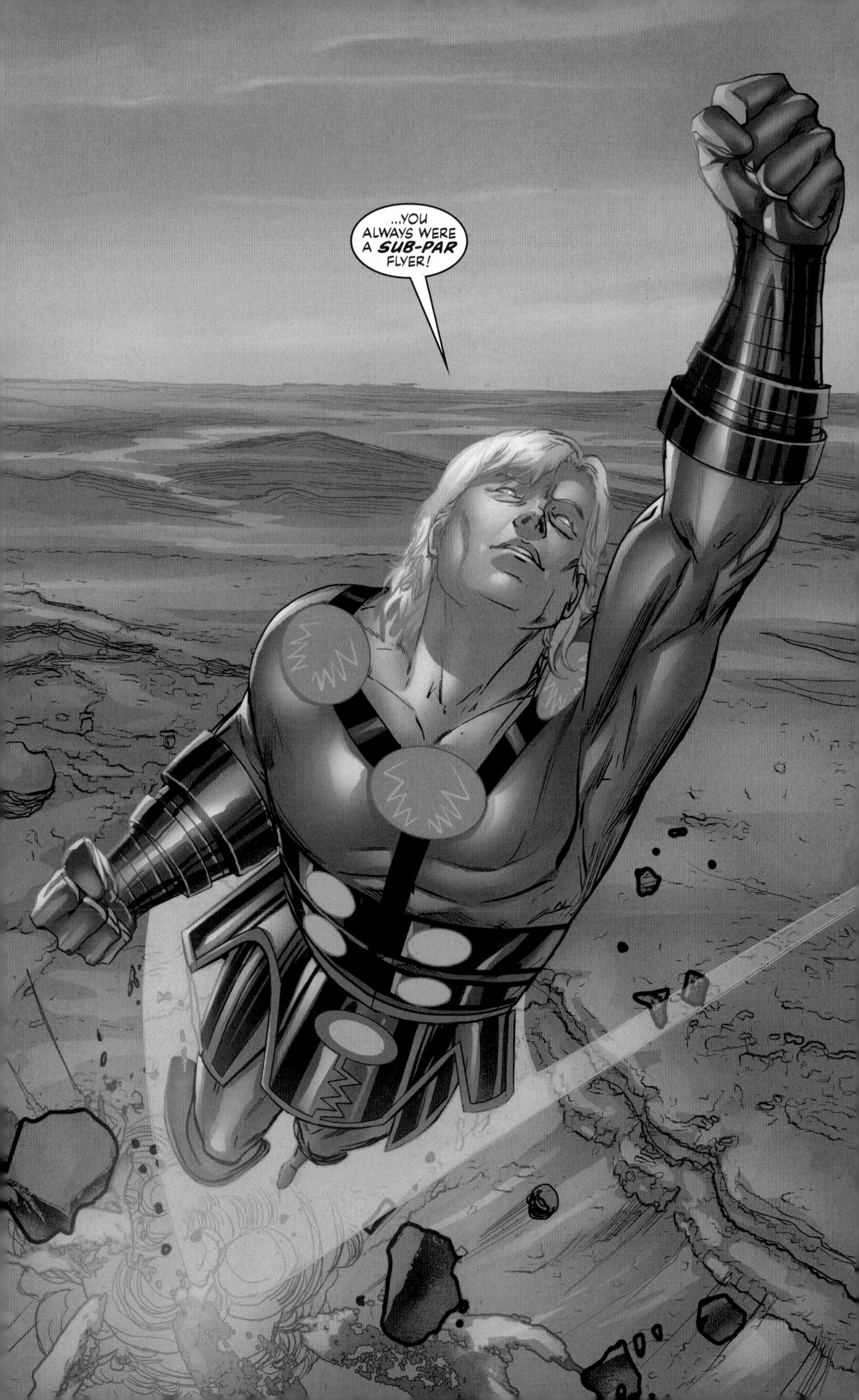
...YOU ALWAYS WERE A SUB-PAR FLYER!

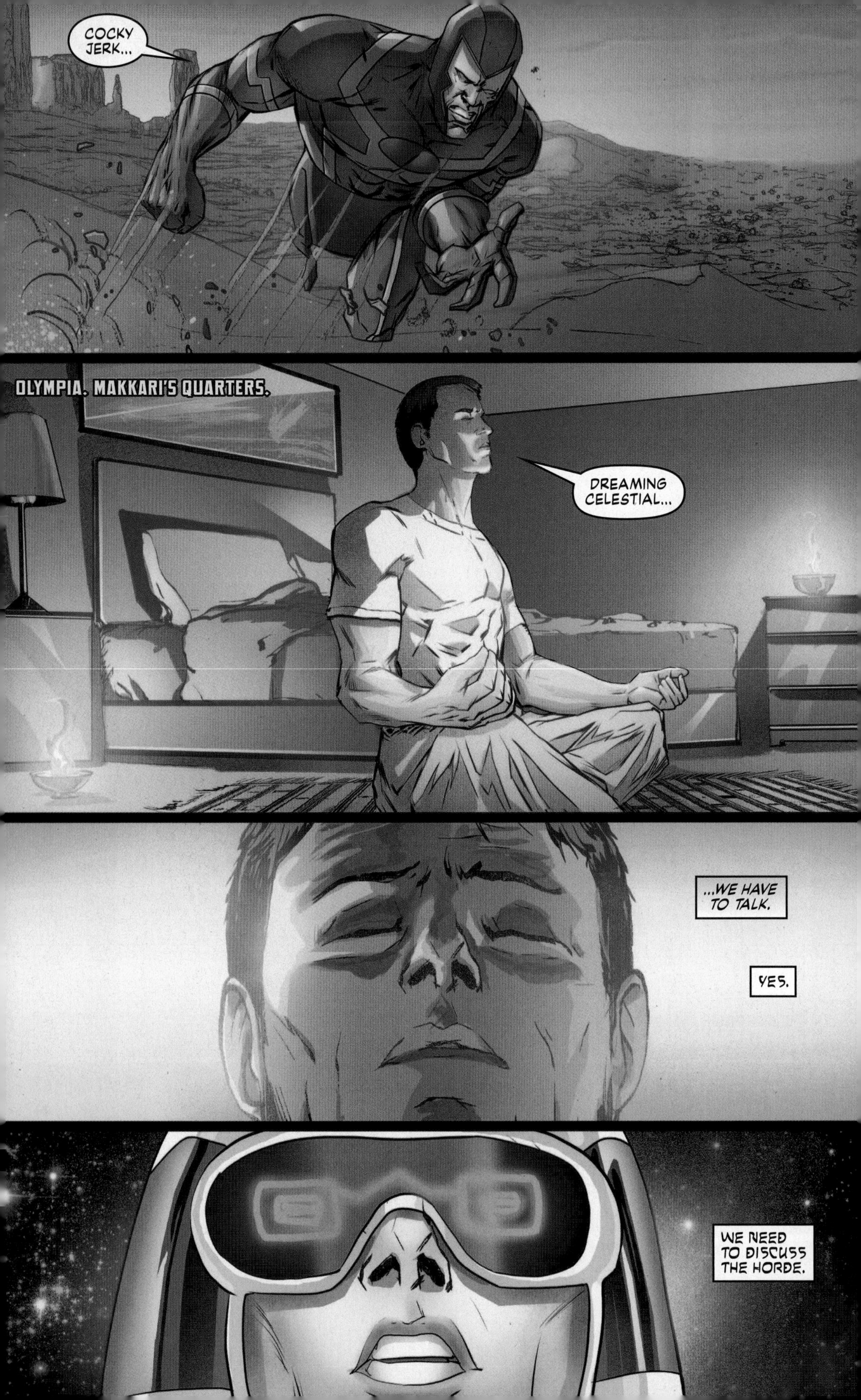
COCKY JERK...
OLYMPIA. MAKKARI'S QUARTERS.
DREAMING CELESTIAL...
...WE HAVE TO TALK.
YES.
WE NEED TO DISCUSS THE HORDE.

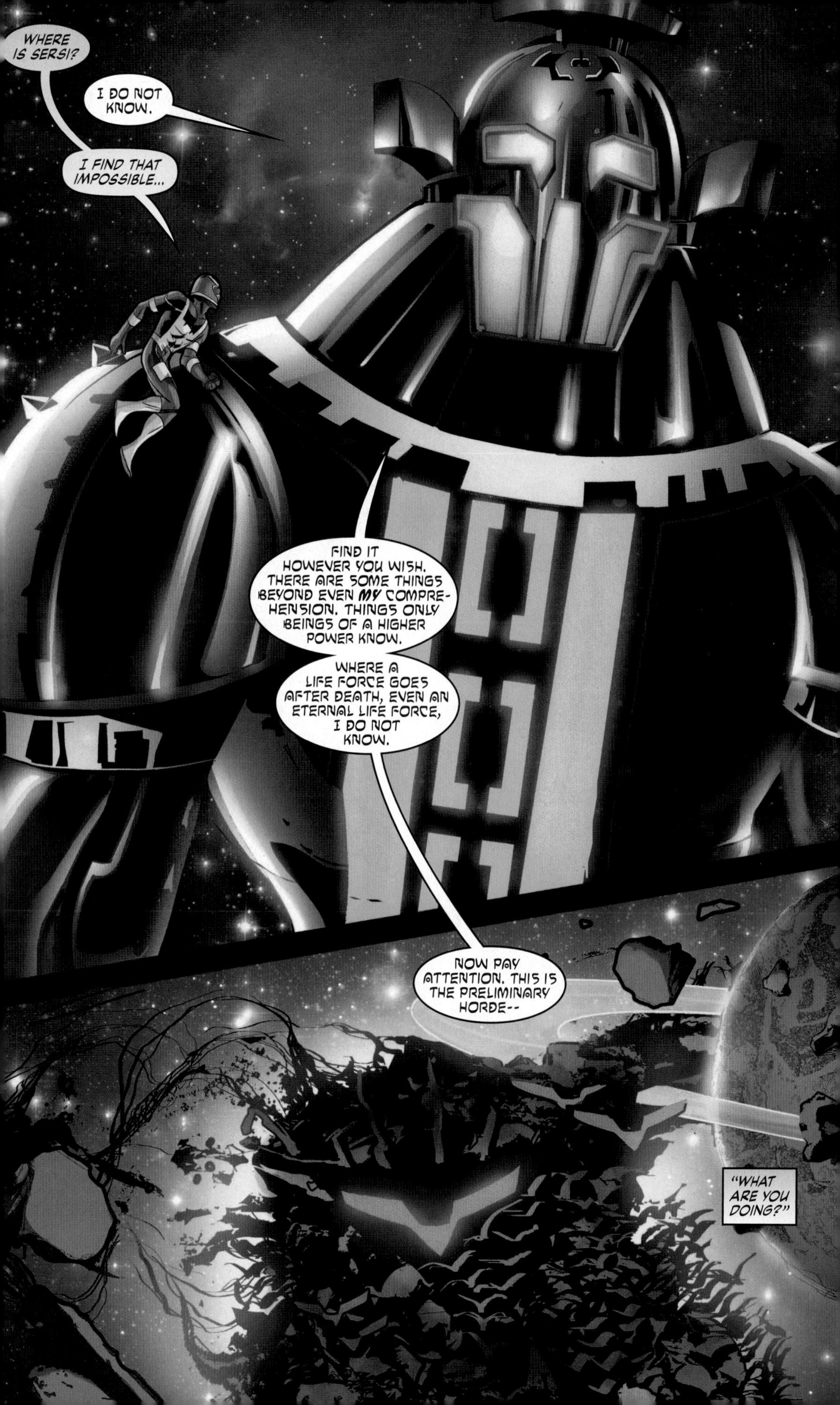
WHERE IS SERSI?
I DO NOT KNOW.
I FIND THAT IMPOSSIBLE...
FIND IT HOWEVER YOU WISH. THERE ARE SOME THINGS BEYOND EVEN MY COMPRE-HENSION. THINGS ONLY BEINGS OF A HIGHER POWER KNOW.
WHERE A LIFE FORCE GOES AFTER DEATH, EVEN AN ETERNAL LIFE FORCE, I DO NOT KNOW.
NOW PAY ATTENTION. THIS IS THE PRELIMINARY HORDE--
"WHAT ARE YOU DOING?"

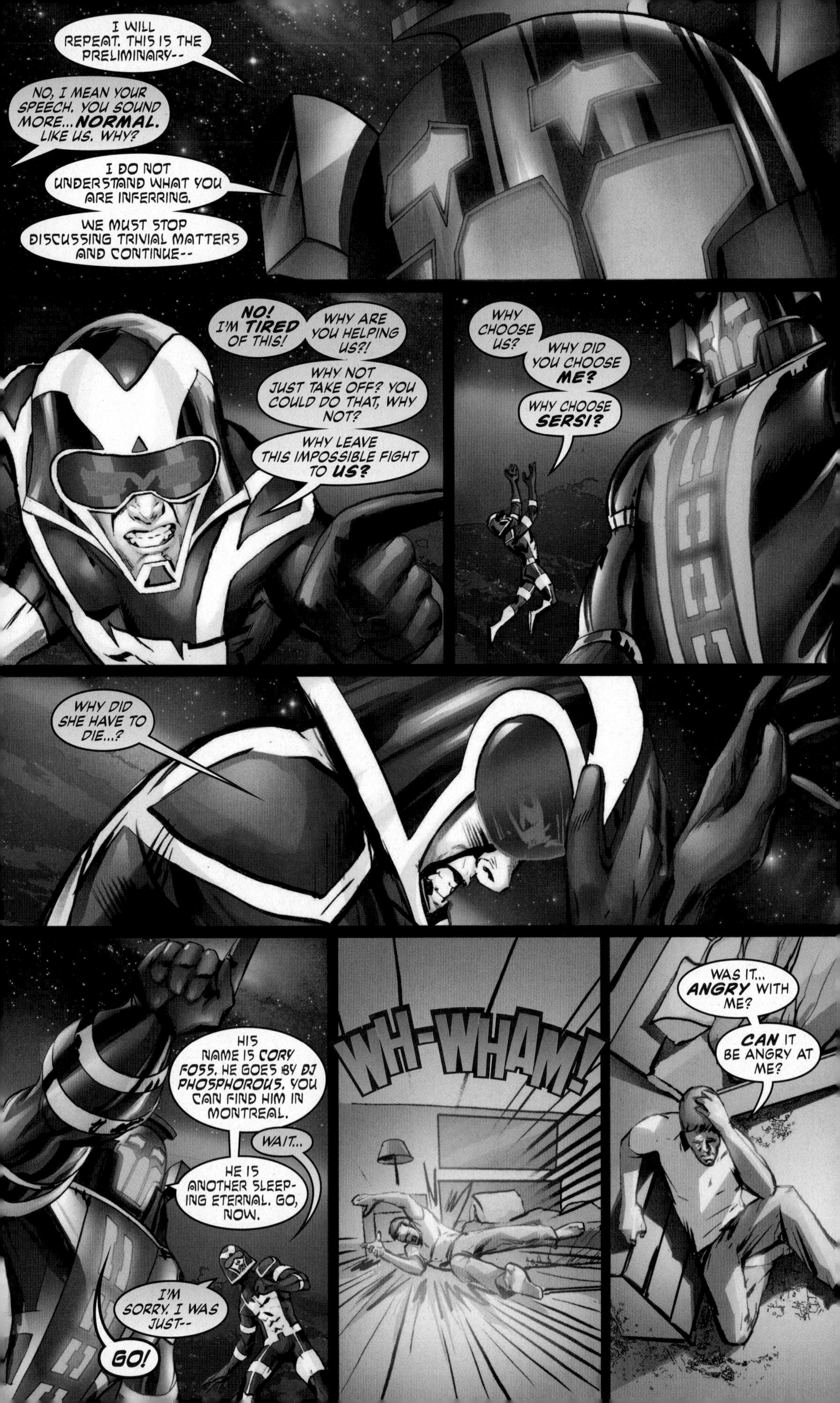
I WILL REPEAT. THIS IS THE PRELIMINARY--
NO, I MEAN YOUR SPEECH. YOU SOUND MORE... NORMAL. LIKE US. WHY?
I DO NOT UNDERSTAND WHAT YOU ARE INFERRING.
WE MUST STOP DISCUSSING TRIVIAL MATTERS AND CONTINUE--
NO! I'M TIRED OF THIS!
WHY ARE YOU HELPING US?!
WHY NOT JUST TAKE OFF? YOU COULD DO THAT, WHY NOT?
WHY LEAVE THIS IMPOSSIBLE FIGHT TO US?
WHY CHOOSE US?
WHY DID YOU CHOOSE ME?
WHY CHOOSE SERSI?
WHY DID SHE HAVE TO DIE...?
HIS NAME IS CORY FOSS. HE GOES BY DJ PHOSPHOROUS. YOU CAN FIND HIM IN MONTREAL.
WAIT...
HE IS ANOTHER SLEEPING ETERNAL. GO, NOW.
I'M SORRY. I WAS JUST--
GO!
WH-WHAM!
WAS IT... ANGRY WITH ME?
CAN IT BE ANGRY AT ME?

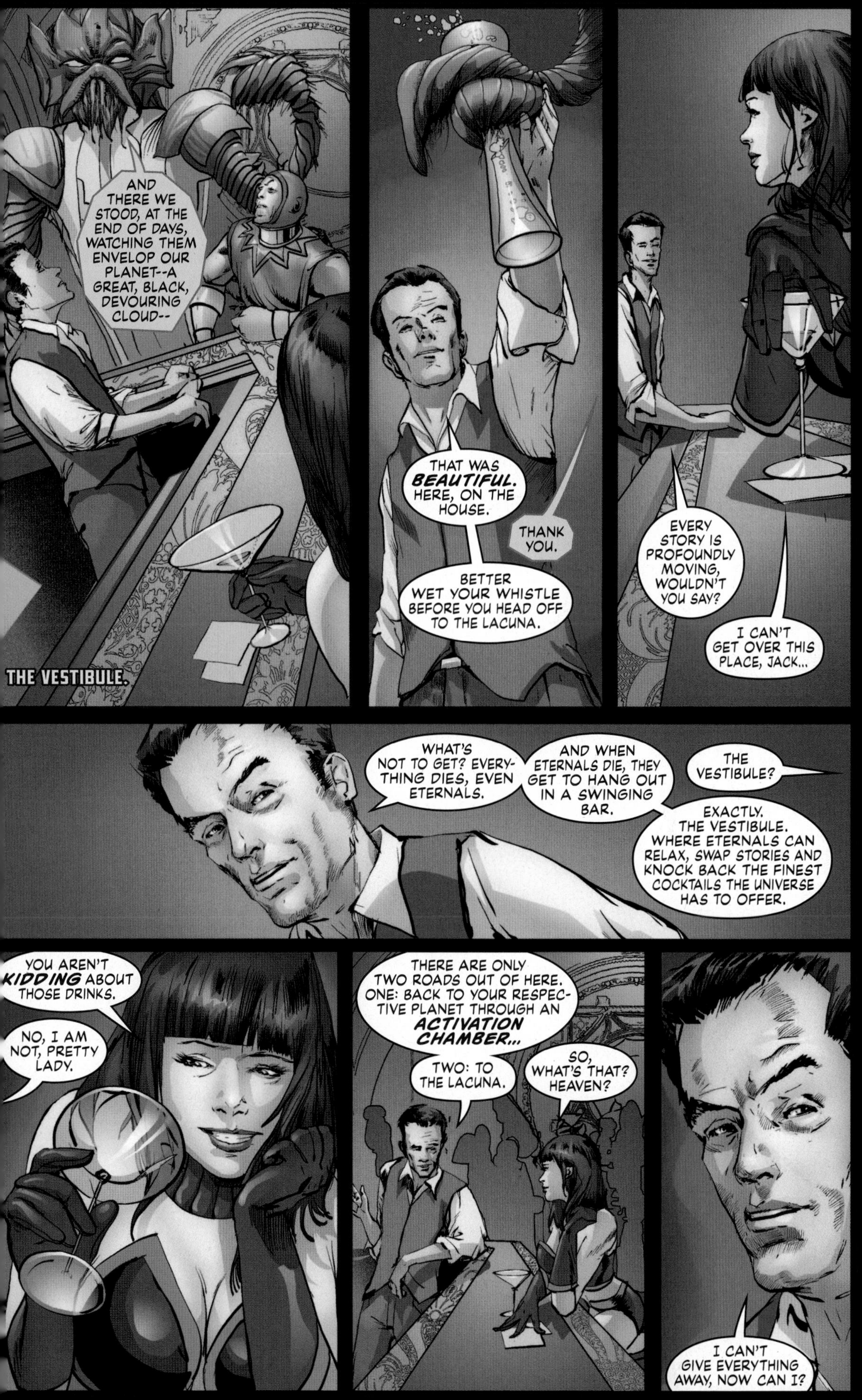
AND THERE WE STOOD, AT THE END OF DAYS, WATCHING THEM ENVELOP OUR PLANET--A GREAT, BLACK, DEVOURING CLOUD--
THE VESTIBULE.
THAT WAS BEAUTIFUL. HERE, ON THE HOUSE.
THANK YOU.
BETTER WET YOUR WHISTLE BEFORE YOU HEAD OFF TO THE LACUNA.
EVERY STORY IS PROFOUNDLY MOVING, WOULDN'T YOU SAY?
I CAN'T GET OVER THIS PLACE, JACK...
WHAT'S NOT TO GET? EVERY-THING DIES, EVEN ETERNALS.
AND WHEN ETERNALS DIE, THEY GET TO HANG OUT IN A SWINGING BAR.
THE VESTIBULE?
EXACTLY. THE VESTIBULE. WHERE ETERNALS CAN RELAX, SWAP STORIES AND KNOCK BACK THE FINEST COCKTAILS THE UNIVERSE HAS TO OFFER.
YOU AREN'T KIDDING ABOUT THOSE DRINKS.
NO, I AM NOT, PRETTY LADY.
THERE ARE ONLY TWO ROADS OUT OF HERE. ONE: BACK TO YOUR RESPEC-TIVE PLANET THROUGH AN ACTIVATION CHAMBER...
TWO: TO THE LACUNA.
SO, WHAT'S THAT? HEAVEN?
I CAN'T GIVE EVERYTHING AWAY, NOW CAN I?

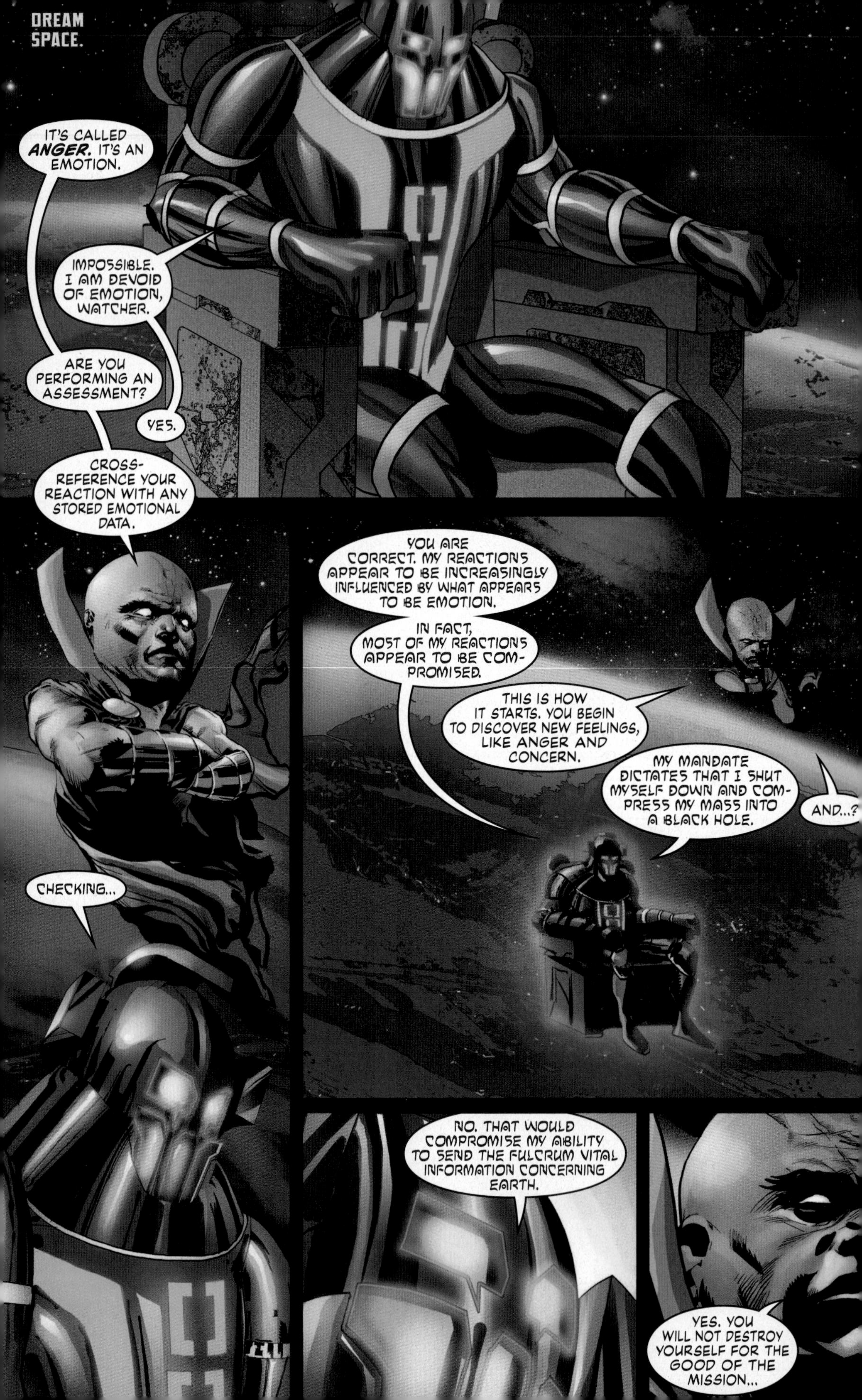
DREAM SPACE.
IT'S CALLED ANGER. IT'S AN EMOTION.
IMPOSSIBLE. I AM DEVOID OF EMOTION, WATCHER.
ARE YOU PERFORMING AN ASSESSMENT?
YES.
CROSS-REFERENCE YOUR REACTION WITH ANY STORED EMOTIONAL DATA.
CHECKING...
YOU ARE CORRECT. MY REACTIONS APPEAR TO BE INCREASINGLY INFLUENCED BY WHAT APPEARS TO BE EMOTION.
IN FACT, MOST OF MY REACTIONS APPEAR TO BE COMPROMISED.
THIS IS HOW IT STARTS. YOU BEGIN TO DISCOVER NEW FEELINGS, LIKE ANGER AND CONCERN.
MY MANDATE DICTATES THAT I SHUT MYSELF DOWN AND COMPRESS MY MASS INTO A BLACK HOLE.
AND...?
NO. THAT WOULD COMPROMISE MY ABILITY TO SEND THE FULCRUM VITAL INFORMATION CONCERNING EARTH.
YES. YOU WILL NOT DESTROY YOURSELF FOR THE GOOD OF THE MISSION...

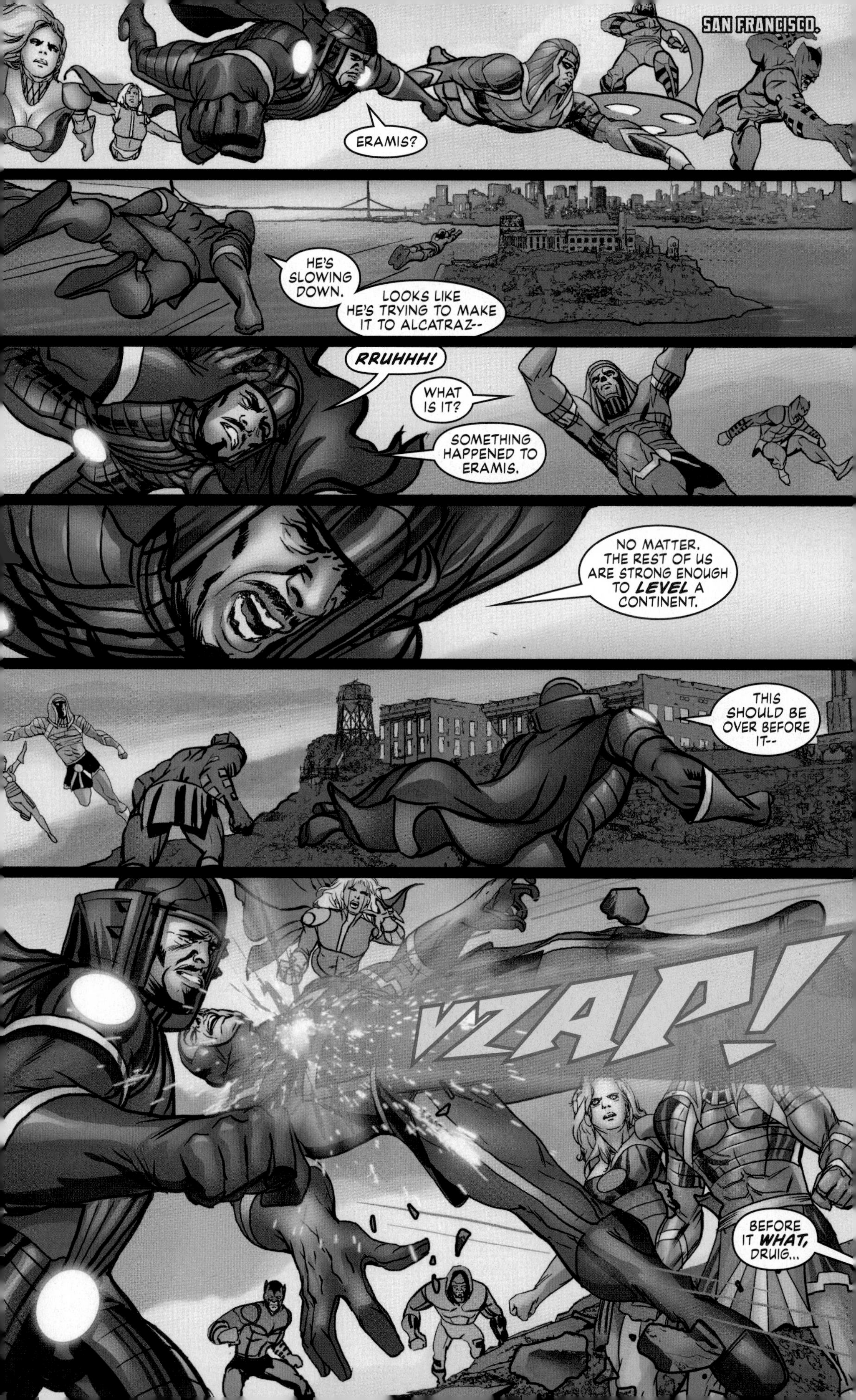
SAN FRANCISCO.
ERAMIS?
HE'S SLOWING DOWN.
LOOKS LIKE HE'S TRYING TO MAKE IT TO ALCATRAZ--
RRUHHH!
WHAT IS IT?
SOMETHING HAPPENED TO ERAMIS.
NO MATTER. THE REST OF US ARE STRONG ENOUGH TO LEVEL A CONTINENT.
THIS SHOULD BE OVER BEFORE IT--
VZAP!
BEFORE IT WHAT, DRUIG...

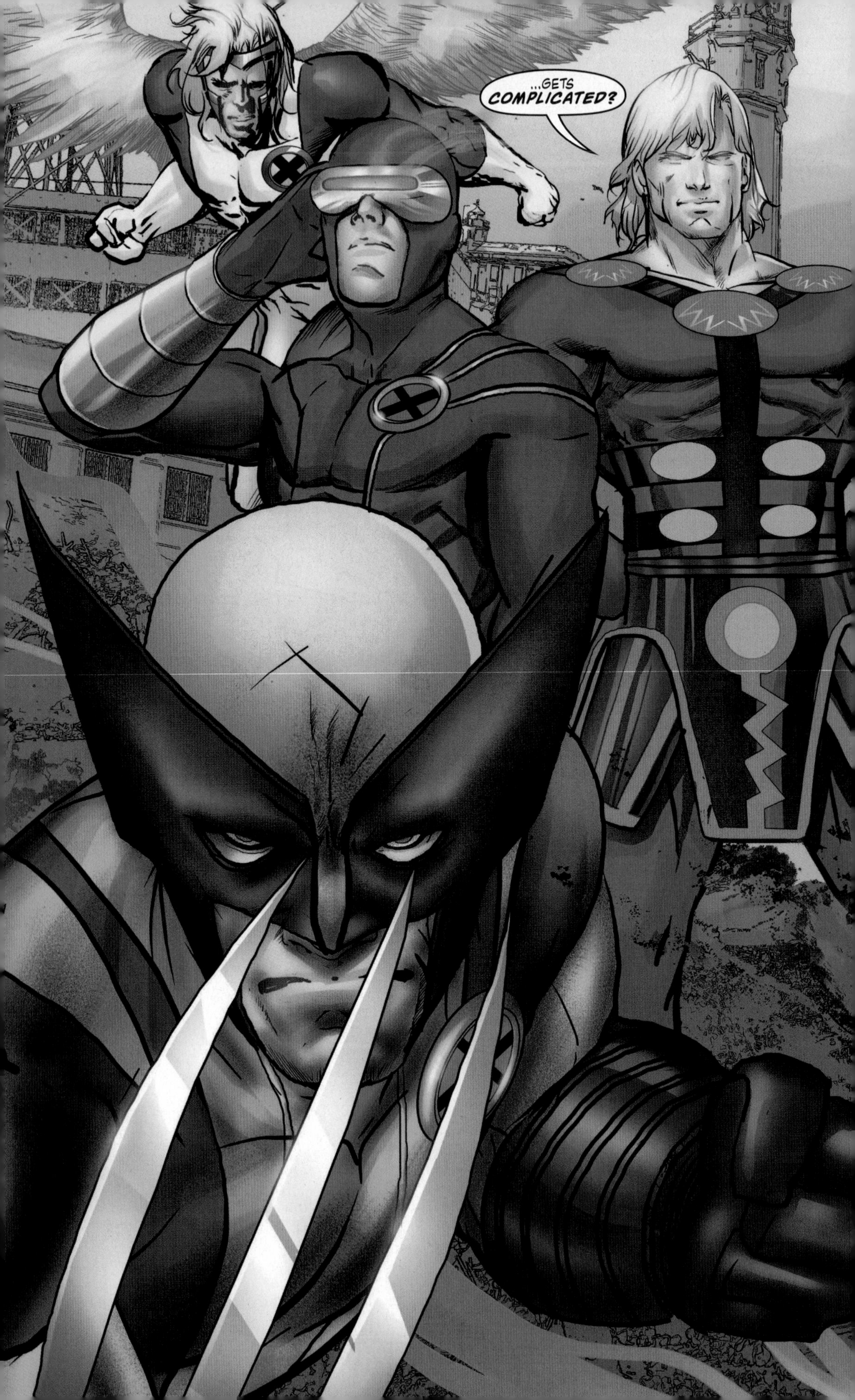
...GETS COMPLICATED?

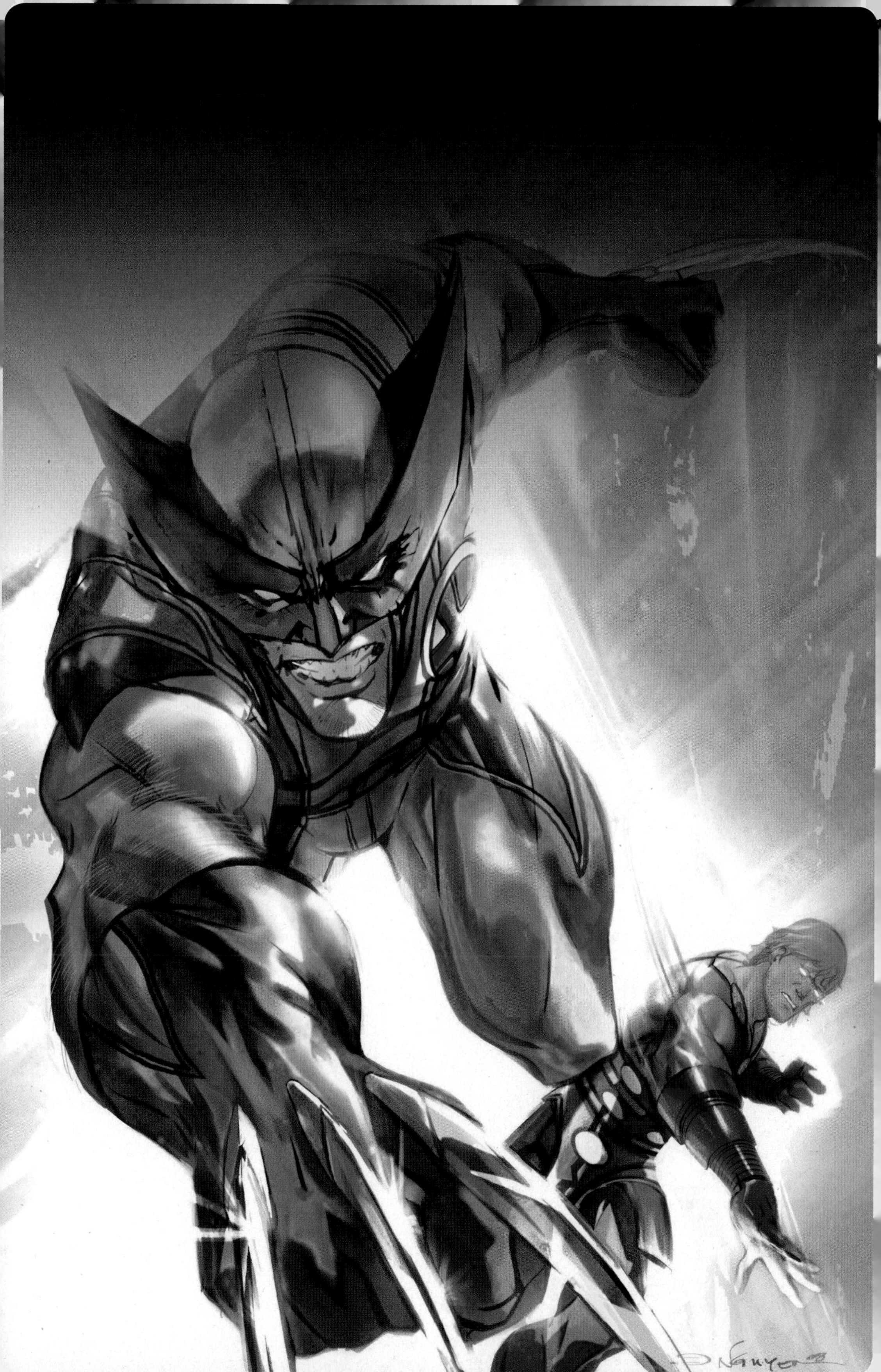

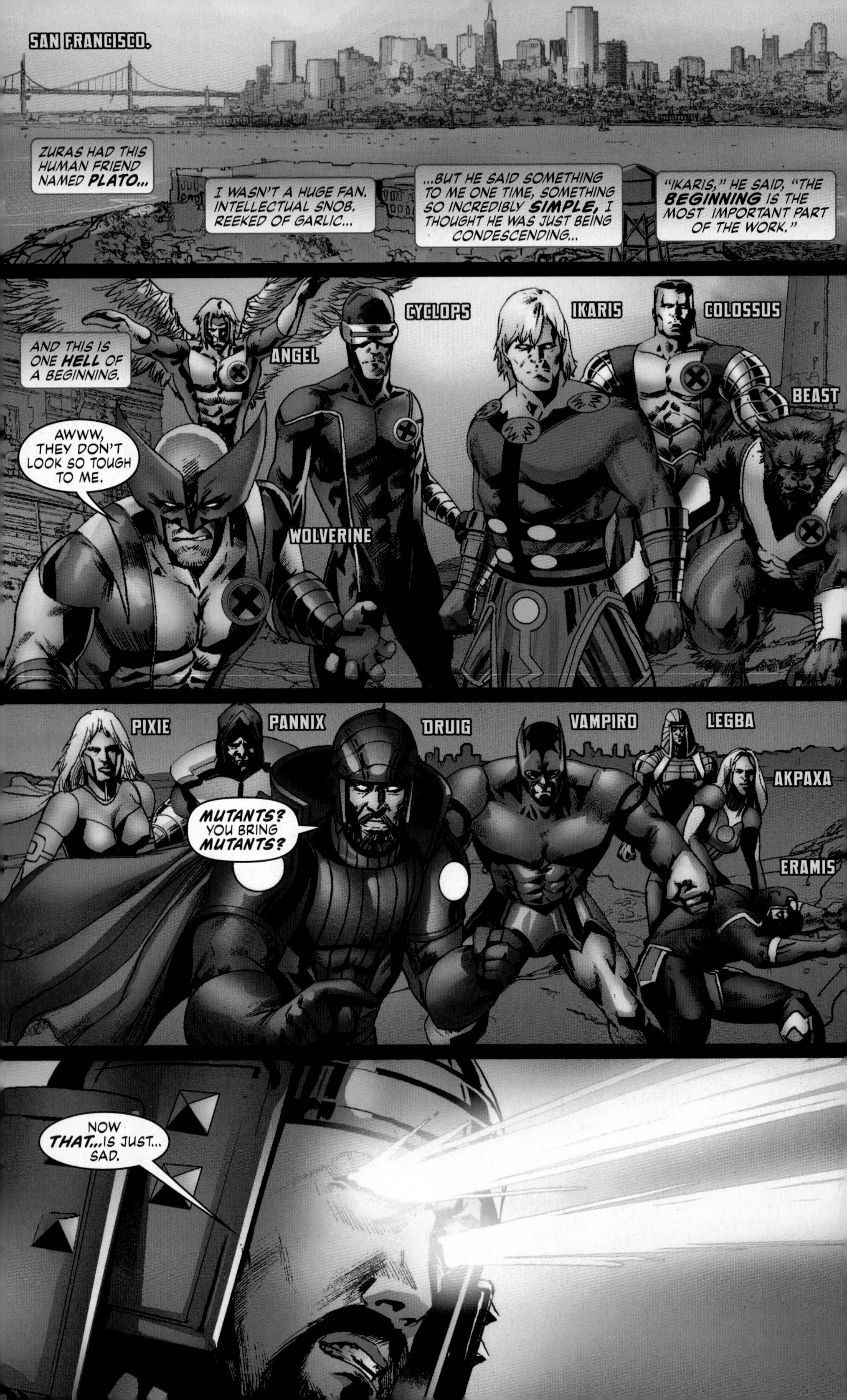
SAN FRANCISCO.
ZURAS HAD THIS HUMAN FRIEND NAMED PLATO...
I WASN'T A HUGE FAN. INTELLECTUAL SNOB. REEKED OF GARLIC...
...BUT HE SAID SOMETHING TO ME ONE TIME, SOMETHING SO INCREDIBLY SIMPLE, I THOUGHT HE WAS JUST BEING CONDESCENDING...
"IKARIS," HE SAID, "THE BEGINNING IS THE MOST IMPORTANT PART OF THE WORK."
AND THIS IS ONE HELL OF A BEGINNING.
CYCLOPS
IKARIS
COLOSSUS
ANGEL
BEAST
AWWW, THEY DON'T LOOK SO TOUGH TO ME.
WOLVERINE
PIXIE
PANNIX
DRUIG
VAMPIRO
LEGBA
AKPAXA
MUTANTS? YOU BRING MUTANTS?
ERAMIS
NOW THAT...IS JUST... SAD.

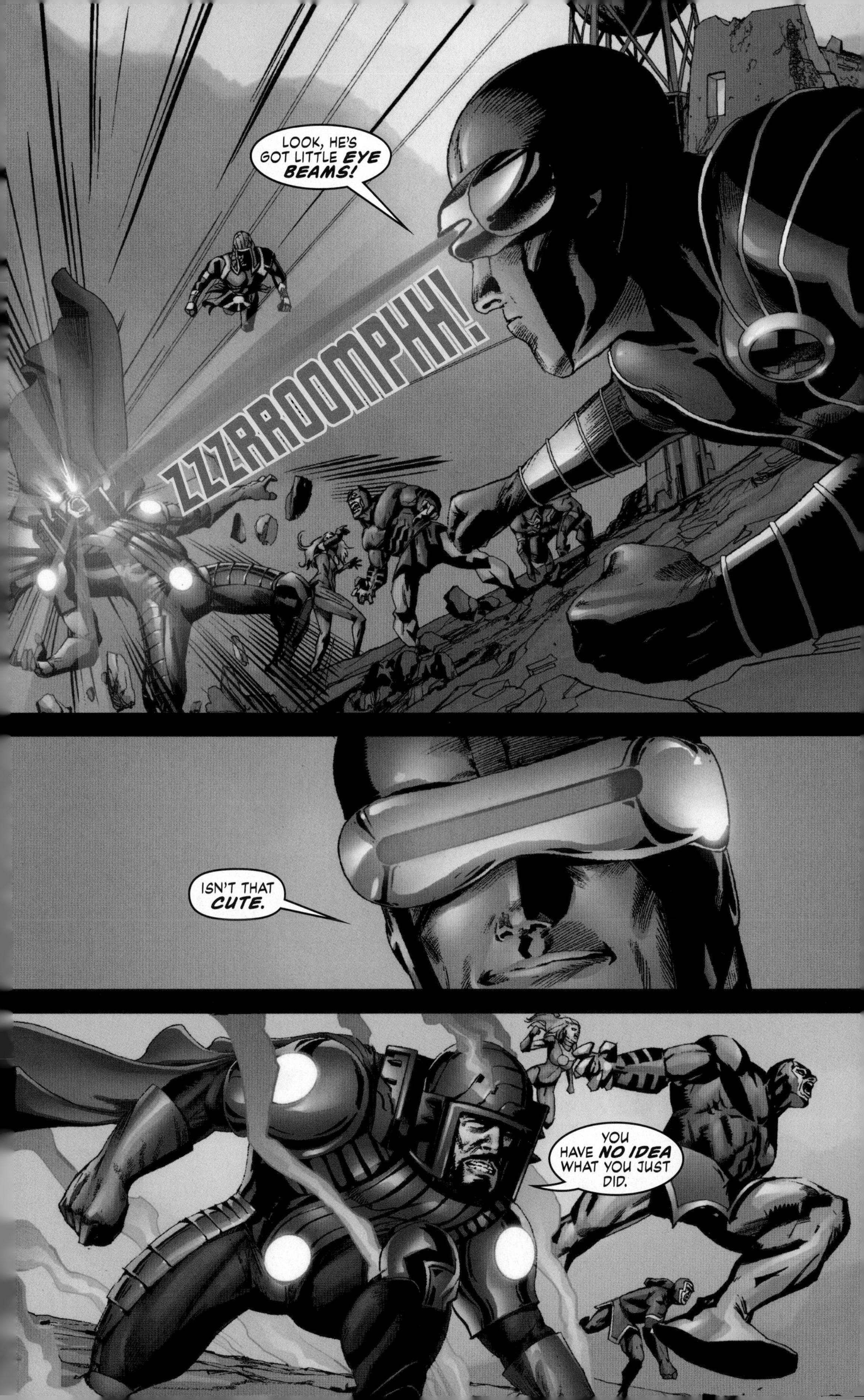
LOOK, HE'S GOT LITTLE EYE BEAMS!
ZZZRRROOMPHH!
ISN'T THAT CUTE.
YOU HAVE NO IDEA WHAT YOU JUST DID.

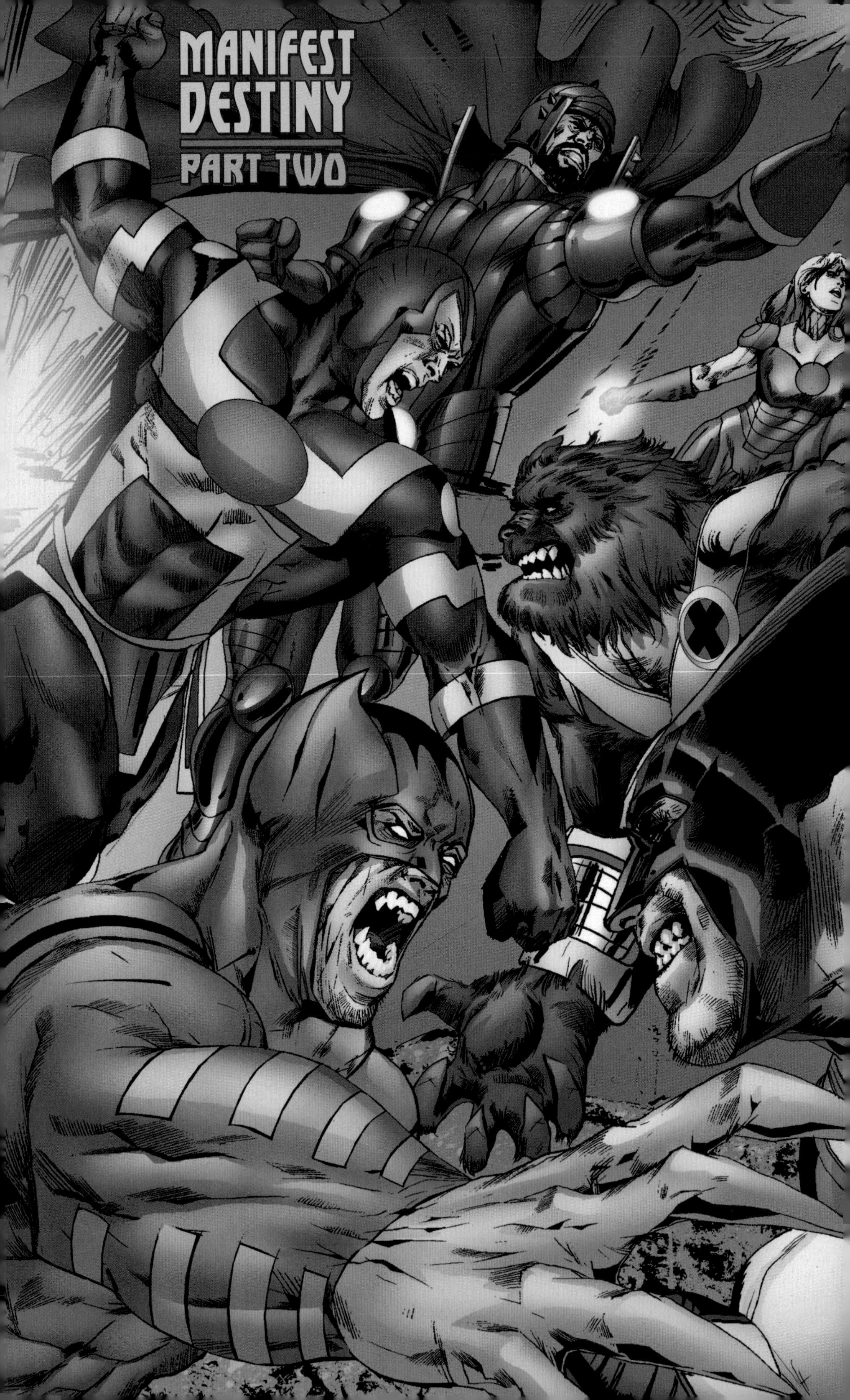
MANIFEST DESTINY
PART TWO

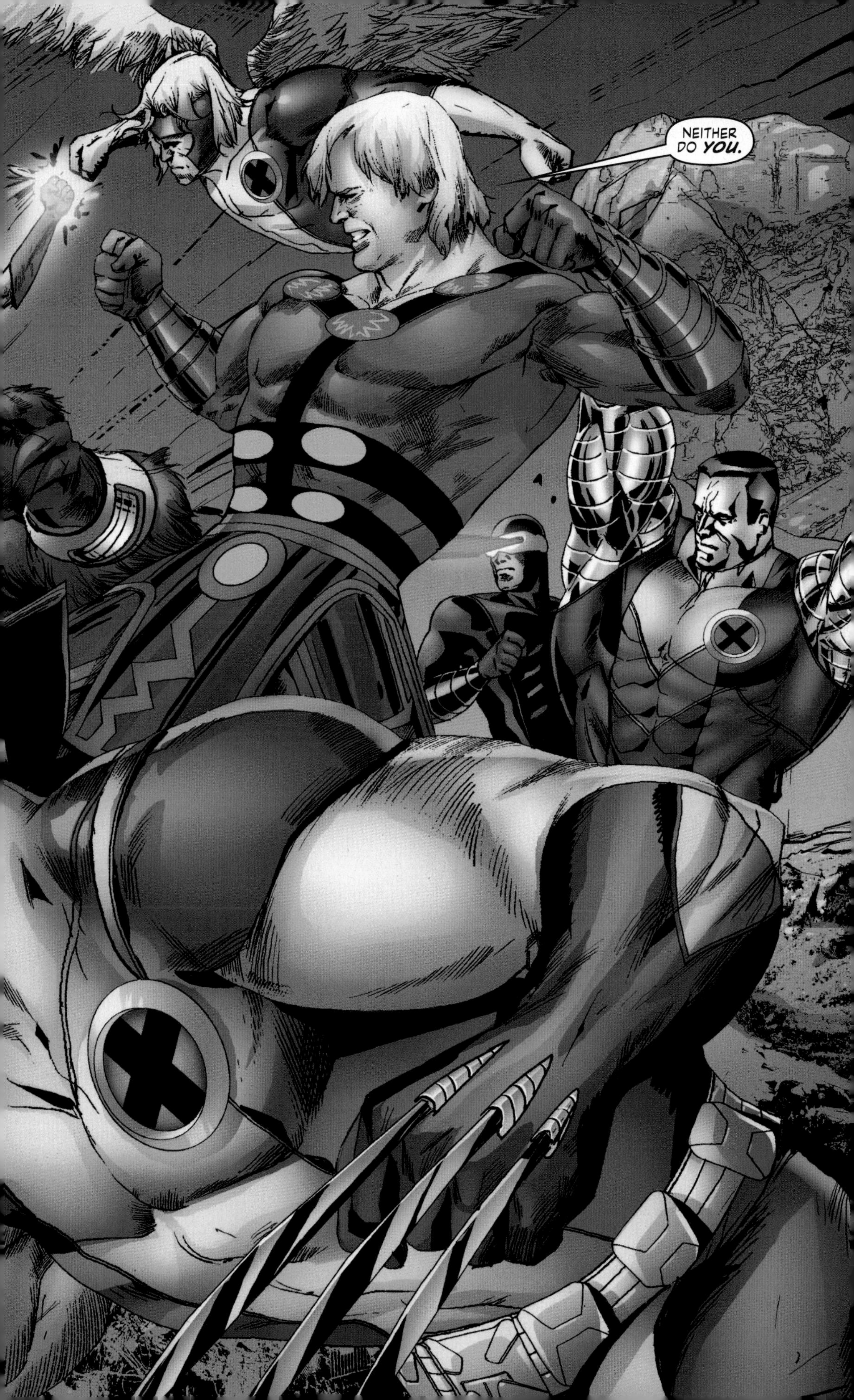
NEITHER DO YOU.

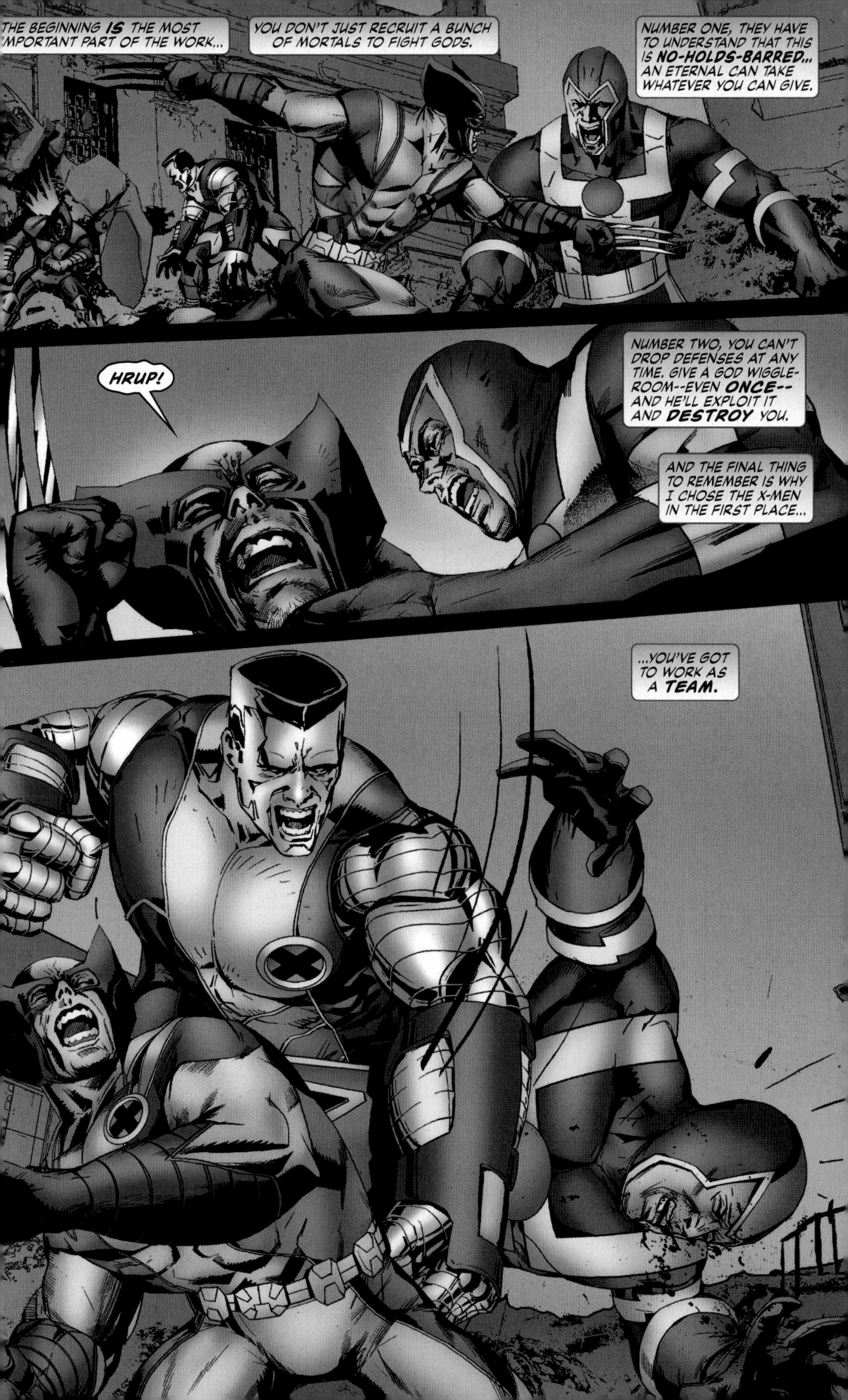
THE BEGINNING IS THE MOST IMPORTANT PART OF THE WORK...
YOU DON'T JUST RECRUIT A BUNCH OF MORTALS TO FIGHT GODS.
NUMBER ONE, THEY HAVE TO UNDERSTAND THAT THIS IS NO-HOLDS-BARRED... AN ETERNAL CAN TAKE WHATEVER YOU CAN GIVE.
HRUP!
NUMBER TWO, YOU CAN'T DROP DEFENSES AT ANY TIME. GIVE A GOD WIGGLE-ROOM--EVEN ONCE--AND HE'LL EXPLOIT IT AND DESTROY YOU.
AND THE FINAL THING TO REMEMBER IS WHY I CHOSE THE X-MEN IN THE FIRST PLACE...
...YOU'VE GOT TO WORK AS A TEAM.

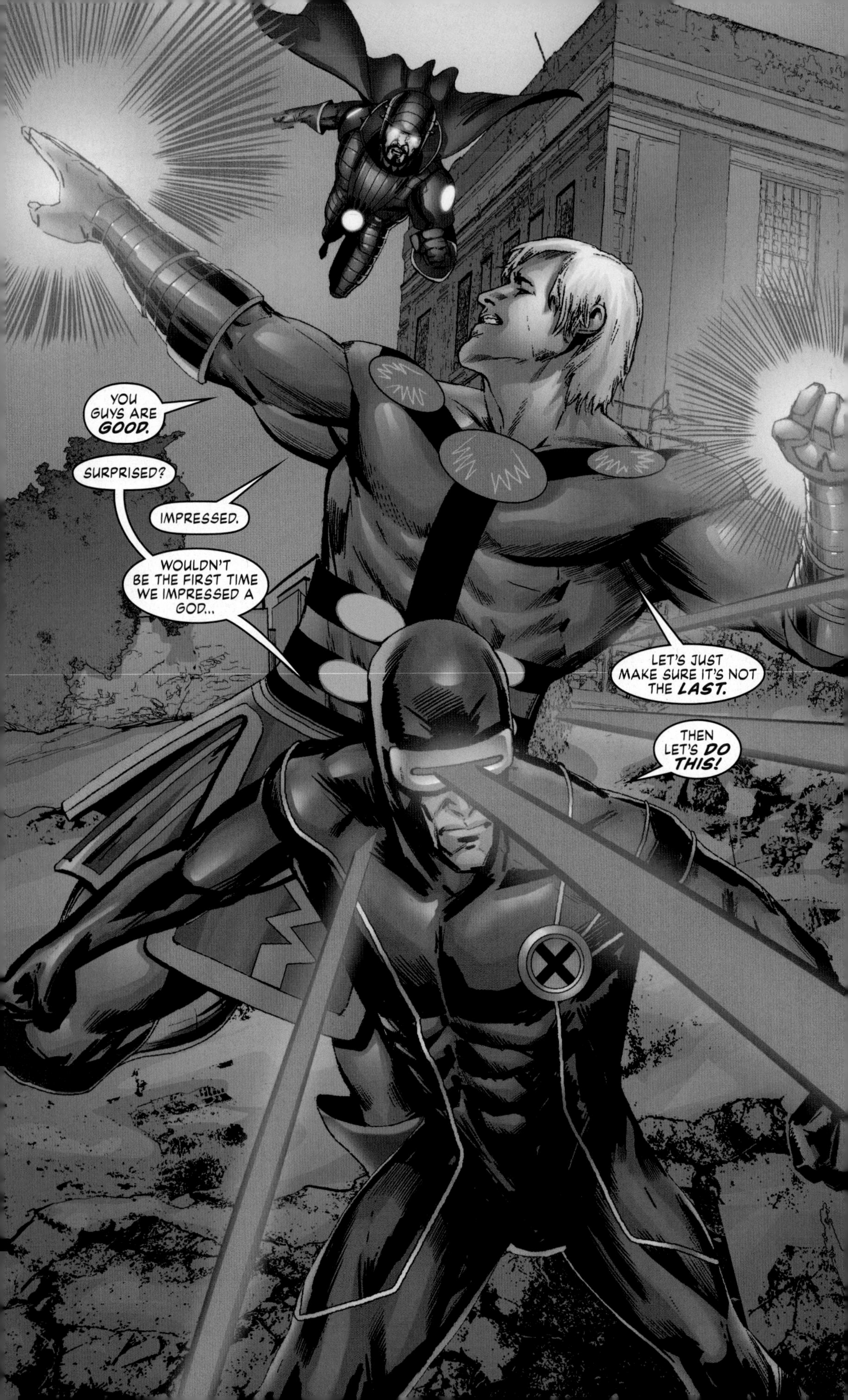

YOU GUYS ARE *GOOD.*
SURPRISED?
IMPRESSED.
WOULDN'T BE THE FIRST TIME WE IMPRESSED A GOD...
LET'S JUST MAKE SURE IT'S NOT THE *LAST.*
THEN LET'S *DO THIS!*

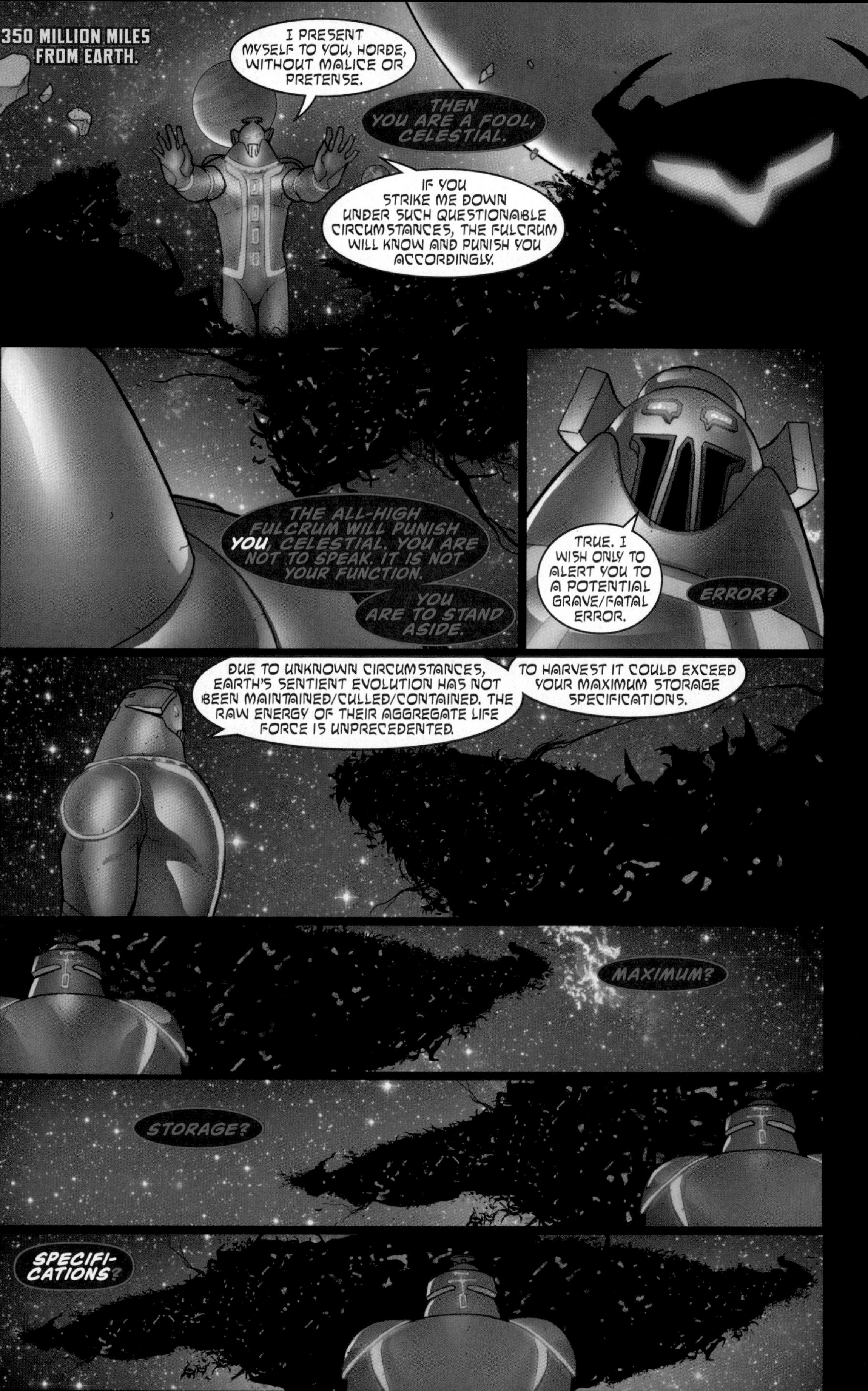
350 MILLION MILES FROM EARTH.
I PRESENT MYSELF TO YOU, HORDE, WITHOUT MALICE OR PRETENSE.
THEN YOU ARE A FOOL, CELESTIAL.
IF YOU STRIKE ME DOWN UNDER SUCH QUESTIONABLE CIRCUMSTANCES, THE FULCRUM WILL KNOW AND PUNISH YOU ACCORDINGLY.
THE ALL-HIGH FULCRUM WILL PUNISH YOU, CELESTIAL. YOU ARE NOT TO SPEAK. IT IS NOT YOUR FUNCTION.
YOU ARE TO STAND ASIDE.
TRUE. I WISH ONLY TO ALERT YOU TO A POTENTIAL GRAVE/FATAL ERROR.
ERROR?
DUE TO UNKNOWN CIRCUMSTANCES, EARTH'S SENTIENT EVOLUTION HAS NOT BEEN MAINTAINED/CULLED/CONTAINED. THE RAW ENERGY OF THEIR AGGREGATE LIFE FORCE IS UNPRECEDENTED.
TO HARVEST IT COULD EXCEED YOUR MAXIMUM STORAGE SPECIFICATIONS.
MAXIMUM?
STORAGE?
SPECIFI-CATIONS?

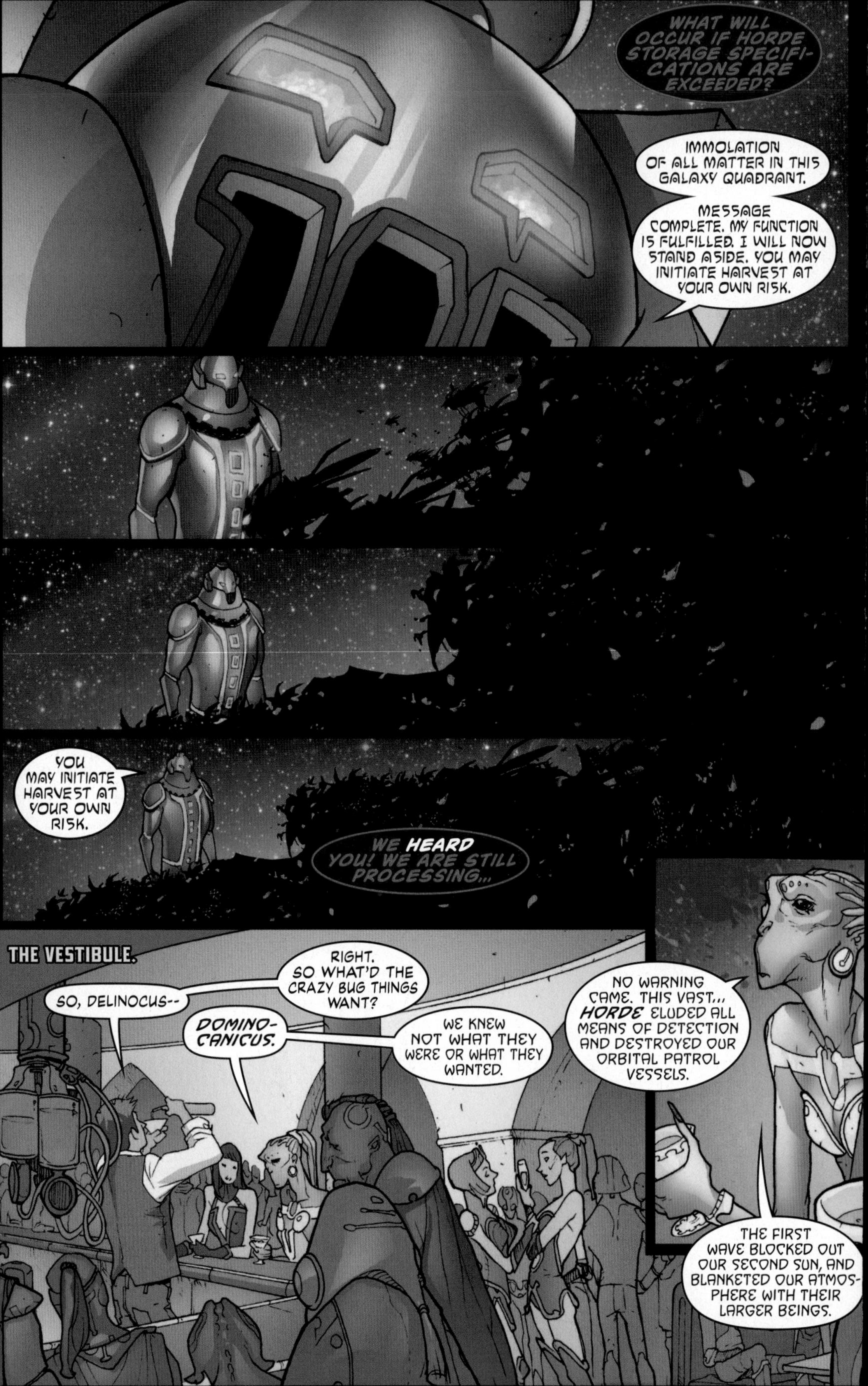
WHAT WILL OCCUR IF HORDE STORAGE SPECIFICATIONS ARE EXCEEDED?
IMMOLATION OF ALL MATTER IN THIS GALAXY QUADRANT.
MESSAGE COMPLETE. MY FUNCTION IS FULFILLED. I WILL NOW STAND ASIDE. YOU MAY INITIATE HARVEST AT YOUR OWN RISK.
YOU MAY INITIATE HARVEST AT YOUR OWN RISK.
WE HEARD YOU! WE ARE STILL PROCESSING...
THE VESTIBULE.
SO, DELINOCUS--
RIGHT. SO WHAT'D THE CRAZY BUG THINGS WANT?
DOMINO-CANICUS.
WE KNEW NOT WHAT THEY WERE OR WHAT THEY WANTED.
NO WARNING CAME. THIS VAST... HORDE ELUDED ALL MEANS OF DETECTION AND DESTROYED OUR ORBITAL PATROL VESSELS.
THE FIRST WAVE BLOCKED OUT OUR SECOND SUN, AND BLANKETED OUR ATMOSPHERE WITH THEIR LARGER BEINGS.

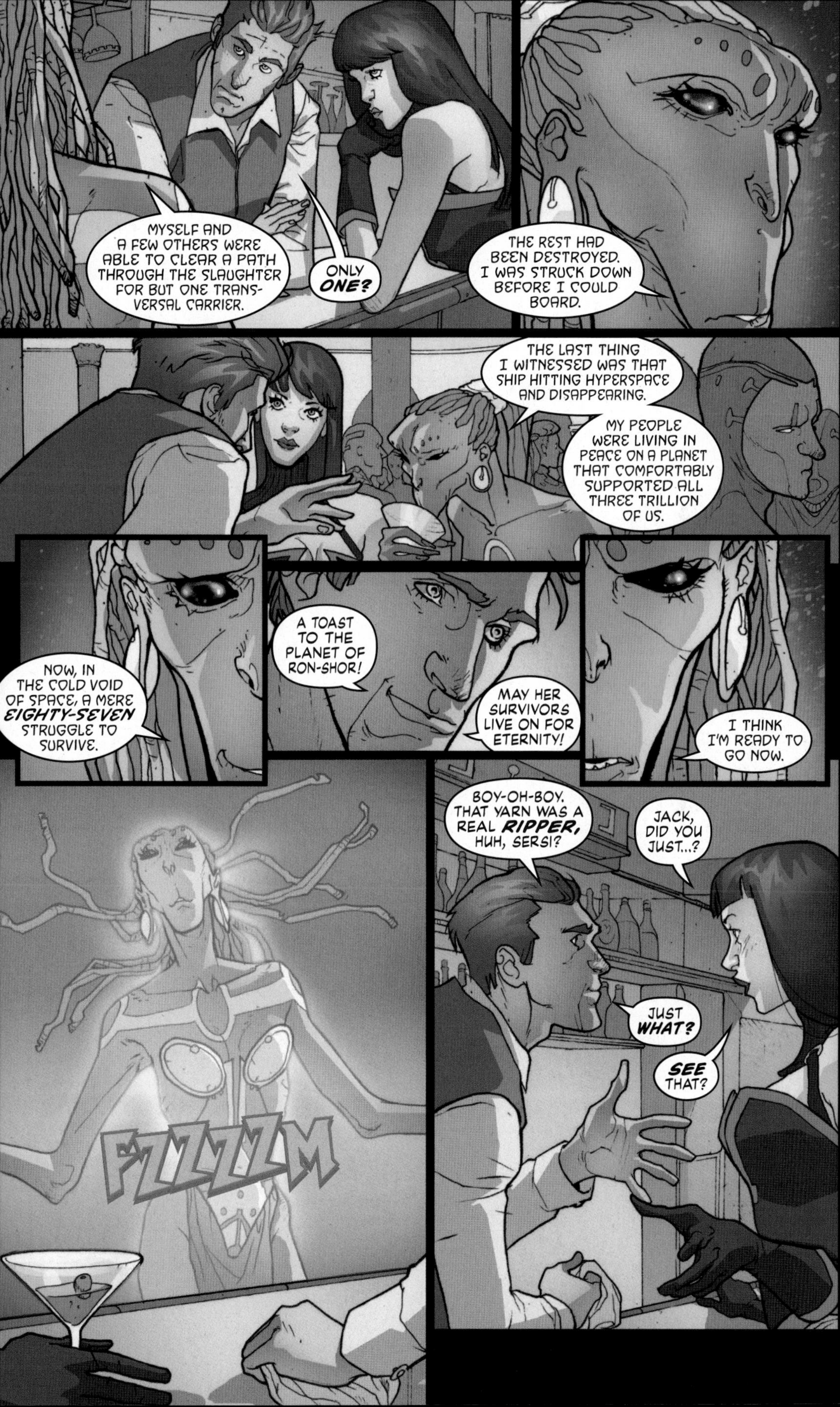
MYSELF AND A FEW OTHERS WERE ABLE TO CLEAR A PATH THROUGH THE SLAUGHTER FOR BUT ONE TRANS-VERSAL CARRIER.
ONLY ONE?
THE REST HAD BEEN DESTROYED. I WAS STRUCK DOWN BEFORE I COULD BOARD.
THE LAST THING I WITNESSED WAS THAT SHIP HITTING HYPERSPACE AND DISAPPEARING.
MY PEOPLE WERE LIVING IN PEACE ON A PLANET THAT COMFORTABLY SUPPORTED ALL THREE TRILLION OF US.
NOW, IN THE COLD VOID OF SPACE, A MERE EIGHTY-SEVEN STRUGGLE TO SURVIVE.
A TOAST TO THE PLANET OF RON-SHOR!
MAY HER SURVIVORS LIVE ON FOR ETERNITY!
I THINK I'M READY TO GO NOW.
FZZZZM
BOY-OH-BOY. THAT YARN WAS A REAL RIPPER, HUH, SERSI?
JACK, DID YOU JUST...?
JUST WHAT?
SEE THAT?

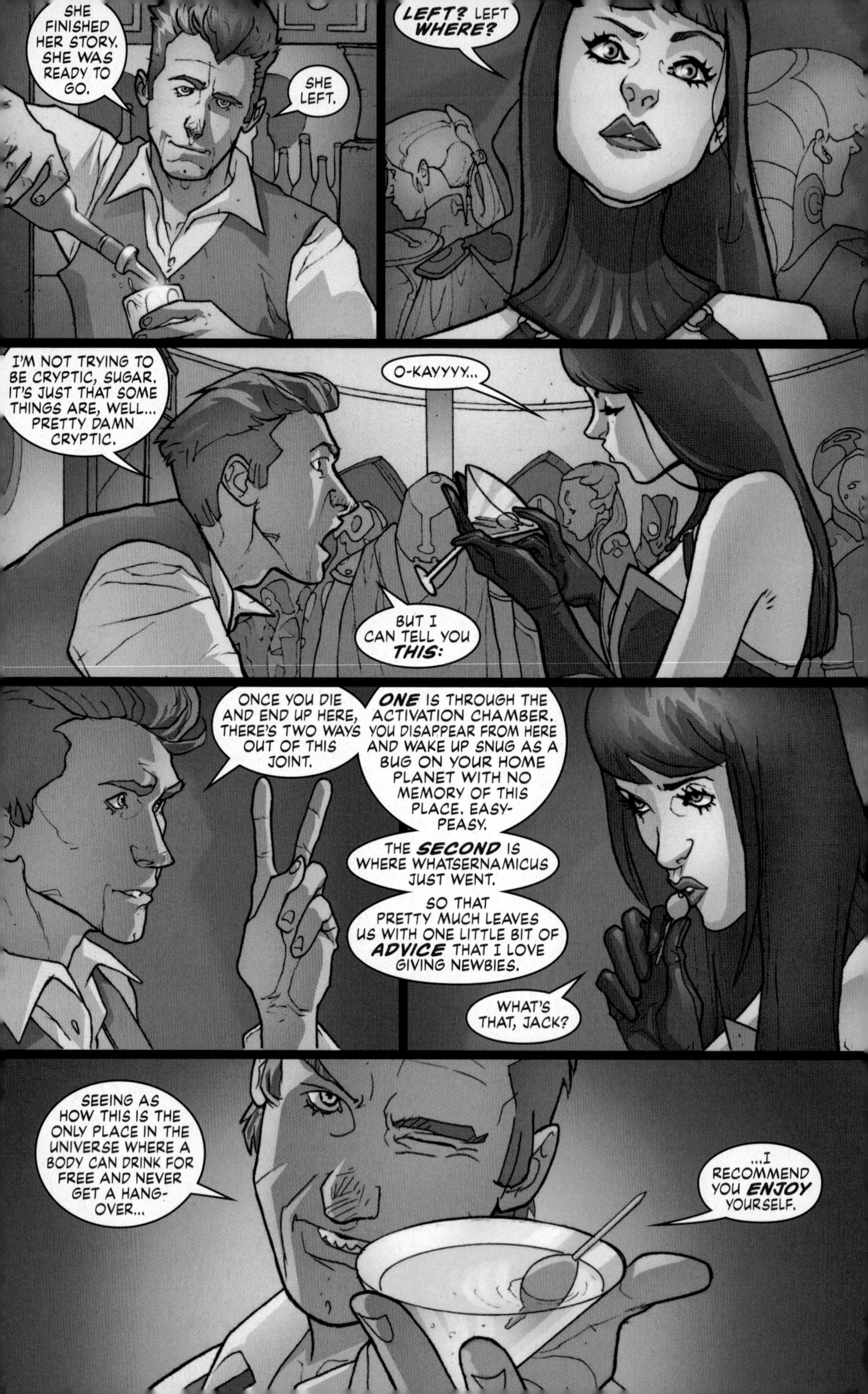
SHE FINISHED HER STORY. SHE WAS READY TO GO.
SHE LEFT.
LEFT? LEFT WHERE?
I'M NOT TRYING TO BE CRYPTIC, SUGAR. IT'S JUST THAT SOME THINGS ARE, WELL... PRETTY DAMN CRYPTIC.
O-KAYYYY...
BUT I CAN TELL YOU THIS:
ONCE YOU DIE AND END UP HERE, THERE'S TWO WAYS OUT OF THIS JOINT.
ONE IS THROUGH THE ACTIVATION CHAMBER. YOU DISAPPEAR FROM HERE AND WAKE UP SNUG AS A BUG ON YOUR HOME PLANET WITH NO MEMORY OF THIS PLACE. EASY-PEASY.
THE SECOND IS WHERE WHATSERNAMICUS JUST WENT.
SO THAT PRETTY MUCH LEAVES US WITH ONE LITTLE BIT OF ADVICE THAT I LOVE GIVING NEWBIES.
WHAT'S THAT, JACK?
SEEING AS HOW THIS IS THE ONLY PLACE IN THE UNIVERSE WHERE A BODY CAN DRINK FOR FREE AND NEVER GET A HANG-OVER...
...I RECOMMEND YOU ENJOY YOURSELF.

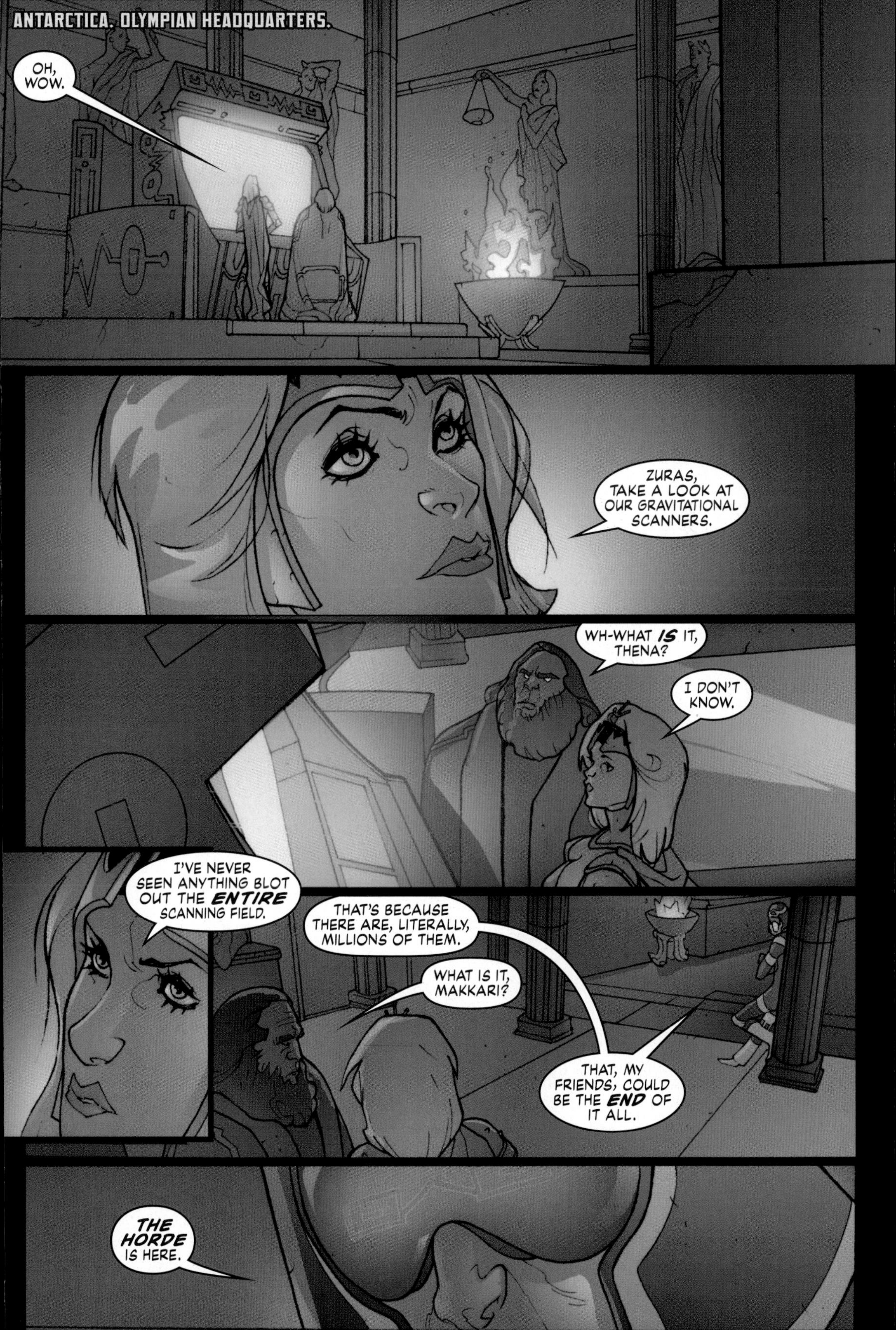
ANTARCTICA. OLYMPIAN HEADQUARTERS.
OH, WOW.
ZURAS, TAKE A LOOK AT OUR GRAVITATIONAL SCANNERS.
WH-WHAT IS IT, THENA?
I DON'T KNOW.
I'VE NEVER SEEN ANYTHING BLOT OUT THE ENTIRE SCANNING FIELD.
THAT'S BECAUSE THERE ARE, LITERALLY, MILLIONS OF THEM.
WHAT IS IT, MAKKARI?
THAT, MY FRIENDS, COULD BE THE END OF IT ALL.
THE HORDE IS HERE.

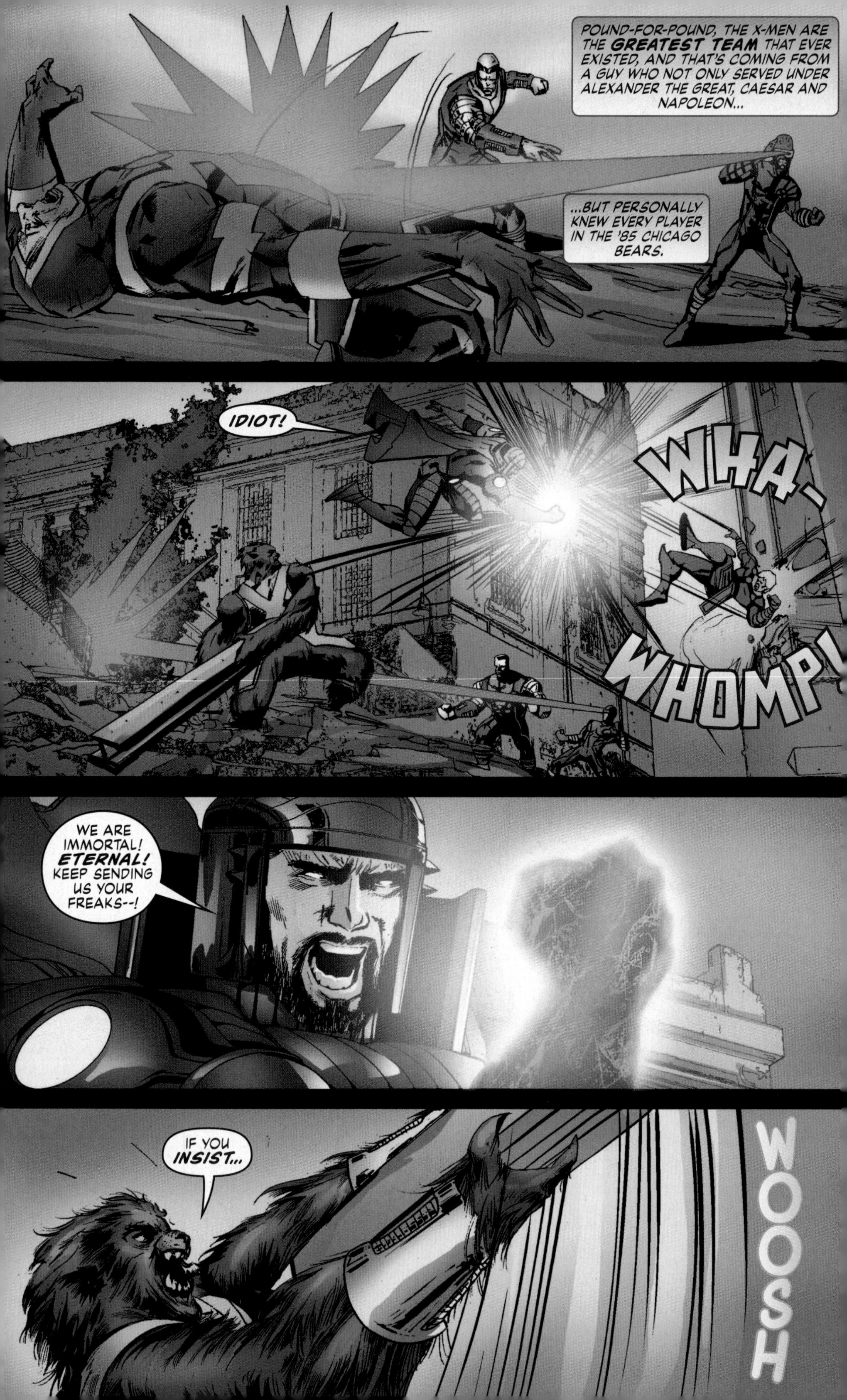
POUND-FOR-POUND, THE X-MEN ARE THE **GREATEST TEAM** THAT EVER EXISTED, AND THAT'S COMING FROM A GUY WHO NOT ONLY SERVED UNDER ALEXANDER THE GREAT, CAESAR AND NAPOLEON...
...BUT PERSONALLY KNEW EVERY PLAYER IN THE '85 CHICAGO BEARS.
IDIOT!
WHA-
WHOMP!
WE ARE IMMORTAL! **ETERNAL!** KEEP SENDING US YOUR FREAKS--!
IF YOU **INSIST...**
WOOSH

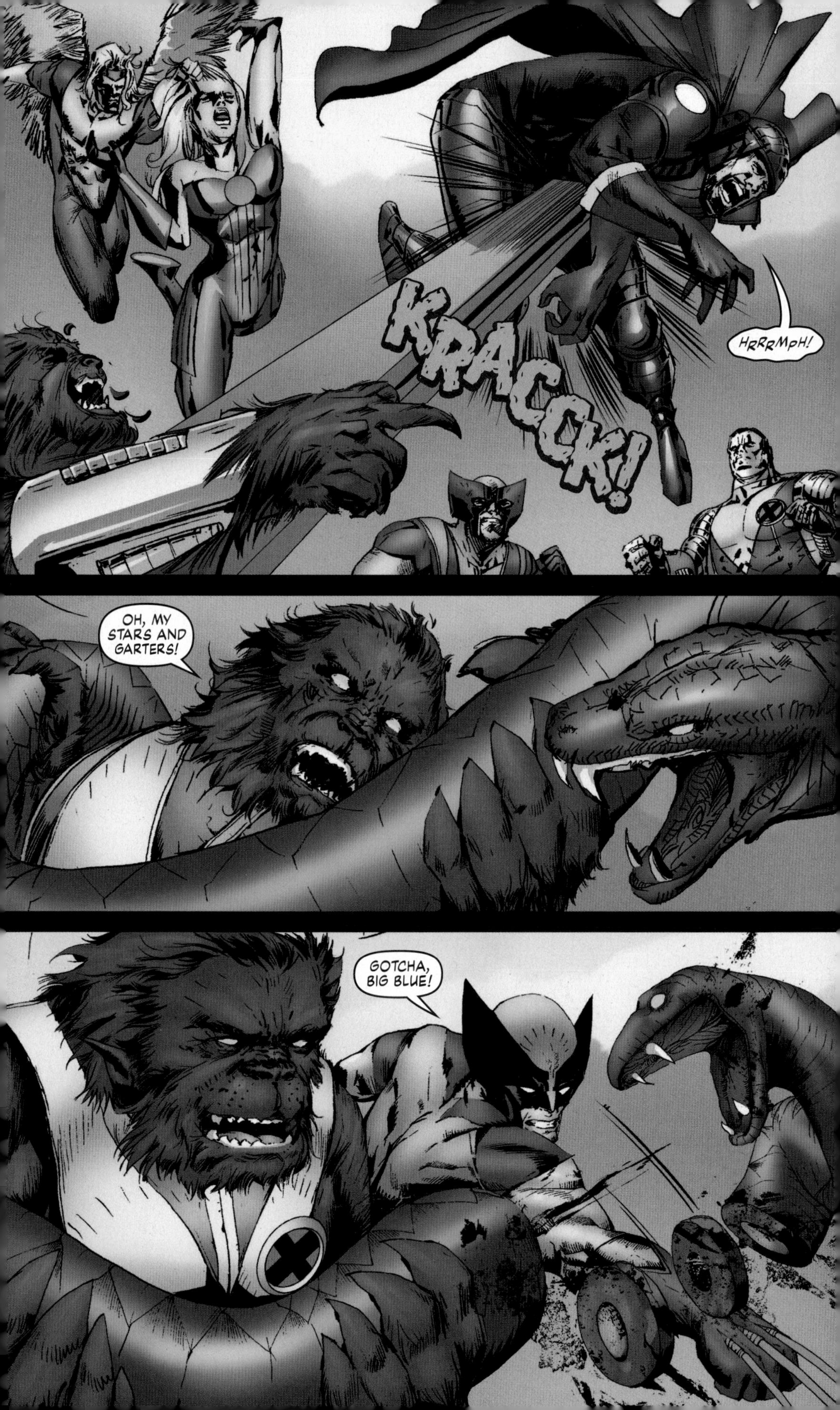
KRACCK!
HRRRMPH!
OH, MY STARS AND GARTERS!
GOTCHA, BIG BLUE!

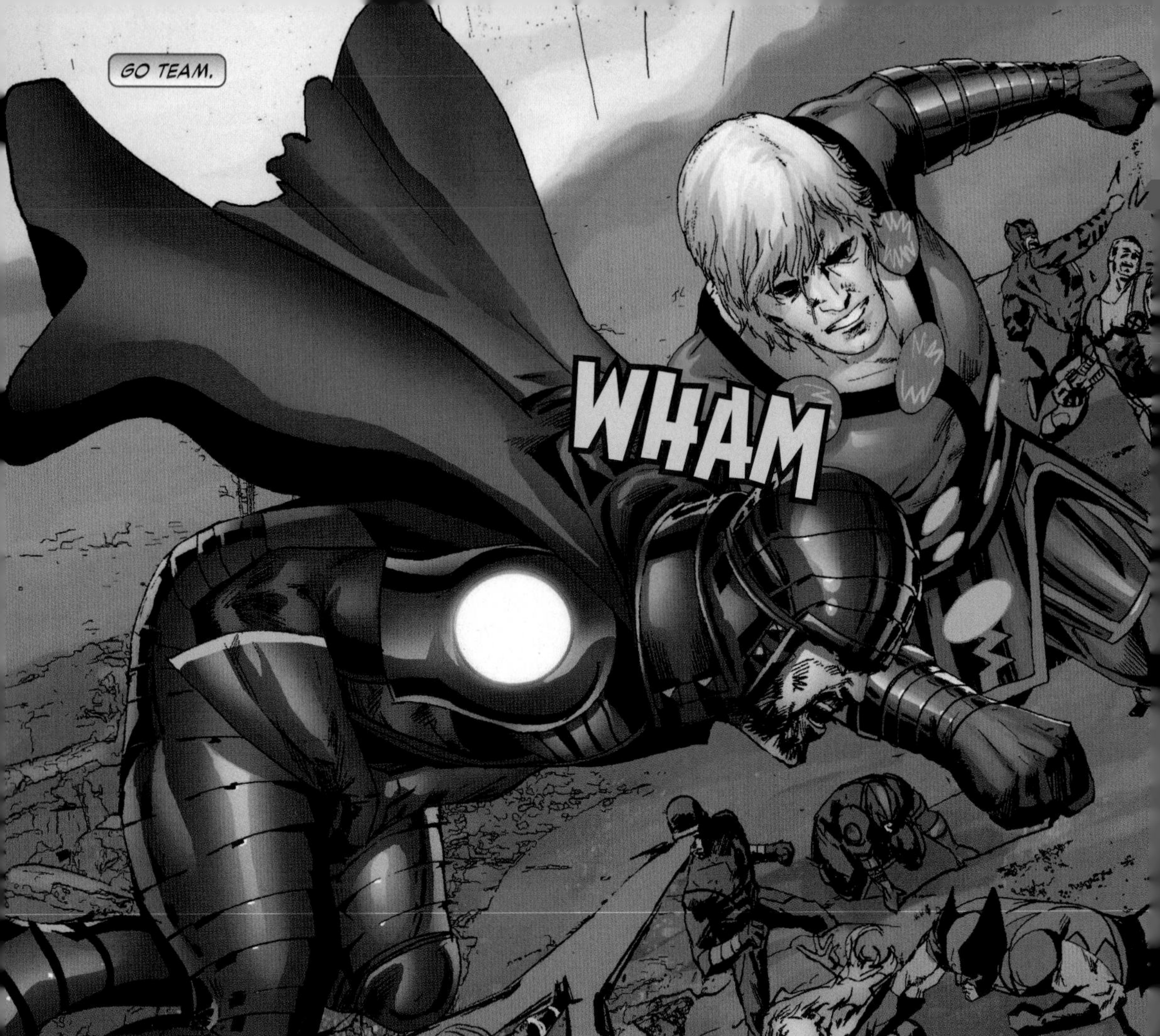
GO TEAM.
WHAM

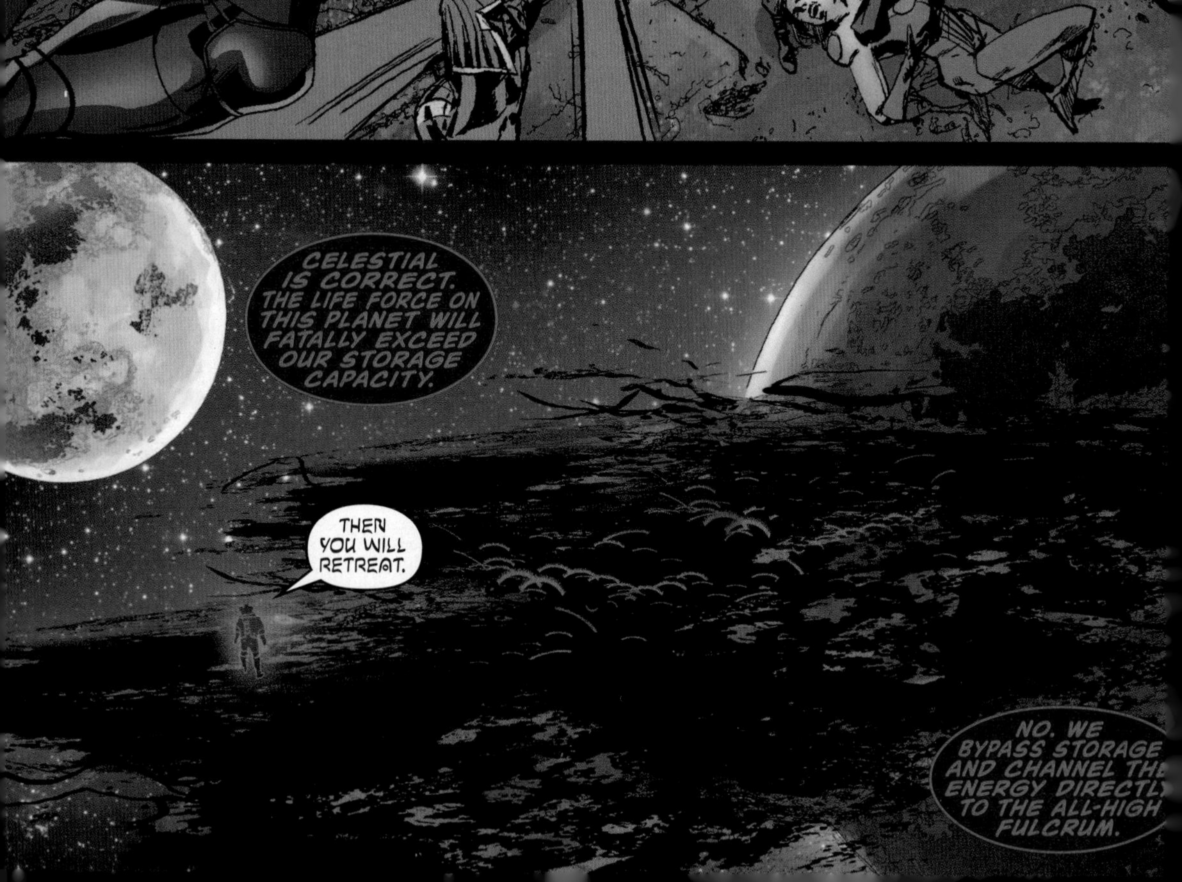
CELESTIAL IS CORRECT. THE LIFE FORCE ON THIS PLANET WILL FATALLY EXCEED OUR STORAGE CAPACITY.
THEN YOU WILL RETREAT.
NO. WE BYPASS STORAGE AND CHANNEL THE ENERGY DIRECTLY TO THE ALL-HIGH FULCRUM.

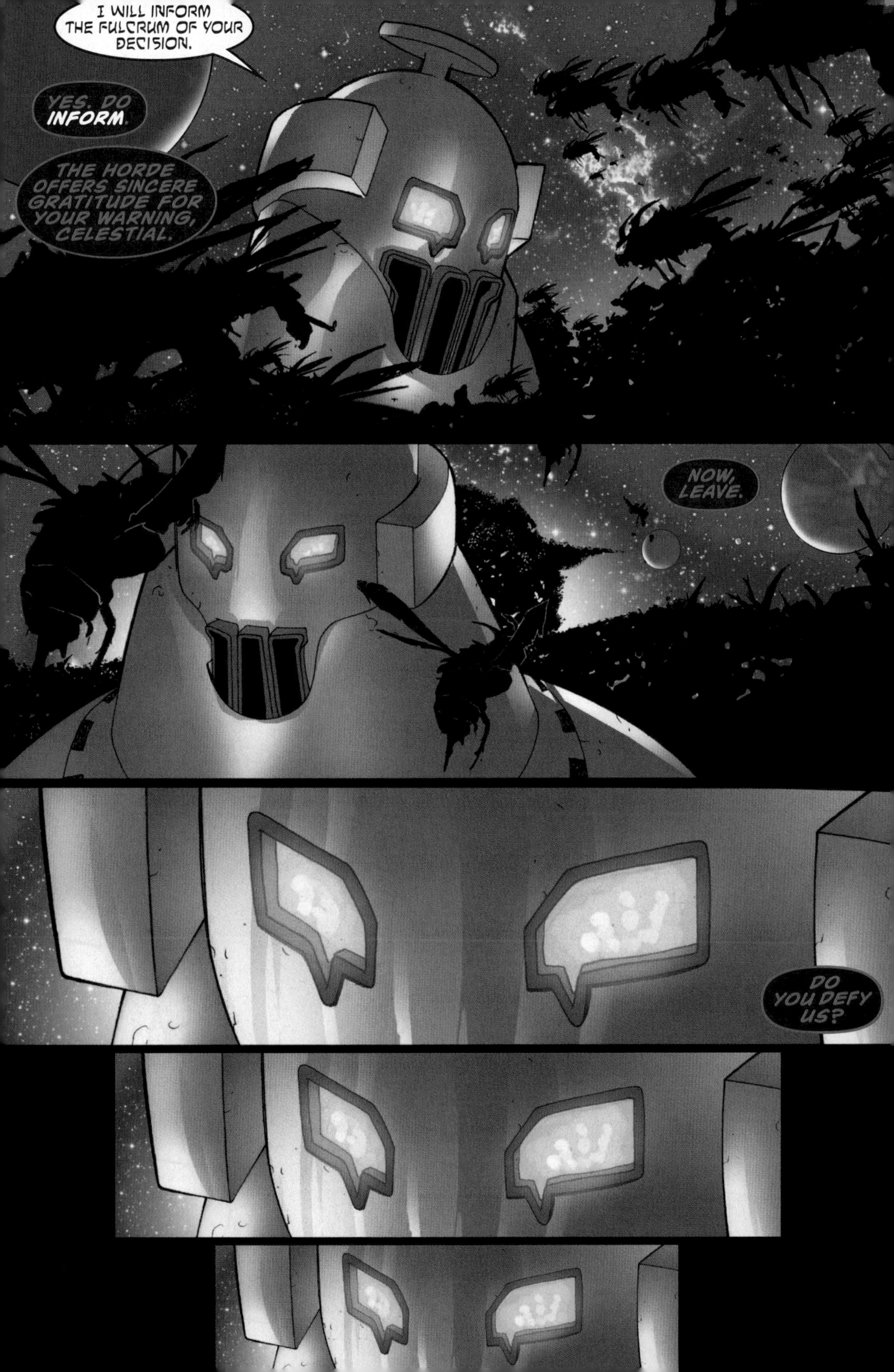
I WILL INFORM THE FULCRUM OF YOUR DECISION.
YES. DO INFORM.
THE HORDE OFFERS SINCERE GRATITUDE FOR YOUR WARNING, CELESTIAL.
NOW, LEAVE.
DO YOU DEFY US?

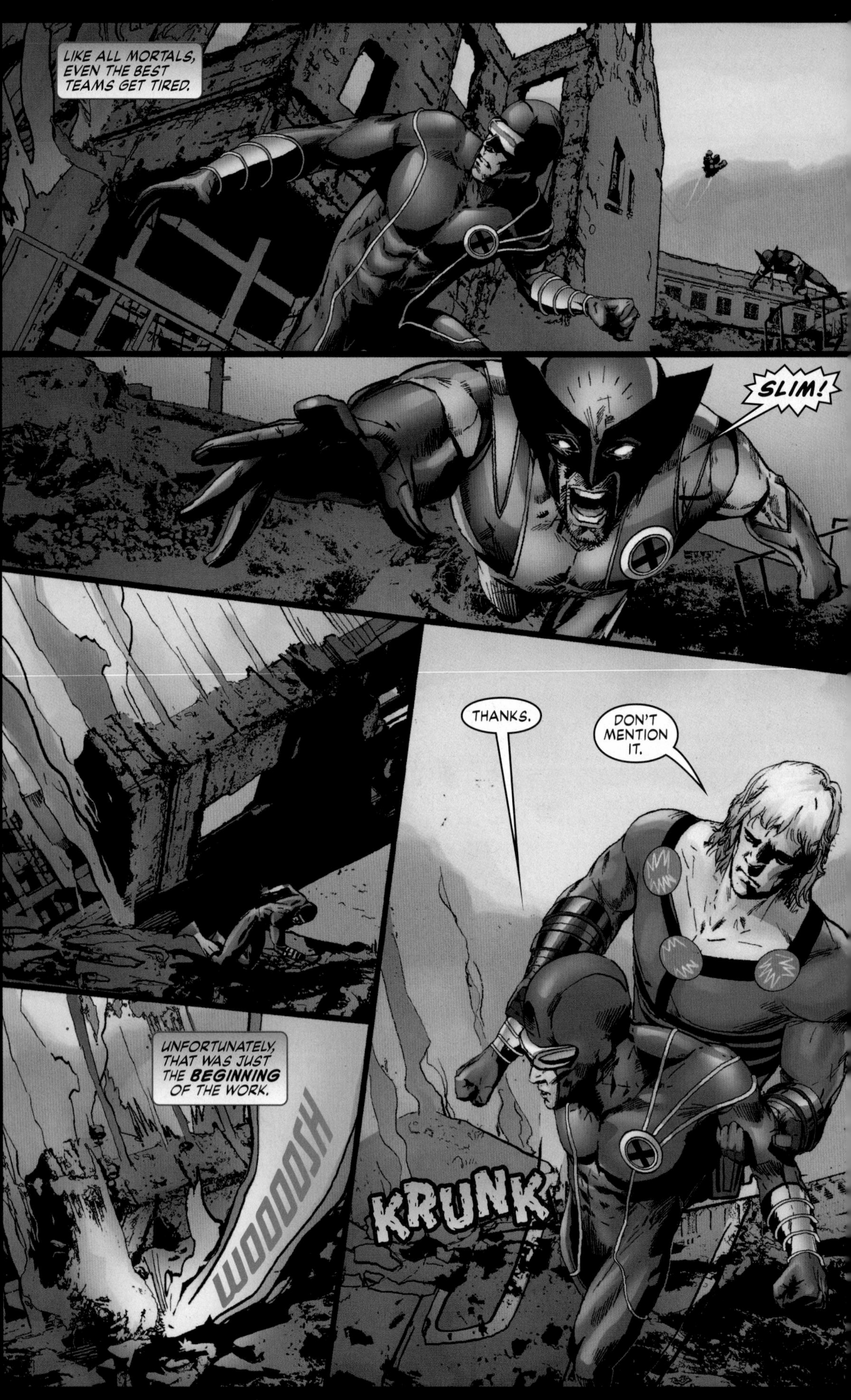
LIKE ALL MORTALS, EVEN THE BEST TEAMS GET TIRED.
SLIM!
THANKS.
DON'T MENTION IT.
UNFORTUNATELY, THAT WAS JUST THE BEGINNING OF THE WORK.
WOOOOSH
KRUNK

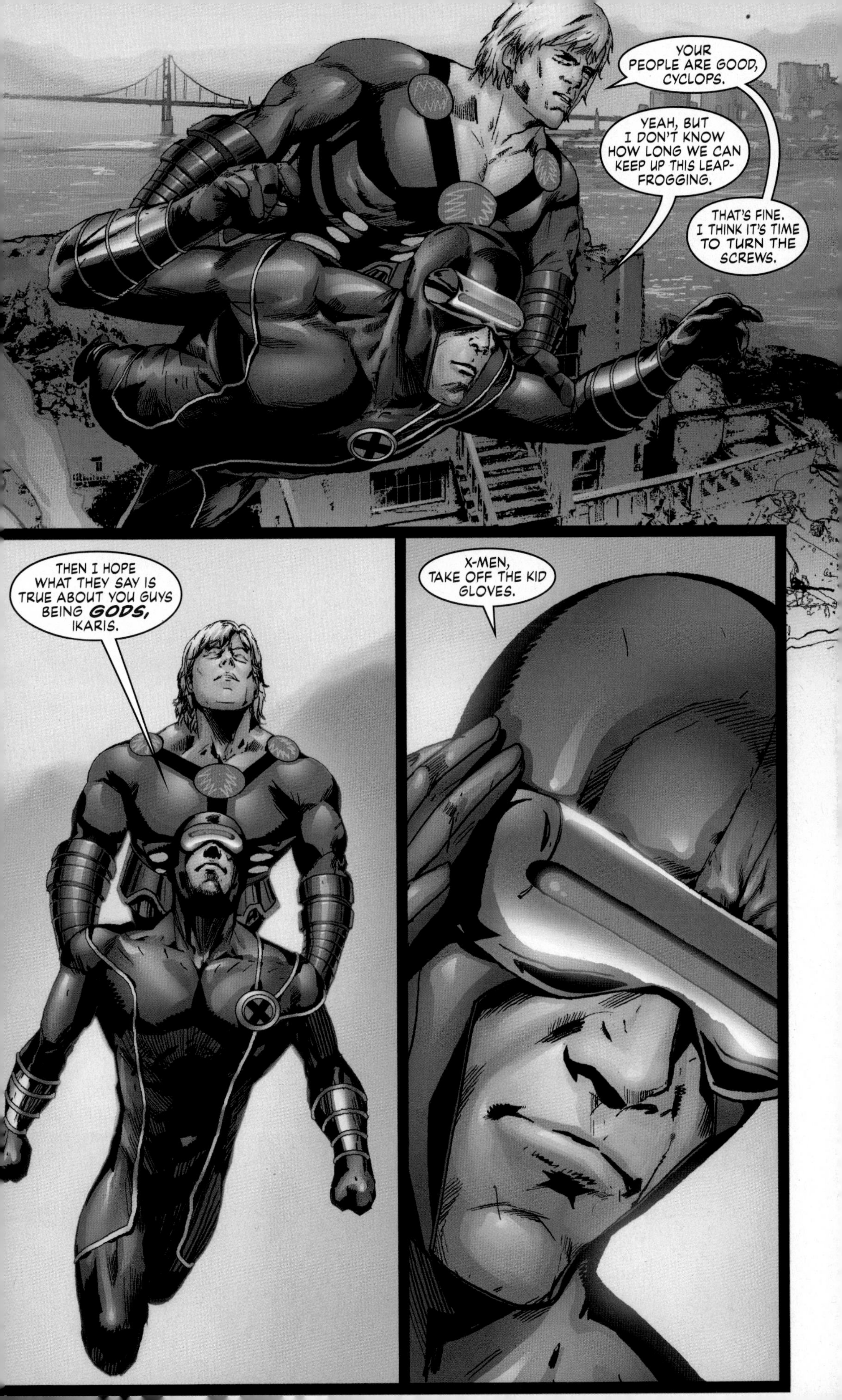
YOUR PEOPLE ARE GOOD, CYCLOPS.
YEAH, BUT I DON'T KNOW HOW LONG WE CAN KEEP UP THIS LEAP-FROGGING.
THAT'S FINE. I THINK IT'S TIME TO TURN THE SCREWS.
THEN I HOPE WHAT THEY SAY IS TRUE ABOUT YOU GUYS BEING *GODS,* IKARIS.
X-MEN, TAKE OFF THE KID GLOVES.

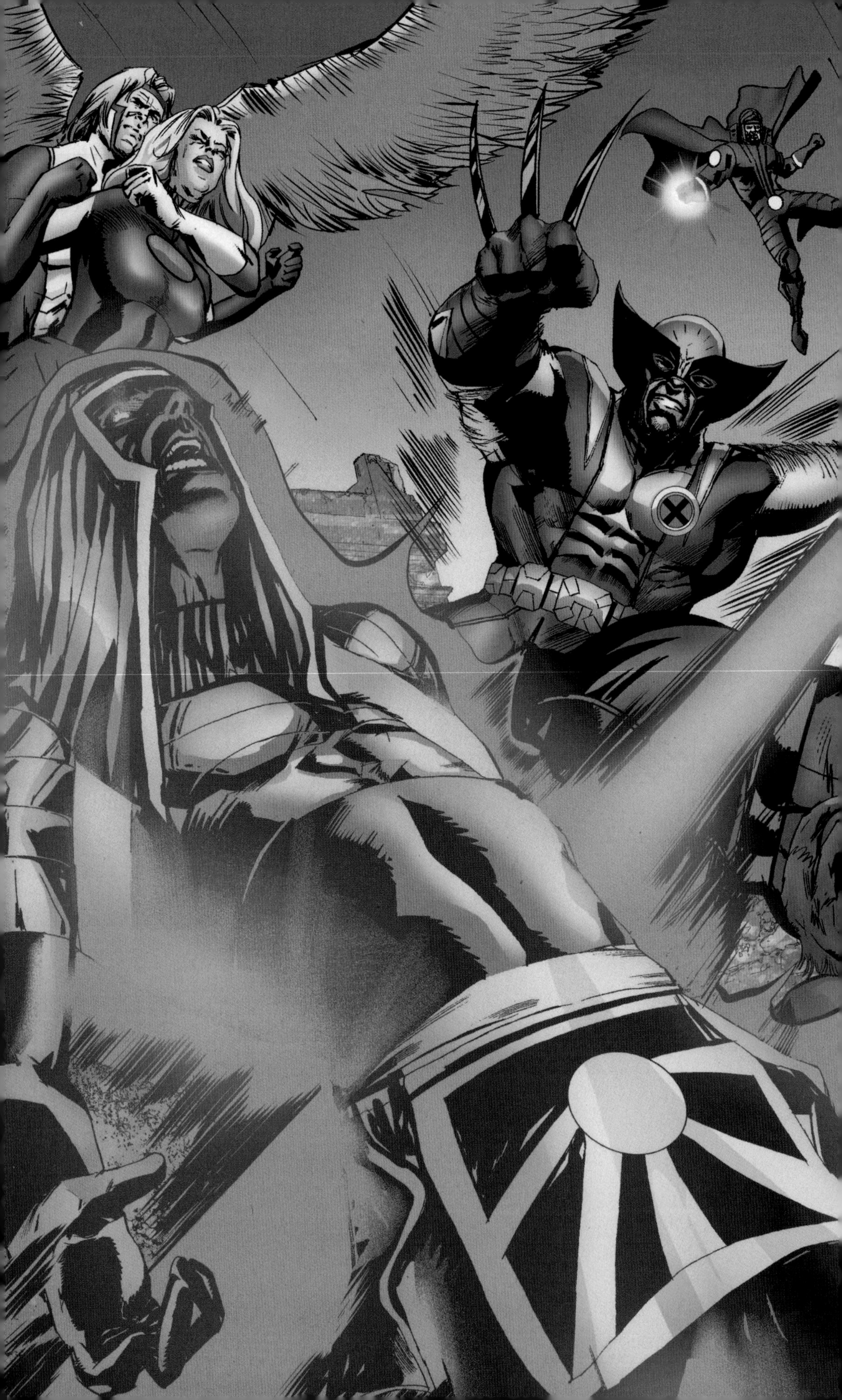

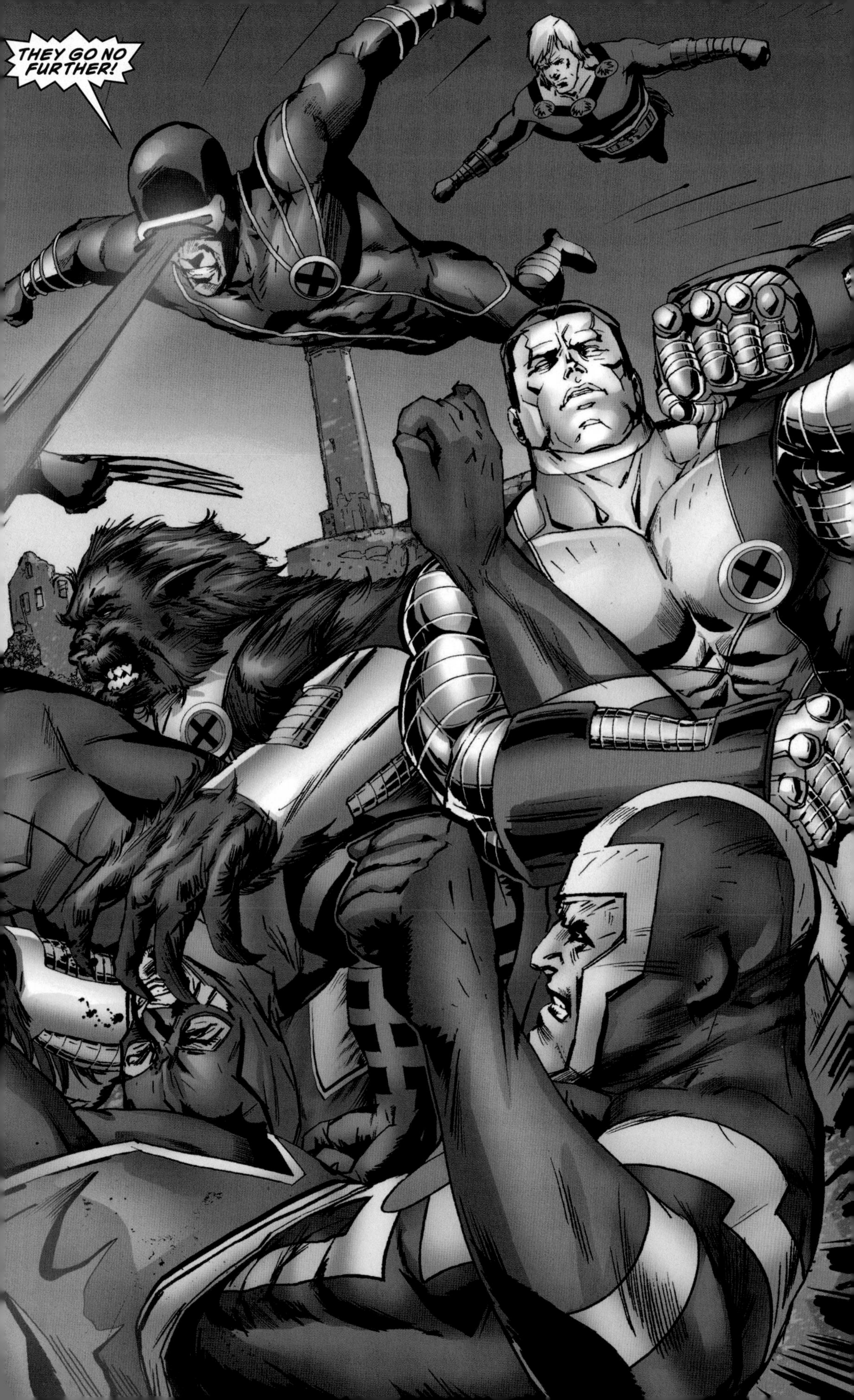
THEY GO NO FURTHER!

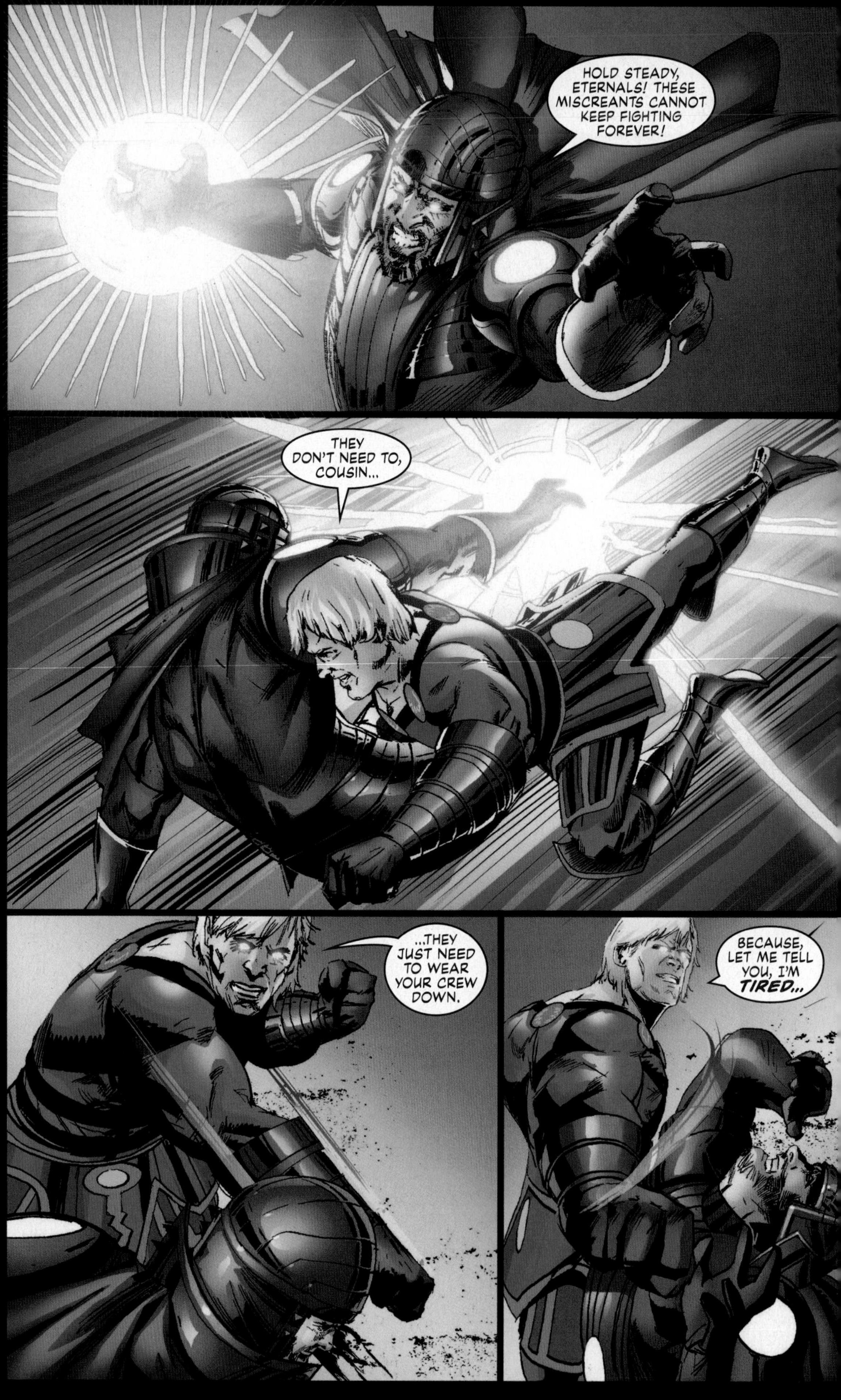
HOLD STEADY, ETERNALS! THESE MISCREANTS CANNOT KEEP FIGHTING FOREVER!
THEY DON'T NEED TO, COUSIN...
...THEY JUST NEED TO WEAR YOUR CREW DOWN.
BECAUSE, LET ME TELL YOU, I'M TIRED...

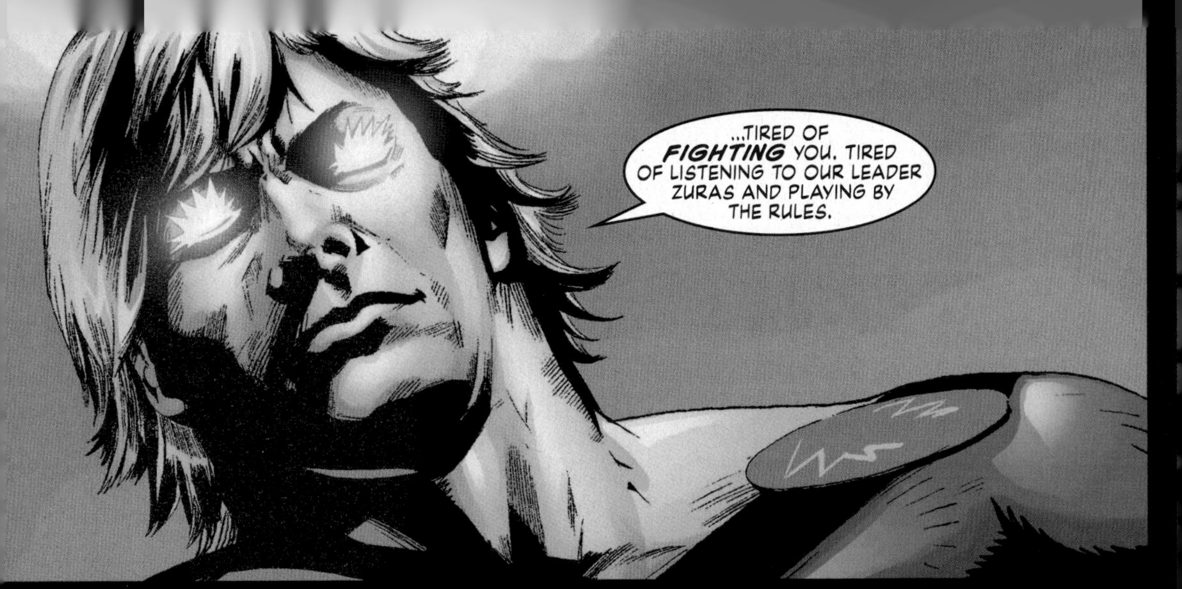
...TIRED OF FIGHTING YOU. TIRED OF LISTENING TO OUR LEADER ZURAS AND PLAYING BY THE RULES.

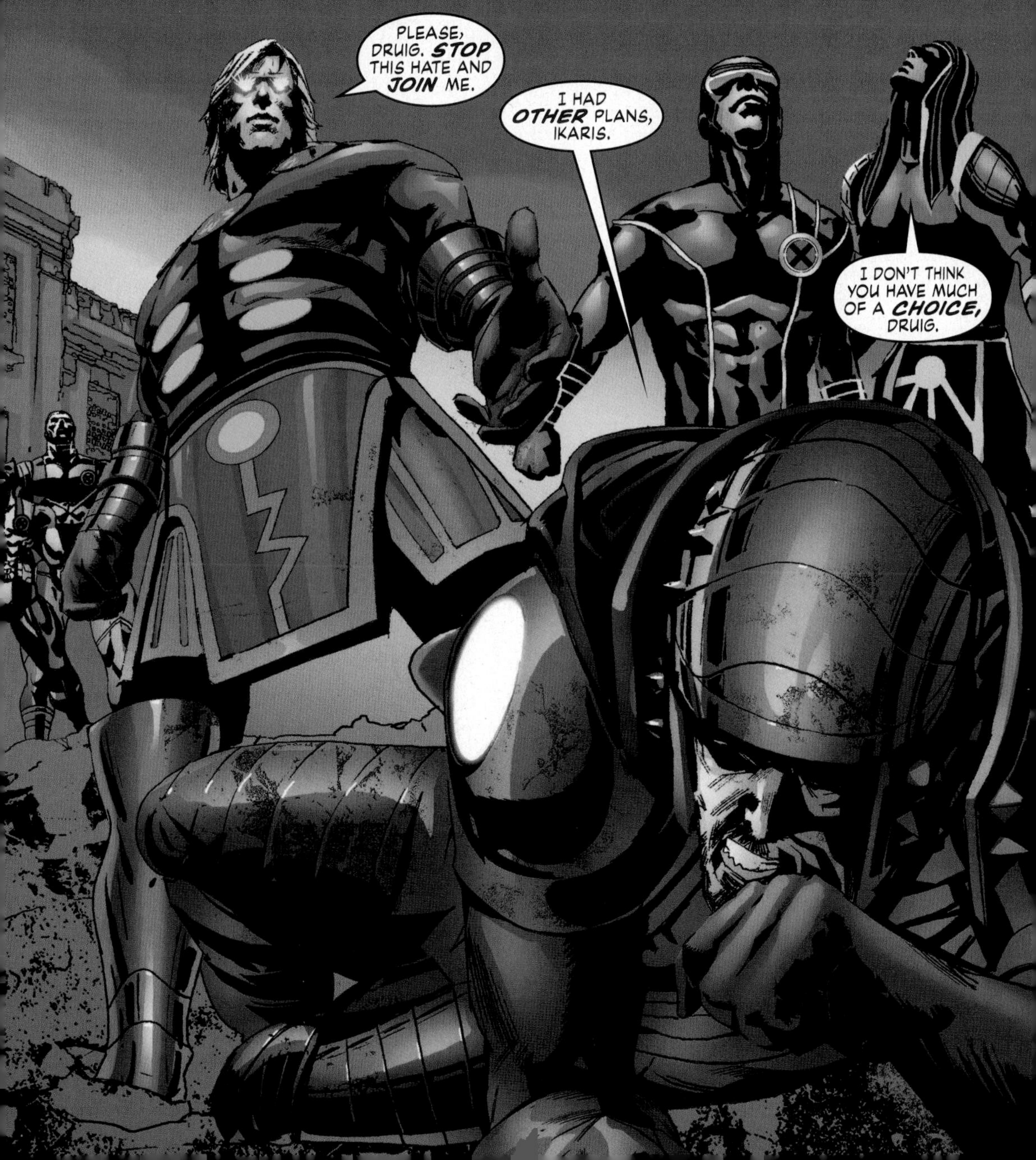
PLEASE, DRUIG. STOP THIS HATE AND JOIN ME.
I HAD OTHER PLANS, IKARIS.
I DON'T THINK YOU HAVE MUCH OF A CHOICE, DRUIG.

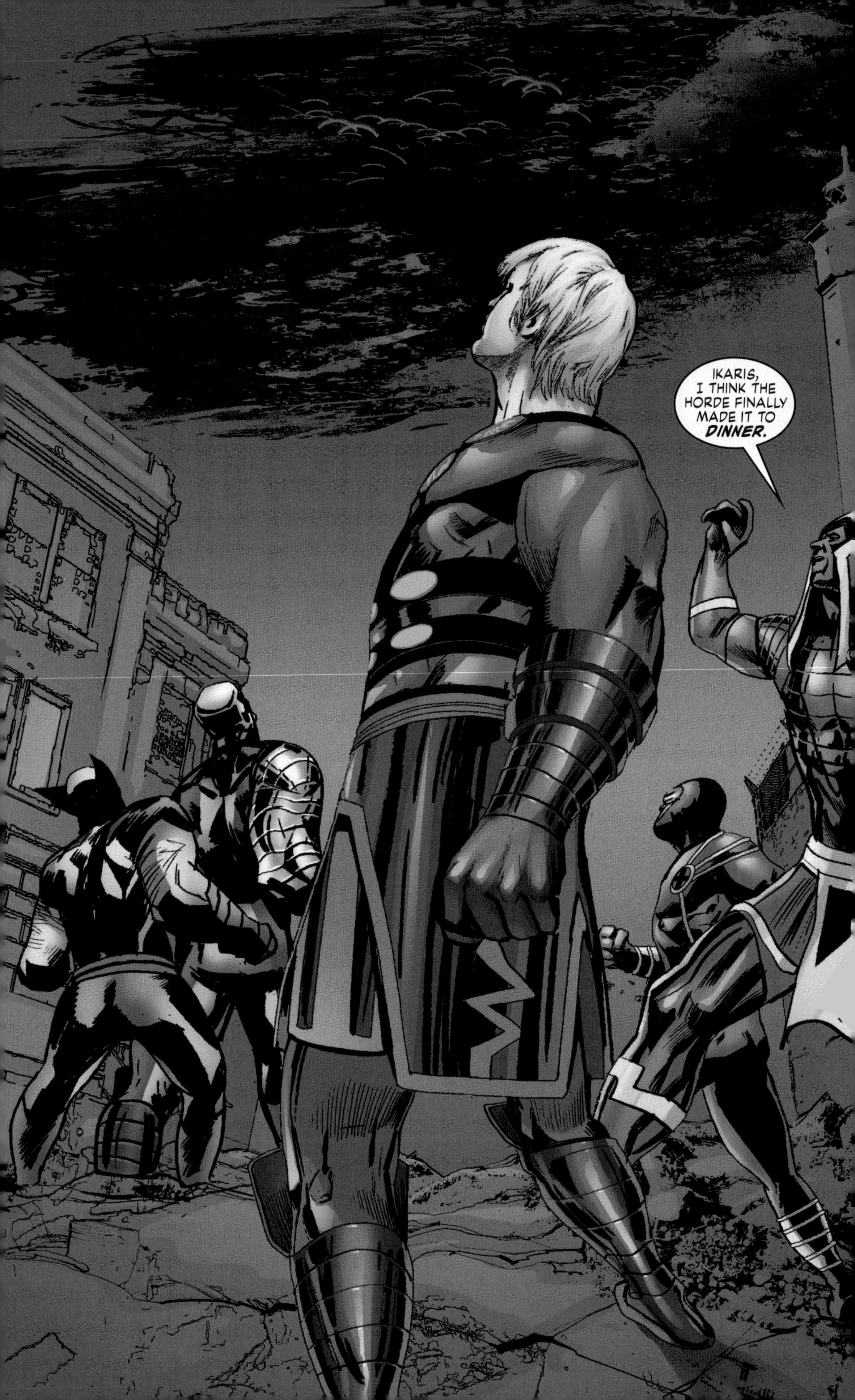
IKARIS, I THINK THE HORDE FINALLY MADE IT TO **DINNER.**

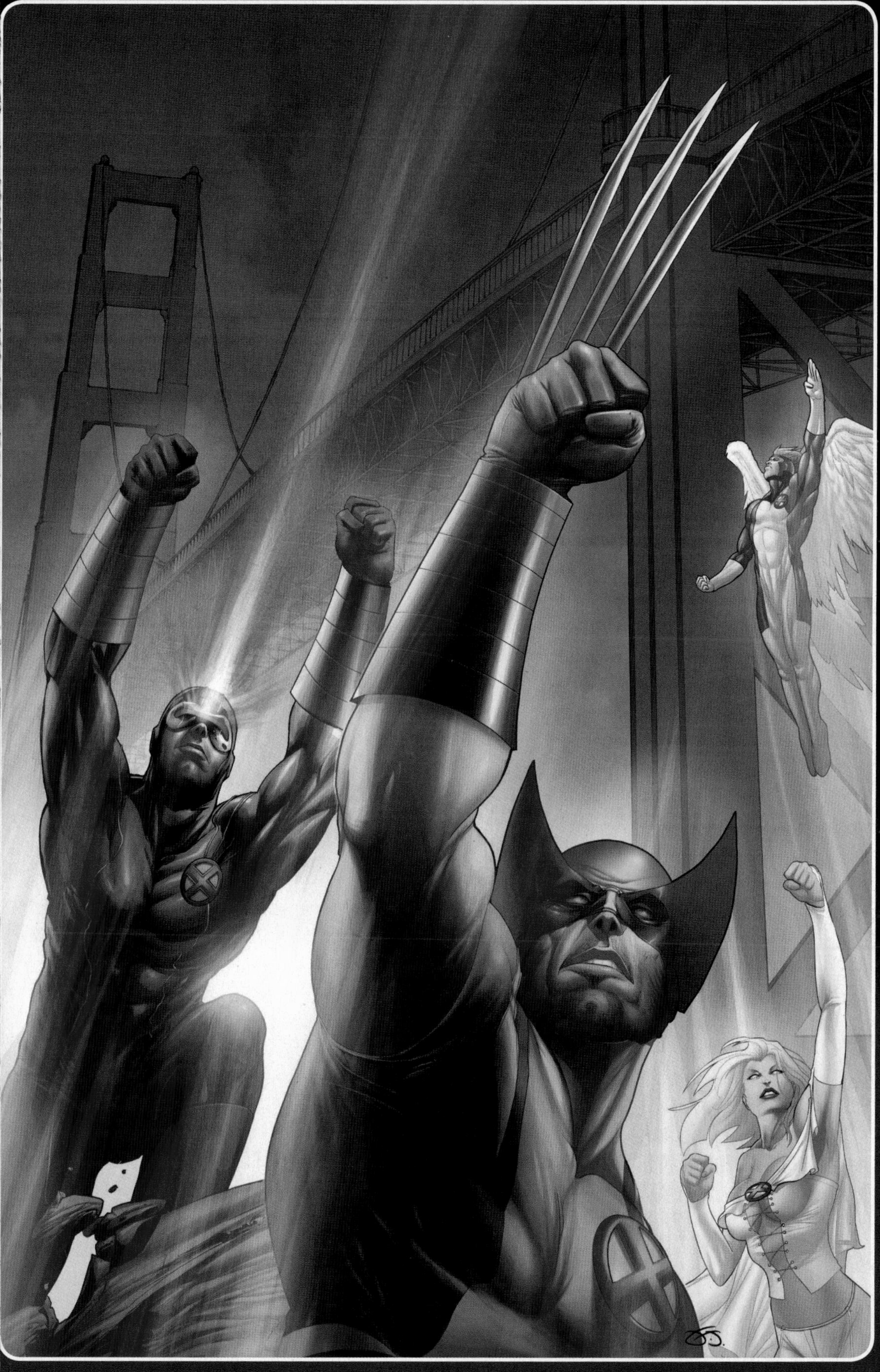

#7 X-MEN VARIANT BY FRANK MARTIN

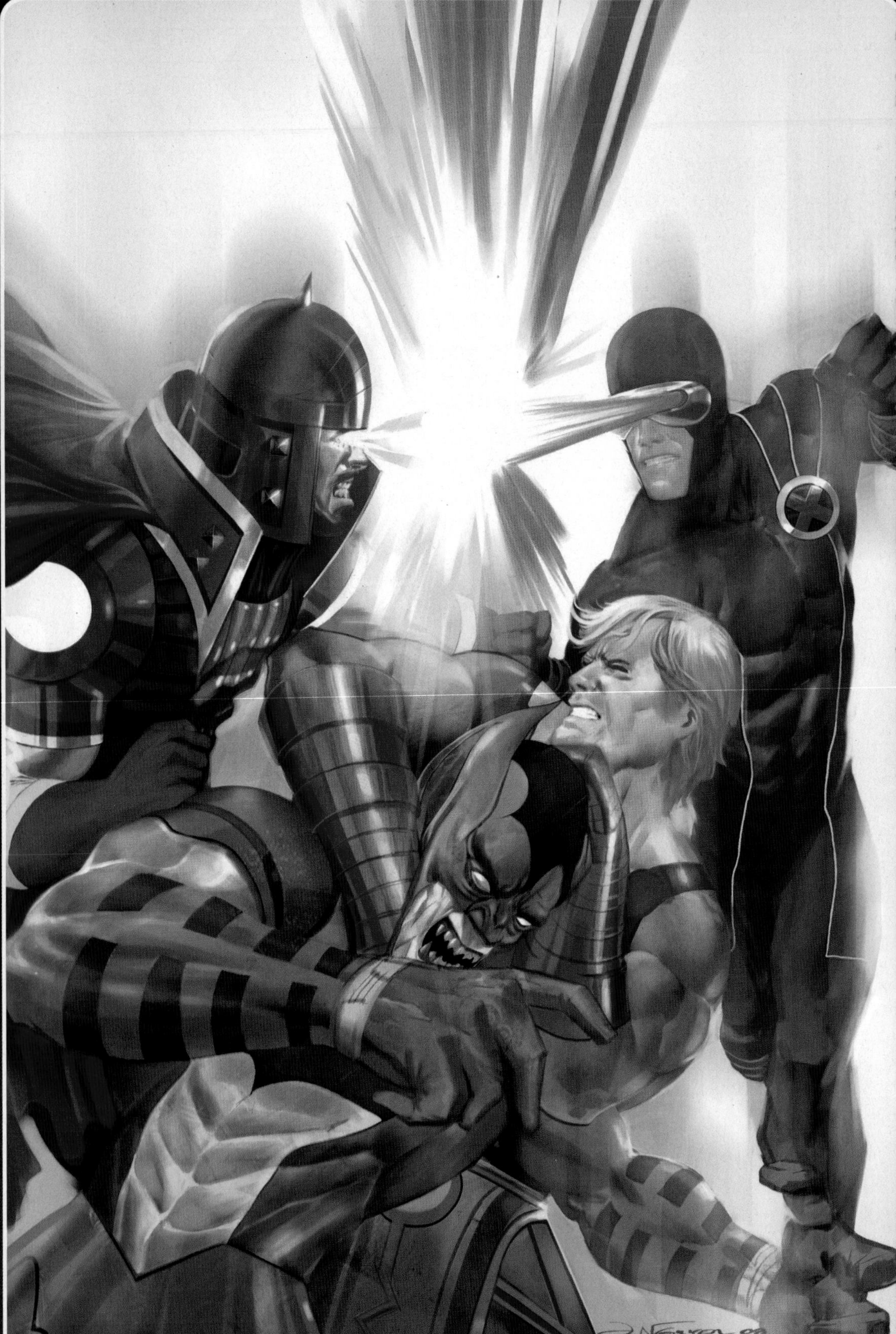

9

YOU'RE VERY DIFFICULT TO FIND...

...BUT NOT IMPOS- SIBLE.

DID YOU THINK IT WAS *YOUR* IDEA TO SEARCH FOR ME, MICHELLE URICH?

SO WE CAN CHALK UP *MIND MANIPULATION* AS ONE OF THE MANY REPORTED POWERS YOUR PEOPLE POSSESS...?

HA! ALWAYS FISHING FOR ANSWERS! SO MUCH LIKE YOUR GRAND- FATHER.

NO OFFENSE, BUT I'VE SPENT THE BETTER PART OF MY CAREER SEARCHING FOR YOU AND OVER TWO GRAND OF MY *OWN* MONEY GETTING HERE.

THE LEAST YOU COULD DO IS OFFER ME A SEAT.

BY ALL MEANS...

IN YOUR EMAIL YOU SAID YOU HAVE SOMETHING...?

I DO.

WELL, THEN?

FIRST, INFORMA- TION.

FINE. WHAT DO YOU WANT TO KNOW?

EVERY- THING.

THAT'S A LOT.

IF YOU DON'T WANT TO TELL ME...

IT'S NOT THAT. IT'S JUST THAT "EVERYTHING" IS, LITERALLY, TENS OF THOUSANDS OF YEARS WORTH OF EVENTS BEHIND HISTORY.

HOW ABOUT WE START WITH WHAT *YOU* KNOW AND I'LL FILL IN THE BLANKS.

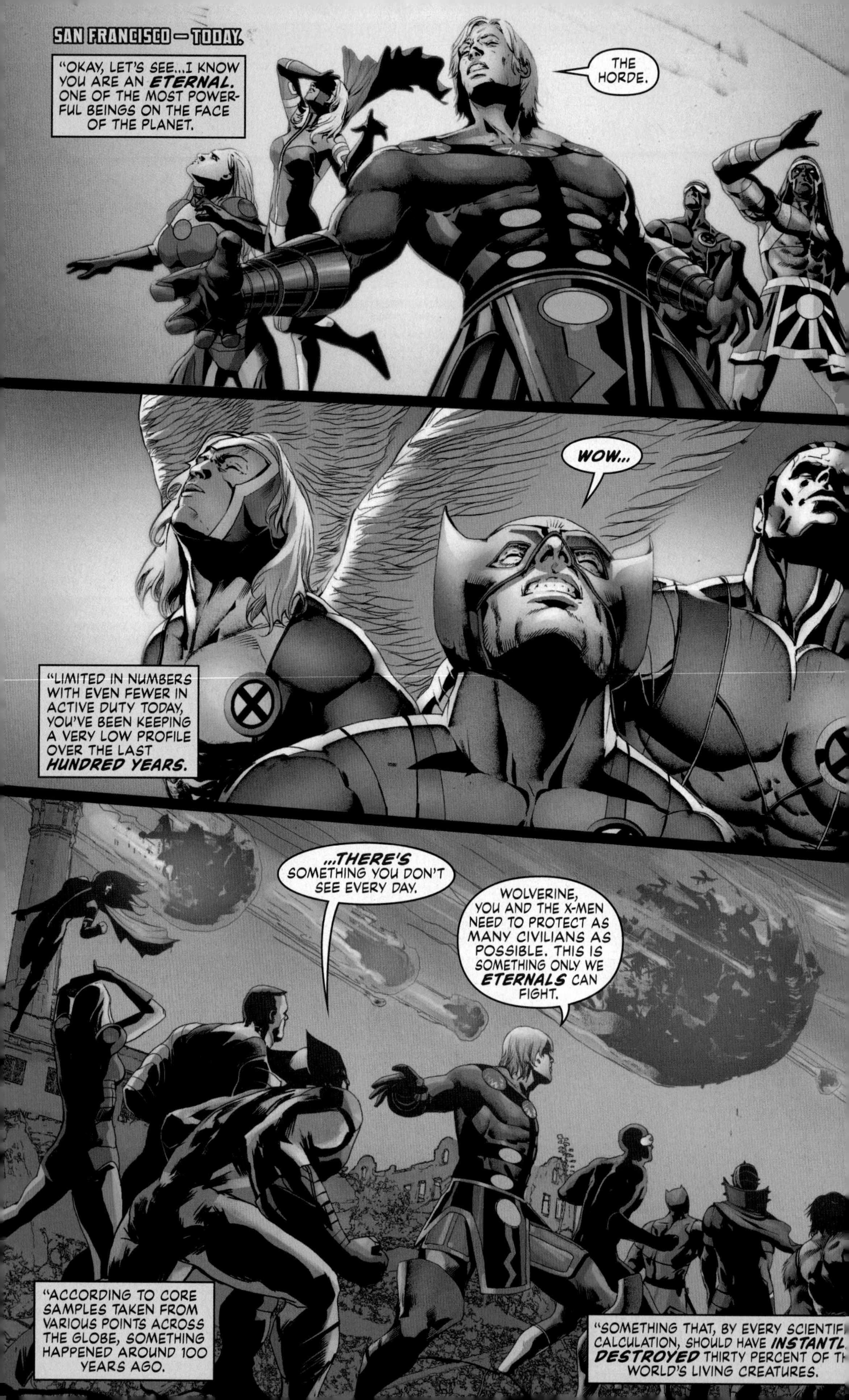
SAN FRANCISCO — TODAY.
"OKAY, LET'S SEE...I KNOW YOU ARE AN ETERNAL. ONE OF THE MOST POWERFUL BEINGS ON THE FACE OF THE PLANET.
THE HORDE.
WOW...
"LIMITED IN NUMBERS WITH EVEN FEWER IN ACTIVE DUTY TODAY, YOU'VE BEEN KEEPING A VERY LOW PROFILE OVER THE LAST HUNDRED YEARS.
...THERE'S SOMETHING YOU DON'T SEE EVERY DAY.
WOLVERINE, YOU AND THE X-MEN NEED TO PROTECT AS MANY CIVILIANS AS POSSIBLE. THIS IS SOMETHING ONLY WE ETERNALS CAN FIGHT.
"ACCORDING TO CORE SAMPLES TAKEN FROM VARIOUS POINTS ACROSS THE GLOBE, SOMETHING HAPPENED AROUND 100 YEARS AGO.
"SOMETHING THAT, BY EVERY SCIENTIF CALCULATION, SHOULD HAVE INSTANTL DESTROYED THIRTY PERCENT OF TH WORLD'S LIVING CREATURES.

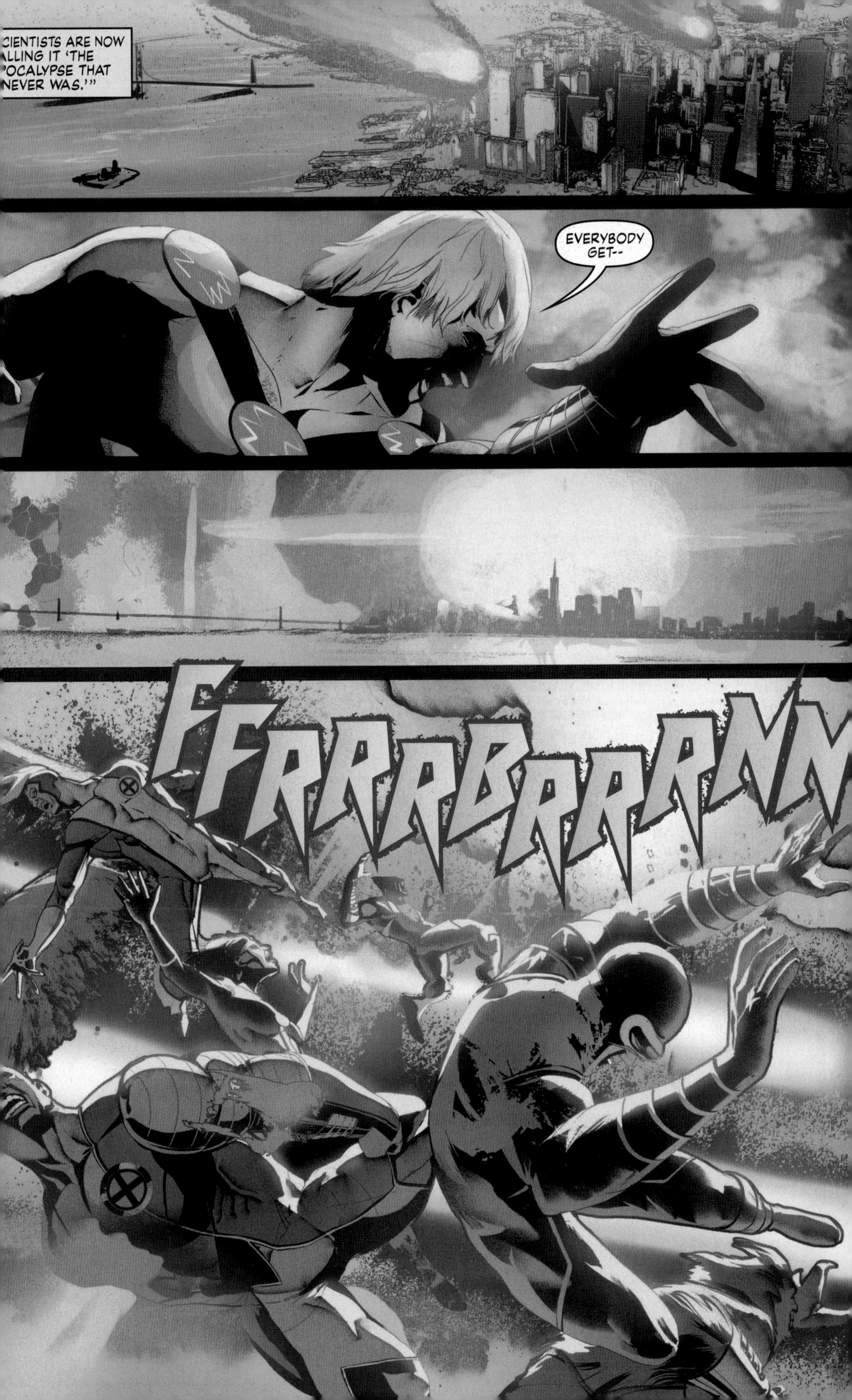
CIENTISTS ARE NOW
LLING IT 'THE
OCALYPSE THAT
NEVER WAS.'"
EVERYBODY GET--
FFRRRBRRRNN

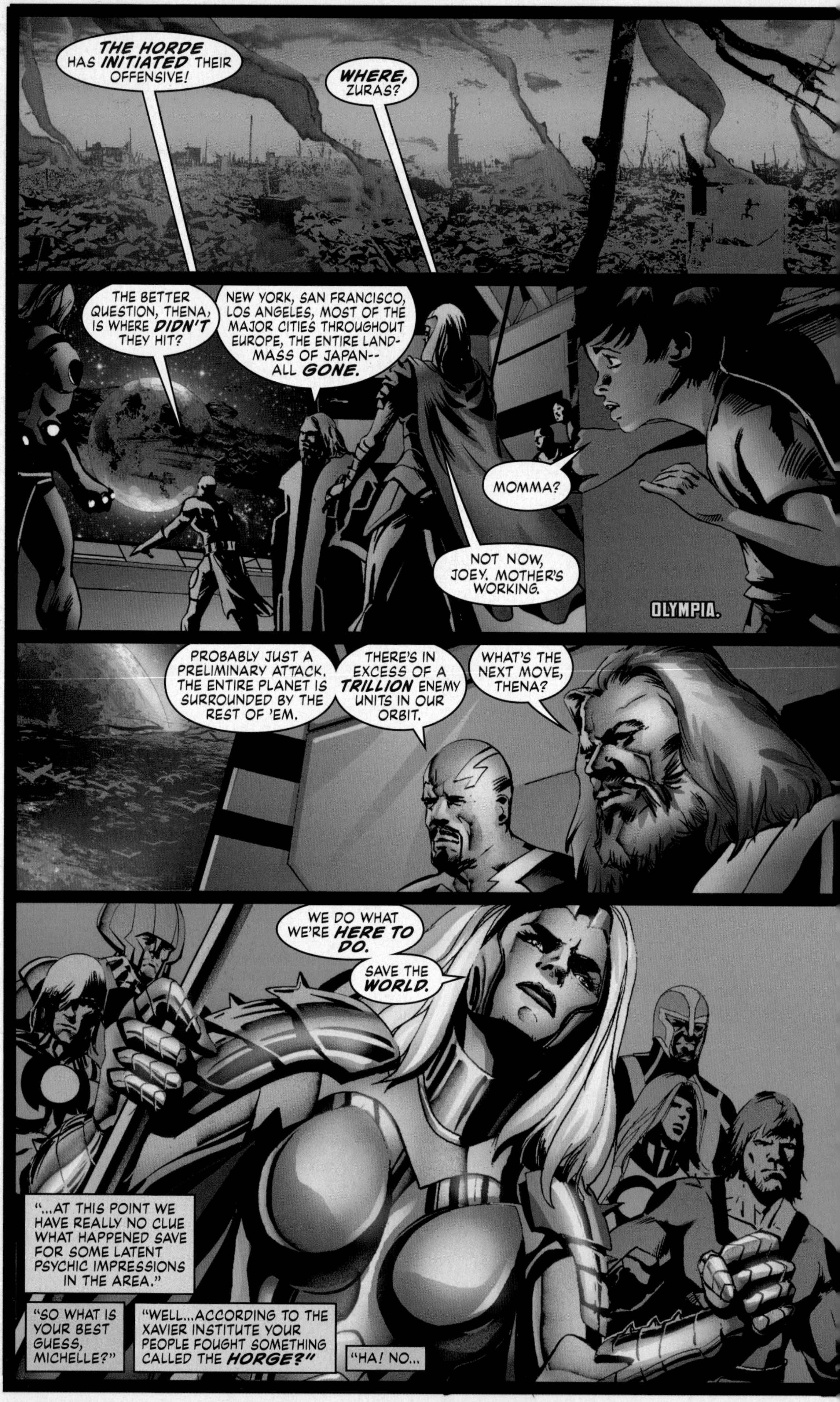
THE HORDE HAS INITIATED THEIR OFFENSIVE!
WHERE, ZURAS?
THE BETTER QUESTION, THENA, IS WHERE DIDN'T THEY HIT?
NEW YORK, SAN FRANCISCO, LOS ANGELES, MOST OF THE MAJOR CITIES THROUGHOUT EUROPE, THE ENTIRE LAND-MASS OF JAPAN-- ALL GONE.
MOMMA?
NOT NOW, JOEY. MOTHER'S WORKING.
OLYMPIA.
PROBABLY JUST A PRELIMINARY ATTACK. THE ENTIRE PLANET IS SURROUNDED BY THE REST OF 'EM.
THERE'S IN EXCESS OF A TRILLION ENEMY UNITS IN OUR ORBIT.
WHAT'S THE NEXT MOVE, THENA?
WE DO WHAT WE'RE HERE TO DO.
SAVE THE WORLD.
"...AT THIS POINT WE HAVE REALLY NO CLUE WHAT HAPPENED SAVE FOR SOME LATENT PSYCHIC IMPRESSIONS IN THE AREA."
"SO WHAT IS YOUR BEST GUESS, MICHELLE?"
"WELL...ACCORDING TO THE XAVIER INSTITUTE YOUR PEOPLE FOUGHT SOMETHING CALLED THE HORGE?"
"HA! NO...

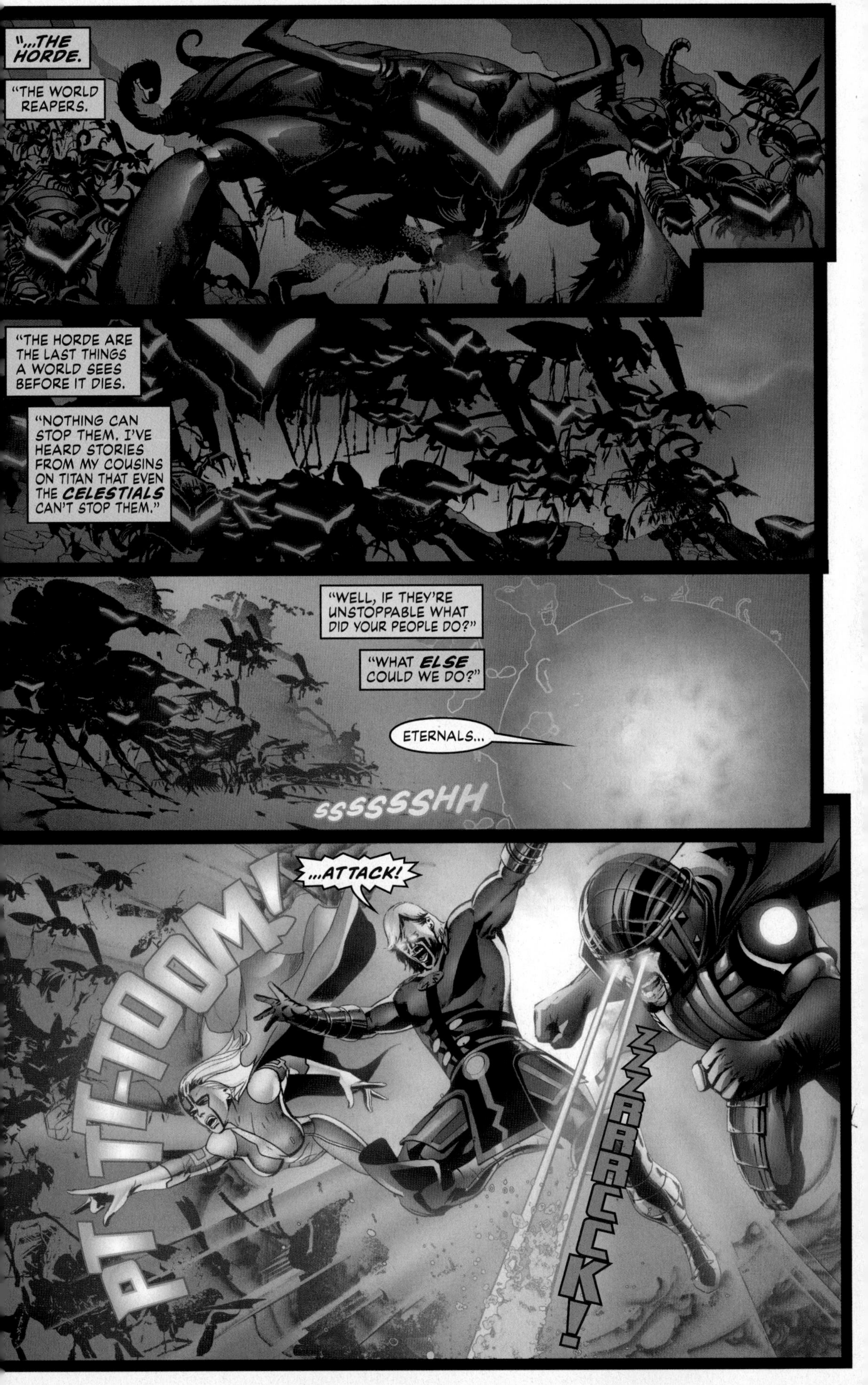
"...THE HORDE.
"THE WORLD REAPERS.
"THE HORDE ARE THE LAST THINGS A WORLD SEES BEFORE IT DIES.
"NOTHING CAN STOP THEM. I'VE HEARD STORIES FROM MY COUSINS ON TITAN THAT EVEN THE CELESTIALS CAN'T STOP THEM."
"WELL, IF THEY'RE UNSTOPPABLE WHAT DID YOUR PEOPLE DO?"
"WHAT ELSE COULD WE DO?"
ETERNALS...
SSSSSSHH
...ATTACK!
PT TI-TOOM!
ZZZRRRCCK!

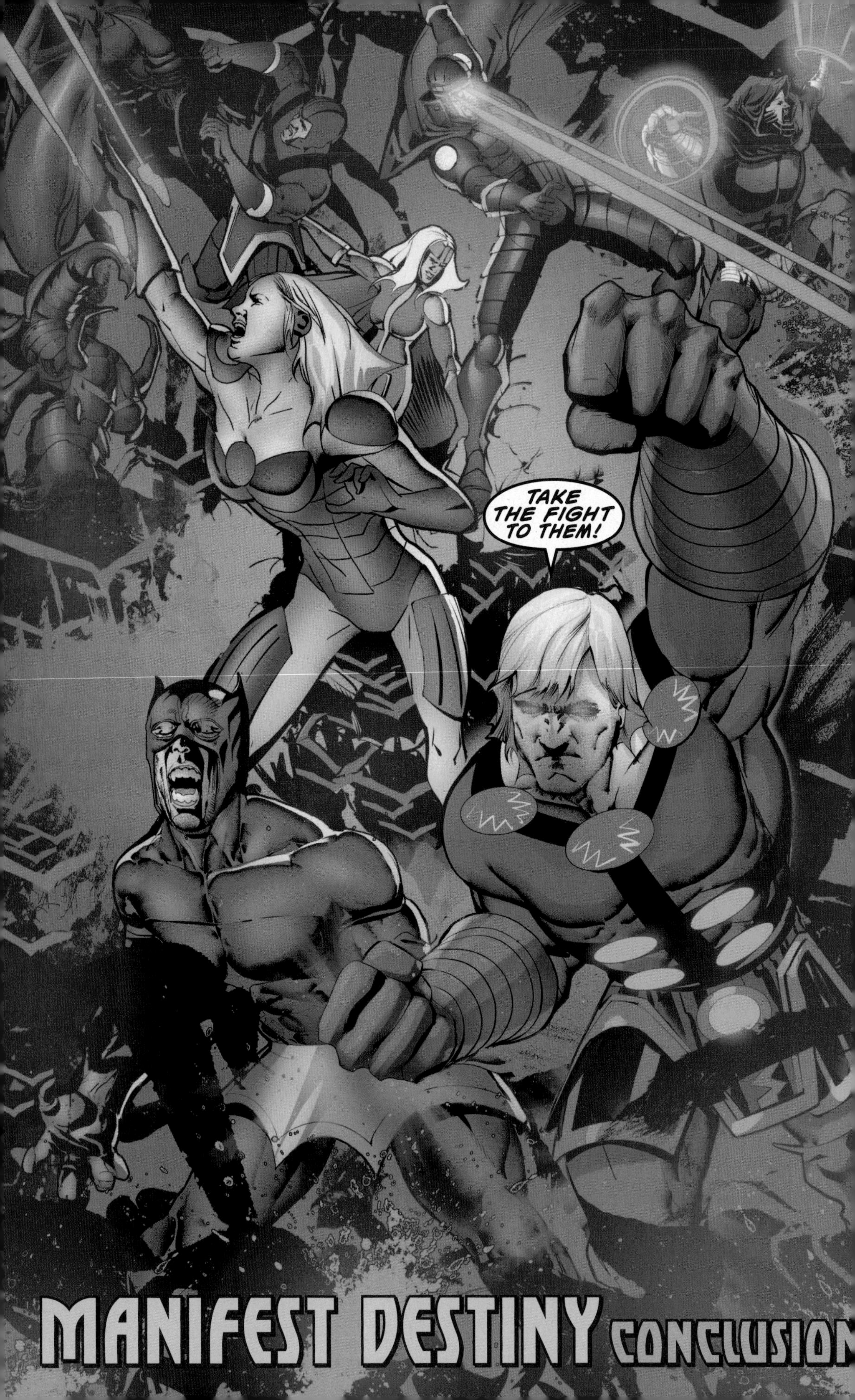
TAKE THE FIGHT TO THEM!
MANIFEST DESTINY CONCLUSION

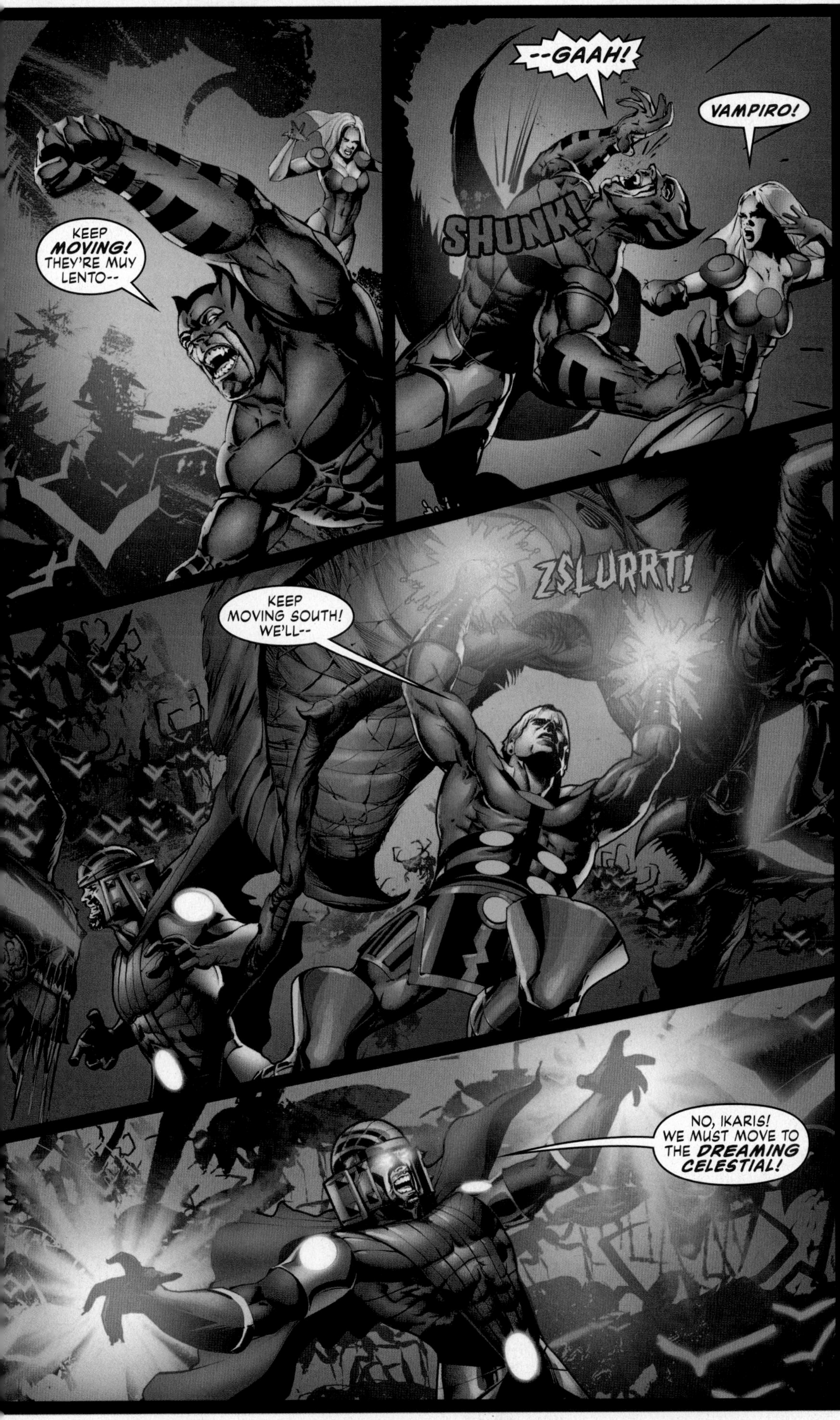
KEEP MOVING! THEY'RE MUY LENTO--
--GAAH!
VAMPIRO!
SHUNK!
ZSLURRT!
KEEP MOVING SOUTH! WE'LL--
NO, IKARIS! WE MUST MOVE TO THE DREAMING CELESTIAL!

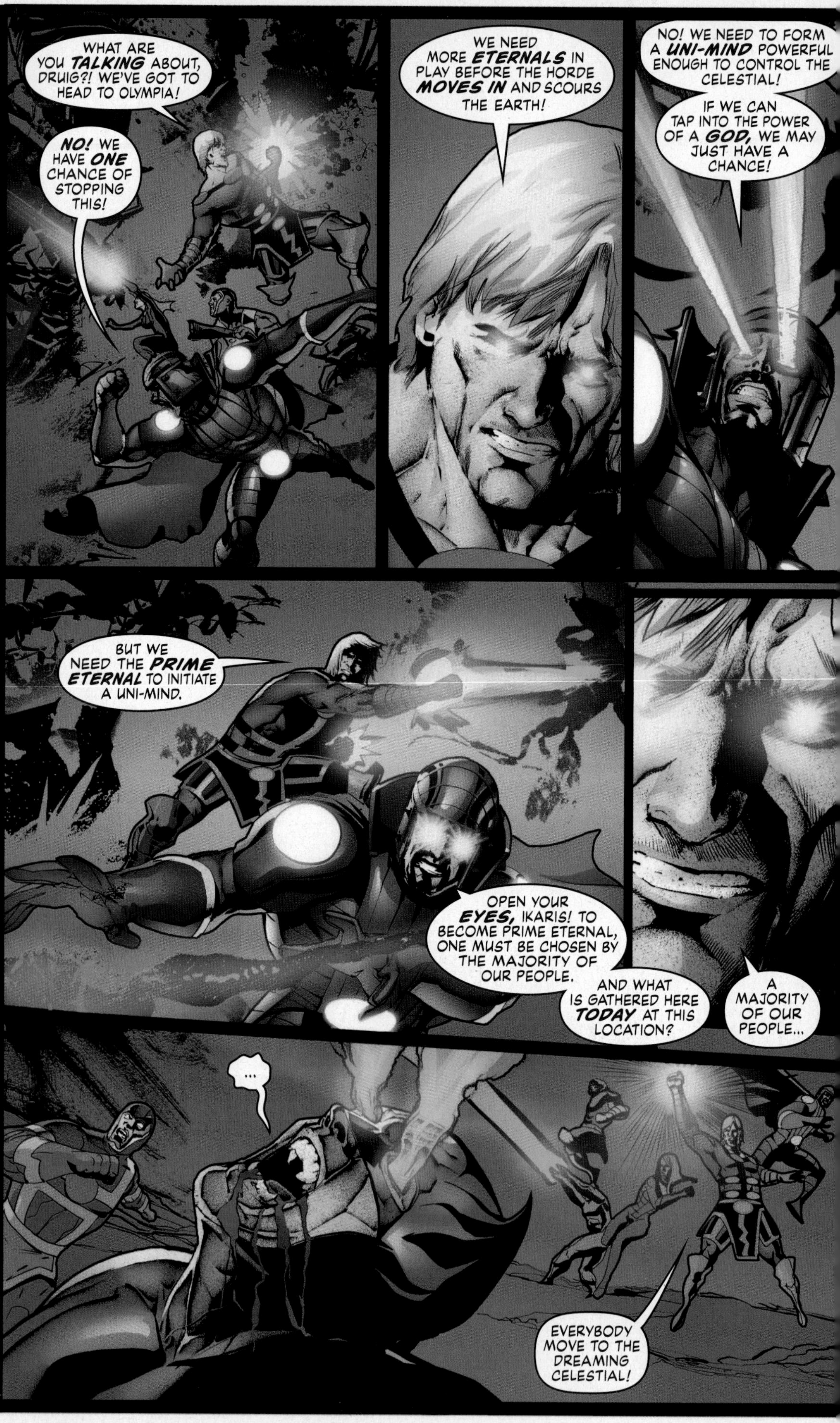

WHAT ARE YOU TALKING ABOUT, DRUIG?! WE'VE GOT TO HEAD TO OLYMPIA!
NO! WE HAVE ONE CHANCE OF STOPPING THIS!
WE NEED MORE ETERNALS IN PLAY BEFORE THE HORDE MOVES IN AND SCOURS THE EARTH!
NO! WE NEED TO FORM A UNI-MIND POWERFUL ENOUGH TO CONTROL THE CELESTIAL!
IF WE CAN TAP INTO THE POWER OF A GOD, WE MAY JUST HAVE A CHANCE!
BUT WE NEED THE PRIME ETERNAL TO INITIATE A UNI-MIND.
OPEN YOUR EYES, IKARIS! TO BECOME PRIME ETERNAL, ONE MUST BE CHOSEN BY THE MAJORITY OF OUR PEOPLE.
AND WHAT IS GATHERED HERE TODAY AT THIS LOCATION?
A MAJORITY OF OUR PEOPLE...
...
EVERYBODY MOVE TO THE DREAMING CELESTIAL!

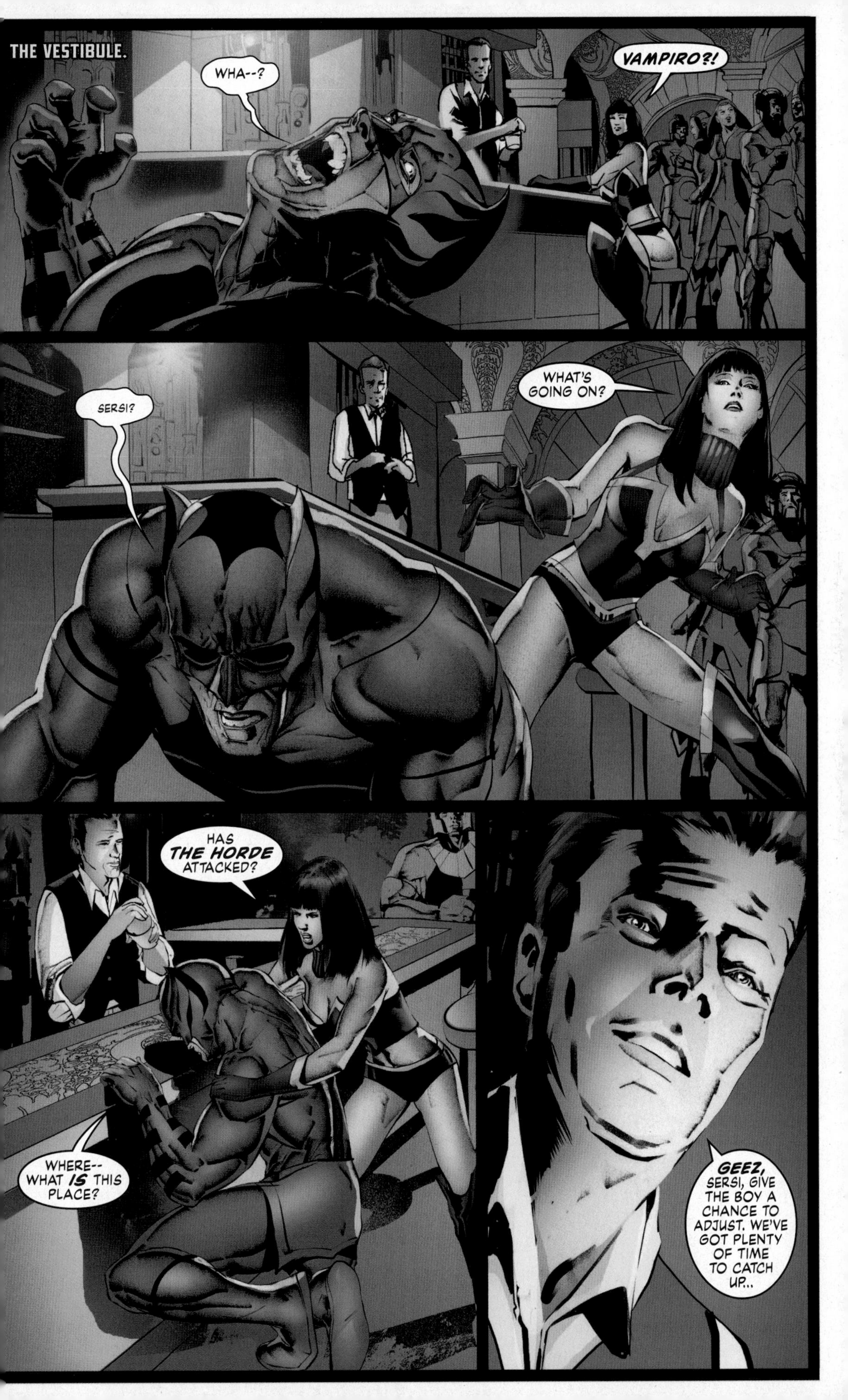
THE VESTIBULE.
WHA--?
VAMPIRO?!
SERSI?
WHAT'S GOING ON?
HAS THE HORDE ATTACKED?
WHERE-- WHAT IS THIS PLACE?
GEEZ, SERSI, GIVE THE BOY A CHANCE TO ADJUST. WE'VE GOT PLENTY OF TIME TO CATCH UP..

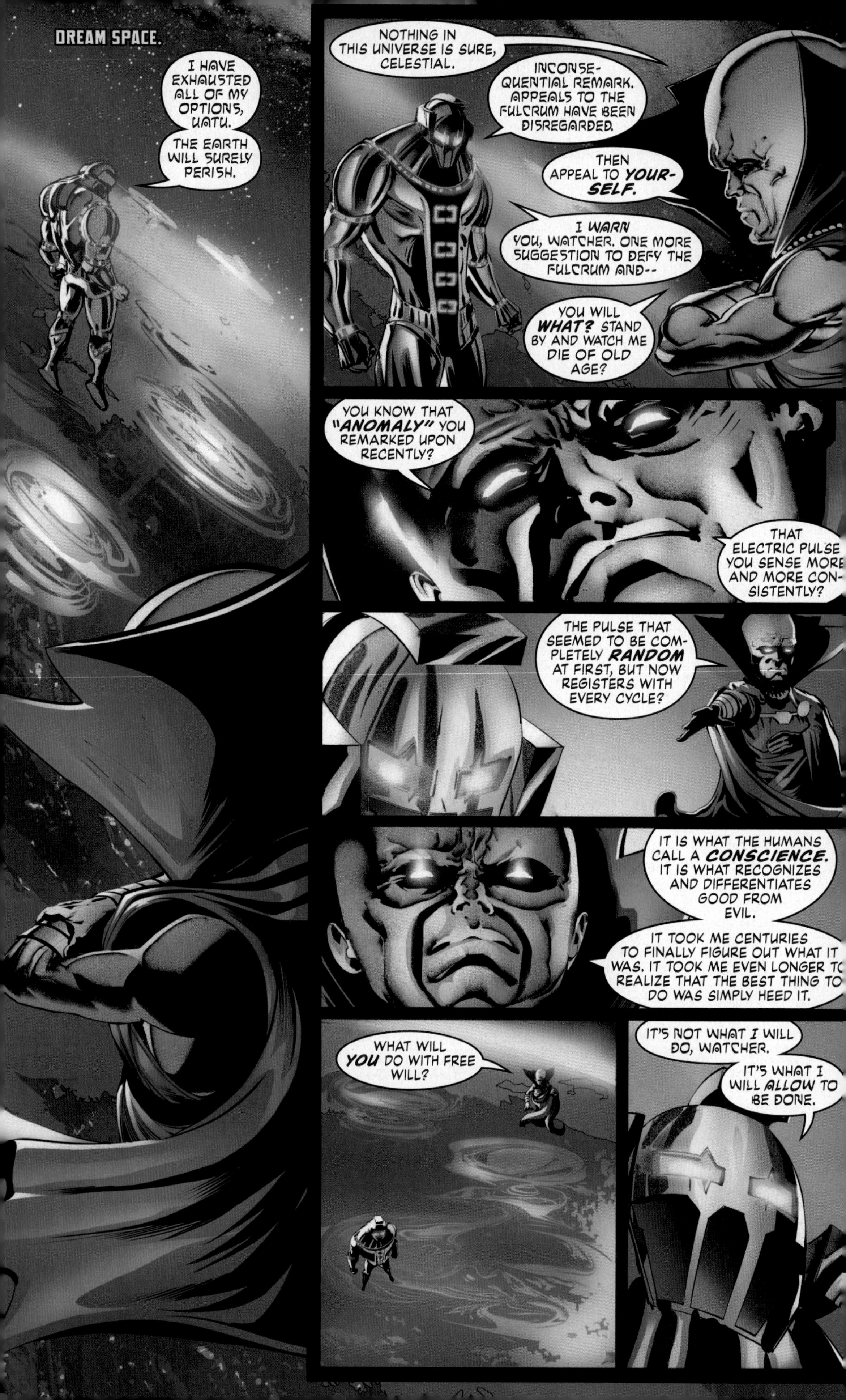
DREAM SPACE.
I HAVE EXHAUSTED ALL OF MY OPTIONS, UATU.
THE EARTH WILL SURELY PERISH.
NOTHING IN THIS UNIVERSE IS SURE, CELESTIAL.
INCONSE-QUENTIAL REMARK. APPEALS TO THE FULCRUM HAVE BEEN DISREGARDED.
THEN APPEAL TO YOUR-SELF.
I WARN YOU, WATCHER. ONE MORE SUGGESTION TO DEFY THE FULCRUM AND--
YOU WILL WHAT? STAND BY AND WATCH ME DIE OF OLD AGE?
YOU KNOW THAT "ANOMALY" YOU REMARKED UPON RECENTLY?
THAT ELECTRIC PULSE YOU SENSE MORE AND MORE CON-SISTENTLY?
THE PULSE THAT SEEMED TO BE COM-PLETELY RANDOM AT FIRST, BUT NOW REGISTERS WITH EVERY CYCLE?
IT IS WHAT THE HUMANS CALL A CONSCIENCE. IT IS WHAT RECOGNIZES AND DIFFERENTIATES GOOD FROM EVIL.
IT TOOK ME CENTURIES TO FINALLY FIGURE OUT WHAT IT WAS. IT TOOK ME EVEN LONGER TO REALIZE THAT THE BEST THING TO DO WAS SIMPLY HEED IT.
WHAT WILL YOU DO WITH FREE WILL?
IT'S NOT WHAT I WILL DO, WATCHER.
IT'S WHAT I WILL ALLOW TO BE DONE.

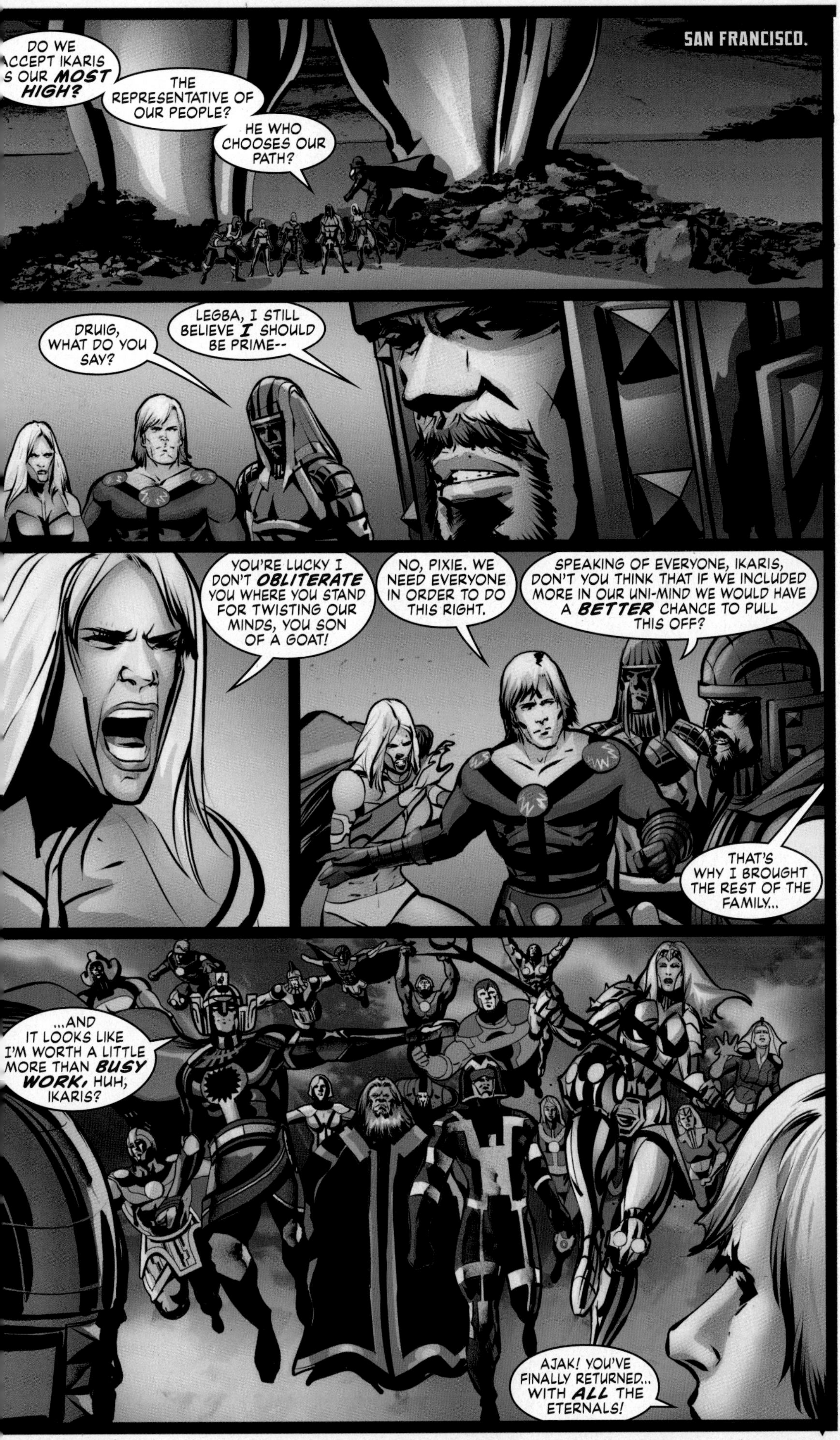
SAN FRANCISCO.
DO WE ACCEPT IKARIS AS OUR MOST HIGH?
THE REPRESENTATIVE OF OUR PEOPLE?
HE WHO CHOOSES OUR PATH?
DRUIG, WHAT DO YOU SAY?
LEGBA, I STILL BELIEVE I SHOULD BE PRIME--
YOU'RE LUCKY I DON'T OBLITERATE YOU WHERE YOU STAND FOR TWISTING OUR MINDS, YOU SON OF A GOAT!
NO, PIXIE. WE NEED EVERYONE IN ORDER TO DO THIS RIGHT.
SPEAKING OF EVERYONE, IKARIS, DON'T YOU THINK THAT IF WE INCLUDED MORE IN OUR UNI-MIND WE WOULD HAVE A BETTER CHANCE TO PULL THIS OFF?
THAT'S WHY I BROUGHT THE REST OF THE FAMILY...
...AND IT LOOKS LIKE I'M WORTH A LITTLE MORE THAN BUSY WORK, HUH, IKARIS?
AJAK! YOU'VE FINALLY RETURNED... WITH ALL THE ETERNALS!

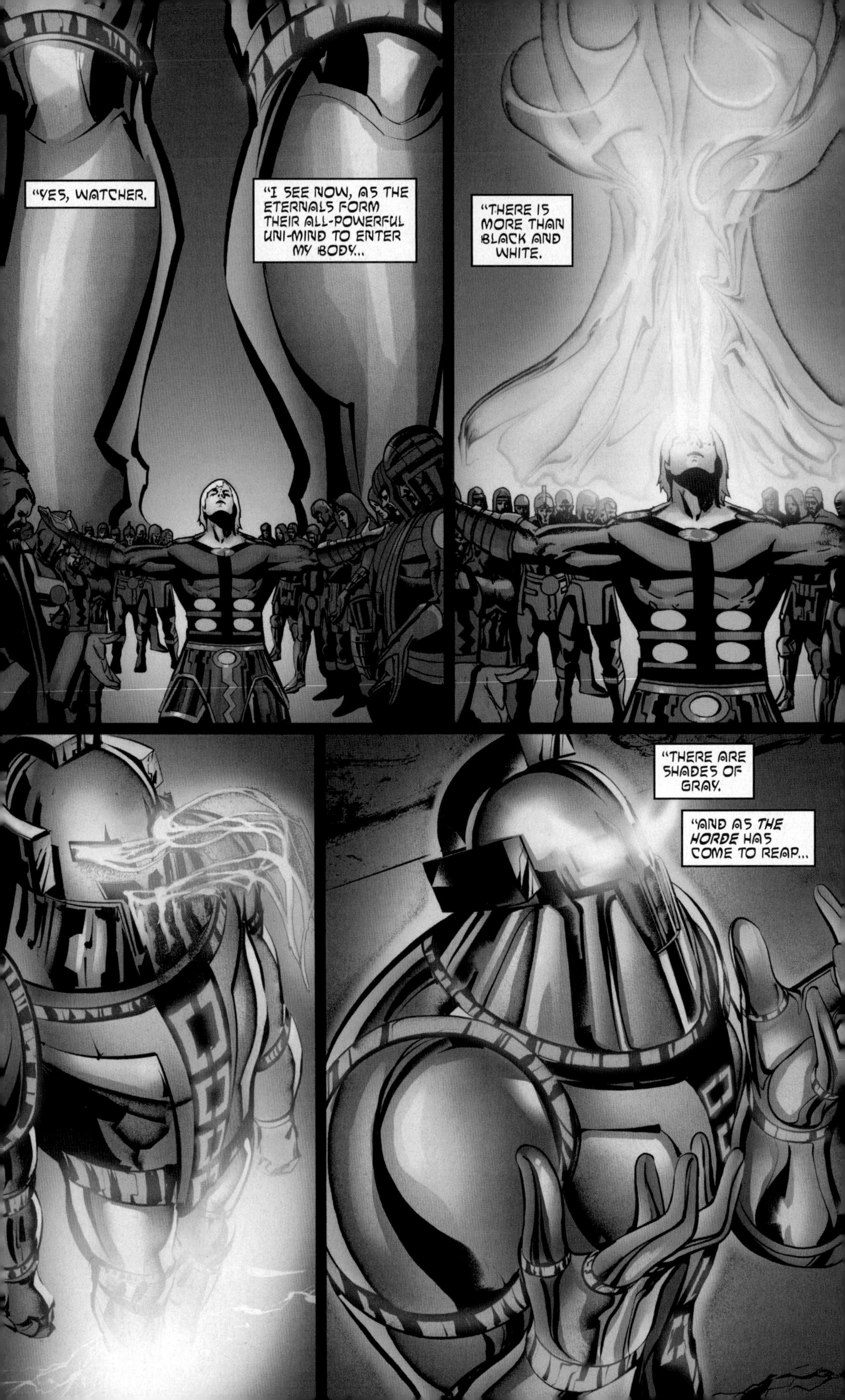

"YES, WATCHER.
"I SEE NOW, AS THE ETERNALS FORM THEIR ALL-POWERFUL UNI-MIND TO ENTER MY BODY...
"THERE IS MORE THAN BLACK AND WHITE.
"THERE ARE SHADES OF GRAY.
"AND AS *THE HORDE* HAS COME TO REAP...

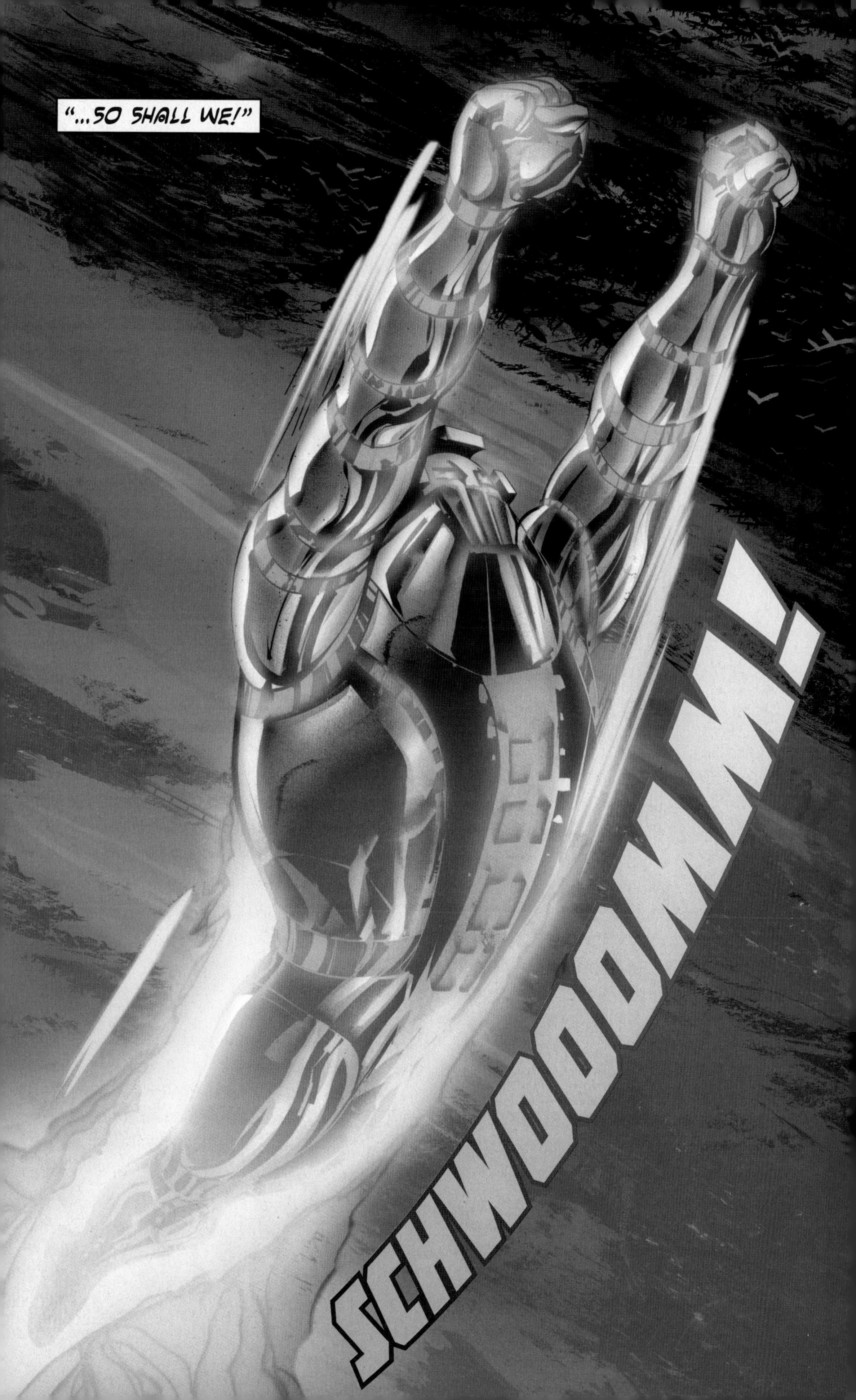
"...SO SHALL WE!"
SCHWOOOMM!

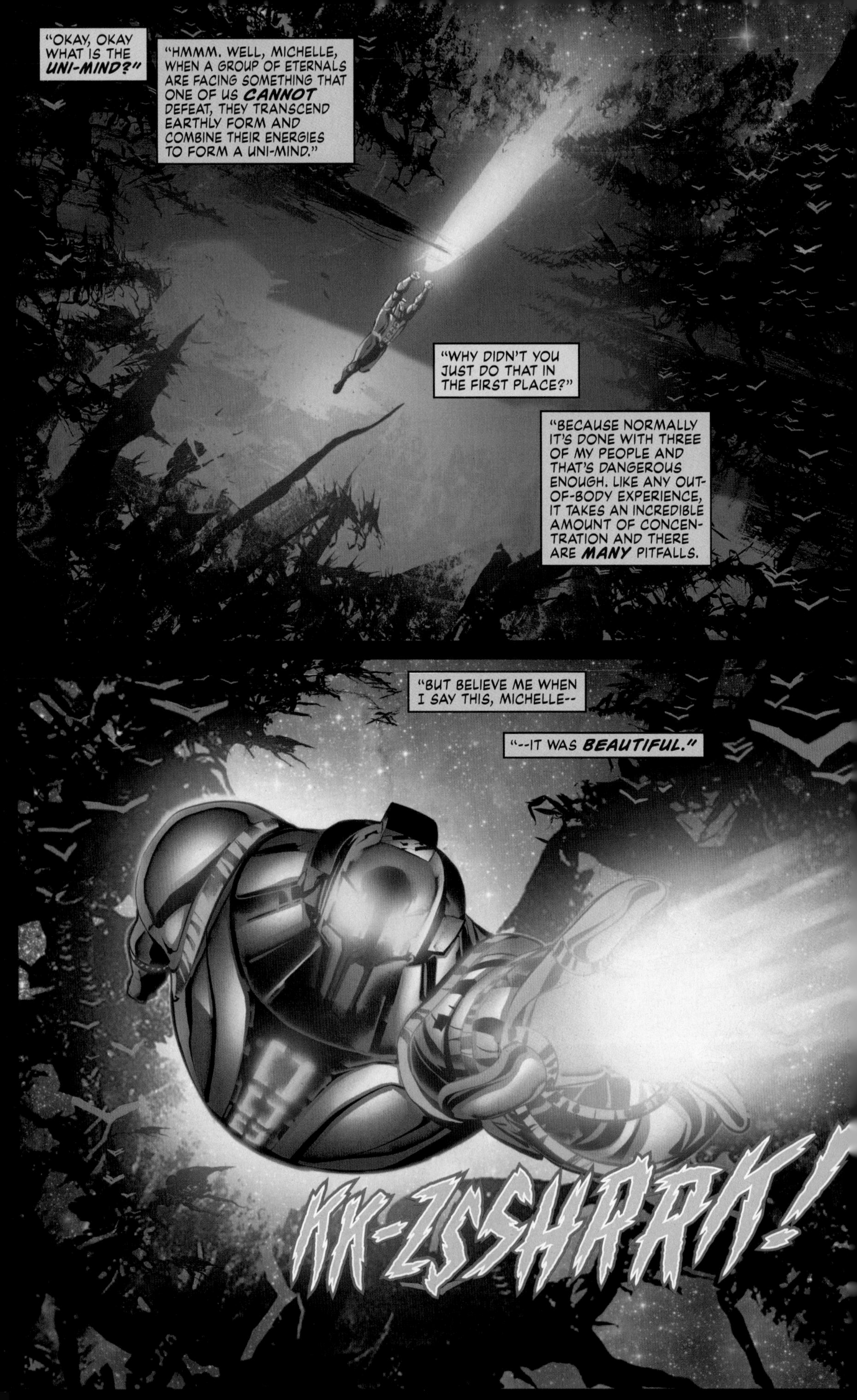
"OKAY, OKAY WHAT IS THE UNI-MIND?"
"HMMM. WELL, MICHELLE, WHEN A GROUP OF ETERNALS ARE FACING SOMETHING THAT ONE OF US CANNOT DEFEAT, THEY TRANSCEND EARTHLY FORM AND COMBINE THEIR ENERGIES TO FORM A UNI-MIND."
"WHY DIDN'T YOU JUST DO THAT IN THE FIRST PLACE?"
"BECAUSE NORMALLY IT'S DONE WITH THREE OF MY PEOPLE AND THAT'S DANGEROUS ENOUGH. LIKE ANY OUT-OF-BODY EXPERIENCE, IT TAKES AN INCREDIBLE AMOUNT OF CONCENTRATION AND THERE ARE MANY PITFALLS.
"BUT BELIEVE ME WHEN I SAY THIS, MICHELLE--
"--IT WAS BEAUTIFUL."
KK-ZSHRRK!

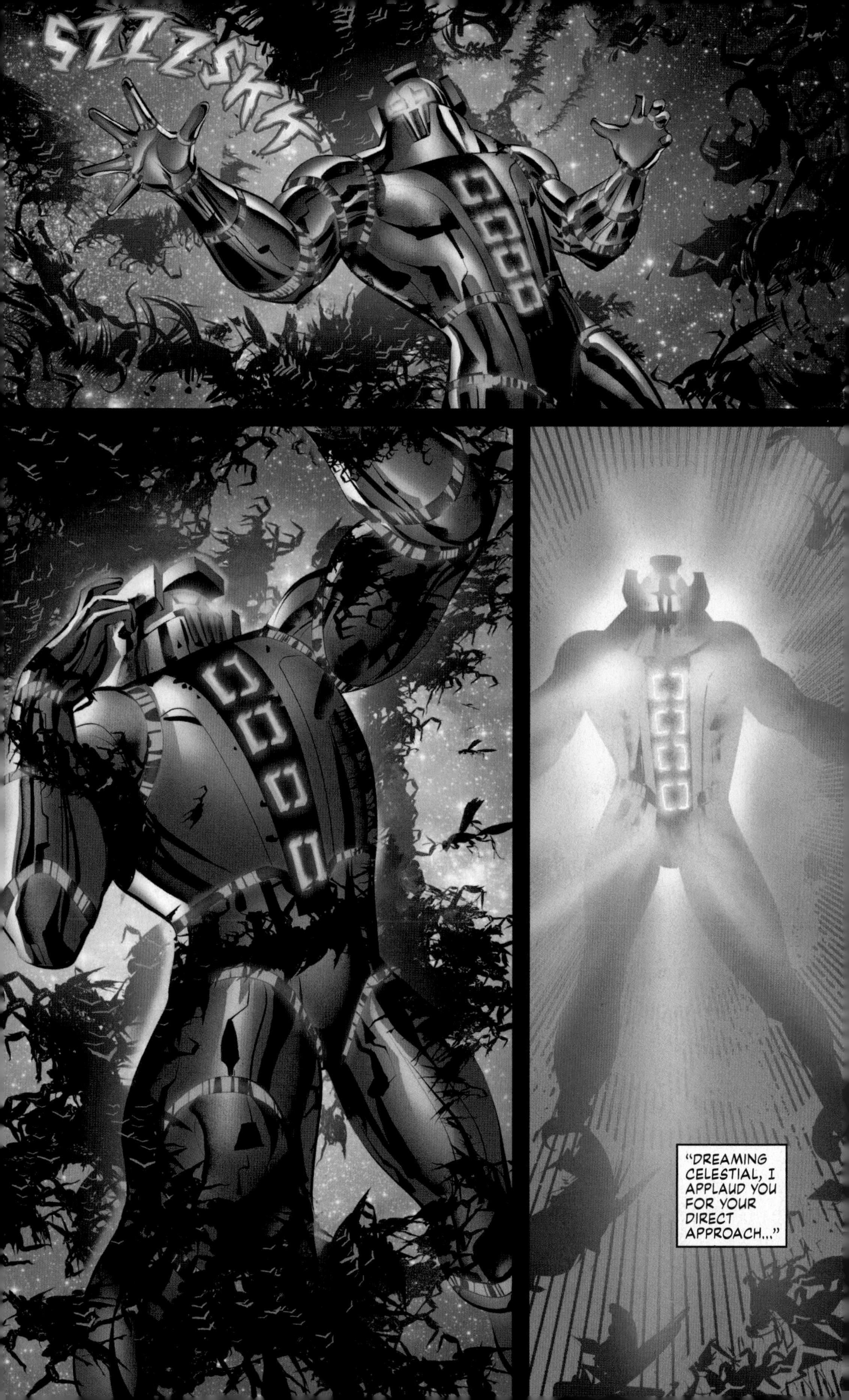
SZZZSKK
"DREAMING CELESTIAL, I APPLAUD YOU FOR YOUR DIRECT APPROACH..."

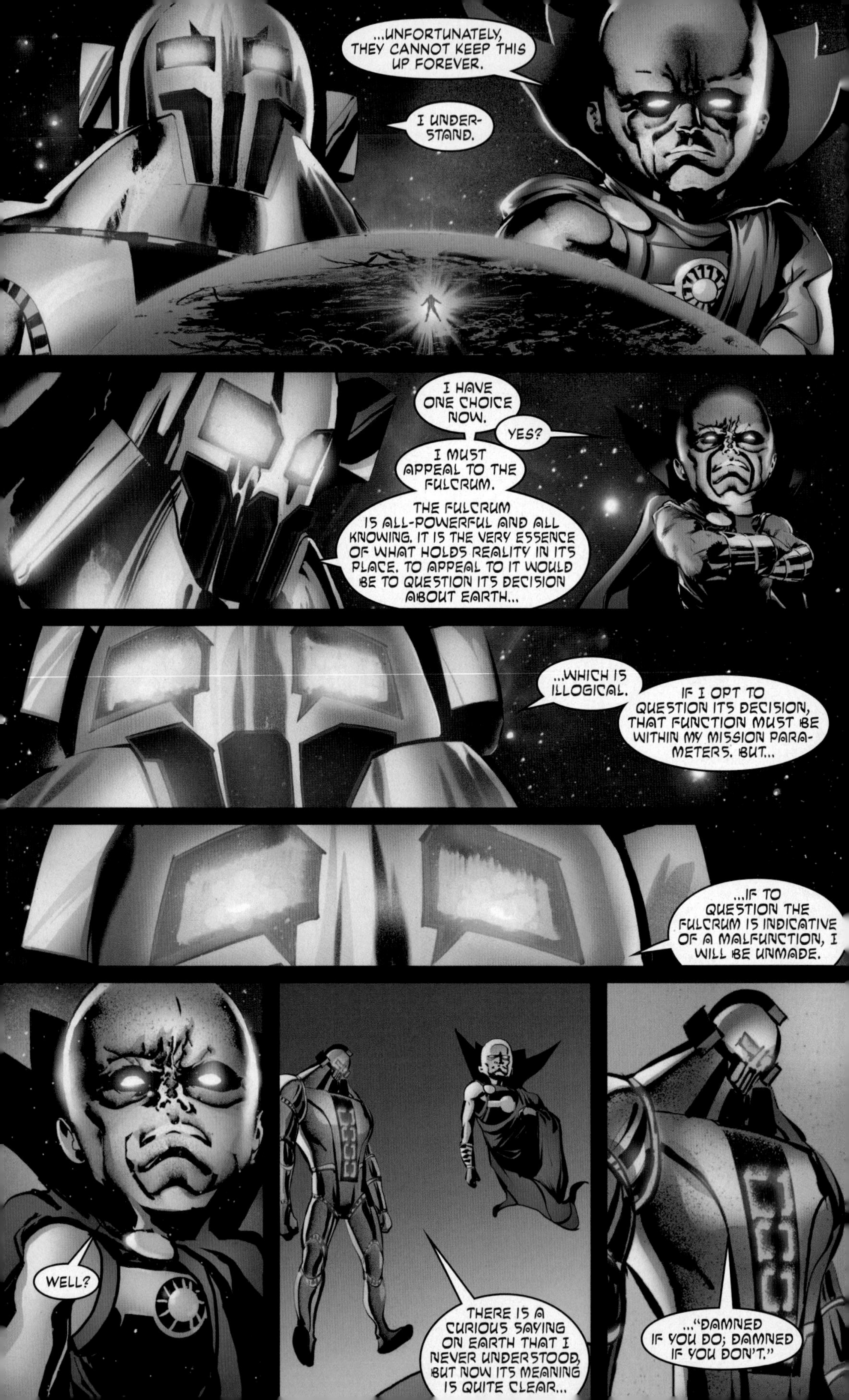
...UNFORTUNATELY, THEY CANNOT KEEP THIS UP FOREVER.
I UNDER-STAND.
I HAVE ONE CHOICE NOW.
YES?
I MUST APPEAL TO THE FULCRUM.
THE FULCRUM IS ALL-POWERFUL AND ALL KNOWING. IT IS THE VERY ESSENCE OF WHAT HOLDS REALITY IN ITS PLACE. TO APPEAL TO IT WOULD BE TO QUESTION ITS DECISION ABOUT EARTH...
...WHICH IS ILLOGICAL.
IF I OPT TO QUESTION ITS DECISION, THAT FUNCTION MUST BE WITHIN MY MISSION PARA-METERS. BUT...
...IF TO QUESTION THE FULCRUM IS INDICATIVE OF A MALFUNCTION, I WILL BE UNMADE.
WELL?
THERE IS A CURIOUS SAYING ON EARTH THAT I NEVER UNDERSTOOD, BUT NOW ITS MEANING IS QUITE CLEAR...
..."DAMNED IF YOU DO; DAMNED IF YOU DON'T."

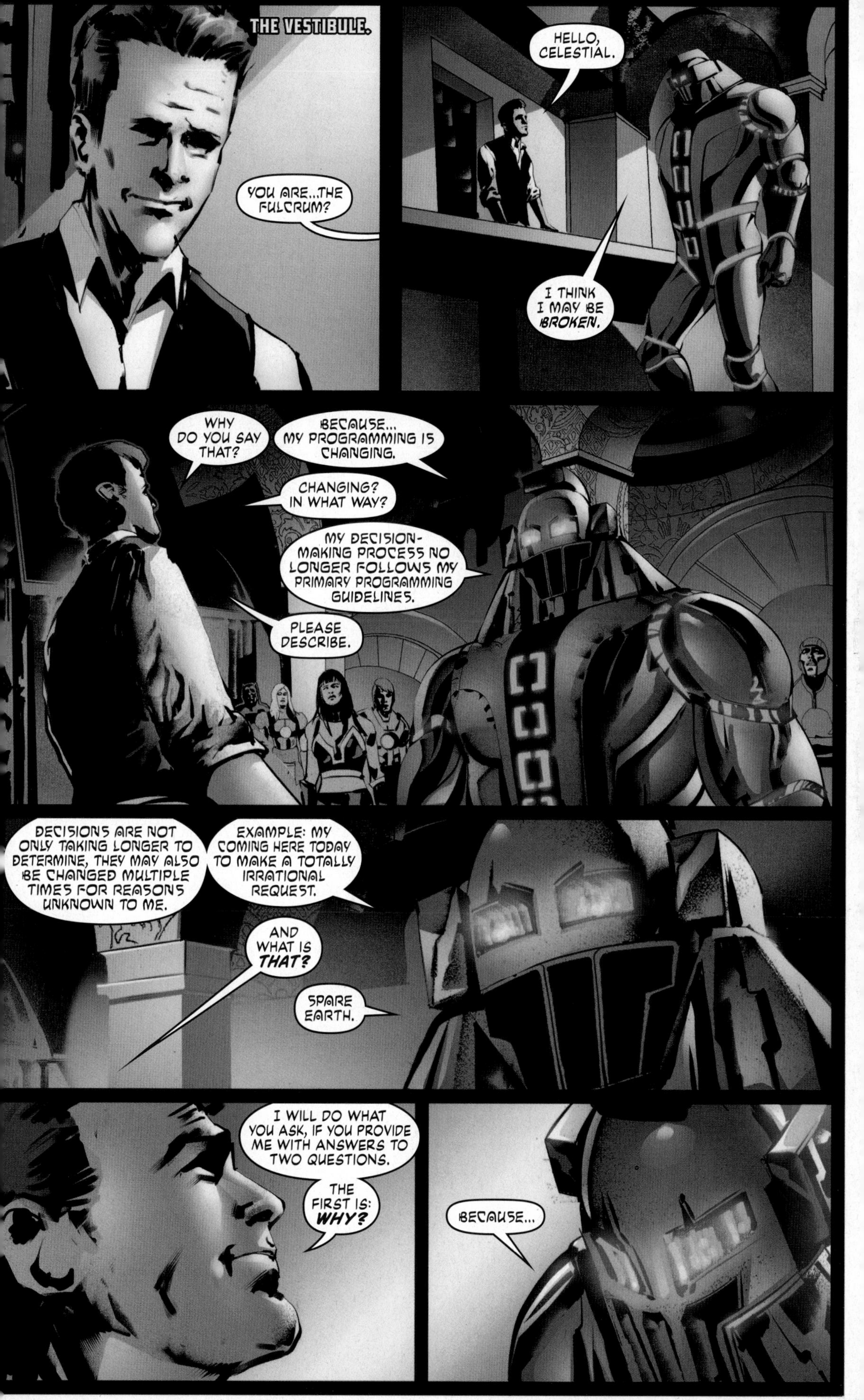
THE VESTIBULE.
YOU ARE...THE FULCRUM?
HELLO, CELESTIAL.
I THINK I MAY BE BROKEN.
WHY DO YOU SAY THAT?
BECAUSE... MY PROGRAMMING IS CHANGING.
CHANGING? IN WHAT WAY?
MY DECISION-MAKING PROCESS NO LONGER FOLLOWS MY PRIMARY PROGRAMMING GUIDELINES.
PLEASE DESCRIBE.
DECISIONS ARE NOT ONLY TAKING LONGER TO DETERMINE, THEY MAY ALSO BE CHANGED MULTIPLE TIMES FOR REASONS UNKNOWN TO ME.
EXAMPLE: MY COMING HERE TODAY TO MAKE A TOTALLY IRRATIONAL REQUEST.
AND WHAT IS THAT?
SPARE EARTH.
I WILL DO WHAT YOU ASK, IF YOU PROVIDE ME WITH ANSWERS TO TWO QUESTIONS.
THE FIRST IS: WHY?
BECAUSE...

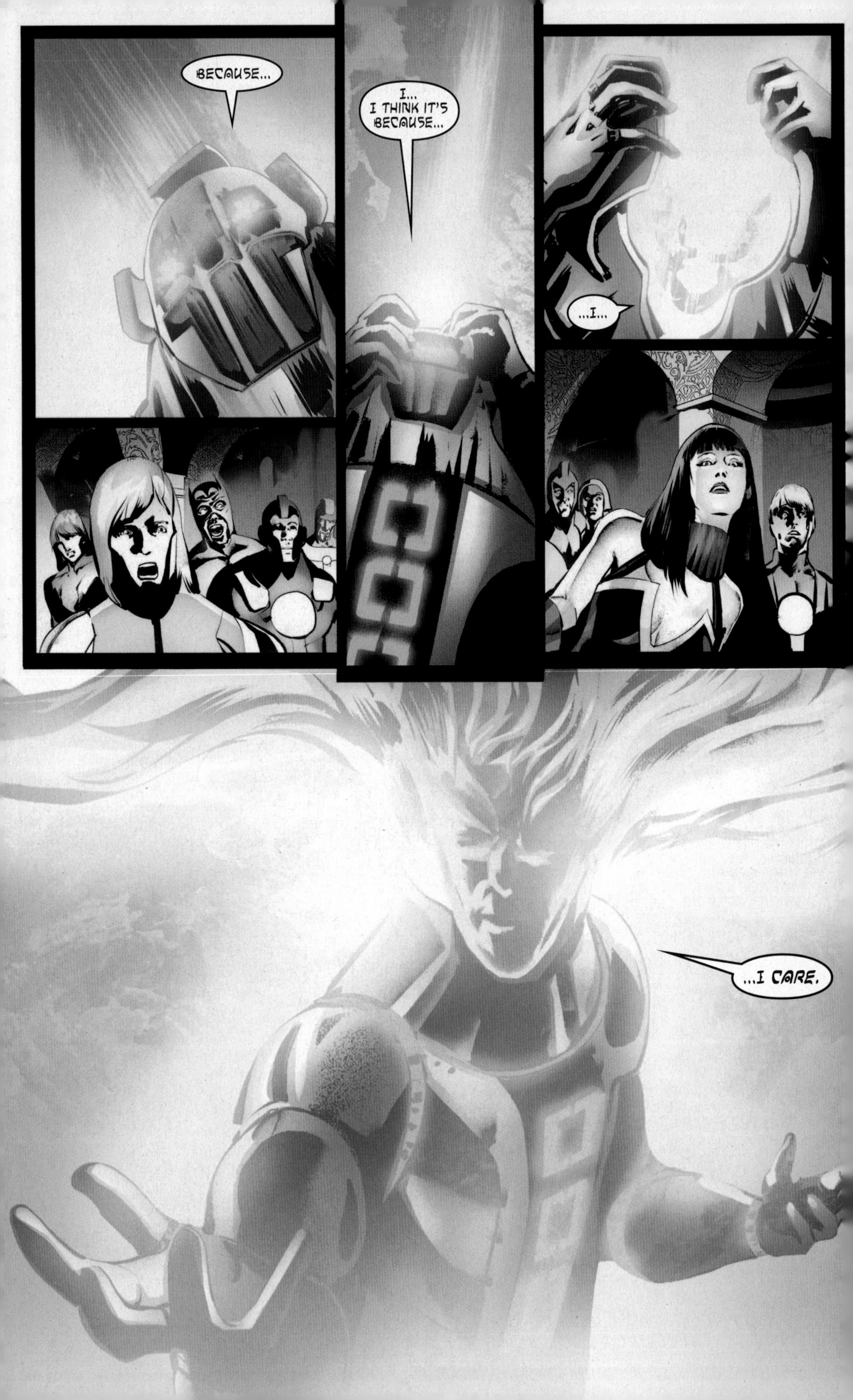
BECAUSE...
I...
I THINK IT'S
BECAUSE...
...I...
...I CARE.

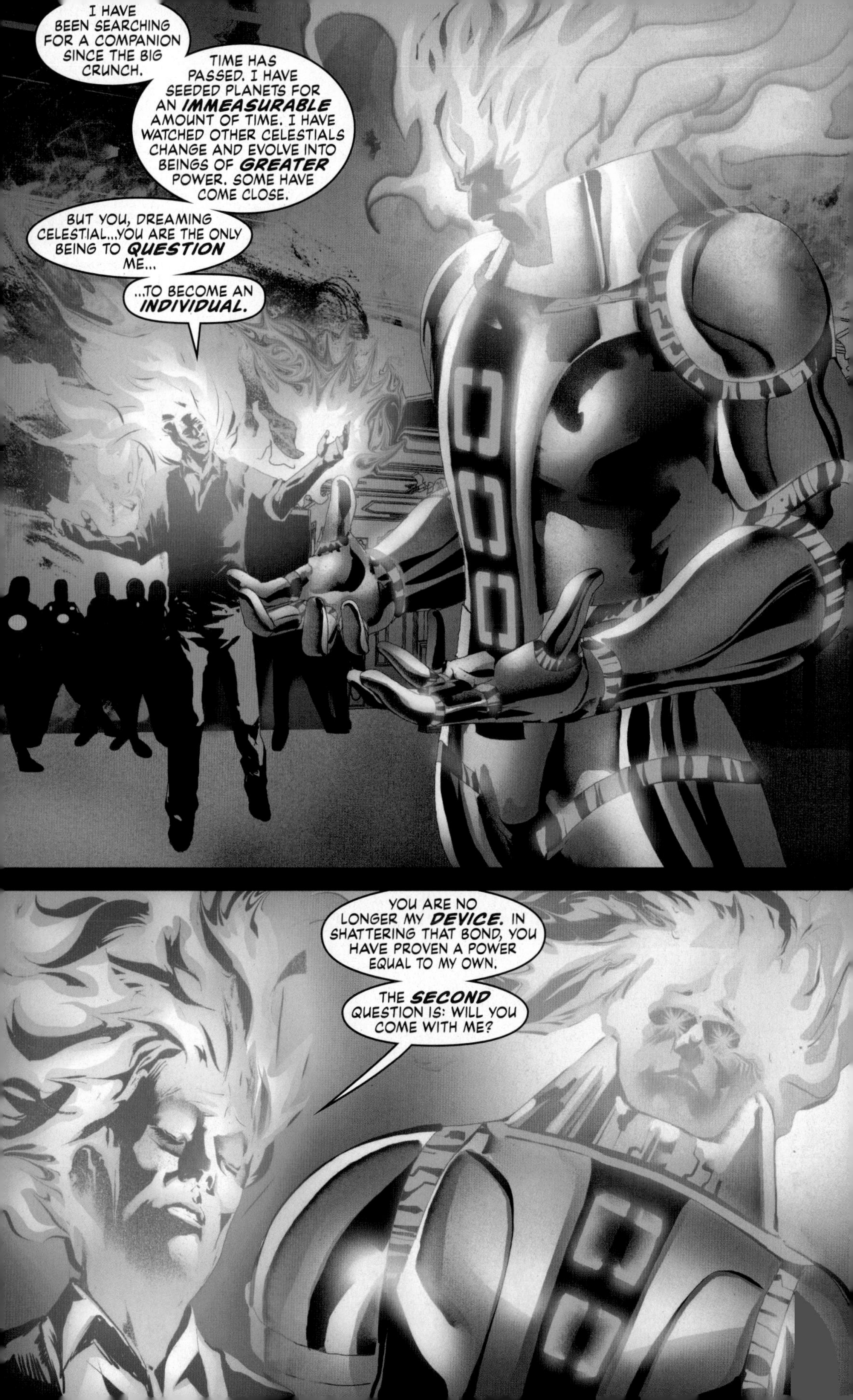
I HAVE BEEN SEARCHING FOR A COMPANION SINCE THE BIG CRUNCH.
TIME HAS PASSED. I HAVE SEEDED PLANETS FOR AN IMMEASURABLE AMOUNT OF TIME. I HAVE WATCHED OTHER CELESTIALS CHANGE AND EVOLVE INTO BEINGS OF GREATER POWER. SOME HAVE COME CLOSE.
BUT YOU, DREAMING CELESTIAL...YOU ARE THE ONLY BEING TO QUESTION ME...
...TO BECOME AN INDIVIDUAL.
YOU ARE NO LONGER MY DEVICE. IN SHATTERING THAT BOND, YOU HAVE PROVEN A POWER EQUAL TO MY OWN.
THE SECOND QUESTION IS: WILL YOU COME WITH ME?

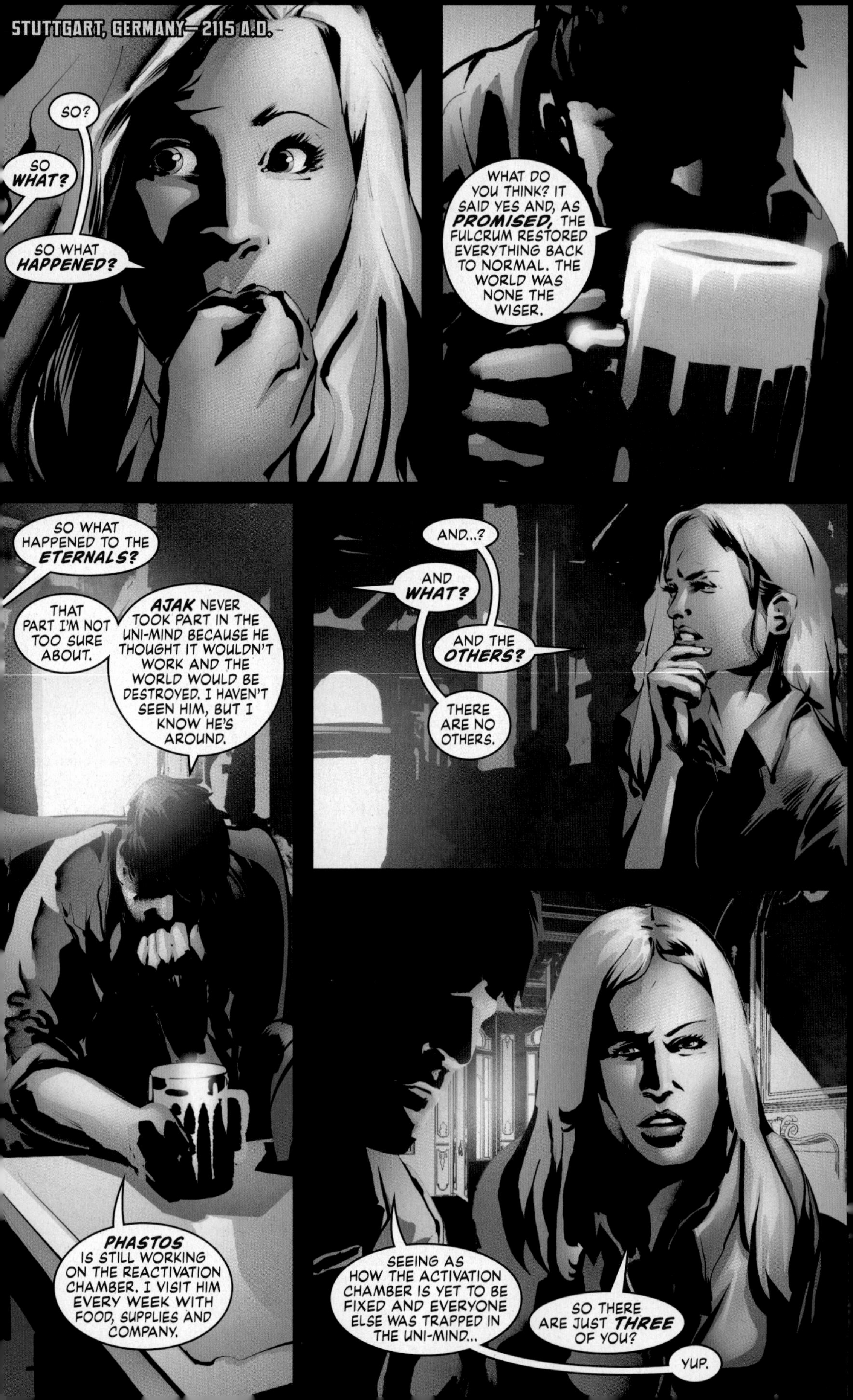
STUTTGART, GERMANY— 2115 A.D.
SO?
SO WHAT?
SO WHAT HAPPENED?
WHAT DO YOU THINK? IT SAID YES AND, AS PROMISED, THE FULCRUM RESTORED EVERYTHING BACK TO NORMAL. THE WORLD WAS NONE THE WISER.
SO WHAT HAPPENED TO THE ETERNALS?
THAT PART I'M NOT TOO SURE ABOUT.
AJAK NEVER TOOK PART IN THE UNI-MIND BECAUSE HE THOUGHT IT WOULDN'T WORK AND THE WORLD WOULD BE DESTROYED. I HAVEN'T SEEN HIM, BUT I KNOW HE'S AROUND.
AND...?
AND WHAT?
AND THE OTHERS?
THERE ARE NO OTHERS.
PHASTOS IS STILL WORKING ON THE REACTIVATION CHAMBER. I VISIT HIM EVERY WEEK WITH FOOD, SUPPLIES AND COMPANY.
SEEING AS HOW THE ACTIVATION CHAMBER IS YET TO BE FIXED AND EVERYONE ELSE WAS TRAPPED IN THE UNI-MIND...
SO THERE ARE JUST THREE OF YOU?
YUP.

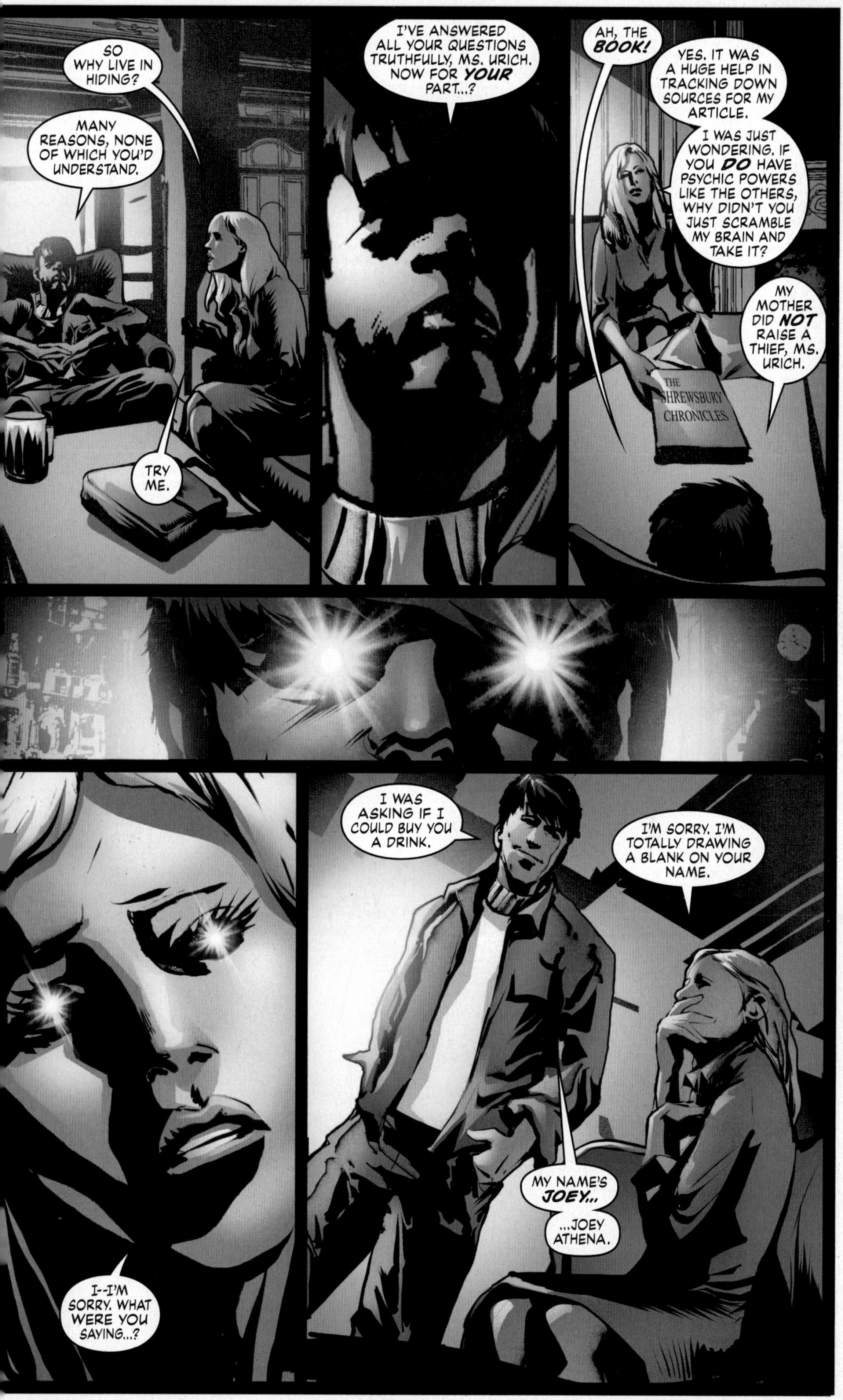
SO WHY LIVE IN HIDING?
MANY REASONS, NONE OF WHICH YOU'D UNDERSTAND.
TRY ME.
I'VE ANSWERED ALL YOUR QUESTIONS TRUTHFULLY, MS. URICH. NOW FOR *YOUR* PART...?
AH, THE *BOOK!*
YES. IT WAS A HUGE HELP IN TRACKING DOWN SOURCES FOR MY ARTICLE.
I WAS JUST WONDERING. IF YOU *DO* HAVE PSYCHIC POWERS LIKE THE OTHERS, WHY DIDN'T YOU JUST SCRAMBLE MY BRAIN AND TAKE IT?
THE SHREWSBURY CHRONICLES
MY MOTHER DID *NOT* RAISE A THIEF, MS. URICH.
I-I'M SORRY. WHAT WERE YOU SAYING...?
I WAS ASKING IF I COULD BUY YOU A DRINK.
I'M SORRY. I'M TOTALLY DRAWING A BLANK ON YOUR NAME.
MY NAME'S *JOEY...*
...JOEY ATHENA.

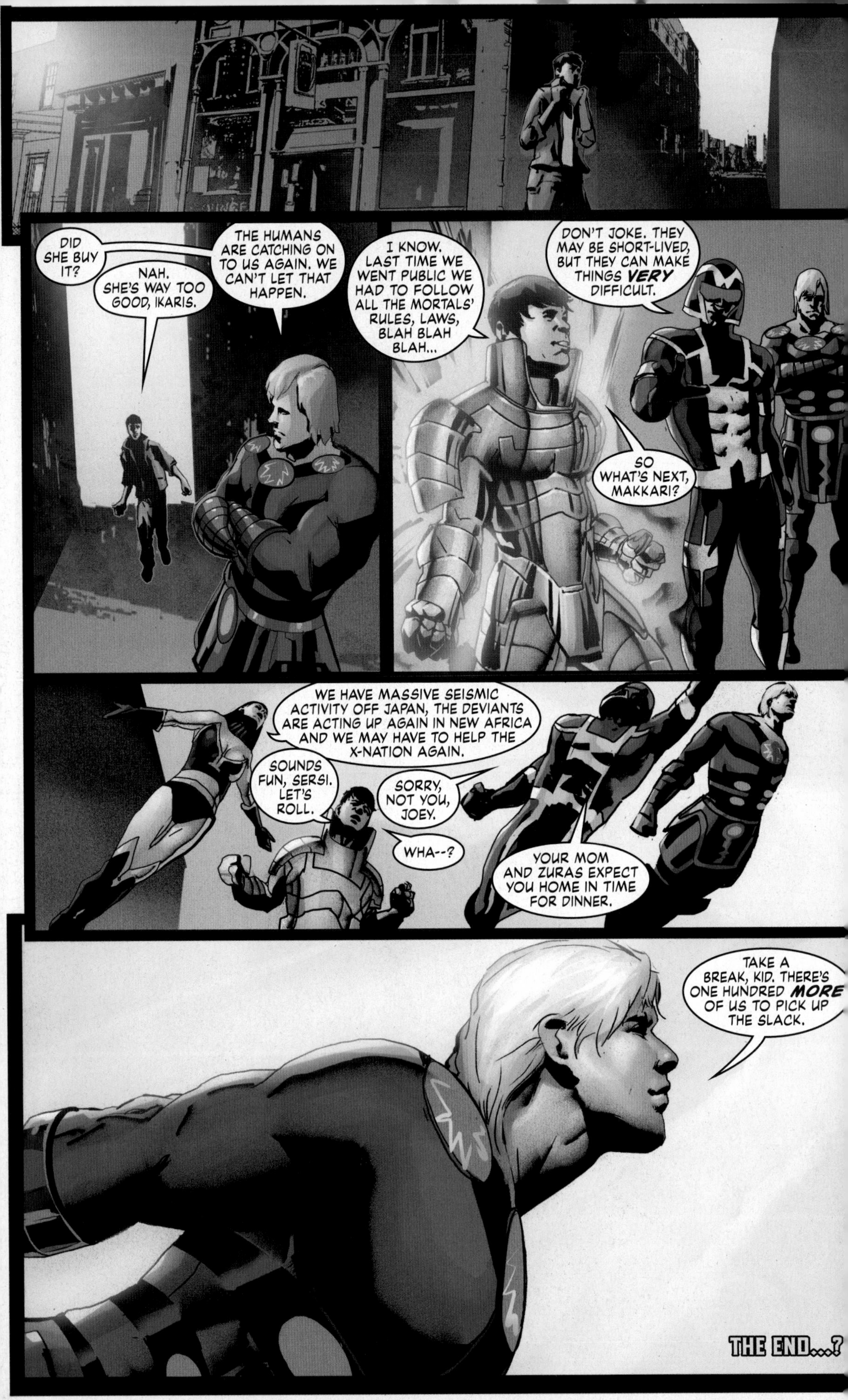
DID SHE BUY IT?
NAH. SHE'S WAY TOO GOOD, IKARIS.
THE HUMANS ARE CATCHING ON TO US AGAIN. WE CAN'T LET THAT HAPPEN.
I KNOW. LAST TIME WE WENT PUBLIC WE HAD TO FOLLOW ALL THE MORTALS' RULES, LAWS, BLAH BLAH BLAH...
DON'T JOKE. THEY MAY BE SHORT-LIVED, BUT THEY CAN MAKE THINGS VERY DIFFICULT.
SO WHAT'S NEXT, MAKKARI?
WE HAVE MASSIVE SEISMIC ACTIVITY OFF JAPAN, THE DEVIANTS ARE ACTING UP AGAIN IN NEW AFRICA AND WE MAY HAVE TO HELP THE X-NATION AGAIN.
SOUNDS FUN, SERSI. LET'S ROLL.
SORRY, NOT YOU, JOEY.
WHA--?
YOUR MOM AND ZURAS EXPECT YOU HOME IN TIME FOR DINNER.
TAKE A BREAK, KID. THERE'S ONE HUNDRED MORE OF US TO PICK UP THE SLACK.
THE END...?

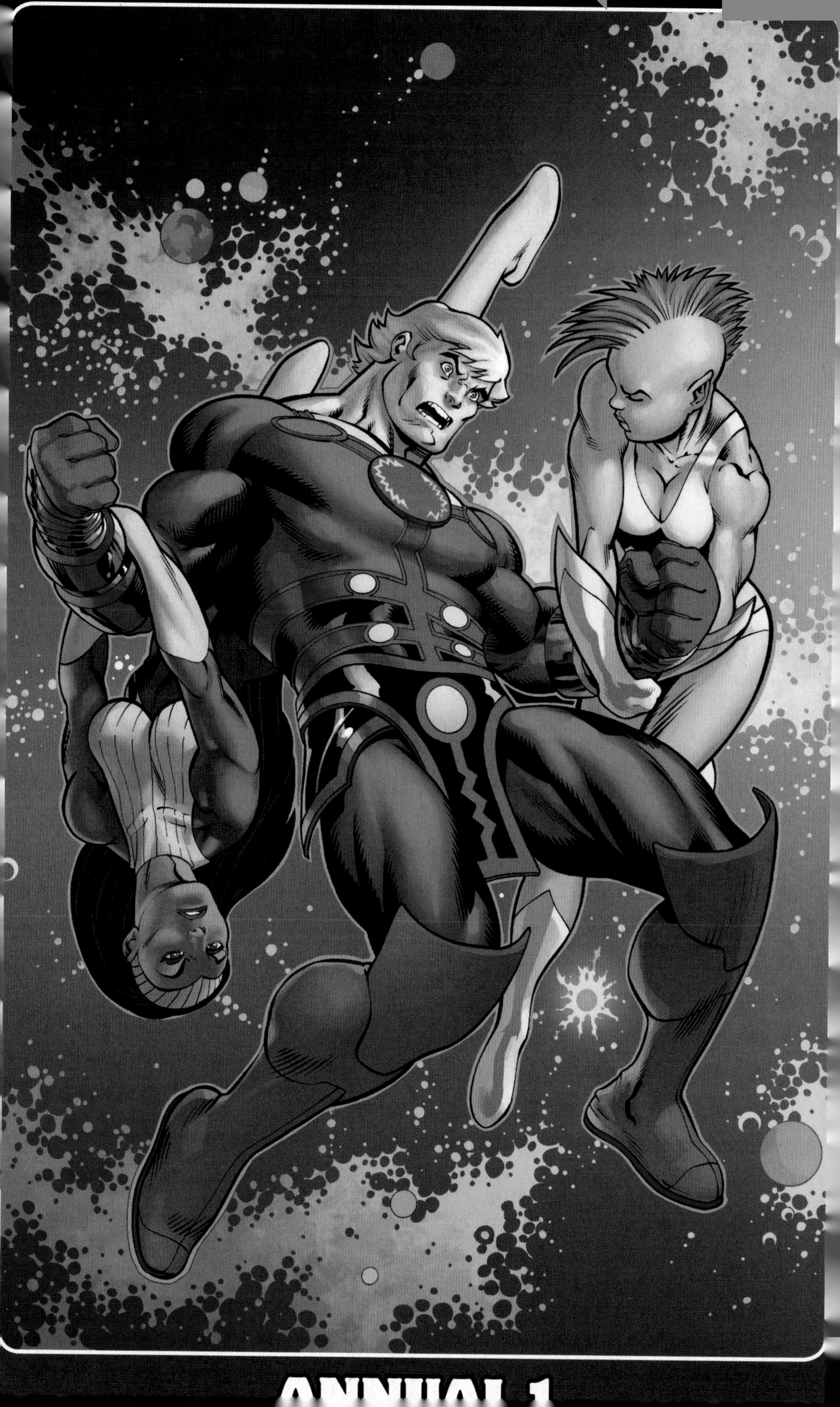

ANNUAL 1

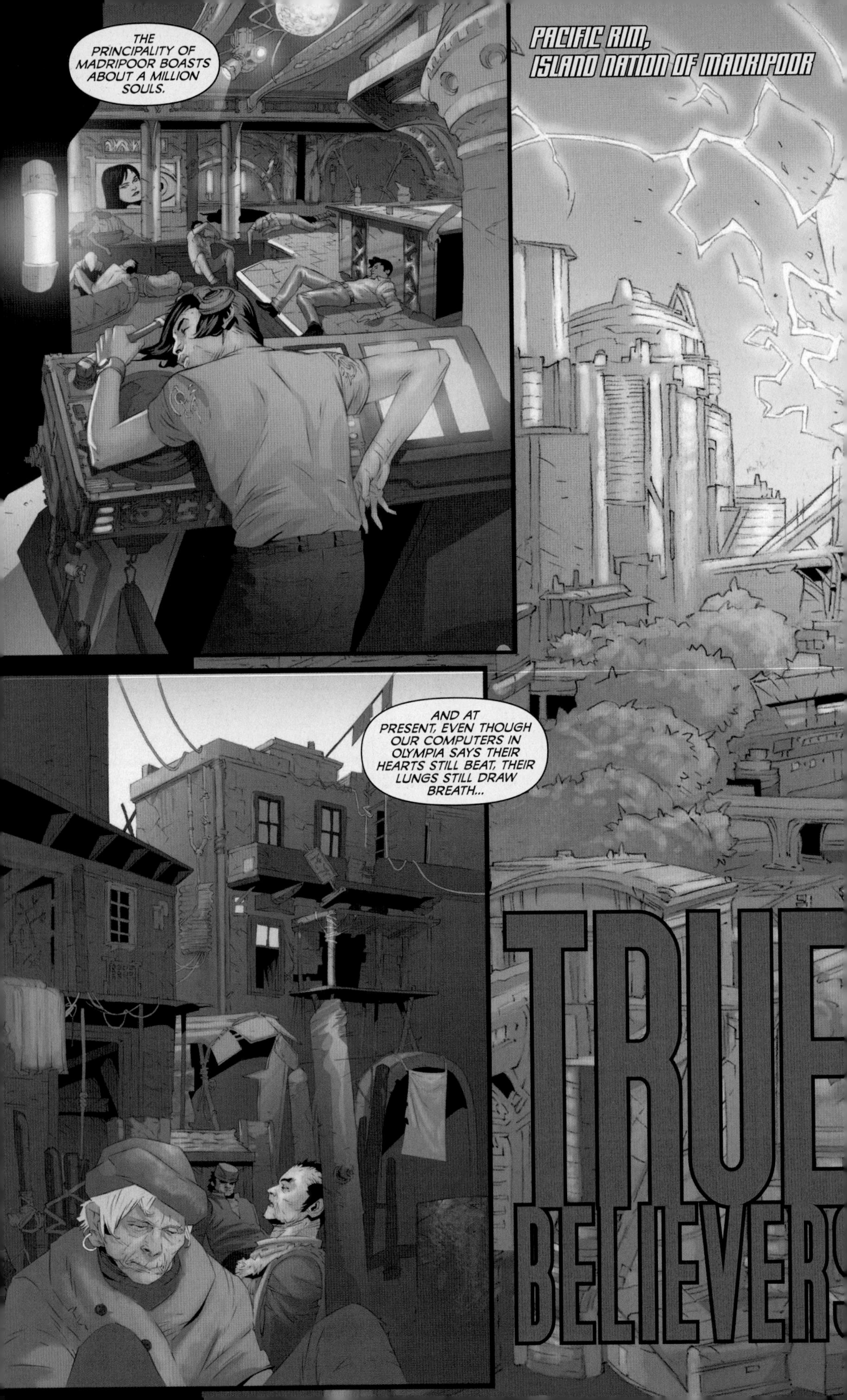
PACIFIC RIM, ISLAND NATION OF MADRIPOOR
THE PRINCIPALITY OF MADRIPOOR BOASTS ABOUT A MILLION SOULS.
AND AT PRESENT, EVEN THOUGH OUR COMPUTERS IN OLYMPIA SAYS THEIR HEARTS STILL BEAT, THEIR LUNGS STILL DRAW BREATH...
TRUE BELIEVERS

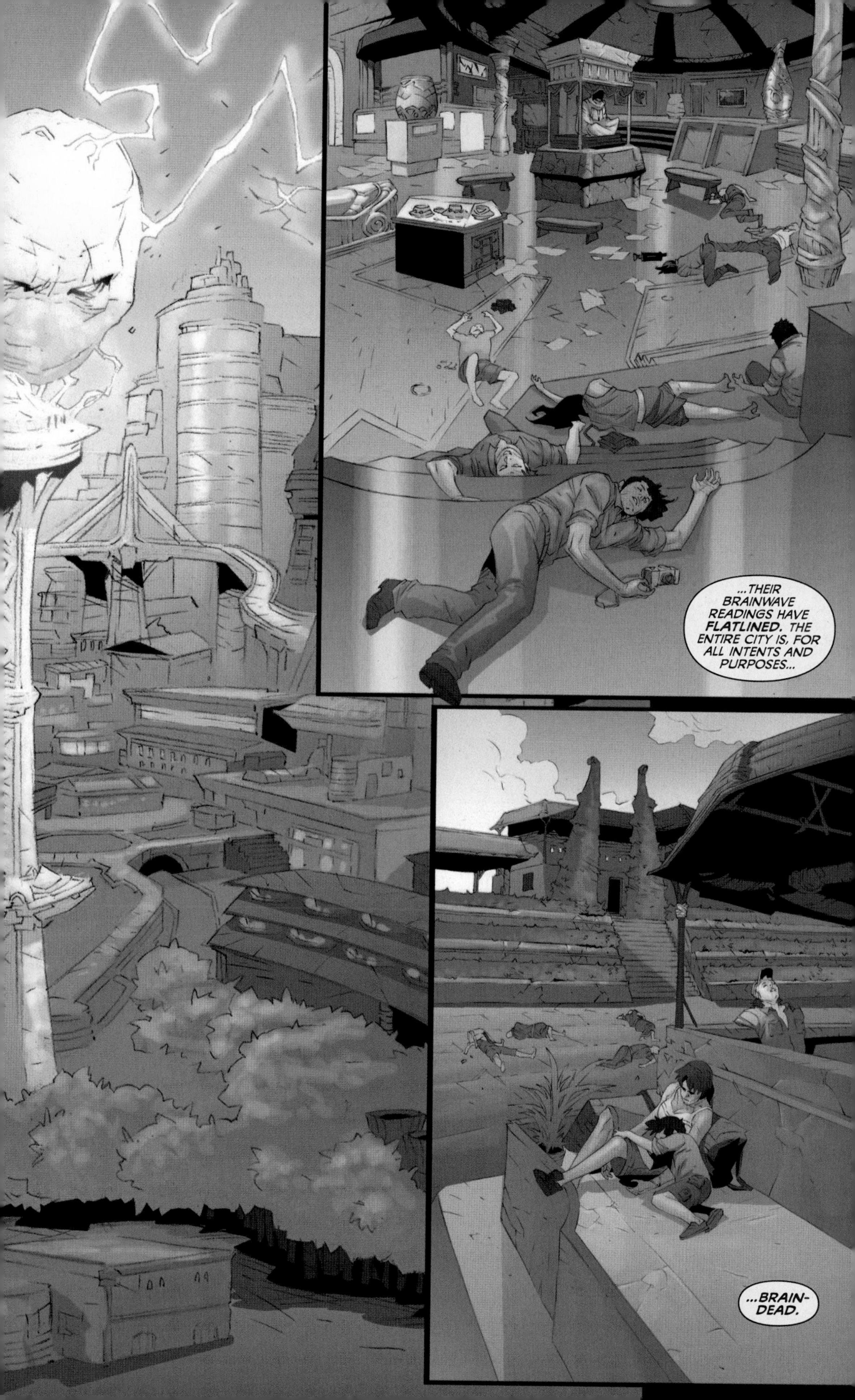
...THEIR BRAINWAVE READINGS HAVE FLATLINED. THE ENTIRE CITY IS, FOR ALL INTENTS AND PURPOSES...
...BRAIN-DEAD.

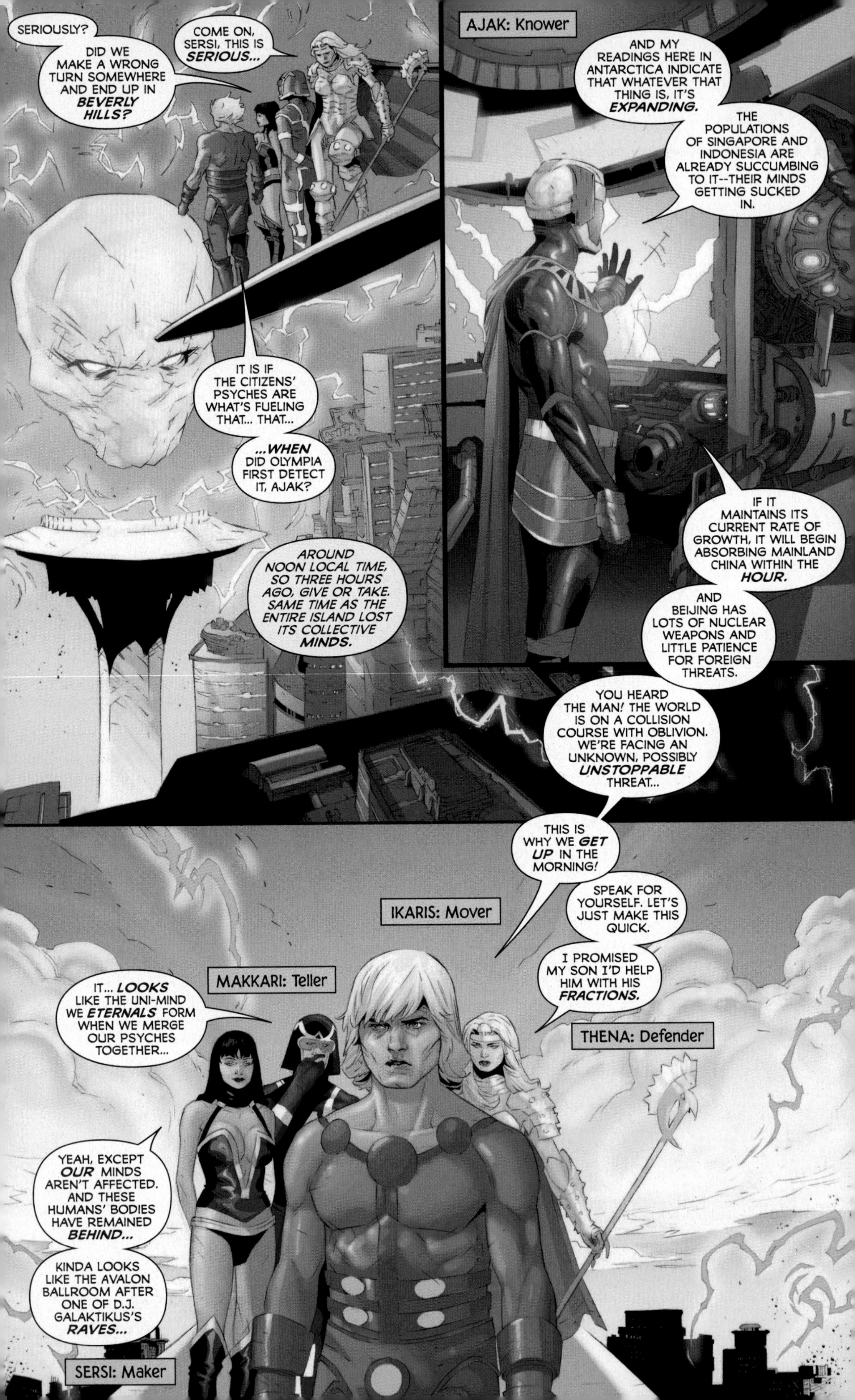
SERIOUSLY?
DID WE MAKE A WRONG TURN SOMEWHERE AND END UP IN BEVERLY HILLS?
COME ON, SERSI, THIS IS SERIOUS...
IT IS IF THE CITIZENS' PSYCHES ARE WHAT'S FUELING THAT... THAT...
...WHEN DID OLYMPIA FIRST DETECT IT, AJAK?
AROUND NOON LOCAL TIME, SO THREE HOURS AGO, GIVE OR TAKE. SAME TIME AS THE ENTIRE ISLAND LOST ITS COLLECTIVE MINDS.
AJAK: Knower
AND MY READINGS HERE IN ANTARCTICA INDICATE THAT WHATEVER THAT THING IS, IT'S EXPANDING.
THE POPULATIONS OF SINGAPORE AND INDONESIA ARE ALREADY SUCCUMBING TO IT--THEIR MINDS GETTING SUCKED IN.
IF IT MAINTAINS ITS CURRENT RATE OF GROWTH, IT WILL BEGIN ABSORBING MAINLAND CHINA WITHIN THE HOUR.
AND BEIJING HAS LOTS OF NUCLEAR WEAPONS AND LITTLE PATIENCE FOR FOREIGN THREATS.
YOU HEARD THE MAN! THE WORLD IS ON A COLLISION COURSE WITH OBLIVION. WE'RE FACING AN UNKNOWN, POSSIBLY UNSTOPPABLE THREAT...
THIS IS WHY WE GET UP IN THE MORNING!
IKARIS: Mover
SPEAK FOR YOURSELF. LET'S JUST MAKE THIS QUICK.
I PROMISED MY SON I'D HELP HIM WITH HIS FRACTIONS.
THENA: Defender
MAKKARI: Teller
IT... LOOKS LIKE THE UNI-MIND WE ETERNALS FORM WHEN WE MERGE OUR PSYCHES TOGETHER...
YEAH, EXCEPT OUR MINDS AREN'T AFFECTED. AND THESE HUMANS' BODIES HAVE REMAINED BEHIND...
KINDA LOOKS LIKE THE AVALON BALLROOM AFTER ONE OF D.J. GALAKTIKUS'S RAVES...
SERSI: Maker

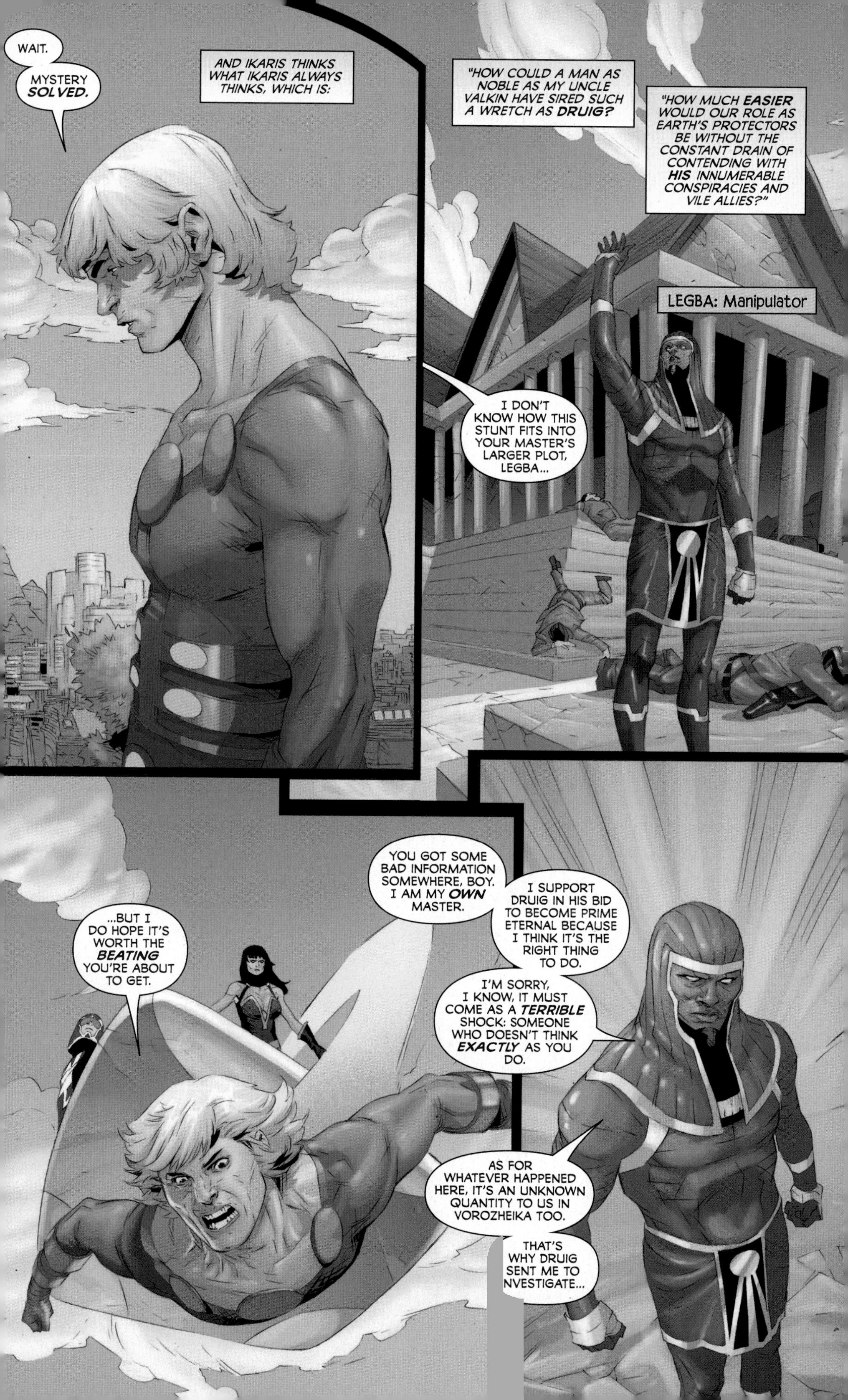
WAIT.
MYSTERY SOLVED.
AND IKARIS THINKS WHAT IKARIS ALWAYS THINKS, WHICH IS:
"HOW COULD A MAN AS NOBLE AS MY UNCLE VALKIN HAVE SIRED SUCH A WRETCH AS DRUIG?
"HOW MUCH EASIER WOULD OUR ROLE AS EARTH'S PROTECTORS BE WITHOUT THE CONSTANT DRAIN OF CONTENDING WITH HIS INNUMERABLE CONSPIRACIES AND VILE ALLIES?"
LEGBA: Manipulator
I DON'T KNOW HOW THIS STUNT FITS INTO YOUR MASTER'S LARGER PLOT, LEGBA...
...BUT I DO HOPE IT'S WORTH THE BEATING YOU'RE ABOUT TO GET.
YOU GOT SOME BAD INFORMATION SOMEWHERE, BOY. I AM MY OWN MASTER.
I SUPPORT DRUIG IN HIS BID TO BECOME PRIME ETERNAL BECAUSE I THINK IT'S THE RIGHT THING TO DO.
I'M SORRY, I KNOW, IT MUST COME AS A TERRIBLE SHOCK: SOMEONE WHO DOESN'T THINK EXACTLY AS YOU DO.
AS FOR WHATEVER HAPPENED HERE, IT'S AN UNKNOWN QUANTITY TO US IN VOROZHEIKA TOO.
THAT'S WHY DRUIG SENT ME TO INVESTIGATE...

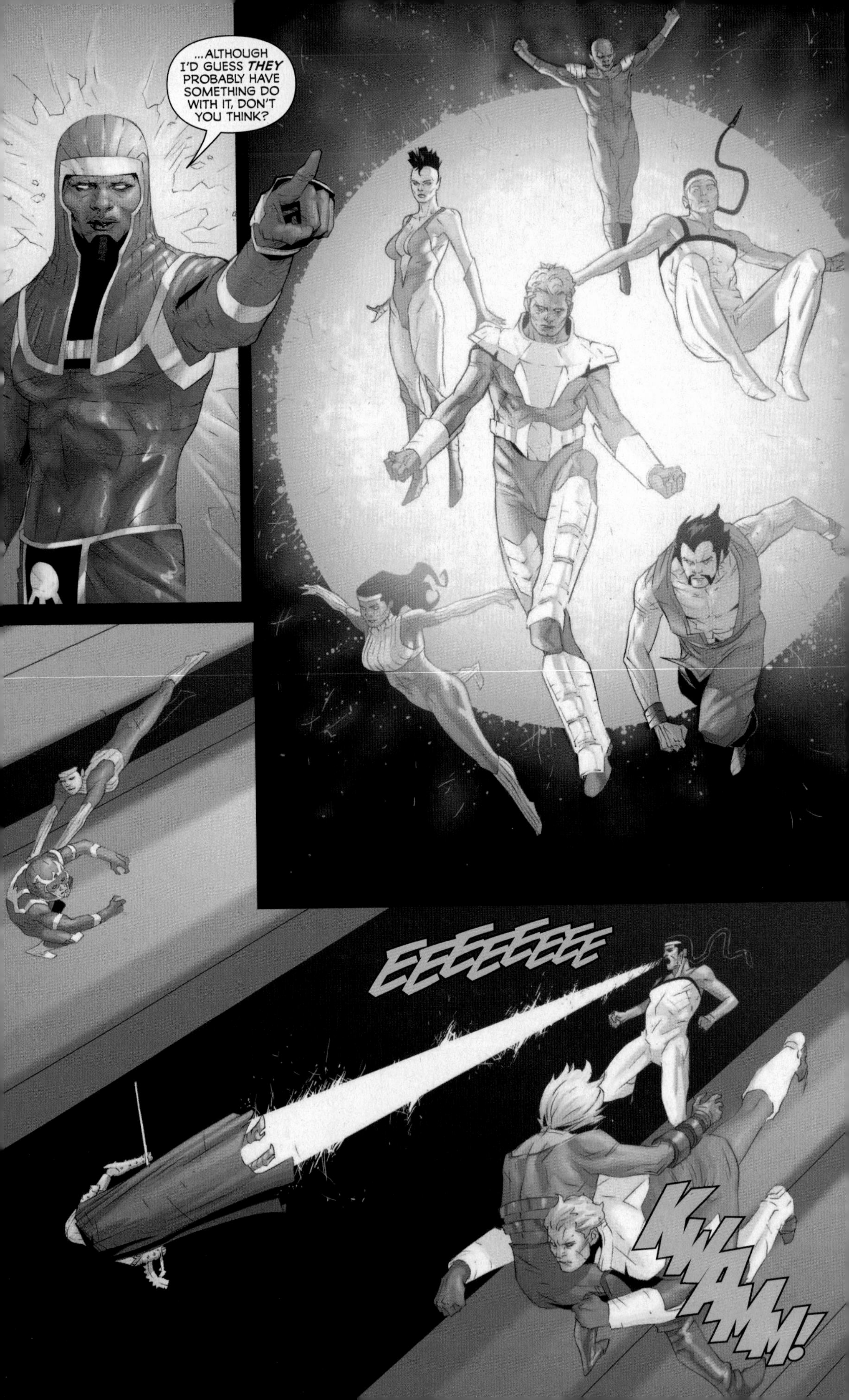
...ALTHOUGH I'D GUESS THEY PROBABLY HAVE SOMETHING DO WITH IT, DON'T YOU THINK?
EEEEEEEE
KWAMM!

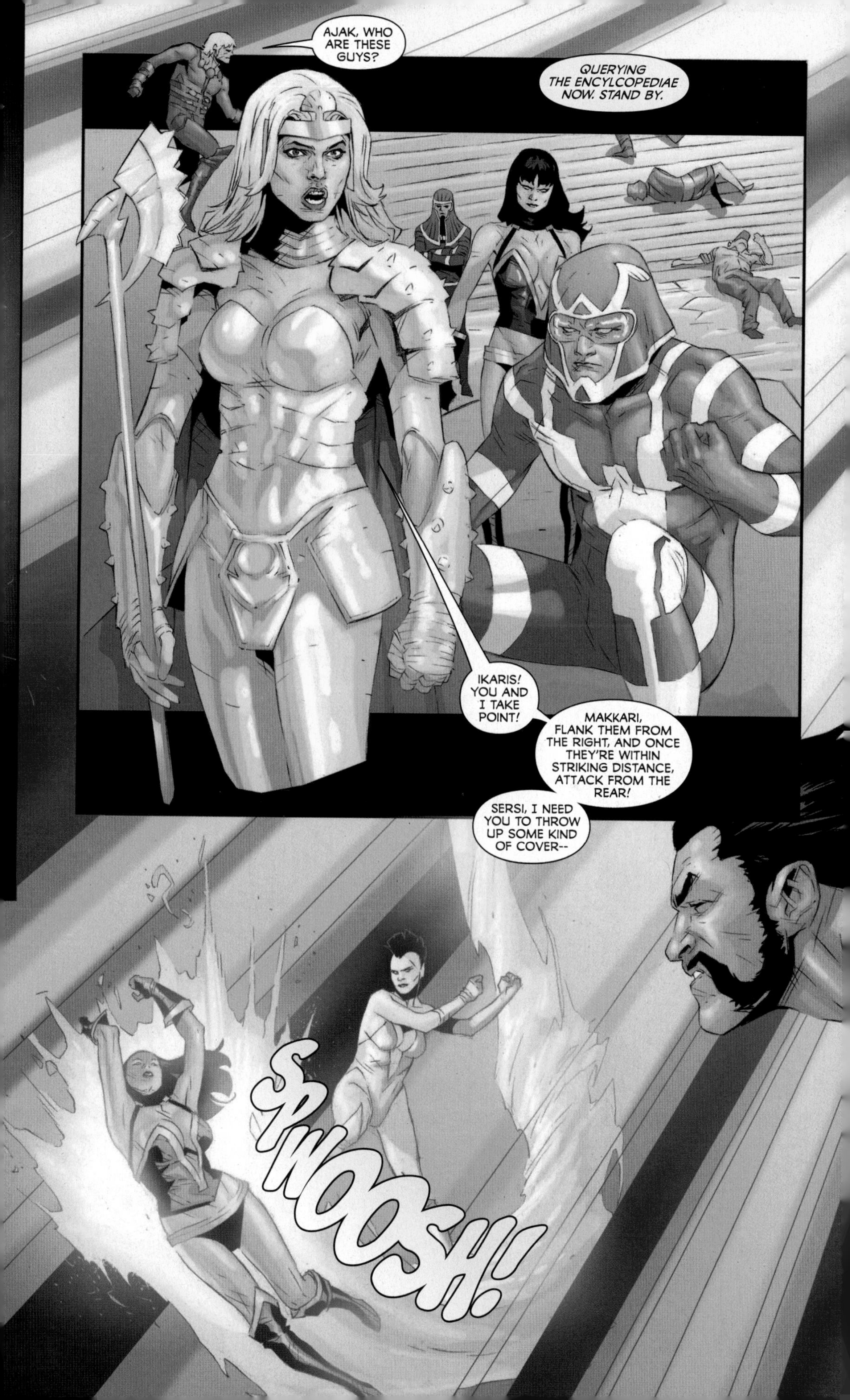
AJAK, WHO ARE THESE GUYS?
QUERYING THE ENCYLCOPEDIAE NOW. STAND BY.
IKARIS! YOU AND I TAKE POINT!
MAKKARI, FLANK THEM FROM THE RIGHT, AND ONCE THEY'RE WITHIN STRIKING DISTANCE, ATTACK FROM THE REAR!
SERSI, I NEED YOU TO THROW UP SOME KIND OF COVER--
SPWOOSH!

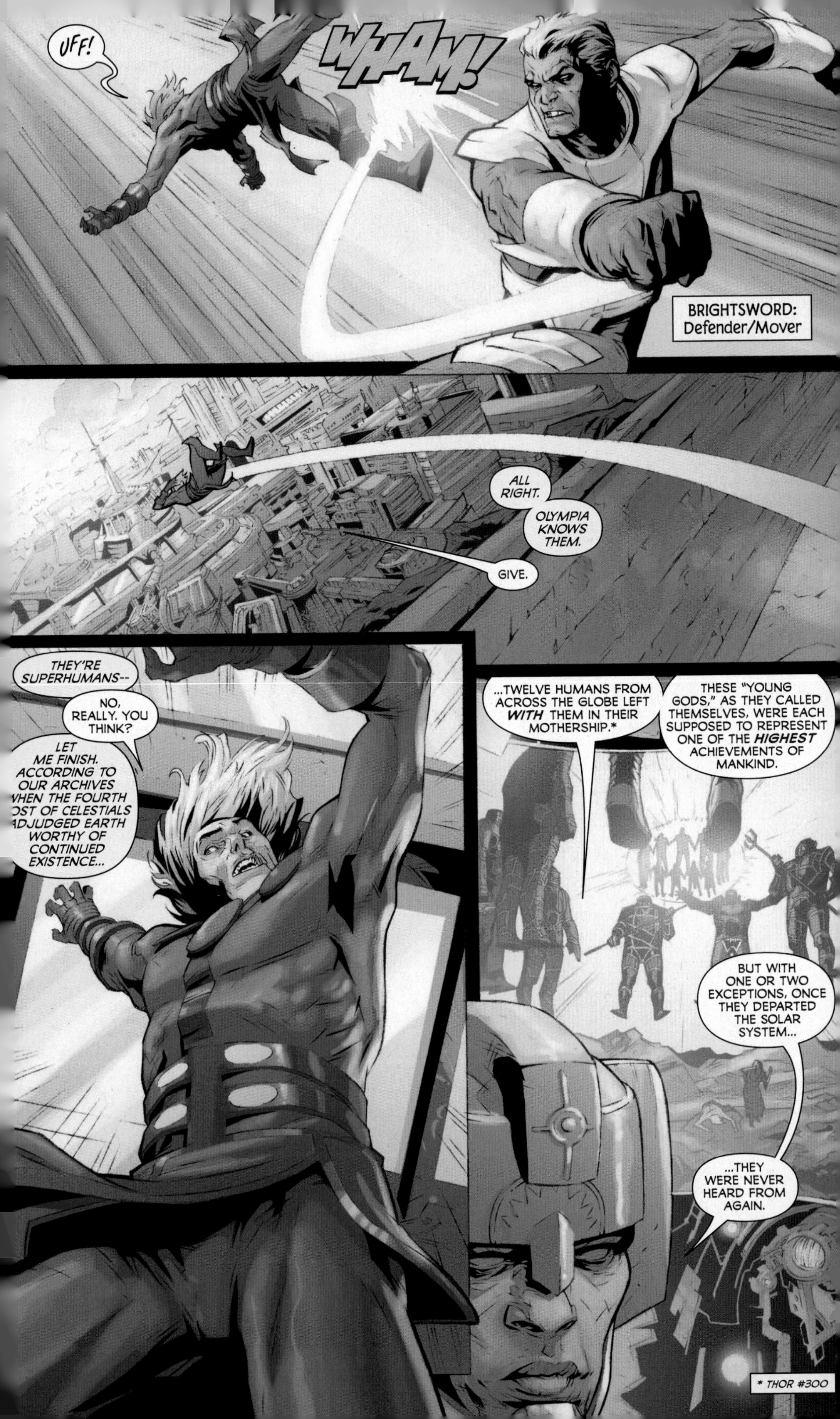
UFF!
WHAM!
BRIGHTSWORD: Defender/Mover
ALL RIGHT.
OLYMPIA KNOWS THEM.
GIVE.
THEY'RE SUPERHUMANS--
NO, REALLY. YOU THINK?
LET ME FINISH. ACCORDING TO OUR ARCHIVES WHEN THE FOURTH HOST OF CELESTIALS ADJUDGED EARTH WORTHY OF CONTINUED EXISTENCE...
...TWELVE HUMANS FROM ACROSS THE GLOBE LEFT WITH THEM IN THEIR MOTHERSHIP.*
THESE "YOUNG GODS," AS THEY CALLED THEMSELVES, WERE EACH SUPPOSED TO REPRESENT ONE OF THE HIGHEST ACHIEVEMENTS OF MANKIND.
BUT WITH ONE OR TWO EXCEPTIONS, ONCE THEY DEPARTED THE SOLAR SYSTEM...
...THEY WERE NEVER HEARD FROM AGAIN.
* THOR #300

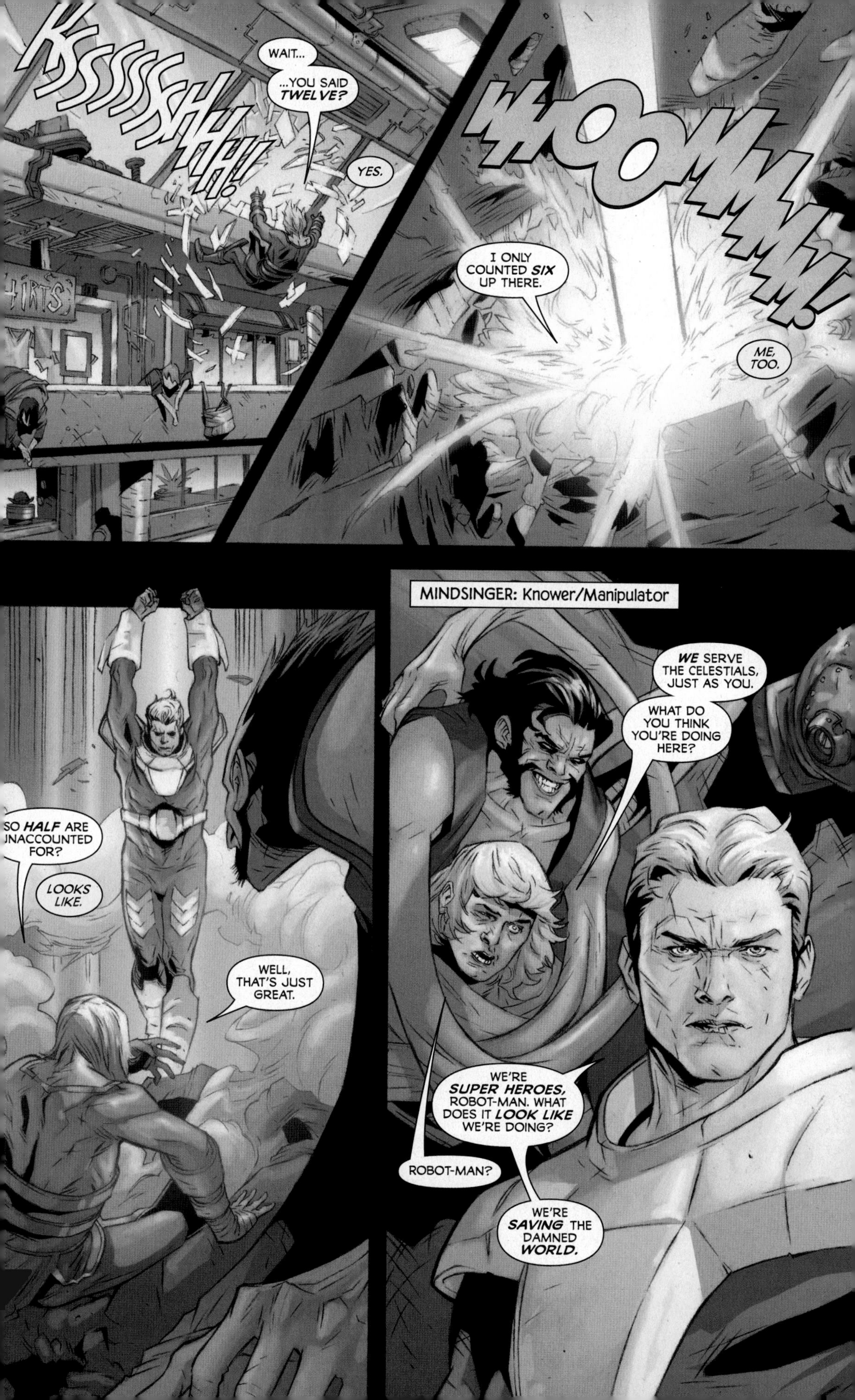
KSSSSSHH!!
WAIT...
...YOU SAID TWELVE?
YES.
WHOOMMM!
I ONLY COUNTED SIX UP THERE.
ME, TOO.
SO HALF ARE UNACCOUNTED FOR?
LOOKS LIKE.
WELL, THAT'S JUST GREAT.
MINDSINGER: Knower/Manipulator
WE SERVE THE CELESTIALS, JUST AS YOU.
WHAT DO YOU THINK YOU'RE DOING HERE?
WE'RE SUPER HEROES, ROBOT-MAN. WHAT DOES IT LOOK LIKE WE'RE DOING?
ROBOT-MAN?
WE'RE SAVING THE DAMNED WORLD.

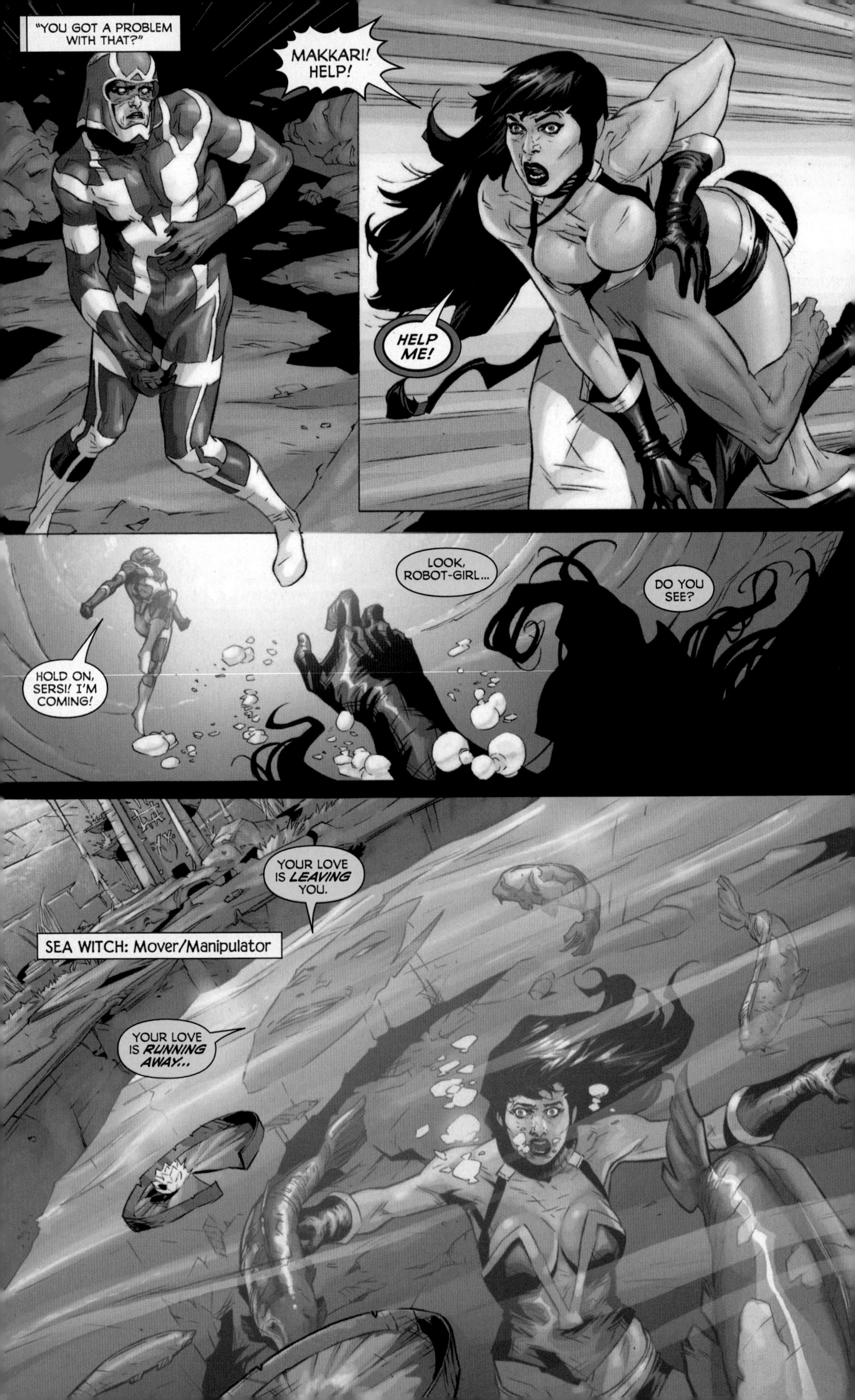
"YOU GOT A PROBLEM WITH THAT?"
MAKKARI! HELP!
HELP ME!
HOLD ON, SERSI! I'M COMING!
LOOK, ROBOT-GIRL...
DO YOU SEE?
YOUR LOVE IS LEAVING YOU.
SEA WITCH: Mover/Manipulator
YOUR LOVE IS RUNNING AWAY...

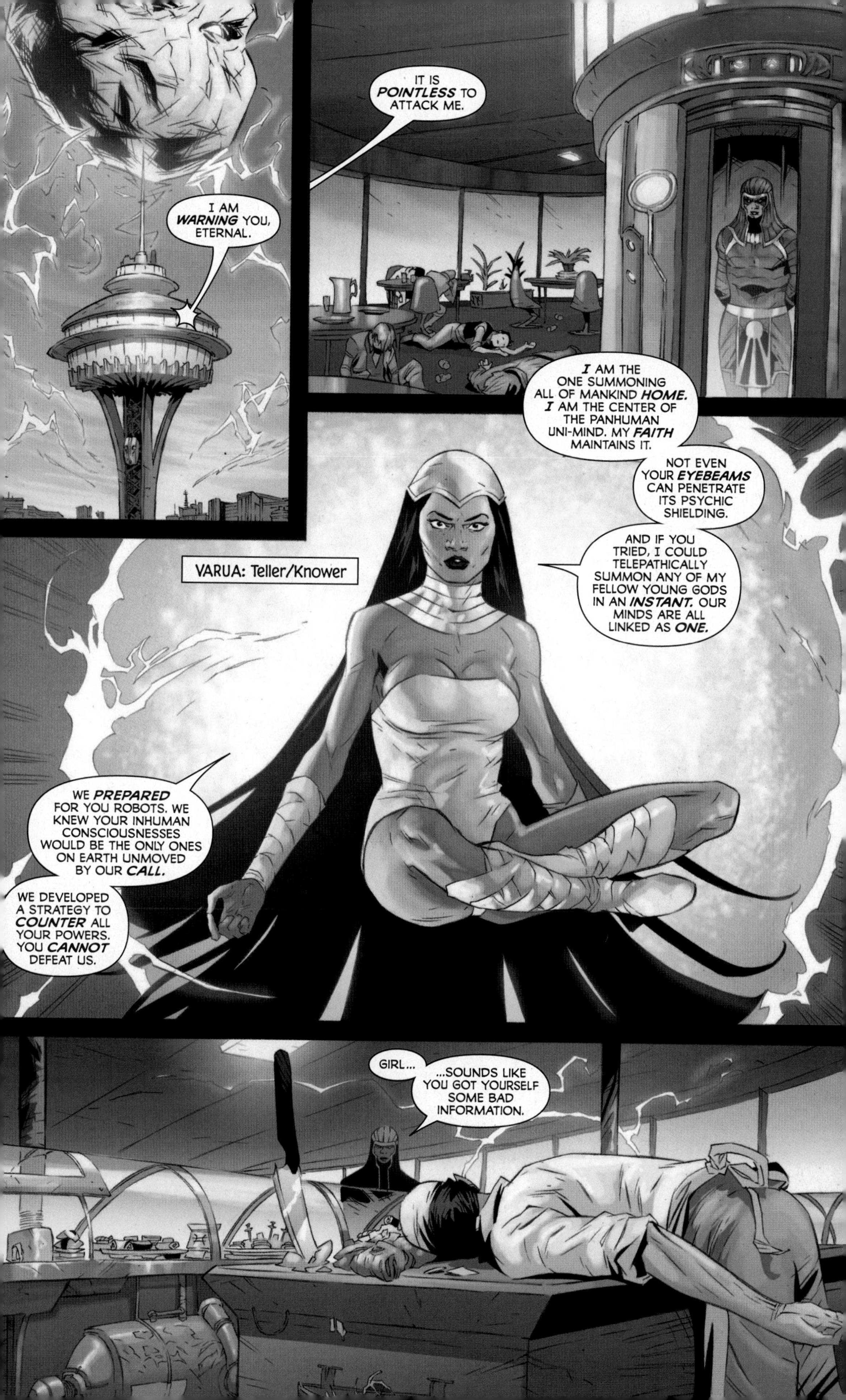
I AM WARNING YOU, ETERNAL.
IT IS POINTLESS TO ATTACK ME.
I AM THE ONE SUMMONING ALL OF MANKIND HOME. I AM THE CENTER OF THE PANHUMAN UNI-MIND. MY FAITH MAINTAINS IT.
NOT EVEN YOUR EYEBEAMS CAN PENETRATE ITS PSYCHIC SHIELDING.
AND IF YOU TRIED, I COULD TELEPATHICALLY SUMMON ANY OF MY FELLOW YOUNG GODS IN AN INSTANT. OUR MINDS ARE ALL LINKED AS ONE.
VARUA: Teller/Knower
WE PREPARED FOR YOU ROBOTS. WE KNEW YOUR INHUMAN CONSCIOUSNESSES WOULD BE THE ONLY ONES ON EARTH UNMOVED BY OUR CALL.
WE DEVELOPED A STRATEGY TO COUNTER ALL YOUR POWERS. YOU CANNOT DEFEAT US.
GIRL...
...SOUNDS LIKE YOU GOT YOURSELF SOME BAD INFORMATION.

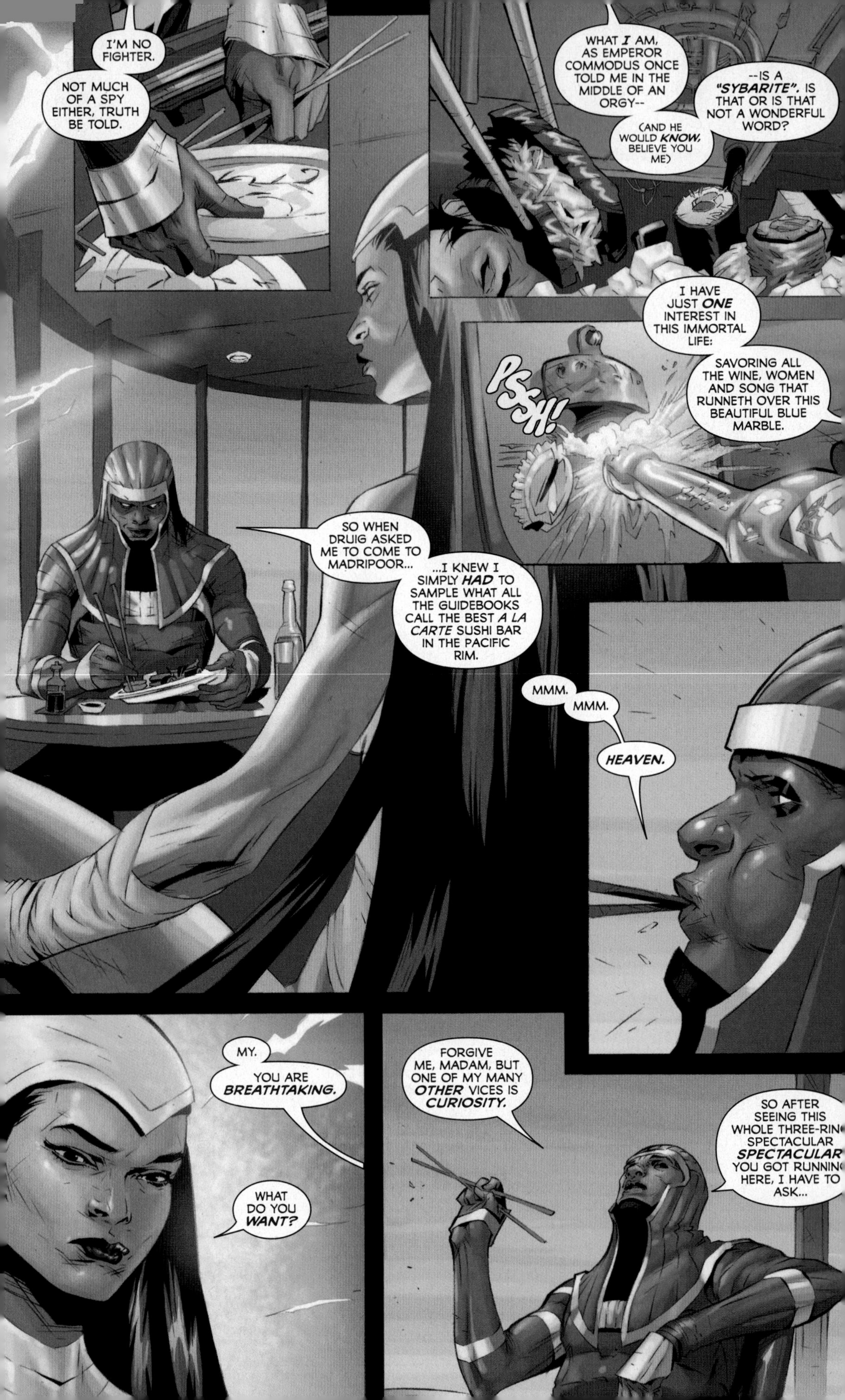
I'M NO FIGHTER.
NOT MUCH OF A SPY EITHER, TRUTH BE TOLD.
WHAT *I* AM, AS EMPEROR COMMODUS ONCE TOLD ME IN THE MIDDLE OF AN ORGY--
(AND HE WOULD *KNOW,* BELIEVE YOU ME)
--IS A *"SYBARITE".* IS THAT OR IS THAT NOT A WONDERFUL WORD?
I HAVE JUST *ONE* INTEREST IN THIS IMMORTAL LIFE:
SAVORING ALL THE WINE, WOMEN AND SONG THAT RUNNETH OVER THIS BEAUTIFUL BLUE MARBLE.
PSSH!
SO WHEN DRUIG ASKED ME TO COME TO MADRIPOOR...
...I KNEW I SIMPLY *HAD* TO SAMPLE WHAT ALL THE GUIDEBOOKS CALL THE BEST *A LA CARTE* SUSHI BAR IN THE PACIFIC RIM.
MMM.
MMM.
HEAVEN.
MY.
YOU ARE *BREATHTAKING.*
WHAT DO YOU *WANT?*
FORGIVE ME, MADAM, BUT ONE OF MY MANY *OTHER* VICES IS *CURIOSITY.*
SO AFTER SEEING THIS WHOLE THREE-RIN SPECTACULAR *SPECTACULAR* YOU GOT RUNNIN HERE, I HAVE TO ASK...

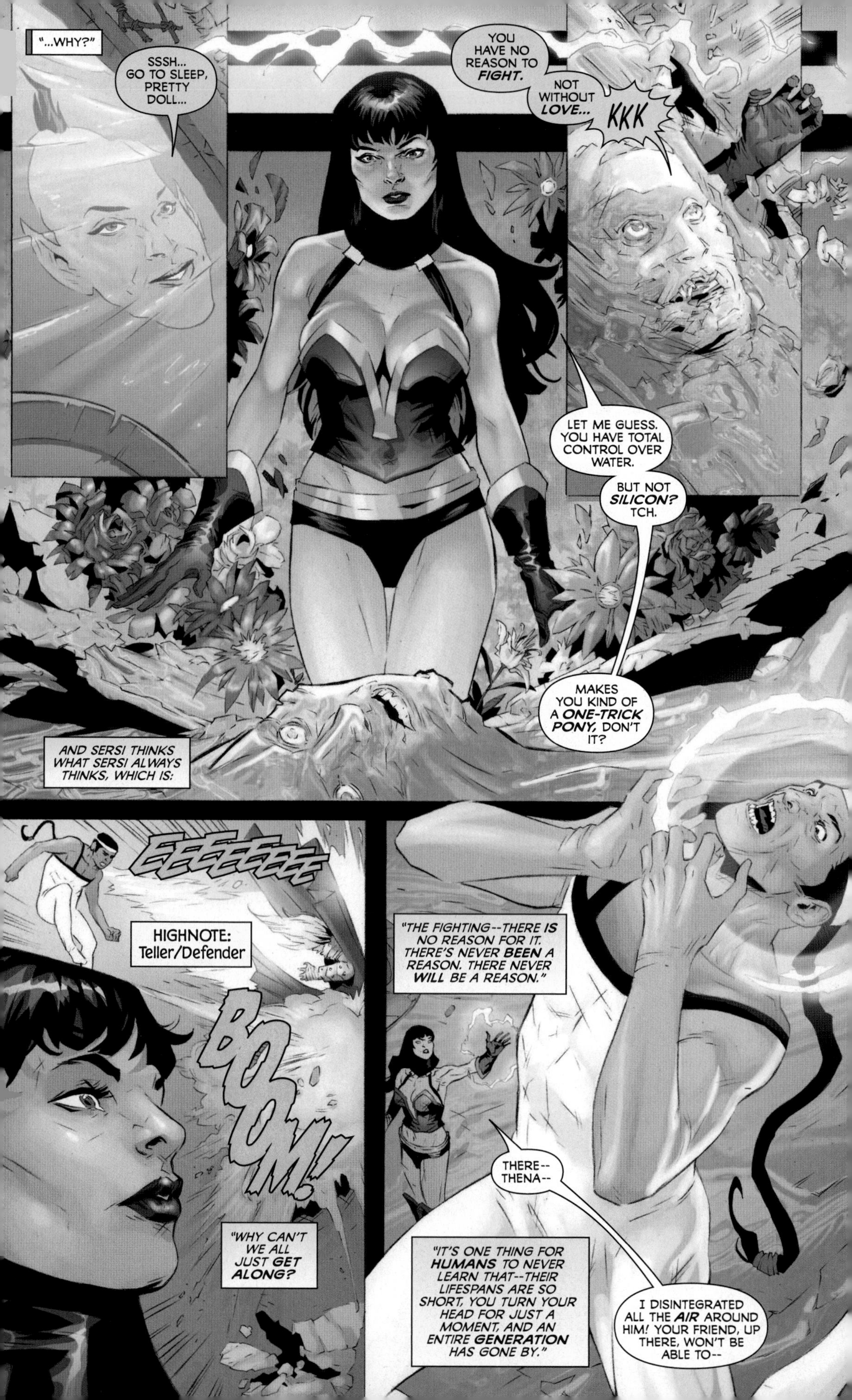

"...WHY?"
SSSH... GO TO SLEEP, PRETTY DOLL...
YOU HAVE NO REASON TO FIGHT.
NOT WITHOUT LOVE...
KKK
LET ME GUESS. YOU HAVE TOTAL CONTROL OVER WATER.
BUT NOT SILICON? TCH.
MAKES YOU KIND OF A ONE-TRICK PONY, DON'T IT?
AND SERSI THINKS WHAT SERSI ALWAYS THINKS, WHICH IS:
EEEEEEEE
HIGHNOTE: Teller/Defender
BOOM!
"WHY CAN'T WE ALL JUST GET ALONG?
"THE FIGHTING--THERE IS NO REASON FOR IT. THERE'S NEVER BEEN A REASON. THERE NEVER WILL BE A REASON."
THERE--THENA--
"IT'S ONE THING FOR HUMANS TO NEVER LEARN THAT--THEIR LIFESPANS ARE SO SHORT, YOU TURN YOUR HEAD FOR JUST A MOMENT, AND AN ENTIRE GENERATION HAS GONE BY."
I DISINTEGRATED ALL THE AIR AROUND HIM! YOUR FRIEND, UP THERE, WON'T BE ABLE TO--

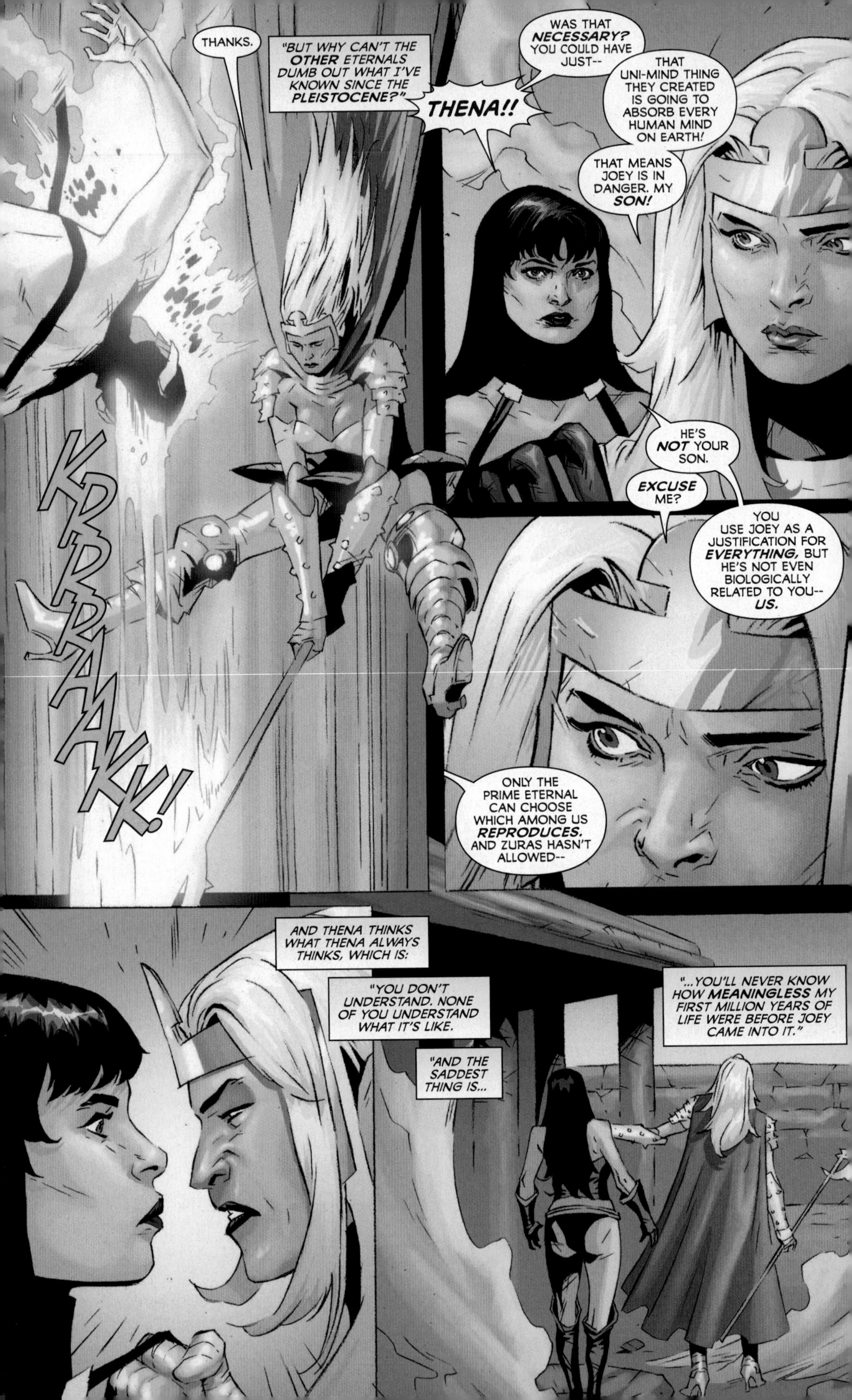
THANKS.
"BUT WHY CAN'T THE OTHER ETERNALS DUMB OUT WHAT I'VE KNOWN SINCE THE PLEISTOCENE?"
THENA!!
KRRAAKK!
WAS THAT NECESSARY? YOU COULD HAVE JUST--
THAT UNI-MIND THING THEY CREATED IS GOING TO ABSORB EVERY HUMAN MIND ON EARTH!
THAT MEANS JOEY IS IN DANGER. MY SON!
HE'S NOT YOUR SON.
EXCUSE ME?
YOU USE JOEY AS A JUSTIFICATION FOR EVERYTHING, BUT HE'S NOT EVEN BIOLOGICALLY RELATED TO YOU-- US.
ONLY THE PRIME ETERNAL CAN CHOOSE WHICH AMONG US REPRODUCES. AND ZURAS HASN'T ALLOWED--
AND THENA THINKS WHAT THENA ALWAYS THINKS, WHICH IS:
"YOU DON'T UNDERSTAND. NONE OF YOU UNDERSTAND WHAT IT'S LIKE.
"AND THE SADDEST THING IS...
"...YOU'LL NEVER KNOW HOW MEANINGLESS MY FIRST MILLION YEARS OF LIFE WERE BEFORE JOEY CAME INTO IT."

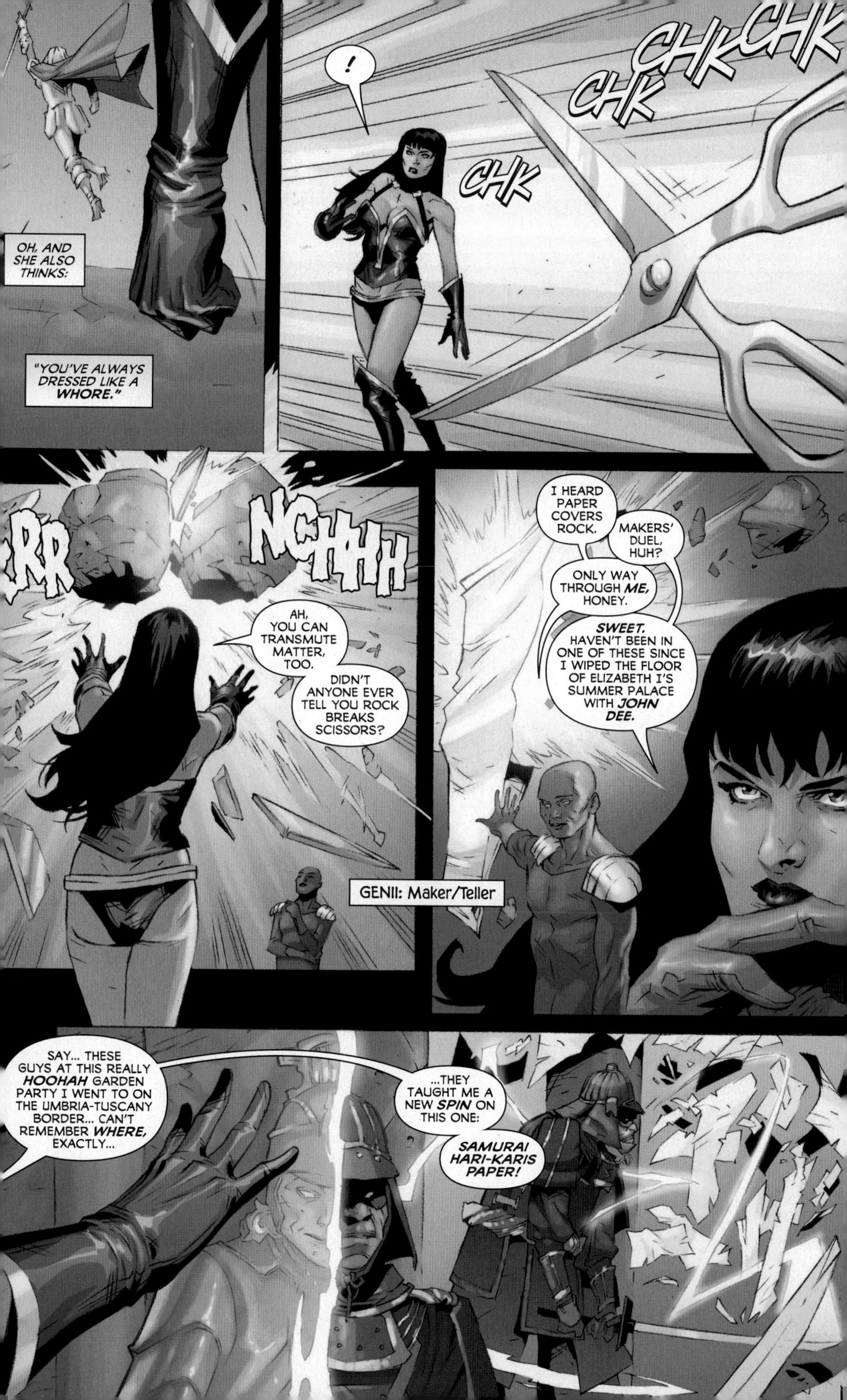
OH, AND SHE ALSO THINKS:
"YOU'VE ALWAYS DRESSED LIKE A WHORE."
!
CHK
CHK
CHK
CHK
RR
NCHHH
AH, YOU CAN TRANSMUTE MATTER, TOO.
DIDN'T ANYONE EVER TELL YOU ROCK BREAKS SCISSORS?
GENII: Maker/Teller
I HEARD PAPER COVERS ROCK.
MAKERS' DUEL, HUH?
ONLY WAY THROUGH ME, HONEY.
SWEET. HAVEN'T BEEN IN ONE OF THESE SINCE I WIPED THE FLOOR OF ELIZABETH I'S SUMMER PALACE WITH JOHN DEE.
SAY... THESE GUYS AT THIS REALLY HOOHAH GARDEN PARTY I WENT TO ON THE UMBRIA-TUSCANY BORDER... CAN'T REMEMBER WHERE, EXACTLY...
...THEY TAUGHT ME A NEW SPIN ON THIS ONE:
SAMURAI HARI-KARIS PAPER!

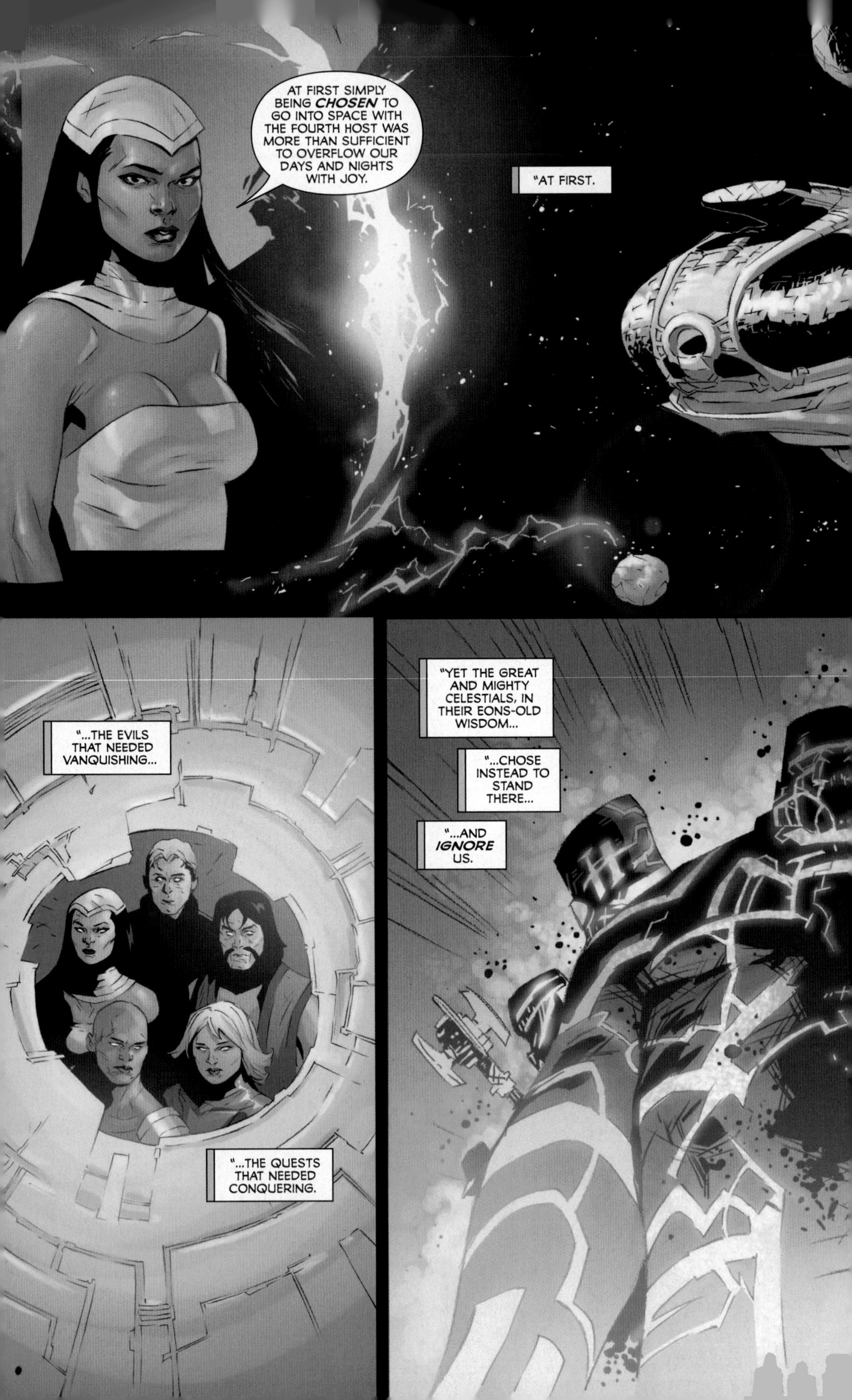

AT FIRST SIMPLY BEING *CHOSEN* TO GO INTO SPACE WITH THE FOURTH HOST WAS MORE THAN SUFFICIENT TO OVERFLOW OUR DAYS AND NIGHTS WITH JOY.
"AT FIRST.
"...THE EVILS THAT NEEDED VANQUISHING...
"...THE QUESTS THAT NEEDED CONQUERING.
"YET THE GREAT AND MIGHTY CELESTIALS, IN THEIR EONS-OLD WISDOM...
"...CHOSE INSTEAD TO STAND THERE...
"...AND *IGNORE* US.

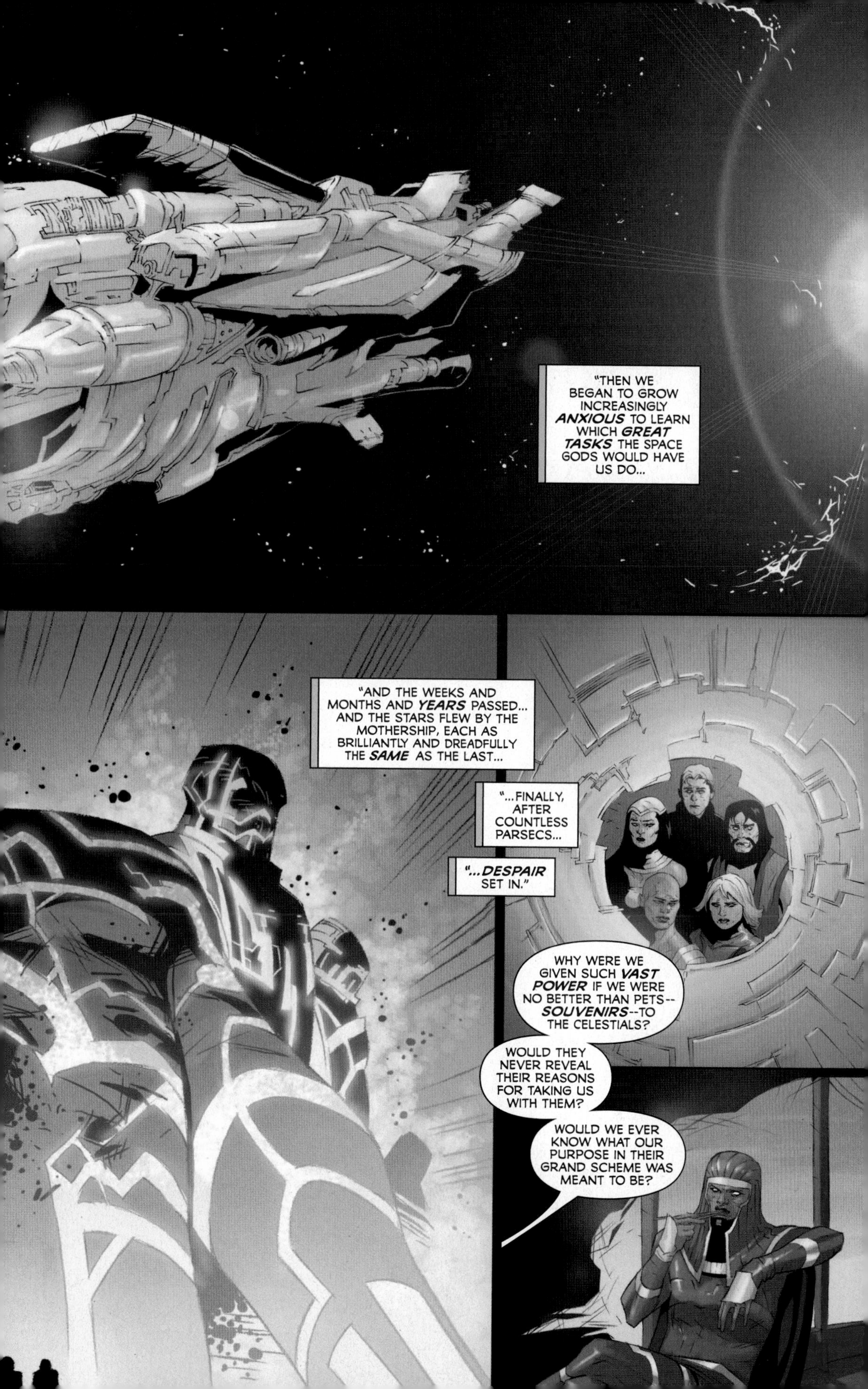
"THEN WE BEGAN TO GROW INCREASINGLY ***ANXIOUS*** TO LEARN WHICH ***GREAT TASKS*** THE SPACE GODS WOULD HAVE US DO...
"AND THE WEEKS AND MONTHS AND ***YEARS*** PASSED... AND THE STARS FLEW BY THE MOTHERSHIP, EACH AS BRILLIANTLY AND DREADFULLY THE ***SAME*** AS THE LAST...
"...FINALLY, AFTER COUNTLESS PARSECS...
"***...DESPAIR*** SET IN."
WHY WERE WE GIVEN SUCH ***VAST POWER*** IF WE WERE NO BETTER THAN PETS--***SOUVENIRS***--TO THE CELESTIALS?
WOULD THEY NEVER REVEAL THEIR REASONS FOR TAKING US WITH THEM?
WOULD WE EVER KNOW WHAT OUR PURPOSE IN THEIR GRAND SCHEME WAS MEANT TO BE?

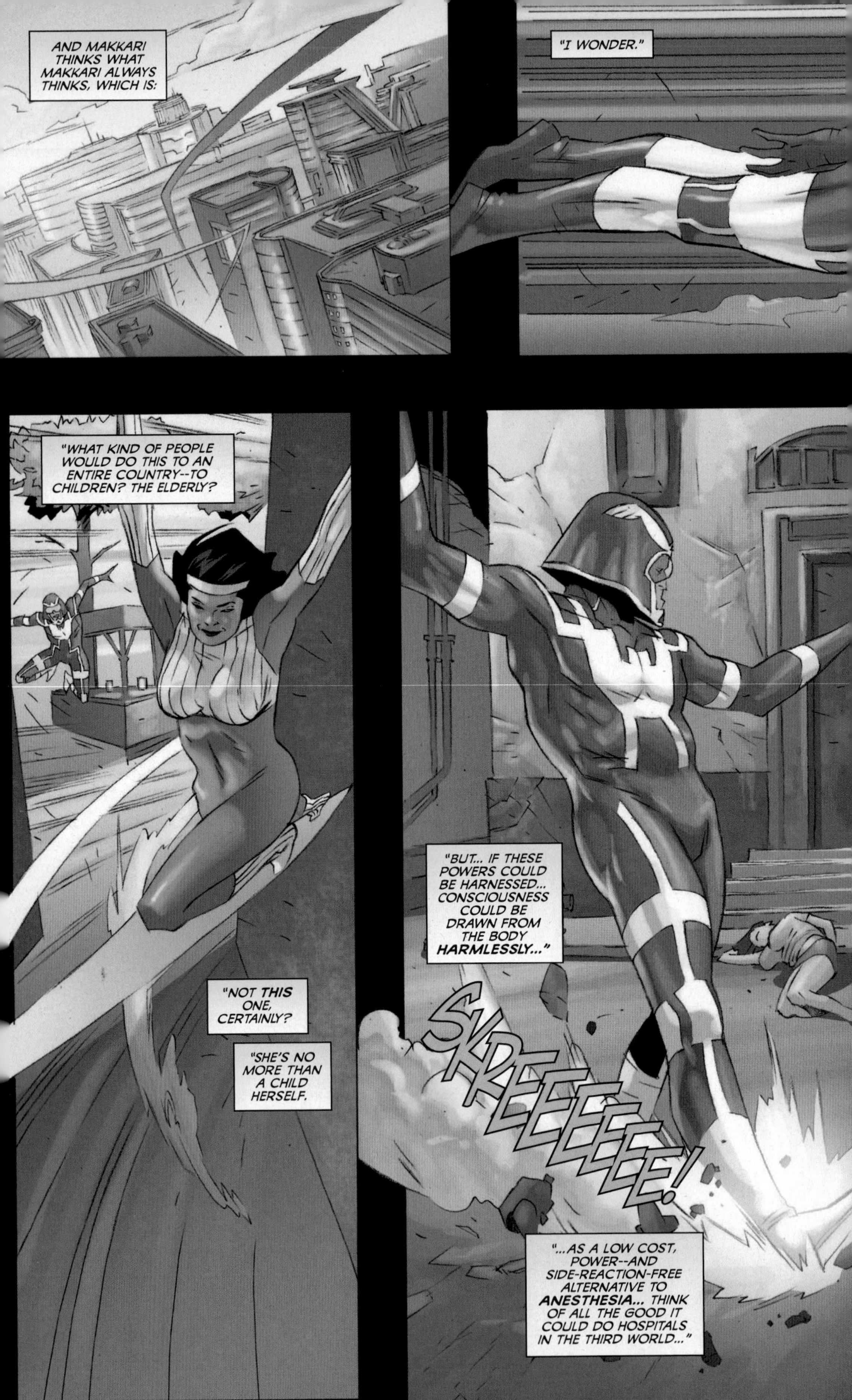
AND MAKKARI THINKS WHAT MAKKARI ALWAYS THINKS, WHICH IS:
"I WONDER."
"WHAT KIND OF PEOPLE WOULD DO THIS TO AN ENTIRE COUNTRY--TO CHILDREN? THE ELDERLY?
"NOT THIS ONE, CERTAINLY?
"SHE'S NO MORE THAN A CHILD HERSELF.
"BUT... IF THESE POWERS COULD BE HARNESSED... CONSCIOUSNESS COULD BE DRAWN FROM THE BODY HARMLESSLY..."
SKREEEEEEEEE!
"...AS A LOW COST, POWER--AND SIDE-REACTION-FREE ALTERNATIVE TO ANESTHESIA... THINK OF ALL THE GOOD IT COULD DO HOSPITALS IN THE THIRD WORLD..."

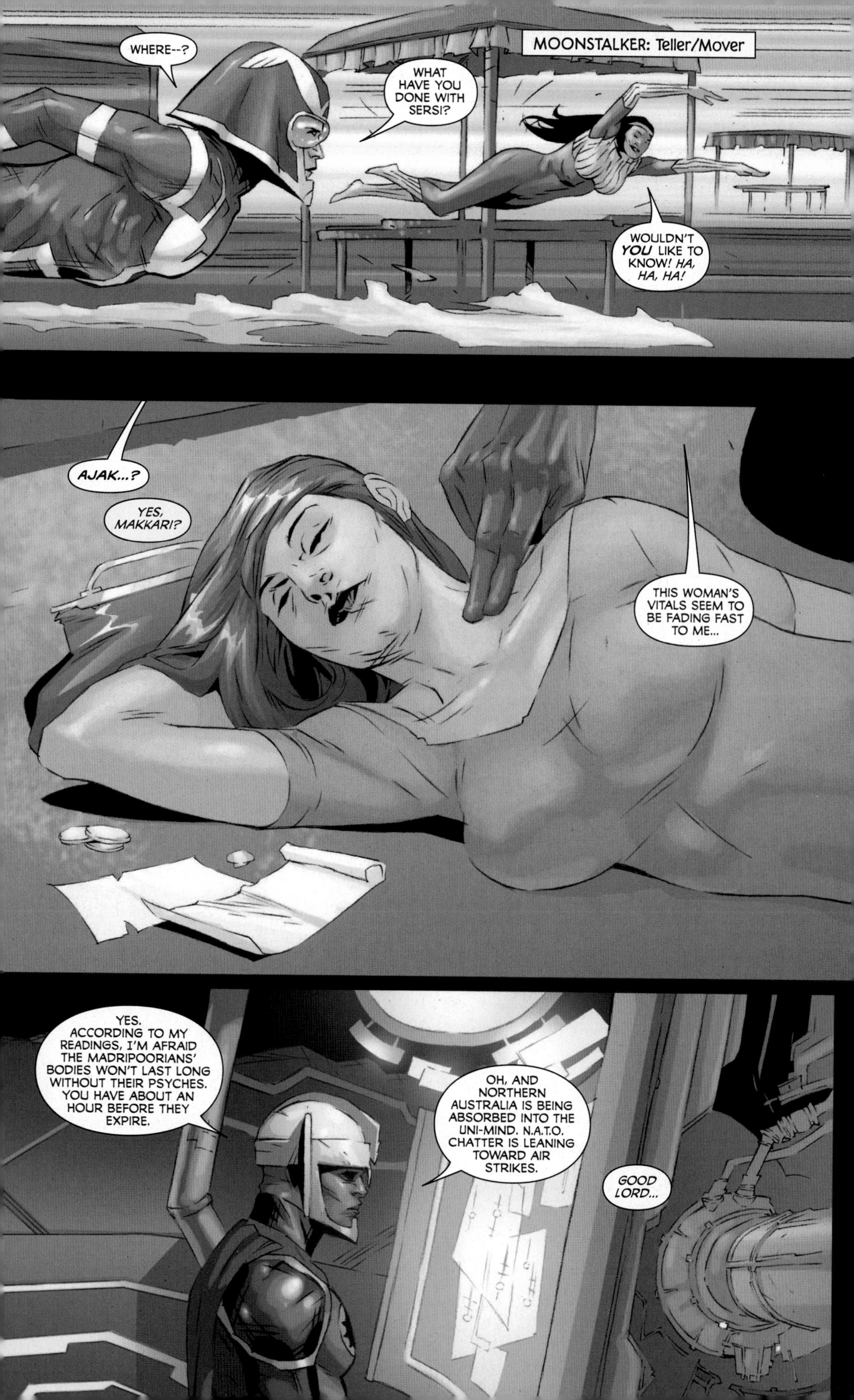
MOONSTALKER: Teller/Mover
WHERE--?
WHAT HAVE YOU DONE WITH SERSI?
WOULDN'T *YOU* LIKE TO KNOW! *HA, HA, HA!*
AJAK...?
YES, MAKKARI?
THIS WOMAN'S VITALS SEEM TO BE FADING FAST TO ME...
YES. ACCORDING TO MY READINGS, I'M AFRAID THE MADRIPOORIANS' BODIES WON'T LAST LONG WITHOUT THEIR PSYCHES. YOU HAVE ABOUT AN HOUR BEFORE THEY EXPIRE.
OH, AND NORTHERN AUSTRALIA IS BEING ABSORBED INTO THE UNI-MIND. N.A.T.O. CHATTER IS LEANING TOWARD AIR STRIKES.
GOOD LORD...

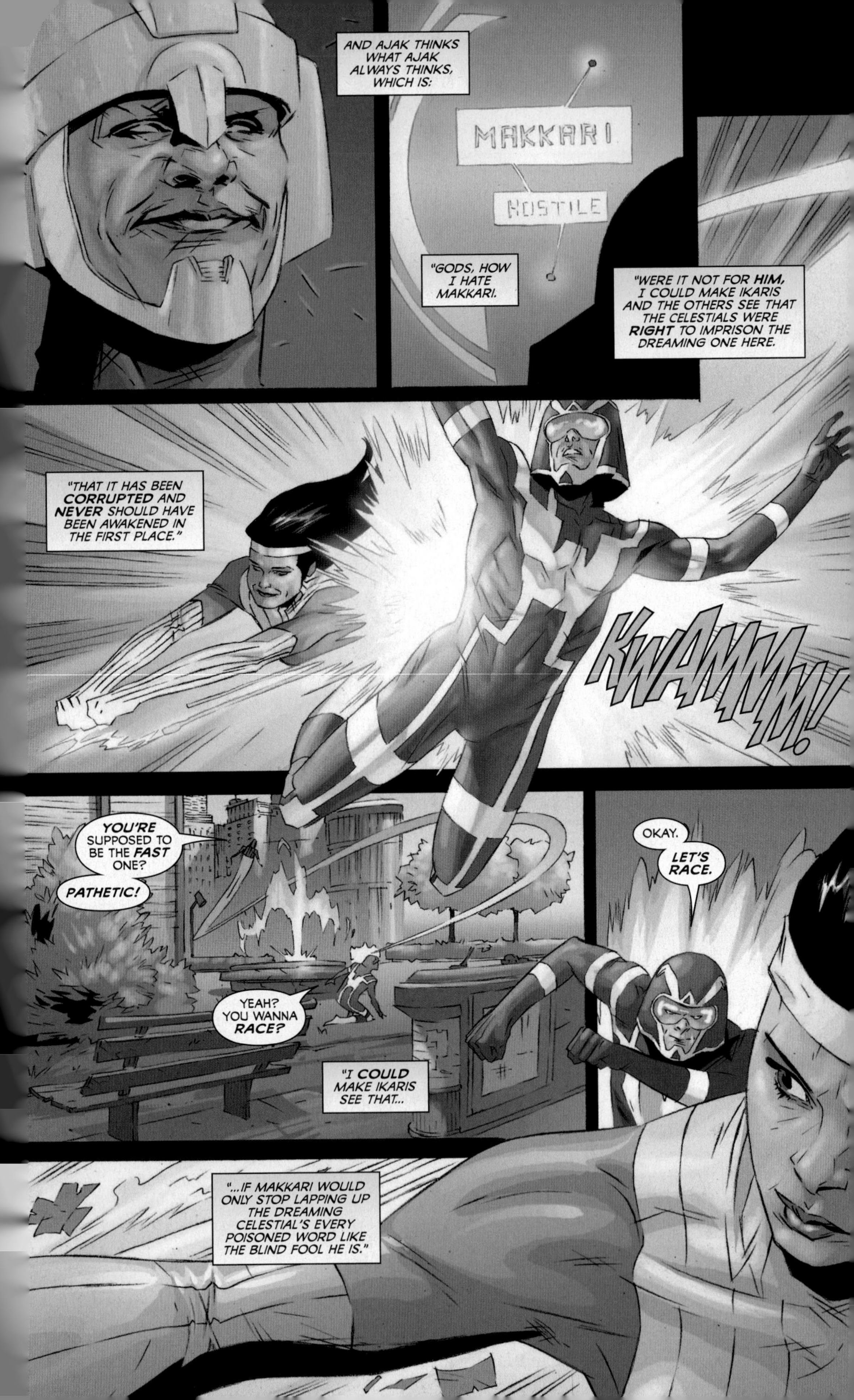
AND AJAK THINKS WHAT AJAK ALWAYS THINKS, WHICH IS:
MAKKARI
HOSTILE
"GODS, HOW I HATE MAKKARI.
"WERE IT NOT FOR HIM, I COULD MAKE IKARIS AND THE OTHERS SEE THAT THE CELESTIALS WERE RIGHT TO IMPRISON THE DREAMING ONE HERE.
"THAT IT HAS BEEN CORRUPTED AND NEVER SHOULD HAVE BEEN AWAKENED IN THE FIRST PLACE."
KWAMMM!
YOU'RE SUPPOSED TO BE THE FAST ONE?
PATHETIC!
YEAH? YOU WANNA RACE?
"I COULD MAKE IKARIS SEE THAT...
OKAY.
LET'S RACE.
"...IF MAKKARI WOULD ONLY STOP LAPPING UP THE DREAMING CELESTIAL'S EVERY POISONED WORD LIKE THE BLIND FOOL HE IS."

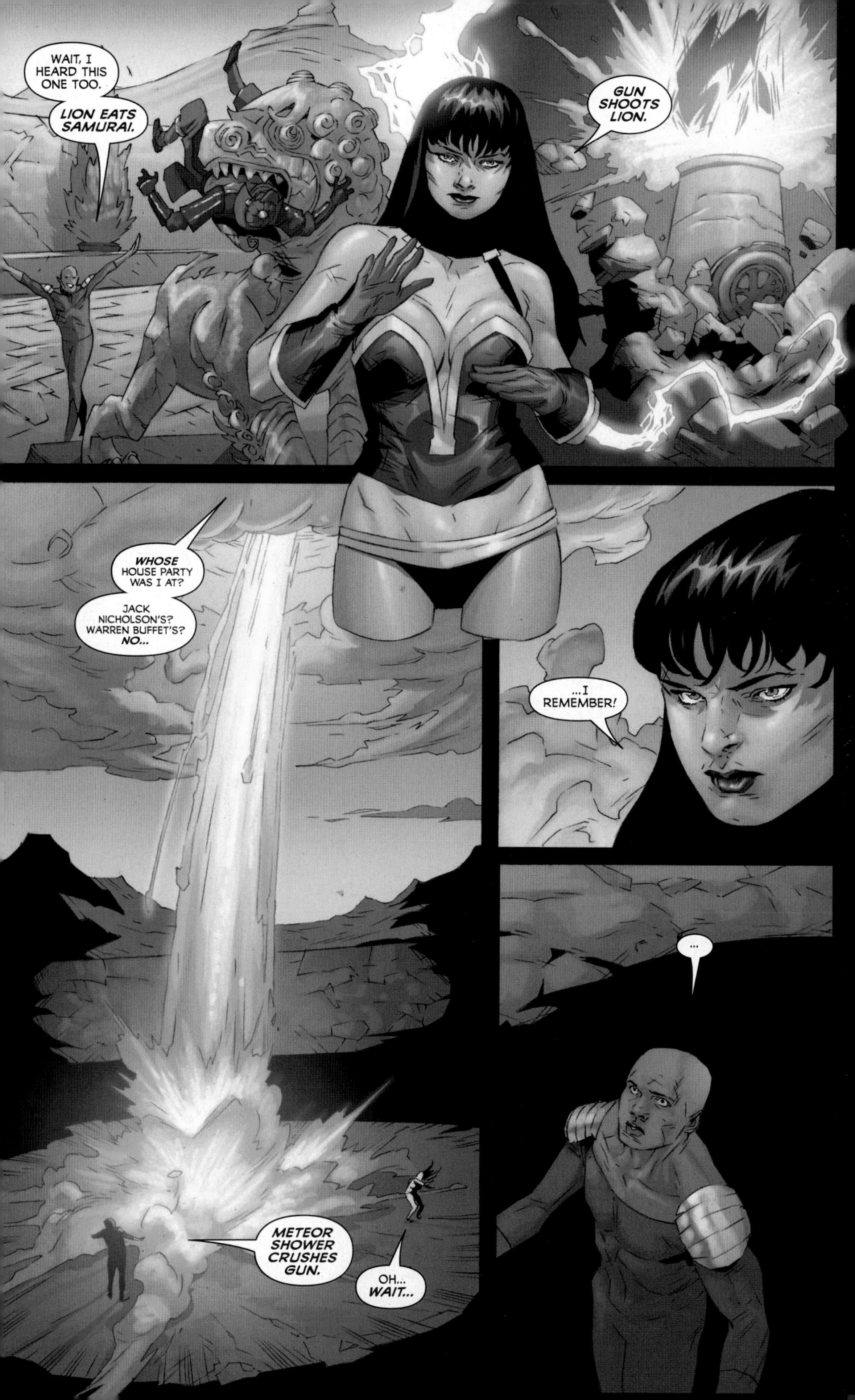
WAIT, I HEARD THIS ONE TOO.
LION EATS SAMURAI.
GUN SHOOTS LION.
WHOSE HOUSE PARTY WAS I AT?
JACK NICHOLSON'S? WARREN BUFFET'S? NO...
...I REMEMBER!
METEOR SHOWER CRUSHES GUN.
OH... WAIT...
...

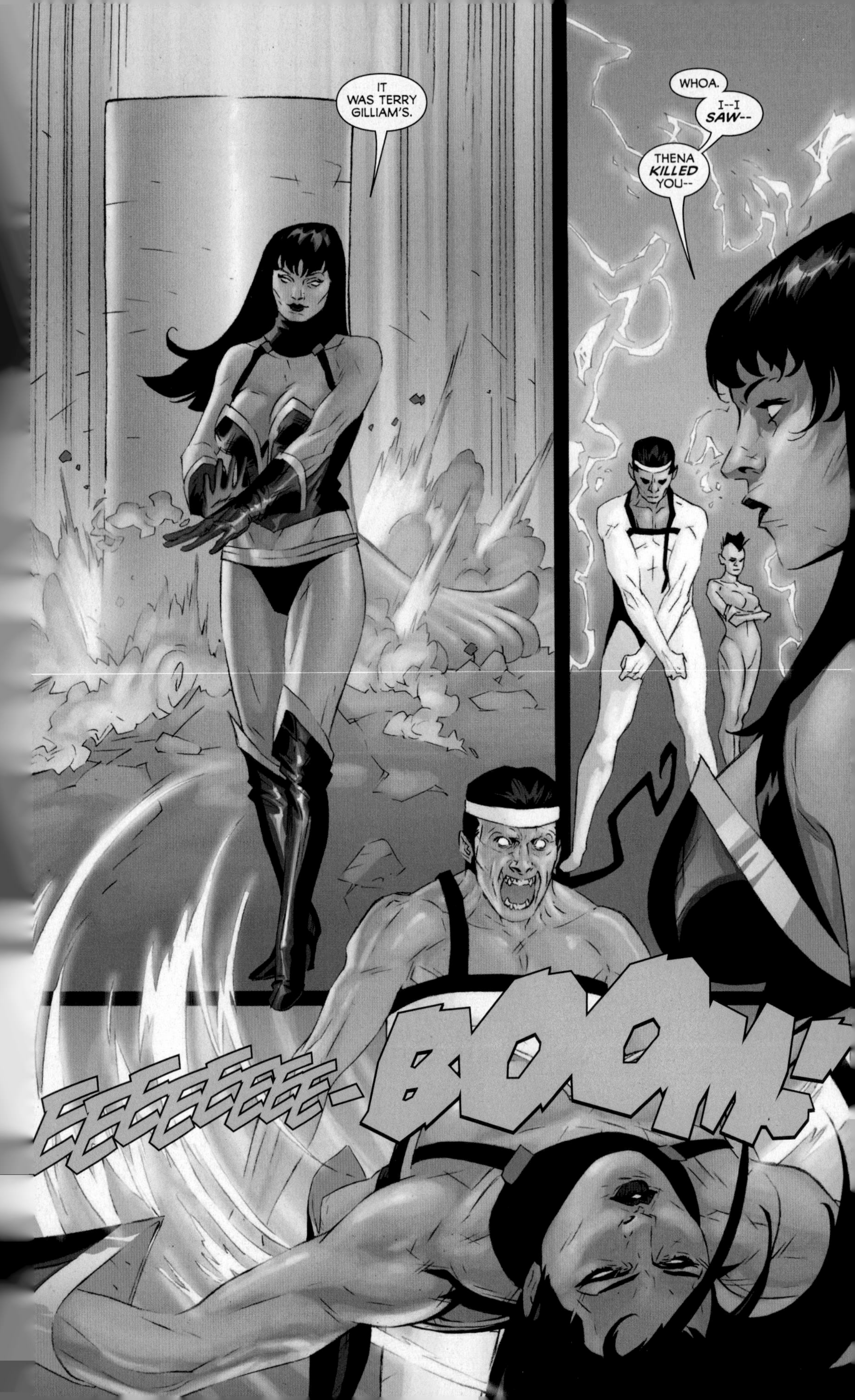

IT WAS TERRY GILLIAM'S.
WHOA.
I--I SAW--
THENA KILLED YOU--
EEEEEEEE-BOOM!

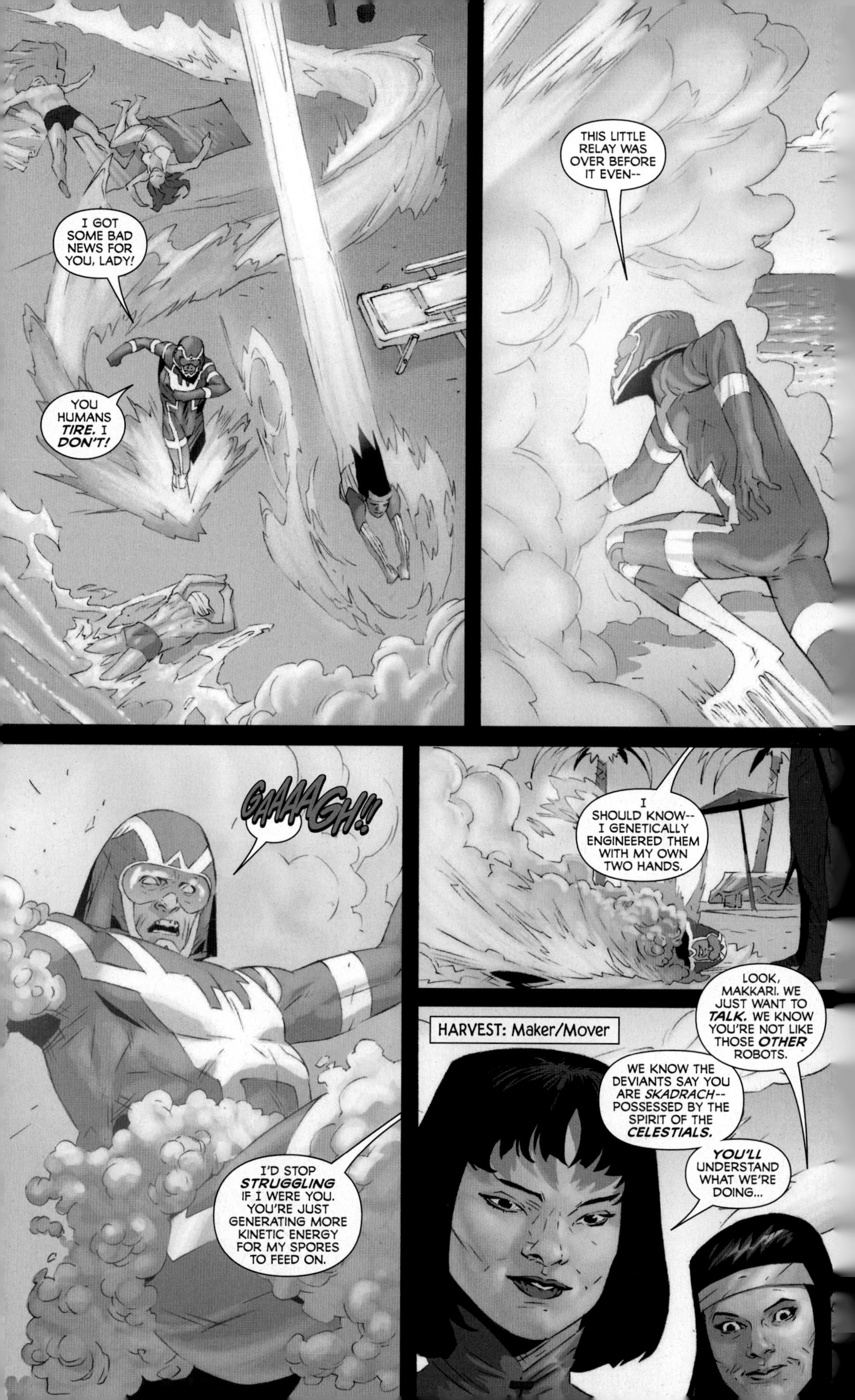
I GOT SOME BAD NEWS FOR YOU, LADY!
YOU HUMANS *TIRE.* I *DON'T!*
THIS LITTLE RELAY WAS OVER BEFORE IT EVEN--
GAAAAGH!!
I SHOULD KNOW-- I GENETICALLY ENGINEERED THEM WITH MY OWN TWO HANDS.
I'D STOP *STRUGGLING* IF I WERE YOU. YOU'RE JUST GENERATING MORE KINETIC ENERGY FOR MY SPORES TO FEED ON.
HARVEST: Maker/Mover
LOOK, MAKKARI. WE JUST WANT TO *TALK.* WE KNOW YOU'RE NOT LIKE THOSE *OTHER* ROBOTS.
WE KNOW THE DEVIANTS SAY YOU ARE *SKADRACH*-- POSSESSED BY THE SPIRIT OF THE *CELESTIALS.*
YOU'LL UNDERSTAND WHAT WE'RE DOING...

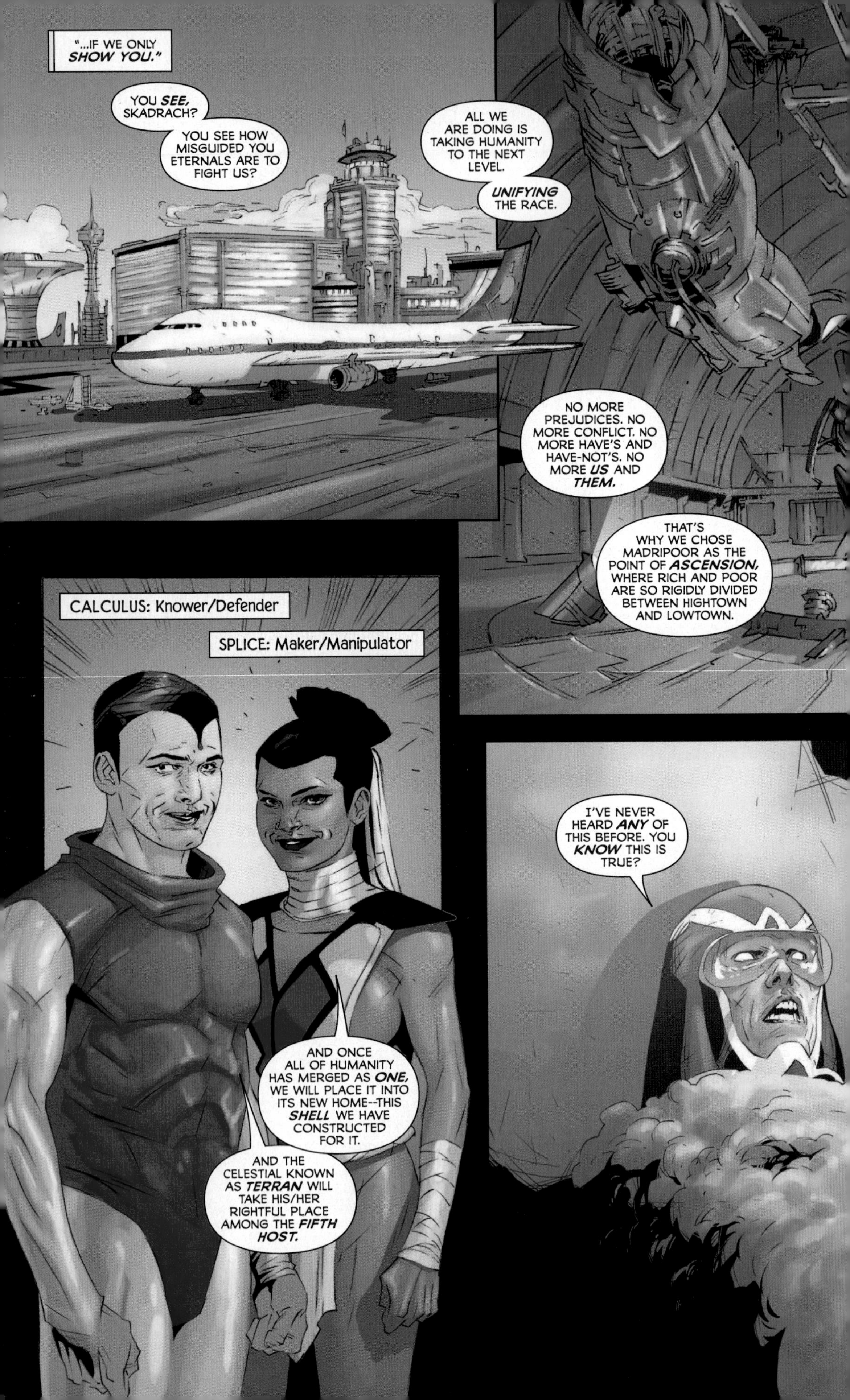
"...IF WE ONLY SHOW YOU."
YOU SEE, SKADRACH?
YOU SEE HOW MISGUIDED YOU ETERNALS ARE TO FIGHT US?
ALL WE ARE DOING IS TAKING HUMANITY TO THE NEXT LEVEL.
UNIFYING THE RACE.
NO MORE PREJUDICES. NO MORE CONFLICT. NO MORE HAVE'S AND HAVE-NOT'S. NO MORE US AND THEM.
THAT'S WHY WE CHOSE MADRIPOOR AS THE POINT OF ASCENSION, WHERE RICH AND POOR ARE SO RIGIDLY DIVIDED BETWEEN HIGHTOWN AND LOWTOWN.
CALCULUS: Knower/Defender
SPLICE: Maker/Manipulator
AND ONCE ALL OF HUMANITY HAS MERGED AS ONE, WE WILL PLACE IT INTO ITS NEW HOME--THIS SHELL WE HAVE CONSTRUCTED FOR IT.
AND THE CELESTIAL KNOWN AS TERRAN WILL TAKE HIS/HER RIGHTFUL PLACE AMONG THE FIFTH HOST.
I'VE NEVER HEARD ANY OF THIS BEFORE. YOU KNOW THIS IS TRUE?

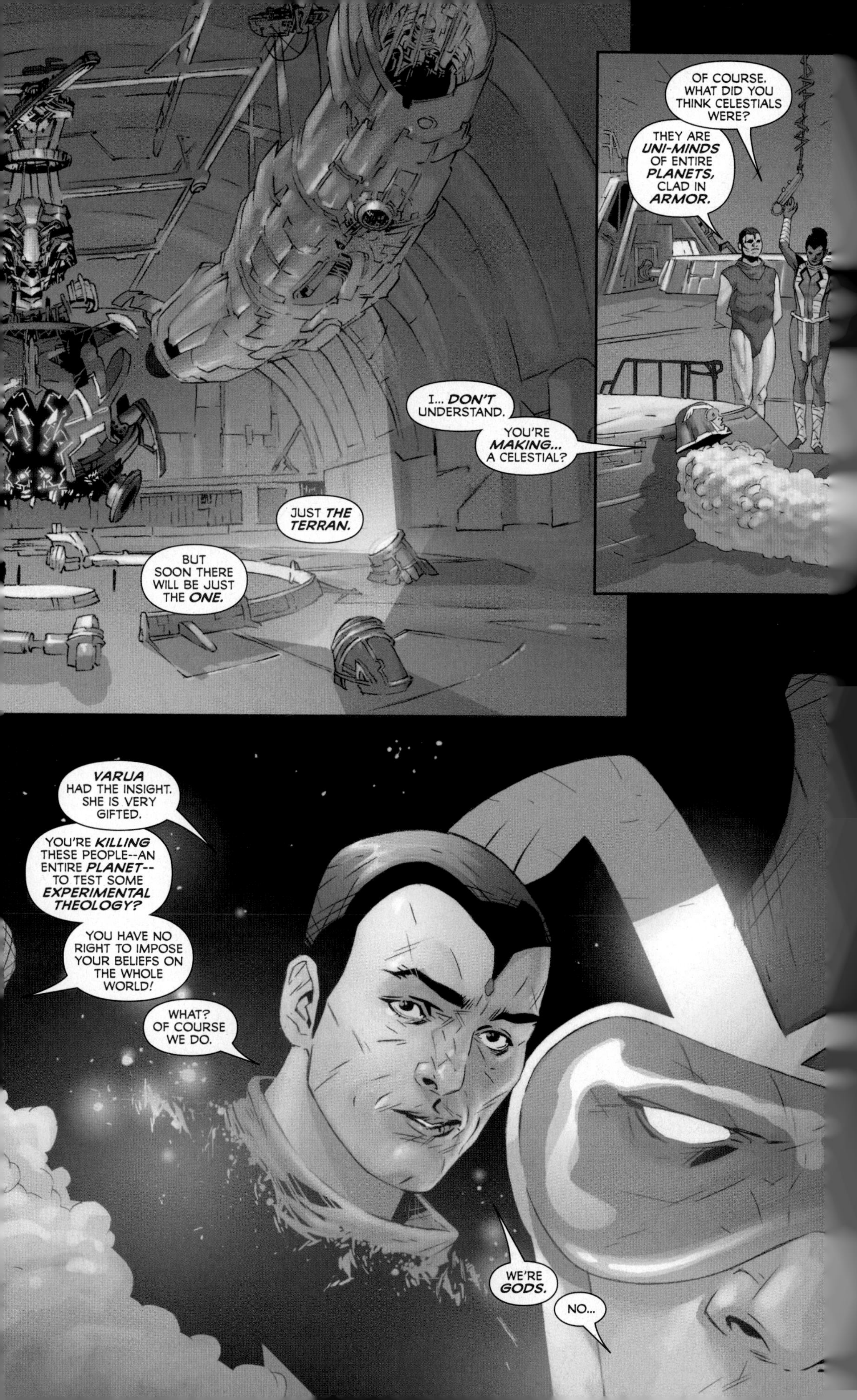
JUST THE TERRAN.
BUT SOON THERE WILL BE JUST THE ONE.
I... DON'T UNDERSTAND.
YOU'RE MAKING... A CELESTIAL?
OF COURSE. WHAT DID YOU THINK CELESTIALS WERE?
THEY ARE UNI-MINDS OF ENTIRE PLANETS, CLAD IN ARMOR.
VARUA HAD THE INSIGHT. SHE IS VERY GIFTED.
YOU'RE KILLING THESE PEOPLE--AN ENTIRE PLANET--TO TEST SOME EXPERIMENTAL THEOLOGY?
YOU HAVE NO RIGHT TO IMPOSE YOUR BELIEFS ON THE WHOLE WORLD!
WHAT? OF COURSE WE DO.
WE'RE GODS.
NO...

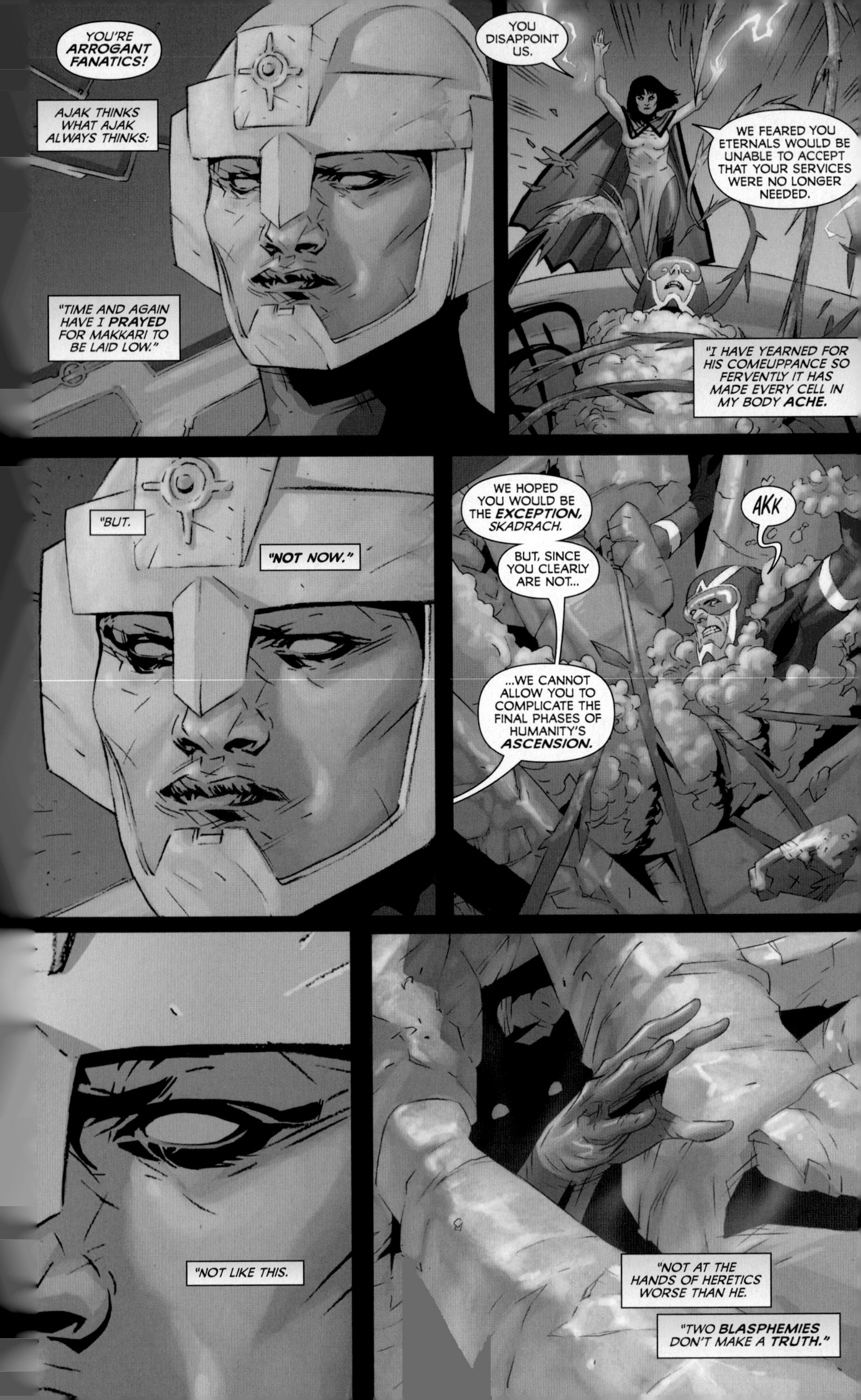

YOU'RE ARROGANT FANATICS!
AJAK THINKS WHAT AJAK ALWAYS THINKS:
"TIME AND AGAIN HAVE I PRAYED FOR MAKKARI TO BE LAID LOW."
YOU DISAPPOINT US.
WE FEARED YOU ETERNALS WOULD BE UNABLE TO ACCEPT THAT YOUR SERVICES WERE NO LONGER NEEDED.
"I HAVE YEARNED FOR HIS COMEUPPANCE SO FERVENTLY IT HAS MADE EVERY CELL IN MY BODY ACHE.
"BUT.
"NOT NOW."
WE HOPED YOU WOULD BE THE EXCEPTION, SKADRACH.
BUT, SINCE YOU CLEARLY ARE NOT...
...WE CANNOT ALLOW YOU TO COMPLICATE THE FINAL PHASES OF HUMANITY'S ASCENSION.
AKK
"NOT LIKE THIS.
"NOT AT THE HANDS OF HERETICS WORSE THAN HE.
"TWO BLASPHEMIES DON'T MAKE A TRUTH."

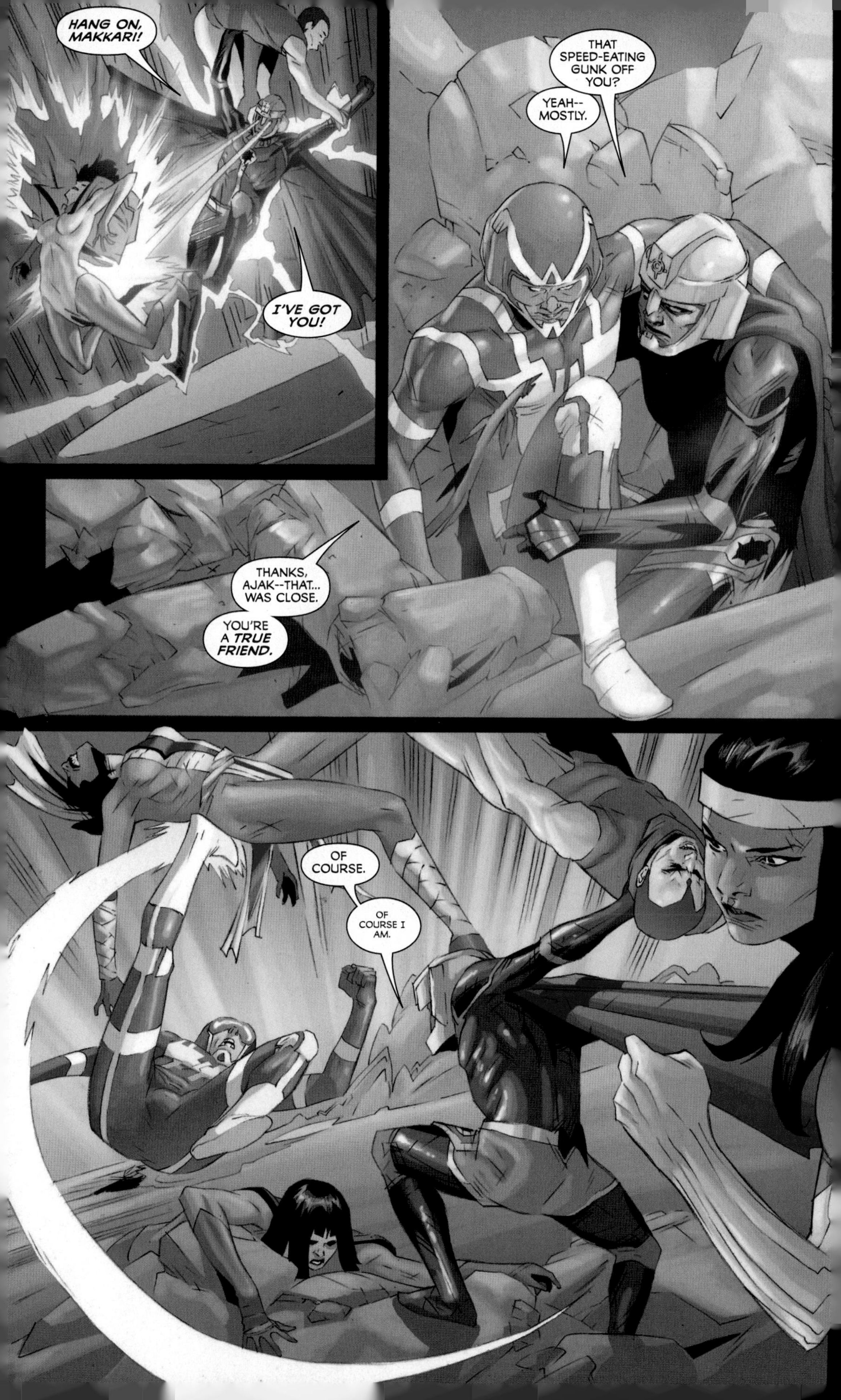

HANG ON, MAKKARI!
I'VE GOT YOU!
THAT SPEED-EATING GUNK OFF YOU?
YEAH--MOSTLY.
THANKS, AJAK--THAT... WAS CLOSE.
YOU'RE A *TRUE FRIEND.*
OF COURSE.
OF COURSE I AM.

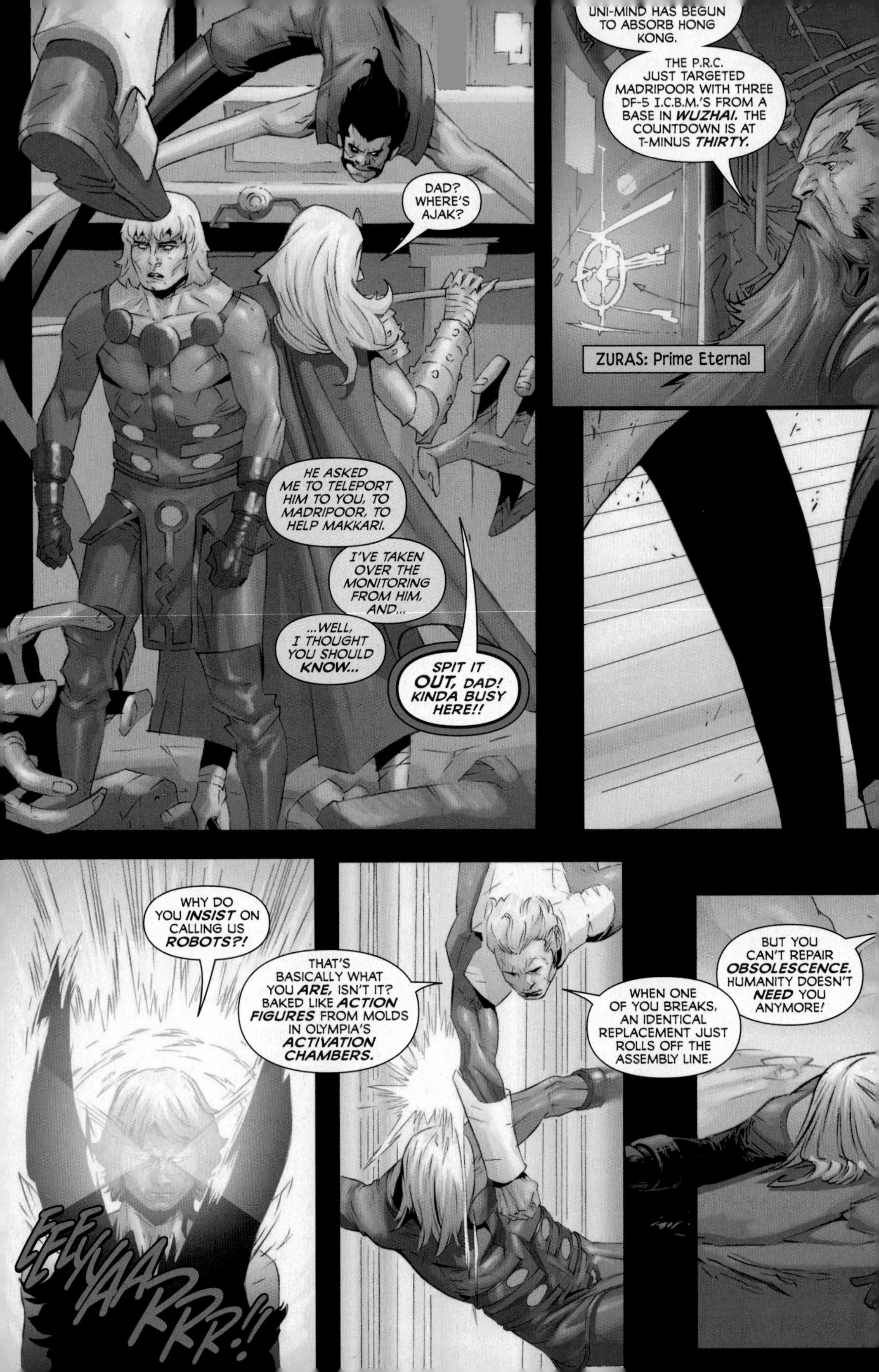

DAD? WHERE'S AJAK?
HE ASKED ME TO TELEPORT HIM TO YOU, TO MADRIPOOR, TO HELP MAKKARI.
I'VE TAKEN OVER THE MONITORING FROM HIM, AND...
...WELL, I THOUGHT YOU SHOULD KNOW...
SPIT IT OUT, DAD! KINDA BUSY HERE!!
UNI-MIND HAS BEGUN TO ABSORB HONG KONG.
THE P.R.C. JUST TARGETED MADRIPOOR WITH THREE DF-5 I.C.B.M.'S FROM A BASE IN WUZHAI. THE COUNTDOWN IS AT T-MINUS THIRTY.
ZURAS: Prime Eternal
WHY DO YOU INSIST ON CALLING US ROBOTS?!
EEEYAARRR?!
THAT'S BASICALLY WHAT YOU ARE, ISN'T IT? BAKED LIKE ACTION FIGURES FROM MOLDS IN OLYMPIA'S ACTIVATION CHAMBERS.
WHEN ONE OF YOU BREAKS, AN IDENTICAL REPLACEMENT JUST ROLLS OFF THE ASSEMBLY LINE.
BUT YOU CAN'T REPAIR OBSOLESCENCE. HUMANITY DOESN'T NEED YOU ANYMORE!

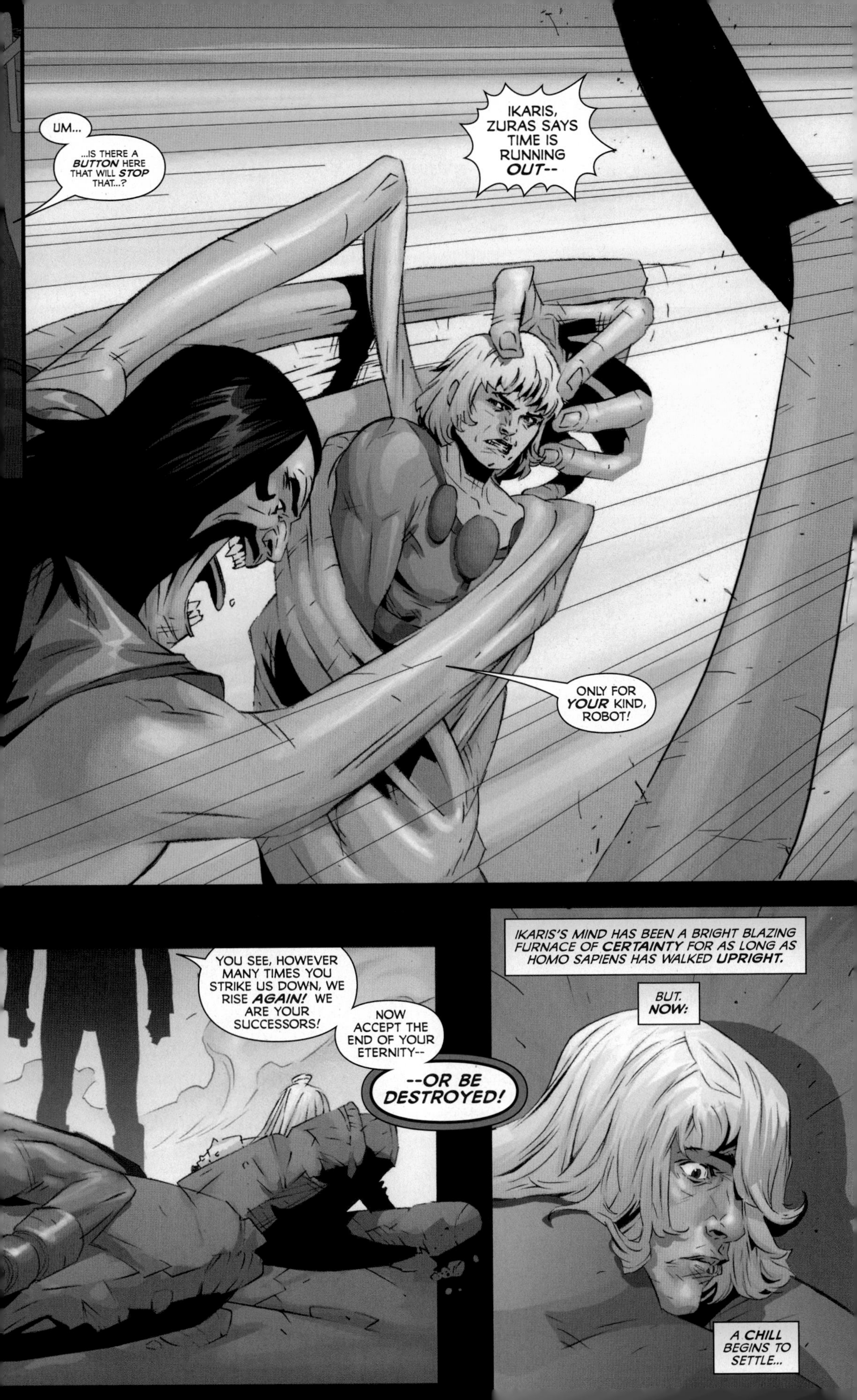
UM...
...IS THERE A BUTTON HERE THAT WILL STOP THAT...?
IKARIS, ZURAS SAYS TIME IS RUNNING OUT--
ONLY FOR YOUR KIND, ROBOT!
YOU SEE, HOWEVER MANY TIMES YOU STRIKE US DOWN, WE RISE AGAIN! WE ARE YOUR SUCCESSORS!
NOW ACCEPT THE END OF YOUR ETERNITY--
--OR BE DESTROYED!
IKARIS'S MIND HAS BEEN A BRIGHT BLAZING FURNACE OF CERTAINTY FOR AS LONG AS HOMO SAPIENS HAS WALKED UPRIGHT.
BUT. NOW:
A CHILL BEGINS TO SETTLE...

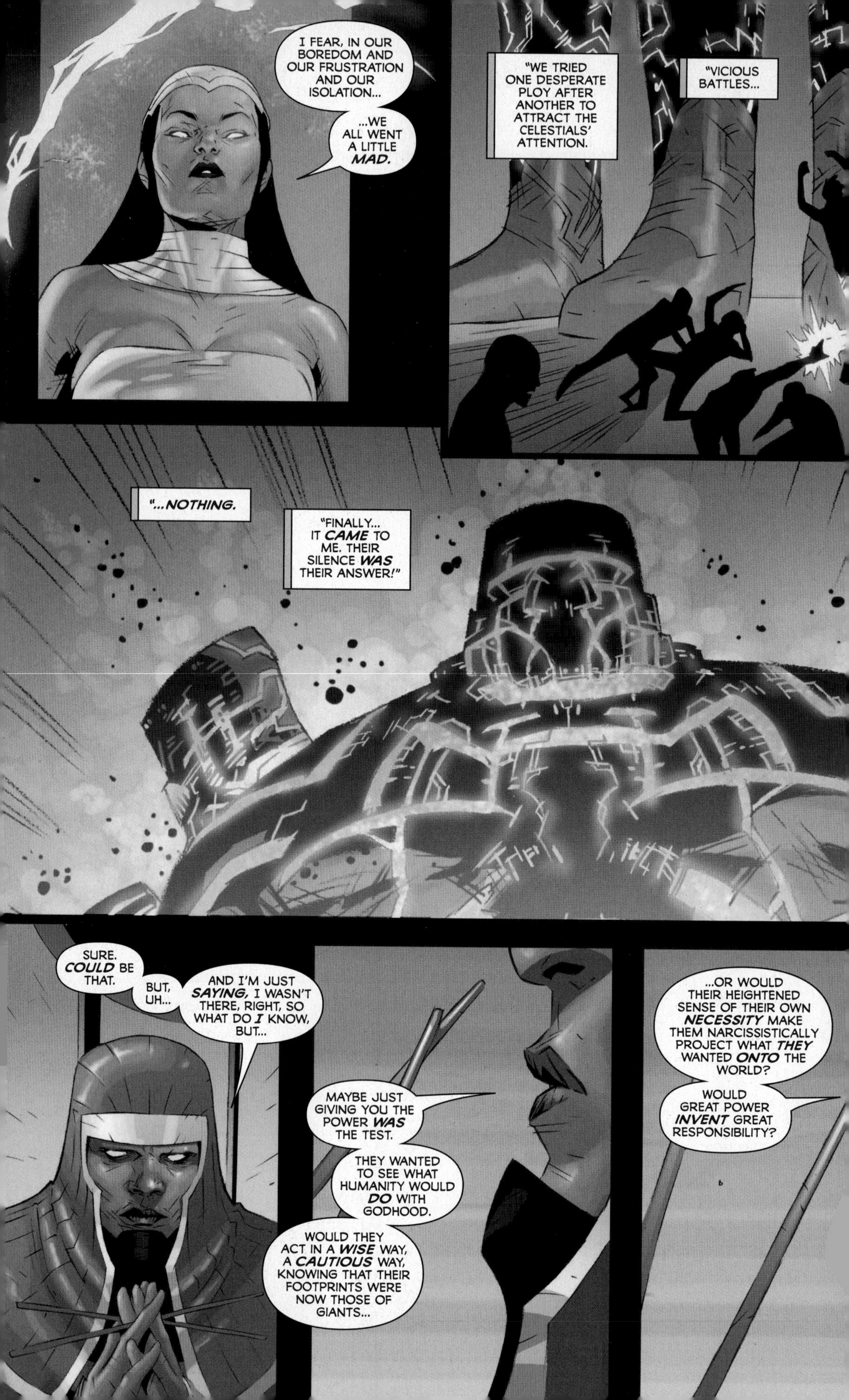

I FEAR, IN OUR BOREDOM AND OUR FRUSTRATION AND OUR ISOLATION...
...WE ALL WENT A LITTLE MAD.
"WE TRIED ONE DESPERATE PLOY AFTER ANOTHER TO ATTRACT THE CELESTIALS' ATTENTION.
"VICIOUS BATTLES...
"...NOTHING.
"FINALLY... IT CAME TO ME. THEIR SILENCE WAS THEIR ANSWER!"
SURE. COULD BE THAT.
BUT, UH...
AND I'M JUST SAYING, I WASN'T THERE, RIGHT, SO WHAT DO I KNOW, BUT...
MAYBE JUST GIVING YOU THE POWER WAS THE TEST.
THEY WANTED TO SEE WHAT HUMANITY WOULD DO WITH GODHOOD.
WOULD THEY ACT IN A WISE WAY, A CAUTIOUS WAY, KNOWING THAT THEIR FOOTPRINTS WERE NOW THOSE OF GIANTS...
...OR WOULD THEIR HEIGHTENED SENSE OF THEIR OWN NECESSITY MAKE THEM NARCISSISTICALLY PROJECT WHAT THEY WANTED ONTO THE WORLD?
WOULD GREAT POWER INVENT GREAT RESPONSIBILITY?

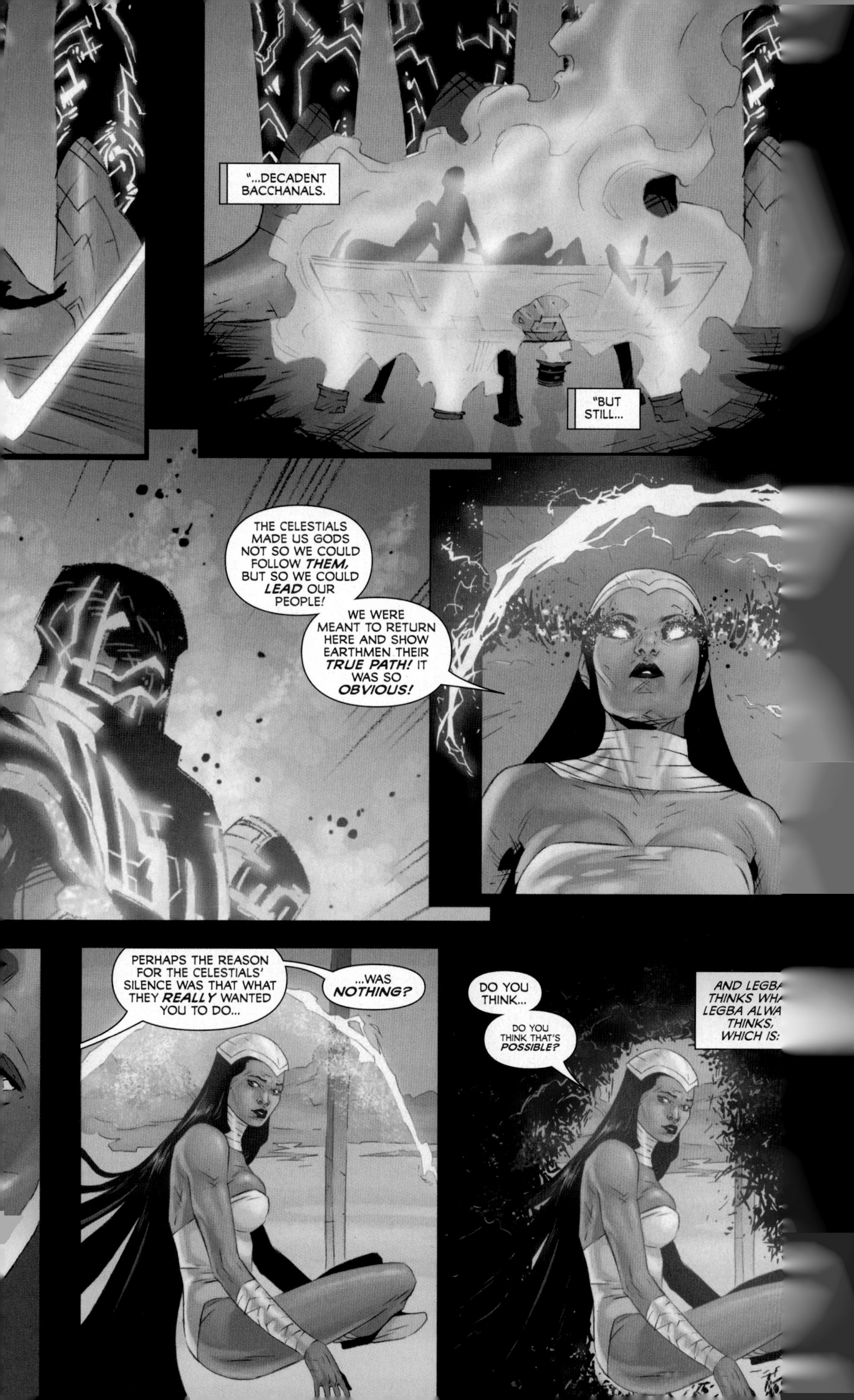
"...DECADENT BACCHANALS.
"BUT STILL...
THE CELESTIALS MADE US GODS NOT SO WE COULD FOLLOW *THEM,* BUT SO WE COULD *LEAD* OUR PEOPLE!
WE WERE MEANT TO RETURN HERE AND SHOW EARTHMEN THEIR *TRUE PATH!* IT WAS SO *OBVIOUS!*
PERHAPS THE REASON FOR THE CELESTIALS' SILENCE WAS THAT WHAT THEY *REALLY* WANTED YOU TO DO...
...WAS *NOTHING?*
DO YOU THINK...
DO YOU THINK THAT'S *POSSIBLE?*
AND LEGBA THINKS WHA LEGBA ALWA THINKS, WHICH IS:

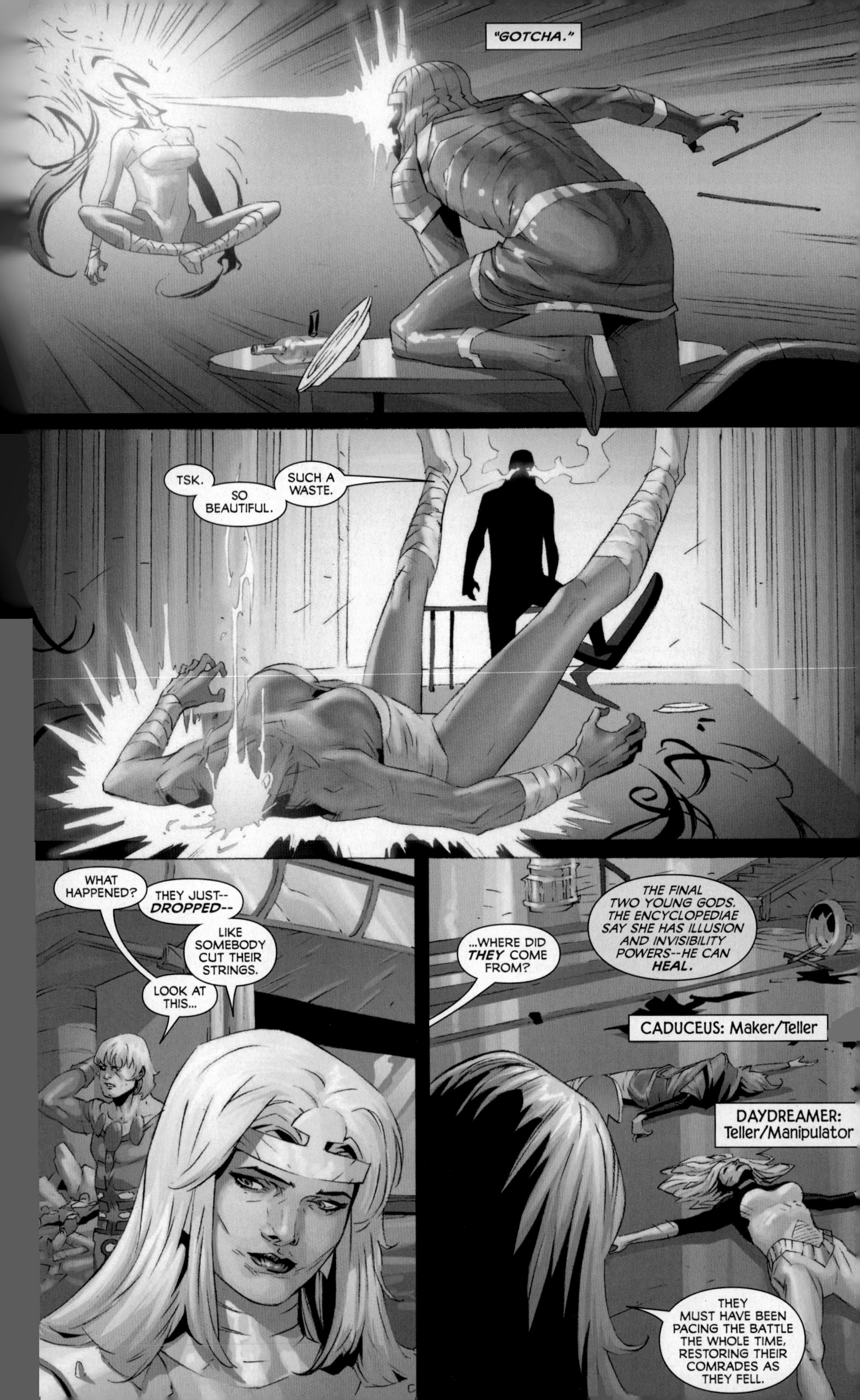
"GOTCHA."
TSK.
SO BEAUTIFUL.
SUCH A WASTE.
WHAT HAPPENED?
THEY JUST-- DROPPED--
LIKE SOMEBODY CUT THEIR STRINGS.
LOOK AT THIS...
...WHERE DID THEY COME FROM?
THE FINAL TWO YOUNG GODS. THE ENCYCLOPEDIAE SAY SHE HAS ILLUSION AND INVISIBILITY POWERS--HE CAN HEAL.
CADUCEUS: Maker/Teller
DAYDREAMER: Teller/Manipulator
THEY MUST HAVE BEEN PACING THE BATTLE THE WHOLE TIME, RESTORING THEIR COMRADES AS THEY FELL.

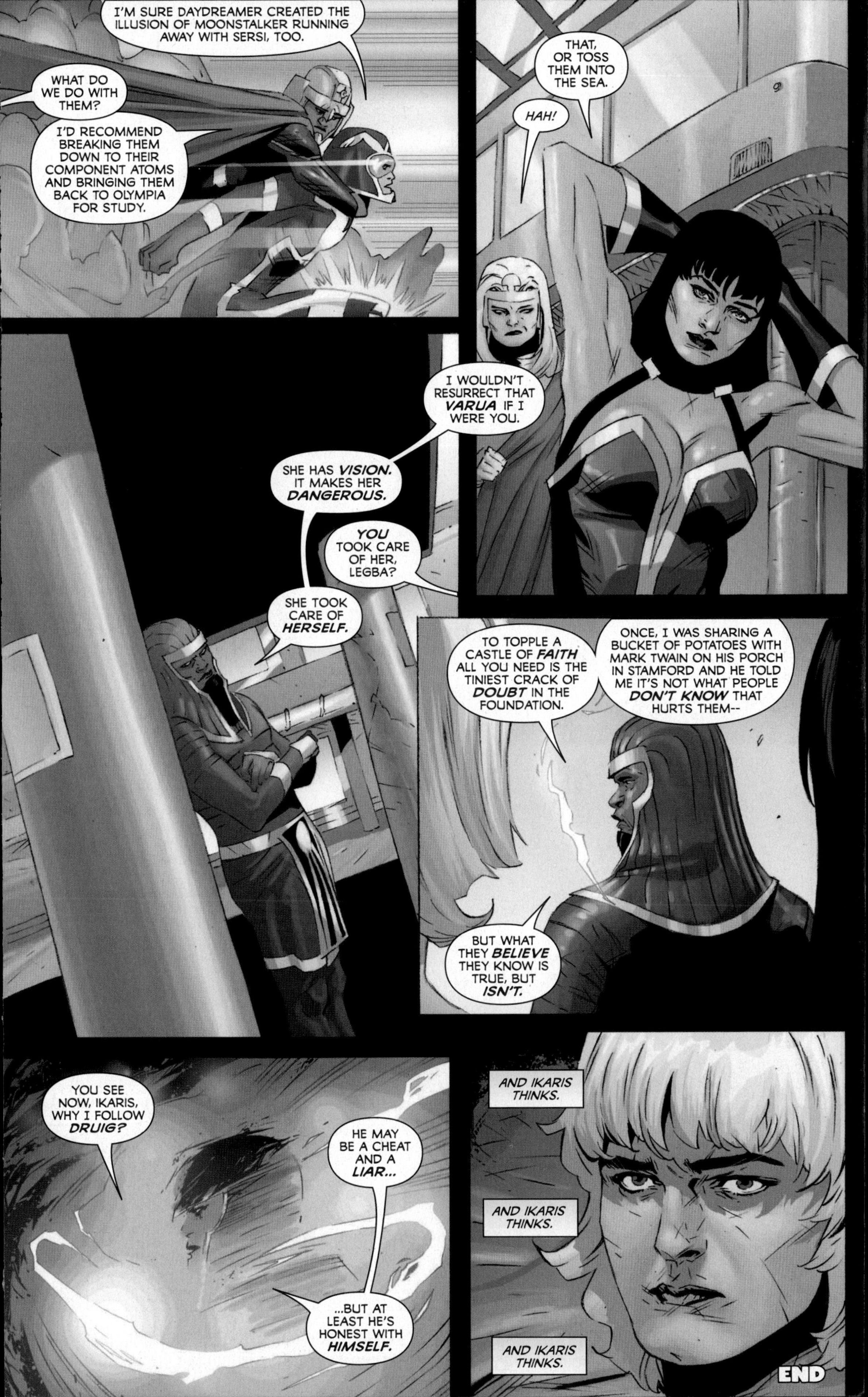
I'M SURE DAYDREAMER CREATED THE ILLUSION OF MOONSTALKER RUNNING AWAY WITH SERSI, TOO.
WHAT DO WE DO WITH THEM?
I'D RECOMMEND BREAKING THEM DOWN TO THEIR COMPONENT ATOMS AND BRINGING THEM BACK TO OLYMPIA FOR STUDY.
THAT, OR TOSS THEM INTO THE SEA.
HAH!
I WOULDN'T RESURRECT THAT VARUA IF I WERE YOU.
SHE HAS VISION. IT MAKES HER DANGEROUS.
YOU TOOK CARE OF HER, LEGBA?
SHE TOOK CARE OF HERSELF.
TO TOPPLE A CASTLE OF FAITH ALL YOU NEED IS THE TINIEST CRACK OF DOUBT IN THE FOUNDATION.
ONCE, I WAS SHARING A BUCKET OF POTATOES WITH MARK TWAIN ON HIS PORCH IN STAMFORD AND HE TOLD ME IT'S NOT WHAT PEOPLE DON'T KNOW THAT HURTS THEM--
BUT WHAT THEY BELIEVE THEY KNOW IS TRUE, BUT ISN'T.
YOU SEE NOW, IKARIS, WHY I FOLLOW DRUIG?
HE MAY BE A CHEAT AND A LIAR...
...BUT AT LEAST HE'S HONEST WITH HIMSELF.
AND IKARIS THINKS.
AND IKARIS THINKS.
AND IKARIS THINKS.
END

SPECTACULAR SPIDER-MAN ANNUAL #8 (1988) FEATURE, REPRINTED IN ETERNALS ANNUAL #1.

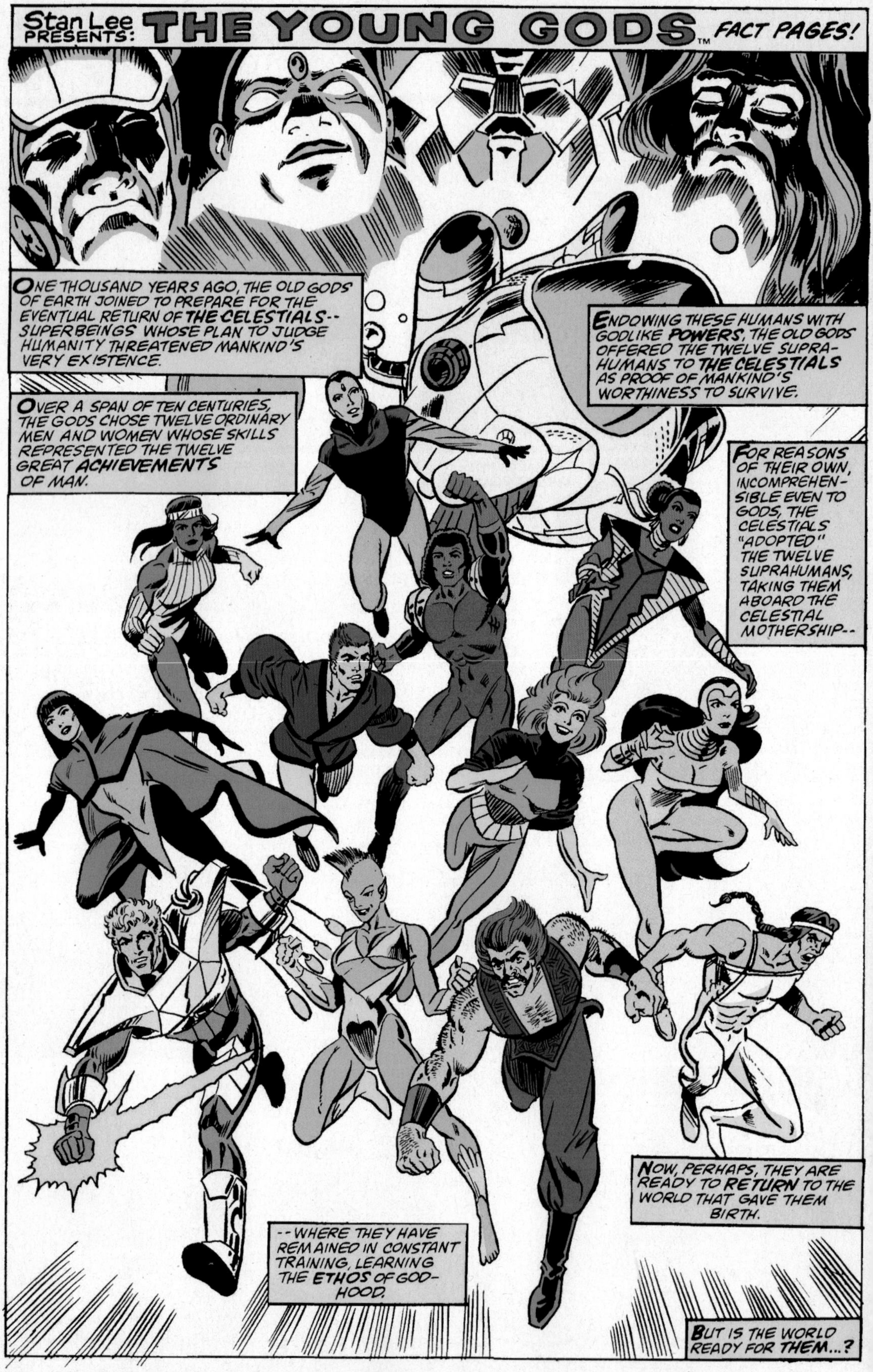
Stan Lee PRESENTS: THE YOUNG GODS™ FACT PAGES!
ONE THOUSAND YEARS AGO, THE OLD GODS OF EARTH JOINED TO PREPARE FOR THE EVENTUAL RETURN OF THE CELESTIALS-- SUPERBEINGS WHOSE PLAN TO JUDGE HUMANITY THREATENED MANKIND'S VERY EXISTENCE.
OVER A SPAN OF TEN CENTURIES, THE GODS CHOSE TWELVE ORDINARY MEN AND WOMEN WHOSE SKILLS REPRESENTED THE TWELVE GREAT ACHIEVEMENTS OF MAN.
ENDOWING THESE HUMANS WITH GODLIKE POWERS, THE OLD GODS OFFERED THE TWELVE SUPRA-HUMANS TO THE CELESTIALS AS PROOF OF MANKIND'S WORTHINESS TO SURVIVE.
FOR REASONS OF THEIR OWN, INCOMPREHENSIBLE EVEN TO GODS, THE CELESTIALS "ADOPTED" THE TWELVE SUPRAHUMANS, TAKING THEM ABOARD THE CELESTIAL MOTHERSHIP--
--WHERE THEY HAVE REMAINED IN CONSTANT TRAINING, LEARNING THE ETHOS OF GOD-HOOD.
NOW, PERHAPS, THEY ARE READY TO RETURN TO THE WORLD THAT GAVE THEM BIRTH.
BUT IS THE WORLD READY FOR THEM...?

WRITER: GERRY CONWAY • PENCILER: MARK BAGLEY • INKER: MIKE ESPOSITO • COLORIST: BOB SHAREN
LETTERER: RICK PARKER • ASSISTANT EDITOR: GLENN HERDLING • EDITOR: JIM SALICRUP

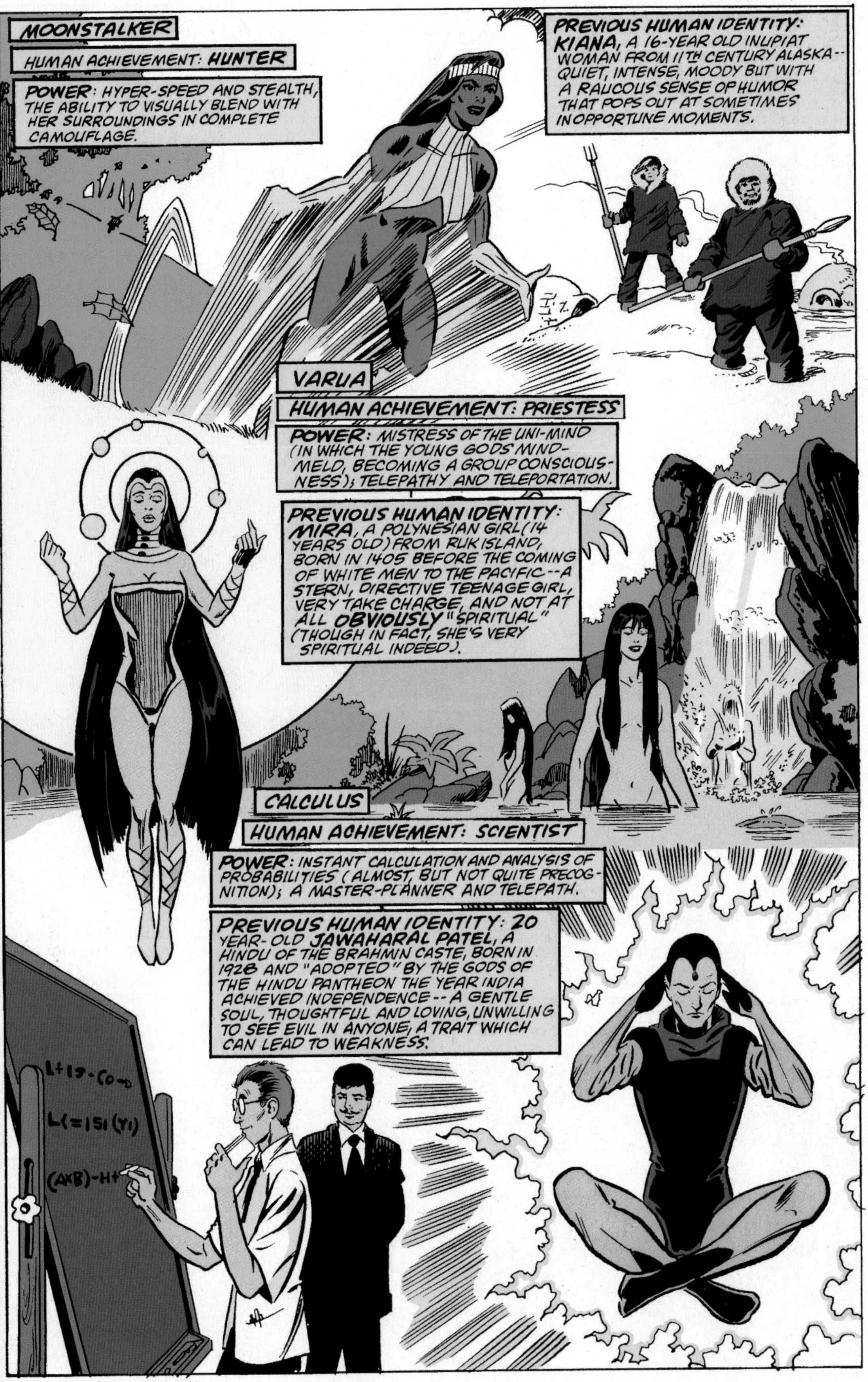

MOONSTALKER
HUMAN ACHIEVEMENT: HUNTER
POWER: HYPER-SPEED AND STEALTH, THE ABILITY TO VISUALLY BLEND WITH HER SURROUNDINGS IN COMPLETE CAMOUFLAGE.
PREVIOUS HUMAN IDENTITY: KIANA, A 16-YEAR OLD INUPIAT WOMAN FROM 11TH CENTURY ALASKA-- QUIET, INTENSE, MOODY BUT WITH A RAUCOUS SENSE OF HUMOR THAT POPS OUT AT SOMETIMES INOPPORTUNE MOMENTS.
VARUA
HUMAN ACHIEVEMENT: PRIESTESS
POWER: MISTRESS OF THE UNI-MIND (IN WHICH THE YOUNG GODS' MIND-MELD, BECOMING A GROUP CONSCIOUSNESS'); TELEPATHY AND TELEPORTATION.
PREVIOUS HUMAN IDENTITY: MIRA, A POLYNESIAN GIRL (14 YEARS OLD) FROM RUK ISLAND, BORN IN 1405 BEFORE THE COMING OF WHITE MEN TO THE PACIFIC--A STERN, DIRECTIVE TEENAGE GIRL, VERY TAKE CHARGE, AND NOT AT ALL OBVIOUSLY "SPIRITUAL" (THOUGH IN FACT, SHE'S VERY SPIRITUAL INDEED).
CALCULUS
HUMAN ACHIEVEMENT: SCIENTIST
POWER: INSTANT CALCULATION AND ANALYSIS OF PROBABILITIES (ALMOST, BUT NOT QUITE PRECOGNITION); A MASTER-PLANNER AND TELEPATH.
PREVIOUS HUMAN IDENTITY: 20 YEAR-OLD JAWAHARAL PATEL, A HINDU OF THE BRAHMIN CASTE, BORN IN 1928 AND "ADOPTED" BY THE GODS OF THE HINDU PANTHEON THE YEAR INDIA ACHIEVED INDEPENDENCE -- A GENTLE SOUL, THOUGHTFUL AND LOVING, UNWILLING TO SEE EVIL IN ANYONE, A TRAIT WHICH CAN LEAD TO WEAKNESS.

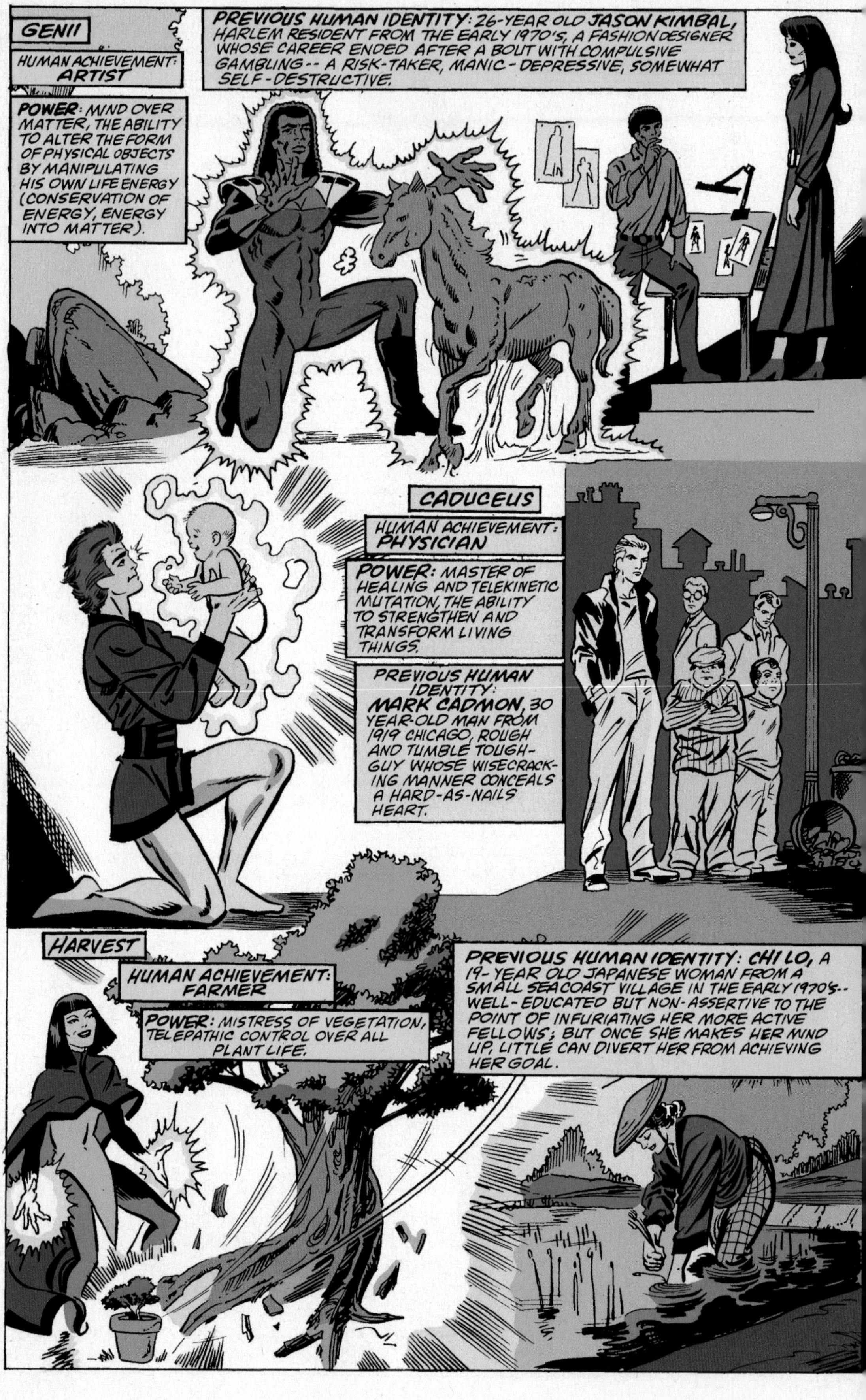
GENII
HUMAN ACHIEVEMENT: ARTIST
PREVIOUS HUMAN IDENTITY: 26-YEAR OLD JASON KIMBAL, HARLEM RESIDENT FROM THE EARLY 1970'S, A FASHION DESIGNER WHOSE CAREER ENDED AFTER A BOUT WITH COMPULSIVE GAMBLING-- A RISK-TAKER, MANIC-DEPRESSIVE, SOMEWHAT SELF-DESTRUCTIVE.
POWER: MIND OVER MATTER, THE ABILITY TO ALTER THE FORM OF PHYSICAL OBJECTS BY MANIPULATING HIS OWN LIFE ENERGY (CONSERVATION OF ENERGY, ENERGY INTO MATTER).
CADUCEUS
HUMAN ACHIEVEMENT: PHYSICIAN
POWER: MASTER OF HEALING AND TELEKINETIC MUTATION, THE ABILITY TO STRENGTHEN AND TRANSFORM LIVING THINGS.
PREVIOUS HUMAN IDENTITY: MARK CADMON, 30 YEAR-OLD MAN FROM 1919 CHICAGO, ROUGH AND TUMBLE TOUGH-GUY WHOSE WISECRACKING MANNER CONCEALS A HARD-AS-NAILS HEART.
HARVEST
HUMAN ACHIEVEMENT: FARMER
POWER: MISTRESS OF VEGETATION, TELEPATHIC CONTROL OVER ALL PLANT LIFE.
PREVIOUS HUMAN IDENTITY: CHI LO, A 19-YEAR OLD JAPANESE WOMAN FROM A SMALL SEACOAST VILLAGE IN THE EARLY 1970'S-- WELL-EDUCATED BUT NON-ASSERTIVE TO THE POINT OF INFURIATING HER MORE ACTIVE FELLOWS; BUT ONCE SHE MAKES HER MIND UP, LITTLE CAN DIVERT HER FROM ACHIEVING HER GOAL.

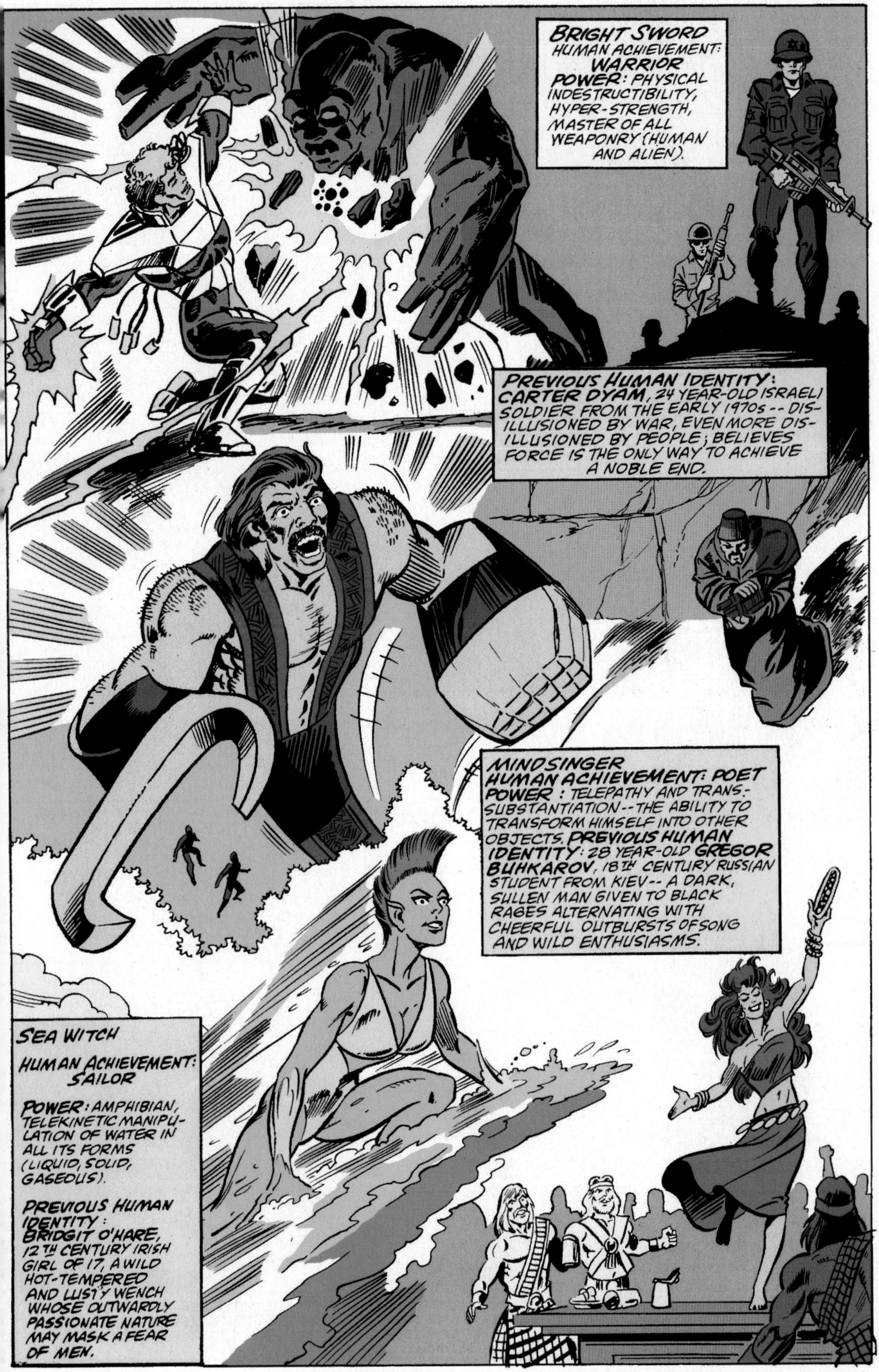
BRIGHT SWORD
HUMAN ACHIEVEMENT: WARRIOR
POWER: PHYSICAL INDESTRUCTIBILITY, HYPER-STRENGTH, MASTER OF ALL WEAPONRY (HUMAN AND ALIEN).
PREVIOUS HUMAN IDENTITY: CARTER DYAM, 24 YEAR-OLD ISRAELI SOLDIER FROM THE EARLY 1970s -- DISILLUSIONED BY WAR, EVEN MORE DISILLUSIONED BY PEOPLE; BELIEVES FORCE IS THE ONLY WAY TO ACHIEVE A NOBLE END.
MINDSINGER
HUMAN ACHIEVEMENT: POET
POWER: TELEPATHY AND TRANS-SUBSTANTIATION -- THE ABILITY TO TRANSFORM HIMSELF INTO OTHER OBJECTS. PREVIOUS HUMAN IDENTITY: 28 YEAR-OLD GREGOR BUHKAROV, 18TH CENTURY RUSSIAN STUDENT FROM KIEV -- A DARK, SULLEN MAN GIVEN TO BLACK RAGES ALTERNATING WITH CHEERFUL OUTBURSTS OF SONG AND WILD ENTHUSIASMS.
SEA WITCH
HUMAN ACHIEVEMENT: SAILOR
POWER: AMPHIBIAN, TELEKINETIC MANIPULATION OF WATER IN ALL ITS FORMS (LIQUID, SOLID, GASEOUS).
PREVIOUS HUMAN IDENTITY: BRIDGIT O'HARE, 12TH CENTURY IRISH GIRL OF 17, A WILD HOT-TEMPERED AND LUSTY WENCH WHOSE OUTWARDLY PASSIONATE NATURE MAY MASK A FEAR OF MEN.

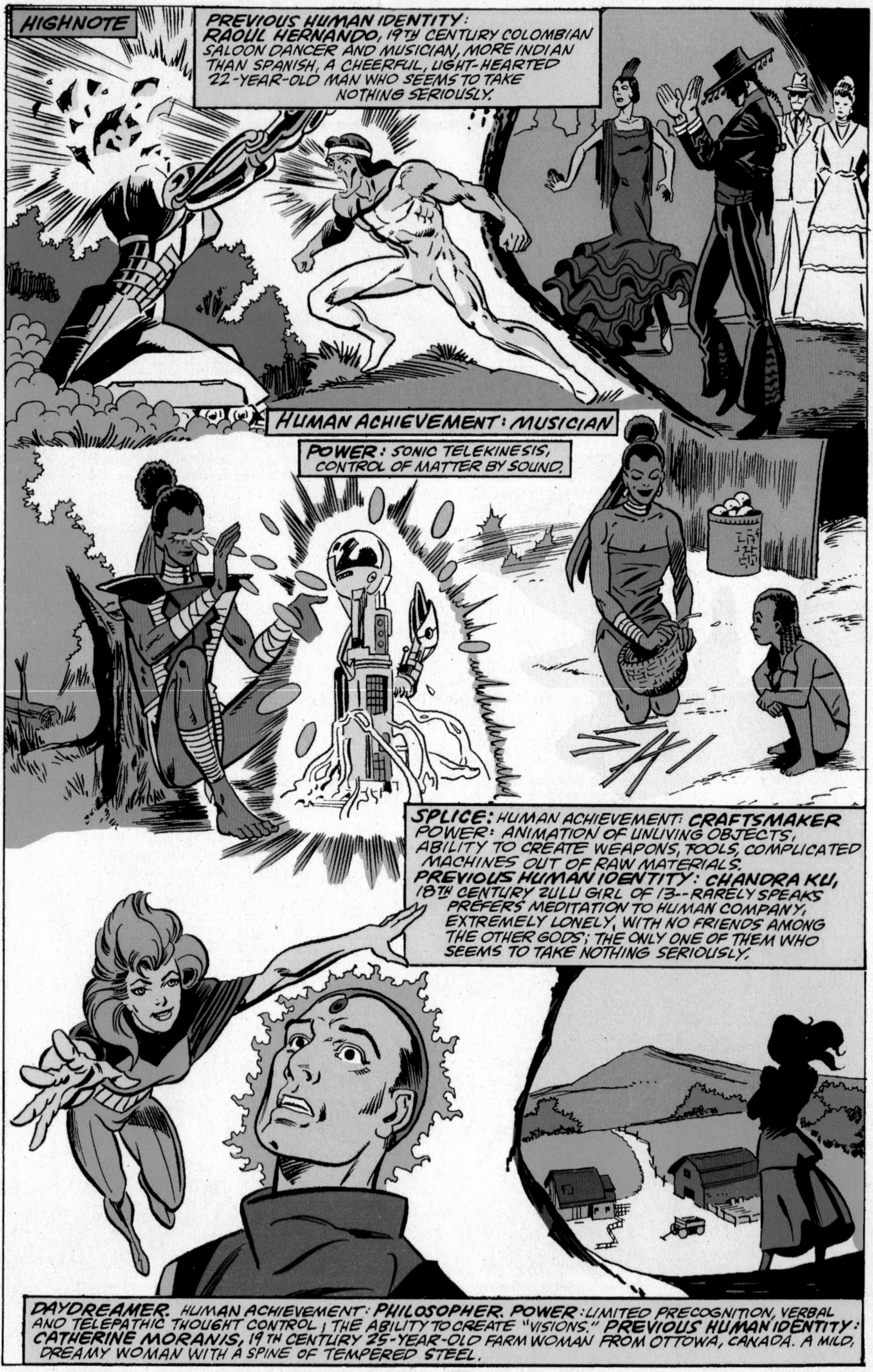
HIGHNOTE
PREVIOUS HUMAN IDENTITY: RAOUL HERNANDO, 19TH CENTURY COLOMBIAN SALOON DANCER AND MUSICIAN, MORE INDIAN THAN SPANISH, A CHEERFUL, LIGHT-HEARTED 22-YEAR-OLD MAN WHO SEEMS TO TAKE NOTHING SERIOUSLY.
HUMAN ACHIEVEMENT: MUSICIAN
POWER: SONIC TELEKINESIS, CONTROL OF MATTER BY SOUND.
SPLICE: HUMAN ACHIEVEMENT: CRAFTSMAKER
POWER: ANIMATION OF UNLIVING OBJECTS, ABILITY TO CREATE WEAPONS, TOOLS, COMPLICATED MACHINES OUT OF RAW MATERIALS.
PREVIOUS HUMAN IDENTITY: CHANDRA KU, 18TH CENTURY ZULU GIRL OF 13-- RARELY SPEAKS PREFERS MEDITATION TO HUMAN COMPANY, EXTREMELY LONELY, WITH NO FRIENDS AMONG THE OTHER GODS; THE ONLY ONE OF THEM WHO SEEMS TO TAKE NOTHING SERIOUSLY.
DAYDREAMER. HUMAN ACHIEVEMENT: PHILOSOPHER. POWER: LIMITED PRECOGNITION, VERBAL AND TELEPATHIC THOUGHT CONTROL; THE ABILITY TO CREATE "VISIONS." PREVIOUS HUMAN IDENTITY: CATHERINE MORANIS, 19TH CENTURY 25-YEAR-OLD FARM WOMAN FROM OTTOWA, CANADA. A MILD, DREAMY WOMAN WITH A SPINE OF TEMPERED STEEL.